HANDBOOK ON MIGRATION AND WELFARE

ELGAR HANDBOOKS IN MIGRATION

The Elgar Handbooks in Migration series provides a definitive overview of recent research in all matters relating to the study of migration, forming an extensive guide to the subject. This series covers research areas including internal migration, the global impact of human trafficking and forced labour and international migration policy, and constitutes an essential new resource in the field. Each volume is edited by an editor recognized as an international leader within the field and consists of original contributions by leading authors. These *Handbooks* are developed using an international approach and contribute to both the expansion of current debates within the field, and the development of future research agendas.
   Titles in the series include:

Handbook of Culture and Migration
Edited by Jeffrey H. Cohen and Ibrahim Sirkeci

Handbook on the Governance and Politics of Migration
Edited by Emma Carmel, Katharina Lenner and Regine Paul

Handbook of Citizenship and Migration
Edited by Marco Giugni and Maria Grasso

Handbook of Migration and Global Justice
Edited by Leanne Weber and Claudia Tazreiter

Research Handbook on International Migration and Digital Technology
Edited by Marie McAuliffe

Handbook on Migration and Welfare
Edited by Markus M. L. Crepaz

Handbook on Migration and Welfare

Edited by

Markus M. L. Crepaz

Josiah Meigs Distinguished Teaching Professor of Political Science, School of Public and International Affairs, University of Georgia, Athens, USA

ELGAR HANDBOOKS IN MIGRATION

Cheltenham, UK • Northampton, MA, USA

© Markus M. L. Crepaz 2022

All rights reserved. No part of this publication may be reproduced, stored in a retrieval system or transmitted in any form or by any means, electronic, mechanical or photocopying, recording, or otherwise without the prior permission of the publisher.

Published by
Edward Elgar Publishing Limited
The Lypiatts
15 Lansdown Road
Cheltenham
Glos GL50 2JA
UK

Edward Elgar Publishing, Inc.
William Pratt House
9 Dewey Court
Northampton
Massachusetts 01060
USA

A catalogue record for this book
is available from the British Library

This book is available electronically in the **Elgar**online
Sociology, Social Policy and Education subject collection
http://dx.doi.org/10.4337/9781839104572

Printed on elemental chlorine free (ECF)
recycled paper containing 30% Post-Consumer Waste

ISBN 978 1 83910 456 5 (cased)
ISBN 978 1 83910 457 2 (eBook)

Typeset by Cheshire Typesetting Ltd, Cuddington, Cheshire
Printed and bound in the USA

Contents

List of contributors viii

Introduction to the *Handbook on Migration and Welfare*: The contours of contested concepts 1
Markus M. L. Crepaz

PART I TAKING STOCK: MIGRATION AND THE STATE OF THE WELFARE STATE

1 Managing migration in modern welfare states: One-size policy does not fit all 13
  Pieter Bevelander and James F. Hollifield

2 Economics or politics? Assessing immigration as a challenge to the welfare state 45
  Maureen A. Eger

3 Migration, diversity, and the welfare state: Moving beyond attitudes 64
  Patrick R. Ireland

PART II IS SOCIAL HOMOGENEITY A PRECONDITION FOR REDISTRIBUTION?

4 Why share with strangers? Reflections on a variety of perspectives 87
  Matthew Wright

5 The boundaries of generosity: Membership, inclusion, and redistribution 102
  Allison Harell, Will Kymlicka, and Keith Banting

6 Immigration and preferences for redistribution: Empirical evidence and political implications of the progressive's dilemma in Europe 118
  Elie Murard

7 When does immigration shape support for a universal basic income? The role of education and employment status 137
  Anthony Kevins

8 Welfare chauvinist or neoliberal opposition to immigrant welfare? The importance of measurement in the study of welfare chauvinism 156
  Edward Anthony Koning

9 Personal and contextual foundations of welfare chauvinism in Western Europe 175
  Conrad Ziller and Romana Careja

PART III POLITICAL INSTITUTIONS AND POLICIES AS SHAPERS OF THE WELFARE-MIGRATION CONTEXT

10 Framing matters: Pathways between policies, immigrant integration, and native attitudes   195
Anita Manatschal

11 The politics of multiculturalism and redistribution: Immigration, accommodation, and solidarity in diverse democracies   210
Keith Banting, Daniel Westlake, and Will Kymlicka

12 The politicization of immigration and welfare: The progressive's dilemma, the rise of far-right parties, and challenges for the left   230
Maureen A. Eger and Joakim Kulin

13 Inclusive solidarity? The social democratic dilemma: Between EU rules and supporters' preferences   255
Zoe Lefkofridi and Susanne Rhein

14 Institutional sources of trust resilience in diverse societies: The mitigating role of inclusive and egalitarian welfare state institutions   276
Elif Naz Kayran and Melanie Kolbe

15 Inequality, immigration, and welfare regimes: Untangling the connections   297
Christel Kesler

16 Welfare states and migration policy: The main challenges for scholarship   321
Frida Boräng, Sara Kalm, and Johannes Lindvall

PART IV POLITICAL CULTURE, MIGRATION, AND REDISTRIBUTION

17 What explains opposition to immigration: Economic anxiety, cultural threat, or both?   338
Hanna Kleider

18 Economic resentment or cultural malaise: What accounts for nativist sentiments in contemporary liberal democracies?   351
Hans-Georg Betz

19 Does contact with strangers matter?   367
Eric M. Uslaner

20 A world to win at work? An integrated approach to meaningful interethnic contact   382
Katerina Manevska, Roderick Sluiter, and Agnes Akkerman

21 Constructing national identity and generalized trust in diverse democracies   405
Patti Tamara Lenard

22	Critically different or similarly critical? The roots of welfare state criticism among ethnic minority and majority citizens in Belgium *Arno Van Hootegem, Koen Abts, and Bart Meuleman*	420

PART V THE VIEW FROM THE GLOBAL SOUTH: THE EFFECTS OF MIGRATION ON ORIGIN COUNTRIES

23	The Janus face of remittances: Do remittances support or undermine development in the Global South? *Farid Makhlouf and Oussama Ben Atta*	442
24	Tracing the links between migration and food security in Bangladesh *Mohammad Moniruzzaman and Margaret Walton-Roberts*	470
25	Migration as a development strategy: Debating the role that migrants and those in diaspora can play *Elizabeth Mavroudi*	488
26	The migration–development nexus under scrutiny *Raúl Delgado Wise*	504
Index		517

Contributors

Koen Abts is Assistant Professor at Tilburg University and research fellow at the Institute of Social and Political Opinion Research (ISPO-KU Leuven), where he is affiliated to the Belgian National Election Study. In his Ph.D. dissertation he examined the relationship between social resentment and ethno-populism. His current research interests include populism, welfare state attitudes, radical right parties, resentment, and cleavage theory.

Agnes Akkerman is Professor of Labour Market Institutions and Labour Relations at the Department of Economics, Institute for Management Research, Radboud University, The Netherlands. Her research interests include industrial conflict, co-determination, and worker participation and voice; protest mobilization and repression. She has published her interdisciplinary research in the *American Journal of Sociology*, *Political Psychology*, *Socio-Economic Review*, and *Comparative Political Studies*.

Oussama Ben Atta is a researcher at the University of Pau and the Pays de L'Adour (UPPA) and an associate researcher at Pau Business School. He holds a master's degree in economics from the UPPA as class major with honors and he is preparing a Ph.D. on empirical development economics. His research work focuses on the economics of migration and of education. He also teaches econometrics, spatial econometrics, statistics, and macroeconomics.

Keith Banting is the Stauffer-Dunning Fellow in the School of Policy Studies and Professor Emeritus in the Department of Political Studies at Queen's University. His research interests focus on the politics of the welfare state and of diversity, and the intersection between them. His books include *Inequality and the Fading of Redistributive Politics* (2013) and *The Strains of Commitment: The Political Sources of Solidarity in Diverse Societies* (2017).

Hans-Georg Betz is Adjunct Professor of Political Science at the University of Zürich. He has taught at various universities in North America, most notably the Johns Hopkins University's School for Advanced International Studies in Washington, DC and York University in Toronto. He has written extensively on the radical populist right, nativism, Islamophobia, and contemporary Western European politics. He is a senior fellow at the Centre for Analysis of the Radical Right. He frequently writes on contemporary sociocultural, socioeconomic, and sociopolitical issues for webportals, such as open Democracy, Fair Observer, and Rantt.

Pieter Bevelander is Professor of International Migration and Ethnic Relations at the Department of Global Political Studies and Director of MIM, Malmö Institute of Studies of Migration, Diversity and Welfare, Malmö University. His main research field is international migration and aspects of immigrant integration as well as reactions and attitudes of receiving society members towards immigrants and minorities. He is Associate Editor for *International Migration Review* and board member of the independent committee The Migration Studies Delegation.

Frida Boräng is Associate Professor in Political Science at the University of Gothenburg. She is the author of *National Institutions – International Migration: Labour Markets, Welfare States and Immigration Policy* (2012) and articles in journals such as the *British Journal of Political Science*, *Governance*, and *European Journal of Political Research*.

Romana Careja is Associate Professor in the Department of Political Science and Public Management at the University of Southern Denmark. Her research addresses issues within the areas of immigration and integration policies, attitudes towards immigrants, and the nexus between social policies and immigration.

Markus M. L. Crepaz is the Josiah Meigs Distinguished Teaching Professor of Political Science in the School of Public and International Affairs at the University of Georgia. His fields of research include comparative political economy, the variety of political institutions and their effects, the role of trust and solidarity in diversifying societies, the causes and consequences of immigration on welfare states, and the determinants of authoritarianism in Western publics as a function of immigration-induced diversity.

Maureen A. Eger is Associate Professor in the Department of Sociology at Umeå University. She holds a Ph.D. and M.A. from the University of Washington and M.A. and B.A. from Stanford University. Her research interests lie broadly in political sociology, with an emphasis on immigration, nationalism, and the welfare state. Eger's work appears in a variety of journals including the *European Sociological Review*, *European Political Science*, *International Journal of Comparative Sociology*, *International Migration Review*, *Nations and Nationalism*, and *Socius*.

Allison Harell is Professor in the Department of Political Science at the University of Quebec in Montreal and holds the UQAM Research Chair in the Political Psychology of Social Solidarity. She co-directs the Consortium on Electoral Democracy and was co-lead of the 2019 Canadian Election Study. Her research focuses primarily on how social diversity influences the political behavior and attitudes of citizens in advanced industrialized democracies.

James F. Hollifield is Ora Nixon Arnold Professor of International Political Economy and Director of the Tower Center at SMU and a Global Fellow at the Wilson Center. Hollifield is a scholar of international and comparative politics and has written widely on issues of political and economic development with a focus on migration. His books include *Understanding Global Migration* (2022), *Controlling Immigration* (2014), and *Migration Theory* (2000).

Patrick R. Ireland is Professor of Political Science at the Illinois Institute of Technology in Chicago, and is trained in comparative politics, modern languages, and public health. Ireland has written extensively on urban-level migrant integration and related themes, employing qualitative and quantitative methods. His publications include several single-authored books and numerous peer-reviewed journal articles and book chapters. His work has been based on extensive fieldwork in Morocco, Senegal, India, Sri Lanka, the Philippines, Australia, Canada, Mexico, and a number of European countries.

Sara Kalm is Senior Lecturer in Political Science at Lund University. Her main research interests include migration policy, citizenship, and social movement mobilization.

Elif Naz Kayran is a Post-Doctoral Fellow at the Faculty of Governance and Global Affairs at Leiden University working for the research program on Citizenship, Migration and Global Transformations. She is also an affiliate member of the European Research Council project "Unequal Democracies" at the University of Geneva. Elif works on comparative political economy, welfare states, immigration, minority integration, voting rights, and citizenship studies. Her research has appeared in *Journal of Ethnic and Migration Studies* and *Journal of European Social Policy*.

Christel Kesler is Associate Professor of Sociology at Colby College. She also currently serves as Faculty Associate Director of Colby's Goldfarb Center for Public Affairs. Kesler's research focuses broadly on issues of inequality and social policy, with a particular emphasis on how political-economic institutions and social policies shape the experiences of immigrants in North America and Western Europe.

Anthony Kevins is Lecturer in Politics and International Studies at Loughborough University's School of Social Sciences and Humanities. His research is focused on the link between public opinion and policy, and his work has appeared in journals such as *Socio-Economic Review*, *Journal of Social Policy*, and *Political Psychology*.

Hanna Kleider is Assistant Professor in the Department of Political Economy at King's College London. She received her Ph.D. from the University of North Carolina Chapel Hill. Her research centers on different aspects of comparative political economy, with a special interest in social policy, preferences for redistribution, and immigration. She has paid particular attention to territorial inequalities and their effect on the welfare state. Some of her research is published in *Comparative Political Studies* and the *European Journal of Political Research*.

Melanie Kolbe is Assistant Professor in the Department of International Relations and Political Science at the Graduate Institute for International and Development Studies, Geneva. Kolbe's work has been published in *Comparative Politics*, *International Migration Review*, *Journal of European Social Policy*, *Ethnic and Racial Studies*, and *Politics and Religion*. Her broader research interests include the study of immigration politics and policy, comparative political economy, social identity politics, and immigrant integration.

Edward Anthony Koning is Associate Professor of Political Science at the University of Guelph. Most of his research investigates the politics of immigration in Western democracies, specifically regarding immigrants' social rights and the role of populist anti-immigrant parties. He is the author of *Immigration and the Politics of Welfare Exclusion* (2019) and has publications in leading academic journals, including *Comparative European Politics*, *Comparative Political Studies*, *Ethnic and Racial Studies*, and *Journal of Public Policy*.

Joakim Kulin is a research fellow in the Department of Sociology at Umeå University, where he also earned his doctorate. A scholar of political sociology, Kulin's research includes cross-national comparisons of attitudes, values, and behaviors related to welfare states, immigration, and the environment. His current project focuses on how government institutions and political ideology influence public views about climate change and climate policies. His work appears in *European Sociological Review*, *Socius*, *Environmental Politics*, *Climate Policy*, and *Global Environmental Change*.

Will Kymlicka is the Canada Research Chair in Political Philosophy in the Philosophy Department at Queen's University in Kingston, Canada, where he has taught since 1998. His research interests focus on issues of democracy and diversity, and in particular on models of citizenship and social justice within multicultural societies. His books include *Multicultural Citizenship: A Liberal Theory of Minority Rights* (1995) and *Multicultural Odysseys: Navigating the New International Politics of Diversity* (2007).

Zoe Lefkofridi is Full Professor of Politics and Gender, Diversity and Equality at the Political Science Department of the University of Salzburg and Editor in Chief of Political Participation, Specialty Section of the new golden open access journal *Frontiers in Political Science*. Lefkofridi's research interests lie in transnational democracy and political representation in Europe, with a focus on inequality. Her work appears in *European Union Politics*, *European Political Science Review*, *Politics and Gender*, and *West European Politics*, among others.

Patti Tamara Lenard is Associate Professor of Ethics in the Graduate School of Public and International Affairs, University of Ottawa. She is the author of *Trust, Democracy and Multicultural* Challenges (2012) and *How Should Democracies Fight Terrorism?* (2020). She is working on the books *Debating Multiculturalism* (with Peter Balint) and *Democracy and Exclusion*. In Ottawa, she runs a small organization called Rainbow Haven, which sponsors, settles, and advocates for LGBTQ refugees: www.facebook.com/rainbowhavenottawa/.

Johannes Lindvall is Professor of Political Science at Lund University, Sweden. His most recent book is *Inward Conquest: The Political Origins of Modern Public Services* (2021, with Ben Ansell). He is also the author of *Reform Capacity* (2017), *Mass Unemployment and the State* (2010), and articles in journals such as the *American Political Science Review*, *Journal of Politics*, and *World Politics*.

Farid Makhlouf is Associate Professor of Economics and Econometrics at Pau Business School and Associate Researcher at the Pau University, France. He specializes in the empirical studies of the remittance phenomenon. His work mainly focuses on the reaction of migrants through their remittances to shocks in their origin and host countries and their effects on the countries of origin. The author holds a Ph.D. (with Distinction) in economics from Pau University.

Anita Manatschal is Assistant Professor of Migration Policy Analysis at the University of Neuchâtel. Previous positions include postdocs at the Universities of California, Berkeley, and Bern, and a visiting scholarship at the European University Institute in Florence. Her research interests embrace comparative migration policy research, integration, immigrants' political engagement, immigration and democracy, and xenophobia and discrimination. Her publications appeared in *West European Politics*, *Regional Studies*, *Journal of European Public Policy*, and various edited volumes and monographs.

Katerina Manevska is Assistant Professor at the Department of Political Science, Institute for Management Research, Radboud University, The Netherlands. She is a cultural and political sociologist with a special interest in cultural and political change, interethnic relations, and employment relations. She has published in the *American Journal of Cultural Sociology*, *Political Psychology*, and *Socio-Economic Review*.

Elizabeth Mavroudi is Reader in Human Geography at Loughborough University. She is a migration scholar with an expertise in the geographies of diaspora. As a qualitative researcher, she has published widely on themes such as theorizations of diaspora, Palestinian and Greek diasporic identity, politics and homeland development, and immigration policy and highly skilled migration in the United Kingdom. Her Leverhulme-funded project focused on Greek, Jewish, and Palestinian young people's identities and politicization in diaspora.

Bart Meuleman is Professor at the Centre for Sociological Research at KU Leuven. His research focuses on cross-national comparisons of value and attitude patterns, such as ethnic prejudice, egalitarianism, and support for the welfare state. He has a special interest in the application of multilevel modeling and structural equation modeling on comparative survey data.

Mohammad Moniruzzaman is a policy and regulatory analyst with graduate education and training in public administration, economics, and economic geography. He holds a Ph.D. in geography from Wilfrid Laurier University, completing his research on household debt, and the impact of international remittances on household consumption and food security. He has held research and teaching posts focused on immigration and development issues, and has expertise in quantitative models and forecasting methods. He is currently an analyst in Canada's Federal Public Service in Ottawa.

Elie Murard is Assistant Professor in Economics at the University of Alicante. He is also a research affiliate at IZA and NOVA SBE. Prior to this, he received his Ph.D. in economics from the Paris School of Economics. His research aims to understand the multifaceted effects of international migration on economic development and social cohesion from the perspective of both the origin and the destination countries.

Susanne Rhein is an M.A. student of political science at the University of Salzburg. She is currently working as a research assistant at the Horizon 2020 project Populism and Civic Engagement. She is also involved in conducting a Youth Survey focusing on digitalization and participation for the project Youth Digitalisation and Participation-Upper Austria. Previously, she worked at the project The Choice for Europe since Maastricht at the Salzburg Center for European Union Studies.

Roderick Sluiter is Postdoctoral Researcher at the Department of Economics, Institute for Management Research, Radboud University, The Netherlands. His research interests include the suppression of employee voice and its consequences. He has recently published in the *American Journal of Sociology, Socio-Economic Review*, and *Political Studies*.

Eric M. Uslaner is Professor of Government and Politics at the University of Maryland-College Park, where he has taught since 1975. His previous positions were at the Australian National University, Canberra and The Hebrew University, Jerusalem. In 2006 he was appointed the first Senior Research Fellow at the Center for American Law and Political Science at the Southwest University of Political Science and Law, Chongqing, China. He was the Fulbright Distinguished Chair in American Political Science at the School of Politics and International Relations at the Australian National University. He is also Honorary Professor of Political Science and Government at Aarhus University.

Arno Van Hootegem is Doctoral Researcher at the Centre for Sociological Research (KU Leuven), where he is conducting a project on public opinion towards distributive justice. His Ph.D. fellowship was awarded by Research Foundation Flanders. Other research interests concern welfare attitudes and anti-refugee sentiments.

Margaret Walton-Roberts is Professor in the Geography and Environmental Studies Department at Wilfrid Laurier University, and affiliated to the Balsillie School of International Affairs, Waterloo, Ontario. She has published widely in issues related to gender and migration, and global health professional migration. Her edited collection *Global Migration, Gender and Health Professional Credentials: Transnational Value Transfers and Losses* is due to be published in 2021.

Daniel Westlake is the Buchanan Post-Doctoral Fellow in Canadian Democracy in the Political Studies Department at Queen's University. He received his Ph.D. from the University of British Columbia and studies the development of multiculturalism policies, political parties' influence over multiculturalism, and Canadian elections. His work has been published in the *Canadian Journal of Political Science* and *Party Politics*.

Raúl Delgado Wise is UNESCO Chair on Migration, Development and Human Rights. He is Professor and Founder of the Doctoral Program in Development Studies at the Autonomous University of Zacatecas, President and Founder of the International Network on Migration and Development, and Co-Director of the Critical Development Studies Network. He is also Editor of the journal *Migración y Desarrollo*.

Matthew Wright earned his Ph.D. in political science from the University of California, Berkeley. Prior to joining their Department of Political Science, he was Associate Professor of Government at American University in Washington, DC. He studies political psychology, and in particular questions how both political identities and core values influence attitudes about immigrants, immigration policy, and diversity more generally. His work has appeared in a number of journals and his book (co-authored with Morris Levy) *Immigration and the American Ethos* was published in 2020.

Conrad Ziller is Assistant Professor in the Department of Political Science at University of Duisburg-Essen. His research interests focus on the role of immigration in politics and society, immigrant integration, policy effects on citizens, and quantitative methods.

Introduction to the *Handbook on Migration and Welfare*: The contours of contested concepts
Markus M. L. Crepaz

The nexus between migration and welfare has hardly ever been more salient than now. On their own, migration and welfare, broadly conceived, have been core themes in the academic fields of political science, international affairs, sociology, economics, and public administration for decades. However, only since the beginning of the new millennium has there been a systematic focus on the many intriguing ways these two central policy fields interact with each other. Scholarly activity has grown exponentially since then and vibrant scholarly debates ensued. However, very little consensus has been achieved and much remains contested. This *Handbook* collects the leading theoretical and empirical contributions based on the central questions and approaches to the field resulting in a stimulating collection of the current state of the art in this diverse field.

Given the scant scholarly agreements in the complex relationships between migration and welfare, it might be prudent to reflect on the dictum of the eminent physicist Werner Heisenberg that "we have to remember that what we observe is not nature in itself, but nature exposed to our method of questioning". In the social sciences, as opposed to the natural sciences, results differ not only on the "method of questioning", such as whether scholars use quantitative or qualitative approaches – both of which are represented in this *Handbook* – but also on the particular field of study that examines the interactions between migration and welfare. As a result, I endeavored to give voice to a variety of disciplines, such as political science, sociology, economics and economic history, human geography, political psychology as well as political philosophy. Moreover, I purposefully solicited chapters representing a wide range of age and reputation of contributors. A number of chapters are written or co-authored by some of the most prominent, senior scholars in the field while others are crafted by up-and-coming, junior colleagues. Finally, I also attempted to achieve gender parity as much as possible. Almost half of the chapters (45 percent) in this *Handbook* are either authored or co-authored by female scholars.

While I attempted to inject diversity in terms of methods, fields, seniority, and gender, I was specific in terms of the task I posed to the contributors. First, I charged the contributors with establishing the state of the art of this research field by reviewing what we know, what we think we know, and what the future contours of research might look like. Readers of this volume are provided with an authoritative summary of the state of play in this tension-filled relationship between migration and welfare.

Second, the contributors were tasked with developing original theoretical but testable hypotheses and/or empirical contributions to push the frontier of our current knowledge. In the most general terms, the central question posed to the contributors in the first four parts of the book is this: will the publics in western societies want to continue funding the welfare state if they perceive, correctly or not, that some of their taxes are going to migrants who look differently, dress differently, speak differently, believe in a different god in addition to a multitude of other visible and behavioral differences, than the native borns? This question was intentionally posed as broadly as possible in order to allow a variety of explanations to flourish. Unsurprisingly, the answers proffered give rise to new questions in turn: does it make a difference how generous the welfare is? Do varying levels of solidarity and trust affect the way native borns are willing to share with migrants? Are political institutions simply a reflection of the migration context or are they actively shaping it? The old question of "do parties matter" comes into play also. Does it matter which parties are in power in terms of how the tension between migration and welfare is resolved, or not? Could the extent to which specific social rights that are extended to migrants mediate the way native borns are more or less willing to share? Do multiculturalism policies engender more tolerance with newcomers or does it lead to the development of "parallel societies"? Fundamentally, at an individual level, how does an individual's education and cultural capital affect the relationship between "them" and "us"? Do native borns react differently in terms of their willingness to disentitle migrants from welfare benefits as a function of whether they are labor migrants or asylum seekers? For those who champion progressive policies an even more profound question presents itself: is it possible to have both, a generous social welfare state and liberal immigration policies? Fortunately, these and many other questions have been either competently answered or at least richly illuminated in this *Handbook*.

The questions raised in the fifth part of the book deal with a much neglected, yet crucial element of migration and welfare, namely the effect of migration on sending countries. There is a vibrant debate among those who conceive of migration as a development strategy insofar as the erstwhile migrants remit significant monies and ideas to their home countries while others consider these remittances as sources of rising economic and ethnic inequality. Do such remittances absolve governments in the Global South to pursue meaningful, lasting development strategies? What is the role of ethnic diasporas abroad and do their social and economic remittances affect some ethnic groups more than others in their homeland? Is the claim that migration as a development strategy is nothing but a form of neo-liberal globalization in disguise? What would a counter-hegemonic or "southern perspective" of development look like? Would global migration regimes be necessary to establish more equity between workers in the Global North and South?

After the introduction, the 26 chapters in the *Handbook* are divided into five parts which are deliberately titled in broad terms. This introduction will provide very brief summaries of each contribution followed by reflections on where there are differences and similarities between the various chapters.

In Part I of the *Handbook* Pieter Bevelander and James Hollifield explore the degree to which immigration poses a threat to the welfare state in comparison with other purported threats to its viability in addition to providing a succinct overview of the *problématique* of this policy field. They argue that immigration generates specific policy challenges to welfare states on account of their claimed ethos of equal treatment and social equality for all legal residents. Finding that while there is tremendous variation in which different countries have employed different strategies to deal with the migration challenge, what appears to be key to successful immigration outcomes are earnest integration policies and the granting of rights to migrants. Nevertheless, more generous welfare states do seem to attract particularly asylum seekers and refugees which turn out to be more difficult to integrate. Whether they represent a particular fiscal burden on the welfare state depends on their age, education level, and the social capital of migrants. Ultimately, whether welfare states can sustain high levels of immigration is a function of political constellations, institutional contexts, and the historical reach of systemic racist and nativist legacies.

Maureen Eger concludes that while there is little evidence that economic issues might undermine the viability of welfare states, the same may not be true for political challenges. Setting the stage by providing a sweeping review of the relevant literature, she highlights various mechanisms that account for the negative association between immigration and welfare state support. The concept of reciprocity is crucial in altruistic concepts such as a redistributive welfare state. However, when native borns believe that out-groups either do not pay taxes or abuse the social welfare system, they might feel less inclined to pay their fair share, thereby undermining the viability of the welfare state. Her empirical analysis across 24 European countries at two time periods (2002 and 2014) indicates that on average, people believe that immigrants are a net burden on welfare states. Other mechanisms, such as in-group bias, or whether native borns consider immigrants as competitors for scarce resources, similarly indicate that people's sentiments tend to favor either disentitling migrants for social benefits, to impose harsher immigration controls, or to reduce redistribution in general. According to Eger, it is natives' attitudes towards migrants and beliefs about their effects on the social cohesion that drives the political challenges to the welfare state.

Noting that much of the public opinion/attitudes-related research has reached a "stalemate", Patrick Ireland laments that the burgeoning welfare-migration cottage industry has generated very few clear answers. He implores readers to go beyond attitudes and to examine not just policy outputs but real-world outcomes. In his view, the causal chain that most quantitative researchers explore stops one link too short, namely at the level of popular attitudes towards redistribution assuming, perhaps erroneously, that attitudes drive actual levels of social benefits. Instead, he argues, scholars should go one more link further, examining how attitudes are connected to actual social spending and benefit levels. However, even social spending is ultimately only a policy output, and still not a policy outcome which is yet one more link removed. In the end, what determines how migrants fare is a matter of the amount and quality of health care, education, and labor market integration they receive, among others. In his words, what matters for migrants is "how welfare delivery truly operates in diversifying societies". To uncover this would require more qualitative approaches, according to Ireland.

Part II of the book raises one of the central questions in the relationship between migration and welfare, namely: why share with strangers, or more specifically: is social homogeneity a precondition for redistribution? Matthew Wright lays out a variety of perspectives based on what human nature is believed to be. He finds that the willingness to share with others depends on whether one takes a view that humans are rational utility maximizers or whether people possess a broader sense of belonging to particular groups with its attendant emphasis on social identity. Sharing, according to Wright, occurs more easily if members of the group share a sense of identity based on either ethnic, national, or racial categories. A yet different perspective is contained in a "values" approach that is centered on a concept of fairness based on norms which have congealed into contractually agreed relationships. This view differs from the group-centered approach insofar as it is not so much about whether immigrants are part of one's group but whether they adhere to broadly accepted social norms. These perspectives, however, appear rarely in their pure form and occur most often in hybrid manifestations.

Allison Harell, Will Kymlicka, and Keith Banting examine the criteria as to who deserves to be included in social benefits and argue for deservingness criteria that are grounded in more than just "civic" and "ethnic" conceptions. Instead, they argue that it is "membership perceptions" upon which natives decide the boundaries of support for redistribution by which they mean the degree to which natives consider immigrants to be willing and committed members of the community. This perception goes beyond just simply conceiving of immigrants as contributors in an economic sense or as sharing the social norms of the host society, as Wright argued above, but whether natives see immigrants as deserving of social benefits based on their beliefs that immigrants are committed members of the community. An empirical analysis indicates that Canada shows a particularly strong association between membership perceptions and inclusive redistribution.

While Wright and Harell et al. examine these issues from a politico-theoretical perspective, Elie Murard and Anthony Kevins were tasked with providing an empirical examination as to whether a redistributive welfare state is compatible with liberal immigration policies. Murard, borrowing from his co-authored, forthcoming work with the late Alberto Alesina and Hillel Rapoport, finds that local exposure to immigration reduces native citizens' support for redistribution. This association is based on a novel dataset consisting of 140 regions across 16 European countries. Murard's finding of course does not mean that the actual size of the welfare state will diminish – rather, reduced public welfare support as a result of exposure to immigration might manifest itself in the rise of anti-immigrant parties, in a systematic disentitling of migrants from social benefits, and even in a rightward shift of the whole party system in a country. While this would not engender the viability of the welfare state per se, it would draw harsher borders between "us" and "them" in terms of who is eligible for protection from the vagaries of the market.

Anthony Kevins argues that immigration might have different effects on the welfare state depending on the type of welfare program, such as whether it is means tested, insurance based, or based on universal benefits. He zeroes in on an item in the 2016 European Social Survey which tapped public support for a universal basic income scheme. Kevins finds that those countries with a higher stock of immigrants show lower support for a universal basic income scheme. However, that relationship only applied to lower-educated individuals suggesting that attitudes are not set in stone and are constantly shaped via socialization, education, and interactions with other members of the community.

Edward Koning focuses on welfare chauvinism which is the argument that social benefits should only accrue to the "rightful" members of the community, based either on ethnic, or national, membership and suggests that opposition to immigrants' access to social programs can be driven by two very different positions: a neo-liberal position which argues that any social programs are inimical to the efficient functioning of capitalist markets and thus should either be abolished or significantly reduced, and a welfare chauvinist position. At the surface, if not conceptually and empirically separated, these two positions are observationally equivalent and, thus, can lead to a number of measurement errors, six of which Koning highlights in his conclusions. Intriguingly, Koning finds, similarly to Kevins, that low education drives welfare chauvinism, but not neo-liberal opposition to the welfare state.

Conrad Ziller and Romana Careja employ a multilevel model using the two waves of the European Social Survey (2008 and 2016) and probe for the individual and contextual correlates of welfare chauvinism. Consistent with the findings by Koning and Kevins, they also find that lower-educated individuals are associated with higher levels of welfare chauvinism. Among other findings, and unsurprisingly, people who live comfortably on their current income show lower welfare chauvinism, while for people who are unemployed the opposite is true. Liberal integration policies, using the MIPEX integration policy measure, depress welfare chauvinism. The variable "proportion of immigrants", however, proved to be sensitive to the type of model specification employed.

Part III shifts the focus to the role of political institutions, broadly understood, and their effects on the migration and welfare nexus. In Part II, political institutions, regimes, and policies were largely argued to be simply bystanders in this push and pull of the migration and welfare vectors. In Part III the authors examine whether policies, types of migration, welfare regimes, political parties, and others can mediate the effects of migration on generalized trust, solidarity, or support for the welfare state more generally. Concepts such as trust and solidarity have become increasingly understood to play a crucial intermediary role between increasing immigration and the natives' willingness to entitle migrants to social benefits as these cultural features may be associated with political institutions, broadly conceived. This part of the *Handbook* hints at a potential for agency suggesting that perhaps multicultural and integration policies, equal or unequal access to social benefits, political parties of different hues, and other contextual factors may shape the migration and welfare context by being more or less adept in generating solidarity and trust between natives and newcomers and affect support for the welfare state more generally.

Anita Manatschal implores scholars to pay attention to what she calls the "indirect" effects of integration policies on native-born attitudes. These indirect effects, such as perceptions on the migrants' part that they are part of the broader society and that they have a stake in society, are a function of the degree to which integration policies extend socioeconomic, civic-political, and cultural rights to migrants. According to Manatschal, generously extending such rights could change the native borns' view of migrants as the "other" to a more inclusive view that sees migrants as part and parcel of society.

Staying with the question of whether policies can make a difference, Keith Banting, Daniel Westlake, and Will Kymlicka empirically examine whether multiculturalist policies weaken support for the welfare state based on newly extending their Multiculturalism Policy Index to 2020, thereby covering five time periods starting in 1980 in ten-year increments. Not only do they not find a reduction in multiculturalist policies, their empirical analysis indicates that both at the individual as well as the state level, there is a positive relationship between support for multiculturalist policies and support for the welfare state. Moreover, they find that multiculturalist policies are not associated with welfare chauvinist behavior. In their own words, "it is time to lay the ghost of the progressive's dilemma to rest".

Maureen Eger and Joakim Kulin, however, disinter that very specter by examining attitudes about immigration and redistribution and associate them with voting behavior for Sweden, the United States, and Germany, paragons of social democratic, liberal, and conservative welfare states. Based on pooled, cross-sectional data from the European Social Survey and the General Social Survey, they find that attitudes consistent with this dilemma have been present in these countries for a long time. While the authors find that progressive attitudes are on the increase in both Germany and the United States, they conclude that only those on the very left in terms of support for immigration and redistribution can be counted on to also vote for left-wing parties.

Zoe Lefkofridi and Susanne Rhein similarly focus on the fate of social democratic parties (SDPs) as they negotiate the tension between redistribution and immigration which they term the "social democratic dilemma". They borrow Peter Mair's conceptual difference between responsiveness and responsibility; the former of which suggests that parties follow the desires of their electorate while the latter means that parties need to honor agreements that they have signed. SDPs, they argue, located in European Union (EU) countries are particularly challenged because EU regulation impedes independent welfare state policy making, as they are losing control over redistribution, an issue they traditionally "owned". This EU-imposed neo-liberal turn makes it more difficult for SDPs to produce a coherent policy stance as far as the rights of migrants to social benefits are concerned. Lefkofridi and Rhein suggest that as long as there are no transnational policies governing redistributive policies, SDPs will be hamstrung in effectively answering the redistribution-immigration tension.

Elif Naz Kayran and Melanie Kolbe also examine the role of institutions broadly understood and focus on whether welfare state institutions can mitigate the widely argued corrosive impact of diversity on trust. Their empirical argument based on nine waves of the European Social Survey initially finds that as the stock of immigrants increases, generalized trust decreases. They then turn their attention to a recently developed measure by Edward Koning, entitled the "Immigrant Exclusion to Social Programs Index" (IESPI). This index measures differential access to social benefits between native borns and immigrants and can be conceived of capturing the variation in "inclusive" or "exclusive" solidarity prevalent across countries. When Kayran and Kolbe statistically interact their diversity measure (percent stock of migrants) with the IESPI, they find that when countries treat migrants more equally with respect to access to social benefits, the negative impact of diversity on trust is significantly reduced.

Are varying levels of inequality and labor market integration, which are themselves resultants of welfare state institutions, systematically associated with more or less support for the welfare state? Similarly, could it be that poor labor market integration of immigrants might have a negative impact on welfare state support? Christel Kesler draws on a variety of data sources such as the International Social Survey Program, the Luxembourg Income Study, and the World Bank's World Development Indicator Database, among others. Applying a pooled cross-sectional, time series model consisting of 20 countries and 54 country years with a total of over 69,000 individuals, she concludes that while overall income inequality measured by the GINI coefficient does not matter much, labor market integration of immigrants in the host country matters. As numbers of immigrants rise and unemployment inequality between immigrants and native borns widens, public support for the welfare state declines. However, where labor market integration of immigrants is successful, larger numbers of immigrants do not affect public support for the welfare state highlighting the crucial role of policies focusing on immigrant integration.

Frida Boräng, Sara Kalm, and Johannes Lindvall identify three challenges in the literature on the nexus between welfare and migration: first, they argue that the differences between labor migration, asylum and refugee policy, as well as immigrant policy are so consequential that they need to be studied on their own terms. Second, they call for a more historically oriented approach since, in their view, the welfare state has co-evolved with migration policy. Third, precisely because the welfare state and migration policy have developed in tandem, they argue, it makes no sense to claim causal connections between migration and the welfare state or vice versa. They provide evidence that while welfare state generosity and openness is positively related for asylum and refugees, the association between welfare state generosity and policy openness is orthogonal for labor migrants. A similar relationship exists when policy openness is plotted over time: after the Second World War policy openness increased for asylum seekers and refugees but declined dramatically for labor migrants, particularly after the mid-1970s. They also remind readers of the rarely achieved high standards of causal inference in empirical studies and make a plea for the relevance of qualitative, historical accounts.

Part IV investigates the effects of contact between native borns and migrants and political culture on the association between welfare and migration. Would it make a difference whether there is more or less meaningful contact between migrants and native borns or whether either one of them is more or less trusting of the "other"? Hanna Kleider confronts the question by taking a broad approach and exploring whether cultural or economic anxieties drive opposition to migration. Her exercise of theory generation borrows concepts from social psychology as she delves into this hotly contested dichotomy of potential explanations. After laying out arguments for the plausibility of both, economic as well as cultural determinants of anti-immigrant attitudes, she concludes that it might be time to move beyond this twofold approach and locates new areas of research such as the role of political parties and various forms of media and their capacity to frame immigrant and welfare issues. Media framing effects could even affect what would otherwise be believed to be "individual-level" characteristics, such as education and religiosity. Moreover, what might be considered "independent" cultural and economic effects might be resultants of how immigrants and their supposed threat are socially constructed by the media, political entrepreneurs, and anybody else with the capacity to leave a public trace.

Hans-Georg Betz focuses on nativism, and, taking a historic view, concludes that over long stretches of time economic and cultural threats have long been employed by various political parties and leaders to gin up anti-immigrant attitudes. However, he argues that more recently economic grievances among the native borns have increased as a function of globalization and modernization which generates a section of the populace without the wherewithal to compete in this neo-liberal, market-driven environment. Combined with the decline of left-wing parties to secure their survival, this *precariat* is increasingly attracted to radical right-wing parties and their attendant media outlets that give voice to their grievances. From there, it is but a small step to make migrants responsible for their plight. According to Betz, nativist attitudes are triggered by four emotions: fear, anger, resentment, and shame – all of which play a crucial role in how sections of the populace are mobilized to support radical right-wing parties.

In a broad sweep, Eric Uslaner examines whether contact with strangers matters. This aptly called "contact theory", despite appearing quite intuitive at first glance, turns out to be rather complex. It may be self-evident that if natives actually knew and interacted with immigrants, they may develop a better sense of their challenges as immigrants or just simply recognize that they share the same joys and fears as the native borns and thus become more acceptant of migrants. But, what type of contact is necessary to trust strangers? Is any contact sufficient, or does it require sustained and meaningful interactions on an equal basis? Could the type of neighborhood, integrated or segregated, affect the degree of stereotype and prejudice? It appears that when people live in integrated neighborhoods they show less ethnic and racial prejudice than otherwise. A venerable literature pioneered by Robert Putnam has argued that trust emerges when people share common interests, such as bowling. Uslaner, however, argues that sharing a common interest is not enough in trusting others; it may be sufficient to tolerate others, but just simply sharing a similar hobby does not mean that others are accepted as part of one's "moral community". Uslaner argues that trust is acquired early in life during the formative years of socialization and, once established, does not vary much in later phases of life. Examining the correlates of trust, he finds that having various forms of interactions with strangers, having friends of different race and ethnicity, or frequency with which in-group and out-group members meet does not increase generalized trust.

Katerina Manevska, Roderick Sluiter, and Agnes Akkerman delve more deeply into the concept of "meaningful contact" and identify the workplace as a locus where meaningful contact might occur given that such interactions depend heavily on interdependence and cooperation, in addition to potentially developing an *esprit de corps* as "colleagues" work towards a common goal. Manevska et al. find that where there are native workers with more interethnic resources, i.e. trust and belief in reciprocity in an out-group co-worker, this tends to morph into general trust for *all* members of that same ethnic out-group in addition to generating more ethnic tolerance. Intriguingly, a further finding is that workplace interethnic ties affect ethnic tolerance at the extremes of the scale: examining changes over time, for those low on prejudice and who already had outside work ties and for those high on prejudice without interethnic ties, having workplace interethnic ties increased ethnic tolerance. Their findings highlight the importance of focusing on workplace dynamics and its importance in shaping interethnic tolerance.

Patti Lenard investigates how bridging trust between native borns and migrants can be constructed and focuses on ways to shape inclusive forms of national identity. Rejecting the idea that there is something inherent or essential to national groups, she emphasizes the functions that individuals and institutions can play in constructing the boundaries of the identity and the groups that define its members. Two "levers" might increase trust among native borns: inclusive welfare state policies and multicultural policies both of which would signal that immigrants are welcome and that efforts are being made to integrate them into their newly chosen society. As a third lever she suggests national identity shaping, meaning that central governments have unique ways to generate trust in an increasingly diverse society assuming that this is what central governments want to do. This national identity shaping could be achieved in four ways: via public pronouncements and declarations, via shaping of naturalization requirements, via educational curricula, and via the construction/reconstruction of national symbols.

Arno Van Hootegem, Koen Abts, and Bart Meuleman are searching for the roots of solidarity in multicultural societies and compare majority as well as minority views (established minorities of Turks and Moroccans) on critiques of the welfare state in Belgium. They focus on moral, economic, and social criticism for institutional arrangements that redistribute towards vulnerable target populations. Comparing minority with majority views on the welfare state should allow them to determine whether these two groups have similar or different attitudes about the role of redistributive schemes – views that could be relevant for bridging trust across different ethnic communities. They find that minorities indicate lower social and moral criticism of the welfare state compared to majorities, which may be explained by their larger dependence on it. Majority groups, however, indicated stronger criticism along the dimensions of egalitarianism, authoritarianism, and left-right placement than the minority groups. This suggests that this type of criticism of the welfare state is more concerned with ensuring market efficiency and the maintenance of neo-liberal arrangements, while also capturing concerns that the welfare state breeds passivity and deviance.

Finally, Part V of the *Handbook* reverses the emphasis from the impact of immigration in receiving countries to the consequences of emigration in sending countries. Recent years have revealed the enormous size of remittances that sending countries have received, far outpacing official development assistance although most recently, remittances have dropped as a result of the Covid-19 pandemic. In addition, migrant diasporas affect sending countries not only via financial resources, but also social and ideological ideas. Farid Makhlouf and Oussama Ben Atta ask whether remittances support or undermine economic growth in the Global South. Their econometric model suggests that remittances, when low, do not positively affect economic growth as such remittances flow directly into consumption rather than investment. However, when remittances exceed a certain threshold, they do significantly affect economic growth in the Global South via investments with long-term, growth-inducing effects.

Mohammad Moniruzzaman and Margaret Walton-Roberts, in a qualitative case study of Bangladesh, find that migrant remittances contribute to higher household income and as a result increase food security. In addition, they find that remittances increase a household's dietary diversity, which tends to lag during economic shocks. Thus, not only do remittances ensure access to food, but also to foods of higher nutritional value which positively affects health outcomes more generally. Finally, remittances also affect food consumption, i.e. the quantity of food that is available, guarding households against food-related shocks and rationing.

Could migration be conceived of as a development strategy in more general terms? Elizabeth Mavroudi examines this complex question by reprising a large amount of literature concluding that migration can have both positive and negative impacts on development outcomes. She argues for a "people-centered" approach recognizing the personal, embodied endeavor that migration entails while at the same time calling for a liberal migration regime that allows for migrants to circulate, i.e. more freely to come and go so as to maximize the impacts of migration on development.

Raúl Delgado Wise critically assesses the migration–development nexus by questioning the, what he calls, "almost sacrosanct belief that migration contributes to the country of origin". He questions the neo-liberal, market-oriented migration policies and their supposed effects on development, and offers, among other contributions, a counter-hegemonic, southern development perspective based on a dialectical, rather than unidirectional, relationship between migration and development. Highlighting global inequality, the continuing unequal development between the Global North and South, human rights infringements of migrants in both the Global North and South, he calls for an international migration regime with the United States as a signatory which, alas, has not happened hitherto. Ultimately, according to Delgado Wise, it is critical to tackle the uneven power relationships between the Global North and South that characterize the world capitalist system, requiring a drastic rethink of the connections between development and migration with an attendant turn from a neo-liberal to a post-liberal perspective.

FROM SEEING TREES TO ENVISIONING FORESTS: IN SEARCH OF PATTERNS

Reading these 26 outstanding contributions it is easy to miss the forest for the trees. What contours do emerge from this collection of chapters? Is it possible to identify patterns, similarities, and contradictions among the chapters? Looking for such patterns is a perilous endeavor, and this is not the place to exhaustively distinguish between agency, structures, cultures, institutions, policies, and methods of inquiry.

However, it appears that when migrants impinge on the welfare state, individually held attitudes, whatever they are, are not necessarily determinative of political outcomes. A number of chapters have highlighted the role of purposive agency in shaping such outcomes via multiculturalism policies and labor market integration policies, allowing more equal access to social benefits to migrants, and extending increased rights to migrants more generally. Such policies tend to bend the needle more towards broader acceptance of migrants than when they are absent.

Another pattern that emerges is the role of education. In a number of contributions, the socioeconomic status of individuals systematically affects their attitudes towards migrants. Specifically, higher-educated individuals tend to have more solidaristic attitudes vis à vis migrants than lower-educated ones. The reason may be that they are less exposed to resource competition from migrants or perhaps they are more sophisticated in giving socially desirable answers to queries tapping issues of nativism or xenophobia.

Structural constraints appear in the form of concerns that extending the fruits of the welfare state to migrants might undermine the efficient functioning of capitalist markets which may in some cases be mistaken as nativism or welfare chauvinism. When examining the impact of emigration on national development strategies, neo-liberal global economic policies are seen as the central obstacle to establishing fairer migration regimes. Constraints also appear in the form of the role the EU plays in restricting the extent to which member states can establish more or less generous welfare states.

Other contributions have zeroed in, some more directly than others, on the role of how politicians, political parties, and their associated media outlets frame the relationship between natives and migrants, suggesting that there is room for socially constructing and shaping this relationship. Such constructions can take various forms generating sentiments among natives ranging from perceiving that migrants are committed members of society to the generation of nativist attitudes. Echoing Heisenberg, that what we observe is a function of our method of questioning, a number of contributions plead for more qualitative, descriptive approaches to the nexus of migration and welfare on account of their conceptual complexity.

The prominent political scientist Karl Deutsch once remarked that "truth lies at the confluence of different streams of evidence", suggesting that when a variety of types of data, and measured at different levels, such as individual-level data, cross-national data,

data collected over time, or even a combination, so-called pooled cross-sectional/time series data point in a similar direction, that the probability of an association between two variables increases. Despite measuring the "progressive's dilemma" with different data and measured at different levels, the relevant chapters in this *Handbook* indicate a lack of consensus as to whether it is possible to have a generous welfare state and liberal immigration policies at the same time. It appears that rumors of the death of the progressive's dilemma are exaggerated. Solving this conundrum with creative theoretical and empirical approaches will keep social scientists busy for the foreseeable future.

Finally, in addition to the factors laid out above, historical constraints such as whether natives believe theirs is a country of immigration or emigration and the long arc of a history of racism and nativism are likely to shape the degree to which native borns consider newcomers as part of their broader moral orbit and whether they are "worthy" receivers of social benefits. It is not set in stone that immigration and a generous welfare state are incompatible as this association is subject to ongoing political contestation. Whether native borns are willing and capable of transcending racial, ethnic, religious, and other differences is a function of their socioeconomic status, variations in institutions, of structural constraints, and the role of political entrepreneurs and their media outlets. Finally, it will require leadership and political will to craft policies to help native borns in recognizing migrants not as "others" but as part of their extended, moral community, but only if this corresponds to the wishes of the government and the people.

PART I

TAKING STOCK: MIGRATION AND THE STATE OF THE WELFARE STATE

1. Managing migration in modern welfare states: One-size policy does not fit all
Pieter Bevelander and James F. Hollifield

INTRODUCTION

International migration and mobility have been steadily increasing since the end of the Second World War.[1] According to United Nations (UN) data, in 2019 approximately 272 million people resided outside of their country of birth for one year or more (barely 3.5 percent of the world's population). Even at the height of the post-war liberal order in the 1980s and 1990s (Hollifield 1992, 2012), emigration remained the exception, not the rule. Until the global pandemic of 2020, tens of millions of people crossed borders on a daily basis, which added up to roughly 2 billion border crossings per year. Human mobility was part of a broader trend of globalization, including trade in goods and services, investments and capital flows, greater ease of travel, and a veritable explosion of information.

Even though the number of international migrants remains relatively low and manageable (at least in the Organisation for Economic Co-operation and Development (OECD) world), migrant flows add up over time and foreign populations have increased in many countries throughout the global north and the global south (Hollifield and Foley 2021). The challenge of "managing migration" has shifted somewhat from issues of immigration control to immigrant integration, and debates about the economic performance and integration of different categories of migrants have intensified. The pace of integration of first-generation immigrants varies widely and states have pursued a range of policies from the most active labor market and welfare policies in Scandinavia to more market-driven, laissez-faire policies in the United States (US).

How immigration affects the social contract and social cohesion in liberal societies is the focus of intense scholarly debate (Brettell and Hollifield forthcoming), and the question of whether welfare states can sustain relatively open immigration and generous asylum policies is at the forefront of political debates. Does the welfare state act as a magnet drawing low-skilled migrants and asylum seekers from the poorer countries of the global south? Are migrants a burden on public finances and will immigration undermine the viability of welfare systems, forcing governments to roll back migrant rights and restrict access to public services? Is there a trade-off between markets (numbers of migrants) and rights (Ruhs 2013)? Rights here can refer to the most basic employment and labor rights, guaranteed in UN and International Labour Organization Conventions (equal pay, work-related benefits, protections against discrimination), as well as more expansive economic and social rights associated with the modern welfare state (access to education, health care, unemployment insurance, social security, and the like). To complete the "Marshallian trilogy" (Marshall 1964), one would expect migrants to be granted basic civil rights (such as due process and equal protection) and as they settle they would acquire political rights as well (Hollifield 2000). However, these "core rights" are more closely associated with naturalization and citizenship, the rules for which will vary from one country to another (Hollifield 2021). This chapter seeks to address these questions about migration and the welfare state from a comparative, historical, and empirical perspective, exploring competing arguments about the relationship between "rights and markets," reviewing strategies for migration management and integration of first-generation immigrants, and offering some policy conclusions about best practices for migration management in modern welfare states.

It would be wise to define upfront what we mean by the *modern welfare state*, which implies high social transfers and public expenditures on such things as health care, pensions, family assistance, unemployment compensation, active labor market spending, and public housing subsidies, among others, as defined by the OECD (see for example, Garfinkel et al. 2010).

One could debate at what level of public expenditures a state qualifies as a "welfare state," but the generally accepted view is when public expenditures exceed 20 percent of gross domestic product (GDP), and should this include spending on public education, for example? Since 1945, about a dozen OECD countries have devoted more than a fifth of their GDP to social transfers, and this number creeps up to a fourth if we include spending on public education. By this measure, the top welfare states in the OECD are, in order of rank, France, Sweden, Austria, Belgium, Denmark, Germany, Finland, Italy, Portugal, and Spain, with Norway, the Netherlands, and the United Kingdom (UK) on the edge of the envelope—all Western European states. By most accounts, the US welfare state is much smaller and policies are radically different from the European social democracies, making comparisons difficult (again Garfinkel et al. 2010; Alesina et al. 2001).

A large body of literature exists on the economics of welfare states and the presumed threats posed by high levels of public expenditures, threats that can be real or imagined. Reviewing the findings of this literature is beyond the scope of this chapter, but we should outline the threats to the viability of welfare states and explain where migration fits into arguments about the sustainability of high levels of public spending and social transfers. Probably the most commonly perceived "threat" to the welfare state is that high levels of social transfers undermine GDP and national income, but economic historians have not been able to find consistent negative effects of welfare spending on the level and growth of GDP (for a review see Lindert 2004). Likewise, there is a concern that high public expenditures, especially for pensions, will lead inevitably to a crisis in public finances as the costs of the welfare state exceed national income and the tax base shrinks. But here again the evidence does not support the argument, as welfare states in Northern Europe have maintained relatively balanced budgets, high levels of economic growth, and lower levels of national debt than states in Southern Europe where public expenditures have undermined public finances. This begs the question, however, why welfare states in Northern Europe are more economically viable than in Southern Europe. Some of the difference can be attributed to the way in which labor markets function in these different regions. Southern European countries have much larger informal economies and segmented or dual labor markets, which reduce the tax base—Greece and Italy are prime examples—whereas fiscal policy is sounder in the countries of Northern Europe.

One of the biggest threats to the viability of welfare states is demographic (aging populations) and migration often is touted as a solution to this problem (Bonin et al. 2000). At the same time migration can be seen as a threat to welfare states because it undermines the legitimacy of social transfers (Freeman 1986) and migration can lead to distributional conflicts and to a political backlash that can weaken the consensus that sustains the welfare state (Facchini and Mayda 2009, 2012); there is a lot of sub-national variation in the backlash, as Money (1999) has shown. Setting aside for the moment the effects of migration on public finances—to be discussed below—by far the biggest threat to the viability of the welfare state is demographic, namely the rapid aging of populations in highly developed welfare states and the rise in the *dependency ratio* of the elderly to the working age population. This trend is especially marked in East Asia, Japan and South Korea for example, and in Europe where Italy and Spain stand out; but no country in the OECD world is immune to the effects of aging and the strains that it places on the welfare state, pension and health-care systems, and on public finances. Until the pandemic of 2020–21, life expectancies were rising in most OECD countries. As pensions for the elderly increase, so does the share of GDP devoted to this segment of the population, which is no longer productive and unable to contribute to financing the welfare state. The only long-term solutions are to raise the age of retirement, increase taxes on the working-age population, and/or to cut pensions and health care for the elderly.

A substantial literature in economics shows that immigration can, under certain circumstances, alleviate the pressure on welfare states, specifically pension systems (Razin and Sadka 1999, 2000; Rowthorn 2008). But the fiscal effects of immigration and whether or not it improves the dependency ratio depend on the mix of migrants (skilled versus unskilled migrants, temporary versus permanent, worker versus family and humanitarian migration, older versus younger migrants, etc.). Moreover, to alter the dependency ratio, levels of immigration would have to be quite large, which is a political non-starter for most countries. Most studies of the fiscal consequences of immigration focus only on first-generation immigrants, but obviously the earnings and contributions of the second generation are key to understanding the long-term costs and benefits of immigration (see NAS 2017; Qi and Bevelander forthcoming, for example). However, the bottom line is that using immigration to manage the age pyramid, to change the dependency ratio, and to alleviate fiscal pressures on pension and health-care systems is not feasible in the short term (Blanchet 1988). We argue that rapid integration of first-generation immigrants into the society and economy is the key to long-term, positive outcomes with respect to immigration, the economy, and the welfare state.

In this respect, slow-moving economic integration by certain categories of migrants (legal categories range from skilled and unskilled workers to accompanying family members, humanitarian migrants, foreign students, and free-movers in the European Union (EU), see Figure 1.1) in recent decades has put pressure on governments to support the labor market and social inclusion of immigrants to maximize the benefits and reduce the costs of immigration and refugee policies. Better labor market integration is beneficial since it allows migrants to contribute to the welfare system through taxes and bring new skills and human capital to the host societies. Improved integration of migrants also helps to reduce the popular backlash against immigrants and refugees and to maintain the legitimacy of immigration policy in general. In the long term, rights remain the key to migration management in liberal and social democracies (Hollifield 1992, 2000, 2021).

To "set the scene" we begin the chapter with an overview of migration trends in the major receiving countries, including forced or refugee migration, with a focus on

16   *Handbook on migration and welfare*

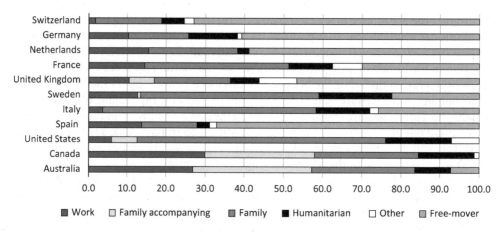

Source: Based on OECD (2020), supplementary tables and figures.

Figure 1.1   Percentage of permanent flows to selected OECD countries, 2018

employment of migrants (as a key indicator of integration) and the factors that affect labor market integration of immigrants and refugees in the host societies. We look next at the fiscal impact of first-generation immigrants before developing a comparison of labor market and social inclusion programs that are designed by receiving countries to enhance the integration of first-generation migrants. Finally, we explore *four national models of migration management* in welfare states to illustrate the policy dilemmas that all receiving countries must face, including the challenges of delivering public services to migrants granted protection under the 1951 Geneva Convention for the Protection of Refugees.

WHAT ARE THE NUMBERS? IMMIGRATION IN THE OECD

According to the latest OECD 2020 International Migration Outlook (OECD 2020), flows of permanent migrants were rising from 2009 until 2016 before levelling off, with about 5.3 million new immigrants arriving to the OECD (see Figure 1.1 for selected countries and intake categories). The top five receiving countries in the OECD in absolute numbers are (in order) the US, Germany, Spain, the UK, and Canada. As for the types of migration flows, the number one category of permanent immigrants in the OECD is family reunion migrants, who make up about 35 percent of all permanent migrants in 2018, and the US is the main destination for this category of migrants. Free-movers in the EU are the second largest category of migrants in the OECD, accounting for 28 percent of migrants in the UK, which until Brexit was a major destination for internal EU migrants. Labor migrants and humanitarian migrants are a far smaller percentage of total immigration, making up 13 and 11 percent, respectively, in 2018, although as we shall see refugees and asylum seekers are more prominent in some highly developed welfare states, and they pose the biggest integration challenge.

Managing migration in modern welfare states 17

As for refugees and forced migration generally, including asylum seekers, the number has fluctuated over the last decades with peaks in asylum seeking in Europe in the early 1990s—when Yugoslavia broke apart—and again in the 2010s with a spike in 2015/16 due to the Syrian civil war and other conflicts in the crescent of instability from the Sahel to South Asia.

A different picture emerges when we calculate the average number of immigrants as a percentage of the total population for the period 2010–18. We find that five small countries in Europe are at the top of the list, whereas a number of traditional so-called immigration countries (Hollifield et al. forthcoming), like the US, the UK, and Israel, have a lower percentage of immigrant intake than the OECD average (Figure 1.2).

Apart from the OECD, another source for migration flows is Eurostat statistics. According to the latest Eurostat reports[2] on migration and migrant population statistics, approximately 2.4 million immigrants moved from non-EU countries to the EU in 2018. In the same period 1.1 million left the EU for a non-EU country, while 1.4 million individuals moved between EU countries. Germany reported the largest number of immigrants with 894,000, followed by Spain with 644,000, France 387,000, and Italy 332,000. Only five EU member states—Bulgaria, Croatia, Latvia, Lithuania, and Romania—experienced net outmigration, mostly emigration by nationals of these states to other EU countries.

A breakdown of the types of residency permits issued, such as family reunions, education (foreign students), employment, or other, shows that in 2019 almost 1.2 million permits were issued for employment, roughly 810,000 for family reasons, and over 400,000 for education-related reasons. Finally, about 546,000 permits were issued for other reasons.[3] Issuance of first-time residency permits by EU countries was stable during the period 2008–17. Permits issued for employment, on the other hand, have been increasing since 2012, reaching a peak of almost 1.2 million in 2019. An outlier among EU states, Poland issued about half of all residence permits for employment with 625,000 permits

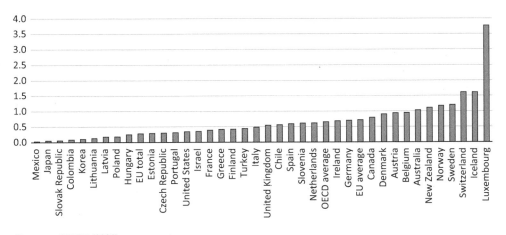

Source: OECD (2020).

Figure 1.2   *Permanent migrants to OECD countries (average percentage of the total population, 2010–18)*

for Ukraine, the non-EU country that received the highest number of residency permits during this period (25.6 percent of the total for all third-country nationals).

A significant share of the migration flow into the OECD countries in the 2010s consists of asylum seekers who subsequently gain access (or not) to temporary or permanent residency, depending on adjudication of the asylum request. According to Eurostat statistics,[4] asylum applications fell from 655,000 applications in 2017 to 581,000 in 2018 and went up again to 676,000 in 2019. This was a decline from the peak years of 2015 and 2016 (Figure 1.3). The main reason for this decline was a drop in the number of applications from Syria and Nigeria.

However one enumerates and breaks down the flows of migrants, it is important to keep in mind that the share of foreign born in the population of most of the OECD countries has increased over the last two decades (Figure 1.4; also Hollifield et al. forthcoming). The increase in foreign populations raises many questions about migration management and the capacity of host societies to integrate newcomers in light of the rise in reactionary populism, nativism, and xenophobia, as reflected in the emergence of anti-immigrant parties in many erstwhile liberal democracies, especially in the UK and the US (Norris and Inglehart 2019).

The US labor economist, George Borjas (1990, 1999b), famously argued that welfare services act as a powerful pull factor (a magnet), which in turn affects the propensity for individuals to emigrate. In Borjas's original formulation of this argument, before the rise of the welfare state, individuals self-selected and they chose to emigrate on the basis of their skills and chances for finding gainful employment. However, following the development of welfare states and the advent of generous social policies in the principal receiving countries after 1945, even migrants with low levels of human and social capital were willing to risk the move, confident that they would be cared for by the host society should they fail to find gainful employment. Poor selection would in turn lower the long-term earnings potential of immigrants and their children.[5] Even before Borjas, the political scientist Gary Freeman (1986) argued that the logic of the modern welfare state is one of

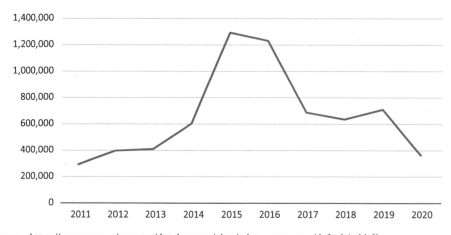

Source: https://ec.europa.eu/eurostat/databrowser/view/migr_asyappctza/default/table?lang=en

Figure 1.3 Number of asylum seekers to EU 27, 2011–20

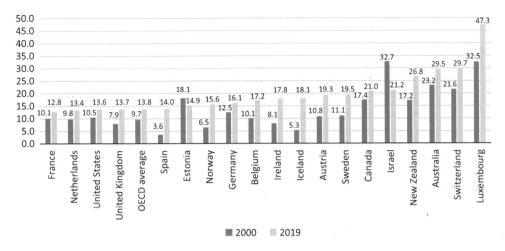

Source: OECD (2020).

Figure 1.4 Share of the foreign born in the total population of OECD countries, 2000 and 2019 (19 largest and OECD average)

closure and that large-scale immigration will ruin public finances, bankrupt social services, and undermine the legitimacy of the welfare state itself (cf. Bommes and Halfmann 1998; Bommes and Geddes 2000). A logical extension of these arguments about "magnets and burdens" is to ask whether there is a trade-off between rights and numbers (markets), as Martin Ruhs (2013) argues. Countries can sustain high levels of migration only if they restrict the rights of migrants and do not allow them access to social services, like the countries of the Persian Gulf, for example (Thiollet 2021). The corollary is that countries with high levels of immigration must restrict rights, and countries with expansive welfare policies must have low levels of immigration. We explore these arguments further below.

Looking at trends in different types (categories) of migration and welfare provisions (rights granted to foreign residents) in the principal receiving states, we must keep in mind that there is a wide range of country-specific work programs to help employers recruit foreign workers. Granting of work and permanent residency permits has the purpose of allowing migrants to integrate and eventually to settle in a new country. As a result, permanent labor migrants contribute upfront to the welfare and social security system in the host country so long as they are employed and paying taxes. It is therefore less controversial that labor migrants have social rights and access to welfare services when they lose their jobs, get sick, or retire. Temporary labor migration, posted (contract), and seasonal workers also contribute to GDP growth and (in liberal and social democracies) they pay taxes directly upon being employed (or posted abroad). Given the nature of temporary employment, most guest workers have fewer benefits and are therefore net contributors to the public finances of the host society, since they come only to work and are unlikely to end up on welfare (Richter 2004). Asylum seekers, who are successful and granted refugee status, either on a temporary or permanent basis, must find employment like any other resident of the receiving country, similar to family reunion migrants who have been admitted and allowed to settle in the host country. Both refugees and family migrants may have equal access to welfare services as soon as they obtain permanent residency in most receiving states although a large variation exists among OECD countries (Thränhardt et al. 2020; Hollifield et al. forthcoming).[6] In looking at the numbers and the gradual shift in the composition of migrant flows and stocks in Europe over time, it is important to keep in mind that many social democracies, like Germany, the Netherlands, and the Scandinavian countries, made a rather dramatic transition from guest worker programs in the 1960s and 1970s to family reunification migrants, refugees, and asylum seekers in the 1980s and 1990s—a trend that has accelerated in the first decades of the twenty-first century. As we shall see, it takes longer for these new migrants, who are not entering as workers, to integrate and to join the labor market. By the same token, the absence of integration policies and lack of social support for immigrants in the US can accelerate employment and labor market integration of first-generation immigrants, compared to Europe (Santel and Hollifield 1998; Orrenius and Zavodny 2012).

The question we explore in this chapter is whether host societies with strong welfare systems can absorb first-generation immigrants, especially those who are not entering as workers. To what extent and how fast are the newcomers able to enter the labor market and at what point do the migrants acquire rights and begin to contribute to the welfare system through taxes? This will allow us to compare rates of integration in the major receiving countries of the OECD. First, however, we review arguments about the effects of immigration on the social contract in modern welfare states.

COMPETING PERSPECTIVES ON MIGRATION AND THE MODERN WELFARE STATE

Gary Freeman (1986) famously posited that the modern welfare state cannot sustain large-scale immigration. In order to maintain the legitimacy of the welfare state, immigration must be kept to a minimum because the logic of welfare systems is one of closure. As summarized above, high levels of immigration will undermine public finances and weaken support for the welfare state among the native population, destroying the normative consensus for social rights and making it impossible to provide public and social goods associated with welfare systems. "When the welfare state is seen as something for 'them' paid by 'us,' its days as a consensual solution to societal problems are numbered" (Freeman 1986: 62). In a similar vein, Robert Putnam argued that diversity undermines trust and is detrimental to civil society. Putnam (2007; cf. Janoski 1998; Hollifield 1999, 2000, 2021) however went on to say that this threat to civil society is a short-term problem and that in the long-term "successful immigrant societies have overcome such fragmentation by creating new, cross-cutting forms of social solidarity and more encompassing identities."

Arguments like this about the relationship between migration, the welfare state, and civil society fall roughly into four categories (Brochmann forthcoming). The *first school of thought* revolves around the issue of economic sustainability following Borjas (1990, 1999b) and Freeman (1986) who argue that *immigration is a burden* for the welfare state. The normative side of this argument can be found in *Spheres of Justice*, where the political theorist Michael Walzer lays out a communitarian argument against open immigration based on "the idea of distributive justice [which] presupposes a bounded world within which distributions take place: a group of people committed to dividing, exchanging and sharing social goods, first of all among themselves" (Walzer 1983: 31). Echoing Walzer, the social theorist, Christian Joppke, in characteristic fashion, puts it more bluntly: "Because rights are costly, they cannot be for everybody" (Joppke 1999: 6). Another political theorist, Seyla Benhabib (2002) advanced the notion of bounded universalism whereby redistributive policies depend on restricted access to welfare.

A *second group of scholars*, following Putnam, insists that "social cohesion" requires ethnic homogeneity. In this school of thought, the diversity that comes with immigration will weaken the normative consensus required to sustain redistributive policies, thereby undermining the foundation of welfare states especially in the Nordic and Scandinavian countries where the social contract revolves around "reciprocity norms" (Alesina and Glaeser 2004; Goodhart 2004).

A *third school* takes issue with the "social cohesion" thesis and the idea that ethnic diversity undermines civil society. Keith Banting and Will Kymlicka find little empirical support for the social cohesion thesis, and they argue that the modern welfare state has the capacity to manage the social and economic costs associated with higher levels of immigration and cultural diversity (Banting and Kymlicka 2006). Markus M.L. Crepaz (2008) also disagrees with the "social cohesion" thesis. He places emphasis on the role of institutions that shape the integration of immigrant populations in welfare states. Crepaz compares the US and Europe, pointing out that the US was a racially divided society when it developed a (relatively weak) welfare state during the New Deal period of the 1930s and again during the Great Society of the 1960s, while in Europe strong welfare states were fully developed and institutionalized long before the waves of post-war immigration (cf. Ellermann 2021). Crepaz disagrees with Freeman and Putnam, stressing that European welfare states are built on a strong institutionalized consensus and are thereby capable of managing diversity, with the capacity to integrate newcomers and make the social investments necessary for a smooth transition to more ethnically diverse societies. Grete Brochmann (forthcoming) agrees with Crepaz that Scandinavian welfare states have the ability to educate and socialize "newcomers through equal treatment and extension of social rights ... to counteract the problems related to low skilled and culturally different immigrants."

A *fourth perspective* extends the social cohesion thesis. Ruud Koopmans (2010, p. 3) finds a fundamental incompatibility between welfare states and multiculturalism, arguing that immigrants do not integrate in welfare states that offer many benefits while promoting multicultural policies, "which do not provide strong incentives for host-country language acquisition and for interethnic contacts." In these instances, according to Koopmans, immigrants end up marginalized in ethnic ghettos or enclaves and they become dependent on welfare handouts. Koopmans hypothesizes that dependence on the dole leads to lower levels of employment, segregation, and increased levels of criminal activity. This school of thought blames multiculturalism and the welfare state for lack of immigrant integration with poor outcomes for migrants and for society as a whole— similar to the argument about segmented assimilation in the US (cf. Portes and Rumbaut 2006) but with radically different policy recommendations. Bloemraad and Wright (2012) test the thesis that multicultural policies inhibit socio-political integration of first-generation immigrants and they find no empirical support for this argument.

Policy debates about migration and the welfare state revolve around these four theoretical perspectives, with those favoring greater restriction relying on the argument that there is a harsh trade-off between numbers and rights (see Ruhs 2013 and for a list of rights associated with migrant integration see Migrant Integration Policy Index (MIPEX), Figure 1.9 in this chapter; Hollifield 2000, 2021) and that welfare dependency hurts immigrant integration. Those supporting liberal immigration and refugee policies contend that the modern welfare state is robust enough to manage more migration and greater diversity and that granting social rights to migrants leads to higher levels of integration and better labor market outcomes (Crepaz 2008; Bevelander 2020; cf. Santel and Hollifield 1998). Restrictionists also worry about the burden that immigration poses for the public purse. Following Borjas (1985, 1990, 1999b) they argue that immigrants lack the skills necessary to succeed in modern, knowledge-based economies and therefore they will be a drag on public finances (cf. Borjas and Friedberg 2009).

OECD data on native- and foreign-born employment rates reveal that immigrants in states with strong welfare systems, like Sweden and Denmark, have worse labor market outcomes, lending support to those who see incompatibility between high numbers of (low-skilled) migrants and generous welfare services. MIPEX (see Figure 1.9) places Sweden at the top of OECD countries with extensive social and economic rights for migrants, putting Sweden and Scandinavian social democracies in the spotlight and raising questions about social rights and how they affect immigrant integration in modern welfare states. Do rights promote or inhibit immigrant integration? To address this and other questions, we must ask which welfare states have been most successful in managing migration and integrating migrants in the long term. Does immigration undermine support for social policy and the welfare state itself?

IMMIGRATION AND LABOR MARKETS: ECONOMIC MIGRANTS AND REFUGEES

One of the key indicators of immigrant integration is the employment rate of the foreign born and how it compares to that of the native born. Many social democracies in Europe have migrant integration policies and for them the employment rate of immigrants is a crude indicator of the effectiveness of integration programs and policies. Measures of the native- and foreign-born employment rates indicate that in almost 70 percent of OECD countries natives have a higher level of employment than foreigners (Figures 1.5 and 1.6). The welfare states of Northern and Western Europe, such as the Netherlands, Belgium, Austria, Germany, and France, have negative employment gaps of over 5 percent and in the case of Sweden and the Netherlands the gap is over 10 percent. Similarly, Mexico records a substantial negative employment gap between natives and the foreign born; but such data for emerging market countries must be taken with a grain of salt because of the large informal sector, which leads to an underestimate of the rate of employment of the foreign born (Hazán 2021). Israel, Luxembourg, and Portugal, as well as Eastern European countries like Poland, Hungary, and the Czech and Slovak Republics show stronger rates of employment among the foreign born. Looking in more detail at the EU countries in 2019, we find a native–migrant employment gap of 6.2 percent overall,

Managing migration in modern welfare states 23

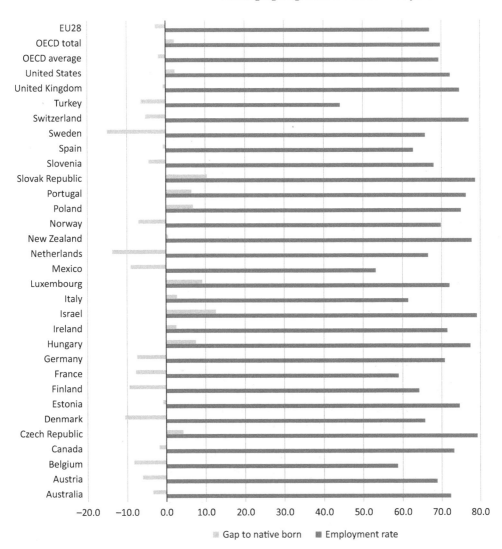

Source: OECD (2020).

Figure 1.5 Employment rate of foreign born and employment gap to native born, 2019

2.4 percent for males, and 8.8 percent for females. However, when we divide the foreign-born group into EU born versus non-EU born, EU-born males and females have higher employment rates than native-born males and females (see Figure 1.6 for selected EU countries). This shows that non-EU born have substantially lower employment rates than both native-born and EU-born migrants. The overall employment gap between native and foreign born is due primarily to the low employment level of non-EU-born men and women (again see Figure 1.6).[7]

24 *Handbook on migration and welfare*

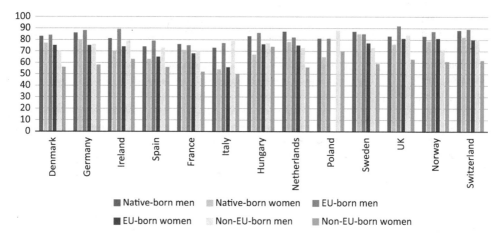

Source: Eurostat (online data code: lfsa_ergacob).

Figure 1.6 Employment rates by country of birth and sex, 2019 (population aged 20–64, selected countries)

Moreover, in the EU the smallest gender employment gap was measured for the native born in 2019 at 10.6 percent. For immigrants from other EU countries this gap is 13.7 percent and for non-EU immigrants the gap is 19.7.[8]

Looking at these descriptive statistics, we can identify four clusters of EU countries with similar employment gaps between natives and migrants: (1) countries with a native–migrant employment gap between 15 and 20 percent have experienced high levels of refugee migration and asylum seeking, mostly advanced welfare states; (2) countries with a long history of immigration have a native–migrant employment gap between 10 and 15 percent; (3) in more recent immigration countries, there is no native–migrant employment gap, or (in most cases) the rate favors the foreign born; and (4) countries with significant migration from neighboring countries have no employment gap between native and foreign born (Grubanov-Boskovic et al. 2017; see Figure 1.7).[9]

A key limitation of these descriptive statistics on employment and other indicators of immigrant integration is that they are at a high aggregate level, and often they do not distinguish between the arrival context and policy designs, including admission status, educational level, or how long the immigrant has been in the country, all key factors for successful labor market integration. As a result, the aggregate data give a misleading picture of the integration of individual migrants and how they and the national or ethnic groups to which they belong fare in the labor market over time.

Figure 1.8 is an example of how employment integration changes for cohorts of refugee groups compared to family reunification migrants and labor migrants in the Swedish labor market. The figure shows both the employment rate over time for male and female immigrants and it illustrates that, independently of legal category and gender, employment levels increase with more years in the country. A further breakdown by country of birth is made in Bevelander and Luik (2020) and shows significant heterogeneity between the labor market integration of refugees of men and women by group.

Managing migration in modern welfare states 25

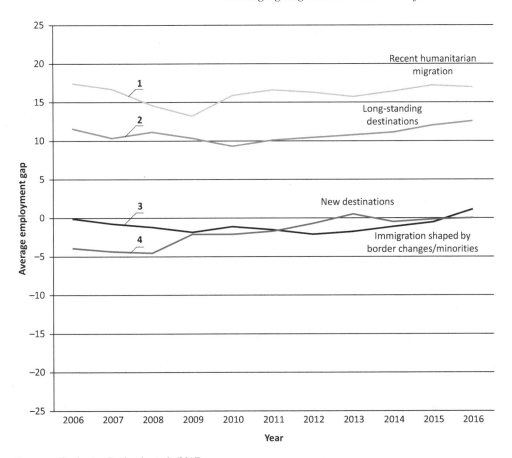

Source: Grubanov-Boskovic et al. (2017).

Figure 1.7 Trends in the native–foreign employment rate gaps for different categories of EU member states, 2006–16

However, just as in Figure 1.8, Bevelander and Luik (2020) show employment levels rise for all migrant groups in Sweden over time. For men from Bosnia, Ethiopia, and Eritrea, employment growth plateaus approximately six years after migration. For women from Bosnia, Ethiopia, and Eritrea the plateau is reached about 8 to 12 years after arrival in the country. Among the men, only male Bosnian refugees show a decline in employment rates after seven years. The same pattern can be observed for Syrians, who start at a lower rate of employment. For male refugees from Iraq, Iran, and Afghanistan, growth is slower but continuous over the 12-year period. For Somalis employment stagnates after two to four years in the country. Women from Afghanistan, Iran, Iraq, Somalia, and Syria have very low employment rates in the first years after migration but the rates increase significantly with more years in the country. Migrants in the Netherlands exhibit similar heterogeneous employment rates (De Vroome and van Tubergen 2010; Bakker et al. 2013), and the same is true for Denmark (Schultz-Nielsen 2017) and Norway (Bratsberg et al. 2017).

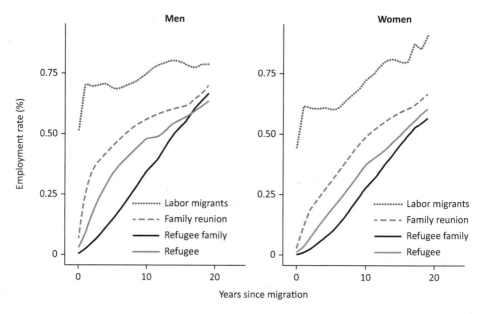

Source: Authors' own calculations based on register data for the years 1997–2016, Statistics Sweden (www.scb.se/en/).

Figure 1.8 Mean employment rate of men/women since first migration, Sweden

In summary, varying employment patterns across migrant groups in EU member states underscore the highly complex process of migrant inclusion in the labor market and other societal domains, especially when we take the fate of asylum seekers and refugees into account. This complexity presents challenges for policy makers working to improve integration and shows that it is hard to generalize about the "migrant experience" across cohorts, in different national contexts, and to discern the relationship between immigration, (employment) rights, integration, and the welfare state. In short, one-size policies do not fit all and broad generalizations about migration and welfare states (see for example Borjas, various works, and Ruhs 2013) can be highly misleading.

UNDERSTANDING THE COMPLEX PROCESS OF IMMIGRANT INTEGRATION IN WELFARE STATES

From an economic perspective, labor market integration of migrants can be influenced by supply-side factors such as migrant skills and qualifications or by the opportunities and restrictions on the demand side, such as the needs of the labor market (for skills), which must be understood in conjunction with migration and integration policies in the receiving country. One of the standard assumptions in the economics of migration is that migrants are favorably self-selected[10] on the basis of their skills, education, age, health, and other traits (Chiswick 1978; Razin and Sadka 2000; Orrenius and Zavodny 2012). When compared to migrants who have been selected on the basis of their skills and qualifications, non-economic migrants, such as family reunion migrants, refugees, and asylum seekers, do not "self-select," which leaves them in a more vulnerable position in the labor markets of host societies (Chiswick 2008; Becker and Ferrara 2019; Chin and Cortes 2015). A key takeaway from these works is that forced migrants present a bigger integration challenge for all states, but especially for welfare states, with fewer low-skilled, entry-level jobs as well as relatively low wage dispersion and/or high minimum wage levels. These countries are attractive for their high living standards and welfare policies but have fewer labor market entry opportunities for newcomers, especially for asylum seekers and refugees (Thränhardt et al. 2020).

Studies in the US (Connor 2010), Canada (Aydemir 2011), the UK (Bloch 2007), the Netherlands (De Vroome and van Tubergen 2010; Bakker et al. 2013), Denmark (Schultz-Nielsen 2017), Norway (Bratsberg et al. 2017), and Sweden (Bevelander and Pendakur 2014) seek to understand the integration of refugees in national labor markets. The findings of these scholars show that, compared to other migrant categories, refugees generally have lower employment rates, especially upon their arrival in the host country. For this reason, many countries, including even the US, have integration policies designed to enhance the entry of refugees into labor markets. Surprisingly, these refugee integration policies have been scarcely evaluated in the scientific literature (Martín et al. 2016; Becker and Ferrara 2019). Refugees arrive under difficult circumstances with few resources and little social capital. Most do not migrate for economic reasons. They are admitted according to other (non-economic) criteria. Clearly, the handicaps associated with forced migration affect the rate and success of refugee integration into the labor market of the host society. Moreover, as both the migration and the admission processes can be lengthy and cumbersome, health issues and the loss of human (and social) capital can hinder individuals' adaptation to the labor market of their new country (Dustmann et al. 2017). Likewise, whether refugees and family migrants obtain permanent or temporary residence creates uncertainty about the future. This uncertainty can affect the investment by migrants in the host-country language, and whether migrants are able to obtain country-specific human capital, which in turn affects the entire labor market integration process (Hainmueller et al. 2016).

Detailed surveys of immigrants find a close relationship between migrant admission categories and economic outcomes. In the case of the Netherlands, De Vroome and van Tubergen (2010) found that host country-specific education, work experience, language proficiency, and contacts with natives were correlated positively with employment outcomes and occupational status. In another study of immigration in the Netherlands, Bakker et al. (2013) showed that post-migration stress or trauma affects the rate of labor market integration. Survey data for the UK also point to the fact that restricting refugees' access to the labor market reduces life chances and has a negative impact on the earnings and long-term employment potential of forced migrants (Bloch 2007).

For Canada, Aydemir (2011) estimates that refugees have lower labor market participation rates than family reunion migrants, but that their earnings are about the same. Assessments of economic outcomes for refugees in the US show that they have lower earnings than other types of migrants, but the difference can be explained partially by variation in language ability, levels of education and family support, mental health, and residential segregation. Some variation in economic and labor market outcomes remains to be explained, however, even after controlling for these factors (Connor 2010). Studies of forced migrants in Norway and Denmark show that refugees and their family members have an initial promising increase in labor market integration but there is a subsequent leveling off and even a reversal of integration after about ten years in the country (Bratsberg et al. 2017; Schultz-Nielsen 2017; Brochmann forthcoming). These national studies underscore the heterogeneity of policies and admission categories, and the importance of country-of-origin schooling as explanatory factors for labor market success. Obviously, the context of reception in the host society matters.

Most of these are country-specific case studies, hence they lack the explanatory power of comparative studies that take the different national contexts of reception into account (Hollifield 1997, 2000; Ellermann 2021). Bevelander and Pendakur (2014) conducted a comparative study of economic integration across admission categories (asylum migrants, resettled refugees, and family reunion migrants) looking at different country-of-origin groups in Sweden and Canada. They reported that, after controlling for socio-economic and demographic characteristics, the probability of gainful employment for these groups was roughly the same in Canada and Sweden. However, there was a difference in earnings between the two countries, higher in Canada than in Sweden, even though differences between admission categories were smaller in Sweden than in Canada. The authors argued that these differences are probably due to the fact that in Sweden all the different types of migrants were entitled to receive the same benefits (social or welfare services) upfront and to participate in identical resettlement programs, whereas in Canada only resettled refugees had access to such broad services and programs, similar to policies in the US.

A principal takeaway from these studies is that refugees are disadvantaged vis à vis other migrant groups in the principal receiving countries when it comes to labor market integration. However, there are some important discrepancies in the findings: a review by Bevelander (2020) shows some studies reporting that the labor market performance of refugees is comparable to that of other migrant groups, while other studies find that the differences between migrant groups are substantial and significant. Among the factors that explain poor economic outcomes and the difficulties of labor market integration for refugees are mental health issues, long waiting periods during the asylum process, uncertainties about the length of stay, different levels of education upon arrival, variation in skills and social capital, and variation in national arrival structures (on the policy context see Thränhardt et al. 2020), including integration programs and receptiveness of the general populations towards immigrants, levels of prejudice, and discrimination. The policy conclusion is clear, however: states that make an upfront investment in forced migrants, granting them rights, reap greater economic rewards in the long term, including higher rates of employment, better health outcomes, human capital improvements, higher tax contributions, and greater public support for immigration and refugee programs. Again, the principal takeaway is that policies and institutions matter and rights are key to immigrant integration and positive economic outcomes.

IS THE WELFARE STATE A MAGNET FOR IMMIGRANTS AND ARE THEY A FISCAL BURDEN?

Although salient in public debates, assessments of the macro-economic consequences of migration in countries with strong welfare systems are limited (Orrenius and Zavodny

2012; Martin forthcoming; NAS 2017; cf. Hansen 2021). Debates revolve around two interrelated questions: *do welfare services act as a magnet for immigrants* and *are they a fiscal burden for the host society*? The premise of the first question is that generous welfare services attract migrants who are unlikely to make a positive contribution to society and the economy. The second question asks whether migrants take more in social transfer payments than they contribute to the welfare system. Here welfare refers to public programs with social transfers or social benefits which can be either contributory and/or non-contributory (Lindert 2004). For example, contributory transfers include unemployment benefits, pensions, or paid parental and sick leave, whereas universal income support programs like social assistance, housing benefits, minimum pension, and children's allowances are non-contributory transfers. Eligibility for and coverage of social services vary widely among OECD countries (Garfinkel et al. 2010).

The welfare magnet hypothesis was developed first by George Borjas. He argues that generous welfare systems act as a pull factor for migration and that they have a negative effect on the skill composition of immigrants. Based on a study of immigration to the US, Borjas (1999a) finds that migrants gravitate to US states with more generous social safety nets and tend to settle there. He purports to show that recent immigrants have a higher risk of unemployment and therefore need welfare support and will choose to reside in states with more generous social services. Since his seminal study, work by other scholars has confirmed the findings of Borjas. Beine et al. (2011) point out that social networks of immigrants can reduce the transaction costs of migration by providing information about employment opportunities in the destination country. They find that immigration policy is an important factor driving the choice of the destination country. In a similar vein, Razin and Wahba (2011) argue that the level of welfare provisions and the type of immigration policy (liberal or restrictive) affect the skill composition of immigrants. *Ceteris paribus*, in an open migration regime both skilled and unskilled migrants will be attracted to states with generous welfare systems. This is especially true for unskilled migrants, who stand to gain the most from emigration to countries with strong welfare services. In a restricted regime, voters will consider how immigrants affect their relative position in the labor market and what impact immigration has on public finances. Razin and Wahba (2011) argue that unskilled migration depresses the wages of low-skilled native workers and increases wages of high-skilled native workers—returns to capital are higher than returns to labor. The opposite is the case with high-skilled immigrants, who have a lower risk of unemployment and pay more into social services than they take out. According to this analysis, natives (voters) of all skills will prefer an immigration policy that favors high-skilled immigration (Krieger 2003). We can draw an analogy with the Stolper–Samuelson (1941) theorem for trade policy. The scarce factor (unskilled, native workers) will seek protection (lower levels of immigration) whereas the abundant factor (capital) will favor a more open immigration regime (cf. Peters 2015). We must be careful, however, not to reduce voters' choices to a pure "political economy" logic, because immigration politics is a multi-dimensional game that involves not just economic choices (markets), but rights (legal status and citizenship) and culture (ethnicity and race), as well as security (Hollifield and Foley 2021; Hollifield and Wong forthcoming; Hollifield et al. forthcoming).

The concentration of the benefits of immigration prompts economists like Borjas and political scientists like Freeman to argue that the major economic issues associated with immigration are distributional, that is, more immigrants increase GDP, but most of this additional GDP accrues to the migrants themselves and to the owners of capital and land. Borjas (1995: 9) concludes:

> If the social welfare function depends on both efficiency gains and the distributional impact of immigration, the slight benefits arising from the immigration surplus may well be outweighed by the substantial wealth redistribution that takes place, particularly since the redistribution goes from workers to owners of capital (or other users of immigrant services).

Immigrant workers expand the economy because their arrival reduces the wages of native-born workers while increasing levels of aggregate demand. Given a negatively sloped demand curve for labor, employers hire more workers at lower wages. However, if immigrants are different in economically important characteristics such as education, they can complement native-born workers, meaning that more immigrants increase the demand for and wages of native-born workers (Martin forthcoming).

Empirical evidence for the "magnet" hypothesis is reviewed by Giulietti and Wahba (2013). It indicates that immigrants in the US had a higher use of social services than natives (see also Borjas 1999a) although the findings are relatively weak in terms of statistical significance. For Europe, De Giorgi and Pellizzari (2009) find a small effect of welfare generosity on the propensity to emigrate, whereas Brücker et al. (2002) find that welfare generosity leads to a negative sorting of immigrants. Trying to control for endogeneity between welfare and immigration, Giulietti and Wahba (2013) find no effect of unemployment benefits in European countries on immigration flows from within (intra-EU) or from outside (third-country nationals) Europe. Again, looking at Europe, Razin and Wahba (2015) find some support for the magnet hypothesis for free-movers, while immigrants from outside Europe (third-country nationals) are more likely to impose a fiscal burden on welfare states, at least in the short term.

Giulietti and Wahba (2013) examine the welfare dependency of migrants versus natives in Europe to measure the magnet effect of welfare services. They review results for Sweden (see also Hansen and Lofstrom 2003) where immigrants move off of welfare the longer they are in the country. For Germany, Riphahn et al. (2010) show that the probability of being on welfare for Turkish immigrants is insignificant when controlling for individual skill levels. Looking at the enlargement of the EU, the EU attracted more "welfare migrants" from Central and Eastern Europe (Boeri 2010; Kahanec et al. 2009; Constant 2011), but the studies show mixed results, and rather small differences in welfare dependency between natives and immigrants. The evidence for a close correlation between immigrant status and use of welfare services is decidedly mixed and again depends heavily on the context.

Later studies by Dustmann and Frattini (2014) indicate that immigrants from the European Economic Area (EEA) made a positive fiscal contribution to the UK, and that non-EEA immigrants made a negative contribution during the period 1994–99. However, both EEA and non-EEA immigrants arriving since 2000 have made positive fiscal contributions to the UK. Looking at the costs of intra-EEA migrants only, Österman et al. (2019) demonstrate the fiscal impact of this group according to different policy regimes (rules and practices that govern the labor market, the tax system, and the welfare state) in the EEA region, but only between the four Western European systems versus the so-called "state insurance" regime common in Eastern Europe. Their findings indicate that in the welfare states of Western Europe the net contribution of EU immigrants is significantly higher, clearly surpassing the per household fiscal contribution: "we do not find any evidence in support of the common idea that migrants generate a greater fiscal burden in more generous welfare states" (Österman et al. 2019: 1). This finding is driven largely by intra-EU Polish migrants, who have a longer history of migration to the west. Overall, although different welfare state regimes are prominent in the EEA region, intra-European migration shows very similar positive fiscal effects for immigrants across the region.

Related to the magnet and dependency literature are studies that analyze the fiscal impact of migration. These studies estimate the net fiscal contribution of first-generation immigrants focusing on the difference between the taxes they pay and the amount of transfer payments they receive in a given period of time, typically a year. According to these studies (Borjas 1985, 1994; International Monetary Fund 2016; Rowthorn 2008; Orrenius and Zavodny 2012; NAS 2017; Martin forthcoming) the net fiscal gain or loss depends heavily on the type of migrant, their demographic profile (age in particular), skill and education levels, and their rate of inclusion in the economy. Again, with the exception of NAS (2017), these studies are focused on first-generation immigrants, and they do not take account of the contribution of subsequent generations. Highly educated migrants—economic migrants as opposed to refugees—and those who are gainfully employed have a positive fiscal impact. Unskilled immigrants can have a positive impact too if they are gainfully employed, are complements rather than substitutes for native workers, and if they do not impose other costs on the welfare state. Characteristics of immigrants like age, employability, year of arrival, as well as the migrant (intake) category can affect the timing and amount of social services received. As we have seen, forced migrants (asylum seekers and refugees) have much greater difficulty in entering the labor market and are therefore more likely to need social services, at least in the early stages of their stay in a new country (cf. Thränhardt et al. 2020; Hansen 2021). The type and (legal) category of the migrant matter a great deal.

Studies of the fiscal impact of first-generation immigrants in countries such as the US, Canada, the UK, or Australia show that the immigrant population tends to be very diverse in terms of age, skills, and reasons for migration. Rowthorn (2008) and others (see, for example, Borjas 1994), Huddle (1995), Lee and Miller (2000), and Passel and Clark (1994) in the US, Somerville et al. (2009) in the UK, Weber and Straubhaar (1996) in Switzerland, or Roodenburg et al. (2003) in the Netherlands all indicate that the net fiscal impact of immigration is small, minimally negative or positive (cf. Nowrasteh and Orr 2018).

For Sweden, Ekberg (1999) found relatively small positive effects of immigration on public finances through the decade of the 1980s at a time when most immigration was economically driven. From the 1990s until the present, permanent immigration to Sweden has consisted mainly of refugees and family migrants and the fiscal impact has been small but negative. Ruist (2015) finds the fiscal cost of refugee migration to be approximately 1 percent of GDP in 2007 and 1.35 percent in 2015, a year when Sweden registered the highest annual per capita refugee immigration in Europe in 30 years. His estimates show that about 80 percent of the fiscal impact of refugee migration in 2007 was due to lower per capita income and lower tax revenues for refugees. The unexplained 20 percent was due to higher per capita costs of refugees in terms of use of social services. By contrast, Hansen (2021) argues that refugee migration in the EU and specifically in

Sweden in 2015–17 was fiscally neutral inasmuch as spending on refugees increased economic growth and investment in municipalities, improving the general welfare.

Other factors to consider when estimating the fiscal contribution of migrants is to look at the use of social services over the lifecycle and to take account of the earnings of the second generation (NAS 2017; Qi and Bevelander forthcoming). Typically, immigrants are self-selected and moving to another country during the early working ages (20s and 30s) and they have been educated in their home countries. When they are entering the labor market in the host country, this lowers the fiscal cost of supporting aging populations by rejuvenating the population and providing additional workers and taxpayers (Qi and Bevelander forthcoming; cf. Blanchet 1988; NAS 2017). Moreover, a substantial share of migrants will see their move as temporary and they may return to their home country to retire. Demographic factors such as changes in the age structure, the permanence of migration, average age at migration, number of years as taxpayers, and country of retirement (see, for example, Borjas 1994; Rowthorn 2008) are important for estimating the net fiscal cost or benefit of immigration to the host society (see also Orrenius and Zavodny 2012; International Monetary Fund 2016; NAS 2017).

INTEGRATION POLICIES AND MULTI-LEVEL GOVERNANCE: INSTITUTIONS MATTER

Policies for migrant integration share the aim of guiding the integration process in a more favorable direction. For countries in the EU, the Qualifications Directive (2011/95/EU), Race Equality Directive (2000/43/EC), and Employment Equality Directive (2000/78/EC) set mandatory minimum standards for integration policies. EU integration policy is made primarily with guidance and support from the European Agenda for Migration and the Action Plan on the integration of third-country nationals. However, integration policies are designed and implemented by individual member states just like other OECD countries and depend on several elements, such as historical migration patterns, intensity of migratory flows, government and institutional structure, and welfare and labor market models (Gregurović and Župarić-Iljić 2018). According to a study by Bevelander and Emilsson (2021), these policies can be classified by the level of national and local authorities' involvement and direction ranging from a national government-led model to a project-based/multi-level governance model, a laissez-faire model, and a non-governmental organization (NGO)-led model (see below for more detail). Irrespective of the model applied, other features determine the inclusion policies adopted by a country. The participation of refugees and beneficiaries of protection in inclusion programs can be voluntary or mandatory, service delivery can be targeted or universal, and the responsibilities between different government levels can be different as well as the number and type of stakeholders involved.

Integration policies are based on different philosophies of integration (Favell 1998). Some systemic forces push integration policies to converge across countries, such as the open method of coordination in the EU and policy diffusion/learning among member states. We can identify two major trends in integration policy making, a national or civic and a local turn (Emilsson 2015; Dekker et al. 2015). These two policy trends are contradictory insofar as the civic turn implies more integration requirements for migrants that are set out at the national level and that have a direct impact on the lives of newcomers. The local turn implies less involvement of national authorities, with cities and localities shouldering greater responsibility for integration policies. In effect we see a lot of institutional variation and multi-level governance in integration policy making in Europe and across the OECD countries (Money 1999; Ellermann 2021; Hollifield et al. forthcoming).

A relatively new feature in immigration policies of the major receiving countries, especially in Europe, is the introduction of *civic integration programs*, consisting of language training and lessons in civics (Goodman 2010, 2012a, 2012b). Successful completion of these programs is often a *requirement for access to long-term or permanent residence and/or citizenship*. Civic integration policies are an integral part of immigration control policies, forcing migrants to meet certain requirements in order to gain permanent residency and to qualify for family reunification (Hollifield et al. forthcoming). The Dutch Newcomers Act of 1998 is considered the first example of a civic integration policy in Europe, but many others have followed this model. Denmark, Germany, Austria, the Netherlands, the UK, and France introduced civic integration programs in the period from 1997 to 2009 (Goodman 2010).

Austria, Flanders in Belgium, the Czech Republic, and France made it mandatory for migrants to pass a level A in the Common European Framework of Reference for Languages[11] in order to obtain permanent residence, while B1 level has to be completed in Austria, Estonia, and France in order to acquire citizenship (European Migration Network 2019). The introduction of such requirements has shifted the burden of integration from the state to the individual migrants. The basic goal of these policies is to promote individual responsibility of the migrant and to establish a common set of values for all newcomers (Groenendijk 2011; Joppke 2017).

Scholars have identified a local turn in integration policies as well, where large cities in particular are entrepreneurial in developing their own integration philosophies and policies (Favell 1998; Scholten and Penninx 2016; De Graauw and Vermeulen 2016). Local governments do not just implement national policies; they are shaping policies as well (Alexander 2003, 2007; Penninx 2009; Penninx et al. 2004; Caponio and Borkert 2010).

IMMIGRANT INTEGRATION IN MODERN WELFARE STATES: MIPEX

MIPEX is a good example of attempts to map, quantify, and compare national integration policies (www.mipex.eu; Solano and Huddleston 2020). In its fifth edition of 2020, it encompasses 52 countries of the world and measures eight integration policy areas—labor market mobility, education, political participation, access to nationality, family reunion, health, permanent residence, and anti-discrimination—for immigrants. The index mainly shows so-called best practices and the development of these policies and the rights associated with them when it comes to integration policies towards immigrants in welfare states more generally. As can be seen in Figure 1.9, both Scandinavian welfare states and traditional immigration countries score high on migrant integration policies. Only 21 out of 52 countries score 50 or above on the MIPEX scale indicating that the majority of the countries have poor migrant arrival policies in place.

34   *Handbook on migration and welfare*

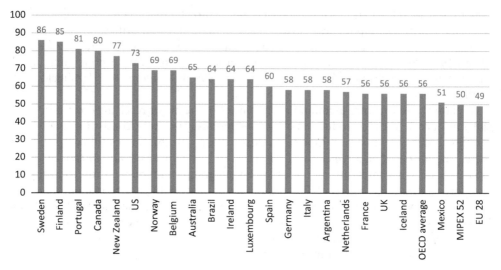

Source: www.mipex.eu; Solano and Huddleston (2020).

Figure 1.9   MIPEX scores by country (weighted by eight areas)

However, with respect to integration for persons granted international protection, MIPEX has two major shortcomings. First, it does not measure integration for different categories of immigrants. Second, it does not really measure integration policies per se, focusing more on equal protection of the rights of migrants compared with citizens (Goodman 2010; cf. Hollifield 1997). Beneficiaries of international protection and those who have received refugee status are entitled to labor market and social support under the same terms as citizens in many countries but there are few measures of integration outcomes.[12] We must be careful not to equate integration policies (outputs) with integration outcomes.

Some studies show that the correlation between integration policy outputs and outcomes are weak and sometimes counter to expectations (Koopmans 2010). Integration outcomes may depend more on the composition of the migrant group (Luik et al. 2018). National integration policies vary according to their underlying ideology, what measures and services they offer, and the governance (implementation) strategies. Bevelander and Emilsson (2021) review the integration policy models in the EU and we reprise their typology here.

First are *national (government-led) models* in Scandinavian countries with "welcoming programs" lasting two or three years, including language training, civic orientation, and other measures to ease access to the labor market—services provided specifically for persons granted international protection. For implementation, these programs rely on national (funding) and local (personnel) authorities, in addition to the involvement of civic organizations and other "social partners." In Norway and Denmark participation in these welcome programs may affect the assessment of future applications for permanent residence, whereas in Sweden participation is seen more as an entitlement. The Swedish model uses local and regional agreements to improve collaboration with important stakeholders, such as employer services, municipalities, universities, and NGOs. While the main advantage of these national models is access to services and resources for new migrants, the downside has been their high cost, the slow pace of labor market entry by migrants, and the fact that only a few of the new measures introduced have proved to be effective, that is leading to positive labor market outcomes.

Under the *project-based/multi-level governance model*, inclusion measures are project based and developed at the local and regional level. The measures can include language courses, skill checks, mentoring programs, apprenticeship, and placement. These project-based models have been used primarily in Austria and Germany. For instance, in Germany, the *Bundesländer* (federal states) and local governments have launched their own programs in response to the refugee crisis of 2015. Even though in this model the national level is not as predominant as in the national government-led models found in Scandinavia, over time there has been an increasing involvement of the national/federal government in Germany as a way to improve coordination and provide a more coherent and strategic approach. Being implemented mainly at the local level, integration measures are targeted to respond to local needs and as a result service delivery varies widely in Germany.

Under the *laissez-faire model*, the national-level government involvement is limited. This approach is followed mainly in Italy, the Netherlands, and the UK. In Italy, the government has slowly moved away from an ad hoc, emergency approach to a more structured approach, providing tailored support to migrants. But delivery of services is mostly dependent on cooperation between local governments and NGOs. In the Netherlands, the delivery of immigrant integration services has been transferred to private companies, and Dutch municipalities can choose which type of assistance to provide to supplement private help. The UK also adopted this model in 2010, stepping back from a national inclusion strategy in order to fund small, multi-level governance projects with NGOs and local governments/councils. The main weakness of the private-sector model is the difficulty of maintaining common/national standards of quality and consistency in service provision.

Lastly, in the *NGO model*, there are no specific resources or infrastructure for inclusion on either the local, regional, or national levels. In countries that follow this approach, NGOs are the main service providers for the inclusion of migrants, using mostly EU funds, especially the Asylum, Migration and Integration Fund. This model is predominant in Central and Eastern European member states.

POLICY DILEMMAS: CONTEXT MATTERS

Notwithstanding the wide variation in integration policies in Europe, all countries must consider if integration programs should be voluntary or mandatory, if service delivery should be targeted or universal, and how formulation and implementation of policy should be carried out across different levels of government. Here we review the range of programs, the criteria by which migrants qualify for them, and the implementation strategies.

Voluntary or Required Participation in Integration Programs

In the Scandinavian model/s, we see that access to services is fairly universal and there is not much variation between Sweden, Norway, and Denmark (Brochmann forthcoming). Nonetheless, there are big differences in the level of integration requirements for getting long-term residence permits and citizenship. According to Lutz (2017), the number of requirements that migrants must fulfil depends on the underlying logic of policy interventions (what he calls a logic of conditioning and a logic of enabling), determining whether the policy interventions are incentive or opportunity based. Moreover, there is no clear evidence to indicate whether or not integration requirements (policy outputs) improve integration outcomes. The main problem with integration metrics is the limited amount of time and support to fulfil existing requirements. For instance, countries such as the Netherlands and the UK have a clear set of requirements, but the state provides little support to persons granted international protection to help them meet the requirements. Scholten et al. (2017) define such countries as having a differential approach, where the state sets up a number of hurdles to delimit the opportunities for integration.

Targeted versus Universal Approaches

Another way to categorize integration measures and programs is to differentiate between universal and targeted approaches, even though some countries like Sweden follow both approaches.

Universal approaches have the overall objective of improving access to basic services through measures that target all those in need of integration assistance. Public agencies are required to provide services in a non-discriminatory way that takes account of cultural diversity of the migrant population.

Targeted approaches, on the other hand, consist of integration programs, often mandatory, with a civics orientation and language courses, and other kinds of integration support tailored to specific groups. Targeted approaches can be temporary and project based as well as widespread and broadly institutionalized.

When the European Migration Network (2019) conducted a survey of integration approaches in the EU member states, they studied eight countries[13] that have a universal approach, five[14] that have a targeted approach, and three[15] that could not be classified either way.

National versus Local Integration Policies

As shown above, some countries have a state-centric top-down integration policy. Sweden and Norway are clear examples where integration programs are implemented by public agencies at the local level, but they are universal, funded and regulated by the national state.

Reviewing the delivery of services for migrants, the European Migration Network (2019) distinguishes between centralized[16] and decentralized[17] models. In the centralized model, responsibilities tend to be concentrated in one or two ministries, some with specialized consultative bodies, whereas in decentralized systems the responsibility for implementing policies is spread across state (national), regional, and local levels. We must be careful not to equate decentralized models with less national oversight, however. Sweden and other Scandinavian countries have, for example, a decentralized service delivery shared between local councils and national agencies. Here again the oversight and funding are carried out by national authorities.

Countries such as Austria and Germany have a more integrated multi-level governance approach to integration, whereas the UK, Italy, Belgium, and the Netherlands have decentralized systems. Integration of migrants is the responsibility of local authorities who must design and implement policy, often in cooperation with NGOs and with some funding from the EU. Other countries have no clear system for designing or implementing integration policies. For example, states in Southern and Eastern Europe rely entirely on NGOs and EU funding for integration programs. From this summary we can see the wide variation of integration policies and programs across the EU.

CONCLUSION: RIGHTS ARE THE KEY TO SUCCESSFUL OUTCOMES

Managing migration is a challenge for all states, not just welfare states. That said, immigration poses a special challenge for welfare states because of their ethos of equal treatment and social equality for all legal residents. The welfare state, as Gösta Esping-Anderson (1996: 2) put it, is as much a moral as a social construct, and it combines liberal individualism with social solidarity, built upon rights and duties, working for everyone so long as everyone works. The dramatic shift in migration flows in the post-war period from (guest) worker and temporary migration to more permanent, worker migration combined with family reunification, as a human right, and ever larger numbers of humanitarian migrants, asylum seekers in particular, poses a special dilemma for welfare states. This dilemma was acute already in the 1990s as humanitarian flows increased across Europe. It reached "crisis" proportions in the 2010s—not because welfare states were incapable of managing and absorbing the large flows of refugees, although this did pose an enormous logistical and humanitarian problem, but because forced migration provoked a political and cultural crisis that risked undermining the legitimacy of immigration and refugee policies and the foundations of the welfare state itself.

In this chapter, we have reviewed the evidence to explore the ever changing relationship between migration and the provision of welfare services in the principal receiving countries. We sought to answer some of the key questions about trade-offs between migrant rights and numbers (absorptive capacity of liberal and social democracies), the extent to which welfare policies act as a magnet for poorly skilled migrants, and whether immigration in general poses a threat to the public finances and is a burden for welfare states. Our findings will be disappointing for those seeking clear answers to these questions. The effect of immigration on welfare states depends on a variety of factors, and there is not a one-size-fits-all policy that allows states to manage the distributional effects of migration, finessing trade-offs between the interests of the migrants, business (capital and land), workers (labor), and so forth—a pure political economy model of migration and welfare remains elusive (Money 1999; Hollifield and Wong forthcoming).

What we found instead is that some states have managed the trade-offs better than others and that national and institutional contexts matter a great deal. Above all, integration and the granting of rights to migrants are key to successful immigration outcomes in liberal and welfare states. While there is a significant gap in the employment rate between the native and the foreign born in the Scandinavian and Western European social democracies, these states, along with Canada, have developed elaborate integration policies to ensure that migrants attain self-sufficiency and that they become productive and active members of society. These states have taken a more proactive, top-down approach to integration with national-level, centralized policies, providing incentives for migrants to assimilate. Some states tie requirements for integration to residency status and ultimately to naturalization. Among advanced welfare states, Sweden has the longest history of immigration and has taken the most liberal, multicultural approach to migration management. Denmark, on the other hand, has taken a more nationalist and assimilationist approach to migrant integration, with Norway somewhere in the middle.

Germany and Austria have elaborate integration policies based on multi-level governance that leave wide latitude for institutional innovations, at the national (federal), state (*Länder*), and local levels, with ample room for cooperation with NGOs and the private sector. The result has been remarkable adaptability and a great capacity for absorbing and integrating a culturally diverse, refugee population. Germany made remarkable progress in managing the influx of refugees and asylum seekers in the mid-2010s and in the integration of the newcomers. At the other end of the spectrum is the US with a largely laissez-faire approach to immigration, if not to formally resettled refugees. US policy shows little concern for the rights of migrants and asylum seekers or their integration, with outright hostility to migrants in broad sectors of society (a new nativism), allowing a black market for migrant labor to develop, which at its height reached almost 12 million unauthorized migrants. This market-driven approach to migration management has resulted in enormous inequalities, exploitation of undocumented migrants, and mistreatment of asylum seekers, especially minors/children, undermining the legitimacy of immigration, refugee, and asylum policies, weakening an already weak welfare state, and threatening the republic itself, with the rise of reactionary populism under Donald Trump, and a new nativism and racism taking the US "back to the future" (Hollifield 2019). The Netherlands and the UK fall somewhere in the middle of the continuum, vacillating between multiculturalism and a more liberal and accommodating immigration policy, on the one hand, and a strongly nationalist and xenophobic policy (Brexit) on the other.

We found considerable support for the thesis that welfare states attract more immigrants, especially humanitarian migrants, and that forced migrants (asylum seekers and refugees) are harder to integrate than highly skilled immigrants. Nothing is particularly surprising in this finding, but what is remarkable is the continued political commitment to the international humanitarian regime by some of the largest social democracies in Europe, especially Sweden and Germany, but also Austria and Norway. It turns out that Chancellor Angela Merkel was correct when she famously said *wir schaffen das* (we can do this), as Germany was able to surmount the crisis of having nearly 1 million humanitarian migrants arriving in a single year. Proportionately, Sweden took in even more refugees and asylum seekers than Germany, and Austria ranked third per capita in granting protection to asylum seekers in 2015–16. Maintaining political support for these liberal policies turned out to be far more difficult than managing the reception and integration of so many forced migrants. In Europe as in the US, immigration and refugee policies have become highly symbolic, bound up with identity politics, as debates about culture and the shifting ethnic composition of societies overwhelm considerations of markets and rights (Hollifield et al. forthcoming).

As for the fiscal burden of immigration, the picture also is mixed. Much depends on the age, human (education), and social capital of migrants. It is more expensive for societies to take care of the young and the old migrants—again no surprises—because the distributional effects of welfare policies are similar to those for the native population. Likewise, it is not surprising that highly educated and skilled immigrants make a larger contribution to social services than those who are poorly skilled, with less than a high school education. Of course, knowledge-based, service economies still have great need of basic manpower, unskilled migrants to pick the crops, build the houses, care workers to look after the sick, the infirmed, and elderly, and change the bed pans, workers now dubbed "essential" in an age of pandemic. Treating migrant workers fairly and avoiding a "harvest of shame" still is a major challenge for welfare states—as it is for all states—but it is a challenge that must be met if these advanced service-based economies are to thrive and if migration is to be win–win–win, contributing to the human development of the migrants themselves and to economic development in the host and sending societies in the long term.

Can welfare states sustain high levels of immigration without undermining the social contract and public finances? The answer to this question depends on politics, whether political coalitions for liberal immigration policies can be put together and sustained over a long period of time. Do states have the institutional capacity to formulate and implement integration (and citizenship) policies that lead migrants to become self-sufficient and productive members of society? As is so often the case in social science, much depends on the social and historical and especially the institutional context, not only at the national but especially at the sub-national levels. Sweden and Germany, for example, managed to cope with a surge in asylum seeking and refugee migration in 2015–16, whereas the US, even with its long history of immigration, has fallen short, in part because of the sad legacies of systemic racism and nativism, and the growth of a large black market for foreign labor that has left over 10 million immigrants in legal limbo, damaging their prospects for integration and those of their children.

NOTES

1. The authors wish to thank Markus M.L. Crepaz, Antje Ellermann, Philip L. Martin, Dietrich Thränhardt, and Natascha Zaun for their invaluable feedback. Errors of course are ours alone.
2. https://ec.europa.eu/eurostat/statistics-explained/index.php?title=Migration_and_migrant_population_statistics.
3. https://ec.europa.eu/eurostat/statistics-explained/index.php/Residence_permits_statistics#First_residence_permits:_an_overview.
4. https://ec.europa.eu/eurostat/statistics-explained/pdfscache/5777.pdf.
5. In fact, Borjas and Friedberg (2009) find that the downward trend in earnings of new immigrants, observed from 1960 to 1990, reversed in the 1990s and by 2000 immigrants were performing just as well as natives in the US labor market. This finding is consistent with the much earlier work of Chiswick (1978).
6. www.mipex.eu/permanent-residence.
7. https://ec.europa.eu/eurostat/statistics-explained/pdfscache/35409.pdf.
8. https://ec.europa.eu/eurostat/statistics-explained/pdfscache/35409.pdf.

9. Country clusters: (1) Denmark, Finland, and Sweden, (2) Austria, Belgium, France, Germany, Luxembourg, the Netherlands, and the United Kingdom, (3) Cyprus, Greece, Ireland, Italy, Malta, Portugal, and Spain, and (4) Bulgaria, the Czech Republic, Estonia, Hungary, Latvia, Lithuania, Poland, the Slovak Republic, and Slovenia.
10. Self-selection means that individuals who migrate are a selection of individuals from a population and have other observed or unobserved characteristics from this population.
11. Read more about the Common European Framework of Reference for Languages here: www.coe.int/en/web/common-european-framework-reference-languages/level-descriptions.
12. The National Integration Evaluation Mechanism project specifically advances an integration policy index for persons granted international protection in 14 EU countries. See: www.forintegration.eu/pl/pub.
13. Austria, Germany, Ireland, Luxembourg, the Netherlands, Spain, Sweden, and the United Kingdom.
14. Belgium, Finland, France, Italy, and Malta.
15. Croatia, Cyprus, and Poland.
16. Bulgaria, Cyprus, Czech Republic, France, Hungary, Latvia, Lithuania, and Malta.
17. Austria, Belgium, Finland, Germany, Ireland, Italy, the Netherlands, Portugal, Slovenia, Spain, and Sweden.

REFERENCES

Alesina, Alberto and Edward L. Glaeser. 2004. *Fighting Poverty in the US and Europe: A World of Difference*, Oxford: Oxford University Press.
Alesina, Alberto, Edward Glaeser, and Bruce Sacerdote. 2001. "Why doesn't the US have a European-style welfare state?" *Harvard Economic Review*, Discussion Paper 1933.
Alexander, M. 2003. "Local policies toward migrants as an expression of host–stranger relations: A proposed typology," *Journal of Ethnic and Migration Studies*, 29/3: 411–30.
Alexander, M. 2007. *Cities and Labor Immigration: Comparing Policy Responses in Amsterdam, Paris, Rome and Tel Aviv*, Aldershot: Ashgate.
Aydemir, A. 2011. "Immigrant selection and short-term labor market outcomes by visa category," *Journal of Population Economics*, 24/2: 451–75.
Bakker, L., J. Dagevos, and G. Engbersen. 2013. "The importance of resources and security in the socio-economic integration of refugees: A study on the impact of length of stay in asylum accommodation and residence status on socio-economic integration for the four largest refugee groups in the Netherlands," *Journal of International Migration and Integration*, 15/3: 431–48.
Banting, Keith and Will Kymlicka. 2006. *Multiculturalism and the Welfare State: Recognition and Redistribution in Contemporary Democracies*, Oxford: Oxford University Press.
Becker, Sascha O. and Andreas Ferrara. 2019. "Consequences of forced migration: A survey of recent findings," *Labor Economics*, 59/August: 1–16.
Beine, M., F. Docquier, and C. Ozden. 2011. "Diasporas," *Journal of Development Economics*, 95/1: 30–41.
Benhabib, Seyla. 2002. "Transformations of citizenship: The case of contemporary Europe," *Government and Opposition*, 37/4: 439–65.
Bevelander, P. 2020. "Integrating refugees into labor markets," *IZA World of Labor*, http://wol.iza.org/articles/integrating-refugees-into-labor-markets.
Bevelander, P. and H. Emilsson. 2021. "One size fits all? Integration approaches for beneficiaries of international protection," MIM Working Paper Series 2021:1.
Bevelander, P and M.A. Luik. 2020. "Refugee employment heterogeneity in Sweden: Evidence from a cohort analysis," *Frontiers in Sociology*, doi: 10.3389/fsoc.2020.00044.
Bevelander, P. and R. Pendakur. 2014. "The labor market integration of refugee and family reunion immigrants: A comparison of outcomes in Canada and Sweden," *Journal of Ethnic and Migration Studies*, 40/5: 689–709.
Blanchet, Didier. 1988. "Immigration et régulation de la structure par âge d'une population," *Population*, 43/2: 293–309.
Bloch, A. 2007. "Refugees in the UK labor market: The conflict between economic integration and policy-led labor market restriction," *Journal of Social Policy*, 37/1: 21–36.
Bloemraad, Irene and Matthew Wright. 2012. "Is there a trade-off between multiculturalism and socio-political integration? Policy regimes and immigrant incorporation in comparative perspective," *Perspectives on Politics*, 10/1: 77–95.
Boeri, T. 2010. "Immigration to the land of redistribution," *Economica*, 77/308: 651–87.
Bommes, Michael and Andrew Geddes, eds. 2000. *Migration and the Welfare State in Contemporary Europe*, London: Routledge.

Bommes, Michael and Jost Halfmann. 1998. *Migration in nationalen Wohlfahrtsstaaten*, Osnabrück: Universitätsverlag Rasch.
Bonin, H., B. Raffelhüschen and J. Walliser. 2000. "Can immigration alleviate the demographic burden?" *FinanzArchiv*, 57/1: 1–21.
Borjas, George J. 1985. "Assimilation, changes in cohort quality, and the earnings of immigrants," *Journal of Labor Economics*, 3/4: 463–89.
Borjas, George J. 1990. *Friends or Strangers: The Impact of Immigrants on the US Economy*, New York: Basic Books.
Borjas, George J. 1994. "The economics of immigration," *Journal of Economic Literature*, 32/4: 1667–717.
Borjas, George J. 1995. "The economic benefits of immigration," *Journal of Economic Perspectives*, 9/2: 3–22.
Borjas, George J. 1999a. "Immigration and welfare magnets," *Journal of Labor Economics*, 17/4: 607–37.
Borjas, George J. 1999b. *Heaven's Door: Immigration Policy and the American Economy*, Princeton, NJ: Princeton University Press.
Borjas, George J. and Rachel M. Friedberg. 2009. "Recent trends in the earnings of new immigrants to the United States," National Bureau of Economic Research, Working Paper 15406: 1–56.
Bratsberg, B., O. Raaum, and K. Røed. 2017. "Immigrant labor market integration across admission classes," *Nordic Economic Policy Review*: 17–54.
Brettell, Caroline B. and James F. Hollifield. forthcoming. *Migration Theory: Talking across Disciplines*, London: Routledge.
Brochmann, Grete. forthcoming. "Governing immigration in advanced welfare states: The Scandinavian 'case,'" in James F. Hollifield, Philip L. Martin, Pia Orrenius, and François Héran, eds, *Controlling Immigration: A Comparative Perspective*, Stanford, CA: Stanford University Press.
Brücker, H., G.S. Epstein, B. McCormick, G. Saint-Paul, A. Venturini, and K. Zimmermann. 2002. "Managing migration in the European welfare state," in T. Boeri, G. Hanson, and B. McCormick, eds, *Immigration Policy and the Welfare System: A Report for the Fondazione Rodolfo Debenedetti*, Oxford: Oxford University Press: 1–167.
Caponio, T. and M. Borkert. 2010. *The Local Dimension of Migration Policymaking*, Amsterdam: Amsterdam University Press.
Chin, A. and K.E. Cortes. 2015. "The refugee/asylum seeker," in B. Chiswick and P. Miller, eds, *The Handbook on the Economics of International Migration*, Volume 1, Amsterdam: Elsevier: 585–658.
Chiswick, B.R. 1978. "The effect of Americanization on the earnings of foreign-born men," *Journal of Political Economy*, 86/5: 897–921.
Chiswick, B.R. 2008. "Are immigrants favorably self-selected? An economic analysis," in C.B. Brettell and J.F. Hollifield, eds, *Migration Theory: Talking across Disciplines*, New York: Routledge: 63–82.
Connor, P. 2010. "Explaining the refugee gap: Economic outcomes of refugees versus other immigrants," *Journal of Refugee Studies*, 23/3: 377–97.
Constant, A.F. 2011. "Sizing it up: Labor migration lessons of the EU enlargement to 27," IZA Discussion Paper 6119.
Crepaz, Markus M.L. 2008. *Trust beyond Borders: Immigration, the Welfare State, and Identity in Modern Societies*, Ann Arbor: University of Michigan Press.
De Giorgi, Giacomo and Michele Pellizzari. 2009. "Welfare migration in Europe." *Labour Economics*, 16/4: 353–63.
De Graauw, Els and F. Vermeulen. 2016. "Cities and the politics of immigrant integration: A comparison of Berlin, Amsterdam, New York City, and San Francisco," *Journal of Ethnic and Migration Studies*, 42/6: 989–1012.
De Vroome, T. and F. van Tubergen. 2010. "The employment experience of refugees in the Netherlands," *International Migration Review*, 44/2: 376–403.
Dekker, R., H. Emilsson, B. Krieger and P. Scholten. 2015. "A local dimension of integration policies? A comparative study of Berlin, Malmö, and Rotterdam," *International Migration Review*, 49/3, https://doi.org/10.1111/imre.12133.
Dustmann, C. and Tomasso Frattini. 2014. "The fiscal effects of immigration to the UK," *The Economic Journal*, 124/580: 593–643.
Dustmann, C., F. Fasani, T. Frattini, L. Minale, and U. Schönberg. 2017. "On the economics and politics of refugee migration," *Economic Policy*, 32: 497–550.
Ekberg, J. 1999. "Immigration and the public sector: Income effects for the native population in Sweden," *Journal of Population Economics*, 12: 411–30.
Ellermann, Antje. 2021. *The Comparative Politics of Immigration: Policy Choices in Germany, Canada, Switzerland, and the United States*, New York: Cambridge University Press.
Emilsson, H. 2015. "A national turn of local integration policy: Multi-level governance dynamics in Denmark and Sweden," *Comparative Migration Studies*, 3/7: 1–17.

Esping-Andersen, Gösta. 1996. "After the golden age? Welfare state dilemmas in a global economy," in Gösta Esping-Andersen, ed., *Welfare States in Transition: National Adaptations in Global Economies*, London: Sage: 1–30.

European Migration Network. 2019. "Labor market integration of third-country nationals in EU member states: Synthesis report," Brussels: European Migration Network.

Facchini, G. and A.M. Mayda. 2009. "Does the welfare state affect individual attitudes towards immigrants? Evidence across countries," *Review of Economics and Statistics*, 91/2: 295–314.

Facchini, G. and A.M. Mayda. 2012. "Individual attitudes towards skilled migration: An empirical analysis across countries," *World Economy*, 35/2: 183–96.

Favell, Adrian. 1998. *Philosophies of Integration: Immigration and the Idea of Citizenship in France and Britain*, New York: St Martin's Press.

Freeman, Gary P. 1986. "Migration and the political economy of the welfare state," *Annals of the American Academy of Political and Social Science*, 485/1: 51–63.

Garfinkel, Irwin, Lee Rainwater, and Timothy M. Smeeding. 2010. *Wealth and Welfare States: Is America a Laggard or Leader?*, Oxford: Oxford University Press.

Giulietti, C. and J. Wahba. 2013. "Welfare migration," in K.F. Zimmermann and A.F. Constant, eds, *International Handbook on the Economics of Migration*, Cheltenham, UK and Northampton, MA, USA: Edward Elgar Publishing: 489–504.

Goodhart, David. 2004. "Too diverse? Is Britain becoming too diverse to sustain the mutual obligations behind good society and the welfare state," *Prospect*, 20/February: 1–14.

Goodman, Sara W. 2010. "Integration requirements for integration's sake? Identifying, categorising and comparing civic integration policies," *Journal of Ethnic and Migration Studies*, 36/5: 753–72.

Goodman, Sara W. 2012a. "Fortifying citizenship: Policy strategies for civic integration in Western Europe," *World Politics*, 64/4: 659–98.

Goodman, Sara W. 2012b. "Measurement and interpretation issues in civic integration studies: A rejoinder," *Journal of Ethnic and Migration Studies*, 38/1: 173–86.

Gregurović, S. and D. Župarić-Iljić. 2018. "Comparing the incomparable? Migrant integration policies and perplexities of comparison," *International Migration*, 56/3: 105–22.

Groenendijk, Kees. 2011. "Pre-departure integration strategies in the European Union: Integration or immigration policy?" *European Journal of Migration and Law*, 13/1: 1–30.

Grubanov-Boskovic, S., F. Natale, and M. Scipioni. 2017. *Patterns of Immigrant Integration in European Labor Markets: What Do Employment Rate Gaps between Natives and Immigrants Tell Us?* Luxembourg: Publications Office of the European Union.

Hainmueller, J., D. Hangartner, and D. Lawrence. 2016. "When lives are put on hold: Lengthy asylum processes decrease employment among refugees," *Science Advances*, 2/1: 1–7.

Hansen, J. and M. Lofstrom. 2003. "Immigrant assimilation and welfare participation," *Journal of Human Resources*, 38/1: 74–98.

Hansen, Peo. 2021. *A Modern Migration Theory: An Alternative Economic Approach to Failed EU Policy*, Newcastle upon Tyne: Agenda Publishing.

Hazán, Miryam. 2021. "International migration and refugee movements in Latin America: Future trends and realities," in James F. Hollifield and Neil Foley, eds, *Understanding Global Migration*, Stanford, CA: Stanford University Press.

Hollifield, James F. 1992. *Immigrants, Markets and States: The Political Economy of Postwar Europe*, Cambridge, MA: Harvard University Press.

Hollifield, James F. 1997. "Immigration and integration in Western Europe: A comparative analysis," in Emek M. Uçarer and Donald J. Puchala, eds, *Immigration into Western Societies: Problems and Policies*, London: Pinter: 28–69.

Hollifield, James F. 1999. "Ideas, institutions and civil society: On the limits of immigration control in liberal democracies," *IMIS-Beiträge*, 10/January: 57–90.

Hollifield, James F. 2000. "Immigration and the politics of rights," in Michael Bommes and Andrew Geddes, eds, *Migration and the Welfare State in Contemporary Europe*, London: Routledge.

Hollifield, James F. 2012. "Migration and international relations," in Marc R. Rosenblum and Daniel J. Tichenor, eds, *The Oxford Handbook of the Politics of International Migration*, Oxford: Oxford University Press: 345–79.

Hollifield, James F. 2019. "The migration challenge," in George P. Shultz, ed., *Governance in an Emerging New World*, 519/Spring, Stanford: Hoover Institution Press: 34–53.

Hollifield, James F. 2021. "General perspectives on membership: Citizenship, migration, and the end of liberalism?" in Marco Giugni and Maria Grasso, eds, *Handbook of Citizenship and Migration*, Cheltenham, UK and Northampton, MA, USA: Edward Elgar Publishing: 101–17.

Hollifield, James F. and Neil Foley. 2021. *Understanding Global Migration*, Stanford, CA: Stanford University Press.

Hollifield, James F. and Tom Wong. forthcoming. "The politics of international migration: How can we 'bring the state back in?'" in James F. Hollifield and Caroline B. Brettell, eds, *Migration Theory: Talking across Disciplines*, London: Routledge.

Hollifield, James F., Philip L. Martin, Pia Orrenius, and François Héran. forthcoming. *Controlling Immigration: A Comparative Perspective*, Stanford, CA: Stanford University Press.

Huddle, Donald L. 1995. "A critique of the Urban Institute's claims of cost-free immigration: Early findings confirmed," *Population and Environment*, 16/6: 507–19.

International Monetary Fund. 2016. "Impact of migration on income levels in advanced economies," *Spillover Notes*, 16/8: 1–26.

Janoski, Thomas. 1998. *Citizenship and Civil Society*, New York: Cambridge University Press.

Joppke, Christian. 1999. *Immigration and the Nation-State*, Oxford: Oxford University Press.

Joppke, Christian. 2017. *Is Multiculturalism Dead? Crisis and Persistence in the Constitutional State*, Cambridge: Polity Press.

Kahanec, M., A. Zaiceva, and K.F. Zimmermann. 2009. "Lessons from migration after EU enlargement," in M. Kahanec and K.F. Zimmermann, eds, *EU Labor Markets after Post-Enlargement Migration*, Berlin: Springer Verlag: 3–46.

Koopmans, R. 2010. "Trade-offs between equality and difference: Immigrant integration, multiculturalism and the welfare state in cross-national perspective," *Journal of Ethnic and Migration Studies*, 36/1: 1–26.

Krieger, T. 2003. "Voting on unskilled immigration under different pension regimes," *Public Choice*, 117/1–2: 51–78.

Lee, R. and T. Miller. 2000. "Immigration, social security, and broader fiscal impacts," *American Economic Review*, 90/2: 350–4.

Lindert, P. 2004. *Growing Public: Social Spending and Economic Growth since the Eighteenth Century*, Cambridge: Cambridge University Press.

Luik, M.A., H. Emilsson, and P. Bevelander. 2018. "The male immigrant–native employment gap in Sweden: Migrant admission categories and human capital," *Journal of Population Research*, 35/4: 363–98.

Lutz, P. (2017). "Two logics of policy intervention in immigrant integration: An institutionalist framework based on capabilities and aspirations," *Comparative Migration Studies*, 5/1: 1–18.

Marshall, T.H. 1964. *Class, Citizenship and Social Development*, Garden City, NY: Doubleday.

Martin, I., A. Arcarons, J. Aumüller, P. Bevelander, H. Emilsson, S. Kalantaryan, A. Maciver, I. Mara, G. Scalettaris, A. Venturini, H. Vidovic, I. Van Der Welle, M. Windisch, R. Wolffberg, and A. Zorlu. 2016. "From refugees to workers: Mapping labor market integration support measures for asylum-seekers and refugees in EU member states," Volume 1: *Comparative Analysis and Policy Findings*; Volume 2: *Literature Review and Country Case Studies*, Gütersloh: Bertelsmann Stiftung.

Martin, Philip L. forthcoming. "Economic aspects of migration," in James F. Hollifield and Caroline B. Brettell, eds, *Migration Theory: Talking across Disciplines*, London: Routledge.

Money, Jeannette. 1999. *Fences and Neighbors: The Geography of Immigration Control*, Ithaca, NY: Cornell University Press.

National Academies of Science (NAS). 2017. *The Economic and Fiscal Consequences of Immigration*, Washington, DC: National Academies Press.

Norris, Pippa and Ronald Inglehart. 2019. *Cultural Backlash: Trump, Brexit, and Authoritarian Populism*, Cambridge: Cambridge University Press.

Nowrasteh, Alex and Robert Orr. 2018. *Immigration and the Welfare State Immigrant and Native Use Rates and Benefit Levels for Means-Tested Welfare and Entitlement Programs*, Washington, DC: CATO Institute.

OECD. 2020. *OECD International Migration Outlook*, Paris: OECD.

Orrenius, Pia M. and Madeline Zavodny. 2012. "Economic effects of migration: Receiving states," in Marc R. Rosenblum and Daniel J. Tichenor, eds, *The Oxford Handbook of the Politics of International Migration*, New York: Oxford University Press: 105–30.

Österman, M., J. Palme, and M. Ruhs. 2019. "National institutions and fiscal effects of EU migrants," Working Paper Reminder Project, European University Institute and Uppsala University.

Passel, Jeffrey and Rebecca Clark. 1994. "How much do immigrants really cost? A reappraisal of Huddle's The costs of immigration," Urban Institute, February, Mimeo.

Penninx, R. 2009. *Decentralising Integration Policies: Managing Migration in Cities, Regions and Localities*, Policy Network Paper, November, London: Policy Network.

Penninx, R., K. Kraal, M. Martiniello, and S. Vertovec. 2004. *Citizenship in European Cities: Immigrants, Local Politics and Integration Policies*, Farnham: Ashgate.

Peters, Margaret E. 2015. "Open trade, closed borders: Immigration policy in the era of globalization," *World Politics*, 67/1: 114–54.

Portes, Alejandro and Ruben G. Rumbaut. 2006. *Immigrant America: A Portrait*, Berkeley, CA: University of California Press.

Putnam, Robert D. 2007. "*E Pluribus Unum*: Diversity and community in the twenty-first century," *Scandinavian Political Studies*, 30/2: 137–74.
Qi, H. and P. Bevelander. forthcoming. "Migration and aging," in Klaus Zimmermann, ed., *Handbook of Labor, Human Resources and Population Economic*, New York: Springer.
Razin, A. and E. Sadka. 1999. "Migration and pension with international capital mobility," *Journal of Public Economics*, 74/1: 141–50.
Razin, A. and E. Sadka. 2000. "Unskilled migration: A burden or a boon for the welfare state?" *Scandinavian Journal of Economics*, 102/3: 463–79.
Razin, A. and J. Wahba. 2011. "Welfare magnet hypothesis, fiscal burden and immigration skill selectivity," NBER Working Paper 17515.
Razin, A. and J. Wahba. 2015. "Welfare magnet hypothesis, fiscal burden, and immigration skill selectivity." *Scandinavian Journal of Economics*, 117/2: 369–402.
Richter, W.F. 2004. "Delaying integration of immigrant labor for the purpose of taxation," *Journal of Urban Economics*, 55/3: 597–613.
Riphahn, R.T., M. Sander, and C. Wunder. 2010. "The welfare use of immigrants and natives in Germany: The case of Turkish immigrants," LASER Discussion Paper 44.
Roodenburg, Hans, Rob Euwals, and Harry ter Rele. 2003. "Immigration and the Dutch economy," CPB Special Publication 47.rdf, CPB Netherlands Bureau for Economic Policy Analysis.
Rowthorn, R. 2008. "The fiscal impact of immigration on the advanced economies," *Oxford Review of Economic Policy*, 24/3: 560–80.
Ruhs, Martin. 2013. *The Price of Rights: Regulating International Labor Migration*, Princeton, NJ: Princeton University Press.
Ruist, J. 2015. "The fiscal cost of refugee immigration: The example of Sweden," *Population and Development Review*, 41: 567–81.
Santel, Bernhard and James F. Hollifield. 1998. "Erfolgreiche Integrationsmodelle? Zur wirtschaftlichen Situation von Einwanderern in Deutschland und den USA," in Michael Bommes and Jost Halfmann, eds, *Migration in nationalen Wohlfartsstaaten*, Osnabrück: Universitätsverlag Rasch: 123–45.
Scholten, P. and R. Penninx. 2016. "The multilevel governance of migration and integration," in Blanca Garcés-Mascareñas and Rinus Penninx, eds, *Integration Processes and Policies in Europe*, Cham: Springer: 91–108.
Scholten, P., F. Baggerman, L. Dellouche, V. Kampen, J. Wolf, and R. Ypma. 2017. *Policy Innovation in Refugee Integration? A Comparative Analysis of Innovative Policy Strategies toward Refugee Integration in Europe*, Rotterdam: Erasmus University Rotterdam.
Schultz-Nielsen, M.L. 2017. "Labor market integration of refugees in Denmark," *Nordic Economic Policy Review*: 55–85.
Solano, Giacomo and Thomas Huddleston. 2020. *Migrant Integration Policy Index (MIPEX)*. Barcelona and Brussels: CIDOB and MPG.
Somerville, Will, Dhananjayan Sriskandarajah, and Maria Latorre. 2009. *United Kingdom: A Reluctant Country of Immigration*, Washington, DC: Migration Policy Institute.
Stolper, Wolfgang Friedrich and Paul A. Samuelson. 1941. "Protection and real wages," *Review of Economic Studies*, 9/1: 58–73.
Thiollet, Hélène. 2021. "Illiberal migration governance in the Arab Gulf," in James F. Hollifield and Neil Foley, eds, *Understanding Global Migration*, Stanford, CA: Stanford University Press.
Thränhardt, Dietrich, Agnieszka Kulesa, Cláudia de Freitas, Tiago Maia, and Bernd Parusel. 2020. *Making Asylum Systems Work in the EU, Four Case Studies: Germany, Poland, Portugal and Sweden*, Gütersloh: Bertelsmann Stiftung.
Walzer, Michael. 1983. *Spheres of Justice: A Defense of Pluralism and Equality*, New York: Basic Books.
Weber, René and Thomas Straubhaar. 1996. "Immigration and the public transfer system: Some empirical evidence for Switzerland," *Weltwirtschaftliches Archiv*, 132: 330–55.

2. Economics or politics? Assessing immigration as a challenge to the welfare state
Maureen A. Eger

INTRODUCTION

Milton Friedman (1999) once asserted, "You cannot simultaneously have free immigration and a welfare state." Opponents of immigration often use this quote to support the claim that immigration is bad for welfare states. However, Friedman (1980) had actually argued that only documented immigration threatens the welfare state, whereas irregular immigration has little economic impact, because undocumented migrants do not qualify for social welfare benefits. Nevertheless, this line of argument implicates immigration as an economic challenge for welfare states, a notion that resonates with a certain proportion of countries' citizens. For instance, recent research from the United States (U.S.) shows that 15 percent of survey respondents believe that the average immigrant receives more than twice the amount in transfers as the average U.S. citizen (Alesina et al. 2019).

While empirical evidence linking immigration inflows to the economic downfall of welfare states is tenuous (Giulietti and Wahba 2013; Kahanec and Pytliková 2017; Rowthorn 2008; Tabellini 2020), the notion that immigration and welfare states are incompatible remains central to a political phenomenon known as the "progressive's dilemma" (Goodhart 2004; Banting 2010; Koopmans 2010). This theoretical tension between supporting both liberal immigration and redistributive social policies (Kulin et al. 2016) stems from the concern that immigration-generated ethnic diversity undermines the trust, cohesion, and solidarity necessary to sustain popular support for the welfare state. Arguably this tension is amplified if citizens believe immigrants take more from the welfare state than they contribute to it (e.g., Boeri 2010), though the progressive's dilemma does not hinge theoretically on immigrants' actual fiscal contributions or welfare use. Based on analyses that link immigration to welfare state attitudes and redistributive political preferences, some scholars identify immigration as a political challenge for European welfare states (e.g., Breznau and Eger 2016; Finseraas 2012; Moriconi et al. 2019).

The goal of this chapter is to assess the extent to which immigration poses a threat to the welfare state. Theoretically, there are two main ways that immigration could negatively impact the welfare state. First is the possibility that immigration economically harms countries by depleting national resources and/or worsening individuals' economic circumstances or the national economy at large. Indeed, anti-immigrant political rhetoric often frames immigration as something countries cannot afford. Not surprisingly, then, the second way that immigration may pose a challenge to the welfare state is political. Actual and/or perceived economic effects may undermine the rational interest and/or social solidarity required to support national welfare states, making political support for left-wing parties less likely, including among those individuals most likely to benefit economically from it.

To provide insight into these theoretical relationships, I synthesize previous research from economics, political science, and sociology that assesses the relationship between immigration and either economics or politics related to the welfare state. There are decades of studies on the economic impact of immigration. Some research is cross-national, while other scholarship relies on case studies of single countries. Some studies take a dynamic approach, investigating the economic effects of immigration over generations, but most examine cross-sectional relationships at a single point in time. Variation in methodological approaches contributes to a literature characterized by mixed findings and different conclusions (Dustmann et al. 2016); yet there is growing evidence that, whether the overall economic benefit of immigration is positive or negative, it is *small* (Rowthorn 2008; OECD 2013). In this chapter, I provide a broad overview of the field with an emphasis on recent research as well as studies that take a longer-term perspective and provide insight into how these relationships fluctuate over time.

Compared to the literature on the fiscal impact of immigration, scholarship evaluating immigration as a political challenge to the welfare state is scant. Despite a growing body of research examining the relationship between immigration and attitudes towards redistribution and the welfare state among the native-born (e.g., Alesina et al. 2021; Burgoon et al. 2012; Brady and Finnigan 2014; Eger and Breznau 2017), there are very few studies connecting immigration to political behavior or policy changes. In this chapter, I discuss relevant scholarship with an emphasis on recent studies that aim to fill this significant gap. Based on my review of these literatures, I conclude that immigration poses a larger political challenge to the welfare state, as there is little evidence that it threatens its economic sustainability.

IMMIGRATION AS AN ECONOMIC CHALLENGE FOR WELFARE STATES

The Fiscal Burden Hypothesis

Two main theoretical accounts understand immigration as an economic challenge for welfare states. The first is the fiscal burden hypothesis, which posits that the net economic effect of immigration is negative. Evidence testing this hypothesis takes two forms: direct and indirect effects. A direct negative effect would be that the contributions immigrants make in the form of taxes are, on average, lower than the transfers they receive (Blau 1984; Borjas 1994). Indirect negative effects would involve a negative relationship between immigration and the labor market activity of the native born, specifically rates of employment and wages, as well as macroeconomic trends such as economic growth (Reder 1963; Butcher and Card 1991; De New and Zimmermann 1994; NASEM 2017). Competing hypotheses are that immigration contributes positively to the efficiency of markets and welfare or that immigration's net positive impact is relatively small (Borjas 1995).

Decades of economic research demonstrates that determining whether immigration is a "boon or bane" (Borjas 1995) for countries largely depends on two broad factors: the composition of the immigrant population vis-à-vis the native-born population and the time horizon under consideration. This is not to suggest that measuring immigration's economic effects is a straightforward task (Dustmann et al. 2016). Variation in the age, education level, and occupational skill of immigrants as well as the size of the immigrant inflow influences both the magnitude and direction of wage and employment effects, which also depend on the composition of the native-born population, the local industry mix, and the overall health of the economy (NASEM 2017). Indeed, the occupational skills of immigrants may be complementary and in demand in one setting (Peri and Sparber 2009), leading to economic benefits for native-born and immigrants alike (Borjas 1995; Winter-Ebmer and Zweimüller 1996; Foged and Peri 2016), while in other settings immigrants may displace native workers or depress their wages (Winter-Ebmer and Zweimüller 1999; Dustmann et al. 2017). The economic impact of immigration also depends on whether it is temporary or permanent (Dustmann 1997) or due to employment or asylum seeking (Ruist 2015).

Immigration's economic effects vary not only by local and national labor markets but also over time (Borjas 2005). Importantly, the economic impact of immigrants shares a commonality with the economic impact of native-born in that any potential contribution of an individual varies throughout the life-course, because children and pensioners are associated with different economic costs and benefits than the working-age population. For instance, if immigrants are near to retirement age when they migrate, on average, their fiscal contribution will be negative, regardless of skill or educational level (Rowthorn 2008). Meanwhile, an increase in immigrants of working age may help sustain "graying" welfare states (Ireland 2004; Crepaz 2008), and to the extent that immigration contributes to population growth, it may also be associated with a general increase in consumer demand, productivity, and long-term macroeconomic growth (NASEM 2017).

With regard to the time horizon, there are two types of analyses that measure the fiscal impact of immigrants: static and dynamic (Rowthorn 2008). A static approach calculates the fiscal impact of immigrants in the short term, typically one year, while a dynamic approach considers the economic impact of immigrants (and their descendants) over the course of their lifetimes. For example, using data from the 1994–2000 waves of the European Community Household Panel, Adsera and Chiswick (2006) find that, on average, immigrant earnings catch up with native-born earnings after 18 years in a European country, demonstrating that the fiscal impact of immigrants varies over time. Further, research indicates that this also varies by education level. Using panel data from the U.S. Census Bureau's Survey of Income and Program Participation, Villarreal and Tamborini (2018) find that college-educated immigrants more quickly close their earnings gap with native-born and experience faster earnings growth.

The National Academies of Sciences, Engineering, and Medicine (NASEM) (2017) examined the fiscal impact of immigrants in the U.S. by generation, specifically first-generation immigrants compared to the second generation (i.e., children of immigrants) and the third generation (i.e., grandchildren of immigrants). Cross-sectional analyses of data from the U.S. Census Bureau's Current Population Survey (CPS) between 1994 and 2013 show that, at any age, the net fiscal impact of the foreign-born was, on average, less than the native-born (i.e., second and third generations). NASEM (2017) also finds that, during this time, foreign-born individuals contributed comparatively less in taxes during working age because they earned, on average, less than native-born. Their analyses also revealed that the second generation (i.e., the children of immigrants) had a larger net positive fiscal contribution than either the first or third generations. However, the size of the differences between groups changes over time due to demographic change and shifting age structures within each generation.

Analyzing cross-national European data from 1985 to 2015, d'Albis et al. (2018) evaluate the economic impact of immigration, and their results challenge the notion that asylum seeking, in particular, is associated with an economic cost to countries. They find that "migration shocks" actually yield an economic benefit to European countries, increasing per capita gross domestic product (GDP), reducing unemployment, and improving the balance of public finances. Their analyses show that an increase in tax revenues offsets the increase in public expenditures. These positive effects are observable in the same year and remain significant for at least two years. However, the positive effect of an inflow of asylum seekers takes longer to kick in. Results show that these significant positive effects on GDP occur three to five years after the migration shock.

Also taking a dynamic approach with an even longer time horizon of 75 years, NASEM (2017) shows that immigration is a net positive at the federal level while a net negative at the state and local levels. This is because localities are financially responsible for social expenditure such as education while the bulk of federal benefits go to the elderly. Young immigrants and immigrant families, therefore, use more state and local benefits while contributing positively to the welfare state at the federal level. Their analysis also shows that because of these investments in education, contemporary immigrants contribute much more than immigrants in previous decades. Moreover, by the second generation, the contributions of the children of immigrants are net positive at the state level. They conclude that a foreign-born and a native-born person with similar education will have, on average, the same fiscal impact because individuals with higher levels of education contribute more positively to government finances regardless of generational status.

That the human capital of immigrants and their reason for migrating are related to their fiscal impact raises questions about how variation in immigration regimes that differ in selectivity (Borjas 1988) and welfare state regimes that differ in degree of universality or generosity (Borjas 1999) are related to cross-national variation in the economic impact of immigrants. *Ceteris paribus*, countries with policies that select high-skilled immigrants and/or limit immigrants' access to social rights are theoretically more likely to experience immigration as an economic advantage in any given year, while countries with policies that select lower-skilled immigrants and/or provide immediate access to social rights are theoretically more likely to experience immigration as an economic disadvantage in any given year (cf. Colas and Sachs 2020). Empirical evidence linking regime type to labor market outcomes for immigrants in Europe is limited (e.g., Gorodzeisky and Semyonov 2017), although studies have shown higher labor force participation among female immigrants in social democratic welfare states (Kesler 2006) and among low-skilled, male immigrants in liberal welfare states (Kogan 2006).

Cross-national differences in immigration policies as well as within-country change over time means that the impact of immigration is neither universal nor immutable. For example, Ekberg (1999, 2009) shows that, due to declining employment, the net contribution of immigrants in Sweden changed from positive in the 1950s through 1970s to negative from the mid-1980s. According to Ekberg (2009), prior to the 1980s immigration to Sweden was dominated by labor migration but this shifted towards asylum seeking in recent decades. Ruist's (2015) analyses of asylum seeking and (2014) intra-EU labor migration to Sweden reveal that, in the same year, the economic impact of refugees, who do not immediately enter the labor market, and labor migrants differ. Economic migrants' contributions are net positive while refugees' are net negative. Ruist (2015) finds that approximately 80 percent of the fiscal cost of refugees stems from lower per capita revenue and only 20 percent comes from higher per capita spending. This implies that increasing the employment rate of refugees is critical for longer-term economic benefits, both direct and indirect.

Though harder to quantify, the indirect costs and benefits of immigration are an important part of the equation. Using municipality and population register data from 1991 to 2008, Foged and Peri (2016) show that an increase in refugees coincided with an increase in employment in less manual labor-intensive occupations among native-borns with lower levels of education. Thus, an increase in asylum seekers yielded positive effects on unskilled native-born Danes' wages, employment, and occupational mobility over time (Foged and Peri 2016). Similarly, Tabellini (2020) connects immigration to occupational upgrading among U.S. natives between 1910 and 1930. He attributes this relationship to two mechanisms: "because of complementarity, natives moved away from occupations that were more exposed to immigrants' competition and specialized in jobs where they had a comparative advantage and, because of discrimination, immigrants did not have access to" (Tabellini 2020, 458).

Using U.S. census data between 1980 and 2007, Piyapromdee (2021) shows that a large increase in the stock of immigrants to cities holds little consequence for the wages of natives and that any real effect is concentrated among previous immigrants. She also finds that internal migration within the U.S. helps equalize the impact of immigration across cities over time. NASEM (2017) finds that the overall long-term impact of immigration on the wages and employment of native-born workers in the U.S. is minimal and that negative effects are concentrated among those with the least education (i.e., less than secondary school). Its analyses suggest that first-generation immigrants are more costly to governments than are the native-born, but the second generation (i.e., the children of immigrants) are among the strongest fiscal and economic contributors in the U.S. They conclude that immigration has an overall positive impact on long-run economic growth in the U.S. Meanwhile, Dustmann et al. (2017) come to different conclusions in their analysis of the impact of Czech workers on bordering local German labor markets; yet their analysis focuses only on the short-term effects of an immigration-induced labor supply shock, leaving open the possibility that longer-term effects might differ.

Nevertheless, the short-term and long-term fiscal contribution of migrants ultimately depends on their degree of integration in the labor market (OECD 2014). If immigrants are unemployed or underemployed, their fiscal contribution will be limited, regardless of skill level or time in the country (Rowthorn 2008). Cross-national research finds lower levels of employment and labor market participation among foreign-born compared to native-born in European countries (Kogan 2006). For instance, using data from the European Social Survey (ESS) and European Union Labour Forces Survey, Gorodzeisky and Semyonov (2017) find that first-generation immigrants from non-European countries and their children (i.e., the second generation) are less likely to be employed than European immigrants and their descendants.

Yet gaps in employment or earnings cannot be fully explained by differences in human capital (Siebers and Koster 2021; Villarreal and Tamborini 2018) and may be attributable to labor market discrimination (Evans and Kelley 1991; Pager and Shepherd 2008) consistent with the segmented assimilation model (Portes and Zhou 1993). According to this account, possibilities and opportunities for immigrants and their children also depend on the social and political characteristics of a country, including existing racial and ethnic stratification and patterns of prejudice. For example, based on their analysis of Vietnamese immigrants in Germany over time, Bösch and Su (2020) conclude that the context of reception plays a more important role for opportunities and outcomes than immigrants' cultural traits or human capital.

Other studies that reveal differences in outcomes by race, ethnicity, or country/region of origin despite the human capital of immigrants are consistent with the segmented assimilation model's predictions. For instance, Rafferty (2012) finds that, in the United Kingdom, the higher education qualifications of immigrants do not translate into labor market outcomes equal to those of comparably educated white native-born. Rafferty describes the disadvantage experienced by minority ethnic groups as an "ethnic penalty." Other recent research finds that, in the U.S., the gap in earnings between Hispanic/black immigrants and white/Asian immigrants is actually larger among college-educated men than among those without tertiary education (Villarreal and Tamborini 2018). According to Van Tubergen et al. (2004), ethnic hierarchies also help explain the underachievement of immigrants with non-European ethnic origins in Western European countries.

Evidence of inequities that cannot be explained by human capital sheds light on a phenomenon known as "the integration paradox," where better economically integrated immigrants with higher levels of education become disenchanted with a host society possibly due to experiences of relative deprivation and labor market discrimination (Verkuyten 2016). For instance, in the Netherlands, Canada, and New Zealand, immigrants with higher levels of education are more likely to report discrimination than those with lower levels of education (de Vroome et al. 2014; OECD 2012). Kogan et al. (2018) show that the immigrants' satisfaction with the host country is related to native-born attitudes towards them. Studies like this are a good reminder that the experiences of immigrants, including their fiscal contributions, do not exist in a vacuum but also depend on interactions with native-born and host-country institutions and policies (Siebers and Koster 2021; Valverde and Latorre 2019).

The Welfare Magnet Hypothesis

The second theoretical account of the relationship between immigration and the welfare state is known as the welfare magnet hypothesis (Borjas 1999). According to this theory, robust welfare states attract more immigrants. Welfare state generosity not only serves as a significant pull factor for immigrants, possibly even attracting individuals and families that would not have otherwise migrated, but also disincentivizes return migration, possibly retaining immigrants who without a social safety net would have otherwise returned to their country of origin. While this hypothesis only predicts demographic trends, the implication is that by attracting more immigrants, a welfare state creates economic challenges for itself, per the fiscal burden hypothesis (e.g., Nannestad 2007).

Cross-national tests of this hypothesis yield mixed findings. For example, Pedersen et al. (2008) find no systematic evidence that social expenditure as a percentage of GDP is related to migration flows from 129 origin countries to 22 Organisation for Economic Co-operation and Development (OECD) destination countries between 1990 and 2000.

Similarly, Giulietti et al. (2013) conclude there is essentially zero causal effect of unemployment benefits on immigration inflows to 19 European countries between 1993 and 2008. However, Brücker et al. (2002) show that the generosity of the welfare state is inversely related to the skill level of immigrants in Western European countries. Moreover, Razin and Wahba (2015) report that, under conditions of free migration within the European Union (EU), the generosity of the welfare state acts as a magnet for unskilled migrants and moves the composition of the immigrant population towards low skill (see also Boeri 2010). Yet under conditions of restricted migration from outside the EU, the generosity of the welfare state attracts high-skilled migrants. Thus, welfare states may make countries more attractive to immigrants, both low and high skilled, but the relationship depends on other factors such as migration policy. Moreover, other factors contribute to decisions to migrate: recent research shows that migrants tend to move to countries where their skills are scarce (Fenoll and Kuehn 2019).

Other scholars argue that welfare use among immigrants, rather than levels of immigration, is evidence of the welfare magnet hypothesis (e.g., Pellizzari 2013). Much like the other literatures reviewed here, the empirical literature on immigrants' use of social welfare relative to the native-born population is also mixed. Arguably this is not only because of variation in the composition of immigrant populations between and within countries but also because of between-country differences in welfare state regimes and within-country changes in social policies affecting immigrants over time. For example, using the U.S. Census Bureau's Survey of Income and Program Participation data, Borjas and Hilton (1996) find that immigrants in the U.S. relied on social welfare more frequently and for longer periods of time than native-born between 1984 and 1991. However, Fix and Passel's (1999) analysis of the CPS reveals that welfare use among immigrants (including refugees) declined sharply after the passage of the 1996 Personal Responsibility and Work Opportunity Reconciliation Act. This legislation mandates, among other things, that non-refugee immigrants who enter the U.S. after 1996 must wait five years before qualifying for federally funded cash assistance. Additionally, the bill limits the length of time refugees qualify for many federal benefits. Fix and Passel show that, by 1997, non-citizens had lower participation rates than citizens, and among poor families with children, non-citizen rates fell to almost half the rate of citizens. Neither naturalization nor rising incomes among immigrants accounts for these patterns.

Recent research indicates that welfare use and associated costs is, on average, lower among immigrants than U.S. natives. Nowrasteh and Orr's (2018) analysis of 2016–17 data from CPS and the 2015 Medical Expenditure Panel Survey reveals that immigrants are less likely than native-born to use every means-tested or welfare program, with the exception of foreign-born being 0.4 percent more likely to use Medicaid. Breaking this down by citizenship status reveals that non-citizen immigrants rely on every welfare program less than U.S. natives do and the difference in participation rates is often quite large. Naturalized immigrants also use less welfare than native-born citizens, with the exception of Medicaid and Supplemental Security Income. Nevertheless, the authors also show that, for every means-tested and entitlement program, the average poor or elderly immigrant costs less than the average poor or elderly native. They report that the average costs for each immigrant eligible for social welfare programs is 27 percent less than for their native-born counterparts. Further, Huang et al.'s (2020) analysis of CPS from 1995 to 2018 indicates that, if immigrants had the same demographic characteristics as native-born, their participation in means-tested programs would have actually been much lower and well below natives' welfare use. Analyzing welfare use at the household rather than individual level, NASEM (2017) also reports that immigrant households have lower utilization rates of means-tested programs compared to native-headed households among households under 200 percent of the federal poverty line.

Cross-national and country case studies from Europe yield mixed results. Using pooled cross-sectional data from the EU Survey of Income and Living Conditions for 12 Western European countries between 2004 and 2007, Boeri (2010) finds that migrants pay proportionally less in taxes and contributions than natives and are also overrepresented among recipients of non-contributory transfers (i.e., social and housing assistance). However, compared to native-born, immigrants are underrepresented among pensioners and recipients of sickness unemployment benefits. Analyses also show that immigrants are overrepresented among recipients of educational allowances but underrepresented in the use of public health care. Boeri reports cross-national differences in welfare dependency. Similarly, Brücker et al. (2002) find variation in welfare dependency with regards to unemployment benefits among immigrants in Austria, Denmark, Finland, France, and the Netherlands, but not in Germany, Greece, Spain, or the United Kingdom. Hansen and Lofstrom (2003, 2009) show higher rates of welfare use among immigrants compared to native-born in Sweden but that immigrants' welfare use declines with time spent in the country, while Nannestad (2004) finds higher welfare use among immigrants even after a decade of residency. Meanwhile, Castronova et al. (2001) find that immigrants, given their eligibility, are no more likely to rely on welfare benefits compared to natives in Germany. Similarly, Zimmermann et al. (2012) show that, while welfare use is higher among immigrants than native-born in much of the EU, this pattern only persists in a few countries once socioeconomic characteristics are considered. Scholars consistently identify the composition of the immigrant population, and characteristics such as skill level (Giulietti and Wahba 2013) and employment status (Wadensjö and Orrje 2002), as key determinants of welfare use.

Taken together, existing empirical research suggests that while it is difficult to claim immigration is an economic threat to national welfare states, it is also unreasonable to describe immigration as a panacea for other welfare state challenges such as "the graying of society." Immigration does contribute to the size of the working-age population but the economic benefit, on average, remains small (OECD 2014). Based on a review of empirical studies, Rowthorn (2008) concluded that the fiscal impact of immigration is modest—falling somewhere between +/− 1 percent of GDP cross-nationally. He argued that this is because the negative fiscal impact of some immigrants is offset by the positive fiscal impact of others. A study of OECD countries came to a similar conclusion: on average, immigrants in the largest economies contribute more in taxes and social contributions than they receive in welfare benefits, but the positive net fiscal impact is small (Liebig and Mo 2013). Indeed, the OECD average is less than 1 percent of GDP. The study concludes that impact of immigration over the past 50 years is broadly neutral, which is consistent with the notion that the negative contribution of some immigrants is counterbalanced by the positive contribution of other immigrants (e.g., Kahanec and Pytliková 2017). In conclusion, the notion that immigration poses a significant challenge to the viability of the welfare state is not supported by the most recent cross-national and longitudinal studies.

IMMIGRATION AS A POLITICAL CHALLENGE FOR WELFARE STATES

That immigration is not an economic detriment to countries does not mean that it cannot pose a political challenge. Sociologists, political scientists, and most recently economists have investigated the relationship between the presence of immigrants and native-born *attitudes* towards the welfare state. Theoretically, there are at least a few different mechanisms that would account for a negative association between immigration and support for a redistributive welfare state. One is reciprocity. Because welfare states depend on mutual obligations among residents of a country, if one believes that welfare recipients do not contribute by paying taxes, it becomes rational not to support the welfare state (Alesina et al. 2001) or to oppose social rights for particular groups perceived as abusing the system. Figure 2.1 reports country averages for perceptions about immigrants' net contribution to the welfare state in countries participating in the ESS in 2002 and 2014. Respondents were asked whether "immigrants take out more than they put in or put in

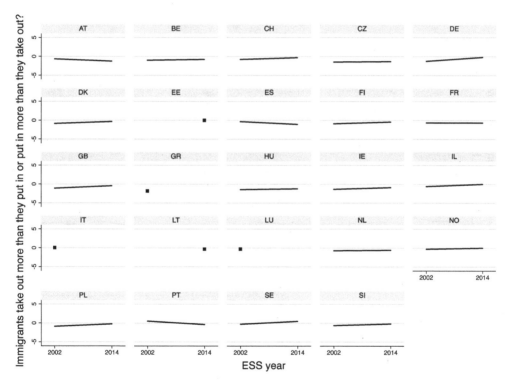

Note: N = 82,544; original variable (IMBLECO) rescaled from 0 to 10 to –5 to 5 to reflect whether the average respondent believes immigrants use more than they contribute (negative values) or contribute more than they use (positive values). In the five countries that only participated in one of these two ESS rounds, the average response is represented by a dot.

Source: European Social Survey (ESS1-9e01).

Figure 2.1 Attitudes about immigrants' impact on the welfare state, 2002 and 2014

more than they take out?" On average, people believe that immigrants' net fiscal contribution is negative, though the extent to which varies cross-nationally.

A second mechanism is out-group prejudice due to economic threat, or concerns that the presence of an out-group engenders competition for scarce economic resources, such as welfare or jobs (Blumer 1958; Blalock 1967). By this account, the belief that immigrants negatively impact a country's economy could weaken support for social spending. Figure 2.2 illustrates country averages over time regarding perceptions about immigrants' impact on the national economy. Like Figure 2.1, these data come from the ESS, but this question has been asked biannually since the start of the survey program. Thus, it is easier to see variation over time as well as between-country differences. It is worth noting that many of the countries where, on average, people believe that immigrants negatively impact the economy have smaller immigrant populations compared to the countries where people, on average, perceive immigrants to positively impact the economy. This picture is consistent with previous scholarship that finds a weak relationship between the proportion of a country that is born abroad and native-born attitudes towards immigrants (e.g., Pottie-Sherman and Wilkes 2017).

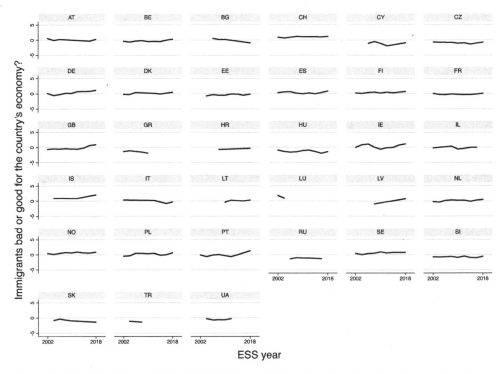

Note: N = 401,884; original variable (IMBGECO) rescaled from 0 to 10 to –5 to 5 to reflect whether the average respondent believes immigration is bad for the national economy (negative values) or good for the national economy (positive values).

Source: European Social Survey (ESS1-9e01).

Figure 2.2 Attitudes about the economic impact of immigration, 2002–18

Economics or politics? 55

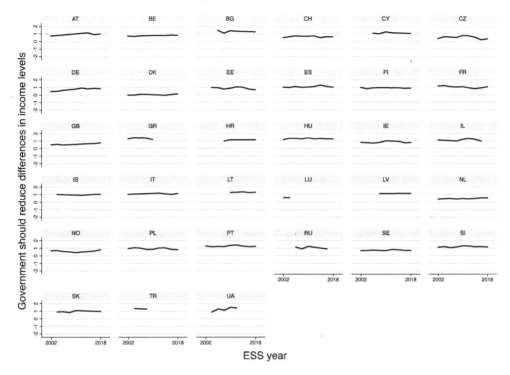

Note: N = 414,432; original variable (GINCDIF) rescaled from 1 to 5 to –2 to 2 to reflect whether the average respondent disagrees (negative values) or agrees (positive values) that the government should reduce income differences.

Source: European Social Survey (ESS1-9e01).

Figure 2.3   Attitudes about redistribution, 2002–18

Figure 2.3 shows average levels of support for redistribution across this same set of countries. On average, people across countries agree to some extent that the government should reduce income inequality.

Is there a relationship between what people think about the economic impact of immigrants and support for redistribution? Figure 2.4 shows the country-level association between perceptions about immigrants' fiscal impact on the national economy and support for redistribution over time. The direction of this bivariate relationship is inconsistent across countries. For example, in Germany, Great Britain, and Greece, more positive attitudes about immigrants' impact on the national economy appears positively associated with support for redistribution, while in Austria, Czech Republic, Norway, Ukraine, and Israel there is a negative association. In other countries, the country-level averages over time are unrelated.

Figure 2.5 illustrates predicted values from an individual-level two-way fixed-effects model, which reveals that the average relationship across countries over time is slightly negative. This means that more positive attitudes about immigrants are actually associated with a small but significant within-country decrease in support for redistribution.

56 *Handbook on migration and welfare*

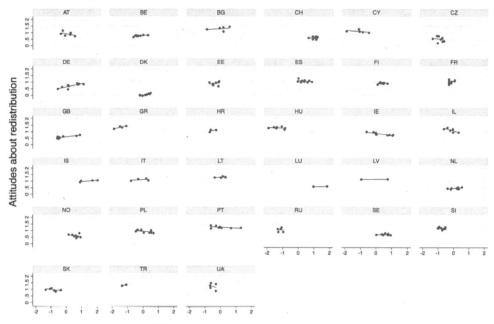

Note: N = 395,895; original variables rescaled from 0 to 10 to –5 to 5 (IMBGECO) and 1 to 5 to –2 to 2 (GINCDIF) to reflect negative and positive attitudes towards immigrants and redistribution.

Source: European Social Survey (ESS1-9e01).

Figure 2.4   Attitudes about immigrants' economic impact and support for redistribution, 2002–18

This negative correlation provides evidence of a literal interpretation of the progressive's dilemma's empirical expectations, specifically the low probability of holding both pro-immigrant and pro-redistribution stances (Kulin et al. 2016).

A third mechanism is in-group bias, or the tendency to favor one's own group. Research from psychology reveals that people prefer allocating resources to in-group members as opposed to out-group members (Brewer 1979; Tajfel et al. 1971; Turner 1975). Based on this experimental evidence, Eger (2010) theorized that, by making national in-group/out-group boundaries salient, increased immigration activates in-group bias and decreases support for social spending. Studies that identify in-group bias as a potential mechanism often analyze the relationship between *objective* immigration and welfare attitudes. Some of these studies have focused on a phenomenon known as welfare chauvinism (Reeskens and Van Oorschot 2012) or welfare nationalism (Eger et al. 2020), where native-born oppose the extension of welfare benefits to immigrants, preferring instead to limit social rights to native-born. However, most studies in this body of research have been concerned with the impact of immigration on support for redistribution, social expenditure, and/or a comprehensive welfare state (Eger 2010; Brady and Finnigan 2014; Breznau and Eger 2016), as a reduction in support for the institution in

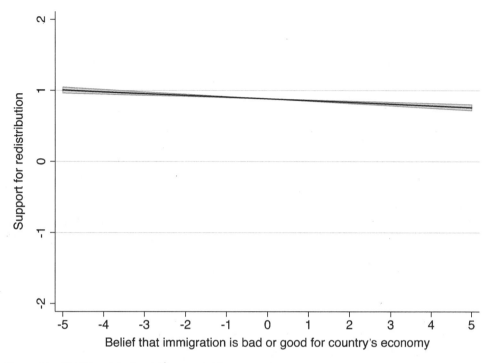

Note: N = 395,895; original variables rescaled from 0 to 10 to –5 to 5 (IMBGECO) and 1 to 5 to –2 to 2 (GINCDIF) to reflect negative and positive attitudes towards immigrants and redistribution; robust standard errors for clustering by country.

Source: European Social Survey (ESS1-9e01).

Figure 2.5 Two-way fixed-effects model of support for redistribution, 2002–18

general would arguably constitute a greater threat to it than a reduction in support for immigrants' social rights specifically. This body of attitudinal research is also characterized by mixed results: cross-national studies, that measure immigration at the country level, find little evidence of a relationship (Brady and Finnigan 2014; Heizmann et al. 2018; Hjerm and Schnabel 2012; Mau and Burkhardt 2009), while studies that analyze the relationship at the sub-national/regional level reveal negative associations between immigrant presence and welfare attitudes (Alesina et al. 2021; Dahlberg et al. 2012; Eger 2010; Eger and Breznau 2017; Stichnoth 2012).

In democracies, public opinion and attitudes are important for voting behavior, electoral politics, and policy outcomes. Thus, the empirical relationship between immigration and welfare attitudes should have implications for political outcomes. To the extent that citizens cast their votes on the basis of these issues, economically left-wing parties that aim to maintain or expand the welfare state could experience a decline in electoral support in reaction to immigration. Research on social democracy between 1918 and 2017 concludes that the decline in electoral support for European social democratic parties is partially due to a decrease in the size of the industrial sector but also to a reduction in these parties' historic core supporters' propensity to vote for them (Benedetto et al. 2020).

Recent studies confirm that views on immigration have contributed to the electoral realignment of working-class voters—those most likely to benefit from redistributive policies (Oesch and Rennwald 2018; Evans and Mellon 2019). As Abou-Chadi and Wagner (2019) point out, in public and academic debates, European social democratic parties' progressive stances on immigration and European integration are often cited as reasons for their electoral decline. According to Goodhart (2004), economically left-wing parties are experiencing a "progressive's dilemma" in that they must decide whether to prioritize social democratic values and voters or immigration and diversity. In other words, because solidarity and diversity are theoretically difficult to combine, social democratic parties risk losing voters and, as a consequence of poor electoral outcomes, undermine the welfare state. Various chapters later in the *Handbook* delve more deeply into the question of whether or to what extent a progressive's dilemma exists in modern welfare states.

Scholarship connecting immigration to electoral support for social democratic parties and redistributive policies is relatively scarce. Yet in recent years empirical studies have begun to examine these relationships. Using ESS data between 2002 and 2008 across 17 European countries, Finseraas (2012) finds that those who oppose immigration but support redistribution are less likely to support a left party than those who support both redistribution and immigration. In Chapter 12 in this *Handbook*, Eger and Kulin also use ESS as well as General Social Survey data to assess the relationship between immigration welfare attitudes and voting behavior in Sweden, Germany, and the U.S. between 2002 and 2018. Their analyses confirm that any attitudinal configuration but the most progressive one (i.e., being pro-redistribution and pro-immigration) makes support for left parties unlikely. Abou-Chadi and Wagner (2019) complicate this picture, however. Combining data from ESS and the Chapel Hill Expert Survey for 13 West European countries between 2002 and 2016, the authors do not find evidence that working-class, less educated, or older voters are less likely to vote for a social democratic party if those parties are more progressive, pro-EU, or pro-immigration. Their analysis also suggests that younger, highly educated, and professional voters may find social democratic parties less attractive if these parties make fewer progressive claims.

Recent research has also investigated how objective immigration affects politics. Using election data from 12 European countries between 2006 and 2017, Moriconi et al. (2019) analyze the impact of immigration on political support for welfare state expansion in Europe. Contrary to expectations, their analyses show that larger inflows of highly skilled immigrants are associated with a significant shift in voting for parties with policy preferences consistent with the expansion—not retrenchment—of the welfare state. Unskilled immigration does not have a significant effect on party vote. However, they also find that inflows of unskilled immigrants are associated with a decline in political parties making pro-welfare state claims. Focusing on the impact of asylum seeking, Dustmann et al. (2019) show that, between 1986 and 1998, refugee placement in Danish municipalities increases anti-immigration parties' vote share in parliamentary and municipal elections and decreases the vote share of center-left parties, except for in the largest localities. They also find that refugee allocation was more strongly associated with voting for anti-immigration parties in municipalities where welfare dependency among immigrants was higher. These results echo findings from studies on the economic impact of immigration, suggesting that the political impact of immigration may also depend on the skill and education levels of immigrants as well as the reason for migrating.

Finally, other research links immigration to policy outcomes, such as social spending. For instance, Tabellini (2020) shows that between 1910 and 1930, immigration negatively impacted both public spending per capita and tax rates in U.S. cities. Analyzing OECD countries, Soroka et al. (2006) show that immigration depressed welfare states' rates of growth between 1970 and 1998. They estimate that if the proportion of countries' population born abroad remained at 1970 levels, these wealthy economies would have spent approximately 17 percent more than they did at the end of the last century. Soroka et al. (2016) revisit this question with data through 2007 and confirm that increased immigration to OECD countries is associated with smaller increases in social spending. Kim and Lee's (2021) panel analysis of 24 OECD destination countries reveals that immigration alters the composition of public spending. Specifically, immigration has a negative impact on social protection and health expenditure, but a positive impact on defense, public order, and economic affairs expenditure. Thus, it appears that immigration may not decrease the overall size of government, but it does affect the extent to which welfare states are redistributive.

CONCLUSION

The goal of this chapter was to assess the extent to which immigration poses an economic and/or political threat to the welfare state. Because immigration is a politically divisive issue, an interest in teasing out the economic impact of immigrants, who comprise only a segment of national populations, from a plethora of other factors has motivated a great deal of economic research. Although there are studies that suggest negative economic effects, other research demonstrates that the fiscal impact of immigration is positive. Further, some scholarship shows immigrants are more likely to be among welfare recipients while other research shows that immigrants rely on welfare to a lesser extent than native-born of similar socioeconomic status. Differences in the time horizon of these studies helps explain these divergent results, as do the demographic characteristics of immigrants, including whether they are members of stigmatized groups in society. Though the most recent cross-national and longitudinal studies indicate that, on average, immigration's net fiscal impact is positive, it is nevertheless small. Scholarship on the political impact of immigration, however, provides clearer evidence that immigration creates challenges for welfare states with regards to welfare attitudes, support for left parties, and redistributive social policies. Arguably, some of these political challenges may be easier to overcome if the myth that immigration is an economic burden is dispelled (d'Albis et al. 2018) and citizens recognize the reciprocal contributions of immigrants. However, this would not necessarily negate the effects of in-group bias, a key theoretical mechanism underlying the progressive's dilemma.

ACKNOWLEDGMENTS

The research in this chapter was supported by the Swedish Research Council for Health, Working Life and Welfare (FORTE 2016-07177).

REFERENCES

Abou-Chadi, Tarik, and Markus Wagner. 2019. "The electoral appeal of party strategies in postindustrial societies: When can the mainstream left succeed?" *Journal of Politics* 81(4): 1405–19.

Adsera, Alicia, and Barry R. Chiswick. 2006. "Divergent patterns in immigrant earnings across European destinations." pp. 85–110 in *Immigration and the Transformation of Europe*, edited by Craig A. Parsons and Timothy M. Smeeding. Cambridge: Cambridge University Press.

Alesina, Alberto, Edward L. Glaeser, and Bruce Sacerdote. 2001. "Why doesn't the U.S. have a European-style welfare system?" *Brookings Papers on Economic Activity* October: 187–248.

Alesina, Alberto, Armando Miano, and Stefanie Stantcheva. 2019. "Immigration and redistribution." *National Bureau of Economic Research* No. w24733, doi: 10.3386/w24733.

Alesina, Alberto, Elie Murard, and Hillel Rapoport. 2021. "Immigration and preferences for redistribution in Europe." *Journal of Economic Geography* lbab002, doi: 10.1093/jeg/lbab002.

Banting, Keith. 2010. "Is there a progressive's dilemma in Canada? Immigration, multiculturalism and the welfare state." *Canadian Journal of Political Science* 43(4): 797–820.

Benedetto, Giacomo, Simon Hix, and Nicola Mastrorocco. 2020. "The rise and fall of social democracy, 1918–2017." *American Political Science Review* 114(3): 928–39.

Blalock, Hubert M. 1967. *Toward a Theory of Minority-Group Relations*. New York: Wiley.

Blau, Francine D. 1984. "The use of transfer payments by immigrants." *ILR Review* 37(2): 222–39.

Blumer, Herbert. 1958. "Race prejudice as a sense of group position." *Pacific Sociological Review* 1(1): 3–7.

Boeri, Tito. 2010. "Immigration to the land of redistribution." *Economica* 77(308): 651–87.

Borjas, George J. 1988. *International Differences in the Labor Market Performance of Immigrants*. Kalamazoo, MI: W.E. Upjohn Institute for Employment Research.

Borjas, George J. 1994. "The economics of immigration." *Journal of Economic Literature* 32(4): 1667–717.

Borjas, George J. 1995. "The economic benefits from immigration." *Journal of Economic Perspectives* 9(2): 3–22.

Borjas, George J. 1999. "Immigration and welfare magnets." *Journal of Labor Economics* 17(4): 607–37.

Borjas, George J. 2005. "The labor-market impact of high-skill immigration." *American Economic Review* 95(2): 56–60.

Borjas, George J., and Lynette Hilton. 1996. "Immigration and the welfare state: Immigrant participation in means-tested entitlement programs." *Quarterly Journal of Economics* 111(2): 575–604.

Bösch, Frank, and Phi Hong Su. 2020. "Competing contexts of reception in refugee and immigrant incorporation: Vietnamese in West and East Germany." *Journal of Ethnic and Migration Studies*, doi:10.1080/1369183X.2020.1724418.

Brady, David, and Ryan Finnigan. 2014. "Does immigration undermine public support for social policy?" *American Sociological Review* 79(1): 17–42.

Brewer, Marilynn B. 1979. "In-group bias in the minimal intergroup situation: A cognitive-motivational analysis." *Psychological Bulletin* 86(2): 307–24.

Breznau, Nate, and Maureen A. Eger. 2016. "Immigrant presence, group boundaries, and support for the welfare state in Western European societies." *Acta Sociologica* 59(3): 195–214.

Brücker, Herbert, Gil S. Epstein, Barry McCormick, Gilles Saint-Paul, Alessandra Venturini, and Klaus F. Zimmermann. 2002. "Managing migration in the European welfare state." pp. 1–168 in *Immigration Policy and the Welfare System*, edited by Tito Boeri, Gordon Hanson, and Barry McCormick. Oxford: Oxford University Press.

Burgoon, Brian, Ferry Koster, and Marcel Van Egmond. 2012. "Support for redistribution and the paradox of immigration." *Journal of European Social Policy* 22(3): 288–304.

Butcher, Kristin F., and David Card. 1991. "Immigration and wages: Evidence from the 1980s." *American Economic Review* 81(2): 292–6.

Castronova, Edward J., Hilke Kayser, Joachim R. Frick, and Gert G. Wagner. 2001. "Immigrants, natives and social assistance: Comparable take-up under comparable circumstances." *International Migration Review* 35(3): 726–48.

Colas, Mark, and Dominik Sachs. 2020. "The indirect fiscal benefits of low-skilled immigration." Opportunity and Inclusive Growth Institute Working Papers 38, Federal Reserve Bank of Minneapolis, doi: 10.21034/iwp.38.

Crepaz, Markus M.L. 2008. *Trust beyond Borders: Immigration, the Welfare State, and Identity in Modern Societies*. Ann Arbor, MI: University of Michigan Press.

d'Albis, Hippolyte, Ekrame Boubtane, and Dramane Coulibaly. 2018. "Macroeconomic evidence suggests that asylum seekers are not a 'burden' for Western European countries." *Science Advances* 4(6): EAAQ0883.

Dahlberg, Matz, Karin Edmark, and Helene Lundqvist. 2012. "Ethnic diversity and preferences for redistribution." *Journal of Political Economy* 120(1): 41–76.

De New, John P., and Klaus F. Zimmermann. 1994. "Native wages impacts of foreign labour: A random effects panel analysis." *Journal of Population Economics* 7(2): 177–92.

de Vroome, Thomas, Borja Martinovic, and Maykel Verkuyten. 2014. "The integration paradox: Level of education and immigrants' attitudes towards natives and the host society." *Cultural Diversity and Ethnic Minority Psychology* 20(2): 166–75.

Dustmann, Christian. 1997. "Return migration, uncertainty and precautionary savings." *Journal of Development Economics* 52(2): 295–316.

Dustmann, Christian, Uta Schönberg, and Jan Stuhler. 2016. "The impact of immigration: Why do studies reach such different results?" *Journal of Economic Perspectives* 30(4): 31–56.

Dustmann, Christian, Uta Schönberg, and Jan Stuhler. 2017. "Labor supply shocks, native wages, and the adjustment of local employment." *Quarterly Journal of Economics* 132: 435–83.

Dustmann, Christian, Kristine Vasiljeva, and Anna Piil Damm. 2019. "Refugee migration and electoral outcomes." *Review of Economic Studies* 86(5): 2035–91.

Eger, Maureen A. 2010. "Even in Sweden: The effect of immigration on support for welfare state spending." *European Sociological Review* 26(2): 203–17.

Eger, Maureen A., and Nate Breznau. 2017. "Immigration and the welfare state: A cross-regional analysis of European welfare attitudes." *International Journal of Comparative Sociology* 58(5): 440–63.

Eger, Maureen A., Christian Albrekt Larsen, and Jan Mewes. 2020. "Welfare nationalism before and after the 'migration crisis.'" pp. 177–98 in *Welfare State Legitimacy in Times of Crisis and Austerity: Between Change and Continuity*, edited by Tijs Laenen, Bart Meuleman, and Wim van Oorschot. Cheltenham, UK and Northampton, MA, USA: Edward Elgar Publishing.

Ekberg, Jan. 1999. "Immigration and the public sector: Income effects for the native population in Sweden." *Journal of Population Economics* 12(3): 411–30.

Ekberg, Jan. 2009. *Invandringen och de offentliga finanserna [Immigration and the public finances]*. Rapport 2009:3 to the Expert Group for Public Finances (ESO). Stockholm: Ministry of Finance.

European Social Survey Cumulative File, ESS 1-9. 2020. Data file edition 1.0. NSD – Norwegian Centre for Research Data, Norway – Data Archive and distributor of ESS data for ESS ERIC. doi:10.21338/NSD-ESS-CUMULATIVE.

Evans, Geoffrey, and Jonathan Mellon. 2019. "Immigration, Euroscepticism, and the rise and fall of UKIP." *Party Politics* 25(1): 76–87.

Evans, M.D.R., and Jonathan Kelley. 1991. "Prejudice, discrimination, and the labor market: Attainments of immigrants in Australia." *American Journal of Sociology* 97(3): 721–59.

Fenoll, Ainoa Aparicio, and Zoë Kuehn. 2019. "Immigrants move where their skills are scarce: Evidence from English proficiency." *Labour Economics* 61: 101748.

Finseraas, Henning. 2012. "Anti-immigration attitudes, support for redistribution and party choice in Europe." In *Changing Social Equality: The Nordic Welfare Model in the 21st Century*, edited by Jon Kvist, Johan Fritzell, Bjørn Hvinden, and Olli Kangas. Bristol: Policy Press: 23–44.

Fix, Michael, and Jeffery S. Passel. 1999. "Trends in noncitizens' and citizens' use of public benefits following welfare reform 1994–97." Washington, DC: The Urban Institute. http://webarchive.urban.org/publications/408086.html.

Foged, Mette, and Giovanni Peri. 2016. "Immigrants' effect on native workers: New analysis on longitudinal data." *American Economic Journal: Applied Economics* 8(2): 1–34.

Friedman, Milton. 1980. "What is America?" Lecture presented at the University of Chicago. www.youtube.com/watch?v=fwDhx1XkXX0.

Friedman, Milton. 1999. Q&A with Milton Friedman at the 18th Annual Institute for Liberty and Policy Analysis (ISIL) World Libertarian Conference, August 20–22, 1999, in San Jose, Costa Rica.

Giulietti, Corrado, and Jackline Wahba. 2013. "Welfare migration." pp. 489–504 in *International Handbook on the Economics of Migration*, edited by Amelie F. Constant and Klaus F. Zimmermann. Cheltenham, UK and Northampton, MA, USA: Edward Elgar Publishing.

Giulietti, Corrado, Martin Guzi, Martin Kahanec, and Klaus F. Zimmermann. 2013. "Unemployment benefits and immigration: Evidence from the EU." *International Journal of Manpower* 34(1): 24–38.

Goodhart, David. 2004. "Too diverse?" *Prospect* February: 30–7.

Gorodzeisky, Anastasia, and Moshe Semyonov. 2017. "Labor force participation, unemployment and occupational attainment among immigrants in West European countries." *PLoS ONE* 12(5): e0176856.

Hansen, Jorgen, and Magnus Lofstrom. 2003. "Immigrant assimilation and welfare participation: Do immigrants assimilate into or out of welfare?" *Journal of Human Resources* 38(1): 74–98.

Hansen, Jorgen, and Magnus Lofstrom. 2009. "The dynamics of immigrant welfare and labor market behavior." *Journal of Population Economics* 22(4): 941–70.

Heizmann, Boris, Alexander Jedinger, and Anja Perry. 2018. "Welfare chauvinism, economic insecurity and the asylum seeker 'crisis.'" *Societies* 8(3): 83.

Hjerm, Mikael, and Annette Schnabel. 2012. "How much heterogeneity can the welfare state endure? The influence of heterogeneity on attitudes to the welfare state." *Nations and Nationalism* 18(2): 346–69.
Huang, Xiaoning, Neeraj Kaushal, and Julia Shu-Huah Wang. 2020. "What explains the gap in welfare use among immigrants and natives?" *Population Research and Policy Review* 40: 819–60.
Ireland, Patrick Richard. 2004. *Becoming Europe: Immigration, Integration, and the Welfare State*. Pittsburgh, PA: University of Pittsburgh Press.
Kahanec, Martin, and Mariola Pytliková. 2017. "The economic impact of east–west migration on the European Union." *Empirica* 44(3): 407–34.
Kesler, Christel. 2006. "Social policy and immigrant joblessness in Britain, Germany and Sweden." *Social Forces* 85(2): 743–70.
Kim, Dowon, and Dongwon Lee. 2021. "Immigration and the pattern of public spending: Evidence from OECD countries." *International Tax and Public Finance*, doi:10.1007/s10797-020-09638-x.
Kogan, Irena. 2006. "Labor markets and economic incorporation among recent immigrants in Europe." *Social Forces* 85(2): 697–721.
Kogan, Irena, Jing Shen, and Manuel Siegert. 2018. "What makes a satisfied immigrant? Host-country characteristics and immigrants' life satisfaction in eighteen European countries." *Journal of Happiness Studies* 19(6): 1783–809.
Koopmans, Ruud. 2010. "Trade-offs between equality and difference: Immigrant integration, multiculturalism and the welfare state in cross-national perspective." *Journal of Ethnic and Migration Studies* 36(1): 1–26.
Kulin, Joakim, Maureen A. Eger, and Mikael Hjerm. 2016. "Immigration or welfare? The progressive's dilemma revisited." *Socius: Sociological Research for a Dynamic World* 2: 1–15.
Liebig, Thomas, and Jeffrey Mo. 2013. "The fiscal impact of immigration in OECD countries." pp. 125–89 in *International Migration Outlook*. Paris: OECD Publishing.
Mau, Steffen, and Christoph Burkhardt. 2009. "Migration and welfare state solidarity in Western Europe." *Journal of European Social Policy* 19(3): 213–29.
Moriconi, Simone, Giovanni Peri, and Riccardo Turati. 2019. "Immigration and voting for redistribution: Evidence from European elections." *Labour Economics* 61: 101765.
Nannestad, Peter. 2004. "Immigration as a challenge to the Danish welfare state?" *European Journal of Political Economy* 20(3): 755–67.
Nannestad, Peter. 2007. "Immigration and welfare states: A survey of 15 years of research." *European Journal of Political Economy* 23(2): 512–32.
National Academies of Sciences, Engineering, and Medicine (NASEM). 2017. "The economic and fiscal consequences of immigration," edited by Francine D. Blau and Christopher Mackie. Washington, DC: National Academies Press, doi: 10.17226/23550.
Nowrasteh, Alex, and Robert Orr. 2018. "Immigration and the welfare state: Immigrant and native use rates and benefit levels for means-tested welfare and entitlement programs." CATO Institute-Immigration Research and Policy Brief, 6: 1–8, www.cato.org/sites/cato.org/files/pubs/pdf/irpb6.pdf.
OECD. 2012. "Settling in: OECD indicators of immigrant integration 2012." Paris: OECD Publishing, doi: 10.1787/9789264171534-en.
OECD. 2013. "The fiscal impact of immigration in OECD Countries." In *International Migration Outlook 2013*. Paris: OECD Publishing, doi: 10.1787/migr_outlook-2013-6-en.
OECD. 2014. "Policy brief: The fiscal and economic impact of migration." *OECD Policy Briefs* May. Paris: OECD Publishing, www.oecd.org/migration/PB-Fiscal-Economic-Impact-Migration-May-2014.pdf.
Oesch, Daniel, and Line Rennwald. 2018. "Electoral competition in Europe's new tripolar political space: Class voting for the left, centre-right and radical right." *European Journal of Political Research* 57(4): 783–807.
Pager, Devah, and Hana Shepherd. 2008. "The sociology of discrimination: Racial discrimination in employment, housing, credit, and consumer markets." *Annual Review of Sociology* 34: 181–209.
Pedersen, Peder J., Mariola Pytlikova, and Nina Smith. 2008. "Selection or network effects? Migration flows into 27 OECD countries, 1990–2000." *European Economic Review* 52(7): 1160–86.
Pellizzari, Michele. 2013. "The use of welfare by migrants in Italy." *International Journal of Manpower* 34(2): 155–66.
Peri, Giovanni, and Chad Sparber. 2009. "Task specialization, immigration, and wages." *American Economic Journal: Applied Economics* 1(3): 135–69.
Piyapromdee, Suphanit. 2021. "The impact of immigration on wages, internal migration, and welfare." *Review of Economic Studies* 88(1): 406–53.
Portes, Alejandro, and Min Zhou. 1993. "The new second generation: Segmented assimilation and its variants." *Annals of the American Academy of Political and Social Science* 530(1): 74–96.
Pottie-Sherman, Yolande, and Rima Wilkes. 2017. "Does size really matter? On the relationship between immigrant group size and anti-immigrant prejudice." *International Migration Review* 51(1): 218–50.
Rafferty, Anthony. 2012. "Ethnic penalties in graduate level over-education, unemployment and wages: Evidence from Britain." *Work, Employment and Society* 26(6): 987–1006.

Razin, Assaf, and Jackline Wahba. 2015. "Welfare magnet hypothesis, fiscal burden, and immigration skill selectivity." *Scandinavian Journal of Economics* 117(2): 369–402.

Reder, Melvin W. 1963. "The economic consequences of increased immigration." *Review of Economics and Statistics* 45(3): 221–30.

Reeskens, Tim, and Wim Van Oorschot. 2012. "Disentangling the 'new liberal dilemma': On the relation between general welfare redistribution preferences and welfare chauvinism." *International Journal of Comparative Sociology* 53(2): 120–39.

Rowthorn, Robert. 2008. "The fiscal impact of immigration on the advanced economies." *Oxford Review of Economic Policy* 24(3): 560–80.

Ruist, Joakim. 2014. "Free immigration and welfare access: The Swedish experience." *Fiscal Studies* 35(1): 19–39.

Ruist, Joakim. 2015. "The fiscal cost of refugee immigration: The example of Sweden." *Population and Development Review* 41(4): 567–81.

Siebers, Hans, and Marissa Koster. 2021. "How official nationalism fuels labour market discrimination against migrants in the Netherlands and its institutional alternatives." *Nations and Nationalism*, doi: 10.1111/nana.12721.

Soroka, Stuart, Keith Banting, and Richard Johnston. 2006. "Immigration and redistribution in a global era." pp. 261–88 in *Globalization and Egalitarian Redistribution*, edited by Pranab K. Bardhan, Michael Wallerstein, and Samuel Bowles. Princeton, NJ: Princeton University Press and Russell Sage Foundation.

Soroka, Stuart N., Richard Johnston, Anthony Kevins, Keith Banting, and Will Kymlicka. 2016. "Migration and welfare state spending." *European Political Science Review* 8(2): 173–94.

Stichnoth, Holger. 2012. "Does immigration weaken natives' support for the unemployed? Evidence from Germany." *Public Choice* 151: 631–54.

Tabellini, Marco. 2020. "Gifts of the immigrants, woes of the natives: Lessons from the age of mass migration." *Review of Economic Studies* 87(1): 454–86.

Tajfel, Henri, Michael G. Billig, Robert P. Bundy, and Claude Flament. 1971. "Social categorization and intergroup behaviour." *European Journal of Social Psychology* 1(2): 149–78.

Turner, John C. 1975. "Social comparison and social identity: Some prospects for intergroup behaviour." *European Journal of Social Psychology* 5(1): 1–34.

Valverde, Gabriela Ortiz, and María C. Latorre. 2019. "The economic impact of potential migration policies in the UK after Brexit." *Contemporary Social Science* 14(2): 208–25.

Van Tubergen, Frank, Ineke Maas, and Henk Flap. 2004. "The economic incorporation of immigrants in 18 Western societies: Origin, destination, and community effects." *American Sociological Review* 69(5): 704–27.

Verkuyten, Maykel. 2016. "The integration paradox: Empiric evidence from the Netherlands." *American Behavioral Scientist* 60(5–6): 583–96.

Villarreal, Andrés, and Christopher R. Tamborini. 2018. "Immigrants' economic assimilation: Evidence from longitudinal earnings records." *American Sociological Review* 83(4): 686–715.

Wadensjö, Eskil, and Helena Orrje. 2002. *Immigration and the Public Sector in Denmark*. Aarhus: Aarhus Universitetsforlag.

Winter-Ebmer, Rudolf, and Josef Zweimüller. 1996. "Immigration and the earnings of young native workers." *Oxford Economic Papers* 48(3): 473–91.

Winter-Ebmer, Rudolf, and Josef Zweimüller. 1999. "Do immigrants displace young native workers: The Austrian experience." *Journal of Population Economics* 12(2): 327–40.

Zimmermann, Klaus F., Martin Kahanec, Corrado Giulietti, Martin Guzi, Alan Barrett, and Bertrand Maître. 2012. *Study on Active Inclusion of Migrants*. IZA Research Report No. 43. Bonn: Institute of Labor Economics.

3. Migration, diversity, and the welfare state: Moving beyond attitudes
Patrick R. Ireland

Migration in its several forms has generated ethnic, cultural, and religious diversity in North America and Europe. Researchers have engaged in intense debate over whether that diversity represents a significant determinant of cross-national differences in the state's redistributive role or even a threat to the Western welfare state. Early on, most studies considered aggregate or macro-level data, exploring the association between measures of migration/migrants and social spending. The focus has since shifted to microlevel analyses scrutinizing both the effects of migration-generated diversity on the ties binding societies together (interpersonal and social trust, social solidarity, social capital, social cohesion) and the reasons for opposing the extension of social benefits to migrants (welfare chauvinism). Notable variations have been observed across countries and policies in these relationships, moderated by such factors as socio-demographic traits, degrees of diversity, residential segregation, interethnic contact, legal statuses, migrant diversity, and national identity in the receiving countries. Strong or weak feelings of shared belonging, in turn, are held to shape attitudes toward redistribution and universal welfare programs.

All told, a massive collection of studies has accumulated. Surprisingly, no consensus has emerged on the nature of the diversity–welfare state nexus, and the crucial link between attitudes and the original dependent variables of interest—social spending and specific policy outputs—has received less scholarly attention. This chapter examines the evolution of this rich, voluminous literature, leading up to the current work in the field that is moving beyond attitudes to probe the connections to social policy responses and welfare benefit allocations and procedures. And to take the next logical step means moving beyond policy outputs to real-world outcomes: how welfare delivery truly operates in diversifying societies. Insights can be gained from comparative analysis of the integration of legal migrants, refugees, asylum seekers, and undocumented migrants into European and North American health systems.

DIVERSITY AND THE WELFARE STATE

The implications of postwar migration for social policy in high-income countries (HICs) in Europe and North America were clear at least by the early 1970s. They have steadily gained in prominence since then, as population aging has thrown the financial viability of welfare programs into doubt and the incorporation of new cultural minorities into them has raised concerns. With globalization and technological change aggravating economic inequality in HICs, political demands for progressive vertical redistribution are interacting and sometimes clashing with those for horizontal redistribution embracing migrant-origin populations (Bisin and Verdier 2017). Because "running contrary to increasing demands, there exists financial and political pressure to stabilize or even retrench welfare state expenditures," the situation becomes a zero-sum game (Enggist 2019, 3).

Even as migrants have been presented as potential guarantors of the welfare state's survival in certain quarters (see Lutz 2020), in others there are fears that they could pose an existential menace to it. Starting in the late 1980s, cross-national comparative studies using aggregate data have shown that cultural (i.e., ethnic, racial, and/or linguistic) diversity often correlates with lower social expenditures and benefits (Mueller and Murrell 1986; Alesina et al. 2003; Alesina and Glaeser 2004; Desmet et al. 2009). At the subnational level, most of the research has been conducted in the United States (U.S.) (although compare Gerdes 2011; Mäkelä and Viren 2017); while results have not always lined up, they have generally suggested that ethnic diversity is related to differences in public spending, especially at the state level (compare Alesina et al. 1999 with Hopkins 2011).

Animating much of this discussion has been the contrast between European welfare states and the U.S. version, whose less distributive character has been attributed in part to its being more culturally fragmented (Alesina et al. 2001). The U.S. has been cast as the "land of opportunity," fairly open to migration but stingy with respect to redistribution; Europe is the more closed but more generous "land of redistribution" (Boeri 2010), "hard on the outside" toward non-European migrants (those from elsewhere in Western Europe not being considered problematic) but "soft on the inside" with inclusive social policies (Bosniak 2006, 4). If it is true that "fractionalization does reduce redistribution," the upshot is "that if Europe becomes more heterogeneous due to immigration, ethnic divisions will be used to challenge the generous welfare state" (Alesina and Glaeser 2004, 11; see Larsen 2011).

National-level studies have been criticized for how they operationalize their dependent (social spending, benefits) and independent (types of diversity) variables (Stichnoth and Van der Straeten 2013). Migration is "the main driver of diversity in most countries" (Dinesen and Sønderskov 2018, 175), save for the U.S., where migration-related changes intertwine more tightly with fraught experiences of longstanding racial and cultural minorities (Alesina et al. 2018, 6). Using a mix of diversity measures, one pair of economists has concluded that redistribution and diversity are related non-linearly: "moderate levels of diversity impede redistribution, while higher levels offset the negative effect" (Gründler and Köllner 2018, 1).

Looking at the HICs included in the Alesina and Glaeser (2004) study, meanwhile, Canadian scholars observed that the size of overall migrant population shares was not associated with changes in social spending levels between 1970 and 2005, although changes in those shares were (Banting et al. 2006; Soroka et al. 2006a). They have likewise argued that there is no evidence of a negative correlation between multicultural policies and changes in social spending and redistribution (Banting and Kymlicka 2004). Countries adopting multicultural policies "have on average fared as well as other countries in maintaining social spending, in maintaining public support for redistributive programs, and in maintaining attitudes of inclusive solidarity" (Kymlicka 2015, 9). Such a conclusion blends together the relationship between migration and outcomes that are both objective (e.g., social spending and benefits levels) and subjective (e.g., public support and solidarity).

An influential hypothesis in political economy posits that cross-country differences in welfare state generosity are owing in large measure to income inequality, higher levels of which heighten preferences for redistribution that translate into household voting behavior supportive of social policy expansion (Meltzer and Richard 1981). This "Meltzer–Richard effect" has by and large been substantiated (Milanovic 2000; Scervini 2012), but ensuing work has indicated that individuals' perceptions and judgments about inequality—implicating culture and diversity—matter in generating preferences, too (Cruces et al. 2013; Durante et al. 2014).

THE FOCUS ON ATTITUDES

In many studies such subjective factors have been portrayed, explicitly or implicitly, as mechanisms through which diversity affects the welfare state—in other words, as intermediary variables. Hundreds of books and articles have by now appeared on these attitudinal factors, yet the results have been inclusive (Stichnoth and Van der Straeten 2013); the literature has reached a "stalemate" (Stolle and Harell 2015).

A subset of this research has looked at migrant-origin voters' possible cultural preferences for privately or communally provided services and how they could weaken the political coalitions sustaining welfare states (Gründler and Köllner 2018). Those alliances could be hurt as well by differences among migrant-origin minorities on this score. There is evidence to suggest that average redistributive preferences in migrants' countries/regions of origin strongly influence their own preferences (Alesina and Fuchs-Schündeln 2007; Luttmer and Singhal 2011), which are "[p]assed on to second generations through cultural transmission" (Bisin and Verdier 2017, 124).

More commonly, migrants themselves are objects and not agents in the research on the attitudinal underpinnings of national welfare states. It is the "native" population's support for redistribution, social policy, public goods provision, and the welfare state—the literature tends to refer to them "as exchangeable outcomes" (Muñoz and Pardos-Prado 2019, 717)—that is primarily at issue: to what degree and how it is affected by diversity. Separating out the attitudinal dimension, debate has roiled the political left for several decades over whether an inverse relationship exists between (a) migration and the resultant ethnocultural diversity and (b) support for redistributive social policies (Banting 2010). The Great Recession and subsequent economic turmoil and so-called refugee and migration crises in Europe and the U.S. have intensified such worries (Reeskens and Van der Meer 2019). Multicultural policies, promoted as the best means of compensating minorities for the harm inflicted on them by the sense of nationhood deemed essential to a welfare state, have come under fire for weakening that very solidarity (Banting et al. 2013).

The Direct Relationship

Efforts to test this "new progressive's dilemma" empirically—like those testing the diversity–spending relationship—have nevertheless yielded "mixed and inconclusive results" (Kymlicka 2015, 1). The connection between ethnoracial diversity and public hostility toward various social policies has been borne out at all levels in the U.S.

(Gilens 1999). Research from the U.S. and Europe has likewise explored the role of anti-migrant sentiment as a predictor of attitudes toward redistribution (Alesina et al. 2001; Schmidt and Spies 2013). Findings that residence in homogeneous neighborhoods raises backing for social spending in the U.S. (Luttmer 2001) have been echoed at least to some degree in European studies (Crepaz 2006; Dahlberg et al. 2012; Eger 2010; Eger and Breznau 2017; Ford 2016; Jofre-Monseny et al. 2016; Senik et al. 2008).

Work done in Canada employing a diversity measure encompassing racial, ethnic, and birthplace differences, on the other hand, has failed to corroborate such conclusions (Soroka et al. 2004, 2006b; see Green and Riddell 2019). They have also been contested by additional analyses dealing with cases from both sides of the Atlantic and beyond (Baldwin and Huber 2010; Banting 2005; Brady and Finnigan 2014). A study of ethnic diversity and individual-level attitudes toward social spending in 91 countries, involving 48 regression models, failed to identify a negative relationship—except with large increases in the migrant population in countries with especially severe economic inequality (Steele 2016). All in all, then, it can be said that existing scholarship "at least demonstrates the absence of a general law-like connection between ethnic diversity and public support for welfare states" (Larsen et al. 2018, 64).

The Mediated Relationship

Further disaggregating that relationship is a branch of this scholarship that has examined the mediating effects of demographic, economic, institutional, political, and other factors. The list of meaningful intervening variables detected is long: the proportion of recent migrants and natives' individual-level characteristics (Eger 2010); within-group or between-group inequality (Lind 2007); in-group bias or loyalty (Dahlberg et al. 2012); negative group loyalty effects and positive labor market effects (Alesina et al. 2018); self-oriented or other-oriented motives (Cavaillé and Trump 2015); pure dislike of migrants or concerns about the economic consequences of migration (Senik et al. 2008); strategic elites (Rugh and Trounstine 2011); type of national identity (Miller and Ali 2014); the interaction of the initial degree of cultural differentiation and fragmentation with income inequality (Bisin and Verdier 2017); and so on. Among the "most promising, yet contested moderating factors in the literature" are "the type of welfare regime and institutional setting" (Muñoz and Pardos-Prado 2019, 719): multicultural policies (Crepaz 2006, 2008; Evans 2006; Kymlicka 2015); "the unique, and very potent, combination of political characteristics in each state" (Fellowes and Rowe 2004, p. 362); the welfare regime, unemployment rate, and gross domestic product (Mau and Burkhardt 2009); and welfare regimes and programs (Crepaz and Damron 2009; Finseraas 2008; Larsen 2008; compare Larsen 2011). Observed effects have tended to be stronger in the U.S. than in Canada or in Europe (Alesina et al. 2018). On the whole, though, not much consensus has been reached on any of the intermediary factors (Muñoz and Pardos-Prado 2019).

Social Cohesion, Social Solidarity, and Social Trust

Moving a level deeper into this scholarly *mise-en-abîme*, another subliterature starts with the argument that public support for the welfare state depends on the good functioning of a society. This social cohesion, in turn, depends on social solidarity, which rests on a foundation of interpersonal trust (subjective social capital), which may be affected by diversity. Although occasionally elided together in pertinent analyses, where literature reviews can be telescoped into a couple of paragraphs, these concepts are in fact quite distinct.

The question becomes whether social cohesion is corroded by weakened social solidarity: the ties holding a society together (Lahusen and Grasso 2018a) that are normally "understood as rights-based" and therefore "delimited by legal entitlements and mutual obligations" (Lahusen and Grasso 2018b, 265–6). The term "social trust" can pertain to that macro-level outcome—in effect, the subjective dimension of social cohesion—or attitudes toward out-groups (Putnam 2007; Abascal and Baldassarri 2015; see Kaufmann and Goodwin 2018; Schaeffer 2014). It can also refer to the micro level involving interpersonal trust or subjective social capital, including assessment of the contact and conflict theories (Luttmer 2001; Finseraas et al. 2019).

Interethnic contact, residential segregation, and a range of other moderating variables "chosen somewhat eclectically" have been put forward at both the individual and contextual levels (Dinesen and Sønderskov 2018, 182). National identity, too, has begun to appear more frequently as a mediator (see Kymlicka and Banting 2015; Stolle and Harell 2015; Sandelind 2018). As with residential segregation, the size of the social context in which diversity is measured—as well as the basis and definition of the groups at issue (including migrants) and how they are tallied—matters: negative relationships between diversity and trust are more common and stronger the smaller the context (Dinesen and Sønderskov 2015).

Taken together, these related lines of inquiry have spawned a veritable academic industrial cottage complex. Not unexpectedly, given Robert Putnam's (1995) prominent early research in the field, ethnic and racial diversity has routinely, albeit not always, been discovered to undermine social trust and other features of social cohesion in the U.S. Evidence of this negative relationship has been weaker in Europe and more mixed in the United Kingdom (U.K.) and Canada—except in smaller, more local settings (Dinesen and Sønderskov 2018). From one perspective, "redistributive social solidarity" results from a stable equipoise between national cultural and institutional frameworks, "produced over long periods of time by historic struggles about social justice," that renders already inclusive social democratic welfare regimes better positioned to respond positively to higher levels of diversity (Hall 2017, 385; see Crepaz 2008). Others, meanwhile, have proposed that such regimes are precisely the ones that recoil the most strongly against increased diversity (Finseraas 2008). To repeat the refrain from the other areas of diversity–welfare investigation, little real agreement has emerged here out of the massive research output.

Welfare Chauvinism and Welfare Deservingness

A parallel avenue of thought considers the belief that migrants "unsettle the fundamental principles of the welfare state by misusing public services for which they are not eligible and have not appropriately contributed" (Bradby et al. 2020, 167; Crepaz and Damron 2009). This concept of welfare chauvinism developed in the context of scholarship on radical right-wing populist parties. Their original opposition to social welfare benefits as the way to discriminate between the hardworking native "us" and the free-loading "others" mutated into insistence that only the former should have access to their rightful benefits—which are being attacked by the elites in the mainstream parties and imperiled by migrants (Kitschelt 1995; Mudde 2007; Schumacher and Van Kersbergen 2016). This pirouette "from domestic neoliberalism to welfare expansion" has characterized the radical populist right in some countries more than others (Swank and Betz 2018, 7).

Many of the efforts undertaken to understand when and under what conditions natives believe that migrants should receive benefits have concentrated on Europe and have relied on European Social Survey data (De Koster et al. 2012; Mewes and Mau 2013; Reeskens and Van Oorschot 2012). With more comprehensive welfare states than North America and multiparty systems that allow for parties combining hostility toward migrants with pro-welfare attitudes, Europe has been more fertile ground for welfare chauvinism (or "welfare populism") (Kriesi 2015; Michel 2017). Overwhelming majorities of respondents there have espoused at best only conditional access for migrants to social benefits (Larsen et al. 2018). The recent refugee and migrant "crises" have only strengthened such preferences (Marx and Naumann 2018).

All the same, there is no agreed-upon definition of "welfare chauvinism," which can refer to a policy orientation, a political agenda, or a conception of who can legitimately lay claim to benefits and services (Keskinen et al. 2016). Reasons given for majorities' reluctance to grant migrants access to social rights have included self-interest; national identity; and people's conception of national interest, which can extend to socio-tropic concerns about the ramifications of migration for the country (Larsen et al. 2018). Welfare regime type appears to inflect welfare chauvinism as well (Nagayoshi and Hjerm 2015; compare Sandelind 2018). Dispute percolates over whether welfare chauvinism is more "related to (a) immigrant status or (b) ethnic difference" (Soroka et al. 2017, 173) and "more strongly correlated with attitudes on an economic-redistributive or socio-cultural dimension" (Enggist 2019, 1).

Increasingly, determining the degree to which welfare chauvinism operates in a given national context bears on the distinction drawn between "deserving" and "undeserving" social groups (Van Oorschot 2006), mirroring the one drawn between desired and undesired migrants and often described as "part of a broader neoliberal restructuring of the welfare state and of welfare retrenchment" (Keskinen et al. 2016, 321). When groups have been ranked according to welfare deservingness in Europe, migrants consistently land at the bottom (Chueri 2020; Van Oorschot 2006). Some studies have distinguished between welfare chauvinism and resentment toward ethnic minority recipients, or "welfare ethnocentrism" (Ford 2016, 4, p. 633).

Welfare deservingness theory argues that when deciding what social benefits should accrue to migrants and other policy target groups, natives refer to the five "CARIN" criteria (Laenen et al. 2019; Van Oorschot et al. 2017):

- control (those who lack control to alter their situation are more deserving);
- attitude (those who are grateful and acquiescent are more deserving);
- reciprocity (those who make contributions to society are more deserving);
- identity (those who belong to one's in-group are more deserving); and
- need (those who have serious financial or health needs are more deserving).

Various of these criteria have been shown to matter the most singly and in combination in determining attitudes regarding different policies and benefits (see Lahusen and Grasso 2018b). Even so, there is no consensus about how to operationalize the criteria, which are "abstract moral principles" to which people adhere "to varying degrees" and "play a mediating role between social-structural characteristics and concrete policy preferences" (Meuleman et al. 2020, 1–2). Researchers have typically relied on proxy variables, causing conceptual confusion and rendering comparative analysis tricky.

Methods and Methodology

A bountiful, multifaceted, and sprawling literature has thus rapidly developed to advance a host of factors as influencing, directly and indirectly, the connections between migration-driven diversity and support for the welfare state. Economists, political scientists, sociologists, and migration and social policy scholars have stood as the primary contributors. Lengthy causal pathways, multiple interacting variables, and noisy feedback loops render predictions about migration's impact on welfare state resilience suspect. Whereas it would be unfair to say that this hefty output has generated more heat than light, it is disappointing that so few clear answers have yet to emerge from it.

Not unrelated to this lack of clarity, by far the lion's share of this scholarship has relied on quantitative techniques of data gathering and data analysis. Regression analyses of original and existing survey data have predominated. Vignettes, conjoint analysis, and similar experiments have also been added to surveys in an attempt to isolate causal mechanisms (e.g., Enggist 2019; Harell et al. 2016; Kootstra 2016; Muñoz and Pardos-Prado 2019; Reeskens and Van der Meer 2019; Soroka et al. 2017). More and more, respondents are recruited online, on occasion by internet-based market research, analytics, and experience management firms and crowdsourcing marketplaces.

With easy opportunities for online surveying and relevant existing data sets (such as the European Social Survey and the International Social Survey Program), the proliferation of quantitative research on the relationship between diversity and popular attitudes toward redistribution becomes understandable. There is no foreseeable end in sight to the analytical one-upmanship and the testing and refinement that relevant theories can undergo. Much of this work has been conducted with funding from national research institutions and governments and the European Union, thereby producing a steady stream of deliverables to policymakers worried about the potentially destabilizing effects of population movements that they have otherwise cheered (Lahusen and Grasso 2018a).

To a large extent, this research remains "siloed" by discipline, and only a handful of exceptionally high-profile scholars are widely cited across the divides. Economists in particular have been criticized for having "hardly begun to draw on knowledge offered by other disciplines about the nature and the consequences of culture and ethnicity" (Gründler and Köllner 2018, 34). Multiculturalism theorists/proponents, on the other hand, often do keep track of the findings from various fields and point to the absence of accord as signaling that "there is no strong evidence for a multiculturalism/redistribution trade-off" (Bloemraad 2015, 3–4). Others cherry-pick conclusions to suit their ideological or policy positions (Steele 2016).

At the same time, there have been growing calls for more methodological diversity. "It would help," Canadian political philosopher Will Kymlicka has remarked, "if we could move beyond bare regression models to uncover some of the actual mechanisms that underpin (or erode) inclusive solidarity" (2015, 9). Besides vignettes and the like, less reliance on survey research and more use of qualitative approaches would be useful in this regard. Accordingly, focus group discussions in Denmark, Germany, and the U.K. have illuminated whether people do apply the CARIN criteria and, if so, which ones. Participants referred explicitly "to a number of context-related criteria extending beyond the deservingness framework" and "to a large extent echoed the normative criteria that are most strongly embedded in the institutional structure of their country's welfare regime" (Laenen et al. 2019, 190). Deliberations in democratic forums in Denmark, Germany, Norway, and the U.K. did not result in less welfare nationalism, disputing the notion that it is the pure creation of radical right-wing populist parties and instead suggesting that it reflects people's conception of national interest (Larsen et al. 2018). Semi-structured interviews of 47 Britons and Swedes, selected through strategic sampling, have proposed "alternative forms of shared identity that may reduce the tension between immigration and solidarity, if such identity is based on contributions or shared institutions" (Sandelind 2018, 198). Ethnographic research, case studies, and comparative institutional analysis (see Hall 2017) as well could shed fresh light on such important, unexplored chapters of the diversity-welfare story. Pulling the field out of its methodological rut could help give it much-needed new momentum.

MOVING BEYOND ATTITUDES

In addition to getting stuck spinning its quantitative wheels, the field has fallen short of its original, stated destination. What was initially a straightforward proposed causal relationship (diversity → welfare state policies) has become a rather involved chain of connections, as seen in Figure 3.1.

Ostensibly the most critical link, the final one between redistributional attitudes to social spending and benefits, has attracted the least attention. For some engaged in attitudinal research, the tie-in with policy outputs is merely incidental: "Empirical evidence for the U.S. shows that lower attitudes to redistribution due to racial heterogeneity even extend to lower actual levels of redistribution allowances across U.S. states" (Alesina et al. 2018, 6). Others acknowledge that social policy and public opinion interact (Mau 2003) but focus more on policies as mediating factors that can affect public support for redistribution (see Muñoz and Pardos-Prado 2019; Reeskens and Van der Meer 2019).

It makes little sense to stop at that support, however, and not make the leap to establishing whether or not it produces the assumed outputs. After all, even widely held popular attitudes do not automatically yield particular policies. Since the mid-1980s, migration scholars have discussed the "gap hypothesis": "the situation in which mass publics take a far more restrictive approach to immigration than governments can or will deliver" (McLaren 2015, 76; see Lutz 2019). It is no stretch to imagine that a comparable gap might exist between public opinion challenging migrant welfare entitlements and real-life social policy responses. Indeed, social services departments and ministries and judiciaries have evidently served as "institutional enclaves" for pro-migrant positions on distributing social benefits, and their decisions can "reshape political dynamics" (Hall 2017, 385).

Figure 3.1 The path from diversity to welfare state policies

Many of the efforts to date addressing the connection between attitudes and policies have honed in on the influence of radical right-wing populist parties on mainstream party positions; pro-welfare political coalitions; and migration, migrant integration, and "law and order" policies. So far, analysts have mostly been dubious as to the strength of their impact (see Mudde 2013; Röth et al. 2018). Fresh data show that outside their "core agenda," those parties' participation in European governments has encouraged "the adoption of welfare chauvinist measures directly and indirectly," especially those financed through general taxation and perhaps in exchange for their acceptance of welfare cuts more generally (Chueri 2020, 20, 29; see also Swank and Betz 2018; Taylor-Gooby et al. 2017; Tyrberg and Dahlström 2018). Social programs on which migrant "outsiders" are disproportionately dependent (such as unemployment insurance) have come under assault (Gordon 2019; Spies 2018). Importantly, research in this subfield has been regularly employing mixed-method designs (e.g., Chueri 2020; Schumacher and Van Kersbergen 2016).

Even when the putative outcomes of concern in this area of research are kept in sight, however, they remain in reality only outputs. The true outcomes are not the levels of spending or policy mix but rather the degree to which all members of a society have access to at least the minimal provisions needed to lead decent lives. If we are interested in how diversity affects the welfare state, then, we have to care about the incorporation of migrants into mainstream social policies and the actual workings of differential inclusion. In short, does migration-driven diversity drive down the degree of welfare state universality? This key aspect of the issue has largely been omitted from the narrative.

On the ground welfare states look far less coherent than in neat and clean macro-level analyses, and the degree to which they include and serve migrant-origin populations can vary within systems as much as they do across them. Above all in the U.S., racial bias in social policy delivery has been "amply demonstrated" (Thomann and Rapp 2017, 531). In Europe, the makeup of social programs and training of social workers would seem positioned to limit discriminatory treatment (Epp et al. 2017; Terum et al. 2018). Content analysis of case files detailing disability benefit procedures in Switzerland has nonetheless revealed that migrants receive poorer treatment, and their place of origin matters in terms of their perceived deservingness (Thomann and Rapp 2017). Using local mapping, resident and provider interviews, ethnographies, and a residents' survey in diverse neighborhoods in four European cities, a team of sociologists has identified the ways in which "apparently universal healthcare systems" can fail migrants (Bradby et al. 2020, 166).

It is critical to recognize that there can be major discrepancies between how ethnic/racial minorities and migrant non-nationals relate to welfare states. Nor are migrants a monolithic group, as "[n]on-citizens' social entitlements differ depending on the nationality, the type of legal status, and the form of employment"; immigration law can thus be guilty of "invalidating the universalism of rights and a residence-based welfare system," leaving some non-nationals "more foreign" than others, and reflecting "the aim of states to redefine the deservingness rather than the personal qualities or characteristics of migrants" (Könönen 2018, 53–5; see Shutes 2016). The "chutes and ladders" of residence and other permits even in a country like Canada—"the epitome of solidarity through multicultural nationalism in the global North" (Bloemraad 2015, 1) whose "experience suggests that immigration, multiculturalism policies, and redistribution can represent a stable political equilibrium" (Banting 2005, 98)—can leave legal as well as undocumented migrants experiencing instability and insecurity (Goldring and Landolt 2013, 8).

Of course, national governments also determine which non-nationals are allowed in to submit to such games in the first place. Canada has followed a selective federal migration policy yielding a sizeable contingent of skilled and economically advantaged "designer immigrants" (Murdie and Ghosh 2010, 304). Before they can enter, migrants undergo thorough vetting by authorities, who assess them as future Canadian citizens; and geographical (oceanic) barriers, the pull of the economic super-magnet to the south, and markedly restrictive visa rules ensure that irregular migration is minimal. Canada has accepted large numbers of resettled refugees from the United Nations High Commissioner for Refugees—some 28,000 in 2017 (Connor and Radford 2019)—but as Prime Minister Justin Trudeau admitted with reference to the 25,000 Syrian refugees it welcomed in 2015: "We were able to actually go and pick and choose and screen and bring over the people we chose. And that gives us a much greater level of control and attention over who's actually going to come in" (CBS News 2016).

Whenever that control is breached, alarm bells sound, as they did when 568 Sri Lankan asylum seekers were intercepted in ships off British Columbia in 2009 and when 20,000 Haitians and others fearing loss of their Temporary Protected Status in the U.S. crossed into Québec outside border checkpoints in 2017 (thereby earning the right to a full hearing on their asylum application). Those whose case is accepted for adjudication receive a range of social benefits. Irregular "economic migrants," like most of the Haitians fleeing the Trump administration's restrictive actions, do not. As the editorial page editor of *The Globe and Mail*, the country's de facto newspaper of record, has put it, "Canada maintains its open-door reputation because it generally has been very selective about whom it allows to approach the door in the first place" (Keller 2018). This stance can be contrasted with those of the U.S., which has a less generous welfare state but until recently has been more open to migrants of varying skill levels and to asylum seekers and refugees, and Germany, which has a more generous welfare state but has been notably open to asylum seekers (and refugees and highly skilled migrants).

MIGRANTS AND HEALTH CARE

All of the aforementioned neglected elements are visible in the ways that migrants have navigated health-care systems, a vital component of modern welfare states. Global health challenges like HIV/AIDS, SARS, H1N1, re-emerging and drug-resistant tuberculosis, and COVID-19 have shined a spotlight on the health effects of mobility in HICs. Health risks of all kinds are greater for migrants than for native-stock populations, yet migration has long loomed in collective imaginations as the source of infectious disease (Hernández-Rosete Martínez 2008). Nowadays, there has allegedly been a "growing trend of states limiting access to health care for migrants, despite commitments to provide 'health for all'" (*The Lancet* 2018).

How receiving countries deal with migrant health depends partly on the type and sources of migration to them. Policies are also affected by their integration and welfare regimes and health system. Cross-national similarities and differences in approaches to migrant health are explored here through a comparison of three country pairs: Austria/Germany, Belgium/France, and Canada/the U.S. The first two countries have been identified as ethnic differentialist migrant integration regimes; the second two, as assimilationist republican regimes (at least in Belgian Wallonia), and the third two, as classical immigration countries with a multicultural approach that is passive (the U.S.) or active (Canada) (Ireland 2014).

National health responses to migrants have diverged widely and changed often (Fakoya et al. 2018). Countries with general taxation-based Beveridge health systems or national health insurance (like Canada) have been presumed to provide greater access to more extensive and responsive services than systems relying more on payroll-based health insurance (like Austria, Germany, Belgium, and France), which are presumed to do better on that score than pluralistic systems (like the U.S.) (Rosano et al. 2017; WHO Europe 2019). Complicating such expectations are beliefs that multiculturalist migrant integration regimes (active ones as in Canada and Belgian Flanders more than the passive American one) are more inclusive than assimilationist regimes (as in France and Wallonia), which are more inclusive than ethnic differential regimes (as in Austria and Germany) (Ireland 2014).

Resident Legal Migrants, Refugees, and Recognized Asylum Seekers

Entry limitations based on health status, firstly, have kept some people out of HICs. As the twenty-first century dawned, for instance, Austria, Belgium, the German federal state of Bavaria, Canada, and the U.S. required longer-term visitors (and short-term visa holders in the U.S.) to be tested for HIV (and sometimes other infections). A positive result for HIV could prevent visa acquisition in Austria, Belgium, Bavaria, and the U.S. Visa policies have since changed, with only Canada and Bavaria retaining HIV testing requirements under certain conditions. In none of the six case countries can a migrant be deported for being HIV positive anymore (Global Database 2020).

Once admitted, legally resident migrants and recognized refugees and their dependents are afforded inclusion into the Belgian, French, and German health systems irrespective of their employment status. Austria focuses on inclusion in areas of dense migrant settlement, gives considerable support to health education and promotion and services responsive to migrants' needs, and involves them more than elsewhere in information efforts and service design and delivery. Care in France and Austria is identical to that provided for nationals. In Belgium it goes beyond the emergency care that Germany extends, but it does not match nationals' entitlements (WHO Europe 2018b, 2019). In France migrants are covered under Universal Sickness Protection (*Protection universelle maladie*), which replaced basic Universal Medical Coverage in 2016 and which allows everyone residing regularly in France to access health care—after three months (KPMG 2019; Simonnot et al. 2016). The waiting period in Germany for migrants and refugees is 15 months (Smith and Levoy 2017).

Asylum seekers sometimes face greater restrictions in Europe. There are no curbs on entitlements for asylum seekers in France and several key exemptions to those that exist for other non-resident non-nationals in Belgium, Austria, and Germany (WHO Europe 2018b). In Belgium, France, and Austria (to those with recognized status in reception centers and certain designated areas), access to medical care is now ensured from the start of the application process and for the duration of the asylum procedure (WHO Europe 2018a). Asylum seekers are exempted from the requirement of residence for three months at a fixed address applied to other non-EU nationals in France; however, in Germany since March 2015, asylum seekers (like refugees) are entitled to welfare benefits under the same conditions as citizens only after 15 months of being covered under the Asylum Seekers Benefits Act (previously this was 48 months). Asylum seekers can receive vaccinations during that period, and the seriously ill and pregnant can access medical treatment. It is necessary in some federal states to get a medical treatment voucher (*Krankenschein*) from a social welfare office (not medical staff) each time care is sought (Smith 2018; Müllerschön et al. 2019). In Germany the children of refugees and migrants receive free health care; in Belgium and France, only the children of refugees; and in Austria, neither group (WHO Europe 2018b, 2019).

The situation in North America is as varied as in Europe. For non-citizens the Canada Health Act (1984)—which defines eligibility for the publicly funded universal insurance system, Medicare (*Assurance maladie*)—requires that it be extended to all those who legally reside in the country, excluding those who are transient or just visiting. Only successful refugees, sponsored spouses, partners, and dependent children—but not other migrants—can obtain permanent residence despite "medical inadmissibility," i.e., constituting a danger to public health or safety or excessive demand on Canada's health and/or social services; in 2018, the threshold for such designation was tripled to CDN$19,965 per year (Pett 2018). While health-care delivery falls to the provinces, most of them cover permanent residents, their sponsored family members, long-term temporary workers, and live-in care workers. British Columbia, New Brunswick, Ontario, and Québec have imposed a three-month post-arrival delay before resettled refugees, people detained under migration legislation, victims of human trafficking, recognized asylum seekers, and resident dependents of all of those groups are included. The national government covers their health-care costs in the interim (Ore 2020).

In 1962, U.S. President John F. Kennedy signed the Migrant Health Act, which "authorized the delivery of primary and supplemental health services to migrant farmworkers and was the beginning of national efforts to improve the health status of the mobile poor" (Kugel and Zuroweste 2010, 422). However, the Immigration Reform and Control Act of 1986 and Personal Responsibility and Work Opportunity Reconciliation Act of 1996 ended the access of certain categories of new legal migrants to the federal state health program for the disabled and families with low incomes and resources (Medicaid) during their first five years in the country (Chavez 2012). The Children's Health Insurance Program Reauthorization Act of 2009 gave states the option to provide coverage (with federal funding support) to legally resident pregnant women and children during that period. California, New York, and Illinois, among the states with the largest migrant populations, were at the forefront of attempts to cover all migrants, children in particular (Kline 2011).

After obtaining an initial health assessment from a local or county public health department, resettled refugees have eight months to become economically independent before losing federal cash assistance and becoming subject to standard Medicaid eligibility requirements. The provisions of the Patient Protection and Affordable Care Act of 2010 have applied to migrants "lawfully present" in the U.S., including people granted asylum, resettled refugees, and income-eligible immigrants with discretionary Temporary Protected Status having lived in the country for seven years or less (Sharrett 2012). The five-year waiting period for Medicaid eligibility remains in effect for low-income non-citizens, but members or veterans of the U.S. Armed Forces and their families, refugees, and asylum seekers are exempt. The U.S. has been noteworthy in deploying targeted migrant health policies usually seen only in national health systems and, like Austria, has championed health education and promotion as concerns asylum seekers (WHO Europe 2019).

Undocumented Migrants

Unauthorized migrants suffer aggravated vulnerability to health risks, and public health officials everywhere have identified them as a priority (O'Donnell 2018). In France, undocumented migrants in the country for more than three months and with a monthly income below a set level are covered for a year under State Medical Aid (*Aide Médicale de l'État*), which until 2001 was part of the standard, universal health insurance system. There are some conditions and restrictions, although exceptions are made for vulnerable and at-risk groups like people with infectious diseases and pregnant women. No limitations apply to children, moreover, since they cannot be considered undocumented. Anyone falling outside the system can access emergency services and care (WHO Europe 2018a).

The state of affairs has been similar in Belgium (Cousin 2019). There the undocumented have the right for three months only to "urgent" medical aid (*Aide Médicale Urgente* (AMU)/*Dringende Medische Hulpverlening* (DMH)), but it encompasses a wide array of emergency, basic, and universal provisions, both curative and preventative. The social welfare office that grants AMU/DMH does cause upset by requiring its social workers to obtain demographic and financial information from undocumented migrants and to make a home visit. A fairly high level of administrative arbitrariness and local variation in Belgium, as in France, characterizes care for the undocumented, reducing access to non-emergency care and compelling a network of non-profit non-governmental organizations (NGOs) to facilitate, fund, and directly dispense services (Smith and Levoy 2017, 14).

In Germany, undocumented migrants have had the same right to receive emergency and essential medical care as asylum seekers (i.e., that treating serious illness or acute pain) since 1998. The law on infectious diseases likewise entitles them to counselling, screening for infectious conditions, and outpatient care for sexually transmitted infections and tuberculosis. Exercising such rights has proved problematic: medical professionals, the social welfare office, and all administrative staff members were originally required by law to report any undocumented migrants they encountered. That regulation was dropped in September 2009 for emergency care yet remains in effect for other health services. Hospitals, for their part, hesitate to treat non-citizens without papers, because the social welfare office frequently refuses to reimburse the costs of their care on technicalities (Müllerschön et al. 2019). Consequently, some health-care providers treat undocumented patients with their own resources to meet their professional ethical commitments. Frustrated with the status quo, more and more cities and regions have stepped into the breach and moved to address the shortfall and, within the bounds of their legal authority, have backed and even funded initiatives to facilitate access to basic health services for undocumented residents. NGOs have joined in such efforts (MacGregor 2019).

NGOs, in fact, play a major role across Europe in the delivery of health care to undocumented migrants. They can access emergency care in Austria but have to pay the incurred fees, which is cost prohibitive for most. Austrian health-related NGOs bear much of the burden of supplying health care to uninsured persons, although they have tended to operate mainly in large cities like Vienna, Graz, and Linz (Karl-Trummer et al. 2009).

In the U.S., the Immigration Reform and Control Act (1986) barred undocumented migrants from most federally funded public health programs. That same year, the Emergency Medical Treatment and Active Labor Act required hospitals to admit and stabilize all individuals seeking care in an emergency room without consideration of their ability to pay or their papers. Emergency Medicaid covers costs related to childbirth and severe complications of chronic diseases; it is likewise obtainable if the failure to receive medical attention would place a person's life in jeopardy. Undocumented and recent legal immigrants can receive emergency care if they meet income and residency requirements and fit in a specified Medicaid-eligible category: children, pregnant women, families with dependent children, elderly, or disabled (Kline 2011; Zuckerman et al. 2011).

The Personal Responsibility and Work Opportunity Reconciliation Act (1996) removed a cash assistance program administered by local governments to serve the undocumented, making it necessary for states to pass their own laws and secure their own funding if they wished to grant benefits to that population (Viladrich 2012). Almost half of the states opted to use state funds to provide additional coverage for recent legal migrants and undocumented children and pregnant women, and cities like San Francisco, Los Angeles, New York, Chicago, and Miami earned reputations for having more generous and inclusive public health-care networks (Joseph and Marrow 2017). Since 2002, some 16 states have embraced the option to deliver prenatal care to women irrespective of their immigration status by extending Children's Health Insurance Program coverage to their unborn child. Six states, including California since mid-2019, use state funds to cover all income-eligible children (Artiga and Diaz 2019).

Undocumented migrants were explicitly excluded from coverage by the Patient Protection and Affordable Care Act (2010). It has reduced federal Disproportionate Share Hospital funds that allow clinics to subsidize care for Medicaid and indigent patients regardless of legal status. Nevertheless, the Act has pumped new funding into federally qualified health centers that afford preventive and primary health services to all income-eligible residents in a local area (Sharrett 2012; Joseph and Marrow 2017).

Health providers in Canada have no legal reason to check migrants' status, but they do ask for a public health insurance card. Undocumented migrants are among those excluded entirely from the system and thus must pay to access public and private services (Ridde et al. 2020). On rare occasions, efforts to access them have resulted in deportation. As in the U.S., the desire to save money, not act as a "welfare magnet," and focus on other groups deemed more deserving of coverage and treatment has done much to determine undocumented migrants' health access (Joseph and Marrow 2017). As in the U.S., too, initiatives by subnational governments have occasionally made care available, such as Ontario's province-supported Community Health Centres and the Toronto City Council's Access T.O. program for undocumented Torontonians (Smith and Levoy 2017).

Rights versus Reality

Having a right to care and exercising it are two different matters. Positive appraisals of the French approach have been tempered by arguments that "social stigmatization, precarious living conditions, and the climate of fear fed by increasingly restrictive immigration policies in practice hinder many from being, or feeling, entitled to that right" (Larchanché 2012, 862). As noted, administrative barriers in several countries prevent some migrants from realizing their due claims. Countries with limited entitlements, conversely, may be more inclusive in practice (see Karl-Trummer et al. 2009).

Further complicating matters are local and regional variations within countries. With legal entitlements codified in national legislation, it is primarily the interpretation and implementation of policies that varies in France. Divergence can be greater in the cases with federal structures: Germany's system is decentralized, and it has developed no national public health priorities; Belgium's health care has undergone a degree of differentiation with the devolution of health care from the federal government to the regions (Brussels, Flanders, and Wallonia) in the areas of health promotion, maternal and child health, elder care, and hospital management; Austria's states differ in regards to the nature and level of migrants' benefits. As already suggested, non-citizens confront disparate health access and conditions across Canada and, especially, the U.S. (Álvarez-del Arco et al. 2014).

There is a relative paucity of structures adapted to migrants' distinctive health needs in all of the case countries. Frequently furnished in cooperation with community-based and national-level NGOs, mediation and translation services, translated information materials for migrants in printed and online form, tailored guidebooks for general practitioners, special meals in hospitals, and so on exist in Austria, Germany, Belgium, France, Canada, and the U.S. These offerings vary in extent and quality across region and locality. Generally speaking, they have been more commonplace in the classical North American migration countries than in Europe—apart from France.

It may seem that overall no discernible pattern of migrant access to health care emerges across the country pairs, except perhaps the mostly strong showing of France and Belgium. A dissimilar and provocative assessment has been provided by the Migration Policy Index (MIPEX), a comparative project overseen by the Barcelona Centre for International Affairs and the Migration Policy Group in Brussels. Not useful for assessing actual integration outcomes, the MIPEX is a tool that can indicate which countries' legal and policy frameworks are open or closed to migrants. In 2015, its health module undertook a longitudinal, mixed-methods survey in 38 HICs. In terms of all types of migrants' legal entitlements and the administrative barriers to them, system accessibility and responsiveness, and measures to achieve change, the scores attributed to the six cases (out of 100 possible) were as follows: U.S. (66—in fifth place overall), Austria (63), Belgium (53), Canada (51), France (49), and Germany (43) (Ingleby 2016; see Ingleby et al. 2019).

Even though one might well quibble with such scores, argue that they ignore or exaggerate this or that factor, or simply point out that they may have changed in the five years since their publication (for example, due to the advent of the Trudeau and Trump administrations in North America and migration-related "crises" in the U.S. and Europe), caution and nuance are clearly advised when speaking broadly about welfare and integration regimes and migrants. And as the analysis in this section has shown, the broad trend line in the health sector, at least in a set of key cases, has been toward greater inclusiveness on paper and in reality. At first glance, it is hard to posit any direct parallel with popular attitudes.

CONCLUSIONS

Even a straightforward cross-national comparative sketch of developments in a single social policy sector, therefore, demonstrates that as endeavors proceed to ferret out the impact of migration on the welfare state, it will be important to take into account the full scope of the implicated policies. Their handling of legal migrants, refugees, recognized asylum seekers, and undocumented migrants cannot be left out of the picture. It is not enough to stop at popular attitudes toward redistribution or to assume that spending levels equate to performance or inclusion. More qualitative and cross-regional work is called for. Even if not much would be gained from getting lost in the policy weeds, it is time for more analysts to come close enough to the ground at least to be able to see the marginalized, vulnerable people who are the reason for caring about this topic in the first place.

REFERENCES

Abascal, Maria, and Delia Baldassarri. 2015. "Love Thy Neighbor? Ethnoracial Diversity and Trust Reexamined." *American Journal of Sociology* 121: 722–82.

Alesina, Alberto, and Nicola Fuchs-Schündeln. 2007. "Good Bye Lenin (or Not?): The Effect of Communism on People's Preferences." *American Economic Review* 97 (4): 1507–28.

Alesina, Alberto, and Edward Glaeser. 2004. *Fighting Poverty in the U.S. and Europe: A World of Difference.* Oxford: Oxford University Press.

Alesina, Alberto, Reza Baqir, and William Easterly. 1999. "Public Goods and Ethnic Divisions." *Quarterly Journal of Economics* 114 (4): 1243–84.

Alesina, Alberto, Edward Glaeser, and Bruce Sacerdote. 2001. "Why Doesn't the United States Have a European-Style Welfare State?" Brookings Papers on Economic Activity No. 2. Washington, DC: Brookings Institution.

Alesina, Alberto, Arnaud Devleeschauwer, William Easterly, Sergio Kurlat, and Romain Wacziarg. 2003. "Fractionalization." *Journal of Economic Growth* 8 (2): 155–94.

Alesina, Alberto, Johann Harnoss, and Hillel Rapoport. 2018. "Immigration and the Future of the Welfare State." Working Paper No. 2018-04. Paris: École d'Économie de Paris, February.

Álvarez-del Arco, Débora, Susana Monge, Ana M. Caro-Murillo, Oriana Ramírez-Rubio, Amaya Azcoaga-Lorenzo, Maria J. Belza et al. 2014. "HIV Testing Policies for Migrants and Ethnic Minorities in EU/EFTA Member States." *European Journal of Public Health* 24 (1): 139–44.

Artiga, Samantha, and Maria Diaz. 2019. "Health Coverage and Care of Undocumented Immigrants." Disparities Policy. San Francisco, CA: Kaiser Family Foundation, July 15.

Baldwin, Kate, and John D. Huber. 2010. "Economic versus Cultural Differences: Forms of Immigration and Public Goods Provision." *American Political Science Review* 104 (4): 644–62.

Banting, Keith G. 2005. "The Multicultural Welfare State: International Experience and North American Narratives." *Social Policy and Administration* 39 (2): 98–115.

Banting, Keith G. 2010. "Is There a Progressive's Dilemma in Canada?" *Canadian Journal of Political Science/ Revue canadienne de science politique* 43 (4): 797–820.

Banting, Keith G., and Will Kymlicka. 2004. "Do Multiculturalism Policies Erode the Welfare State? In *Cultural Diversity Versus Economic Solidarity*, ed. Philippe Van Parijs, 227–84. Brussels: De Boeck.

Banting, Keith G., Richard Johnston, Will Kymlicka, and Stuart N. Soroka. 2006. "Do Multicultural Policies Erode the Welfare State?" In *Multiculturalism and the Welfare State*, eds. Keith G. Banting and Will Kymlicka, 49–91. Oxford: Oxford University Press.

Banting, Keith G., Stuart N. Soroka, and Edward Koning. 2013. "Multicultural Diversity and Redistribution." In *Inequality and the Fading of Redistributive Politics*, eds. Keith Banting and John Myles, 165–86. Vancouver: University of British Columbia Press.

Bisin, Alberto, and Thierry Verdier. 2017. "Inequality, Redistribution and Cultural Integration in the Welfare State." *European Journal of Political Economy* 50 (C): 122–40.

Bloemraad, Irene. 2015. "Definitional Debates, Mechanisms and Canada: Comment on Will Kymlicka's Article: 'Solidarity in Diverse Societies.'" *Comparative Migration Studies* 3: 16.

Boeri, Tito. 2010. "Immigration to the Land of Redistribution." *Economica* 77 (308): 651–87.

Bosniak, Linda S. 2006. *The Citizen and the Alien*. Princeton, NJ: Princeton University Press.

Bradby, Hannah, Rachel Humphris, and Beatriz Padilla. 2020. "Universalism, Diversity and Norms: Gratitude, Healthcare and Welfare Chauvinism." *Critical Public Health* 30 (2): 166–78.

Brady, David, and Ryan Finnigan. 2014, "Does Immigration Undermine Public Support for Social Policy?" *American Sociological Review* 79 (1): 17–42.

Cavaillé, Charlotte, and Kris-Stella Trump. 2015. "The Two Facets of Social Policy Preferences." *Journal of Politics* 77 (1): 146–60.

CBS News. 2016. "Prime Minister Trudeau." 60 Minutes, March 6. www.cbsnews.com/news/60-minutes-prime-minister-trudeau/.

Chavez, Leo R. 2012. "Undocumented Immigrants and Their Use of Medical Services in Orange County, California." *Social Science and Medicine* 74 (6): 887–93.

Chueri Barbosa Correa, Juliana. 2020. "Who Deserves the Welfare? The Populist Radical Right's Transformation of Social Policy." PhD dissertation, Université de Genève.

Connor, Phillip, and Jynnah Radford. 2019. "These Are the Countries That Accept the Most Refugees in the World." World Economic Forum, June 27. www.weforum.org/agenda/2019/06/canada-now-leads-the-world-in-refugee-resettlement-surpassing-the-u-s/.

Cousin, Mathilde. 2019. "Non, la France n'est pas le seul pays à prendre en charge des soins pour les migrants en situation irrégulière." *20 Minutes Société*, September 14. www.20minutes.fr/societe/2611335-20190924-non-france-seul-pays-prendre-charge-soins-migrants-situation-irreguliere.

Crepaz, Markus M.L. 2006. "If You Are My Brother, I May Give You a Dime! Public Opinion on Multiculturalism, Trust, and the Welfare State." In *Multiculturalism and the Welfare State*, eds. Keith G. Banting and Will Kymlicka, 92–117. Oxford: Oxford University Press.

Crepaz, Markus M.L. 2008. *Trust beyond Borders: Immigration, the Welfare State, and Identity in Modern Societies*. Ann Arbor, MI: University of Michigan Press.

Crepaz, Markus M.L., and Regan Damron. 2009. "Constructing Tolerance: How the Welfare State Shapes Attitudes about Immigrants." *Comparative Political Studies* 42 (3): 437–63.

Cruces, Guillermo, Ricardo Perez-Truglia, and Martin Tetaz. 2013. "Biased Perceptions of Income Distribution and Preferences for Redistribution." *Journal of Public Economics* 98: 100–12.

Dahlberg, Matz, Karin Edmark, and Helène Lundqvist. 2012. "Ethnic Diversity and Preferences for Redistribution." *Journal of Political Economy* 120 (1): 41–76.

De Koster, Willem, Peter Achterberg, and Jeroen Van der Waal. 2012. "The New Right and the Welfare State." *International Political Science Review* 34 (1): 3–20.

Desmet, Klaus, Ignacio Ortuño-Ortí, and Shlomo Weber. 2009. "Linguistic Diversity and Redistribution." *Journal of the European Economic Association* 7 (6): 1291–318.

Dinesen, Peter Thisted, and Kim Mannemar Sønderskov. 2015. "Ethnic Diversity and Social Trust: Evidence from the Micro-Context." *American Sociological Review* 80 (3): 550–73.

Dinesen, Peter Thisted, and Kim Mannemar Sønderskov. 2018. "Ethnic Diversity and Social Trust: A Critical Review of the Literature and Suggestions for a Research Agenda." In *The Oxford Handbook of Social and Political Trust*, ed. Eric M. Uslaner, 175–204. Oxford: Oxford University Press.

Durante, Ruben, Louis Putterman, and Joël Van der Weele. 2014. "Preferences for Redistribution and Perception of Fairness." *Journal of the European Economic Association* 12 (4): 1059–86.

Eger, Maureen A. 2010. "Even in Sweden: The Effect of Immigration on Support for Welfare State Spending." *European Sociological Review* 26 (2): 203–17.

Eger, Maureen A., and Nate Breznau. 2017. "Immigration and the Welfare State: A Cross-Regional Analysis of European Welfare Attitudes." *International Journal of Comparative Sociology* 58 (5): 440–63.

Enggist, Matthias. 2019. "Welfare Chauvinism—Who Cares? Evidence on Priorities and the Importance the Public Attributes to Expanding or Retrenching Welfare Entitlements of Immigrants." Paper presented at the 26th International Conference of Europeanists, Madrid, June 20–22. http://welfarepriorities.eu/ wp-content/uploads/2020/01/22-Enggist-Welfare-Chauvinism-Who-Cares.pdf.

Epp, Charles R., Steven Maynard-Moody, and Donald Haider-Markel. 2017. "Beyond Profiling: The Institutional Sources of Racial Disparities in Policing." *Public Administration Review* 77 (2): 168–78.

Evans, Geoffrey. 2006. "Does Multiculturalism Reduce Support for Welfare Provision? A Case Study of British Social Attitudes." In *Multiculturalism and the Welfare State*, eds. Keith G. Banting and Will Kymlicka, 152–76. Oxford: Oxford University Press.

Fakoya, Ibidun, Débora Álvarez-Del Arco, Susana Monge, Andrew J. Copas, Anne-Francoise Gennotte, Alain Volny-Anne et al. 2018. "HIV Testing History and Access to Treatment among Migrants Living with HIV in Europe." *Journal of the International AIDS Society* 21 (S4): 60–73.

Fellowes, Matthew C., and Gretchen Rowe. 2004. "Politics and the New American Welfare States." *American Journal of Political Science* 48 (2): 362–73.

Finseraas, Henning. 2008. "Immigration and Preferences for Redistribution: An Empirical Analysis of European Survey Data." *Comparative European Politics* 6 (4): 407–31.

Finseraas, Henning, Tørbjørn Hanson, Åshild A. Johnsen, Andreas Kotsadam, and Gaute Torsvik. 2019. "Trust, Ethnic Diversity, and Personal Contact: A Field Experiment." *Journal of Public Economics* 5 (1): 72–84.

Ford, Robert. 2016. "'Who Should We Help?' An Experimental Test of Discrimination in the British Welfare State." *Political Studies* 64 (3): 630–50.

Gerdes, Christer. 2011. "The Impact of Immigration on the Size of Government." *Scandinavian Journal of Economics* 113 (1): 74–92.

Gilens, Martin. 1999. *Why Americans Hate Welfare: Race, Media, and the Politics of Anti-Poverty Policy.* Chicago, IL: University of Chicago Press.

Global Database on HIV-Related Travel Restrictions. 2020. Berlin: Deutsche AIDS-Hilfe e.V. www.hivtravel.org/.

Goldring, Luin, and Patricia Landolt. 2013. "The Conditionality of Legal Rights and Status." In *Producing and Negotiating Non-Citizenship: Precarious Legal Status in Canada*, eds. Luin Goldring and Patricia Landolt, 3–27. Toronto: University of Toronto Press.

Gordon, Joshua C. 2019. "The Perils of Vanguardism: Explaining Radical Cuts to Unemployment Insurance in Sweden." *Socio-Economic Review* 17 (4): 947–68.

Green, David A., and W. Craig Riddell. 2019. "Is There a Tradeoff between Ethnic Diversity and Redistribution?" Institut zur Zukunft der Arbeit Discussion Paper No. 12098. Bonn: IZA, January.

Gründler, Klaus, and Sebastian Köllner. 2018. "Culture, Diversity, and the Welfare State." CESifo Working Paper No. 6856. Munich: Center for Economic Studies and Ifo Institute, Ludwigs-Maximilians-Universität.

Hall, Peter A. 2017. "The Political Sources of Social Solidarity." In *The Strains of Commitment: The Political Sources of Solidarity in Diverse Societies*, eds. Keith Banting and Will Kymlicka, 349–98. Oxford: Oxford University Press.

Harell, Allison, Stuart Soroka, and Shanto Iyengar. 2016. "Race, Prejudice and Attitudes toward Redistribution: A Comparative Experimental Approach." *European Journal of Political Research* 55 (4): 723–44.

Hernández-Rosete Martínez, Daniel. 2008. "La otra migración: Historias de discriminación de personas que vivieron con VIH en México." *Salud Mental* 31 (4): 253–60.

Hopkins, Daniel J. 2011. "The Limited Local Impacts of Ethnic and Racial Diversity." *American Politics Research* 39 (2): 344–79.

Ingleby, David. 2016. "Summary Report on the MIPEX Health Strand and Country Reports." Brussels: Migration Health Division, Regional Office Brussels, International Organization for Migration.

Ingleby, David, Roumyana Petrova-Benedict, Thomas Huddleston, and Elena Sanchez, and MIPEX Health Strand Consortium. 2019. "The MIPEX Health Strand: A Longitudinal, Mixed-Methods Survey of Policies on Migrant Health in 38 Countries." *European Journal of Public Health* 29 (3): 458–62.

Ireland, Patrick R. 2014. "Welfare States and Migrant Incorporation Trajectories." In *An Introduction to Immigrant Incorporation Strategies*, eds. Marco Martiniello and Jan Rath, 345–70. Amsterdam: University of Amsterdam Press.

Jofre-Monseny, Jordi, Pilar Sorribas-Navarro, and Javier Vázquez-Grenno. 2016. "Immigration and Local Spending in Social Services." *International Tax and Public Finance* 23 (6): 1004–29.

Joseph, Tiffany D., and Helen B. Marrow. 2017. "Health Care, Immigrants, and Minorities." *Journal of Ethnic and Migration Studies*, 43 (12): 1965–84.

Karl-Trummer, Ursula, Birgit Metzler, and Sonja Novak-Zezula. 2009. "Health Care for Undocumented Migrants in the EU." Brussels: International Organization for Migration.

Kaufmann, Eric, and Matthew J. Goodwin. 2018. "The Diversity Wave: A Meta-Analysis of the Native-Born White Response to Ethnic Diversity." *Social Science Research* 76 (November): 120–31.

Keller, Tony. 2018. "Canada Has Its Own Ways of Keeping Out Unwanted Immigrants." *The Atlantic*, July 12. www.theatlantic.com/ideas/archive/2018/07/ canada-immigration-success/564944/.

Keskinen, Suvi, Ov Cristian Norocel, and Martin Bak Jørgensen. 2016. "The Politics and Policies of Welfare Chauvinism under the Economic Crisis." *Critical Social Policy* 36 (3): 321–29.

Kitschelt, Herbert. 1995. *The Radical Right in Western Europe*. Ann Arbor, MI: University of Michigan Press.

Kline, Michelle. 2011. "National Immigration Policy and Access to Health Care." Philadelphia, PA: American College of Physicians.

Könönen, Jukka. 2018. "Differential Inclusion of Non-Citizens in a Universalistic Welfare State." *Citizenship Studies* 22 (1): 53–69.

Kootstra, Anouk. 2016. "Deserving and Undeserving Welfare Claimants in Britain and the Netherlands." *European Sociological Review* 32 (3): 325–38.

KPMG. 2019. "Ending the Epidemic: France." London: KPMG LLP, March.

Kriesi, Hanspeter. 2015. "Enlightened Understanding, Empowerment and Leadership: Three Ways to Enhance Multiculturalism." *Comparative Migration Studies* 3: 18.

Kugel, Candace, and Edward L. Zuroweste. 2010. "The State of Health Care Services for Mobile Poor Populations." *Journal of Health Care for the Poor and Underserved* 21 (2): 422–29.

Kymlicka, Will. 2015. "Solidarity in Diverse Societies: Beyond Neoliberal Multiculturalism and Welfare Chauvinism." *Comparative Migration Studies* 3: 17.

Kymlicka, Will, and Keith G. Banting. 2015. "The Political Sources of Solidarity in Diverse Societies." European University Institute Working Paper RSCAS 2015/73. Fiesole: EUI, October.

Laenen, Tijs, Federica Rossetti, and Wim Van Oorschot. 2019. "Why Deservingness Theory Needs Qualitative Research." *International Journal of Comparative Sociology* 60 (3): 190–216.

Lahusen, Christian, and Maria T. Grasso. 2018a. "Solidarity in Europe–European Solidarity: An Introduction." In *Solidarity in Europe: Citizens' Responses in Times of Crisis*, eds. Christian Lahusen and Maria T. Grasso, 1–18. Cham: Palgrave Macmillan.

Lahusen, Christian, and Maria T. Grasso. 2018b. "Solidarity in Europe: A Comparative Assessment and Discussion." In *Solidarity in Europe: Citizens' Responses in Times of Crisis*, eds. Christian Lahusen and Maria T. Grasso, 253–81. Cham: Palgrave Macmillan.

The Lancet. 2018. "Editorial: Harmful, Unfounded Myths about Migration and Health." *Science Daily*, December 5. www.sciencedaily.com/releases/2018/12/ 181205232658.htm.

Larchanché, Stéphanie. 2012. "Intangible Obstacles: Health Implications of Stigmatization, Structural Violence, and Fear among Undocumented Immigrants in France." *Social Science and Medicine* 74 (6): 858–63.

Larsen, Christian A. 2008. "The Institutional Logic of Welfare Attitudes: How Welfare Regimes Influence Public Support." *Comparative Political Studies* 41 (2): 145–68.

Larsen, Christian A. 2011. "Ethnic Heterogeneity and Public Support for Welfare: Is the American Experience Replicated in Britain, Sweden and Denmark?" *Scandinavian Political Studies* 34 (4): 332–53.

Larsen, Christian A., Morten Frederiksen, and Mathias Herup Nielsen. 2018. "European Welfare Nationalism: A Democratic Forum Study in Five Countries." In *Attitudes, Aspirations and Welfare: Social Policy Directions in Uncertain Times*, eds. Peter Taylor-Gooby and Benjamin Leruth, 63–91. Cham: Palgrave Macmillan.

Lind, Jo T. 2007. "Fractionalization and the Size of Government." *Journal of Public Economics* 91 (1–2): 51–76.

Luttmer, Erzo F.P. 2001. "Group Loyalty and the Taste for Redistribution." *Journal of Political Economy* 109 (3): 500–28.

Luttmer, Erzo F.P., and Monica Singhal. 2011. "Culture, Context, and the Taste for Redistribution." *American Economic Journal: Economic Policy* 3 (1), 157–79.

Lutz, Philipp. 2019. "Reassessing the Gap-Hypothesis: Tough Talk and Weak Action in Migration Policy?" *Party Politics*, April 24. doi: 10.1177/1354068819840776.

Lutz, Philipp. 2020. "Welfare States, Demographic Transition, and Immigration Policies." In *The European Social Model under Pressure*, eds. Romana Careja, Patrick Emmenegger, and Nathalie Giger, 331–47. Wiesbaden: Springer VS.

MacGregor, Marion. 2019. "Germany: Sick without Papers." *InfoMigrants*, November 11. www.infomigrants.net/en/post/20743/germany-sick-without-papers.

Mäkelä, Erik, and Matti Viren. 2017. "Migration Effects on Municipalities' Expenditures." *Review of Economics* 69 (1): 59–86.

Marx, Paul, and Elias Naumann. 2018. "Do Right-Wing Parties Foster Welfare Chauvinistic Attitudes?" *Electoral Studies* 52 (April): 111–16.

Mau, Steffen. 2003. *The Moral Economy of Welfare States: Britain and Germany Compared.* London: Routledge.

Mau, Steffen, and Christoph Burkhardt. 2009, "Migration and Welfare State Solidarity in Western Europe." *Journal of European Social Policy* 19 (3): 213–29.

McLaren, Lauren M. 2015. *Immigration and Perceptions of National Political Systems in Europe.* Oxford: Oxford University Press.

Meltzer, Allan H., and Scott F. Richard. 1981. "A Rational Theory of the Size of Government." *Journal of Political Economy* 89 (5): 914–27.

Meuleman, Bart, Femke Roosma, and Koen Abts. 2020. "Welfare Deservingness Opinions from Heuristic to Measurable Concept: The CARIN Deservingness Principles Scale." *Social Science Research* 85: 102352.

Mewes, Jan, and Steffen Mau. 2013. "Globalization, Socio-Economic Status, and Welfare Chauvinism: European Perspectives on Attitudes Towards the Exclusion of Immigrants." *International Journal of Comparative Sociology* 54 (3): 228–45.

Michel, Elie. 2017. "Welfare Politics and the Radical Right: The Relevance of Welfare Politics for the Radical Right's Success in Western Europe." PhD dissertation, European University Institute.

Milanovic, Branko. 2000. "The Median-Voter Hypothesis, Income Inequality, and Income Redistribution." *European Journal of Political Economy* 16 (3): 367–410.

Miller, David, and Sundas Ali. 2014. "Testing the National Identity Argument." *European Political Science Review* 6 (2): 237–59.

Mudde, Cas. 2007. *Populist Radical Right Parties in Europe.* Cambridge: Cambridge University Press.

Mudde, Cas. 2013. "Three Decades of Populist Radical Right Parties in Western Europe: So What?" *European Journal of Political Research* 52 (1): 1–19.

Mueller, Dennis C., and Peter Murrell. 1986. "Interest Groups and the Size of Government." *Public Choice* 48 (2): 125–45.

Müllerschön, Johanna, Carmen Koschollek, Claudia Santos-Hövener, Anna Kuehne, Jacqueline Müller-Nordhorn, and Viviane Bremer. 2019. "Impact of Health Insurance Status among Migrants from Sub-Saharan Africa on Access to Health Care and HIV Testing in Germany." *BMC International Health and Human Rights* 19: 10.

Muñoz, Jordi, and Sergi Pardos-Prado. 2019. "Immigration and Support for Social Policy: An Experimental Comparison of Universal and Means-Tested Programs." *Political Science Research and Methods* 7 (4): 717–35.

Murdie, Robert, and Sutama Ghosh. 2010. "Does Spatial Concentration Always Mean a Lack of Integration?" *Journal of Ethnic and Migration Studies* 36 (2): 293–311.

Nagayoshi, Kikuko, and Mikael Hjerm. 2015. "Anti-Immigration Attitudes in Different Welfare States: Do Types of Labor Market Policies Matter?" *International Journal of Comparative Sociology* 56 (2): 141–62.

O'Donnell, Catherine A. 2018. "Health Care Access for Migrants in Europe." *Oxford Research Encyclopedias.* doi: 10.1093/acrefore/9780190632366.013.6.

Ore, Jonathan. 2020. "Pay-As-You-Go Health Care." CBC Radio, January 17. www.cbc.ca/radio/whitecoat/pay-as-you-go-health-care-uninsured-people-in-canada-face-sky-high-bills-delays-in-treatment-doctors-say-1.5426679.

Pett, William. 2018. "Travel Restrictions for People with HIV." AIDSmap. London: National AIDS Manual, December. www.aidsmap.com/about-hiv/travel-restrictions-people-hiv.

Putnam, Robert D. 1995. "Bowling Alone: America's Declining Social Capital." *Journal of Democracy* 6 (1): 65–78.

Putnam, Robert D. 2007. "*E Pluribus Unum*: Diversity and Community in the Twenty-First Century." *Scandinavian Political Studies* 30 (2): 137–74.

Reeskens, Tim, and Tom Van der Meer. 2019. "The Inevitable Deservingness Gap: A Study into the Insurmountable Immigrant Penalty in Perceived Welfare Deservingness." *Journal of European Social Policy* 29 (2): 166–81.

Reeskens, Tim, and Wim Van Oorschot. 2012. "Disentangling the 'New Liberal Dilemma': On the Relations between General Welfare Distribution Preferences and Welfare Chauvinism." *International Journal of Comparative Sociology* 53 (2): 120–39.

Ridde, Valéry, Joséphine Aho, Elhadji Malick Ndao, Magalie Benoit, Jill Hanley, Solène Lagrange et al. 2020. "Unmet Healthcare Needs among Migrants without Medical Insurance in Montreal, Canada." *Global Public Health* 15 (11): 1603–16.

Rosano, Aldo, Marie Dauvrin, Sandra C. Buttigieg, Elena Ronda, Jean Tafforeau, and Sonia Dias. 2017. "Migrants' Access to Preventive Health Services in Five EU Countries." *BMC Health Services Research* 17: 588.

Röth, Leonce, Alexandre Afonso, and Dennis C. Spies. 2018. "The Impact of Populist Radical Right Parties on Socio-economic Policies." *European Political Science Review* 10 (3): 325–50.

Rugh, Jacob S., and Jessica Trounstine. 2011. "The Provision of Local Public Goods in Diverse Communities." *Journal of Politics* 73 (4): 1038–50.

Sandelind, Clara N. (2018). "Constructions of Identity, Belonging and Exclusion in the Democratic Welfare State." *National Identities* 20 (2): 197–218.

Scervini, Francesco. 2012. "Empirics of the Median Voter: Democracy, Redistribution, and the Role of the Middle Class." *Journal of Economic Inequality* 10 (4): 529–50.

Schaeffer, Merlin. 2014. *Ethnic Diversity and Social Cohesion: Immigration, Ethnic Fractionalization and Potentials for Civic Action*. Aldershot: Ashgate.

Schmidt, Alexander W., and Dennis C. Spies. 2013. "Do Parties 'Playing the Race Card' Undermine Natives' Support for Redistribution? Evidence from Europe." *Comparative Political Studies* 47 (4): 519–49.

Schumacher, Gijs, and Kees Van Kersbergen. 2016. "Do Mainstream Parties Adapt to the Welfare Chauvinism of Populist Parties?" *Party Politics* 22 (3): 300–12.

Senik, Claudia, Holger Stichnoth, and Karine Van der Straeten. 2008. "Immigration and Natives' Attitudes towards the Welfare State: Evidence from the European Social Survey." *Social Indicators Research* 91: 345–70.

Sharrett, Luke. 2012. "Limits Placed on Immigrants in Health Care Law." *New York Times*, September 17. www.nytimes.com/2012/09/18/health/policy/limits-placed-on-immigrants-in-health-care-law.html?pagewanted=all&_r=0.

Shutes, Isabel. 2016. "Work-Related Conditionality and the Access to Social Benefits of National Citizens, EU and Non-EU Citizens." *Journal of Social Policy* 45 (4): 691–707.

Simonnot, Nathalie, Annabel Rodriguez, Mabel Nuenberg, François Fille, Patricio-Ezequiel Aranda-Fernandez, and Pierre Chauvin. 2016. "Access to Healthcare for People Facing Multiple Vulnerabilities in Health in 31 Cities in 12 Countries." Paris: Médecins du Monde.

Smith, Alyna C., and Michele Levoy. 2017. "Cities of Rights: Ensuring Health Care for Undocumented Residents." Brussels: Platform for International Cooperation on Undocumented Migrants.

Smith, Peter. 2018. "HIV-bei Flüchlingen oft ein Tabu-Thema." *Ärtzeitung*, March 27. www.aerztezeitung.de/Panorama/HIV-bei-Fluechtlingen-oft-ein-Tabu-Thema-229066.html.

Soroka, Stuart N., Richard Johnston, and Keith G. Banting. 2004. "Ethnicity, Trust and the Welfare State." In *Cultural Diversity versus Economic Solidarity*, ed. Philippe Van Parijs, 33–57. Brussels: De Boeck.

Soroka, Stuart N., Keith G. Banting, and Richard Johnston. 2006a. "Immigration and Redistribution in a Global Era." In *Globalization and Egalitarian Redistribution*, eds. Pranab Bardhan, Samuel Bowles, and Michael Wallerstein, 261–88. Princeton, NJ: Princeton University Press.

Soroka, Stuart N., Richard Johnston, and Keith G. Banting. 2006b. "Ties That Bind: Social Cohesion and Diversity in Canada." In *The Art of the State III: Belonging? Diversity, Recognition and Shared Citizenship in Canada*, eds. Keith Banting, Thomas J. Courchene, and F. Leslie Seidle, 561–600. Montreal: Institute for Research in Public Policy.

Soroka, Stuart N., Matthew Wright, Richard Johnston, Jack Citrin, Keith Banting, and Will Kymlicka. 2017. "Ethnoreligious Identity, Immigration, and Redistribution." *Journal of Experimental Political Science* 4 (3): 173–82.

Spies, Dennis C. 2018. *Immigration and Welfare State Retrenchment*. Oxford: Oxford University Press.

Steele, Liza G. 2016. "Ethnic Diversity and Support for Redistributive Social Policies." *Social Forces* 94 (4): 1439–81.

Stichnoth, Holger, and Karine Van der Straeten. 2013. "Ethnic Diversity, Public Spending, and Individual Support for the Welfare State." *Journal of Economic Surveys* 27 (2): 364–89.

Stolle, Dietlind, and Allison Harell. 2015. "The Consequences of Ethnic Diversity: Advancing the Debate." In *Social Cohesion and Immigration in Europe and North America: Mechanisms, Conditions, and Causality*, eds. Ruud Koopmans, Bram Lancee, and Merlin Schaeffer, 105–22. London: Routledge.

Swank, Duane, and Hans-Georg Betz. 2018. "Globalization, Institutions of Social Solidarity, and Radical Right-Wing Populism in Western Europe." Paper presented at the Annual Meetings of the American Political Science Association, Boston, August 30–September 2.

Taylor-Gooby, Peter, Benjamin Leruth, and Heejung Chung. 2017. "Liberalism, Social Investment, Protectionism, and Chauvinism." In *After Austerity: Welfare State Transformation in Europe after the Great Recession*, eds. Peter Taylor-Gooby, Benjamin Leruth, and Heejung Chung, 201–19. Oxford: Oxford University Press.

Terum, Lars Inge, Gaute Torsvik, and Einar Øverbye. 2018. "Discrimination against Ethnic Minorities in Activation Programme? Evidence from a Vignette Experiment." *Journal of Social Policy* 47 (1): 39–56.

Thomann, Eva, and Carolin Rapp. 2017. "Who Deserves Solidarity? Unequal Treatment of Immigrants in Swiss Welfare Policy Delivery." *Policy Studies Journal* 46 (3): 531–52.

Tyrberg, Maria, and Carl Dahlström. 2018. "Policy Effects of Anti-Immigrant Party Representation on Aid to Vulnerable European Union/European Economic Area Citizens." *Political Studies* 66 (1): 3–22.

Van Oorschot, Wim. 2006. "Making the Difference in Social Europe: Deservingness Perceptions among Citizens of European Welfare States." *Journal of European Social Policy* 16 (1): 23–42.

Van Oorschot, Wim, Femke Roosma, Bart Meuleman, and Tim Reeskens, eds. 2017. *The Social Legitimacy of Targeted Welfare: Attitudes to Welfare Deservingness*. Cheltenham, UK and Northampton, MA, USA: Edward Elgar Publishing.

Viladrich, Anahí. 2012. "Beyond Welfare Reform: Reframing Undocumented Immigrants' Entitlement to Health Care in the United States." *Social Science and Medicine* 74 (6): 822–9.

World Health Organization Regional Office for Europe (WHO Europe). 2018a. "Health of Refugees and Migrants: Practices in Addressing the Health Needs of Refugees and Migrants." Copenhagen: WHO Europe.

WHO Europe. 2018b. "Report on the Health of Refugees and Migrants in the WHO European Region." Copenhagen: WHO Europe.

WHO Europe. 2019. "Health Diplomacy: Spotlight on Refugees and Migrants." Copenhagen: WHO Europe.

Zuckerman, Stephen, Timothy A. Waidmann, and Emily Lawton. 2011. "Undocumented Immigrants, Left Out of Health Reform." *Health Affairs* 30 (10): 1997–2004.

PART II

IS SOCIAL HOMOGENEITY A PRECONDITION FOR REDISTRIBUTION?

4. Why share with strangers? Reflections on a variety of perspectives
Matthew Wright

The willingness to give up resources of one's own to others whom he or she has never met is the beating heart of modern political communities. We all make sacrifices to gain, both individually, and in the aggregate, from collective action. The political community, in the aggregate and, at least in democracies, as the product of political contestation, defines not only what its citizens get in return for such sacrifices, but also sets the rules for who may join and on what terms. All of this – the parties with whom potential community members are expected to deal, what gets redistributed and to whom, and the nature of the institutions governing the transaction – is contingent on time and place. Developed democracies have, in the years since the Second World War, furnished their citizens with a relatively expansive social safety net. Yet as these democracies have become more ethnically, religiously, and culturally diverse, mainly through large-scale immigration, debates have emerged over whether the old order can stand and, if it can, whether or not immigrants should be allowed to benefit from it. Large blocs of citizens, and those who claim to speak for them, are no longer willing to share with strangers or, at any rate, with *those* strangers (e.g. Gest 2016; Kaufmann 2019).

This chapter explores some of the reasons why people share, and why they might refuse to. I will proceed as follows. First, I take a moment to define the scope of my analysis, and do a bit of conceptual brush-clearing. Following this, I examine three "ideal-typic" approaches to the question: economic self-interest, group identity and group primacy, and political values. Following this, because reality is never as clean as the ideal-types suggest, I look at three "hybrid" theories, which is to say explanations that recombine elements of the ideal-types in different ways. I then compare and contrast the theories. Finally, I close with a number of critical questions on this literature.

SCOPE OF THE CHAPTER

The prompt "Why share with strangers?" is extremely broad, and answering it comprehensively would require anyone taking on the task to travel well beyond the bounds of the typical review essay. As such, I want to delineate the scope of the present endeavor in two ways. First, the question of sharing with *whom*? Of course, "strangers" are all around us: the neighbors next door we've never exchanged a word with, the people with whom we share public transit, and indeed people living in different cities, states, and nations around the world. Here, I mainly explore "strangerhood" through the prism of immigration. On a national scale, immigrant-driven diversity – ethnic, religious, and linguistic – has fundamentally reshaped the demographic landscape in Europe, North America, and elsewhere, and this process shows no sign of slowing (Cornelius and Rosenblum 2005;

Hooghe et al. 2008). It has made the issue of "strangerhood" salient to an unprecedented degree, and, accordingly, debates over the various *consequences* of immigration occupy an increasingly large piece of the political and social landscape. So, when I speak here of giving to "strangers," I am (unless otherwise specified) speaking of giving to immigrants.

Second, what do we mean by "sharing"? Here, I am mainly thinking of support for government redistribution. One could envisage all kinds of "sharing with strangers" that do not fit this category: giving money to a beggar on the street, putting money in a church collection basket, or donating to an international charitable organization. One might also think of "sharing" in non-monetary terms, for instance harboring people whose lives are in peril (Monroe 1998), or supporting the provision of political rights to individuals that would not have otherwise had them. Since we are speaking of immigration, one might argue (and not without merit) that even support for liberal immigration policies counts as "sharing with strangers" in the sense that we are allowing migrants to share in the benefits of national citizenship. While there is some overlap, I try to avoid the broader discussion of what drives anti-immigrant sentiment, which has been well covered elsewhere (e.g. Ceobanu and Escandell 2010; Hainmueller and Hopkins 2014; Wright and Levy 2020).

Taken together, these two qualifications essentially redefine "sharing with strangers" as *welfare chauvinism* (Kitschelt 1997), sometimes referred to as the 'Progressive's' or 'New Liberal Dilemma' (Goodhart 2004; Reeskens and Van Oorschot 2012). What is it, in short, that leads people to be *less* willing to share with immigrants than they are to their fellow countrymen? If this seems narrow and arbitrary, nothing could be further from the truth. As we shall see, a variety of interrelated perspectives has emerged to tackle this question. Some I refer to as "ideal-typic" theories and others as "hybrids"; the distinction here is that the former draw on one major school of thought whereas the latter tends to spread across them. I take each in turn in the following sections.

APPROACHES: IDEAL-TYPIC THEORIES

Homo Economicus

The signal assumption underpinning the "rational actor" model of behavior is that individuals function as utility maximizers. While discussion of what constitutes "utility" and, for that matter, what is "rational" are beyond the scope of this chapter, for our purpose the standard approach suggests that people are primarily interested in supporting policies that maximize their economic well-being. Along these lines, the broader conversation about redistributive preferences – i.e. the extent to which governments should reduce economic inequality via social welfare – in economics invokes a number of different principles: income maximization, prospects of upward mobility (Benabou and Ok 2001; Alesina and La Ferrara 2005; Alesina et al. 2018b), inequality aversion (Bolton and Ockenfels 2000; Fehr and Schmidt 1999), reciprocity (Dufwenberg and Kirchsteiger 2004; Rabin 1993), and risk aversion (Beck 1994; Fisman et al. 2020; Giuliano and Spilimbergo 2014).

The link from utility maximization to immigration *per se* occurs when people link immigration policies to economic gains and losses. In the narrowest sense, people care about immigration to the degree that they think it alters their wages and job prospects, the prices they pay at the supermarket, the tax increases they might be expected to sustain, or immigrants "crowding out" the benefits to which they might be entitled. As it happens, though, this kind of thinking is uncommon, a figment of a "zombie theory," Hainmueller and Hopkins' review of immigration attitudes goes so far as to say (2014, 241). People simply do not reliably reject immigrants who would threaten their job and accept immigrants who would complement their skills and raise their marginal product of labor (Citrin et al. 1997). With some important exceptions such as native-born software engineers in Silicon Valley (Malhotra et al. 2013), the concentration of immigrants in the industry that people work in is only weakly related to preferences about immigration (Hainmueller et al. 2014; though see Dancygier and Donnelly 2013). And, insofar as exposure to higher tax burdens or exclusion from benefits are concerned, there is at most a weak, contingent, complex, and indeterminate relationship between the size of immigrant populations in people's own states and localities and opposition to immigration (Citrin et al. 1997; Hopkins 2010).

Things get more interesting if we allow that people might think beyond their pocketbook, and more about the financial well-being of some broader social aggregate (more on this later). They may care about the impact of immigration on the national economy out of a Tocquevillian sense of "enlightened self-interest," believing that a strong economy will in the long run personally benefit themselves and those they care about. Or, such motivations might rest on selfless commitments to the well-being of an ethnic group or the nation, something I consider in depth further on. Either way, when it comes to welfare chauvinism, the argument here is that people resent immigration if they believe that immigrants "take out" more in government services than they "put in" through taxes, *regardless of whether they themselves will benefit*. This assumption – that people are thinking about what kinds of immigrants are economically beneficial to the nation as a whole – remains somewhat undertheorized but is at any rate consistent with findings from a number of recent studies. For example, Hainmueller and Hopkins (2015) demonstrate a wide-ranging "hidden consensus" over an immigrant admissions policy that favors those who come legally, work hard, speak English, and (if at all possible) hold an advanced degree in science, technology, engineering, or medicine. And, while this and other complementary studies (i.e. Levy et al. 2016; Wright et al. 2016) are United States (U.S.)-focused, this is consistent with comparative work showing broad support for higher-skilled rather than lower-skilled immigrants and, at the same time, little or no evidence that this support is conditioned on individuals' own exposure to labor market competition (Valentino et al. 2017).

Group-Centrism

Another, quite different, perspective on why we might include or exclude immigrants from access to redistribution is driven by group allegiance over rational utility maximization. The lead actor in these accounts, *homo sociologicus*, is a social animal embedded in a political community and invested in its integrity – not only its economic flourishing but the preservation of its way of life. People's political judgments are at root all about preserving "us." One (but not the only) prominent expression of this view is in Social Identity Theory (Tajfel and Turner 1979), which stipulates that people seek pride and self-esteem from their group affiliations, and that identification with other group members solidifies their sense of belonging in a complicated social world. Greater feelings of shared identity and solidarity with those *inside* a salient group boundary makes people want to share resources within the group. Hostility or indifference to those *outside* of that boundary fuels exclusion. In short, people think and act with an eye to either maintaining or enhancing the status of some salient group identity they hold (the "in-group") versus whomever they consider to be outside of that boundary. This is especially so when people are primed to see out-groups as "threatening."

For present purposes, the group-centrist argument is that immigration politics, including (but not limited to) welfare chauvinism, hinge upon deeply rooted group identifications. Some care more about in-group favorability, as in numerous recent accounts of "white identity" or "white working class" backlash to mass immigration among other things (e.g. Abrajano and Hajnal 2015; Gest 2016; Jardina 2019; Kaufmann 2019). Others emphasize perceived status differentials and group hierarchy (Carter 2019; Masuoka and Junn 2013). Still others focus more sharply on out-group hostility as such, whether this is group-specific animus against, say, Latinos or Muslims (e.g. Sides and Gross 2013; Valentino et al. 2013), or broader ethnocentric orientations against "outsiders" (Kalkan et al. 2009; Kinder and Kam 2009). And, finally, some examine them from the standpoint of subjective definitions of the boundaries of national identity (Citrin and Sears 2014; Schildkraut 2011, 2014; Theiss-Morse 2009; Wong 2010; Wright 2011).

There is an enormous body of research loosely centered on the notion that concerns over "cultural threat" – broadly construed as threat to dominant group status – are key drivers of anti-immigrant sentiment (Ceobanu and Escandell 2010; Hainmueller and Hopkins 2014). Where welfare chauvinism is concerned, the argument is simple: insofar as immigrants are (a) seen as outside of some salient in-group identification and (b) seen as a threat to the status or prestige of that identification, members of that group will respond with hostility. Welfare chauvinism, then, comes from the perception that redistribution is a zero-sum game, and that government benefits that are finding their way into immigrants' hands must, by necessity boost their status *at the expense of* the native born.[1]

Values

If the group-centrist view is all about who belongs (and who doesn't), a different point of view on *homo sociologicus* asks: on what terms? Here the emphasis is more strictly deontological, which is to say based on the idea that political communities are groups of people bound by an understanding of the unofficial and official reciprocal obligations of subjects to one another and to the sovereign.[2] They call to mind a social contract. Contractarian philosophies diverge sharply over what the specific rules and obligations are or ought to be, yet such distinct renderings as Hobbesian absolutism, Lockeian liberalism, and Rousseauist public-spirited direct democracy all share the assumption that the basis for legitimate political authority is a legal compact. As with membership in most clubs and associations that involve repeated interactions between members, the social contract has both formal and informal components, and these may be near consensual or politically contested.

This kind of argument suggests that people think about immigration policy in terms of what is fair for immigrants, rather than whether they identify immigrants as part of "us" or part of "them." Fairness judgments are rendered on the basis of whether a policy (or an immigrant who may benefit from said policy) strikes people as consonant with their understanding of what immigrants owe their adoptive political community and what it owes them in return. For instance, in the American case, we have argued that people judge immigrants and immigration policy on the basis of whether or not they seem to violate basic norms about assimilation, which are themselves tied to bedrock beliefs about egalitarianism, legalism, and individualism (Levy and Wright 2020).

Where do these rules and norms come from? A big part of the story is historical, and in the political, legal, and cultural development of a community's "political culture." Sociologist T.H. Marshall, for instance, pioneered the notion that support for the expansion of citizenship rights required a kind of national community in which co-citizens respected each others' adherence to obligations derived from the social contract (Marshall 1992 [1950]). In the American case, there is a long tradition of work debating the origin and significance of "Americanness" and "American Exceptionalism" (i.e. Schafer 1999), much of which informs subsequent discussions about how various aspects of the American political tradition – liberal assimilationist values, individualism and the so-called "Protestant work ethic," and egalitarianism – go on to define the social contract immigrants are ostensibly joining (Levy and Wright 2020).

At the same time, people seem to act on more "universalist" tendencies – that is, values and norms that are not obviously tied to one political community and its particular social contract. Here I have in mind typically pro-immigrant tendencies like humanitarianism, which leads people to support immigrants to the degree that the latter are perceived as suffering political, social, or economic persecution (Levy and Wright 2020; Newman et al. 2015; Pantoja 2006). But one might also point to other basic human tendencies that push in a more anti-immigrant direction, for example germ aversion (Aarøe et al. 2017; Brown et al. 2019).

Either way, the implication is that people will support access to redistribution for immigrants who "play by the rules" – be they formal or informal, and be they sociohistorical or more closely tied to evolutionary biology – and hostile to redistribution for those who do not. Critically, this process should play out independently from (or at least net of) group-specific traits that make immigrants "like" or "unlike" in the sense discussed earlier.

APPROACHES: HYBRID THEORIES

The preceding section outlined three approaches to "sharing with strangers" that were, at least in principle, more or less distinct. People might reason along economic lines (either egocentrically or sociotropically), they might think predominantly about what will benefit the status of their "in-group," or they might care most about whether or not putative beneficiaries are in good standing with respect to the social contract. Here, I outline a few additional approaches that mix and match across perspectives.

Economic Group-Centrism

Much of the economics-based work on diversity and welfare chauvinism is rooted firmly in sociotropic ideas about utility maximization, but also assumes that ethnicity plays an important role in the cost–benefit calculus. Whereas earlier I mentioned that sociotropic optimization occurred with reference to "social aggregates," here we can specify further that the relevant social aggregate is the majority group's ethnicity. Along these lines, the core observation is that altruistic preferences for redistribution do not travel well across ethnic lines. For example, Alesina et al. (2001) compare social spending across levels of racial fragmentation to illustrate that racial prejudice in the U.S. undermines policy support for redistribution to the poor, who are disproportionately black and widely stereotyped as such.[3] Similarly, Luttmer (2001) used survey data to demonstrate both negative exposure effect (reduced support for redistribution as the rate of welfare recipients in their community rises), as well as the racial group loyalty effect, which argues that support for redistribution rises as the percentage of local welfare recipients from their own racial group increases.

With an eye to the issue of immigrants and welfare chauvinism, Dahlberg et al. (2013) leveraged randomized refugee placement in Sweden to show that immigrant inflows undermine public support for social welfare policies.[4] Elsewhere, Alesina et al. (2018a) showed that even priming subjects to *think* about immigration reduced their support for redistribution. Finally, through a more historical lens, Tabellini (2020) uses settlement data from 1910 to 1930 to argue that immigrants were seen as a burden, which decreased demand for redistribution among the existing Protestant population.

What makes this approach distinct from more "identity"-grounded explanations is that scholars play up the economic side of the ledger and tend to leave the social psychology of in-group identification in the background. There is nothing intrinsically "ethnic" about the basic notions underpinning the rational actor, and one might imagine such notions leading people to want to restrict immigrants' access to social programs for entirely non-racial reasons. Yet economic group-centrism makes the added assumptions that (a) people prefer to associate with similar others, a notion derived from homophily theory (McPherson et al. 2001), and (b) that "likeness" is meaningfully determined along ethnoreligious lines. Utility maximization, then, occurs through the prism of zero-sum conflict between ethnic groups. From this follows expectations – usually pessimistic ones – not only about welfare chauvinism, but about the prospects for "social cohesion" in diversifying societies more generally.

Deservingness and Belonging

Another hybrid approach to welfare chauvinism centers on judgments about whether or not those that would benefit have appropriately earned it. This "deservingness" framework (Petersen 2012; Aaroe and Petersen 2017) stipulates that, for our purposes here, people support welfare immigrants deemed "deserving" of it (e.g. Van Oorschot 2000; Reeskens and Van Oorschot 2012).

A twist on the "deservingness" idea focuses more on the communitarian side of the political community. It leaves aside certain "deservingness" criteria (primarily the considerations of whether people control their own economic circumstances, and how much they actually need the help) and plays up others that more closely reflect more communitarian concerns. These include: *identity*, or the perception of the extent that the individuals in need are "like"; *attitude*, or whether the individuals are viewed as grateful for the support they receive; and *reciprocity*, or the extent to which individuals are perceived as likely to "give back" or contribute to society. In essence, scoring recipients highly on these dimensions indicates that they are viewed as members of a shared ethical community, and thus entitled to its benefits (Banting et al. 2019).

Theories that predicate welfare support on judgments of "deservingness" or "belonging" (especially the latter) are hybrid theories because they draw freely on the power of social identity and group identification as engines of in-group solidarity and, by extension, support for redistribution to in-group members. At the same time, they rely heavily on judgments of attitudes and behaviors that tie back to conceptions of the social contract.

Group Empathy

The last "hybrid" theory I will examine here is the "group empathy" argument. This argument is that empathy, which is akin to humanitarian values as outlined earlier, also functions as a kind of group-level process. For example, Sirin et al. build on the idea that majority members may feel some compassion towards oppressed groups (2016a, 2016b, 2017). From this, they derive two main implications: (1) welfare chauvinism is likely to be tamped down when majority members view immigrants (or some subset thereof) as an oppressed population worthy of help; and (2) members of historically oppressed groups should be better able to understand the suffering of *other* minority groups, which should encourage the willingness to redistribute even when these groups compete for resources (Sirin et al. 2017, 430).

COMPARING/CONTRASTING APPROACHES

Where do all the explanations I've collected here agree, and where do they disagree? First the similarities: (1) while I have defined some as principally "group-centric" and others not, virtually all posit some kind of judgment based on a salient group boundary.[5] (2) Unsurprisingly, given that we want to explain sharing with (or excluding) strangers, virtually all involve a target beneficiary's position in or outside of that salient boundary. Does a given immigrant, a particular group of immigrants (African versus European, say, or legal versus undocumented), or even all immigrants as a category fit – for redistributive purposes – as one of "us" or one of "them"? (3) Since all judgments about strangers are made on the basis of little information – if not, it is hard to see how they'd count as "strangers" in a definitional sense – all rely on stereotypes about what members of the target group are like. While the notion that stereotypes matter seems especially obvious with respect to the more group-centrist approaches, even economic or values-based theories rely on group stereotypes; indeed, such stereotypes are precisely what informs people's thinking about who absorbs more in government benefits than they pay in taxes, or who follows "the rules" and who doesn't. (4) All suggest theories about which psychological predispositions are called to the fore when people form judgments about redistribution; group-centrist approaches highlight in-group attachment and "linked fate" with other in-group members, for instance, whereas values-based approaches elevate core ideological principles about egalitarianism, individualism, legalism, and so on. (5) All, whether they say so explicitly or not, work with the concept of *salience*, in that they all presuppose that the psychological linkages people form in their minds – e.g. the link between redistribution and immigration, or the link between particular kinds of immigrants and violations of core principles – are not innate but rather politically constructed. In short, people may harbor predispositional loyalty to their ethnic in-group, or long-standing devotion to economic utility maximization or some other economic principle. But only in discourse can these become linked to how people think about immigration. (6) Finally, all deal – again, either implicitly or explicitly – with the concept of *threat*: economic well-being, group attachments, or values-based concerns only become relevant to immigration when immigrants (or some subcategory thereof) are perceived as threatening to them.[6]

The *contrast* across these approaches lies in two main factors. First, they differ in terms of how they view people's understanding of the political community they find themselves in. The closer we get to a purely individualistic, economic utility maximization model, the more agnostic we get on this question. But most other views outlined above either take or imply a position. Group-centrist theories (and the hybrid approaches that invoke group-centric considerations) are premised on the idea that people regard the political community as a kind of family that elicits strong feelings of "tribal" loyalty and mutual obligation to kin and suspicion or protectiveness against outsiders. Values-based theories, on the other hand, are a matter of contract rather than kin: a political community is in spirit a kind of chartered club or association whose members have agreed upon formal rules and evolved informal understandings that guide behavior even where familial loyalties do not exist and overpower them where they do. It is, in short, a community of norms, principles, and values that extend well beyond "family first."

The second key point of disagreement is over the issue of what motivates people, and in particular what they are acting to maintain or enhance. Everyone, we think, is optimizing *something*. The question is, what? Economic theories highlight either pocketbook, group-specific, or even national economic well-being as a key driver. Group-centrist theories are, at root, predicated on the notion that what people care about most is maximizing the status (broadly defined) of their own group in the broader social hierarchy. Finally, values-based thinkers are generally thinking along the lines of some broader ideological conception of the "good society," although as we will see later this is tricky because one's vision of a "good society" could be rooted in either deontological concerns or in identity-based ones. The relative scope and force of these various arguments matters both as a matter of intellectual interest and because they shed very different kinds of light on real-world political debates. Most obviously, they give us purchase over the vital question of what policies people are likely to support and why. They can therefore help us understand the trajectory of policy support over time, the distinctions people make across policies, and the relationship between public opinion and policy outcomes (e.g. Levy and Wright 2020; Levy et al. 2016; Wright and Levy 2020). Second, and relatedly, the relative power of various theories helps delineate what avenues of persuasion are possible; for example, a "group-centric" attitude rooted in ethnic animus is likely much harder to dislodge than one based on the perceived economic consequences of immigration, or based on perceptions about whether or not immigrants are successfully "assimilating" to the social contract. Third, they help us understand the relationship between immigration and ethnic change, on the one hand, and broader political developments, such as the rise of the so-called populist right in Europe and elsewhere, on the other (Gest 2016; Kaufmann 2019). Finally, they help us understand the prospects for democratic, meaningfully redistributive societies in an age defined by ethnic change. In particular, the dual questions of whether "solidarity" (or social cohesion) is required to sustain a redistributive state and whether ethnic diversity undermines that solidarity have been hotly debated for decades (Harell and Stolle 2010). And, as it turns out, one comes up with markedly different answers depending on which theory is doing the heavy lifting.[7]

FURTHER ISSUES

At this point, I turn my focus to several long-standing issues in research on this topic. My aim in doing so is not simply critique for the sake of it; rather, I hope in so doing to underline precisely how persistently they can befuddle the cleverest of researchers.

The Conceptual Interplay of Groups and Values

The first thorny issue is conceptual, and stems from the interrelatedness of group identity (a group-centrist factor) and group norms (a values-based one). Ostensibly, group-centrist and values-based theories each put explanatory weight on different aspects of *homo sociologicus*: on the one hand, we have group attachments and group loyalty, while, on the other, we have the values and norms that govern good behavior. The problem is that these things are easier to separate in theory than in practice. Norms and values are created, packaged, imparted, and reinforced by social groups. They evolve and are sustained, at least in part to lubricate intra-group relationships and, what is more, to improve the group's standing versus others. They are promulgated and diffused (sometimes formally, sometimes informally), and they are enforced by sanction. In the U.S., a challenging case precisely *because* it is often identified as a nation of "values" and yet, at the same time, bears a long legacy of racial conflict, elements of political culture such as individualism, equality, and the rule of law are deeply intertwined with the country's history of racial stratification and oppression, and they can obviously serve as tools of social control and enforced conformity.

Part of the solution is to take greater care in interpreting empirical findings, on which more in the subsection that follows. But a deeper problem, and one that cannot be solved with the sorts of empirical techniques typically deployed in public opinion studies, is that the values-driven conceptions of attitude formation have evolved over centuries alongside, and sometimes in furtherance of, the interests and status of racial groups, nations, and other social collectives. Particular "modules" of social values may be hardwired into human beings through evolution (Graham et al. 2009) but their cultural adaptation into systems of belief that prioritize some and demote others is of course attributable in no small part to human beings' multiple and overlapping group memberships, which is to say sociological.

Interpreting Empirical Findings

Unsurprisingly, given the conceptual knottiness of the motivators in question, it is often quite difficult to see, in a given empirical model of immigration attitudes, what is actually driving people's preferences. One part of the problem is measurement. I've raised this elsewhere in the context of ascertaining the "stuff" of national identity using established (but problematic) survey questions about the boundaries of national identity, and on the difficulty of what exactly "cultural threat" is supposed to mean (Wright 2019). Here, I'd take this a bit further by questioning the active ingredients in measurement scales that feature in some of the hybrid theories discussed above, namely those designed to tap "nationhood," "belongingness," and "group empathy." With respect to nationhood and national identity, one frequently sees claims based on the correlation between items asking people about whether "following rules and laws is important to being truly American" and some putative consequence. But it isn't altogether clear that people would answer differently, or that their answer would have different correlates, if we asked the same question without the "truly American" part. And if – hypothetically speaking – the same results obtain whether or not we mention anything about the nation or national identity, it would follow that people's response was keyed more to "rules" than the nation as such. In a similar vein, survey items designed to tap "belongingness" (Banting et al. 2019) all reflect an admixture of group identity, norms, and national identity, and as a result are also vulnerable to these kinds of interpretive questions.[8] Finally, in Sirin et al.'s (2016a, 2016b, 2017) indices of "group empathy," we have measures designed to tap the extent to which people express various norms (such as perspective-taking) along with nods to "other racial groups." For example, one item reads: "If I'm sure I'm right about something, I don't waste much time listening to the arguments of people, particularly those of other racial or ethnic groups." Would things change if we asked people the same question without the last clause? One way of putting the issue underlying all of these examples is this: how much of what's in these "intermediate" explanations boils down to the "fundamentals," and how much represents something qualitatively unique?

A related issue often emerges when one interprets the results of survey experiments designed to cue one kind of explanation versus another. One example I've explored elsewhere is the ubiquitous, yet somewhat nebulous, notion of cultural threat. The difficulty is that culture as such folds together both group identification as well as norms and values; accordingly, whatever threat is perceived and acted upon by *homo sociologicus* might be from either or both, and it is often difficult if not impossible to tell the difference (Wright 2019). Another interpretive challenge lies in distinguishing sociotropic economic motivations, on the one hand, from assimilationist values on the other. To elaborate, consider Hainmueller and Hopkins' (2015) "hidden consensus" argument, namely that Americans favor immigrants who are skilled, well educated, and speak English well. The results are, in a sense, unambiguous. Yet the question of *why* they should do so is not. It could be that they are picking the immigrants that would enhance the country's prosperity in a big-picture sense, as some variants of economic utility maximizers ought.[9] But it could also be that such concerns reflect a more values-based logic tied to norms of assimilation. On this thinking, favoring immigrants who are well educated and good English speakers is placing a bet on immigrants who are more able (and willing) to smoothly integrate into the host country's social fabric (Levy and Wright 2020). These different interpretations are, here and elsewhere, difficult to pry apart because even the cleverest experimental vignettes and primes can often be seen in multiple ways. One part of the solution lies in research design, and in particular crafting scenarios where competing root motives are "cross-pressured." But this isn't always possible, and so it makes sense to keep an open mind about why people respond as they do.

Psychology of Acquisition

Most of what I've discussed to this point has taken people's core motives as a given. A deeper question is where, when, and how do people acquire whatever theoretical lens they apply to these issues? How do they learn what is good or bad for their own (or their country's) business? How do they come to understand who "deserves" what, or who "belongs" and who doesn't? A variety of possibilities have been floated, from evolutionary theory and genetic advantage, to macro-level accounts based on political culture and national policy regime (e.g. Crepaz 2008; Weldon 2006; Levy and Wright 2020; Wright 2011), micro-level accounts of personality and political socialization (i.e. civic education, or more informal socializing from parents or extended social networks), among many others. What makes nailing this down difficult is that such things tend not to be especially (or at all) amenable to survey experiments and other "tools of the trade" for those who have studied these issues. Generally speaking, we need to take the world as given and assess the correlation between people's outlook and the composition of their social network, the political culture they grew up in, and so on. Such an approach can be useful, but the tradeoff is that serious causal inference becomes impossible in most cases.

Another, related question is how, once these predispositions – utility maximization, group attachments, the social contract, or for that matter judgments of "belonging" or "deservingness" – have taken root, do people come to link them to more proximate judgments about immigrants and welfare? Here we can think of, again, socialization in some vague sense, political communication (news media and political advertising), and political contestation at the elite level as likely mediators. All of these things work to shape people's opinions, and crystallize the link between predisposition and proximate judgments. Such information effects can be simulated to some degree by surveys that present an issue framed or primed in different ways, although one always needs to keep in mind issues of external validity. A more difficult issue is that the relationship between elites and masses on this issue and others is not entirely top-down. Indeed, it is likely that public opinion feeds back into the system by constraining elite action, or presenting opportunities for elite mobilization (e.g. Levy et al. 2016; Levy and Wright 2020). To the degree that this is so, it is difficult to generate direct evidence. Yet it seems impossible to understand the political dynamics of nationalist populism, either manifested as welfare chauvinism in Europe or as nativist "Trumpism" in the U.S., without understanding *both* how entrepreneurs at the elite level use political communication to mobilize constituencies and how these constituencies go on to encourage or constrain their rhetoric and policy choices once they have attained power.

CONCLUSION

In this chapter, I have taken on a relatively narrow version of an extremely broad question: why share with strangers? As it turns out, even this narrow slice brought forth numerous theories, from various kinds of economic rationalization, through group loyalty, through norms and values, and everywhere in between. It turns out that, beneath the relatively banal assertion that people support "sharing with strangers" when they believe that strangers deserve it, there is a great deal of ambiguity and disagreement about what shapes these kinds of deservingness judgments and why. Sometimes we are in a position to take a strong position one way or the other. But often we are not, both for reasons elaborated here and elsewhere. The good news is that our approach to answering these questions has gotten ever more sophisticated, and the cost of collecting and analyzing data of all kinds has decreased. Concomitantly, the quality of the answers we have come up with has, by and large, improved. No doubt that, as they continue to do so, our understanding of welfare chauvinism – not just who is right but what kinds of forces prevail for what kinds of individuals, and under what circumstances – will continue to evolve apace.

NOTES

1. This argument is usually made with respect to white majorities. But it applies as well to non-immigrant minorities, who might view immigrants and immigration as a threat to their own status (Carter 2019).
2. "De-ontological" here is inherited from de-ontological ethics, in which actions are deemed right or wrong based on rules rather than consequences. Both the economic and identity-based arguments outlined so far highlight, by contrast, more "consequentialist" thinking about pocketbook labor competition, or relative group status.
3. In a more comparative setting, Alesina and Glaeser (2004) argued that European countries have more progressive redistribution policies – in much part – due to relative racial homogeneity (Alesina and Stantcheva 2020).
4. The validity of the authors' choice of an instrumental variable and the causal relationship highlighted in their results has been debated. See Nekby and Pettersson-Lidbom (2014) and Dahlberg et al. (2013).
5. The exceptions would be a purely atomistic utility rational utility maximizer or somebody who thinks purely in terms of universally applied values. In either case judgments about immigrants and access to social benefits might be rendered with no conception at all that immigrants are a social category that needs to be understood on its own terms.
6. One could plausibly imagine a version of these arguments that does invoke a threat to something cherished. For instance, one might strongly support redistribution for immigrants because society benefits in some way. Whether the "active ingredient" in such a position is a genuinely pro-immigrant outlook or merely the absence of threat is conceptually quite difficult to resolve and, fortunately, not really essential to the present discussion.
7. See, for example, outstanding edited volumes by Banting et al. (2019) as well as Gustavsson and Miller (2019). Both of these volumes debate the question of "welfare solidarity" and "welfare chauvinism," and amass a variety of perspectives.
8. For example, the "fairness" element of the belongingness index is worded as follows: "One way citizens contribute to society is by working and paying taxes. Given the resources available in each community, do you think the following groups are contributing their fair share, or more or less than their fair share?" There is a lot that makes answers to this question hard to interpret, not least of which the blending of rules and norms with group references.
9. As noted earlier, there is vanishingly little support for the idea that people think in terms of individual self-interest by, say, opposing labour market substitutes or supporting compliments.

REFERENCES

Aarøe, Lene, Michael Bang Petersen, and Kevin Arceneaux. 2017. "The Behavioral Immune System Shapes Political Intuitions: Why and How Individual Differences in Disgust Sensitivity Underlie Opposition to Immigration." *American Political Science Review* 111(2): 277–294.

Abrajano, Marissa, and Zoltan L. Hajnal. 2015. *White Backlash: Immigration, Race, and American Politics.* Princeton, NJ: Princeton University Press.

Alesina, A., and E. Glaeser. 2004. *Fighting Poverty in the US and Europe.* Oxford: Oxford University Press.

Alesina, Alberto, and Eliana La Ferrara. 2005. "Preferences for Redistribution in the Land of Opportunities." *Journal of Public Economics* 89(5–6): 897–931.

Alesina, A., and S. Stantcheva. 2020. "Diversity, Immigration, and Redistribution." *AEA Papers and Proceedings* 110: 329–334.

Alesina, Alberto, Edward Glaeser, and Bruce Sacerdote. 2001. "Why Doesn't the U.S. Have a European-Style Welfare System?" *National Bureau of Economic Research*, No. w8524.

Alesina, Alberto, Armando Miano, and Stefanie Stantcheva. 2018a. "Immigration and Redistribution." *National Bureau of Economic Research*, No. w24733.

Alesina, Alberto, Stefanie Stantcheva, and Edoardo Teso. 2018b. "Intergenerational Mobility and Preferences for Redistribution." *American Economic Review* 108(2): 521–554.

Beck, John H. 1994. "An Experimental Test of Preferences for the Distribution of Income and Individual Risk Aversion." *Eastern Economic Journal* 20(2): 131–145.

Benabou, Roland, and Efe A. Ok. 2001. "Social Mobility and the Demand for Redistribution: The POUM Hypothesis." *Quarterly Journal of Economics* 116(2): 447–487.

Bolton, Gary E., and Axel Ockenfels. 2000. "ERC: A Theory of Equity, Reciprocity, and Competition." *American Economic Review* 90(1): 166–193.

Brown, Mitch, Lucas A. Keefer, Donald F. Sacco, and Aaron Bermond. 2019. "Is the Cure a Wall? Behavioral Immune System Responses to a Disease Metaphor for Immigration." *Evolutionary Psychological Science* 5: 345–356.

Carter, Niambi. 2019. *American While Black: African Americans, Immigration, and the Limits of Citizenship.* New York: Oxford University Press.

Ceobanu, Alin M., and Xavier Escandell. 2010. "Comparative Analyses of Public Attitudes toward Immigrants and Immigration Using Multinational Survey Data: A Review of Theories and Research." *Annual Review of Sociology* 36(1): 309–328.

Citrin, Jack, and David O. Sears. 2014. *American Identity and the Politics of Multiculturalism.* New York: Cambridge University Press.

Citrin, Jack, Donald P. Green, Christopher Muste, and Cara Wong. 1997. "Public Opinion toward Immigration Reform: The Role of Economic Motivations." *Journal of Politics* 59(3): 858–881.

Cornelius, Wayne A., and Marc R. Rosenblum. 2005. "Immigration and Politics." *Annual Review of Political Science* 8: 99–119.

Crepaz, Markus M.L. 2008. *Trust beyond borders: Immigration, the Welfare State, and Identity in Modern Societies.* Ann Arbor, MI: University of Michigan Press.

Dahlberg, Matz, Karin Edmark, and Heléne Lundqvist. 2013. "Ethnic Diversity and Preferences for Redistribution: Reply." *Working Paper Series* 4, Uppsala University, Department of Economics.

Dancygier, Rafeala M., and Michael J. Donnelly. 2013. "Sectoral Economies, Economic Contexts, and Attitudes toward Immigration." *Journal of Politics* 75(1): 17–35.

Dufwenberg, Martin, and Georg Kirchsteiger. 2004. "A Theory of Sequential Reciprocity." *Games and Economic Behavior* 47(2): 268–298.

Fehr, Ernst, and Klaus M. Schmidt. 1999. "A Theory of Fairness, Competition, and Cooperation." *Quarterly Journal of Economics* 114(3): 817–868.

Fisman, Raymond, Ilyana Kuziemko, and Silvia Vannutelli. 2020. "Distributional Preferences in Larger Groups: Keeping Up with the Joneses and Keeping Track of the Tails." *Journal of the European Economic Association.* https://doi.org/10.1093/jeea/jvaa033.

Gest, Justin. 2016. *The New Minority: White Working Class Politics in an Age of Immigration and Inequality.* New York: Oxford University Press.

Giuliano, P., and A. Spilimbergo. 2014. "Growing Up in a Recession." *Review of Economic Studies* 81(2): 787–817.

Goodhart, David. 2004. "Too Diverse?" *Prospect*, February: 30–37.

Graham, J., J. Haidt, and B.A. Nosek. 2009. "Liberals and Conservatives Rely on Different Sets of Moral Foundations." *Journal of Personality and Social Psychology* 96(5): 1029–1046.

Gustavsson, G., and Miller, D., eds, 2019. *Liberal Nationalism and Its Critics: Normative and Empirical Questions.* New York: Oxford University Press.

Hainmueller, Jens, and Daniel J. Hopkins. 2014. "Public Attitudes toward Immigration." *Annual Review of Political Science* 17: 225–249.

Hainmueller, Jens, and Daniel J. Hopkins. 2015. "The Hidden Immigration Consensus: A Conjoint Analysis of Attitudes toward Immigrants." *American Journal of Political Science* 59(3): 529–548.

Hainmueller, Jens, Michael J. Hiscox, and Yotam Margalit. 2014. "Do Concerns about Labor Market Competition Shape Attitudes toward Immigration? New Evidence." *Journal of International Economics* 97: 193–207.

Harell, Alison, and Dietlind Stolle. 2010. "Diversity and Democratic Politics: An Introduction." *Canadian Journal of Political Science* 43(2): 384–400.

Harell, Alison, Keith Banting, and Will Kymlicka. 2021. "Shared Membership Beyond National Identity: Deservingness and Solidarity in Diverse Societies," *Political Studies*. Online first, doi: https://doi.org/10.1177/0032321721996939

Hooghe, Marc, Ann Trappers, Bart Meuleman, and Tim Reeskens. 2008. "Migration to European Countries: A Structural Explanation of Patterns, 1980–2004." *International Migration Review* 42(2): 476–504.

Hopkins, Daniel J. 2010. "Politicized Places: Explaining Where and When Immigrants Provoke Local Opposition." *American Political Science Review* 104(1): 40–60.

Jardina, Ashley. 2019. *White Identity Politics*. New York: Cambridge University Press.

Kalkan, K.O., G.C. Layman, and E.M. Uslaner. 2009. "Bands of Others? Attitudes toward Muslims in Contemporary American Society." *Journal of Politics* 71(3): 847–862.

Kaufmann, Eric. 2019. *Whiteshift: Populism, Immigration, and the Future of White Majorities*. New York: Abrams Press.

Kinder, D.R., and C.D. Kam. 2009. *Us against Them: Ethnocentric Foundations of American Opinion*. Chicago, IL: University of Chicago Press.

Kitschelt, Herbert. 1997. *The Radical Right in Western Europe: A Comparative Analysis*. Ann Arbor, MI: University of Michigan Press.

Levy, Morris, and Matthew Wright. 2020. *Immigration and the American Ethos*. New York: Cambridge University Press.

Levy, Morris, Matthew Wright, and Jack Citrin. 2016. "Mass Opinion and Immigration Policy in the United States: Re-assessing Clientelist and Elite Perspectives." *Perspectives on Politics* 14(3): 660–680.

Luttmer, Erzo F.P. 2001. "Group Loyalty and the Taste for Redistribution." *Journal of Political Economy* 109(3): 500–528.

Malhotra, Neil, Yotam Margalit, and Cecilia M. Mo. 2013. "Economic Explanations for Opposition to Immigration: Distinguishing Between Prevalence and Magnitude." *American Journal of Political Science* 57(2): 391–410.

Marshall, T.H. 1992 [1950]. *Citizenship and Social Class*. Concord, MA: Pluto Press.

Masuoka, Natalie, and Jane Junn. 2013. *The Politics of Belonging: Race, Public Opinion, and Immigration*. Chicago, IL: University of Chicago Press.

McPherson, Miller, Lynn Smith-Lovin, and James M. Cook. 2001. "Birds of a Feather: Homophily in Social Networks." *Annual Review of Sociology* 27: 415–444.

Monroe, K. 1998. *The Heart of Altruism: Perceptions of a Common Humanity*. Princeton, NJ: Princeton University Press.

Nekby, L., and P. Pettersson-Lidbom. 2014. "Comment on Dahlberg, Edmark and Lundqvist (2012)." *Research Papers in Economics* 5.

Newman, Benjamin J., Todd K. Hartman, Patrick Lown, and Stanley Feldman. 2015. "Easing the Heavy Hand: Humanitarian Concern, Empathy, and Opinion on Immigration." *British Journal of Political Science* 45(3): 583–607.

Pantoja, Adrian. 2006. "Against the Tide? Core American Values and Attitudes Toward U.S. Immigration Policy in the Mid-1990s." *Journal of Ethnic and Migration Studies* 32(3): 515–531.

Petersen, Michael B. 2012. "Social Welfare as Small-Scale Help: Evolutionary Psychology and the Deservingness Heuristic." *American Journal of Political Science* 56(1): 1–16.

Rabin, Matthew. 1993. "Incorporating Fairness into Game Theory and Economics." *American Economic Review* 83(5): 1281–1302.

Reeskens, Tim, and Wim Van Oorschot. 2012. "Disentangling the 'New Liberal Dilemma': On the Relation between General Welfare Redistribution Preferences and Welfare Chauvinism." *International Journal of Comparative Sociology* 53: 120–139.

Schafer, Byron E. 1999. "American Exceptionalism." *Annual Review of Political Science* 2: 445–463.

Schildkraut, Deborah J. 2011. *Americanism in the Twenty-First Century: Public Opinion in the Age of Immigration*. New York: Cambridge University Press.

Schildkraut, Deborah J. 2014. "Boundaries of American Identity: Evolving Understandings of 'Us.'" *Annual Review of Political Science* 17: 441–460.

Sides, John, and Kimberly Gross. 2013. "Stereotypes of Muslims, and Support for the War on Terror." *Journal of Politics* 75(3): 583–598.

Sirin, Cigdem V., Nicholas A. Valentino, and José D. Villalobos. 2016a. "Group Empathy in Response to Nonverbal Racial/Ethnic Cues: A National Experiment on Immigration Policy Attitudes." *American Behavioral Scientist* 60(14): 1676–1697.

Sirin, Cigdem V., Nicholas A. Valentino, and José D. Villalobos. 2016b. "Group Empathy Theory: The Effect of Group Empathy on U.S. Intergroup Attitudes and Behavior in the Context of Immigration Threats." *Journal of Politics* 78(3): 893–908.

Sirin, Cigdem V., Nicholas A. Valentino, and José D. Villalobos. 2017. "The Social Causes and Political Consequences of Group Empathy." *Political Psychology* 38(3): 427–448.

Tabellini, Marco. 2020. "Gifts of the Immigrants, Woes of the Natives: Lessons from the Age of Mass Migration." *Review of Economic Studies* 87(1): 454–486.

Tajfel, H., and J.C. Turner. 1979. "An Integrative Theory of Intergroup Conflict," in W.G. Austin and S. Worchel (eds), *The Social Psychology of Intergroup Relations*. Monterey, CA: Brooks/Cole, 33–37.

Theiss-Morse, Elizabeth. 2009. *Who Counts as an American? The Boundaries of National Identity*. New York: Cambridge University Press.

Valentino, N.A., T. Brader, and A.E. Jardina. 2013. "Immigration Opposition among U.S. Whites: General Ethnocentrism or Media Priming of Attitudes about Latinos?" *Political Psychology* 34: 149–166.

Valentino, Nicholas A., Stuart N. Soroka, Shanto Iyengar, Toril Aalberg, Raymond Duch, Marta Fraile, Kyu S. Hahn, Kasper M. Hansen, Allison Harell, Marc Helbling, Simon Jackman, and Tetsuro Kobayashi. 2017. "Economic and Cultural Drivers of Immigrant Support Worldwide." *British Journal of Political Science* 49: 1201–1226.

Van Oorschot, W.J.H. 2000. "Who Should Get What, and Why? On Deservingness Criteria and the Conditionality of Solidarity among the Public." *Policy and Politics: Studies of Local Government and Its Services* 28(1): 33–48.

Weldon, Steven A. 2006. "The Institutional Context of Tolerance for Ethnic Minorities: A Comparative, Multilevel Analysis of Western Europe." *American Journal of Political Science* 50(2): 331–349.

Wong, Cara J. 2010. *Boundaries of Obligation in American Politics: Geographic, National, and Racial Communities*. New York: Cambridge University Press.

Wright, Matthew. 2011. "Diversity and the Imagined Community: Immigrant Diversity and Conceptions of National Identity." *Political Psychology* 32(5): 837–862.

Wright, Matthew. 2019. "Identity and Immigration: What We Think We Know, and Why We Might Not Actually Know It." *Nations and Nationalism* 25: 467–477.

Wright, Matthew, and Morris Levy. 2020. "American Public Opinion on Immigration: Nativist, Polarized, or Ambivalent?" *International Migration* 58(6): 77–95.

Wright, Matthew, Morris Levy, and Jack Citrin. 2016. "Public Attitudes Toward Immigration Policy across the Legal/Illegal Divide: The Role of Categorical and Attribute-Based Decision-Making." *Political Behavior* 38: 229–253.

5. The boundaries of generosity: Membership, inclusion, and redistribution
Allison Harell, Will Kymlicka, and Keith Banting

The development of modern welfare systems in the twentieth century has been intimately connected to the nation-state. As a result, questions of who is included or excluded from the welfare state have been inextricably linked to questions of inclusion and exclusion from the nation. Indeed, on many accounts, the welfare state is fundamentally a vehicle of national solidarity. The welfare state presupposes and helps to reproduce a sense of forming a national "we", and calls upon this sense of we-ness as the source of a commitment to protection and redistribution amongst co-nationals. This link between the welfare state and nationhood helps explain why people are willing to share with co-nationals even if they are strangers. However, the focus on a national "we" raises the question of the boundaries of inclusion: who is included in the charmed circle of the national "we"? How do individuals or groups gain admission to this circle? In this chapter, our focus is on public attitudes towards who should be admitted to the national "we", and in particular attitudes regarding migrants' claims to the welfare state.

In much of the literature, the inclusion of migrants is answered by reference to ideas about "civic" versus "ethnic" nationalism. Civic nationalism is said to be relatively open to newcomers joining the nation, whereas ethnic nationalism makes it difficult or impossible for newcomers to join the nation. We will discuss below some of the limits of this civic/ethnic distinction as a way of understanding how newcomers gain inclusion into the national welfare state. The distinction between ethnic and civic nationalism is not always easy to draw, but even if we can draw it, it does not capture the broader dynamics of inclusion and exclusion. The civic/ethnic distinction focuses on the outer boundary of the nation, which is understood as a single line that separates the solidaristic "in-group" from various "out-groups" (aliens, foreigners). Once inside the line, individuals are assumed to become part of the in-group, an equal member of the nation, with full claim to national solidarity. In reality, the "boundaries of generosity" not only involve *external boundaries*, but also *internal hierarchies* of deservingness, and both of these affect the way immigrants are included in the welfare state. A "civic nation" may allow immigrants and other minorities to become national citizens – to cross the external boundary of nationhood – yet they may not be seen as equally deserving of national solidarity, perhaps because they are seen as not authentically "one of us", or not fully committed to being "one of us". As we will see, even within "civic nations", immigrants can be subject to harsh judgments of being undeserving or unworthy.

In this chapter, we will focus on three bases on which inclusion within redistributive schemes can be conceptualized: national identity, deservingness judgments, and membership perceptions. These three bases of inclusion represent forms of bounded solidarity, and as such differ from pure humanitarianism. The attitudes examined here embody the mutual concern and obligation to each other that we have as members of a society, which in the contemporary era is reflected in the structures of a welfare state. The first of our bases of inclusion, national identity, is fundamentally about external boundaries – i.e., who is admitted into the circle of the nation. The second and third – deservingness judgments and membership perceptions – reflect internal hierarchies within the circle of the nation. There is now a vibrant literature on the role of deservingness judgments in shaping generosity towards various groups, and this literature shows that immigrants are consistently seen as less deserving than other groups in society; indeed, they are often at the bottom of the "deservingness ladder". However, the explanation for this remains controversial. We will argue that one important and understudied source of these deservingness judgments is what we will call "membership perceptions" – that is, perceptions of whether individuals and groups are committed to the larger society. We believe that these perceptions of membership commitment are a powerful criterion on which individuals decide the boundaries of their support for redistribution. We conclude with a discussion of how these various dimensions each provide a part of the larger puzzle for understanding how publics view the inclusion of immigrants within the welfare state.

INCLUSION THROUGH NATIONAL IDENTITY

Through formal inclusion within a state's jurisdiction, people gain access to a variety of rights and protections, and as the welfare state developed in the twentieth century, to various redistributive programs. Citizenship can be defined as full membership within a political community with access to all the civil, political, and social rights afforded by the state (Marshall 1963). Formal inclusion within the state creates obligations (such as loyalty in times of war, requirements to pay taxes, willingness to adhere to laws and being subject to the state's enforcement of them) as well as benefits (freedom of entry, civil and political rights, access to redistributive schemes). The modern welfare state, in this sense, becomes the intermediary in which a more general form of generosity is operationalized. All members who are able must contribute, and the state serves as the intermediary through which these resources are shared.

Yet the question remains: what sustains the motivation to share with co-citizens? For Marshall, the expanding range of rights and benefits associated with citizenship were fundamentally sustained by "a direct sense of community membership based on a civilization that is a common possession" (1963, 96). In the contemporary world, the most expansive shared community is the nation, and national identity has traditionally been seen as central to understanding how resources are distributed. Insofar as generosity is tied to a shared identity, the crucial question with respect to migrants is whether they can become a member of this shared community. In many countries, membership has historically been intimately intertwined with an ethnic conception of political community, making it hard for immigrants with diverse ethnic, racial, and religious backgrounds to be accepted as co-nationals. To use Anthony Smith's language (1986, 1991), co-nationals share a common historical core or dominant *ethnie*. At its extreme, a strict ethnic conception of the nation would limit membership to those who share, through blood and descent, a link to a historic community. The ethnic conception sees the nation "as a fictive 'superfamily'" (Smith 2005, 180), and defines national identity in terms of shared culture, language and history, and perhaps even descent. In this sense, the boundary of the political community – and the corresponding boundaries of generosity – are restricted to imagined co-ethnics within the state. Status within the sharing community is based on meeting ascriptive characteristics that by their nature are exclusive.

Across the West, ethnic conceptions of nationhood have gradually been repudiated, at least at the level of public policy, even if public attitudes are more ambiguous (Bloemraad et al. 2019). If access to the national community is limited to co-ethnics, immigrants and their children are condemned to permanent second-class status, and this is now widely seen as unjust and undemocratic. People have therefore called for a more "civic" conception of national identity, which defines the nation in terms of shared political institutions and political values (Brubaker 1999, 2004). Membership within the political community, in this sense, has more open and fluid boundaries, open to all who are willing to commit to these political institutions and values regardless of their ethnicity or ancestry. It is through the adoption and acceptance of these shared values and institutions that political community is created. The simple imagining of a "we" defined on non-exclusive terms is argued to create the same types of cross-group solidarity and mutual dependence that underpins more generous redistribution schemes (Brubaker 2004, 121).

In the West, these political values and institutions are rooted in liberal democracy, and so "civic" nationalism is also sometimes referred to as "liberal" nationalism. Liberal nationalists argue that the transition from an exclusive ethnic nationalism to an inclusive civic nationalism requires a twofold change. On the one hand, majority citizens need to reject purely ethnic definitions of the nation that automatically exclude people of other backgrounds. On the other hand, there need to be opportunities for newcomers and minorities to show that they do indeed share a commitment to the country's political values and institutions, and that they are willing participants in the polity (Miller 2006, 332, 2017, 73; Miller and Ali 2014). Such a two-way process of rejecting exclusionary attitudes and accepting others' willingness to join in a shared collective project underpins a collective imagining of we-ness that is at the heart of national identity. As scholars of nationalism point out, national identity is a form of "imagined community" that is constructed (Anderson 2006). The nation-state, then, becomes a way of thinking about and appraising political and social membership through the tying of citizenship status to the normative content of these identities (Brubaker 1992).

Despite the rich and varied literature that has emerged around the civic/ethnic dichotomy, it faces both conceptual and empirical limits in its ability to explain the boundaries of generosity. As a conceptual framework, Brubaker (1999) argues that the analytic distinction is difficult to employ, because real-world nationalisms are neither purely "ethnic" nor purely "civic". Take for example the importance of knowing the national language, which in most countries is a requirement for gaining citizenship. From an ethnic nationalist perspective, language is a defining feature of the *ethnie*'s culture. From a civic nationalist perspective, the capacity to speak a common language provides equal access to shared political life. This is just one of many examples of the fact that even "liberal" or "civic" nations are always embedded in particular cultural forms, and so require particular cultural skills and commitments. Liberal-democratic politics is always culturally "formatted", in Patten's terminology (Patten 2016), using culturally specific languages, idioms, narratives, norms, and practices. And this in turn means that someone can endorse "civic" nationalism and yet be skeptical about whether immigrants – or certain subgroups of immigrants – are able and willing to master the culturally specific version of liberal democracy that prevails in a given country. Native-born citizens may agree that the nation is defined in terms of political values, not ancestry, and yet be skeptical that immigrants are able to master the prevailing culturally specific political traditions in a country: for example, the specifically French tradition of *laïcité*, or the Danish tradition of irreverence, or the Canadian tradition of civility and compromise. Mouritsen calls this "particularist universalism" (2006) – the tendency of civic nationalists to link universal political values to local cultural idioms that require lengthy periods of socialization to acquire, and hence not easily picked up by immigrants. Indeed, survey evidence shows that defenders of civic nationalism can be as exclusionary towards immigrants – particularly Muslims – as defenders of ethnic nationalism (Simonsen and Bonikowski 2020; Turgeon et al. 2019).

The civic/ethnic distinction fails to capture the ways that liberal-democratic politics is always already culturally embedded, and the challenges this raises for how immigrants enter the circle of nationhood. Attempts to measure public attitudes regarding civic and ethnic nationalism continually founder on this problem, with no consistency in how scholars assign these cultural dimensions (such as language) to either the "civic" or "ethnic" side of the divide. Not surprisingly, the measures themselves have faced serious criticism for being poorly related to the underlying concept or failing to load consistently into two distinct, reliable subdimensions that work across contexts (Reeskens and Hooghe 2010; Kunovich 2009; Wright 2011; Wright et al. 2012).

A deeper problem, for the purposes of our chapter, is that even if we can define and measure support for civic and ethnic nationalism, it is not in fact an empirically reliable basis for predicting the boundaries of generosity. As we noted earlier, there is a widespread assumption that the crucial issue for national solidarity is the external boundary of nationhood, and that once someone crosses the line into the charmed circle of the nation, they thereby acquire clear entitlement to social protection. This assumption is deeply rooted in the study of nationalism, captured most famously in Benedict Anderson's claim that the nation is "always conceived as a deep horizontal comradeship" (Anderson 2006, 7). Once one crosses the external boundary of the nation, it is assumed, one becomes part of the "deep horizontal comradeship" that is embodied in the welfare state. This helps explain why so much attention has been paid to whether citizens define this external boundary in terms of ethnicity or political values.

In reality, people's attitudes towards the external boundary of the nation tells us surprisingly little about their views regarding solidarity or "comradeship" within the nation. Civic or liberal measures of national identity have not been found to be reliably associated with support for redistribution (Johnston et al. 2017; Breidahl et al. 2018; Miller and Ali 2014; Reeskens and Wright 2013; Citrin et al. 2012; Theiss-Morse 2009; Gustavsson 2019). While some defenders of civic nationalism support extending the bonds of national solidarity to immigrants, others are in favor of weakening the bonds of national solidarity for everyone, endorsing a more "neoliberal" conception of the civic nation (Gugushvili et al. 2021). There is indeed a vibrant debate about whether more open conceptions of the nation necessarily lead to a weakening of the strength of national solidarity – what is sometimes called the progressive's dilemma (Goodhart 2006; Pearce 2004; Kymlicka 2015). Civic nationalists also disagree about whether immigrants need to "earn" access to the welfare state, and hence what sorts of conditions can or should be placed on immigrants' access to social programs, including residency requirements, work requirements, and integration requirements, such as knowledge of the national language (Banting and Koning 2017; Reeskens and van Oorschot 2012; Wright and Reeskens 2013; Koning 2019).

In short, where people draw the external boundary of the nation radically underdetermines their views about the boundaries of generosity within the nation. Whether immigrants can gain the legal status of citizenship is obviously important, for many reasons, but this does not ensure that they are then securely covered by the "deep horizontal comradeship" of national solidarity. National solidarities involve not only external boundaries, but also internal hierarchies of worth and deservingness. To understand these dynamics of inclusion and exclusion, therefore, we need to attend to questions of deservingness.

INCLUSION THROUGH DESERVINGNESS

While studies of nationalism have emphasized the idea of a deep horizontal comradeship amongst co-nationals, the literature on deservingness emphasizes instead the existence of steep vertical hierarchies of perceived worth and deservingness within the nation. There is a rich comparative literature that focuses on how people's attitudes toward social programs are linked to evaluations of program recipients' deservingness. When policies evoke sympathetic beneficiaries in the public's mind, support for these programs tends to be higher, but if the beneficiaries are seen as unworthy or underserving, public support drops.

As we noted earlier, studies to date suggest that immigrants are often at the bottom of the ladder of perceived deservingness. When asked about a range of possible beneficiaries of the welfare state – the elderly, single mothers, people who are sick or unemployed, people with disabilities, immigrants – immigrants are typically ranked last. This ranking is so ubiquitous that van Oorschot calls it "a truly universal element in the popular welfare culture of present Western welfare states" (2006, 25). Some commentators interpret this ranking as evidence that immigrants are seen as falling outside the circle of the nation – which in turn is often interpreted as evidence of "ethnic nationalism" – but in fact, as we will see, deservingness judgments also apply to groups who fall securely within the (civic) nation.

Indeed, deservingness, as a concept, has been studied most extensively in relationship to poverty and people's willingness to support targeted assistance to those facing economic hardship, a central feature of a robust welfare state (see, for example, Coughlin 1980; Golding and Middleton 1982; Gans 1995). Deservingness generally refers to evaluations and perceptions of the behavior and characteristics of various groups in helping themselves and/or helping others. These perceptions are seen as critical in explaining who is viewed as worthy of support in society. Unlike entitlement, which depends on the legal norms governing eligibility for specific social benefits, deservingness entails a critical assessment of a group's actions and their consequences in determining whether they should receive social support (Feather 2003).

Deservingness assessments tend to be shared. Evident in diverse social and political communities, Aaroe and Petersen (2014) maintain that a deservingness heuristic operates cross-nationally as a universal and automatic process of human cognition which broadly affects who is deemed worthy of social support. In a similar vein, van Oorschot (2006) finds that Europeans appear to share a "deservingness culture", with consistent patterns across several European countries in the groups that are perceived as most deserving of social inclusion and support.

While the broad outlines of this "deservingness culture" are well known, there is more disagreement about the causes of these deservingness judgments. To date, most of the literature has focused on two factors: perceived need and perceived control or responsibility. Need captures the idea that we tend to be more generous to those who we see as requiring more support. If faced with two people, and one has enough to eat and shelter and the other does not, the latter would have a higher need, and all else equal, should be helped first. By its nature, need is comparative. Faced with limited resources and a choice between who should benefit from them, level of need is an efficient decision rule.

Yet, we know that support for poverty reduction measures often do not receive the same level of support as universal programs like universal healthcare, and indeed, means-based programs targeting the needy are often viewed least favorably by the public. This is because the poor are sometimes seen as responsible for their plight. If they just worked harder, or behaved more prudently, they could escape their poverty. These perceptions of responsibility or control are highly influential in shaping public opinions on who deserves help (Cook 1979; Weiner 1993; De Swaan 1988; Will 1993; Feather and Dawson 1998; van Oorschot 2000). As Applebaum (2001) observes, public perceptions of poorer groups largely attribute their economic disadvantage to individual deficits, such as laziness or poor life choices.

These perceptions of need and control are clearly important, but we do not believe that they capture the full range of factors shaping deservingness judgments, and in particular do not fully explain why immigrants and racial minorities are often at the bottom of the deservingness ladder. It is certainly true that some ethnic or racial groups are stereotyped as lazy: Gilens' seminal work on welfare attitudes in the United States showed that perceptions of Blacks as undeserving are rooted in stereotypes about Blacks as "lazy" and accountable for their own economic circumstances (Gilens 1999). Comparative work has extended these findings about perceived control to the Canadian and United Kingdom cases and to a wider range of racialized minority groups (Harell et al. 2013; Ford 2015; Harell et al. 2016; Ford and Kootstra 2016).

However, perceptions of control/responsibility do not fully capture why people view immigrants as undeserving. For one thing, not all immigrant groups are seen as lazy. In the Canadian case, several surveys have shown that most Canadians "agree with the statement that immigrants tend to work harder than people born in Canada" (Environics Institute for Survey Research 2019, 5). Moreover, recent research has confirmed that host societies see immigrants as less deserving even after controlling for control: they favor hard-working native-born citizens compared to hard-working immigrants (Reeskens and van der Meer 2019).

So there must be other factors shaping these hierarchies of deservingness. Van Oorschot (2000) suggests three additional criteria of deservingness, beyond control and need:

- identity: perceptions of the extent that the individuals in need are "like us";
- attitude: whether the individuals are grateful for support they receive; and

- reciprocity: the extent to which individuals are perceived as likely to "give back" or contribute to society.

Some important new research has been conducted on these additional criteria, and why they might operate to penalize immigrants. Regarding identity and attitude, studies suggest that likeability and proximity to "us" matter for deservingness in some contexts (van Oorschot 2000; Applebaum 2002; Kootstra 2016; Reeskens and van der Meer 2019), and that lack of acceptance of mainstream norms or values is considered detrimental to deservingness (Applebaum 2001). Regarding reciprocity, immigrants are sometimes perceived to be "taking advantage" of the social security system, relocating to America to "cash in" on welfare benefits and "gaming" the system (Yoo 2008). Other studies have focused on narratives regarding immigrants as either economic contributors or "burdens" and their assimilation in the majority society (Yukich 2013; Huber 2015; Jørgensen and Thomsen 2016; Nicholls et al. 2016).

In our view, these additional criteria beyond need and control are indeed essential to understanding the inclusion and exclusion of immigrants. However, as various critics have noted, this list of additional criteria seems rather ad hoc, and is not tied to any underlying theory. The criteria are also operationalized in inconsistent ways: researchers use very different questions to try to measure "identity", for example, or "attitude" (Knotz et al. 2020). We believe that we can make progress here by linking these criteria of deservingness to a deeper theory about the meaning of membership, and the obligations that flow from membership. Immigrants, we will suggest, are often seen as undeserving, not because they fall outside the circle of the nation, nor because they are seen as lazy, but because they are seen as not adequately committed to the larger society, and not adequately motivated by an ethics of membership.

INCLUSION THROUGH PERCEPTIONS OF MEMBERSHIP COMMITMENT

The idea of an "ethics of membership" has not been clearly articulated in either the nationalism literature or the deservingness literature, but we believe it is implicit in both. Recall our previous discussion of liberal nationalism. For liberal nationalists, inclusion is a two-step process: the majority must reject exclusionary ethnic definitions of the nation, and minorities in turn must show their willingness to join in a shared national political project. Much has been written about the challenges of the first step: how to overcome deep historical legacies of ethnicized and racialized definitions of the nation. But much less has been written about the second step: how do minorities, particularly newcomers, show their commitment to the larger society? How do minorities show that they are in fact willing and committed participants in the civic nation? And do others in society perceive this commitment?

As noted earlier, some definitions of "civic" nationalism imply that all that is required is for immigrants to make a commitment to universal liberal-democratic values. But a civic nation is not just a set of abstract values, it is always embedded in a particular culture and emplaced in a particular territory, and commitment to a civic nation requires concerns for *this* community and *this* territory, not just a concern for universal values. Liberal nationalists have argued that nationhood is rooted in a people's shared sense that they form a bounded community, and it is this shared sense of membership that does the work in fostering trust and solidarity. This idea of nationhood is well captured by David Miller (1995), who defines nationhood as having five features: (1) a sense that there is a "we" that *belongs together*, and would find it objectionable for the "we" to be divided into two separate countries or merged into a larger country; (2) a sense that the "we" has *historical continuity*; it extends backwards and forwards in time, and current members have a duty to pass on the national patrimony in good shape to future members of the nation; (3) a sense that the "we" wishes to *act collectively*, and so seeks means of collective agency, such as political self-government; (4) a sense that the "we" occupies a particular *territory* or homeland, and has a distinctive relationship to that territory; and (5) a sense that the "we" shares a *common public culture*, which in turn provides the cultural basis for collective agency. In virtue of these five features, nationhood becomes an "ethical community" (Tamir 1993), in which members recognize distinctive obligations to co-members. This sense of "us" and the desire for collective action lies at the heart of social solidarity, understood as the willingness to support each other through a redistributive welfare state.

In the case of immigrants, then, inclusion in the solidaristic "we" requires not only rejecting ethnic definitions of the nation and racist stereotypes about laziness, but also some channel by which immigrants can affirm their commitment to being full and willing members in a collective "we", with its associated ideas of belonging together, historical continuity, collective action, territorial attachment, and public culture. This second step has received very little empirical scrutiny, in part because there are few existing measures that fully capture the idea of a shared commitment to the collective. In the nationalism literature, measures of civic nationhood focus largely on shared values and respect for laws, but not on the nature of the social fabric that ties society together. In the deservingness literature, membership is partially captured by van Oorschot's (2000) criteria of attitude, reciprocity, and identity, but as we have seen, critics argue these are somewhat ad hoc criteria, not explicitly tied to an underlying idea of membership. We would argue that we need more explicit questions that capture the extent to which immigrants are seen as willing members of the larger society, committed to the nation as an "ethical community".

Capturing this sense of shared membership in society comparatively requires questions that focus on the extent that people think immigrants are committed to and care about society. We have proposed a short-version scale that succinctly captures this sentiment.[1] Built from a longer scale developed in this Canadian context, the four-item scale of membership perceptions was fielded in both Canada in May 2020 (Harell et al. 2020) and a cross-national survey conducted the University of Siena in eight European countries in September–October 2020, which included France, Germany, Italy, the Netherlands, Spain, Romania, Poland, and the UK.[2] In both datasets, data were collected with quota-based online sampling, and weights were created using an iterative ranking procedure. The four items in the scale include:

- IDENTIFY: Compared to other people living in [COUNTRY], how much do you think immigrants identify with [COUNTRY]?
- CARES: Compared to other people living in [COUNTRY], how much do you think immigrants care about the concerns and needs of other [NATIONALITY citizens]?

- SACRIFICE: Compared to other people living in [COUNTRY], how willing do you think immigrants are to make sacrifices for others in our society?
- CONTRIBUTE: One way citizens contribute to society is by working and paying taxes. Compared to other people living in [COUNTRY], do you think immigrants are contributing their fair share, or more or less than their fair share?

The response categories include a five-point scale running from much less (–1) to much more (1), where 0 represents an evaluation that places immigrants on par with other people in the country.

In the first column of Table 5.1, we provide the mean score in each country on the membership scale. We can immediately observe that membership scores in every country are significantly below 0 on the –1 to 1 scale. Recall that a 0 score would mean that respondents, on average, think that immigrants care, identify, sacrifice, and contribute at a level that is about the same as others in the country. Negative scores, then, represent what we call a "membership penalty" for immigrants. Consistently across these nine countries, immigrants are evaluated comparatively poorly compared to others in society in terms of their commitment to the larger society.

This is not an objective evaluation, of course. Immigrants make myriad contributions to collective life. Yet, the membership scale captures an important dimension of public perceptions: on balance, people view immigrants as just not as fully committed to others in society. We also note that there is important cross-national variation in the size of this penalty. Canada, and to a lesser extent the UK, have relatively more positive views, at least at the aggregate level, compared to some of the continental European countries in the study that cluster more closely together.

Table 5.1 also presents a measure of support for inclusive redistribution in each country. We capture the concept of inclusive redistribution, measured with a three-item scale that asks people their level of (dis)agreement with the idea that the government should be responsible for (1) ensuring immigrants have access to social welfare programs when they need them, (2) providing a decent standard of living for newcomers, and (3) reducing income differences between immigrants and other nationals (Cronbach's alpha ranges from 0.799 to 0.859 in each country). Table 5.1 displays the mean on this scale by

Table 5.1 Attitudes toward membership and inclusive redistribution

	Inclusive redistribution	Membership perceptions	Pairwise correlation		Coefficient		Country N
Canada	–0.168	0.589	0.506	***	0.320	***	2220
France	–0.481	0.563	0.326	***	0.222	***	2478
Germany	–0.441	0.582	0.425	***	0.330	***	2740
Italy	–0.442	0.613	0.382	***	0.249	***	2865
Poland	–0.438	0.598	0.314	***	0.205	***	2815
Romania	–0.331	0.731	0.129	***	0.098	***	2125
Spain	–0.363	0.645	0.396	***	0.233	***	2753
The Netherlands	–0.442	0.572	0.362	***	0.239	***	2310
United Kingdom	–0.279	0.586	0.482	***	0.332	***	2461

country, which are all within a relatively small range on the scale (0.56 and 0.64) with the exception of Romania which appears to be a clear outlier.

These differences in the size of membership penalties are interesting, but for the purposes of this chapter, the crucial question is whether they affect the boundaries of generosity: that is, do perceptions of membership commitment affect the willingness to share? Our hypothesis is that membership perceptions are indeed predictors of generosity toward immigrants, above and beyond perceptions of control and need. At the individual level, this appears to be the case. In Table 5.1, there is a clear relationship between the membership scale and support for inclusive redistribution. The two are significantly correlated together. The estimated effect of a one-point shift on the membership scale is between 0.205 and 0.332 on inclusive redistribution, again with the exception of Romania. We illustrate this relationship by mapping the means on each scale in Figure 5.1.

This preliminary evidence at the cross-national level is supported by more comprehensive analysis of the Canadian case. In past work, we have shown that at least in Canada, membership attitudes are powerful predictors of support for inclusive redistribution, even after controlling for more traditional explanations of support for redistribution, as well as controls for perceptions of need and laziness (Banting et al. 2020; Harell et al. 2021). Figure 5.2 gives an indication of the scale of these effects in the Canadian context. This work demonstrates that membership has a large, robust effect on support for

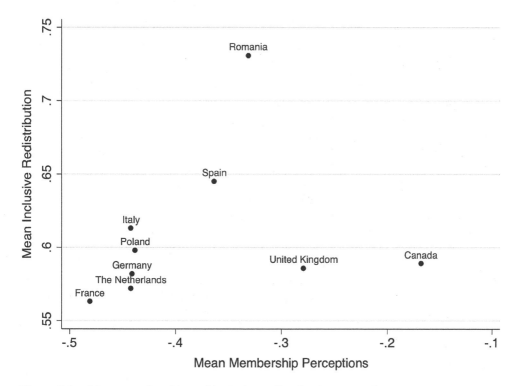

Figure 5.1 Mean membership and inclusive redistribution scores by country

112   *Handbook on migration and welfare*

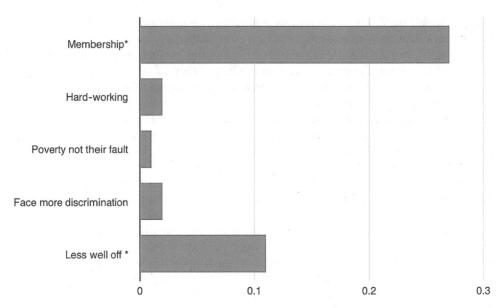

Note: The figure reports standardized coefficients in a multivariate linear regression model predicting support for inclusive redistribution. Model controls for attitudes toward group distance, national identity, multiculturalism, sociodemographic controls, and partisanship (not shown). Model limited to non-immigrant respondent (n = 1497). * indicates variables that are significant at the p < .01 level.

Figure 5.2   The relative impact of membership perceptions compared to other deservingness factors in support of redistribution in Canada

redistribution toward immigrants (Figure 5.2), as well as other types of spending that target immigrant integration in society (not shown), even when controlling for a host of more traditional measures of deservingness.

It is interesting to note that while these membership perceptions do clearly affect the willingness to share with immigrants, they have relatively small direct effects on more general support for the welfare state. That is to say, where citizens view immigrants as lacking the desired membership commitment, this does not lead to a general retreat from support for the welfare state, but rather takes the form of expressing opposition to immigrants' access to social programs.

This is obviously just preliminary evidence, though the findings in Canada appear robust. Much work remains to be done to confirm that membership perceptions affect the boundaries of generosity more generally, and if so, to then think about what the sources of these membership perceptions are. For example, why do immigrants in France face a much larger "membership penalty" than in the UK or Canada? However, we are convinced that membership perceptions provide a fruitful and promising avenue for asking new questions about the relationship between immigration and redistribution.

CONCLUSION: TOWARDS INCLUSIVE SOLIDARITY

If we want to fully understand the extent to which people are willing to extend the social safety net to immigrants, we need to think about many different dimensions of inclusion and exclusion. In this chapter, we have laid out several possible approaches that are often studied in isolation or have received insufficient empirical examination. In this concluding section, we step back and return to our opening premise. If we wish to understand when and why people are prepared to share with strangers, we need to think about both *external boundaries* and *internal hierarchies*. Both are essential to understanding the "we" that forms the bonds of solidarity in a society.

The first dimension concerns *external boundaries*: who is considered outside the political community and therefore outside the bounds of membership-based obligation? There may be certain humanitarian obligations that are truly universal – duties of rescue and asylum – but the welfare state is typically understood as a vehicle by which the members of society care for each other. A Canadian national (at least one without dual citizenship) has no imagined obligation to contribute to redistributive schemes in another country. The question then becomes how immigrants enter the circle of membership-based obligation. From a legal perspective, formal membership status is conveyed by the state, which is a matter of both (a) admission policy (which types of immigrants are admitted into the territory of the country); and (b) settlement and naturalization policy (how immigrants gain secure legal status, permanent residency, and citizenship). However, our primary interest is in how citizens understand the external boundaries of their *political community*, which as we have seen is often tied to a particular image of nationhood as an obligation-generating "ethical community". Citizens' perceptions of the external boundaries of the ethical community may differ from the formal statuses accorded by the state, in ways that are either more inclusive or more exclusionary. In the recent Windrush scandal, for example, many citizens were appalled that the British government was treating people from the Caribbean who had been living in the UK for 40 years as if they fell outside the external boundaries of the political community due simply to a legal glitch about their citizenship status (White 2019). In other cases, however, citizens may think governments are too quick to include migrants or minorities within the boundaries of the ethical community.

In addition to these *external boundaries*, the political community also has *internal hierarchies* that structure how willing citizens are to support social programs that benefit others, generating complex gradations in who is seen as deserving of the full benefits of membership within the political community. The interaction between external boundaries and internal hierarchies has not been sufficiently studied in the literature. The nationalism literature has not adequately captured this complexity, because it views the external boundary as the only or main barrier to the "deep horizontal comradeship" of national solidarity. The deservingness literature has done a better job of capturing these internal hierarchies, but it pays less attention to external boundaries, and has tended to assume that deservingness is about need and control, when in fact perceptions of "we"-ness are equally important.

This reconceptualization sees the political community as essentially a meta category. The state regulates who has a formal status in the country, and this status itself can have gradations that are more or less salient across different countries (citizen, permanent resident, denizen, etc.). However, access to legal status within a country does not guarantee admission into the prevailing public conception of the boundaries of the "ethical community" within which norms of mutual support and solidarity normally prevail.

Assessments of deservingness happen at *both* the external and internal levels. Generosity can be restricted because people are viewed as outside of the community (e.g., do not have the status of community member), and comparatively, there is variation in how political communities define and maintain this boundary. This variation is often analyzed in terms of a "civic versus ethnic" dichotomy, but since political values and institutions are always culturally embedded, it might be more accurate to say that within each country citizens invoke their own idiosyncratic mix of cultural and political elements in determining how immigrants earn the right to cross the external border of the nation and gain obligation-generating membership.

Generosity can also be restricted based on internal boundaries that capture salient distinctions *within* the political community. These internal boundaries reflect attitudes toward other groups, or to use the language of intergroup relations, the extent of out-group hostility. If there are high levels of intergroup prejudice, this serves as a barrier to extending generosity. Certain groups who clearly fall within the political community may nonetheless be seen as undeserving because of prejudice. Indeed, the rich literature on how racial attitudes shape welfare support makes evident that prejudicial thinking often permeates evaluations of deservingness, either directly or indirectly by activating biased evaluations of other deservingness criteria. Another internal boundary, which is less studied, is the extent to which other groups are viewed as committed to the larger political community. Rather than ask about how out-groups are viewed, this internal boundary captures the extent to which each group is seen as a committed member of the larger community. This is captured, in part, by what van Oorschot calls "reciprocity", which focuses on the willingness to contribute to a shared project. Yet, as we have argued elsewhere (Banting et al. 2020; Harell et al. 2021), membership perceptions are not just about "contribution", particularly not if this is understood in a narrowly economic sense. It is not just the perception that people are contributing, but also that they *care* about others in the political community and think of themselves as such. Indeed, in our battery of questions regarding membership perceptions, the "care" question was a more powerful predictor of support for redistribution than the "contribute" question. Our respondents were looking for evidence of moral commitment to the larger society, not just economic contribution.

This framework provides the foundation for an exploration of the sources of a more inclusive solidarity. Countries can be compared not just on the nature and ease of access to formal legal categories of entitlement, but also on public perceptions about both the external boundaries of the political community and its internal hierarchies of deservingness. At a minimum, a more inclusive solidarity requires the rejection of explicit out-group discrimination (in policy) and the reduction of out-group prejudice (in perceptions). This is a necessary, but we would argue insufficient, condition. For a society to be willing to fully share the benefits of social cooperation with newcomers, immigrants also need to be accepted as willing and committed members of the political community. They need to lose their out-group status and be viewed on the same footing as other insiders. Again, this has a policy dimension: are immigrants given full political, social, and economic rights? In addition, it requires citizens to both reject xenophobia but also see immigrants as willing members of a shared society. It is this last dimension that has received the least consideration by both normative and empirical scholars to date.

NOTES

1. Note that the four-item measure is a short form of a longer battery that we have previously released in Banting et al. (2020) and Harell et al. (2021). In a third working paper, we also demonstrate that the four-item measure is the most powerful and efficient scale (Harell et al. n.d.).
2. We also ran a previous study in Canada in 2017 with an alternative question format that included these four questions. See Banting et al. (2020) and Harell et al. (2021) for analyses of the 2017 data.

REFERENCES

Aaroe, Lene, and Michael Bang Petersen. 2014. "Crowding Out Culture: Scandinavians and Americans Agree on Social Welfare in Face of Deservingness Cues". *Journal of Politics* 76(3): 684–97.

Anderson, Benedict. 2006. *Imagined Communities: Reflections on the Origin and Spread of Nationalism*. New York: Verso Books.

Applebaum, Lauren. 2001. "The Influence of Perceived Deservingness on Policy Decisions Regarding Aid to the Poor". *Political Psychology* 22(3): 419–42.

Applebaum, Lauren. 2002. "Who Deserves Help? Students' Opinions about the Deservingness of Different Groups Living in Germany to Receive Aid". *Social Justice Research* 15(3): 201–25.

Banting, Keith, and Edward Koning. 2017. "Just Visiting? The Weakening of Social Protection in a Mobile World". In *Multicultural Governance in a Mobile World*, ed. Anna Triandafyllidou. Edinburgh: Edinburgh University Press, 108–35.

Banting, Keith, Will Kymlicka, Allison Harell, and Rebecca Wallace. 2020. "Beyond National Identity: Liberal Nationalism, Shared Membership and Solidarity". In *Liberal Nationalism and Its Critics: Normative and Empirical*, eds. Gina Gustavsson and David Miller. Oxford: Oxford University Press, 205–25.

Bloemraad, Irene, Will Kymlicka, Michèle Lamont, and Leanne S. Son Hing. 2019. "Membership Without Social Citizenship? Deservingness and Redistribution as Grounds for Equality". *Daedalus* 148(3): 73–104.

Breidahl, Karen Nielsen, Nils Holtug, and Kristian Kongshøj. 2018. "Do Shared Values Promote Social Cohesion? If So, Which? Evidence from Denmark". *European Political Science Review* 10(1): 97–118.

Brubaker, Rogers. 1992. *Citizenship and Nationhood in France and Germany*. Cambridge, MA: Harvard University Press.

Brubaker, Rogers. 1999. "The Manichean Myth: Rethinking the Distinction between 'Civic' and 'Ethnic' Nationalism". In *Nation and National Identity: The European Experience in Perspective*, eds. Hanspeter Kriesi, Klaus Armington, and Hannes Siegrist. West Lafayette, IN: Purdue University Press, 55–72.

Brubaker, Rogers. 2004. "In the Name of the Nation: Reflections on Nationalism and Patriotism". *Citizenship Studies* 8(2): 115–27.

Citrin, Jack, Richard Johnston, and Matthew Wright. 2012. "Do Patriotism and Multiculturalism Collide? Competing Perspectives from Canada and the United States". *Canadian Journal of Political Science* 45(3): 531–52.

Cook, Fay Lomax. 1979. *Who Should Be Helped? Public Support for Social Services*. Beverly Hills, CA: Sage.

Coughlin, Richard. 1980. *Ideology, Public Opinion and Welfare Policy: Attitudes towards Taxes and Spending in Industrial Societies*. Berkeley, CA: Institute of International Studies, University of California.

De Swaan, Abram. 1988. *In Care of the State*. Amsterdam: Bakker.

Environics Institute for Survey Research. 2019. *Canadian Public Opinion about Immigration and Refugees*. Toronto.

Feather, Norm. 2003. "Distinguishing between Deservingness and Entitlement: Earned Outcomes versus Lawful Outcomes". *Journal of Social Psychology* 33(3): 367–85.

Feather, Norm, and Sara Dawson. 1998. "Judging Deservingness and Affect in Relation to Another's Employment or Unemployment: A Test of a Justice Model". *European Journal of Social Psychology* 28: 361–81.

Ford, Robert. 2015. "Who Should We Help? An Experimental Test of Discrimination in the British Welfare State". *Political Studies* 64(3): 630–50.

Ford, Robert, and Anouk Kootstra. 2016. "Do White Voters Support Welfare Policies Targeted at Ethnic Minorities? Experimental Evidence from Britain". *Journal of Ethnic and Migration Studies* 43(1): 80–101.
Gans, Herbert. 1995. *The War against the Poor*. New York: Basic Books.
Gilens, Martin. 1999. *Why Americans Hate Welfare: Race, Media, and the Politics of Anti-Poverty Policy*. Chicago, IL: University of Chicago Press.
Golding, Peter, and Sue Middleton. 1982. *Images of Welfare: Press and Public Attitudes to Poverty*. Oxford: Robertson.
Goodhart, David. 2006. *Progressive Dilemma*. London: Demos.
Gugushvili, Dimitri, Laura Ravazzini, Michael Ochsner, Martin Lukac, Orsolya Lelkes, Marcel Fink, Peter Grand, and Wim van Oorschot. 2021. "Welfare Solidarities in the Age of Mass Migration: Evidence from European Social Survey 2016". *Acta Politica*: 1–25.
Gustavsson, Gina. 2019. "National Attachment–Cohesive, Divisive, or Both? A Reconsideration of the National Identity Argument through the Lens of Social Identity Theory". In *Liberal Nationalism and Its Critics: Normative and Empirical Questions*, eds. Gina Gustavsson and David Miller. Oxford: Oxford University Press, 59–77.
Harell, Allison, Stuart Soroka, and Shanto Iyengar. 2016. "Race, Prejudice and Attitudes toward Redistribution: A Comparative Experimental Approach". *European Journal of Political Research* 55(4): 723–44.
Harell, Allison, Stuart Soroka, and Kierra Ladner. 2013. "Public Opinion, Prejudice and the Racialization of Welfare in Canada". *Racial and Ethnic Studies* 37(4): 2580–97.
Harell, Allison, Laura Stephenson, Daniel Rubenson, and Peter Loewen. 2020. *Democracy Check-Up Survey*. Dataset.
Harell, Allison, Keith Banting, Will Kymlicka, and Rebecca Wallace. 2021. "Shared Membership beyond National Identity: Deservingness and Solidarity in Diverse Societies". *Political Studies*. doi:10.1177/0032 321721996939.
Harell, Allison, Colin Scott, and Rebecca Wallace. n.d. "Decoding Deservingness: Testing the Reliability and Validity of Deservingness Criteria in the Canadian Context".
Huber, Lindsay Pérez. 2015. "Constructing 'Deservingness': DREAMers and Central American Unaccompanied Children in the National Immigration Debate". *Association of Mexican American Educators Journal* 9(3): 22–34.
Johnston, Richard, Matthew Wright, Jack Citrin, and Stuart Soroka. 2017. "Diversity and Solidarity: New Evidence from Canada and the US". In *The Strains of Commitment: The Political Sources of Solidarity in Diverse Societies*, eds. Keith Banting and Will Kymlicka. Oxford: Oxford University Press, 152–76.
Jørgensen, Martin Bak, and Trine Lund Thomsen. 2016. "Deservingness in the Danish Context: Welfare Chauvinism in Times of Crisis". *Critical Social Policy* 36(3): 330–51.
Knotz, Carlo, Mia Gandenberger, Giuliano Bonoli, and Flavia Fossati. 2020. *R.I.C.E.: An Integrated Model of Welfare Deservingness Perceptions*. National Centres of Competence in Research Working Paper 26.
Koning, Edward. 2019. *Immigration and the Politics of Welfare Exclusion*. Toronto: University of Toronto Press.
Kootstra, Anouk. 2016. "Deserving and Undeserving Welfare Claimants in Britain and the Netherlands: Examining the Role of Ethnicity and Migration Status Using a Vignette Experiment". *European Sociological Review* 32(3): 325–38.
Kunovich, Robert M. 2009. "The Sources and Consequences of National Identification". *American Sociological Review* 74(4): 573–93.
Kymlicka, Will. 2015. "Solidarity in Diverse Societies: Beyond Neoliberal Multiculturalism and Welfare Chauvinism". *Comparative Migration Studies* 3(1): 1–19.
Marshall, Thomas Humphrey. 1963. *Sociology at the Crossroads*. London: Heinemann.
Miller, David. 1995. *On Nationality*. Oxford: Clarendon Press.
Miller, David. 2006. "Multiculturalism and the Welfare State: Theoretical Reflections". In *Multiculturalism and the Welfare State*, eds. Keith Banting and Will Kymlicka. Oxford: Oxford University Press, 332–38.
Miller, David. 2017. "Solidarity and Its Sources". In *The Strains of Commitment: The Political Sources of Solidarity in Diverse Societies*, eds. Keith Banting and Will Kymlicka. Oxford: Oxford University Press, 61–79.
Miller, David, and Sundas Ali. 2014. "Testing the National Identity Argument". *European Political Science Review* 6(2): 237–59.
Mouritsen, Per. 2006. "The Particular Universalism of a Nordic Civic Nation". In *Multiculturalism, Muslims and Citizenship: A European Approach*, eds. Tariq Modood and Anna Triandafyllidou. New York: Routledge, 81–104.
Nicholls, Walter J., Marcel Maussen, and Laura Caldas De Mesquita. 2016. "The Politics of Deservingness: Comparing Youth-Centered Immigrant Mobilizations in the Netherlands and the United States". *American Behavioral Scientist* 60(13): 1590–612.

Patten, Alan. 2016. *Equal Recognition: The Moral Foundations of Minority Rights*. Princeton, NJ: Princeton University Press.

Pearce, Nicholas. 2004. "Diversity versus Solidarity: A New Progressive Dilemma?" *Renewal: A Journal of Labour Politics* 12(3): 79–87.

Reeskens, Tim, and Marc Hooghe. 2010. "Beyond the Civic–Ethnic Dichotomy: Investigating the Structure of Citizenship Concepts across Thirty-Three Countries". *Nations and Nationalism* 16(4): 579–97.

Reeskens, Tim, and Tom van der Meer. 2019. "The Inevitable Deservingness Gap: A Study into the Insurmountable Immigrant Penalty in Perceived Welfare Deservingness". *Journal of European Social Policy* 29(2): 166–81.

Reeskens, Tim, and Wim van Oorschot. 2012. "Disentangling the 'New Liberal Dilemma': On the Relation between General Welfare Redistribution Preferences and Welfare Chauvinism". *International Journal of Comparative Sociology* 53(2): 120–39.

Reeskens, Tim, and Matthew Wright. 2013. "Nationalism and the Cohesive Society: A Multilevel Analysis of the Interplay between Diversity, National Identity, and Social Capital across 27 European Societies". *Comparative Political Studies* 46(2): 153–81.

Simonsen, Kristina Bakkaer, and Bart Bonikowski. 2020. "Is Civic Nationalism Necessarily Inclusive? Conceptions of Nationhood and Anti-Muslim Attitudes in Europe". *European Journal of Political Research* 59(1): 114–36.

Smith, Anthony D. 1986. *The Ethnic Origins of Nations*. Oxford: Blackwell Publishing.

Smith, Anthony D. 1991. *National Identity*. Reno, NV: University of Nevada Press.

Smith, Anthony D. 2005. "Civic and Ethnic Nationalism". In *Nations and Nationalism: A Reader*, eds. Philip Spencer and Howard Wollman. Edinburgh: Edinburgh University Press, 177–83.

Tamir, Yael. 1993. *Liberal Nationalism*. Princeton, NJ: Princeton University Press.

Theiss-Morse, Elizabeth. 2009. *Who Counts as an American?* Cambridge: Cambridge University Press.

Turgeon, Luc, Antoine Bilodeau, and Stephen E. White. 2019. "A Tale of Two Liberalisms? Attitudes toward Minority Religious Symbols in Quebec and Canada". *Canadian Journal of Political Science* 52(2): 247–65.

van Oorschot, Wim. 2000. "Who Should Get What and Why? On Deservingness Criteria and the Conditionality of Solidarity among the Public". *Policy and Politics* 28(1): 33–49.

van Oorschot, Wim. 2006. "Making the Difference in Social Europe". *Journal of European Social Policy* 16(1): 23–42.

Weiner, Bernard. 1993. "On Sin versus Sickness: A Theory of Perceived Responsibility and Social Motivation". *American Psychologist* 48(9): 957–65.

White, Robin. 2019. "The Nationality and Immigration Status of the 'Windrush Generation' and the Perils of Lawful Presence in a 'Hostile Environment'". *Journal of Immigration, Asylum and Nationality Law* 33(3): 218–39.

Will, Jeffry A. 1993. "The Dimensions of Poverty: Public Perceptions of the Deserving Poor". *Social Science Research* 22(3): 312–32.

Wright, Matthew. 2011. "Diversity and the Imagined Community: Immigrant Diversity and Conceptions of National Identity". *Political Psychology* 32(5): 837–62.

Wright, Matthew, and Tim Reeskens. 2013. "Of What Cloth Are the Ties That Bind? National Identity and Support for the Welfare State across 29 European Countries". *Journal of European Public* 20(10): 1443–63.

Wright, Matthew, Jack Citrin, and Jonathan Wand. 2012. "Alternative Measures of American National Identity: Implications for the Civic-Ethnic Distinction". *Political Psychology* 33(4): 469–82.

Yoo, Grace J. 2008. "Immigrants and Welfare: Policy Constructions of Deservingness". *Journal of Immigrant and Refugee Studies* 6(4): 490–507.

Yukich, Grace. 2013. "Constructing the Model Immigrant: Movement Strategy and Immigrant Deservingness in the New Sanctuary Movement". *Social Problems* 60(3): 302–20.

6. Immigration and preferences for redistribution: Empirical evidence and political implications of the progressive's dilemma in Europe
Elie Murard

INTRODUCTION

"You cannot simultaneously have free immigration and a welfare state." This famous quote, uttered by Milton Friedman during a libertarian conference in 1999, is perhaps the best-known expression of the concern of an inherent tension between immigration and a redistributive welfare state. The challenge immigration poses for modern welfare states has been a fundamental research topic in social sciences. It is often argued that the United States (U.S.) has a less generous welfare state than most European countries because of its immigration history, which resulted in an ethnically diverse society (Alesina and Glaeser, 2004; Freeman, 1986). The hypothesis that solidarity, public and private, travels better within the same ethnic, cultural or racial group than across groups has sparked a debate about the future of the welfare state in Europe. As immigration is making European societies more and more diverse, will it inevitably lead to the demise of the welfare state as we know it? The possibility that diversity undermines the collective identity and solidarity required to maintain popular support for welfare has become a commonly expressed fear, especially among social progressives, who see *both* immigration *and* a generous welfare state as essential ideals.[1] Will this potential tension between immigration and redistribution – often called "the progressive's dilemma" or the "new liberal dilemma" (Koopmans, 2010; Kumlin and Rothstein, 2010; Reeskens and Van Oorschot, 2012) – remain theoretical or will it materialize in an actual retrenchment of the European welfare state?

To evaluate whether immigration poses an actual threat to the national welfare state, I begin by reviewing empirical studies across the social sciences. I focus on the empirical evidence on the effect of immigration on support for the welfare state in the European context. Much of the previous research on the relationship between ethnic diversity and redistribution comes from analyses of the U.S. and scholarship on the American case usually reveals a negative effect of racial and ethnic heterogeneity on welfare attitudes. Given the recent unprecedented rates of immigration to European countries, I review the growing body of work that examines whether the American pattern will be replicated in Europe. I then extensively discuss the results of the recent study by Alesina et al. (forthcoming) which overcome the methodological limitations of previous cross-country studies by using a new unique dataset of immigrant population matched with attitudes towards redistribution in a sample of 140 regions in 16 European countries. Finally, I discuss the possible implications of the immigration-redistribution dilemma both in terms of actual policy setting and change in the structure of the political landscape.

My main conclusions are the following. Cross-country studies find virtually no correlation between immigration and redistribution, but this is likely the result of omitted confounders due to immigrants' endogenous location choices (notably based on the generosity of the national welfare system). In contrast, within-country studies that provide more credible causal evidence tend to confirm the hypothesis that immigration and diversity reduce support for redistribution. In line with previous literature, Alesina et al. (forthcoming) find that, within country, native citizens display lower support for redistribution when the share of immigrants in their residence region is higher. This reaction against redistribution is driven by low-educated voters at the center or the right of the political spectrum living in countries with relatively large welfare systems and with high levels of residential segregation between immigrants and natives. In contrast, the anti-redistribution effect of immigration is less pronounced when immigrants are more skilled and come from origin countries that are culturally more similar to the destination.

Whether and how this change in preferences for redistribution translates into actual policy change remains largely unanswered by the existing literature. The little empirical evidence that exists in Europe does not indicate large negative effects of immigration on the level of redistribution. However, the fact that immigration is unlikely to cause important across-the-board cuts in the welfare system does not imply that there will be no consequences in the political arena or the policy-making process. The recent rise of far-right populist parties in Europe can certainly be interpreted as a nativist political response to the growing tension between immigration and welfare. The new political platform of these parties consists in an original combination of restrictive immigration policies with redistributive policies meant to protect native citizens against the economic (and cultural) threat of globalization. Curbing the inflow of immigrants into the nation state is not yet the only political response of the far right in its attempt to reserve welfare benefits to native citizens. Even more troubling is the growing public support for welfare chauvinistic positions (mostly but not exclusively endorsed by the far right) to exclude immigrants from accessing welfare. Reforms that purely and simply disentitle certain categories of immigrants or make the requirements for access to welfare harder and more onerous for newcomers have been already implemented in the Netherlands, United Kingdom (U.K.) and Denmark (Koning, 2019). Even if far-right parties have not always gained enough power to significantly influence the policy-making process, there is evidence that their political instrumentalization of the immigration-redistribution dilemma has shifted the entire political spectrum to the right, in particular on immigration. The consequence of this shift is that conservative anti-redistributive parties may have an incentive to play the immigration card (i.e., activate natives' stereotypes against "lazy undeserving immigrants") to generate backlash against redistribution. Another consequence may also be that left-wing parties will have a harder time attracting voters when they propose policies that are at the same time open to immigration and strongly redistributive. More generally, the "globalists versus nativists" cleavage (opposing those favoring to those against open immigration and free trade policies) is likely to complement (or even gradually replace) the conventional left–right divide.

In conclusion, the traditional socially generous and inclusive policies of European countries will face the dilemma of natives favoring welfare for themselves but opposing them for immigrants. How to maintain and strengthen the bonds of solidarity in ethnically diverse societies is certainly one of the major and most pressing challenges facing the European welfare state (Banting and Kymlicka, 2006).

LITERATURE

This chapter builds upon earlier literature reviews by Nannestad (2007), Stichnoth and Van der Straeten (2013) and especially on the excellent review by Elsner and Concannon (2020).

Given that the question that this chapter attempts to address is centered on Europe – will immigration make Europeans less supportive of welfare? – I concentrate on reviewing the existing empirical evidence in European countries. I also focus on the evidence on the effect of immigration, as distinct from ethnic diversity, which has been the focal point of a related strand of literature. Although immigration and ethnic diversity are inextricably linked, both are not the same. Ethnic diversity is often the result of migration over many generations. But places with a high ethnic diversity need not have many immigrants, at least not if immigrants are defined as people who are foreign-born (and not second or third generation).[2]

Over the last decades a substantial body of empirical work has examined the relationship between immigration and redistribution. This literature has mostly focused on natives' preferences for redistribution, rather than on the actual level of redistribution, which depends on governments' decisions on taxation and spending. Preferences for redistribution are a crucial step to understanding how immigration affects the setting of redistributive policies. Not only do people's preferences for redistribution affect the design of social policy, but they also have a broader influence on social norms and social cohesion in a society and, thus, determine many political and individual decisions. Preferences also offer many more practical advantages for researchers as they can be observed in much more frequent regular intervals. In contrast, tax and spending policies are the result of slow political processes and may react to immigration with great delay. Another advantage is that preferences are measured at the individual level, and this allows the analysis of heterogeneous reaction to immigration depending on individual characteristics, which is crucial to test and uncover causal mechanisms through which immigrants affect support for welfare.

Methodological Challenges

Before reviewing the existing literature on immigration and preferences for redistribution, I discuss the important methodological challenges that the empirical literature usually confronts.

Data and measurement
Preferences for redistribution are typically measured through survey responses. Surveys differ substantially in their questions, with some asking very broadly about the government's role in reducing income inequality, while others ask specifically about different domains of welfare. The survey modules on preferences typically ask respondents for their desired level of government involvement in domains such as unemployment

insurance, healthcare, pensions, childcare, old-age care, education and housing. Respondents typically give answers on a scale ranging from "only the individual is responsible" to "only the government is responsible". Other surveys also ask broader questions such as whether "the government should take measures to reduce differences in income levels", or whether they think that "social benefits make people lazy". There are no objective criteria nor scientific consensus for what is the most relevant measure of an individual's support for redistribution, which ultimately depends on the context and the researcher's question. This is far from being an immaterial issue as, using the European Social Survey (ESS), Alesina et al. (forthcoming) show that different measures of preferences (eight questions on views on income redistribution, government responsibility and social benefits) are not strongly correlated with each other, with correlation coefficients of typically below 0.5. The same goes for the measurement of exposure to immigrants. A typical statistical model relates individual attitudes to redistribution to the individual's exposure to immigration. But the way exposure is measured is extremely important as individuals can be exposed in many different ways: in their residential neighborhood, in the workplace, or in the traditional or social media for example. Also, it is crucial to know which migrants are more relevant for individual responses; for example, immigrants from similar cultural backgrounds or from more distant ones? Immigration is likely to trigger different responses among the host population depending on the context, and interpreting the impact of immigration requires good knowledge of the context as well as the measurement of exposure to immigrants that is the most appropriate for the research question.

Identification of causality

Studies that examine the impact of immigration on the receiving community face an inherent endogeneity problem. While producing descriptive correlations is often straightforward, establishing causality is challenging because migration is not a random process. In particular, migrants face choices between several destinations and tend to select places that offer favorable economic and social conditions. A correlation between the number of migrants, and various economic or social variables of the host community is thus difficult to interpret: does it reflect the causal impact of the immigrant inflow, or rather the fact that certain areas attract more migrants? For example, cross-country studies about immigration and redistribution typically suffer from the important drawback that they do not control for the endogenous sorting of immigrants across countries based on the generosity of their welfare systems, i.e., for "welfare magnet" effects. Establishing causality becomes inherently difficult because a country's welfare system may attract migrants as well as shape its citizens' preferences for redistribution.

Evidence Across and Within Countries

Cross-country evidence

A natural point to start to explore the relationship between immigration and preferences for redistribution is to examine whether natives' preferences differ between countries with high and low levels of immigration. Cross-country studies are useful as they provide stylized facts, but, given their methodological limitations (aforementioned), their evidence should be considered as mostly descriptive and not conclusive. Given these empirical drawbacks, it is rather unsurprising that the relationship between immigration and preferences for redistribution seems weak and sensitive to the chosen specification. Brady and Finnigan (2014) exploits individual-level International Social Survey Programme panel data from 17 countries over 20 years. Based on multilevel and two-way fixed-effect models, they find a weak positive correlation between immigration and native preferences for redistribution, which holds after controlling for welfare expenditures and employment rates. Kwon and Curran (2016), using the same data, find a more subtle pattern. In countries with more multiculturalist policies – policies fostering a multicultural society – the correlation between immigration and preferences for redistribution tends to be positive, whereas in countries without these policies it tends to be negative. Work by Burgoon et al. (2012), using ESS data, underlines the importance of the geographic level at which immigration is measured. For the share of immigrants at the national level – the standard measure in this literature – they find a weak correlation between immigration and preferences for redistribution. However, interesting patterns emerge when they instead look at the share of immigrants in a person's occupation. Workers in occupations with a high concentration of immigrants display higher support for redistribution. This finding is in line with the view that immigration increases natives' labor market risk, explaining which natives demand more redistribution as an insurance/compensation mechanism.

Some of these studies attempt to address the aforementioned problem of endogeneity of immigrant location choices by controlling for features of a country's welfare state, such as the share of social spending in gross domestic product (GDP) or tax revenues relative to GDP. However, accounting for a limited number of confounders is unlikely to fully address the endogeneity problem, as there are many unobserved aspects of the welfare state (and of the country's idiosyncratic characteristics) that jointly determine immigration and preferences. A more promising approach is to measure immigration at a more disaggregated subnational level, and use variation in exposure to immigrants within countries. This is the approach that Alesina et al. (forthcoming) use by comparing preferences of people who live under the same welfare regime but in different regions with varying shares of immigrants in the population. Eger and Breznau (2017) follow a similar approach by measuring the concentration of immigrants at the NUTS-2 level in Europe and find that the proportion of the regional population that is foreign-born is negatively associated with native-born support for the government provision of social welfare. However, the empirical analysis in Eger and Breznau (2017) is potentially contaminated by the same confounders plaguing cross-country studies, as the authors use regressions without country fixed effects, which implies that their estimates are driven not only by within-country variation in exposure to immigrants, but also by cross-country variation.

Within-country evidence
Within-country studies allow us to examine whether the U.S. – the prototypical multicultural society among high-income countries – is exceptional in its attitudes towards redistribution. Evidence from European countries rejects the idea of U.S. exceptionalism and suggests that the negative relationship between population diversity and redistribution prevails in both the New and the Old Worlds. Eger (2009) considers the case of Sweden, one of the countries with the most generous welfare states in the world. Using variation in the share of immigrants across Swedish counties, she documents a significant negative

relationship between the number of immigrants and preferences for redistribution. Dahlberg et al. (2012), also using Swedish data, successfully establish causality by taking advantage of the existence between 1985 and 1994 of a refugee placement program which exogenously allocates refugees to municipalities in Sweden, essentially without refugees having a say as to where they can be placed. The authors analyze changes in natives' attitudes to redistribution resulting from the arrival of refugees and find a strong negative effect on support for redistribution, especially among high-income earners. Similar results are found by Schmidt-Catran and Spies (2016) with German data, who, using panel data to isolate within-regional variation in immigration, show that an increase in the share of immigrants reduces support for welfare spending. Interestingly, their estimates suggest that immigration has smaller effects in areas with higher shares of foreigners – consistent with Allport's (1954) contact hypothesis – and larger effects in areas with high unemployment – supporting Forbes's (1997) group conflict theory. While immigration seems to affect attitudes to general welfare spending in Germany, there appears to be no impact on support for the unemployed. Stichnoth (2012) finds a strong negative correlation between the regional share of immigrants and native support for the unemployed, but this correlation becomes small and insignificant when he uses panel data and accounts for the endogenous location choices of immigrants.

Mechanisms: Why Immigration Affects Preferences for Redistribution

As Alesina and Giuliano (2011) emphasize, individual preferences for redistribution not only depend on self-centered economic interest, but more broadly on socio-tropic considerations about acceptable levels of inequality in the society, or perceptions of fairness, e.g., the perception of whether economic success is the result of luck or effort. Immigration may influence natives' support for the welfare state because it affects their individual economic situation through labor market competition, pensions, or fiscal leakage (the notion that taxes paid by the natives finance the welfare benefits of poorer immigrants). But immigration may also affect natives' preferences for non-economic reasons, for example if they fear that their native culture is threatened by immigrants "importing" their culture, or if they believe that immigrants are less deserving of welfare than natives.

Perceptions of immigrants

Cross-country studies in Europe by Finseraas (2008), Senik et al. (2009), Magni-Berton (2014) and Burgoon and Rooduijn (2021) provide evidence that natives' support for redistribution is greatly influenced by their perceptions and attitudes towards migrants. Using ESS data in 22 countries, Finseraas (2008) finds that natives who believe that immigrants should not have equal rights compared to natives are less in favor of redistribution. Senik et al. (2009) make a similar point, also based on the ESS. They find that natives who believe that immigration reduces native employment and wages and/or express a strong dislike towards immigrants display lower support for redistribution when they perceive a greater share of immigrants in the country. For individuals who do not hold such views, the correlation between perceived immigration and preferences for redistribution is close to zero. Magni-Berton (2014) and Burgoon and Rooduijn (2021) perform a similar analysis based on later waves of the ESS and find that natives who believe that immigrants drain the welfare system are less in favor of redistribution. All of these studies also tend to find evidence of a compensation effect among natives who perceive immigration as an economic threat: immigration may awaken people's economic insecurities that in turn spur support for welfare protection and redistribution.

While these cross-country studies provide interesting correlations, several recent experimental studies aim at establishing the causal effect of natives' perceptions of immigrants. The research design of these studies is based on priming natives about immigration. A randomly assigned treatment group receives information about immigrants – for example, the share of immigrants in their country, or the average tax contribution of immigrants – before answering questions about preferences for redistribution. This design allows researchers to isolate causal effects of information about immigrants on preferences. Naumann and Stoetzer (2018) find that only respondents with high incomes and facing low labor market competition show reduced support for redistribution when primed about migration. Runst (2018) uncovers similar results: high-income individuals lower their demand for redistribution when primed with information on immigration because they are the ones who pay a large share of overall taxes. A survey experiment by Avdagic and Savage (2019) points to the importance of how the information about immigration is framed. When respondents are presented with negative information suggesting that immigrants are a drain on public finances they show lower support for welfare spending compared to a control group. The experiment of Alesina et al. (2018a) reveals that natives are vastly misinformed about immigrants, regarding their number, country of origin, education level and reliance on the welfare state. In an information experiment, the authors provide the respondents with randomized information treatments about immigration. These include randomizing the order of question blocks – making immigration more salient by asking the immigration questions before those about redistribution. Interestingly, the authors find significantly lower levels of support for redistribution among respondents that were "primed" to think about immigration before answering the questions on redistribution. Taken together, this set of results suggests that it is not the facts about immigrants that are important determinants of preferences for redistribution, but rather people's perceptions about immigrants.

Welfare chauvinism
Social identity is a potentially important determinant explaining preferences for redistribution. Natives may show less solidarity with poor immigrants than with equally poor natives, simply because the immigrants are seen as not belonging to the same identity group, which characterizes people either of the same race, culture or religion, or all of these dimensions combined. As natives prefer to redistribute to the in-group and less towards the out-group, greater population diversity reduces support for redistribution since it decreases the share of in-group members among the recipients of welfare. Luttmer (2001) is the first study that empirically established the existence of such differential altruism based on social identity between white and black populations in the U.S. and coined the term *group loyalty*. In Europe, several studies show that natives support less redistribution if the main beneficiaries are immigrants rather than natives (Ford, 2016; Harell et al., 2016) – a distinction that is often termed welfare chauvinism (Andersen and Bjørklund, 1990). Cappelen and Midtbø (2016) focus on intra-European Union (EU) migration to Norway and combine list experiments with vignettes, whereby they randomize both the list items used for measuring welfare chauvinism as well as information

treatment. The authors find evidence of widespread welfare chauvinism towards immigrants, and in particular that natives become less supportive of the welfare state when being informed that intra-EU immigrants have rights to claim welfare benefits.

There is no consensus on the exact causal mechanism driving welfare chauvinism. The reluctance to redistribute towards immigrants may be due to views that immigrants are less deserving of social benefits than natives, probably because of the stereotypical views of immigrants as "free-riders" of the welfare system. Using European survey data, Van Oorschot (2006) analyzes survey responses which measure the extent to which a respondent believes that a social group deserves welfare support. While the data reveal large support for elderly, sick or disabled people as well as for the unemployed, respondents view immigrants as less deserving of support. Ford's (2016) experimental study in the U.K. confirms that white British respondents view immigrants as well as non-white British as less deserving of social benefits. Two studies from Sweden directly investigate the driving forces behind welfare chauvinism and find that individuals' prejudice is a key factor (Hjorth, 2016; Goldschmidt and Rydgren, 2018). Building on rational choice theory, other studies argue that the lack of solidarity with immigrants reflects humans' unwillingness to engage in reciprocal relations they expect not to benefit from (Fong, 2007; Lee et al., 2006).

Social cohesion
More generally, immigration may affect redistribution because the population diversity it creates can potentially erode mutual trust, weakens social norms of cooperation and reciprocity and undermines the social cohesion on which the welfare state is built on. As a large literature has shown, higher diversity is often associated with lower social capital (Alesina and La Ferrara, 2000, 2002; Putnam, 2007), social anomia (Algan et al., 2016), lower welfare spending and poorer quality of public goods (Alesina et al., 1999; Desmet et al., 2009) – see Alesina and La Ferrara (2005) for a review.

NEW EVIDENCE FROM EUROPEAN REGIONS

Since 1980 the share of the foreign-born population has more than doubled in Western Europe, with about two thirds of the increase generated by immigration from outside Europe. As Europe is becoming more diverse, one may therefore ask whether immigration will make Europeans less supportive of redistribution. For this section I draw from a forthcoming co-authored piece with Alberto Alesina and Hillel Rapoport in which we assembled a unique dataset of immigrant population matched with attitudes towards redistribution in a sample of 140 regions in 16 European countries.

Methodology

The new dataset assembled by Alesina et al. (forthcoming) is a set of fully harmonized population census and register data at the regional level (in the years 1990, 2000 and 2010) which is matched with attitudinal data from the 2008 and 2016 rounds of the ESS. The authors construct a composite index of attitudes towards redistribution taken from the answers to eight different questions elicited in the ESS survey. These questions measure different dimensions of redistribution, for example "Do you favor a reduction in income differences?", or "Should the government be responsible for the standard of living of the poor/old/unemployed", or "do you agree/disagree that social benefits make people lazy?". With this index in hand, we then investigate the relationship between immigration and natives' attitudes to redistribution by exploiting within-country, i.e., regional, variation in the share of immigrants. We estimate multivariate regressions that include country fixed effects, which implies that they compare regions within the same country and thereby control for any time-invariant country characteristics such as geographic size, and most importantly, for welfare and redistribution policies set at the national level. This approach neutralizes any potential "welfare magnet effects" (that is, immigrants' choice of a destination country based on the generosity of its welfare system) which usually plague cross-country studies because they potentially generate a spurious positive correlation between levels of immigration and support for redistribution, as it would the case if immigrants choose to go to the more generous countries that also happen to be those where natives' support for redistribution is higher.

The assumption of the empirical analysis is that the welfare system of a country is relatively homogeneous across regions and therefore the choice of location of immigrants within a country does not depend on the level of redistribution at the subnational local level. This assumption may not be a safe one in federal countries (e.g., Germany), where regions have more fiscal autonomy to set the welfare policy, but the results hold even if these countries are excluded. In any event, we check the robustness of the results to various potential confounders related to the non-random location choices of immigrants. In particular, immigrants may self-select into regions with better economic opportunities and higher prospects for upward income mobility. Since people have lower support for redistribution when the prospects for upward mobility are higher (Alesina et al., 2018b), this could generate a spurious negative correlation between support for redistribution and the share of immigrants. We address this concern by controlling for proxies of economic growth or decline (such as regional GDP growth, negative trade shocks and industrial decline) and by using the share of immigrants in 1990 (instead of 2010), that is, many decades before attitudes to redistribution are measured, and therefore, likely independent of local economic conditions prevailing at the time of the ESS survey.

Main Results: Average Effect

First, local (i.e., regional) exposure to immigration in the residence region appears to affect natives' perceptions of the number of immigrants at the national level and, therefore, also their perception about the identity (natives versus immigrants) of the potential beneficiaries of the welfare state. This result is not surprising, perhaps, but it buttresses the idea of using local immigration data to assess preferences of natives about national policies, like welfare. We then show that native respondents in their sample display lower support for redistribution when the share of immigrants in their residence region is higher. This effect is sizable, comparable to the effect of individual variables such as education or income that are important determinants of preferences for redistribution (Alesina and Giuliano, 2011). For example, the anti-redistribution effect of increasing a region's share of immigrants from the bottom to the top quintile of the immigration size distribution is two-thirds as large as the attitudinal effect of an equivalent increase in

Table 6.1 Immigration and attitudes towards redistribution

Dep var.:	\multicolumn{5}{c}{Index of welfare attitudes}				
	(1)	(2)	(3)	(4)	(5)
Share of immigrants in 2010	−2.711*** (0.728)	−2.802*** (0.665)	−2.842*** (0.655)	−2.670*** (0.658)	−2.323*** (0.606)
Share of immigrants in 2010, squared	6.865*** (2.022)	5.372*** (1.941)	5.201*** (1.985)	4.848** (1.986)	4.088** (1.812)
R^2	0.10	0.11	0.13	0.15	0.28
N	31,230	31,230	31,230	31,230	31,230
Immigrants' share minimizing dependent variable	.197	.261	.273	.275	.284
Country year fixed effects	X	X	X	X	X
Regional control		X	X	X	X
Basic individual controls			X	X	X
Income controls				X	X
Ideology controls					X

Note: This table presents the estimates of regressions where the dependent variable *Index of welfare attitudes* is constructed as the first component of a principal component analysis using height attitudinal variable measuring support for redistribution. The different columns correspond to regressions with a different set of control variables on the right-hand side. Regional controls include: native population (log), GDP per capita (log), unemployment rate, share of tertiary educated among the native population. Individual controls include: year of birth*sex, sex*education, household composition, employment status (unemployed, self-employed, retired …), education of parents and country of birth of parents, type of respondent's domicile (big city, suburbs, small town, village). Individual income controls include: current or former occupation (isco88 2 digits), household income quintile in the country and feeling about current household's income. Ideology controls include: placement on left–right scale, opinions about whether people should be treated equally and have equal opportunities, opinions about the importance to help people and care for others' well-being, opinions about whether most people try to take advantage of you or try to be fair. Standard errors (in parenthesis) are clustered at the NUTS regional level. *** $p<0.01$, ** $p<0.05$, * $p<0.1$.

household income. So, the answer to the question – Is immigration reducing support for redistribution in Europe? – seems to be "yes", on average. This is shown in Table 6.1, which reveals a significantly negative effect of immigration on support for redistribution at the regional level. Also, the attitudinal effect of immigrants appears non-linear and tends to taper off gradually with the share of immigrants (i.e., is marginally decreasing, as shown by the significant positive quadratic term in the table). Going from 0 to, say, 5 percent of immigrants in a region may be more salient and visible for the natives – and the perception of this increase more obvious – than moving from 20 to 25 percent.

Heterogeneity

The average negative effect described above hides considerable heterogeneity along a number of dimensions: type of receiving countries, type of respondents and type of migrants. First, the anti-redistribution impact of immigration is mainly driven by destination countries with more generous welfare states (e.g., Nordic countries and France) relative to countries with smaller welfare states (e.g., the U.K. or Ireland). This may be because natives of the countries with larger social services may be more concerned about the fiscal cost of immigrants, and more precisely by the fear of a "fiscal leakage effect", diverting public revenues from native tax payers to foreign welfare recipients (Razin et al., 2002, 2011).

Second, the reaction against redistribution is significantly stronger among native individuals placing themselves at the center or the right of the political spectrum, while the attitudes of leftist individuals are not much affected by immigration. The reaction against redistribution is also significantly stronger among natives who hold negative views about immigrants or think that immigrants should not be entitled to welfare benefits. This is consistent with welfare chauvinism and anti-solidarity effects, i.e., the belief that immigrants are less deserving of social benefits than natives (Andersen and Bjørklund, 1990; Ford, 2016). In contrast, the attitudinal response to immigration is less pronounced among the more educated individuals – in line with the "educated preferences" theory, i.e., the fact that more educated respondents are significantly less intolerant towards immigrants and place greater value on cultural diversity (Hainmueller and Hiscox, 2007). The attitudinal response to immigration is also less pronounced among households in the bottom quintile of the income distribution, which are of greater risk of downward income mobility, possibly due to tighter labor market competition with immigrants. This is inline with the compensation hypothesis that predicts that, with more immigration, workers should demand more redistribution to insure them against labor market risks.

Third, the attitudinal effect of immigration greatly depends on immigrants' countries of origin and skills. Immigrants originating from the Middle East (North Africa included), as well as from Eastern and Central European countries (that joined the EU after 2004), generate a much larger anti-redistribution effect relative to immigrants from other origin countries. This suggests that the cultural, linguistic or religious background of the immigrants is an important determinant of natives' attitude. Also, immigrants' skills, both in terms of formal education and labor market occupation, shape natives' attitudinal reaction: a higher proportion of high-skilled immigrants significantly mitigates the anti-redistribution effect of immigration. This can be due either to the fact that highly educated immigrants rely less on the welfare system, or because they assimilate more easily and thus are culturally closer to natives. Finally, for a given share of immigrants in a region, a higher residential segregation of immigrants (likely due to a lower degree of integration) is associated, *ceteris paribus*, with a significant reduction in the support for redistribution in that region.

Overall, these results are broadly consistent with group loyalty effects, that is, with the fact that individuals prefer to redistribute towards the in-group (people of the same race, culture or nationality) and less so towards the out-group. However, they are not exclusive of other channels that determine natives' attitudinal responses to immigration. As discussed, immigration may influence attitudes because it affects individuals' economic situation through labor market competition or through fiscal leakage. Because we use observational and not experimental data, we cannot disentangle these different mechanisms.

POLITICAL IMPLICATIONS

Redistributive Policies

Consistent with the literature on preferences of redistribution, our results suggest that immigration erodes support for welfare in Europe. Does this shift in preferences translate into actual policy changes? Compared to the literature on preferences, the body of work on the effect of immigration on actual policy setting is much smaller and the evidence more mixed. In the economic literature, some studies find that immigration to Europe can lead to a small reduction in social spending and in particular in public education spending (Tanaka et al., 2018; Jofre-Monseny et al., 2016; Speciale, 2012), while other studies find no effect on municipal public spending (Gerdes, 2011). In the political science literature, there is even less evidence that migration has led to actual welfare retrenchment (Finseraas, 2012; Crepaz, 2008; Soroka et al., 2006). Overall, the empirical evidence is ambiguous and no study finds a large reduction in the level of redistribution due to immigration. These null findings may not be unsurprising for at least three reasons. First, there are institutional obstacles to welfare reduction (Huber and Stephens, 2010; Pierson, 1994; Brooks and Manza, 2008) and, as the median voter usually benefits from the welfare state, any plans for widespread reductions in benefits are likely to face an opposing majority. Second, the strongest reaction against immigration tends to be found among low-educated workers and the unemployed, exactly those groups of voters who can also be expected to support redistribution (Scheve and Slaughter, 2001; Crepaz, 2008; Svallfors, 2006). Third, the effect of migration on policy setting crucially depends on whether immigrants have voting rights and can directly influence policy. As some studies show, immigration can actually lead to higher local taxes and spending in contexts in which immigrants have voting rights (Ferwerda, 2020; Chevalier et al., 2018).

But the fact that immigration is unlikely to cause important across-the-board welfare cuts does not mean that it will have no effect on any aspect of the welfare system, or no consequence on the political landscape in general. I discuss three possible non-mutually exclusive consequences of the immigration-redistribution dilemma: (1) increasing support for populist anti-immigrant parties with an agenda of restricting admission policies; (2) discrimination against immigrants in terms of social rights to welfare and/or access to social programs; and (3) changes in the structure of the political conflict.

Rise of Populist Parties

One obvious way to tackle the (perceived) tension between immigration and welfare could be to restrict the admission of immigrants into European destination countries. In fact, tapping into natives' concerns of the economic and social effects of immigration (as expressed in various opinion surveys), far-right populist parties, such as La Lega in Italy, Le Rassemblement (ex-Front) National in France, or Alternative für Deutschland, have received increasing support over the last decade. While usually proponents of tightening immigrant admission policy, these new political parties tend to defend a more centrist or even leftist position on issues of redistribution (Andersen and Bjørklund, 2000; Ignazi, 2003; Ivarsflaten, 2005; De Lange, 2007). The entrance of these new parties on the political scene seems to have met the demand of an increasing share of the electorate for anti-immigration policies combined with pro-redistributive policies. The recent electoral success of Rassemblement National's strategy to move the party's manifesto away from the free market and towards redistributive and protectionist policies is a case in point.

Using empirical analyses accounting for migrants' endogenous location choices, some studies have provided causal evidence that, in some contexts, local exposure to immigration increases natives' support for nativist populist parties. Dustmann et al. (2019) show that the Danish government's quasi-random assignment of refugees from 1986 to 1998 increased anti-immigrant voting, in particular in small municipalities. Halla et al. (2017) find a positive impact of immigration on the vote share of Jörg Haider's far-right Freedom Party (FPO) in Austria. Likewise, Edo et al. (2019) find that immigration (especially low skilled and from non-Western countries) increased the vote share of far-right presidential candidates in France from 1988 to 2017. Hangartner et al. (2019) and Dinas et al. (2019) also show that, in the aftermath of the Syrian conflict, the arrival of refugees on Greek islands increased the vote share of the far-right Golden Dawn party. Interestingly, immigrants seem to cause different reactions depending on their skill composition. Moriconi et al. (2018) examine the role of immigrants' skills using data from elections in 12 European countries from 2007 to 2016. They find that the arrival of low-skilled immigrants increases votes for nationalist parties, while the influx of high-skilled immigrants has the opposite effect. Using the same data, Murard (2017) reaches similar conclusions using self-reported attitudes towards immigrants as the outcome variable instead of voting. Mayda et al. (forthcoming) carry out a similar exercise for the U.S. and also find that low-skilled immigration increases the Republican vote share while high-skilled immigration decreases it. An interpretation of these findings is that the desirability of immigrants crucially hinges on natives' perceptions about immigrants' welfare dependency. While low-skilled migrants are typically seen as a burden or cost for the welfare system – because they consume more in social benefits than they pay in taxes – the opposite is likely to be true for high-skilled migrants, who tend to be net contributors. In other words, since high-skilled immigrants are unlikely to be the beneficiaries of redistribution, the immigration-redistribution trade-off is much less salient for them than for low-skilled immigrants.

Welfare Exclusion of Immigrants

Another possible outcome of the tension between immigration and generous welfare institutions is the (partial) exclusion of immigrants from the welfare system (Koning, 2019). The growing support for such radical discriminating measures does not necessarily entail opposition to redistribution but rather a belief that native-born citizens are entitled to more generous welfare programs than newcomers to the political community. Many political science studies find that large portions of the population believe that native-born citizens should be privileged in the welfare system and a non-significant minority even favor indefinite categorical exclusion of non-natives (Gorodzeisky and Semyonov, 2009; Van der Waal et al., 2010; Mewes and Mau, 2013; De Koster et al., 2013). Restrictions on immigrants' access to welfare benefits is not an abstract possibility, as a wide variety of countries, including Denmark, the Netherlands, the U.K. and the U.S., have in recent years made it harder for immigrants to qualify for benefits and social programs (Wilkinson et al., 2012; Sainsbury, 2012). Reforms aimed at restricting welfare benefits differ in the form of exclusion they entail. Some reforms disentitle certain categories of migrants, making them altogether ineligible – as with the U.K.'s exclusion of temporary migrants from non-contributory benefits – while others make immigrants receive lower benefits – such as Denmark's coupling of social assistance to duration of residence. Still other reforms make the requirements for access more onerous for newcomers than for native-born citizens (e.g., Germany's requirement to attend integration courses). Finally, even if immigrants are legally entitled to the same benefits, more subtle forms of exclusion can still impede access to benefits. There is evidence that immigrants' take-up of welfare benefits is hindered by discrimination (Barrett et al., 2013; Sabates-Wheeler and Feldman, 2011) and, more frequently, by cultural and linguistic barriers (Simich et al., 2005; Ma and Chi, 2005).

Unsurprisingly, the most virulent proponents of immigrants' exclusion from welfare are far-right populist parties, not only because of their hostility towards the immigrant population, but also because their platforms support a redistributive welfare state, whose benefits should in their view be restricted to native citizens only. Such a welfare chauvinistic position allows populist parties to combine attacks both against the dangerous "other" (immigrants) and the pro-market liberal establishment: right-wing populists can blame the elite for cutting the welfare rights of "deserving natives" and blame the immigrants for their "excessive claims" on the welfare state. For example, Front National's Marine Le Pen stated: "We must reserve our welfare and our social policy for our compatriots, as well as give them priority access to employment and housing".[3]

More worrisome is the fact that the attempt of discriminating immigrants in their access to welfare seems to gain traction in mainstream politics. Analyzing the manifestoes of 61 parties in 11 European countries in 2012, Koning (2017) finds that more than three in five parties explicitly note the potential for immigration to burden the social security system.

The notion of limiting immigrants' access to welfare benefits is present not only in far-right parties' manifestoes but also in the manifestoes of 50 percent of the liberal conservative parties and 30 percent of Christian Democratic parties. These numbers are certainly not trivial. This apparent contagion effect, i.e., the adoption of populist parties' political agenda by mainstream parties, led us to examine the third possible consequence of the immigration-redistribution dilemma, namely changes in the structure of the political landscape.

Changing Structure of the Political Conflict

Some studies document that the electoral success of far-right parties put pressure on mainstream parties to adopt an anti-immigration rhetoric and advocate restrictive immigration policies. Minkenberg (2001) and Van Spanje (2010) report an "agenda-setting effect" leading the other parties to co-opt the agenda of far-right parties, notably in Germany with the major parties embracing the right-wing definition of the "asylum problem" in 1992. In the same vein, Pettigrew (1998, 95) states that "while far-right efforts have gained only minimal power directly, they have shifted the entire political spectrum to the right on immigration". Abou-Chadi and Krause (2020) provide convincing causal evidence that the electoral success of far-right parties has changed mainstream party positions towards a more anti-immigrant and culturally protectionist stance. Employing a regression discontinuity design, the authors exploit exogenous variation in electoral thresholds that determine which vote share will lead to parliamentary representation of parties in the form of seats. As parliamentary representation provides additional resources and media attention, radical right parties that passed the electoral thresholds constitute a more credible challenger for established parties. When exposed to higher competition with far-right parties, the mainstream parties are more likely to shift their political platform to the right. If such contagion effects exist, as these findings strongly suggest, then the emergence of anti-immigration parties could potentially affect the overall policy-making process throughout Western Europe.

More generally, the focus on immigration issues in the current political debate can also benefit (and be strategically fueled by) parties with an anti-redistribution agenda who can play the immigration card to generate backlash against redistribution. As Alesina and Glaeser (2004) have convincingly shown in the U.S. context, "playing the race card", that is, the instrumental use and activation of natives' racial prejudices to undermine redistributive policies, might be a valuable strategy to mobilize political support. For Europe, a similar pattern has been discussed extensively in the literature (Arzheimer, 2008; Schmidt and Spies, 2014; Mudde, 2013, 2015). As Alesina et al. (2018a) document, native citizens in Europe hold stereotypical views of immigrants as undeserving recipients of the welfare state, which is seen as mostly benefiting non-natives, thus leaving them in what they perceive as the role of mere payers for unjustified claims. These misperceptions echo the deeply rooted stereotype of the "lazy black" in the U.S. public discourse (Gilens, 1995). Conservative politicians have an incentive to maintain and exaggerate these misperceptions to undermine citizens' support for redistributive policies.

The immigration-redistribution tension is also likely to affect left-wing parties, which will have a harder time attracting voters when they propose policies at the same time open to immigration and strongly redistributive. Their hard-core base may agree with those, but with such policies left-wing parties are unlikely to attract moderate swing center-right voters. The general decline in the electoral support for leftist parties holding pro-immigrant and pro-redistribution positions illustrates the point. More generally, the "globalists versus nativists" cleavage is likely to complement (or even gradually replace) the conventional left–right divide – traditionally structured as opposing egalitarian to inegalitarian principles of distributive justice – as the main dimension of political conflict (Algan et al., 2018; De Vries, 2018). The rise of the globalization/migration cleavage can also contribute to explaining the emergence of a "multiple elite" party system in which high-education elites now vote for the "left", while high-income/high-wealth elites still vote for the "right" (Piketty, 2018).

NOTES

1. The idea that society requires some form of collective identity is a central tenet of political philosophy. According to John Stuart Mill (1960), ethnic homogeneity is vital to the existence of free and democratic institutions, as a common nationality facilitates sympathy, loyalty and cooperation among co-ethnics. Baldwin (1990, 196) maintains that demographic homogeneity facilitated the emergence of universal welfare states in the Scandinavian countries and Britain – that "social insurance, especially of a solidaristic bent, was only possible given a certain degree of homogeneity".

2. Elsner and Concannon (2020) provide the example of the Turkish community in Germany: over 3 million people in Germany are of Turkish descent but the majority of these people were born in Germany and it was their parents or grandparents who immigrated from Turkey. Their presence contributes to ethnic diversity in Germany, but they are not immigrants because they were born in Germany.
3. "Marine Le Pen reprend le credo de la 'préférence nationale', *Le Monde*, January 17, 2011, www.lemonde. fr/politique/article/2011/01/17/marine-le-pen-reprendle-credo-de-la-preference-nationale 1466519.

REFERENCES

Abou-Chadi, Tarik, and Werner Krause. 2020. "The causal effect of radical right success on mainstream parties' policy positions: A regression discontinuity approach". *British Journal of Political Science* 50(3): 829–847.

Alesina, Alberto, and Paola Giuliano. 2011. "Preferences for redistribution". In *Handbook of Social Economics*, Vol. 1. New York: Elsevier, 93–131.

Alesina, Alberto, and Edward Glaeser. 2004. *Fighting Poverty in the U.S. and Europe: A World of Difference*. Oxford: Oxford University Press.

Alesina, Alberto, and Eliana La Ferrara. 2000. "Participation in heterogeneous communities". *Quarterly Journal of Economics* 115(3): 847–904.

Alesina, Alberto, and Eliana La Ferrara. 2002. "Who trusts others?". *Journal of Public Economics* 85(2): 207–234.

Alesina, Alberto, and Eliana La Ferrara. 2005. "Preferences for redistribution in the land of opportunities". *Journal of Public Economics* 89(5–6): 897–931.

Alesina, Alberto, Reza Baqir, and William Easterly. 1999. "Public goods and ethnic divisions". *Quarterly Journal of Economics* 114(4): 1243–1284.

Alesina, Alberto, Armando Miano, and Stefanie Stantcheva. 2018a. "Immigration and redistribution". Working Paper 24733, National Bureau of Economic Research.

Alesina, Alberto, Stefanie Stantcheva, and Edoardo Teso. 2018b. "Intergenerational mobility and preferences for redistribution". *American Economic Review* 108(2): 521–554.

Alesina, Alberto, Elie Murard, and Hillel Rapoport. forthcoming. "Immigration and preferences for redistribution in Europe". *Journal of Economic Geography*.

Algan, Yann, Camille Hémet, and David D. Laitin. 2016. "The social effects of ethnic diversity at the local level: A natural experiment with exogenous residential allocation". *Journal of Political Economy* 124(3): 696–733.

Algan, Yann, Elizabeth Beasley, Daniel Cohen, and Martial Foucault. 2018. "The rise of populism and the collapse of the left-right paradigm: Lessons from the 2017 French presidential election". VOX EU, https://voxeu.org/article/rise-populism-and-collapse-left-right-paradigm.

Allport, Gordon. 1954. *The Nature of Prejudice*. Cambridge, MA: Harvard University Press.

Andersen, Jørgen Goul, and Tor Bjørklund. 1990. "Structural changes and new cleavages: The progress parties in Denmark and Norway". *Acta Sociologica* 33(3): 195–217.

Andersen, Jørgen Goul, and Tor Bjørklund. 2000. "Radical right-wing populism in Scandinavia: From tax revolt to neo-liberalism and xenophobia". In *Politics of the Extreme Right: From the Margins To the Mainstream*. London: Bloomsbury, 193–223.

Arzheimer, Kai. 2008. "Protest, neo-liberalism or anti-immigrant sentiment: What motivates the voters of the extreme right in Western Europe?" *Zeitschrift für vergleichende Politikwissenschaft* 2(2): 173–197.

Avdagic, Sabina, and Lee Savage. 2019. "Negativity bias: The impact of framing of immigration on welfare state support in Germany, Sweden and the U.K.". *British Journal of Political Science* 51(2): 624–45.

Baldwin, Peter. 1990. *The Politics of Social Solidarity: Class Bases of the European Welfare State, 1875–1975*. Cambridge: Cambridge University Press.

Banting, Keith G., and Will Kymlicka, eds. 2006. *Multiculturalism and the Welfare State: Recognition and Redistribution in Contemporary Democracies*. Oxford: Oxford University Press.

Barrett, Alan, Martin Kahanec, Klaus F. Zimmermann, and Anna Myung-Hee Kim. 2013. "Pitfalls of immigrant inclusion into the European welfare state". *International Journal of Manpower* 34(1): 39–55.

Brady, David, and Ryan Finnigan. 2014. "Does immigration undermine public support for social policy?" *American Sociological Review* 79(1): 17–42.

Brooks, Clem, and Jeff Manza. 2008. *Why Welfare States Persist: The Importance of Public Opinion in Democracies*. Chicago, IL: University of Chicago Press.

Burgoon, Brian, and Matthijs Rooduijn. 2021. "'Immigrationization' of welfare politics? Anti-immigration and welfare attitudes in context". *West European Politics* 44(2): 177–203.

Burgoon, Brian, Ferry Koster, and Marcel Van Egmond. 2012. "Support for redistribution and the paradox of immigration". *Journal of European Social Policy* 22(3): 288–304.

Cappelen, Cornelius, and Tor Midtbø. 2016. "Intra-EU labour migration and support for the Norwegian welfare state". *European Sociological Review* 32(6): 691–703.
Chevalier, Arnaud, Benjamin Elsner, Andreas Lichter, and Nico Pestel. 2018. "Immigrant voters, taxation and the size of the welfare state". IZA Discussion Papers, August.
Crepaz, Markus M.L. 2008. *Trust beyond Borders: Immigration, the Welfare State, and Identity in Modern Societies*. Ann Arbor, MI: University of Michigan Press.
Dahlberg, M., K. Edmark, and H. Lundqvist. 2012. "Ethnic diversity and preferences for redistribution". *Journal of Political Economy* 120: 41–76.
De Koster, Willem, Peter Achterberg, and Jeroen Van der Waal. 2013. "The new right and the welfare state: The electoral relevance of welfare chauvinism and welfare populism in the Netherlands". *International Political Science Review* 34(1): 3–20.
De Lange, Sarah L. 2007. "A new winning formula? The programmatic appeal of the radical right". *Party Politics* 13(4): 411–435.
De Vries, Catherine E. 2018. "The cosmopolitan-parochial divide: Changing patterns of party and electoral competition in the Netherlands and beyond". *Journal of European Public Policy* 25(11): 1541–1565.
Desmet, Klaus, Shlomo Weber, and Ignacio Ortuño-Ortín. 2009. "Linguistic diversity and redistribution". *Journal of the European Economic Association* 7(6): 1291–1318.
Dinas, Elias, Konstantinos Matakos, Dimitrios Xefteris, and Dominik Hangartner. 2019. "Waking up the golden dawn: Does exposure to the refugee crisis increase support for extreme-right parties?". *Political Analysis* 27(2): 244–254.
Dustmann, Christian, Kristine Vasiljeva, and Anna Piil Damm. 2019. "Refugee migration and electoral outcomes". *Review of Economic Studies* 86(5): 2035–2091.
Edo, Anthony, Yvonne Giesing, Jonathan Oztunc, and Panu Poutvaara. 2019. "Immigration and electoral support for the far-left and the far-right". *European Economic Review* 115: 99–143.
Eger, Maureen A. 2009. "Even in Sweden: The effect of immigration on support for welfare state spending". *European Sociological Review* 26(2): 203–217.
Eger, Maureen A., and Nate Breznau. 2017. "Immigration and the welfare state: A crossregional analysis of European welfare attitudes". *International Journal of Comparative Sociology* 58(5): 440–463.
Elsner, Benjamin, and Jeff Concannon. 2020. "Immigration and redistribution". *IZA DP No. 13676*.
Ferwerda, Jeremy. 2020. "Immigration, voting rights, and redistribution: Evidence from local governments in Europe". *Journal of Politics* 83(1): 321–39.
Finseraas, H. 2008. "Immigration and preferences for redistribution: An empirical analysis of European survey data". *Comparative European Politics* 6: 407–431.
Finseraas, Henning. 2012. "Anti-immigration attitudes, support for redistribution and party choice in Europe". In *Changing Social Equality: The Nordic Welfare Model in the 21st Century*. Bristol: Policy Press, 103–32.
Fong, Christina M. 2007. "Evidence from an experiment on charity to welfare recipients: Reciprocity, altruism and the empathic responsiveness hypothesis". *The Economic Journal* 117(522): 1008–1024.
Forbes, Hugh Donald. 1997. *Ethnic Conflict: Commerce, Culture, and the Contact Hypothesis*. New Haven, CT: Yale University Press.
Ford, Robert. 2016. "Who should we help? An experimental test of discrimination in the British welfare state". *Political Studies* 64(3): 630–650.
Freeman, Gary P. 1986. "Migration and the political economy of the welfare state". *Annals of the American Academy of Political and Social Science* 485(1): 51–63.
Gerdes, Christer. 2011. "The impact of immigration on the size of government: Empirical evidence from Danish municipalities". *Scandinavian Journal of Economics* 113(1): 74–92.
Gilens, Martin. 1995. "Racial attitudes and opposition to welfare". *Journal of Politics* 57(4): 994–1014.
Goldschmidt, Tina, and Jens Rydgren. 2018. "Social distance, immigrant integration, and welfare chauvinism in Sweden". Discussion Papers, Research Unit: Migration, Integration, Transnationalization.
Gorodzeisky, Anastasia, and Moshe Semyonov. 2009. "Terms of exclusion: Public views towards admission and allocation of rights to immigrants in European countries". *Ethnic and Racial Studies* 32(3): 401–423.
Hainmueller, Jens, and Michael J. Hiscox. 2007. "Educated preferences: Explaining attitudes toward immigration in Europe". *International Organization* 61(2): 399–442.
Halla, Martin, Alexander F. Wagner, and Josef Zweimüller. 2017. "Immigration and voting for the far right". *Journal of the European Economic Association* 15(6): 1341–1385.
Hangartner, Dominik, Elias Dinas, Moritz Marbach, Konstantinos Matakos, and Dimitrios Xefteris. 2019. "Does exposure to the refugee crisis make natives more hostile?" *American Political Science Review* 113(2): 442–455.
Harell, Allison, Stuart Soroka, and Shanto Iyengar. 2016. "Race, prejudice and attitudes toward redistribution: A comparative experimental approach". *European Journal of Political Research* 55(4): 723–744.
Hjorth, Frederik. 2016. "Who benefits? Welfare chauvinism and national stereotypes". *European Union Politics* 17(1): 3–24.

Huber, Evelyne, and John D. Stephens. 2010. *Development and Crisis of the Welfare State: Parties and Policies in Global Markets*. Chicago, IL: University of Chicago Press.

Ignazi, Piero. 2003. *Extreme Right Parties in Western Europe*. Oxford: Oxford University Press.

Ivarsflaten, Elisabeth. 2005. "The vulnerable populist right parties: No economic realignment fuelling their electoral success". *European Journal of Political Research* 44(3): 465–492.

Jofre-Monseny, Jordi, Pilar Sorribas-Navarro, and Javier Vázquez-Grenno. 2016. "Immigration and local spending in social services: Evidence from a massive immigration wave". *International Tax and Public Finance* 23(6): 1004–1029.

Koning, Edward A. 2017. "Selecting, disentitling, or investing? Exploring party and voter responses to immigrant welfare dependence in 15 West European welfare states". *Comparative European Politics* 15(4): 628–660.

Koning, Edward A. 2019. *Immigration and the Politics of Welfare Exclusion*. Toronto: University of Toronto Press.

Koopmans, Ruud. 2010. "Trade-offs between equality and difference: Immigrant integration, multiculturalism and the welfare state in cross-national perspective". *Journal of Ethnic and Migration Studies* 36(1): 1–26.

Kumlin, Staffan, and Bo Rothstein. 2010. "Questioning the new liberal dilemma: Immigrants, social networks, and institutional fairness". *Comparative Politics* 43(1): 63–80.

Kwon, Ronald, and Michaela Curran. 2016. "Immigration and support for redistributive social policy: Does multiculturalism matter?" *International Journal of Comparative Sociology* 57(6): 375–400.

Lee, Woojin, John Roemer, and Karine Van der Straeten. 2006. "Racism, xenophobia, and redistribution". *Journal of the European Economic Association* 4(2–3): 446–454.

Luttmer, Erzo. 2001. "Group loyalty and the taste for redistribution". *Journal of Political Economy* 109: 500–528.

Ma, Ambrose, and Iris Chi. 2005. "Utilization and accessibility of social services for Chinese Canadians". *International Social Work* 48(2): 148–160.

Magni-Berton, Raul. 2014. "Immigration, redistribution, and universal suffrage". *Public Choice* 160(3–4): 391–409.

Mayda, Anna Maria, Giovanni Peri, and Walter Steingress. forthcoming. "The political impact of immigration: Evidence from the United States". *American Economic Journal: Applied Economics*.

Mewes, Jan, and Steffen Mau. 2013. "Globalization, socio-economic status and welfare chauvinism: European perspectives on attitudes toward the exclusion of immigrants". *International Journal of Comparative Sociology* 54(3): 228–245.

Mill, John Stuart. 1960. *On Liberty, Representative Government, the Subjection of Women; Three Essays*. Oxford: Oxford University Press.

Minkenberg, Michael. 2001. "The radical right in public office: Agenda-setting and policy effects". *West European Politics* 24(4): 1–21.

Moriconi, Simone, Giovanni Peri, and Riccardo Turati. 2018. "Skill of the immigrants and vote of the natives: Immigration and nationalism in European elections 2007–2016". Technical Report, National Bureau of Economic Research.

Mudde, Cas. 2013. "Three decades of populist radical right parties in Western Europe: So what?" *European Journal of Political Research* 52(1): 1–19.

Mudde, Cas. 2015. "Populist radical right parties in Europe today". In *Transformations of Populism in Europe and the Americas: History and Recent Trends*. London: Bloomsbury, 295–305.

Murard, Elie. 2017. "Less welfare or fewer foreigners? Immigrant inflows and public opinion towards redistribution and migration". Technical Report IZA DP No. 10805.

Nannestad, Peter. 2007. "Immigration and welfare states: A survey of 15 years of research". *European Journal of Political Economy* 23(2): 512–532.

Naumann, Elias, and Lukas F. Stoetzer. 2018. "Immigration and support for redistribution: Survey experiments in three European countries". *West European Politics* 41(1): 80–101.

Pettigrew, Thomas F. 1998. "Reactions toward the new minorities of Western Europe". *Annual Review of Sociology* 24(1): 77–103.

Pierson, Paul. 1994. *Dismantling the Welfare State? Reagan, Thatcher and the Politics of Retrenchment*. Cambridge: Cambridge University Press.

Piketty, Thomas. 2018. "Brahmin left vs merchant right: Rising inequality and the changing structure of political conflict". *WID*, World Working Paper 7.

Putnam, Robert D. 2007. "*E pluribus unum*: Diversity and community in the twenty-first century: The 2006 Johan Skytte Prize Lecture". *Scandinavian Political Studies* 30(2): 137–174.

Razin, Assaf, Efraim Sadka, and Phillip Swagel. 2002. "Tax burden and migration: A political economy theory and evidence". *Journal of Public Economics* 85: 167–190.

Razin, Assaf, Efraim Sadka, and Benjarong Suwankiri. 2011. *Migration and the Welfare State: Political-Economy Policy Formation*. Cambridge, MA: MIT Press.

Reeskens, Tim, and Wim Van Oorschot. 2012. "Disentangling the 'new liberal dilemma': On the relation between general welfare redistribution preferences and welfare chauvinism". *International Journal of Comparative Sociology* 53(2): 120–139.

Runst, Petrik. 2018. "Does immigration affect demand for redistribution? An experimental design". *German Economic Review* 19(4): 383–400.

Sabates-Wheeler, Rachel, and Rayah Feldman. 2011. *Migration and Social Protection: Claiming Social Rights beyond Borders*. New York: Springer.

Sainsbury, Diane. 2012. *Welfare States and Immigrant Rights: The Politics of Inclusion and Exclusion*. Oxford: Oxford University Press.

Scheve, Kenneth F., and Matthew J. Slaughter. 2001. "Labor market competition and individual preferences over immigration policy". *Review of Economics and Statistics* 83: 133–145.

Schmidt, Alexander W., and Dennis C. Spies. 2014. "Do parties 'playing the race card' undermine natives' support for redistribution? Evidence from Europe". *Comparative Political Studies* 47(4): 519–549.

Schmidt-Catran, Alexander W., and Dennis C. Spies. 2016. "Immigration and welfare support in Germany". *American Sociological Review* 81(2): 242–261.

Senik, C., H. Stichnoth, and K. Van der Straeten. 2009. "Immigration and natives? Attitudes towards the welfare state: Evidence from the European Social Survey". *Social Indicators Research* 91: 345–370.

Simich, Laura, Morton Beiser, Miriam Stewart, and Edward Mwakarimba. 2005. "Providing social support for immigrants and refugees in Canada: Challenges and directions". *Journal of Immigrant and Minority Health* 7(4): 259–268.

Soroka, Stuart, Keith Banting, and Richard Johnston. 2006. "Immigration and redistribution in a global era". In *Globalization and Egalitarian Redistribution*. Berlin: De Gruyter, 261–288.

Speciale, Biagio. 2012. "Does immigration affect public education expenditures? Quasiexperimental evidence". *Journal of Public Economics* 96(9–10): 773–783.

Stichnoth, Holger. 2012. "Does immigration weaken natives' support for the unemployed? Evidence from Germany". *Public Choice* 151(3–4): 631–654.

Stichnoth, Holger, and Karine Van der Straeten. 2013. "Ethnic diversity, public spending, and individual support for the welfare state: A review of the empirical literature". *Journal of Economic Surveys* 27(2): 364–389.

Svallfors, Stefan. 2006. *The Moral Economy of Class: Class and Attitudes in Comparative Perspective*. Stanford, CA: Stanford University Press.

Tanaka, Ryuichi, Lidia Farre, and Francesc Ortega. 2018. "Immigration, assimilation, and the future of public education". *European Journal of Political Economy* 52: 141–165.

Van der Waal, Jeroen, Peter Achterberg, Dick Houtman, Willem De Koster, and Katerina Manevska. 2010. "'Some are more equal than others': Economic egalitarianism and welfare chauvinism in the Netherlands". *Journal of European Social Policy* 20(4): 350–363.

Van Oorschot, Wim. 2006. "Making the difference in social Europe: Deservingness perceptions among citizens of European welfare states". *Journal of European Social Policy* 16(1): 23–42.

Van Spanje, Joost. 2010. "Contagious parties: Anti-immigration parties and their impact on other parties? Immigration stances in contemporary Western Europe". *Party Politics* 16(5): 563–586.

Wilkinson, Mick, Gary Craig, E. Carmel, A. Cerami, and T. Papadopoulos. 2012. "Wilful negligence: Migration policy, migrants' work and the absence of social protection in the U.K.". In *Migration and Welfare in the New Europe: Social Protection and the Challenges of Integration*. Bristol: Policy Press, 177–98.

7. When does immigration shape support for a universal basic income? The role of education and employment status
Anthony Kevins

For Milton Friedman, open borders and universal welfare programmes were inherently incompatible. In an attempt to explain the American public's turn against liberal immigration policies, for example, Friedman argued that "[i]t is one thing to have free immigration to jobs", but "another thing to have free immigration to welfare". The tension was clear to him, as:

> you cannot have both. If you have a welfare state, if you have a state in which every resident is promised a certain minimal level of income, or a minimum level of subsistence, regardless of whether he works or not, produces it or not. Well then it really is an impossible thing. (Friedman 1977)

In Friedman's view, then, opposition to mass immigration was a logical consequence of welfare state expansion – and immigration should pose a particularly large challenge to welfare state support wherever social programmes offer benefit access to natives and newcomers alike. Whether or not more generous welfare states are actually more likely to suffer from these tensions, however, is much less clear (see, for example, Brandt and Svendsen 2019; Fenwick 2019; Römer 2017) – and research suggests that certain programmes should be more susceptible to immigration effects than others (e.g. Muñoz and Pardos-Prado 2019; Soroka et al. 2016).

To explore these dynamics, this chapter looks at public opinion toward one social policy innovation that has been garnering increased attention in recent years: a universal basic income (UBI) (see Dermont and Weisstanner 2020; Gentilini et al. 2020). Though it is rare for social policy programmes to take an approach to granting benefit access that is as open as that described by Friedman (see Kevins and van Kersbergen 2018; Simola and Wrede 2020), UBI schemes offer the closest example of what he appears to have had in mind. At the same time, studying attitudes toward the introduction of such a programme can give us a good sense of how the social solidarity that undergirds the welfare state may be shaped by immigration (see, for example, Bay and Pedersen 2006).

In order to unpack this relationship, the chapter begins by laying out the theoretical and empirical reasons we might expect immigration to have different effects on different types of welfare programmes. It then sketches an overview of the literature related to two other likely sources of variation: the broader context, discussing immigration-related policies, the size and distribution of the immigrant population, and economic factors; and individual-level characteristics, homing in on labour market vulnerability and anti-immigrant attitudes. The second half of the chapter then empirically explores how education levels, employment status, and the size of the immigrant population might interact to shape support for UBI. This analysis is carried out using survey data from 21 countries that participated in the 2016 wave of the European Social Survey.

The results, based on hierarchical analysis, indicate that while larger immigrant populations may decrease support for implementing a UBI scheme, we only see clear evidence of such an effect among individuals with lower education levels. Furthermore, the scope of these effects varies based on employment status: while immigration is associated with reduced support for UBI among a substantial proportion of low-educated workers in standard employment, similar effects are concentrated among atypically employed or unemployed individuals with especially low levels of education. All in all, the findings of this investigation suggest that larger immigrant populations may weaken support for a UBI scheme, but only among a relatively small subset of the population.

PUBLIC OPINION, IMMIGRATION, AND THE WELFARE STATE

Disaggregating the Welfare State

A wide array of studies have examined the broad impact that immigration might have on support for the welfare state, coming to mixed results (c.f. Auspurg et al. 2019; Crepaz 2008; Dahlberg et al. 2012; Schmidt-Catran and Spies 2016; Steele 2016). Yet as the literature on welfare chauvinism has highlighted (e.g. Cappelen and Peters 2018b; Schumacher and van Kersbergen 2016), many people maintain their support for social programmes in the face of immigration – on the condition that immigrant access to those programmes is restricted. Real and perceived immigrant use patterns have thus been a central component of this debate (e.g. Bratsberg et al. 2014; Larsen 2011), and evidence suggests that citizens intrinsically take these concerns into account as well (see Albrekt Larsen 2020).

Given that access patterns will almost always vary across different sorts of welfare state programmes, however, there are strong *a priori* reasons to expect that some programmes will be more susceptible than others to immigration-related attitudinal effects. Indeed, it seems far more probable that any such variation will exist within and across countries, based on *welfare programme* types, rather than simply across *welfare state* types, based on the so-called "worlds of welfare" (see van Kersbergen and Vis 2015). A three-fold distinction is likely to matter here.

First, targeted spending and means-tested programmes appear to be especially prone to immigration-related effects (e.g. Muñoz and Pardos-Prado 2019). Unemployment benefits, for example, present a series of challenges – in particular when they take the form of social assistance, funded by general taxation (as opposed to unemployment insurance, funded by insurance contributions): worries about moral hazard, misuse, and fraud, with undeserving claimants seeking out benefits that they do not truly need, are a recurring theme (see, for example, Careja et al. 2016; Soroka et al. 2016). Arguably as a direct consequence of these anxieties, perceptions of recipient deservingness play a central role in shaping who does and does not deserve access to these benefits. Yet immigrants tend to be rather uniformly treated as an undeserving group, assessed more harshly than their native-born equivalents (see Nielsen et al. 2020; Van Oorschot 2006). Experimental

The role of education and employment status   139

evidence from Canada, the United Kingdom, and the United States, for example, suggests that immigrant status – even more than ethnicity – is likely to shape beliefs about who should and should not have access to welfare benefits (Soroka et al. 2017). Indeed, related work suggests that a recipient's place of birth is among the most important factors shaping public perceptions of deservingness (Kootstra 2016; Reeskens and van der Meer 2019).

Second, although similar dynamics may shape public opinion on whether or not immigrants deserve access to social insurance (e.g. Thomann and Rapp 2018), the broader impact of immigration on attitudes toward these programmes is less clear (see Finseraas et al. 2017). In general, however, one would expect that immigration's impact on support for contributory, insurance-based programmes should depend on benefit access rules: given the role of contribution requirements in shaping access to these benefits, *de facto* restrictions on access may serve to restrict immigrant take-up even where *de jure* restrictions are absent (see Koning 2020; Simola and Wrede 2020). The underlying insurance logic – with benefits "earned" through contributions – may thus help these programmes sidestep many of the immigration-related concerns that are raised vis-à-vis other sorts of benefits (e.g. Burkhardt and Mau 2011).

Third, and finally, the effect of immigration on support for universal benefits is likely to fall between those of insurance-based programmes and targeted ones (c.f. Muñoz and Pardos-Prado 2019). Characterized by an indiscriminate access to benefits for all citizens or residents (see, for example, Carey and Crammond 2017), universalism helps minimize the concerns around deservingness and fraud, for example, that lend themselves well to anti-immigrant sentiment; yet generous universal schemes also risk reinforcing a focus on in-group/out-group boundaries, given that letting someone into the universal community entails granting them access to "community perks" (Kevins and van Kersbergen 2018). The spread of welfare chauvinism across Scandinavia would thus appear relatively unsurprising (e.g. Frederiksen 2018). Furthermore, and importantly for the study presented here, similar dynamics have been shown to impact attitudes toward *proposed* universal programmes, including UBI – with support for the proposition undercut by discourses that foreground immigrant access (Bay and Pedersen 2006).

On the one hand, then, it is difficult to abstract away from the exact contours of welfare state programmes: within a given country, for example, immigration could simultaneously (1) undermine support for targeted benefits that have a high take-up by immigrants, (2) lead to a push for increased welfare chauvinism vis-à-vis universal programmes, and (3) have no impact on attitudes toward insurance benefits that *de facto* exclude (recent) immigrants. On the other hand, however, the sum total of these shifts may undercut broad support for the welfare state, with (in the most likely best-case scenario) foreign-born recipients being the sole targets of the native-born public's ire. What is more, in situations where immigrant use patterns are harder to control (as with, perhaps most notably, intra-European Union migration[1]), welfare chauvinism may eventually be replaced by reduced support for the welfare state (Cappelen and Peters 2018a).

The Broader Context

As the above section has made clear, the specific constellation of welfare programmes should be central to shaping how immigration impacts support for the welfare state. Yet these contextual effects of course go well beyond the social policy landscape. I summarize just a few of the most relevant and commonly cited factors here, drawing out research and debates related to immigration policies, the size and distribution of immigrant populations, and the broader economic context.

Turning first to what is arguably the most obvious of these factors, immigration- and integration-related policies should play a key role in explaining the effects of migration on social policy preferences. At the most general level, rules around naturalization often shape when foreign-born individuals are granted access to different social programmes – with additional variation across different migrant groups (see Sainsbury 2006 for a discussion). Yet immigration policies are liable to matter in other ways, too: immigrant selection processes will shape factors – such as immigrant skill profiles, recourse to government transfers, and intercultural differences – that likely have knock-on effects on welfare state attitudes (Gorodzeisky 2013; Pardos-Prado 2020; Spies and Schmidt-Catran 2016); while the mix of different types of migrants (e.g. economic migrants, asylum seekers) will affect perceptions of the deservingness and need of would-be benefit claimants (Nielsen et al. 2020). Multiculturalism policies have similarly attracted much attention. For some, combining generous welfare states with a multiculturalist approach reinforces the divide between native- and foreign-born populations, and hence undercuts the social solidarity and trust that make welfare states viable (e.g. Koopmans 2010); yet other work variously suggests either the opposite relationship, with multiculturalism having a positive impact (e.g. Crepaz 2007; Kymlicka 2015), or no relationship whatsoever (e.g. Hooghe et al. 2007; Kesler and Bloemraad 2010).

Moving beyond the policy context, the size and territorial distribution of migrant populations and the interactions (or lack thereof) of foreign- and native-born individuals are another recurring theme in the literature. At the most fine-grained level, research on daily interactions has built on the broader "contact" literature focused on anti-immigrant sentiment (e.g. Allport 1954; Kotzur et al. 2019): work in this vein looking at social policy preferences suggests, for instance, that intergroup contact may decrease levels of welfare chauvinism (Cappelen and Peters 2018b), and living in a more diverse neighbourhood has been tied to stronger pro-welfare state attitudes (Steele and Perkins 2018). Research focused on immigrant population sizes, by contrast, typically finds that immigration has a negative impact on social policy preferences, with immigrant influxes and high levels of migrant stock weakening welfare state support and/or increasing levels of welfare chauvinism (e.g. Dahlberg et al. 2012; Meer and Reeskens 2021; Stichnoth 2012). To take but one example, cross-national research from Eger and Breznau (2017), examining public opinion across Europe, suggests that regional migrant stock levels shape support for both redistribution and a more comprehensive welfare state.

Finally, the broader economic context has attracted considerable attention as well. This is of course unsurprising in light of widespread fears that immigrants will not only undercut the wages of native-born workers and "steal" their jobs, but also reduce the available social support by "using up" state resources (Taylor-Gooby et al. 2019). These worries appear to be reflected in social policy preferences in predictable ways. Research looking at public opinion in Europe, for instance, has found that immigration is especially likely to have a negative impact on welfare state attitudes in countries with higher rates of unemployment and benefit take-up among immigrants (Burgoon 2014). Insofar as general economic circumstances shape perceptions of immigration's effect on the labour market, of broader resource availability, and of immigrants' benefit use patterns, they are likely to also impact how immigration affects social policy preferences. The exact nature of these effects are nevertheless subject to considerable debate: deteriorating economic circumstances could push potential native-born recipients toward favouring stronger welfare states to compensate for increased risk; or they could push potential native-born recipients toward favouring a dualistic approach to welfare protection – with extra protection for natives and less protection for immigrants (c.f. Brady and Finnigan 2014; Finseraas et al. 2017; Valentova and Callens 2018).

Individual-Level Variation

In exploring how immigration might impact social policy preferences, I have thus far concentrated exclusively on contextual-level factors – yet immigration's effect on these attitudes will clearly vary systematically across individuals as well. This section lays out a few themes in the research on this topic, focusing on unpacking the potential overlap between economic vulnerability, anti-immigrant sentiment, and social policy preferences.

It has been widely suggested that immigration is especially likely to shape the welfare state attitudes of the economically vulnerable, with self-interest playing an important role (e.g. Degen et al. 2019). Evidence from Gerber et al. (2017), to highlight but one study in this vein, suggests that lower-skilled individuals tend to be more concerned that immigration will further reduce their economic standing and jeopardize their access to the welfare state. Yet for reasons alluded to above, it could also be that immigration – to the extent that it renders the vulnerable even more likely to rely on state benefits – has the exact opposite effect, pushing these individuals to be even more supportive of welfare programmes (e.g. Finseraas 2008). Empirical work provides some evidence in support of this position as well: working in an occupation with higher levels of exposure to competition from immigrants, for instance, has been tied to increased support for redistribution – as these workers seek compensation for their weakened labour market position (Burgoon et al. 2012).

The exact nature of these dynamics is muddled, however, by the fact that an individual's broader take on immigration should clearly affect the dynamics highlighted here. A study of American public opinion by Garand et al. (2017), for example, found that welfare state attitudes were profoundly shaped by broader attitudes toward immigration; and while Senik et al. (2009) uncovered only weak evidence of an overall relationship between immigration and social policy preferences in Europe, their results suggested that respondents who either disliked immigrants or expressed concerns about immigration's economic consequences were more likely to be critical of the welfare state. Similarly, several studies focused on attitudes in Europe have concluded that the saliency of in-group/out-group (native-/foreign-born) boundaries moderates the relationship between immigration and the welfare state (e.g. Breznau and Eger 2016; Larsen 2011). As a consequence, various individual-level factors that have been tied to anti-immigrant sentiment – ranging from relative group deprivation to labour market vulnerability itself (see Kevins and Lightman 2020; Meuleman et al. 2020) – are liable to shape how immigration impacts social policy preferences.

At this point, clearly, the relationship between the factors discussed in this chapter becomes highly complicated – with multiple potential linkages between, on the one hand, economic vulnerability and anti-immigrant sentiment and, on the other, social policy design, immigration patterns, and economic context. Offering perhaps the clearest illustration of this complexity, Burgoon and Rooduijn (2021) found that the impact anti-immigrant attitudes have on support for redistribution in Europe cannot be properly understood unless we also take into account levels of migrant stock, welfare state generosity, and immigrant use of social programmes. And in the closest study to this one, Parolin and Siöland (2020) found that welfare chauvinism decreases support for UBI in European countries with higher levels of social expenditure; while similar research from Stadelmann-Steffen and Dermont (2020) concluded that Finns and Swedes react more favourably to generous UBI schemes that explicitly restrict access for non-nationals (for a related discussion on the relevance of cultural divides on these attitudes, see Dermont and Weisstanner 2020). The remainder of the chapter builds directly on these studies. And while it cannot possibly, of course, aim to parse out all of the dynamics highlighted above, I home in on the extent to which labour market vulnerability – measured in terms of education levels and employment status – might shape how immigration affects UBI preferences.

LABOUR MARKET VULNERABILITY, IMMIGRATION, AND SUPPORT FOR A UNIVERSAL BASIC INCOME

Data

In carrying out this study, I rely primarily on data from the 2016 wave of the European Social Survey (ESS 2016). Given the focus of the analysis, the sample excludes respondents who (1) were not on the labour market (whether employed or unemployed) at the time of the survey or (2) were themselves born abroad. After accounting for missing data at the individual and national levels, the final sample includes 20,403 respondents from 21 European countries (see Table 7A.1 for details).

I focus on the 2016 round of the ESS since it incorporated a special module on welfare attitudes – including a question on support for the introduction of a UBI scheme. As Bay and Pedersen (2006) have argued, attitudes toward UBI offer a good sense of social solidarity via the welfare state – and they also have the benefit of encapsulating the potential trade-off highlighted by Friedman. The wording for this item integrated a brief overview of what a basic income programme would entail, with the exact text reading as follows:

> Some countries are currently talking about introducing a basic income scheme. In a moment I will ask you to tell me whether you are against or in favour of this scheme. First, I will give you some more details. The highlighted box at the top of this card shows the main features of the scheme. A basic income scheme includes all of the following:
>
> - The government pays everyone a monthly income to cover essential living costs.
> - It replaces many other social benefits.
> - The purpose is to guarantee everyone a minimum standard of living.

- Everyone receives the same amount regardless of whether or not they are working.
- People also keep the money they earn from work or other sources.
- This scheme is paid for by taxes.

Respondents were then asked whether they would "be against or in favour of having this scheme" in their country, with response options ranging from "Strongly against" (1) to "Strongly in favour" (4). The mean (weighted) response was 2.46 on this four-point scale, with a standard deviation of 0.80.

Reflecting the discussion above, the regression analysis then explores the potential interactive effect of labour market vulnerability – assessed by looking at education and employment status – and migrant stock on attitudes toward UBI. First, education is measured using a variable that captures the total number of years spent in (full-time equivalency) education – with a weighted mean of 13.6 years and a standard deviation of 3.8. Second, labour market positions are assessed using a three-category measure of employment status, divided into: "standard employment" (employees with full-time, open-ended contracts – 51.7 per cent of the sample), "non-standard employment" (individuals whose work patterns are marked by one or more of the following: part-time employment; solo self-employment (i.e. self-employed with no employees); fixed-term employment; and/or contract-less work – 40.9 per cent of the sample); and the "unemployed" (respondents who described themselves as having been unemployed in the week prior to the survey – 7.4 per cent of the sample). Finally, immigrant population size is measured at the national level (to maximize the number of countries in the analysis) using Organisation for Economic Co-operation and Development (OECD) data on the percentage of the population that was born abroad (OECD 2016) – with a mean of 11.9 per cent and a standard deviation of 4.6.

Figure 7.1 presents a first cut at unpacking how education, labour market position, and immigration levels might interact to shape attitudes on UBI. The panels illustrate the percentage of migrant stock versus the (weighted) mean stance on introducing a basic income scheme, alongside a line of best fit. The within-country samples are divided up according to respondents' labour market positions and education levels – with the education split separating respondents who have completed less than the mean number of years in education in their country ("Low Education") from those who have completed the mean number of years in education or more ("High Education").

These preliminary analyses suggest that larger immigrant populations are broadly associated with lower levels of support for introducing a UBI scheme. This dynamic is present most notably among respondents who have lower levels of education, for whom the bivariate relationship consistently attains statistical significance regardless of employment status. The relationship is less predominant among higher-educated individuals: we only see a clear, statistically significant relationship for respondents in standard employment.

In the full analysis below, I also incorporate a series of controls that reflect past work on the topic (e.g. Parolin and Siöland 2020; Roosma and Van Oorschot 2020; Schwander and Vlandas 2020; Shin et al. 2021; Vlandas 2021. These are: a binary gender variable (with females coded as (1); age and its square (to account for a potential non-linear

144   *Handbook on migration and welfare*

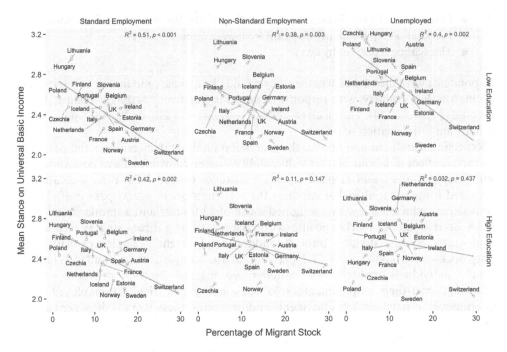

Note: Data from ESS (2016) and OECD (2016). Respondents split based on whether they have completed less than ("low education") or at least ("high education") the weighted mean number of years in education in a given country. The figure incorporates post-stratification survey weights.

Figure 7.1   Mean stance on universal basic income, by employment status, education, and migrant stock

effect); household income decile, with decile brackets adjusted to reflect country-level income distributions; the number of people regularly living in a given household (to complement the household income measure); marital/civil partnership status; whether the respondent belongs to a minority ethnic group; trade union membership; gross domestic product (GDP) per capita at current prices; the national unemployment rate; and social expenditure as a percentage of GDP. Note that all national-level data are taken for the closest year (2015 or 2016) available from the OECD (2020a, 2020b) or Eurostat (2020). For a descriptive overview of each of the variables included in the analysis, see Table 7A.2.

Analysis

The empirical investigation is based on a set of models using maximum likelihood estimation, with population and post-stratification weights incorporated into the analysis. The full regression results are included in Table 7A.3, with four models presenting: (1) an individual-level only regression, excluding the national-level variables; (2) the standard full model; (3) the standard full model with cluster robust standard errors; and (4) the standard full model with random slopes for education and employment status. The results are consistent across the various full-model specifications, despite some small shifts in effect sizes. I also confirm that the findings are robust to converting the dependent variable into a binary "against versus in favour" measure and running logistic regressions instead. Since the core results remain unchanged, I present the findings below using the linear models for ease of interpretation.

As the main focus here is on interactive effects, results are illustrated using a series of plots that present predicted values and marginal effects.[2] Note that the predicted value plots incorporate 83.5 per cent confidence intervals, allowing readers to quickly visualize when and where values are statistically distinguishable at the $p < 0.05$ confidence level – with a lack of overlapping intervals indicating significant differences (see Bolsen and Thornton 2014). The marginal effect plots, in turn, incorporate 95 per cent confidence intervals, and thus also illustrate statistically significant differences at the $p < 0.05$ level. In both cases, extreme values of the explanatory variables – those in the lowest and highest five percentiles – are excluded from the illustrations so as to focus our attention on representative effects.

To begin, Figure 7.2 presents the results of the individual-level only regression analysis (i.e. before accounting for variation in migrant population sizes). Predicted values are illustrated in the left-hand panel (with education on the x-axis) while the marginal effect of education is illustrated in the right-hand panel (with employment status on the x-axis). In this first stage of the investigation, we see evidence of a division between employed persons – be they in standard or non-standard employment – and unemployed persons. Findings thus highlight that the unemployed often express a greater openness to UBI programmes than their employed counterparts. Yet they also suggest that this difference is only present among respondents with lower levels of education (specifically, those with fewer than the median number of years in education – i.e. 12 and under); at higher levels of education, the predicted attitudes of the employed and unemployed become statistically indistinguishable. Notably, results suggest that this shift is due to the positive effect education has on the employed: lower educated persons in standard or non-standard employment are less likely than their more educated counterparts to be in favour of a UBI programme, all else being equal. Among the unemployed, by contrast, education does not appear to impact stances before national-level variation is taken into account.

Figure 7.3 presents the results after cross-country differences in the (relative) immigrant population sizes are incorporated into the analysis. The top panels illustrate predicted responses to the question based on the size of the migrant population (on the x-axes), education (divided across three panels at illustrative low (10th percentile), average (50th percentile), and high (90th percentile) values), and employment status (plotted with separate lines on each panel). The bottom panels, in turn, show the marginal effect of the percentage of migrant stock, broken down by education (on the x-axes) and employment status (each illustrated separately across the three panels).

Turning first to the top set of panels, we see that the major distinction is once again between the unemployed and those in employment (be it standard or non-standard), but that this effect is only discernible at lower levels of education: when we look at average- or highly educated individuals, employment status is not associated with a meaningful difference. At the same time, the results also suggest that larger immigrant populations are

146 *Handbook on migration and welfare*

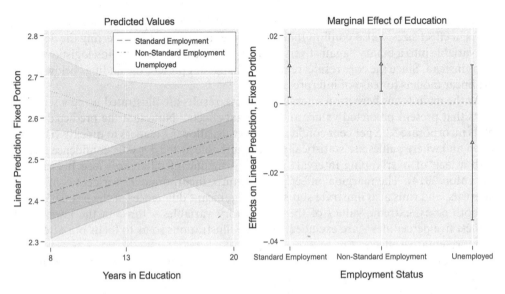

Note: Plots based on "individual-level only regression" (see Table 7A.3). In the predicted values plot, the x-axis ticks mark the 5th, 50th, and 95th percentile values of years in education.

Figure 7.2   Effects of employment status and education on stance toward universal basic income

correlated with weaker support for introducing UBI – though once again only among individuals with below-average levels of education.

The bottom panels confirm this effect of migrant stock and allow us to better evaluate the scope of its effect. Among those in standard employment, larger immigrant population sizes are associated with a statistically significant ($p < 0.05$) reduction in support for UBI among individuals with 13 years of education or less; this is the median level of education in the sample and amounts to the (lower) 36 per cent of respondents in standard employment. This effect is less prevalent among those in more precarious labour market positions: for the unemployed, we see a similar decrease only among those with 11 years or less of education (25 per cent of the unemployed); while for those in non-standard employment, the relationship is only visible among those with eight years or less of education (5 per cent of those in non-standard employment). The size of these effects varies modestly, but is largest among the unemployed: for an individual at the 10th percentile of educational values (nine years), moving across the interquartile range of migrant stock (from 8 to 15 per cent of a country's population) would be associated with a reduction of 0.17 on the response scale if they were in standard employment, 0.09 if they were in non-standard employment, and 0.23 if they were unemployed. (Recall that possible responses to the question ranged from 1 to 4, with a mean of 2.46 and a standard deviation of 0.80.) I draw out the significance of these findings in the final section of the chapter.

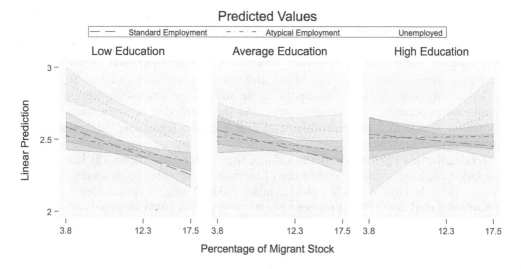

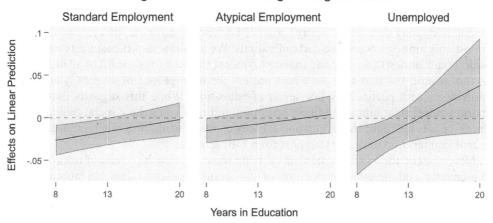

Note: Plots based on "standard full regression" (see Table 7A.3). Predicted values plots are illustrated at three illustrative values of education: low (9 years, the 10th percentile value); average (13 years, the 50th percentile value); and high (16 years, the 90th percentile value). The x-axis ticks mark the 5th, 50th, and 95th percentile values of percentage of migrant stock (in the top panels) or years in education (in the bottom panels).

Figure 7.3 *Effects of employment status, education, and migrant stock on stance toward universal basic income*

DISCUSSION AND CONCLUSION

This chapter set out to examine Milton Friedman's argument that welfare states are inherently incompatible with free immigration. It began by highlighting that empirical work on this topic is divided (c.f. Brandt and Svendsen 2019; Fenwick 2019; Römer 2017) and that there are good reasons to expect that any effects immigration might have on social policy preferences should be far from uniform (e.g. Muñoz and Pardos-Prado 2019; Soroka et al. 2016). The chapter then discussed some of the main potential sources of heterogeneity debated in the literature: variation across different sorts of welfare programmes (means-tested, insurance-based, and universal benefits); variation tied to the wider context (immigration-related policies, the size and geographic distribution of the immigrant population, and the economy); and the interaction between these broader contextual factors and key individual-level characteristics (economic vulnerability and anti-immigrant sentiment).

To shed further light on Friedman's claim, the chapter then empirically investigated the factors shaping attitudes toward one of the rare social policy programmes that may in fact reflect the kind of benefit he had in mind: a UBI. Using survey data from a special module included in the 2016 European Social Survey (ESS 2016), this analysis explored how an individual's education and labour market status might interact with immigration levels to shape attitudes toward the introduction of a UBI scheme. Crucially, the focus on this particular programme allowed us to investigate how labour market vulnerability and immigration may, taken together, shape the social solidarity that undergirds the welfare state (see, for example, Bay and Pedersen 2006).

The results of this analysis provide some support for the claim that larger immigrant populations may decrease support for a UBI scheme – however, this relationship was found only among lower-educated individuals. We also saw that these effects were most widespread among those in standard employment (affecting over a third of all individuals in this group), but that they were also present for unemployed or atypically employed individuals with particularly low levels of education. While this suggests that labour market vulnerability may condition how immigration shapes these social policy preferences, results highlight that education is a key component shaping whether and to what extent immigration undercuts support for a UBI scheme.

Nevertheless, the exact mechanisms driving these relationships remain unexplored in this chapter, and the assessed measures of immigrant population sizes and labour market vulnerability are relatively crude (see, for example, Gorodzeisky and Semyonov 2020; Marx and Picot 2020). At the same time, the attitudinal effects among unemployed persons raise particular questions. Are these results driven, for example, by an assumption among the unemployed that a UBI scheme will go against their interests by weakening existing benefits? Further work exploring these dynamics in greater detail would therefore be especially valuable.

NOTES

1. Within the European Union, non-discrimination rules have pushed member states to offer equal access to social security regimes for all EU citizens residing in a given country, regardless of nationality – though in practice member states nevertheless have room for manoeuvre (see Simola and Wrede 2020).
2. The figures in the chapter are drawn with the help of several packages (Bischof 2017; Kassambara 2020; Slowikowski 2019; Wickham 2016; Wickham et al. 2019).

REFERENCES

Albrekt Larsen, Christian. 2020. "The Institutional Logic of Giving Migrants Access to Social Benefits and Services". *Journal of European Social Policy* 30(1): 48–62.
Allport, Gordon W. 1954. *The Nature of Prejudice*. Reading, MA: Addison-Wesley.
Auspurg, Katrin, Josef Brüderl, and Thomas Wöhler. 2019. "Does Immigration Reduce the Support for Welfare Spending? A Cautionary Tale on Spatial Panel Data Analysis". *American Sociological Review* 84(4): 754–63.
Bay, Ann-Helén, and Axel West Pedersen. 2006. "The Limits of Social Solidarity: Basic Income, Immigration and the Legitimacy of the Universal Welfare State". *Acta Sociologica* 49(4): 419–36.
Bischof, Daniel. 2017. "New Figure Schemes for Stata: Plotplain and Plottig". *The Stata Journal* 17(3): 748–59.
Bolsen, Toby, and Judd R. Thornton. 2014. "Overlapping Confidence Intervals and Null Hypothesis Testing". *The Experimental Political Scientist* 4(1): 12–16.
Brady, David, and Ryan Finnigan. 2014. "Does Immigration Undermine Public Support for Social Policy?" *American Sociological Review* 79(1): 17–42.
Brandt, Urs Steiner, and Gert Tinggaard Svendsen. 2019. "How Robust Is the Welfare State When Facing Open Borders? An Evolutionary Game-Theoretic Model". *Public Choice* 178: 179–195.
Bratsberg, Bernt, Oddbjørn Raaum, and Knut Røed. 2014. "Immigrants, Labour Market Performance and Social Insurance". *Economic Journal* 124(580): F644–83.
Breznau, Nate, and Maureen A. Eger. 2016. "Immigrant Presence, Group Boundaries, and Support for the Welfare State in Western European Societies". *Acta Sociologica (United Kingdom)* 59(3): 195–214.
Burgoon, Brian. 2014. "Immigration, Integration, and Support for Redistribution in Europe". *World Politics* 66(3): 365–405.
Burgoon, Brian, and Matthijs Rooduijn. 2021. "'Immigrationization' of Welfare Politics? Anti-Immigration and Welfare Attitudes in Context". *West European Politics* 44(2): 177–203.
Burgoon, Brian, Ferry Koster, and Marcel van Egmond. 2012. "Support for Redistribution and the Paradox of Immigration". *Journal of European Social Policy* 22(3): 288–304.
Burkhardt, Christoph, and Steffen Mau. 2011. "Challenges of Ethnic Diversity: Results from a Qualitative Study". In *Worlds of Welfare? British and German Social Policy in the 21st Century*, ed. Jochen Clasen. Oxford: Oxford University Press, 52–73.
Cappelen, Cornelius, and Yvette Peters. 2018a. "Diversity and Welfare State Legitimacy in Europe: The Challenge of Intra-EU Migration". *Journal of European Public Policy* 25(9): 1336–56.
Cappelen, Cornelius, and Yvette Peters. 2018b. "The Impact of Intra-EU Migration on Welfare Chauvinism". *Journal of Public Policy* 38(3): 389–417.
Careja, Romana, Christian Elmelund-Præstekær, Michael Baggesen Klitgaard, and Erik Gahner Larsen. 2016. "Direct and Indirect Welfare Chauvinism as Party Strategies: An Analysis of the Danish People's Party". *Scandinavian Political Studies* 39(4): 435–57.
Carey, Gemma, and Brad Crammond. 2017. "A Glossary of Policy Frameworks: The Many Forms of 'Universalism' and Policy 'Targeting'". *Journal of Epidemiology and Community Health* 71: 303–7.
Crepaz, Markus M.L. 2007. "'If You Are My Brother, I May Give You a Dime!' Public Opinion on Multiculturalism, Trust, and the Welfare State". In *Multiculturalism and the Welfare State: Recognition and Redistribution in Contemporary Democracies*, eds. Keith G Banting and Will Kymlicka. Oxford: Oxford University Press, 92–100.
Crepaz, Markus M.L. 2008. *Trust beyond Borders: Immigration, the Welfare State, and Identity in Modern Societies*. Ann Arbor, MI: University of Michigan Press.
Dahlberg, Matz, Karin Edmark, and Heléne Lundqvist. 2012. "Ethnic Diversity and Preferences for Redistribution". *Journal of Political Economy* 120(1): 41–76.
Degen, Daniel, Theresa Kuhn, and Wouter van der Brug. 2019. "Granting Immigrants Access to Social Benefits? How Self-Interest Influences Support for Welfare State Restrictiveness". *Journal of European Social Policy* 29(2): 148–65.
Dermont, Clau, and David Weisstanner. 2020. "Automation and the Future of the Welfare State: Basic Income as a Response to Technological Change?" *Political Research Exchange* 2(1) doi.org/10.1080/24747 36X.2020.1757387.
Eger, Maureen A., and Nate Breznau. 2017. "Immigration and the Welfare State: A Cross-Regional Analysis of European Welfare Attitudes". *International Journal of Comparative Sociology* 58(5): 440–63.
ESS. 2016. "European Social Survey Round 8 Data", ed. Norwegian Social Science Data Services, Data Archive and Distributor of ESS Data.
Eurostat. 2020. "European Labour Force Survey".
Fenwick, Clare. 2019. "The Political Economy of Immigration and Welfare State Effort: Evidence from Europe". *European Political Science Review* 11(3): 357–75.

Finseraas, Henning. 2008. "Immigration and Preferences for Redistribution: An Empirical Analysis of European Survey Data". *Comparative European Politics* 6(4): 407–31.

Finseraas, Henning, Marianne Røed, and Pål Schøne. 2017. "Labor Market Competition with Immigrants and Political Polarization". *Quarterly Journal of Political Science* 12(3): 347–73.

Frederiksen, Morten. 2018. "Varieties of Scandinavian Universalism: A Comparative Study of Welfare Justifications". *Acta Sociologica* 61(1): 3–16.

Friedman, Milton. 1977. *"What Is America?" Milton Friedman Speaks. Lecture Sponsored by the University of Chicago*. Chicago, IL.

Garand, James C., Ping Xu, and Belinda C. Davis. 2017. "Immigration Attitudes and Support for the Welfare State in the American Mass Public". *American Journal of Political Science* 61(1): 146–62.

Gentilini, Ugo, Margaret Grosh, Jamele Rigolini, and Ruslan Yemtsov. 2020. "Exploring Universal Basic Income: A Guide to Navigating Concepts, Evidence, and Practices". In *Exploring Universal Basic Income A Guide to Navigating*, eds. Ugo Gentilini, Margaret Grosh, Jamele Rigolini, and Ruslan Yemtsov. Washington, DC: International Bank for Reconstruction and Development and World Bank, 1–16.

Gerber, Alan S., Gregory A. Huber, Daniel R. Biggers, and David J. Hendry. 2017. "Self-Interest, Beliefs, and Policy Opinions: Understanding How Economic Beliefs Affect Immigration Policy Preferences". *Political Research Quarterly* 70(1): 155–71.

Gorodzeisky, Anastasia. 2013. "Mechanisms of Exclusion: Attitudes toward Allocation of Social Rights to Out-Group Population". *Ethnic and Racial Studies* 36(5): 795–817.

Gorodzeisky, Anastasia, and Moshe Semyonov. 2020. "Perceptions and Misperceptions: Actual Size, Perceived Size and Opposition to Immigration in European Societies". *Journal of Ethnic and Migration Studies* 46(3): 612–30.

Hooghe, Marc, Tim Reeskens, and Dietlind Stolle. 2007. "Diversity, Multiculturalism and Social Cohesion: Trust and Ethnocentrism in European Societies". In *Belonging? Diversity, Recognition and Shared Citizenship in Canada*, eds. Keith Banting, Thomas Courchene, and Leslie Seidle. Montreal: Institute for Research on Public Policy, 387–410.

Kassambara, Alboukadel. 2020. "'Ggpubr': 'ggplot2' Based Publication Ready Plots". *R package version 0.2.5*.

Kesler, Christel, and Irene Bloemraad. 2010. "Does Immigration Erode Social Capital? The Conditional Effects of Immigration-Generated Diversity on Trust, Membership, and Participation across 19 Countries, 1981–2000". *Canadian Journal of Political Science* 43(2): 319–47.

Kevins, Anthony, and Naomi Lightman. 2020. "Immigrant Sentiment and Labour Market Vulnerability: Economic Perceptions of Immigration in Dualized Labour Markets". *Comparative European Politics* 18(3): 460–84.

Kevins, Anthony, and Kees van Kersbergen. 2018. "The Effects of Welfare State Universalism on Migrant Integration". *Policy and Politics* 47(1): 115–32.

Koning, Edward A. 2020. "Accommodation and New Hurdles: The Increasing Importance of Politics for Immigrants' Access to Social Programmes in Western Democracies". *Social Policy and Administration*. https://doi.org/10.1111/spol.12661.

Koopmans, Ruud. 2010. "Trade-Offs between Equality and Difference: Immigrant Integration, Multiculturalism and the Welfare State in Cross-National Perspective". *Journal of Ethnic and Migration Studies* 36(1): 1–26.

Kootstra, Anouk. 2016. "Deserving and Undeserving Welfare Claimants in Britain and the Netherlands: Examining the Role of Ethnicity and Migration Status Using a Vignette Experiment". *European Sociological Review* 32(3): 325–38.

Kotzur, Patrick F., Sarina J. Schäfer, and Ulrich Wagner. 2019. "Meeting a Nice Asylum Seeker: Intergroup Contact Changes Stereotype Content Perceptions and Associated Emotional Prejudices, and Encourages Solidarity-Based Collective Action Intentions". *British Journal of Social Psychology* 58(3): 668–90.

Kymlicka, Will. 2015. "Solidarity in Diverse Societies: Beyond Neoliberal Multiculturalism and Welfare Chauvinism". *Comparative Migration Studies* 3: 17.

Larsen, Christian Albrekt. 2011. "Ethnic Heterogeneity and Public Support for Welfare: Is the American Experience Replicated in Britain, Sweden and Denmark?" *Scandinavian Political Studies* 34(4): 332–53.

Marx, Paul, and Georg Picot. 2020. "Three Approaches to Labor-Market Vulnerability and Political Preferences". *Political Science Research and Methods* 8(2): 356–61.

Meer, Tom Van Der, and Tim Reeskens. 2021. "Welfare Chauvinism in the Face of Ethnic Diversity: A Vignette Experiment across Diverse and Homogenous Neighbourhoods on the Perceived Deservingness of Native and Foreign-Born Welfare Claimants". *European Sociological Review* 37(1): 89–103.

Meuleman, Bart, Koen Abts, Peter Schmidt, Thomas F. Pettigrew, and Eldad Davidov. 2020. "Economic Conditions, Group Relative Deprivation and Ethnic Threat Perceptions: A Cross-National Perspective". *Journal of Ethnic and Migration Studies* 46(3): 593–611.

Muñoz, Jordi, and Sergi Pardos-Prado. 2019. "Immigration and Support for Social Policy: An Experimental Comparison of Universal and Means-Tested Programs". *Political Science Research and Methods* 7(4): 717–35.

Nielsen, Mathias Herup, Morten Frederiksen, and Christian Albrekt Larsen. 2020. "Deservingness Put into Practice: Constructing the (Un)Deservingness of Migrants in Four European Countries". *British Journal of Sociology* 71(1): 112–26.
OECD. 2016. "Database on Immigrants in OECD and Non-OECD Countries (DIOC-E)". Paris: OECD.
OECD. 2020a. "National Accounts Statistics". Paris: OECD.
OECD. 2020b. "Social Expenditure: Aggregated Data". Paris: OECD.
Pardos-Prado, Sergi. 2020. "Labour Market Dualism and Immigration Policy Preferences". *Journal of European Public Policy* 27(2): 188–207.
Parolin, Zachary, and Linus Siöland. 2020. "Support for a Universal Basic Income: A Demand–Capacity Paradox?" *Journal of European Social Policy* 30(1): 5–19.
Reeskens, Tim, and Tom van der Meer. 2019. "The Inevitable Deservingness Gap: A Study into the Insurmountable Immigrant Penalty in Perceived Welfare Deservingness". *Journal of European Social Policy* 29(2): 166–81.
Römer, Friederike. 2017. "Generous to All or 'Insiders Only'? The Relationship between Welfare State Generosity and Immigrant Welfare Rights". *Journal of European Social Policy* 27(2): 173–96.
Roosma, Femke, and Wim Van Oorschot. 2020. "Public Opinion on Basic Income: Mapping European Support for a Radical Alternative for Welfare Provision". *Journal of European Social Policy* 30(2): 190–205.
Sainsbury, Diane. 2006. "Immigrants' Social Rights in Comparative Perspective: Welfare Regimes, Forms of Immigration and Immigration Policy Regimes". *Journal of European Social Policy* 16(3): 229–44.
Schmidt-Catran, Alexander W., and Dennis C. Spies. 2016. "Immigration and Welfare Support in Germany". *American Sociological Review* 81(2): 242–61.
Schumacher, Gijs, and Kees van Kersbergen. 2016. "Do Mainstream Parties Adapt to the Welfare Chauvinism of Populist Parties?" *Party Politics* 22(3): 300–312.
Schwander, Hanna, and Tim Vlandas. 2020. "The Left and Universal Basic Income: The Role of Ideology in Individual Support". *Journal of International and Comparative Social Policy* 36(3): 237–68.
Senik, Claudia, Holger Stichnoth, and Karine Straeten. 2009. "Immigration and Natives' Attitudes towards the Welfare State: Evidence from the European Social Survey". *Social Indicators Research* 91(3): 345–70.
Shin, Young Kyu, Teemu Kemppainen, and Kati Kuitto. 2021. "Precarious Work, Unemployment Benefit Generosity and Universal Basic Income Preferences: A Multilevel Study on 21 European Countries". *Journal of Social Policy* 50(2): 323–45.
Simola, Anna, and Sirpa Wrede. 2020. "Young EU Migrant Citizens' Access to Financial Independence in Conditions of Precarious Work: A Tripartite Approach to Welfare Conditionality". *Journal of European Social Policy*. https://doi.org/10.1177/0958928720950625.
Slowikowski, Kamil. 2019. "Ggrepel: Automatically Position Non-Overlapping Text Labels with 'Ggplot2'". *R Package Version 0.8.1.*
Soroka, Stuart N., Richard Johnston, Anthony Kevins, Keith Banting, and Will Kymlicka. 2016. "Migration and Welfare State Spending". *European Political Science Review* 8(2): 174–93.
Soroka, Stuart N., Matthew Wright, Richard Johnston, Jack Citrin, Keith Banting, and Will Kymlicka. 2017. "Ethnoreligious Identity, Immigration, and Redistribution". *Journal of Experimental Political Science* 4(3): 173–82.
Spies, Dennis, and Alexander Schmidt-Catran. 2016. "Migration, Migrant Integration and Support for Social Spending: The Case of Switzerland". *Journal of European Social Policy* 26(1): 32–47.
Stadelmann-Steffen, Isabelle, and Clau Dermont. 2020. "Citizens' Opinions about Basic Income Proposals Compared: A Conjoint Analysis of Finland and Switzerland". *Journal of Social Policy* 49(2): 383–403.
Steele, Liza G. 2016. "Ethnic Diversity and Support for Redistributive Social Policies". *Social Forces* 94(4): 1439–81.
Steele, Liza G., and Krystal Perkins. 2018. "The Effects of Perceived Neighborhood Diversity on Preferences for Redistribution: A Pilot Study". *Societies* 8(3): 82–106.
Stichnoth, Holger. 2012. "Does Immigration Weaken Natives' Support for the Unemployed? Evidence from Germany". *Public Choice* 151(3–4): 631–54.
Taylor-Gooby, Peter, Bjørn Hvinden, Steffen Mau, Benjamin Leruth, Mi Ah Schoyen, and Adrienn Gyory. 2019. "Moral Economies of the Welfare State: A Qualitative Comparative Study". *Acta Sociologica* 62(2): 119–34.
Thomann, Eva, and Carolin Rapp. 2018. "Who Deserves Solidarity? Unequal Treatment of Immigrants in Swiss Welfare Policy Delivery". *Policy Studies Journal* 46(3): 531–52.
Valentova, Marie, and Marie Sophie Callens. 2018. "Did the Escalation of the Financial Crisis of 2008 Affect the Perception of Immigration-Related Threats? A Natural Experiment". *Journal of Ethnic and Migration Studies* 44(3): 439–61.
van Kersbergen, Kees, and Barbara Vis. 2015. "Three Worlds' Typology: Moving beyond Normal Science?" *Journal of European Social Policy* 25(1): 111–23.

Van Oorschot, Wim. 2006. "Making the Difference in Social Europe: Deservingness Perceptions among Citizens of European Welfare States". *Journal of European Social Policy* 16(1): 23–42.

Vlandas, Tim. 2021. "The Political Economy of Individual Level Support for the Basic Income in Europe". *Journal of European Social Policy* 31(1): 62–77.

Wickham, Hadley. 2016. *Ggplot2: Elegant Graphics for Data Analysis*. New York: Springer.

Wickham, Hadley, Mara Averick, Jennifer Bryan, Winston Chang, Lucy D'Agnostino McGowan, Romain Francois et al. 2019. "Welcome to the Tidyverse". *Journal of Open Source Software* 4(43): 1686–92.

APPENDIX

Table 7A.1 Number of respondents (per country) included in analysis

Country	Respondents
Austria	896
Belgium	1033
Czech Republic	1112
Estonia	1180
Finland	1287
France	1138
Germany	1740
Hungary	578
Iceland	636
Ireland	1251
Italy	830
Lithuania	982
Netherlands	1030
Norway	1032
Poland	792
Portugal	716
Slovenia	600
Spain	901
Sweden	920
Switzerland	707
United Kingdom	1042
Total	20403

Table 7A.2 Descriptive statistics, incorporating survey weights for individual-level variables

	Mean	Standard deviation	Minimum	Maximum
Support for a universal basic income	2.456	0.803	1	4
Years in education	13.625	3.803	0	54
Employment situation	0.622	0.636	0	2
Female	0.501	0.500	0	1
Age	45.433	15.782	15	98
Household income decile	5.793	2.760	1	10
Number of people in household	2.802	1.289	1	12
Lives with spouse	0.536	0.499	0	1
Belongs to a minority ethnic group	0.024	0.153	0	1
Member of trade union	0.158	0.365	0	1
GDP per capita at current prices	36371.835	12769.492	12348.915	79766.945
Unemployment rate	7.966	4.513	3.000	19.600
Social expenditure at % of GDP	24.830	4.362	15.482	31.982
Percentage of migrant stock	11.888	4.558	1.604	29.387
Observations	20403			

Table 7A.3 Results of regression analysis

	(1) Individual-level only regression	(2) Standard full regression	(3) Cluster robust standard errors regression	(4) Random slopes regression
	\multicolumn{4}{c}{Dependent variable: Support for a universal basic income}
Years in education (centred)	0.0111* (0.005)	0.0109** (0.004)	0.0109** (0.004)	0.0117** (0.004)
Atypical employment	0.0291 (0.031)	0.0281 (0.031)	0.0281 (0.031)	0.0241 (0.030)
Unemployed	0.143** (0.044)	0.140*** (0.041)	0.140*** (0.041)	0.133** (0.044)
Atypical employment # years in education (centred)	0.000421 (0.004)	0.000357 (0.004)	0.000357 (0.004)	−0.000303 (0.004)
Unemployed # years in education (centred)	−0.0227** (0.008)	−0.0196* (0.008)	−0.0196* (0.008)	−0.0191** (0.007)
Female	−0.0164 (0.013)	−0.0158 (0.013)	−0.0158 (0.013)	−0.0167 (0.013)
Age	−0.00684** (0.002)	−0.00721*** (0.002)	−0.00721*** (0.002)	−0.00750*** (0.002)
Age # age	0.0000443+ (0.000)	0.0000473+ (0.000)	0.0000473+ (0.000)	0.0000511+ (0.000)
Household income decile	−0.0326*** (0.006)	−0.0321*** (0.006)	−0.0321*** (0.006)	−0.0322*** (0.006)
Number of people in household	0.00888 (0.010)	0.00791 (0.009)	0.00791 (0.009)	0.00807 (0.009)
Lives with spouse	−0.00940 (0.024)	−0.00943 (0.024)	−0.00943 (0.024)	−0.00980 (0.023)
Belongs to minority ethnic Group	0.0247 (0.048)	0.0167 (0.050)	0.0167 (0.050)	0.0157 (0.050)
Trade union member	−0.00295 (0.026)	0.000190 (0.026)	0.000190 (0.026)	−0.00246 (0.026)
% of migrant stock (centred)		−0.0147+ (0.008)	−0.0147+ (0.008)	−0.0151+ (0.008)
Years in education (centred) # % of migrant stock (centred)		0.00206* (0.001)	0.00206* (0.001)	0.00186* (0.001)
Atypical employment # % of migrant stock (centred)		0.00895*** (0.002)	0.00895*** (0.002)	0.00883*** (0.002)
Unemployed # % of migrant stock (centred)		0.0129 (0.010)	0.0129 (0.010)	0.0123 (0.010)

Table 7A.3 (continued)

	Dependent variable: Support for a universal basic income			
	(1) Individual-level only regression	(2) Standard full regression	(3) Cluster robust standard errors regression	(4) Random slopes regression
Atypical employment # years in education (centred) # % of migrant stock (centred)		−0.000468 (0.001)	−0.000468 (0.001)	−0.000537 (0.001)
Unemployed # years in education (centred) # % of migrant stock (centred)		0.00438+ (0.003)	0.00438+ (0.003)	0.00458+ (0.002)
GDP per capita at current prices		−0.00000396 (0.000003)	−0.00000396 (0.000003)	−0.00000396 (0.000003)
Unemployment rate		−0.000939 (0.007)	−0.000939 (0.007)	−0.000316 (0.007)
Social expenditure at % of GDP		−0.00788 (0.006)	−0.00788 (0.006)	−0.00796 (0.006)
Constant	2.842*** (0.061)	3.184*** (0.210)	3.184*** (0.210)	3.188*** (0.210)
Variance				
Country level	0.194*** (0.039)	0.121*** (0.019)	0.121*** (0.019)	0.122*** (0.018)
Residual	0.786*** (0.010)	0.786*** (0.010)	0.786*** (0.010)	0.785*** (0.010)
Country (years in education)				0.00739*** (0.002)
Country (employment status)				0.0356*** (0.012)
Observations	20403	20403	20403	20403

Note: Cells contain maximum likelihood regression coefficients, with standard errors in parentheses. All models incorporate survey weights. $^+ p < 0.10$, $^* p < 0.05$, $^{**} p < 0.01$, $^{***} p < 0.001$.

8. Welfare chauvinist or neoliberal opposition to immigrant welfare? The importance of measurement in the study of welfare chauvinism
Edward Anthony Koning

INTRODUCTION

In academic research on the connection between migration and welfare, a large and growing literature examines welfare chauvinism, the sentiment that newcomers should have less access to the benefits of a redistributive welfare system than native-born citizens. This growth in attention is not surprising. Welfare chauvinist rhetoric permeates contemporary anti-immigrant rhetoric – for example, it was key to the "Leave" camp in the Brexit referendum, featured frequently in the campaign that brought Donald Trump to the White House, and helped Alternative for Germany enter parliament in 2017. Moreover, while much early research examined whether migration would bring about overall reductions in welfare generosity and public support for the welfare system, recent research has revealed that a more likely outcome is the exclusion of migrants from welfare benefits and an increased traction of welfare chauvinist sentiment (for a review, see Koning 2019, 11–16).

The general agreement in the blossoming literature on welfare chauvinism seems to be that large portions of the electorate across Western welfare states support placing restrictions on immigrants' access to social programs, and that more general theories of xenophobia help to explain where this sentiment comes from. This chapter reviews this literature and concludes that many contributions ignore that opposition to immigrants' access to social programs can be rooted in two very different positions: a neoliberal position, which opposes immigrant welfare out of more general opposition to state intervention in the market, and a welfare chauvinist position, which supports the welfare system in general but opposes immigrant welfare based on the belief that only "true members" of the nation-state should be allowed to draw from it. This distinction is crucial for understanding not only where opposition to immigrants' access to social programs comes from, but also what consequences it might have. Using data from the 2016 European Social Survey, this chapter demonstrates that neoliberals and welfare chauvinists are motivated by different concerns and have very different effects on the balance of power. More generally, this chapter shows that without distinguishing between neoliberal opposition and welfare chauvinist opposition to immigrant welfare, we risk overestimating the size of the welfare chauvinist electorate, underestimating the explanatory power of existing theories on the origins of welfare chauvinism, underestimating the importance of this sentiment for political outcomes, and introducing considerable unreliability in cross-national empirical investigations.

I pursue this argument as follows. The following section reviews how existing literature tends to conceptualize and operationalize welfare chauvinism, and demonstrates the merit of distinguishing between neoliberal opposition and welfare chauvinism. I then turn the attention to explanations of welfare chauvinism and show that the two types of opposition to immigrant welfare are driven by different variables. The subsequent section examines the consequences of welfare chauvinist sentiment for voting behavior and reveals that previous research has likely overestimated how "right-wing" welfare chauvinist voters really are and underestimated how important they are in changing the balance of political power. The conclusion summarizes the argument and identifies six reasons to incorporate the distinction between neoliberal and welfare chauvinist opposition to immigrant welfare in future research.

CONCEPTUALIZATION AND MEASUREMENT OF WELFARE CHAUVINISM

The term welfare chauvinism was coined by Jørgen Andersen and Tor Bjørklund, who used it to qualify the depiction of the Danish and Norwegian Progress Parties and their constituents as right wing:

> Progress Party voters are less hostile towards the welfare state than other right-wing voters. Furthermore, several groups highly dependent on the welfare state in Denmark and Norway are among the supporters of the Progress Party. Thus, it is probably more correct to speak of "welfare state chauvinism" than of anti-welfare attitudes: the expenditure should be restricted to "our own". (Andersen and Bjørklund 1990, 214)

The importance of this observation is difficult to overstate. Not only does it signal a key manifestation of anti-immigrant rhetoric in contemporary politics, but it also detects important party movement in the electoral space and the fragmentation of welfare state supporters in the electorate. Understandably, therefore, much research on welfare chauvinism followed Andersen and Bjørklund's foundational contribution.

With the blossoming of research on welfare chauvinism, however, also came divergence in its conceptualization. Some researchers have used the term to denote a set of prejudicial beliefs about immigrants' interaction with the welfare state, in particular that newcomers are prone to take advantage of social programs and are unreasonably reliant on government assistance (Crepaz and Damron 2009; Grdesic 2019; Wright and Reeskens 2013). In keeping with such a definition, this scholarship tends to rely on survey questions probing views on immigrants' effect on the economy or perceptions of the level of immigrants' benefit use. There is no question about the value of this type of inquiry. However, *prejudice* about immigrants' position in the welfare system is conceptually and theoretically distinct from the *policy position* that a welfare system should not grant easy access to newcomers. After all, knowing that someone is concerned about the effect of immigration on the welfare system does not tell us what, if anything, that person would propose as a policy response (Koning 2017).

In other research, the term welfare chauvinism does appear as indicating a preference for limiting social services and programs for immigrants. However, the bulk of this literature conceptualizes and, even more frequently, operationalizes this in absolute terms, i.e. it investigates whether people oppose generous programs and services for immigrants without considering whether they favor such programs for native-born in the first place (for recent examples, see Cappelen and Midtbo 2016; Kros and Coenders 2019; Larsen 2019; Marx and Naumann 2018). As a result, this approach does not allow one to assess whether a respondent favors cutting immigrants' benefits for welfare chauvinist reasons (i.e. because they do not believe immigrants are deserving) or for neoliberal reasons (i.e. because they do not believe in the merits of state intervention in the market for anyone).

Only a minority of studies truly measure the sentiment to which Andersen and Bjørklund so rightly drew attention: the policy position that combines support for a redistributive welfare state with a desire to restrict its benefits to native-born citizens. Several of these studies are clever experiments that primarily aim to demonstrate that people are inclined to discriminate against immigrants when it comes to preferences on benefit extension (Bay and Pedersen 2006; Buss 2019; Ford 2015; Luttmer 2001; Stadelmann-Steffen and Dermont 2020). Others have, in the absence of perfect indicators, relied on indirect measurements capturing the sentiment that the state owes more to native-born than to immigrant residents (Gorodzeisky and Semyonov 2009; Koning 2019; Mau and Burkhardt 2009). The only observational study of which I am aware that includes a precise question on welfare chauvinism is a Dutch survey from 2006, which explicitly asked whether immigrants should have fewer entitlements to social assistance than Dutch natives (De Koster et al. 2012; Van der Waal et al. 2010).

In sum, even though the large literature on welfare chauvinism includes much valuable insight, it does not always measure its key concept carefully. To overcome this challenge, I propose distinguishing between welfare chauvinist and neoliberal opposition to immigrant welfare. Both these positions favor the exclusion of migrants from benefits, but the key distinction is that the former comes with a favorable view of a redistributive welfare system while the latter does not.

An empirical illustration demonstrates that this distinction is not merely academic. I rely on data for all Western European countries that are included in the 2016 European Social Survey: Austria, Belgium, Finland, France, Germany, Iceland, Ireland, Italy, Netherlands, Norway, Portugal, Spain, Sweden, Switzerland, and the United Kingdom.[1] To measure attitudes on immigrant welfare access, I use the question on which most studies of welfare chauvinism rely:

> Thinking about people coming to live in [country] from other countries, when do you think they should obtain the same rights to social benefits and services as citizens already living here? Immediately on arrival, after living in [country] for a year, after they have worked and paid taxes for at least a year, once they become a [country] citizen, or never?

There is some disagreement in the literature about the most appropriate interpretation of the five answer options (see e.g. Mewes and Mau 2013; Reeskens and Van Oorschot 2012). In the following, I will consider the answers "Once they become a citizen" and "Never" as signaling an exclusionary position.[2]

To measure general attitudes on the desirability of a redistributive welfare system, I rely on an index of nine questions that tap neoliberal sentiment (see Table 8A.1).[3] By means of simplification, I will consider any respondent with at least half the maximum score on this index as neoliberal and everyone else as socialist.

Table 8.1 Typology of political orientation based on views on desirability of welfare state and immigrants' access to benefits, with average estimated size in 15 West European countries

	Neoliberal	Socialist
Inclusionary on immigrant access	*Inclusionary neoliberal* 34.9 percent	*Inclusionary socialist* 34.9 percent
Exclusionary on immigrant access	*Neoliberal opponent* 17.6 percent	*Welfare chauvinist* 12.6 percent

Source: Data from European Social Survey (2016); estimated size weighted for survey design characteristics and population size.

Combining these two indicators allows for an assessment of the relative size of those who favor exclusionary approaches to immigrants' welfare rights for neoliberal and welfare chauvinist reasons in the countries under study. Table 8.1 divides all respondents in four categories, depending on their positions on the desirability of a welfare state and immigrants' access to benefits. The European Social Survey suggests that about 30 percent of the electorate in Western European countries holds an exclusionary position on immigrants' access to social benefits. More importantly, about 60 percent of those individuals do not express strong support for a welfare state in the first place. The importance of incorporating more general views on a redistributive welfare system in any operationalization of welfare chauvinism is obvious. In this case, not doing so would lead to a misclassification of most respondents.

As one might expect, there are large cross-national differences in both the overall support for the exclusion of migrants from benefits and the relative size of welfare chauvinists and neoliberal opponents. As Figure 8.1 illustrates, overall support for exclusion ranges from only about 20 percent in Spain to as much as 52 percent in the Netherlands. And while neoliberal opponents take up almost three quarters of exclusionists in France and the United Kingdom, their relative size is less than 40 percent in Finland and Iceland. The implication is that the size of measurement error resulting from operationalizing welfare chauvinism without considering more general views on the welfare state is variable across countries. Many existing cross-national studies of welfare chauvinism, therefore, face a double complication: not only do they overestimate the number of welfare chauvinists; their cross-national comparisons are also troubled because the degree of that overestimation differs dramatically from one country to another.

Of course, none of this would pose serious problems if neoliberal opposition and welfare chauvinism were driven by largely the same factors and influenced politics in largely the same ways. As the next two sections show, however, this is not the case.

THE DRIVERS OF WELFARE CHAUVINISM

Much research has been dedicated to understanding why some individuals but not others are attracted to welfare chauvinist sentiment. (There are several studies pursuing

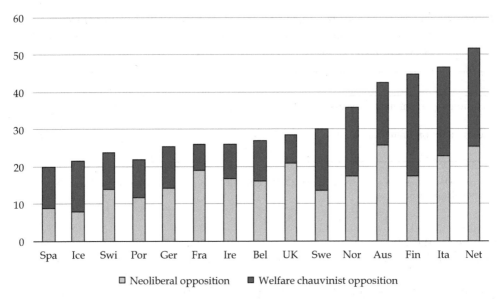

Source: Data from European Social Survey (2016); estimated size weighted for survey design characteristics.

Figure 8.1 Neoliberal and welfare chauvinist opposition to immigrant welfare access, 15 countries

country-level explanations as well, but a discussion of that literature is beyond the scope of this chapter.) Taken together, the literature suggests that three sets of variables are most important.

First, and most obviously, welfare chauvinism is closely associated with more general views about immigration. Unsurprisingly, anti-immigrant attitudes (such as prejudice towards immigrants, preference for social distance, perception of ethnic threat, and racial intolerance) appear as a significant driver of welfare chauvinism in every study that includes them (see e.g. Gorodzeisky 2013; Hjorth 2016; Van der Waal et al. 2013). Similarly unsurprising is the persistent finding that native-born citizens without any immigrant background are more likely to be welfare chauvinist than newcomers (see e.g. Heizmann et al. 2018; Kolbe and Crepaz 2016).

A second type of explanation points at factors that encourage individuals to think of immigrants as belonging to an "outgroup" and/or as occupying a lower position in a hierarchy of deservingness. Nationalism, for example, might drive welfare chauvinism, not because it necessarily produces anti-immigrant attitudes but because it encourages the sentiment that membership to the nation should come with privileges (Mierina and Koroleva 2015; Wright and Reeskens 2013). We can hypothesize Euroscepticism to function similarly, although interestingly the two existing studies that have investigated the connection between opposition to European integration and welfare chauvinism reached mixed conclusions (Cappelen and Peters 2018; Kuhn and Kamm 2019). Next, authoritarian sentiment likely increases welfare chauvinism: the preferences for conformity and traditions and the belief in a natural hierarchy of rights likely leads to high comfort levels with differentiation between social groups (Reeskens and Van Oorschot 2012). We can also include the role of social and institutional distrust, especially the lack of what Markus Crepaz (2008) calls "universal trust", in this category of explanation: in this line of reasoning, an inclination to expect the worst of people and of government institutions encourages thinking of immigrants as an undeserving outgroup (Cappelen and Peters 2018; Crepaz and Damron 2009; Fernandez 2019; Mierina and Koroleva 2015). And finally, several scholars have hypothesized that individuals who live in rural areas and experience limited exposure to (immigrant-induced) diversity are more likely to consider immigrants as an outgroup and therefore to favor granting them fewer welfare rights than native-born citizens. Interestingly, however, while some studies find that rural and isolated residents indeed exhibit more welfare chauvinism (Mewes and Mau 2013; Reeskens and Van Oorschot 2012; Van der Waal et al. 2010), others do not (Cappelen and Peters 2018; Eger and Breznau 2017; Gorodzeisky and Semyonov 2009; Grdesic 2019).

Finally, much existing literature looks for explanations in individuals' socio-economic status. Most researchers expect individuals with high levels of education, efficacy, and income to be much less welfare chauvinist than their counterparts who experience income insecurity and depend on the welfare state for their income. Most often, the explanation is rooted in conflict theory: those who are economically insecure, so the argument goes, are most affected by immigrants in their economic prospects because they compete with them for jobs and social benefits, and therefore are more likely to favor economic support for themselves than for non-natives in their position. Virtually all existing evidence suggests that these types of socio-economic indicators are indeed powerful predictors of welfare chauvinism: of all the studies reviewed in this chapter, only four (Bay and Pedersen 2006; Hjorth 2016; Kolbe and Crepaz 2016; Kuhn and Kamm 2019) find no significant effects for any of the socio-economic variables they include in their investigation.

Beyond these three sets of variables, many studies include other demographic variables, especially age, gender, marital status, union membership, and religiosity. However, the inclusion of these variables is rarely justified on theoretical grounds. And when their effects are explicitly hypothesized, they usually are related to the key variables mentioned above and therefore cannot be considered truly independent (for example, some hypothesize that older individuals are more likely to be welfare chauvinist because previous research has shown that age is positively correlated with xenophobia and authoritarianism). Much in keeping with the limited theoretical basis for their inclusion, existing evidence on the effects of these variables is decidedly mixed.

In sum, existing research has provided much insight into the possible drivers of welfare chauvinist sentiment. However, some of this insight might have to be qualified because of the above-mentioned tendency to treat any opposition to offering generous services and programs to immigrants as welfare chauvinism. Many of the explanations reviewed above are much more clearly about welfare chauvinist opposition than neoliberal opposition to immigrant welfare, and therefore existing research might have underestimated their importance. More generally, if these variables have different effects on welfare chauvinist opposition than on neoliberal opposition, the conflation of the two has likely produced misleading results.

The analysis below investigates whether neoliberal opposition and welfare chauvinism can be explained by the same variables. It does so with multinomial regression models, in which the dependent variable is the classification in Table 8.1 and the two inclusionary positions (inclusionary socialist and inclusionary neoliberal) are combined as the reference category. As independent variables, it includes country dummies to control for country-specific effects, the neoliberalism index to allow for a clean comparison between the two exclusionary positions, and 19 variables that existing literature identifies as the most pertinent: xenophobia, status as native-born, nationalism, Euroscepticism, authoritarianism, institutional distrust, social distrust, residence in a rural environment, residence in an isolated environment with a small immigrant population, low education, inefficacy, benefit dependence, low income, concern about household income, age, gender, living without partner, union membership, and religiosity. To facilitate the interpretation of results, I recoded all variables to range from 0 to 1, except for four variables that turned out to have exceptionally large effects: xenophobia (coded to range from 0 to 4), Euroscepticism (0–2), institutional distrust (0–2), and social distrust (0–2). Table 8A.1 provides information on operationalization and descriptive statistics for each variable.

Table 8.2 reports the results from a model with eight independent variables (apart from the country dummies and neoliberalism index). The other variables are excluded from this model in order to avoid multicollinearity (Euroscepticism, social distrust, institutional distrust, isolated residence, inefficacy, and low income are highly correlated with other variables in this model)[4] and to reduce saturation (concern about household income, gender, living without partner, union membership, and religiosity did not have a significant effect on either neoliberal opposition or welfare chauvinism).

Figure 8.2 presents these findings graphically: it plots the independent effect of each variable as the predicted percentage change in probability of neoliberal opposition and welfare chauvinism with a maximum increase in each independent variable, with 95 percent confidence intervals. For example, Figure 8.2 shows that, while holding all other variables constant, maximally nationalist respondents are about 50 percent more

Table 8.2 Multinomial regression predicting neoliberal opposition and welfare chauvinism

	Neoliberal opposition		Welfare chauvinism	
	Exp(b)	Sign.	Exp(b)	Sign.
Xenophobia (coded 0–4)	2.257	<0.001	2.436	<0.001
Native-born	1.720	<0.001	2.377	<0.001
Nationalism	1.055	0.616	1.475	0.001
Authoritarianism	1.035	0.781	1.404	0.009
Rural residence	1.117	0.228	1.441	<0.001
Low education	1.083	0.286	1.260	0.003
Dependence on benefits as main income	1.189	0.003	1.016	0.786
Age	0.750	0.053	0.647	0.004
N	21,269			
Nagelkerke Pseudo R-square	0.383			
Likelihood Ratio Test	<0.001			

Source: Data from European Social Survey (2016); reference category for dependent variable is inclusive position on immigrant access to welfare; coefficients for country dummies and neoliberalism index not shown.

Welfare chauvinist or neoliberal opposition 163

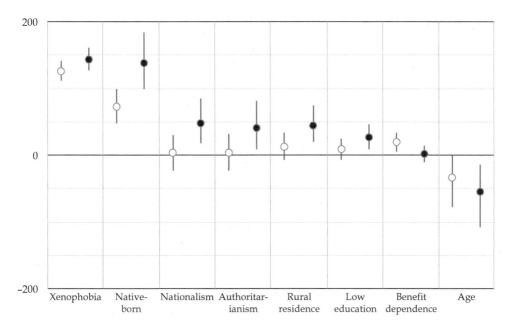

Note: Figure depicts predicted percentage change in probability of neoliberal opposition (open markers) and welfare chauvinism (closed markers) with a maximum increase in the value of the independent variable, with 95 percent confidence interval, while controlling for all other variables, country-fixed effects, and views on neoliberalism. For the variable xenophobia, the figure depicts the predicted change in probability with an increase of a quarter of the maximum range; see multinomial regression model in Table 8.2.

Figure 8.2   Predictors of neoliberal opposition (open markers) and welfare chauvinism (closed markers)

likely to be welfare chauvinist than minimally nationalist respondents. In contrast, nationalism does not seem to affect neoliberal opposition, considering the confidence interval crosses the "0" line indicating no change in probability.

The findings strongly suggest that welfare chauvinism and neoliberal opposition have different origins. The two variables that are most directly related to immigration (how one feels about immigration and whether one has immigrant roots) have a larger effect on welfare chauvinism than on neoliberal opposition, suggesting the former sentiment stems more from a desire to differentiate between immigrants and native-born than the latter. The results for the variables that have been theorized to encourage the depiction of migrants as an "outgroup" – nationalism, authoritarianism, and rural residence – suggest a similar conclusion. They have a clear and statistically significant effect on welfare chauvinism, but not on neoliberal opposition. Surprisingly, older respondents appear less likely to be neoliberal opponents, and much less likely to be welfare chauvinist.[5]

Perhaps the most interesting finding is the distinct effect of two socio-economic variables that existing literature tends to treat similarly: low education seems to drive welfare chauvinism but not neoliberal opposition, whereas depending on social benefits as the main source of income significantly (albeit modestly) increases neoliberal opposition but has no effect on welfare chauvinism. Speculatively, we might explain these countervailing effects as follows. On the one hand, education likely encourages ideological consistency, which means that it should make socialists but not neoliberals more opposed to reducing immigrants' access to benefits. On the other hand, being dependent on the welfare state might force neoliberals to draw sharper contrasts between groups of people in their deservingness of social benefits (and thus to start thinking more harshly about immigrants), whereas there is less reason to expect such an effect for socialists who already think favorably about the principle of a redistributive welfare state.

We reach much the same overall conclusions when we turn our attention to the variables that are not included in Table 8.2. Figure 8A.1 plots the effects of the six variables that were omitted to avoid multicollinearity as estimated by six separate regression models in which each variable was switched for the variable(s) with which they were highly correlated (see also note 4). Euroscepticism, social distrust, institutional distrust, residence in an isolated region, and inefficacy all have a much larger and more significant effect on welfare chauvinism than on neoliberal opposition.[6] Somewhat surprisingly, low income does not seem to drive either sentiment. This is likely the result of countervailing effects: low income is related to low education and skills, which bolsters welfare chauvinism, but also to likely dependence on the state, which increases neoliberal opposition.

Figure 8A.2 plots the effects of the five variables that were omitted to reduce saturation, based on a regression model that adds them to the model in Table 8.2. The lack of any effect of gender, being single, religiosity, and trade union membership is well in line with existing theory, which offers little reason why they should matter independently. That concern about household income has no significant effects is more surprising but might be explained again by the presence of countervailing effects.

All in all, the findings in this section show that operationalizing welfare chauvinism without considering more general views on a redistributive welfare state has had two negative implications for our understanding of the origins of this sentiment. First, it has made us underestimate the importance of the most invoked explanations for welfare chauvinism. It has been impossible to appreciate just how much nationalism, authoritarianism, and rural residence matters for welfare chauvinism because most research has included a sentiment in the measurement of the dependent variable that is not influenced by these factors. Second, it has led to a misidentification of the relevance of socioeconomic variables: the current analysis at least suggests that welfare chauvinism has more to do with low education levels and feelings of inefficacy than with economic dependence on the state.[7]

THE CONSEQUENCES OF WELFARE CHAUVINISM FOR VOTING BEHAVIOR

Compared to the large literature investigating the drivers of welfare chauvinist sentiment, the scholarship on its effects on voting behavior is quite small. Welfare chauvinism occasionally appears as an independent variable in attempts to explain support for populist anti-immigrant parties, but few studies have investigated the relationship between welfare chauvinism and vote choice more broadly. Willem De Koster and his colleagues (2012) pursued such an investigation in a case study of the Netherlands, and found that welfare chauvinism had a larger effect on support for the anti-immigrant Freedom Party than on

Welfare chauvinist or neoliberal opposition 165

the support for any other party. Another study (which does not incorporate more general views on redistribution) found that support for welfare exclusion is more associated with support for right-wing parties, and more specifically, for parties that champion immigrant welfare exclusion as well (Koning 2017).

The analysis in this section investigates whether welfare chauvinism and neoliberal opposition to immigrant welfare have similar effects on the choice voters make in the voting booth. This analysis is of particular importance for understanding the fortunes of modern anti-immigrant parties and their effect on the balance of power. As many observers have noted, these parties tend to occupy an ambiguous position on welfare issues: they have moved to the center in order to capture the welfare chauvinist vote, but have rarely embraced the label "left wing" (De Lange 2007; Rathgeb 2020). On the one hand, we might therefore expect neoliberal opponents to be drawn more to such parties than welfare chauvinists. On the other hand, however, opposition to immigrants' welfare rights should have a larger effect on those who have generally supportive views of the welfare state than on neoliberals, who are likely to vote for a right-wing party anyway. The implication of such a finding would be that welfare chauvinist sentiment shifts the balance of political power in a right-wing direction, much in line with the predictions Tim Bale (2003) made in an early contribution to this literature. The observation that anti-immigrant parties tend to enter a coalition with right-wing parties when they make it into government[8] further underlines that implication.

The European Social Survey asked all respondents for which party they voted in the last national elections. To enable aggregate analysis, I categorized all political parties in these countries as socialist/green, center-left, center-right, or anti-immigrant. Table 8A.2 lists the classification for each party.[9] Table 8.3 depicts the bivariate relationship between the typology in Table 8.1 and vote choice by broad category of political party. It confirms our two key expectations.

First, there are large differences in the voting preferences of neoliberal opponents and welfare chauvinists. As a focused comparison of the fourth and fifth columns reveals, neoliberal opponents are much more likely to vote for center-right and anti-immigrant parties than welfare chauvinists. (More elaborate analysis which is not shown here reveals, however, that this pattern is much more pronounced in some countries, in particular France, Germany, Norway, and the United Kingdom, and much less in others, in particular Belgium, Finland, Italy, and Spain.) Second, differences in the voting behavior of inclusionary socialists and welfare chauvinists are much larger than the differences

Table 8.3   Vote choice by position on welfare state and immigrant access to benefits (%)

	Inclusionary neoliberal	Inclusionary socialist	Neoliberal opponent	Welfare chauvinist	Total
Socialist/green	8.6	24.3	6.9	16.6	15.3
Center-left	29.7	43.0	28.6	40.3	36.0
Center-right	52.8	28.7	49.5	32.4	40.2
Anti-immigrant	8.9	4.0	15.0	10.8	8.4
Total	100	100	100	100	100

Note: $\lambda = 0.108$; Cramer's V = 0.180; χ^2 p < 0.001.

between inclusionary neoliberals and neoliberal opponents. In other words, favoring a restrictive position on immigrants' access to welfare benefits has a much larger effect on the voting behavior of those who are generally in favor of a redistributive welfare state in the first place.

Figure 8.3 demonstrates this latter conclusion more systematically. For each country under study, it compares the strength and direction of the relationship between views on immigrant welfare (using the original five-point question when immigrants should be allowed to access social benefits) and vote choice (using the four-point ordinal scale of broad party family) for respondents with neoliberal views with the strength of that relationship for respondents with socialist views. The relationship is consistently more positive and more significant for socialists than for neoliberals (except in Ireland, where the relationship is weak and insignificant for both categories of voters). Opposing immigrants' access to social programs, therefore, pushes voters who generally like a welfare state more to the right than their counterparts who do not like a welfare state to begin with. The size of this difference, however, varies considerably between countries. It is minimal in France, Germany, and the United Kingdom, but massive in Belgium, Spain, and Sweden.

All in all, these results again demonstrate the merit of distinguishing between neoliberal opposition and welfare chauvinism. Studies that do not likely generate a considerable right-wing bias when estimating the voting preferences of welfare chauvinist respondents. Moreover, they likely underestimate the effect of welfare chauvinism on voting behavior and the balance of political power. And because the scope of these biases

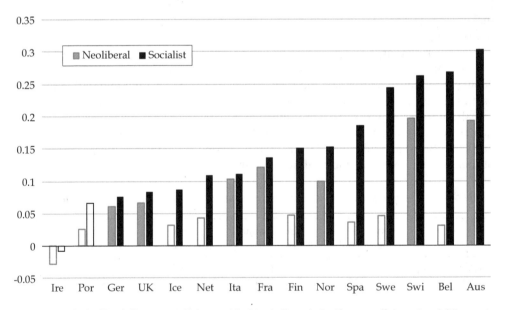

Note: Bars depict Kendall's tau-c coefficients; white bars indicate insignificant coefficients ($p > 0.05$).

Figure 8.3 Effect of position regarding immigrant welfare access on vote choice, neoliberal and socialist respondents

is variable across countries, the distinction is crucial in any pursuit of reliable cross-national comparisons.

CONCLUSIONS

The literature on welfare chauvinism has come a long way. We now know much about the foundations and importance of the policy position that combines support for a redistributive welfare system with a desire to limit the extent to which newcomers can access it. In order to move this well-developed literature forward, closer attention to measurement is key. The main argument of this chapter is that a careful analysis of welfare chauvinism (including its origins and consequences) requires the systematic incorporation of more general views about a redistributive welfare state, so that we can distinguish truly welfare chauvinist sentiment from opposition to immigrant welfare that is rooted in broader opposition to an interventionist state. As we have seen, research that does not incorporate this distinction might run into six types of measurement error.

First, it will likely overestimate the number of welfare chauvinists. Many of those who wish to limit the available services for immigrants cannot really be considered welfare chauvinist because they do not support a redistributive welfare system for anyone. Their view that immigrants should take care of themselves and not ask for taxpayer support is no different from their views on other economically vulnerable groups. According to the examination in this chapter, only about two in five of those with exclusionary positions on immigrant welfare combine such a perspective with an otherwise favorable view of redistribution and economic intervention.

Second, it will likely underestimate how well existing theory can explain individual variation in welfare chauvinist sentiment. Nationalism, authoritarianism, Euroscepticism, social and institutional distrust, and residence in rural and/or isolated areas have large effects on welfare chauvinist sentiment, but little to none on neoliberal opposition. Conflating those two positions has therefore made these effects seem much smaller. This observation has an obvious theoretical implication as well: existing insights that draw attention to these variables should be understood as explanations of welfare chauvinism, not of opposition to immigrant welfare in general.

Third, it might have led to a misidentification of the role of socio-economic variables. Much existing research tends to treat income, income insecurity, welfare dependence, education, occupational status, and human capital as more or less interchangeable indicators to support the argument rooted in conflict theory that the economically insecure are more welfare chauvinist because they are more likely facing competition from newcomers on the labor market and in the welfare offices. The analysis in this chapter, however, suggests we might have to rethink our explanation for the covariation between opposition to immigrant welfare and socio-economic status: while low education and efficacy seem to drive welfare chauvinism, economic dependence on the state only affects neoliberal opposition to immigrant welfare. While this surprising finding clearly requires further corroboration in future research, an implication could be that the dampening effect of education on welfare chauvinism is not so much about avoiding likely economic conflict but rather about encouraging ideological consistency (i.e. the explanation would be that the highly educated are less likely to be welfare chauvinist because such sentiment is internally inconsistent).

Fourth, it likely introduces a considerable right-wing bias in estimates of the vote choice of welfare chauvinists. The analysis in this chapter reveals that welfare chauvinist respondents are considerably more likely to vote for left-wing parties than their counterparts who oppose immigrant welfare for neoliberal reasons, and in fact, even tend to vote more left wing than neoliberals who do *not* oppose immigrant welfare.

Fifth, it will likely underestimate how much welfare chauvinism encourages a right-wing shift in the balance of power. For neoliberal respondents, it makes little difference whether they want to restrict immigrants' access to the welfare state or not: these individuals will likely vote for a right-wing party anyway. The story is very different, however, for those who are otherwise supportive of redistribution: opposition to immigrant welfare is likely to make them switch their vote from a left-wing to a right-wing party (as Table 8.3 reveals, for example, it more than doubles their probability of supporting an anti-immigrant party).

Sixth, and finally, it likely introduces unreliability in cross-national research. The size of the bias of each of the five issues above varies considerably between countries. Therefore, the importance of avoiding them counts double for studies that aim to make clean comparisons between different countries.

All in all, there is no doubt that existing research has taught us much about welfare chauvinism. But as the analyses in this chapter reveal, a more careful measurement of this key sentiment will likely qualify some of our empirical observations and theoretical conclusions. There is thus a clear agenda for future research on this sentiment that has so crucially transformed electoral and partisan politics.

NOTES

1. In order to avoid difficult comparisons with countries that have a very different history of migration and welfare state development, this analysis excludes Czech Republic, Estonia, Hungary, Israel, Lithuania, Poland, Russia, and Slovenia.
2. This decision is based on two considerations. First, survey respondents are likely to understand the answer options as a five-point Likert scale, and therefore the selection of one of the two last options – regardless of their exact formulation – likely signals support for a restrictive position (Casper et al. 2020). Second, these two answers most clearly suggest an exclusionary departure from current policy arrangements. While the 15 countries under study differ considerably in the extent to which they open their systems of social policy to immigrants, none of them indefinitely exclude all foreigners, let alone all foreign-born individuals (while they all do pose residence and/or work history requirements for at least some benefits) (Koning 2021).
3. For all indexes in this chapter, I used exploratory factor analyses to determine which survey items could be meaningfully combined. These analyses are not shown, but can be made available upon request. Table 8A.1 reports the Cronbach Alpha coefficient indicating the reliability of combining the composite items for every index.
4. The variables Euroscepticism, social distrust, and institutional distrust were excluded because of their high correlations with the variable xenophobia (0.461, 0.314, and 0.338, respectively); the variable isolated residence because of its high correlation with the variable rural residence (0.336); the variable inefficacy because of its high correlation with education (0.376); and the variable income because of its high correlations with education (0.407) and benefit dependency (0.374).
5. The explanation is unclear, but it is worth repeating that these are estimated effects independent of the other variables in the model: when we exclude all the other variables in Figure 8.2, we find that older people are both more likely to be a neoliberal opponent and more likely to be a welfare chauvinist, and if we exclude

the three attitudinal variables (xenophobia, nationalism, and authoritarianism), the effects are insignificant. In any event, this surprising finding underlines the limited basis for expecting older age to independently increase welfare chauvinism.
6. While it is true that the effects of Euroscepticism, social distrust, and institutional distrust on neoliberal opposition are still large and statistically significant, this is most likely because these variables are indirectly picking up more general views about immigration now that the variable xenophobia is omitted.
7. An additional problem is, again, cross-national reliability. In some countries (especially Austria, Italy, and the Netherlands) the multinomial regression models have a very high fit, suggesting that the differences in the extent to which these variables explain neoliberal opposition and welfare chauvinism are sizeable, and therefore, that a conflation of the two is very problematic. In other countries (in particular Belgium, Ireland, and Portugal), the models have a lower fit, and therefore the conflation poses smaller problems.
8. At the time of writing, Western European anti-immigrant parties have entered a formal or informal coalition 19 times, and only once was this without involving a right-wing party: the short-lived coalition in Italy between the anti-immigrant (Northern) League and the Five Star Movement. (The other instances are four coalitions in Austria, four informal coalitions in Denmark, one coalition in Finland, four coalitions in Italy, one coalition and one informal coalition in the Netherlands, and two coalitions and one informal coalition in Norway.) Switzerland includes all major parties in its Federal Council and is therefore not considered here.
9. I excluded any party that was selected by fewer than 10 respondents. The use of only four broad categories made the classification of most parties straightforward. The most debatable decisions were to (1) categorize "social liberal" parties (such as the Liberal Democrats in the United Kingdom) as center-left parties; and (2) to force a label on arguably unclassifiable parties, i.e. to classify the Belgian New Flemish Alliance as center-right and to label the German Pirate Party, the Icelandic Pirate Party, the Italian Five Star Movement, and the Dutch 50+ as center-left parties. I reran the analyses after excluding the parties that are difficult to classify and categorizing social liberal parties as center-right, and the results do not challenge the two main conclusions in this section. In these alternative analyses, neoliberal opponents are still more likely to vote for right-wing parties (including anti-immigrant parties) than welfare chauvinists, and the position on immigrant exclusion still has a larger effect on vote choice for socialists than for neoliberals (although this is no longer the case in France and the United Kingdom when classifying social-liberal parties as center-right). These results are not shown but can be made available upon request.

REFERENCES

Andersen, Jørgen Goul, and Tor Bjørklund. 1990. "Structural Changes and New Cleavages: The Progress Parties in Denmark and Norway". *Acta Sociologica* 33 (3): 195–217.

Bale, Tim. 2003. "Cinderella and Her Ugly Sisters: The Mainstream and Extreme Right in Europe's Bipolarising Party Systems". *West European Politics* 26 (3): 67–90.

Bay, Ann-Helén, and Axel West Pedersen. 2006. "The Limits of Social Solidarity: Basic Income, Immigration, and the Legitimacy of the Universal Welfare State". *Acta Sociologica* 49 (4): 419–436.

Buss, Christopher. 2019. "Public Opinion towards Targeted Labour Market Policies: A Vignette Study on the Perceived Deservingness of the Unemployed". *Journal of European Social Policy* 29 (2): 228–240.

Cappelen, Cornelius, and Tor Midtbo. 2016. "Intra-EU Labour Migration and Support for the Norwegian Welfare State". *European Sociological Review* 32 (6): 691–703.

Cappelen, Cornelius, and Yvette Peters. 2018. "The Impact of Intra-EU Migration on Welfare Chauvinism". *Journal of Public Policy* 38 (3): 389–417.

Casper, W. Camron, Bryan D. Edwards, J. Craig Wallace, Ronald S. Landis, and Dustin A. Fife. 2020. "Selecting Response Anchors with Equal Intervals for Summated Rating Scales". *Journal of Applied Psychology* 105 (4): 390–409.

Crepaz, Markus M. 2008. *Trust Beyond Borders: Immigration, the Welfare State, and Identity in Modern Societies*. Ann Arbor, MI: University of Michigan Press.

Crepaz, Markus M., and Regan Damron. 2009. "Constructing Tolerance: How the Welfare State Shapes Attitudes about Immigrants". *Comparative Political Studies* 42 (3): 437–463.

De Koster, Willem, Peter Achterberg, and Jeroen Van der Waal. 2012. "The New Right and the Welfare State: The Electoral Relevance of Welfare Chauvinism and Welfare Populism in the Netherlands". *International Political Science Review* 34 (1): 3–20.

De Lange, Sarah L. 2007. "A New Winning Formula? The Programmatic Appeal of the Radical Right". *Party Politics* 13 (4): 411–435.

Eger, Maureen A., and Nate Breznau. 2017. "Immigration and the Welfare State: A Cross-Regional Analysis of European Welfare Attitudes". *International Journal of Comparative Sociology* 58 (5): 440–463.

Fernandez, E.G.G. 2019. "Migration Incorporation Regimes and Institutionalized Forms of Solidarity: Between Unconditional Institutional Solidarity and Welfare Chauvinism". *American Behavioral Scientist* 63 (4): 506–522.

Ford, Robert. 2015. "Who Should We Help? An Experimental Test of Discrimination in the British Welfare State". *Political Studies* 64 (3): 630–650.

Gorodzeisky, Anastasia. 2013. "Mechanisms of Exclusion: Attitudes toward Allocation of Social Rights to Out-Group Population". *Ethnic and Racial Studies* 36 (5): 795–817.

Gorodzeisky, Anastasia, and Moshe Semyonov. 2009. "Terms of Exclusion: Public Views towards Admission and Allocation of Rights to Immigrants in European Countries". *Ethnic and Racial Studies* 32 (3): 401–423.

Grdesic, Marko. 2019. "Neoliberalism and Welfare Chauvinism in Germany: An Examination of Survey Evidence". *German Politics and Society* 37 (2): 1–22.

Heizmann, Boris, Alexander Jedinger, and Anja Perry. 2018. "Welfare Chauvinism, Economic Insecurity and the Asylum Seeker 'Crisis'". *Societies* 8 (3): 1–18.

Hjorth, Frederik. 2016. "Who Benefits? Welfare Chauvinism and National Stereotypes". *European Union Politics* 17 (1): 3–24.

Kolbe, Melanie, and Markus M.L. Crepaz. 2016. "The Power of Citizenship: How Immigrant Incorporation Affects Attitudes towards Social Benefits". *Comparative Politics* 49 (1): 105–123.

Koning, Edward Anthony. 2017. "Selecting, Disentitling, or Investing? Exploring Party and Voter Responses to Immigrant Welfare Dependence in Fifteen West European Welfare States". *Comparative European Politics* 15 (4): 628–660.

Koning, Edward Anthony. 2019. *Immigration and the Politics of Welfare Exclusion: Selective Solidarity in Western Democracies*. Toronto: University of Toronto Press.

Koning, Edward Anthony. 2021. "Social Protection of Migrants and Citizenship Rights". In *Handbook on Citizenship and Migration*, edited by Marco Giugni and Maria Grasso. Cheltenham, UK and Northampton, MA, USA: Edward Elgar Publishing, pp. 223–225.

Kros, Mathijs, and Marcel Coenders. 2019. "Explaining Differences in Welfare Chauvinism between and within Individuals over Time: The Role of Subjective and Objective Economic Risk, Economic Egalitarianism, and Ethnic Treat". *European Sociological Review* 35 (6): 860–873.

Kuhn, Theresa, and Aaron Kamm. 2019. "The National Boundaries of Solidarity: A Survey Experiment on Solidarity with Unemployed People in the European Union". *European Political Science Review* 11: 179–195.

Larsen, Christian Albrekt. 2019. "The Institutional Logic of Giving Migrants Access to Social Benefits and Services". *Journal of European Social Policy* 30 (1): 48–62.

Luttmer, Erzo F. 2001. "Group Loyalty and the Taste for Redistribution". *Journal of Political Economy* 109 (3): 500–528.

Marx, Paul, and Elias Naumann. 2018. "Do Right-Wing Parties Foster Welfare Chauvinistic Attitudes? A Longitudinal Study of the 2015 'Refugee Crisis' in Germany". *Electoral Studies* 52: 111–116.

Mau, Steffen, and Christoph Burkhardt. 2009. "Migration and Welfare State Solidarity in Western Europe". *Journal of European Social Policy* 19 (3): 213–229.

Mewes, Jan, and Steffen Mau. 2013. "Globalization, Socio-economic Status and Welfare Chauvinism: European Perspectives on Attitudes toward the Exclusion of Immigrants". *International Journal of Comparative Sociology* 54 (3): 228–245.

Mierina, Inta, and Ilze Koroleva. 2015. "Support for Far Right Ideology and Anti-Migrant Attitudes among Youth in Europe: A Comparative Analysis". *Sociological Review* 63 (2): 183–205.

Rathgeb, Philip. 2020. "Makers against Takers: The Socio-economic Ideology and Policy of the Austrian Freedom Party". *West European Politics* 44 (3): 635–660.

Reeskens, Tim, and Wim Van Oorschot. 2012. "Disentangling the 'New Liberal Dilemma': On the Relation between General Welfare Redistribution Preferences and Welfare Chauvinism". *International Journal of Comparative Sociology* 53 (2): 120–139.

Stadelmann-Steffen, Isabelle, and Clau Dermont. 2020. "Citizens' Opinions about Basic Income Proposals Compared: A Conjoint Analysis of Finland and Switzerland". *Journal of Social Policy* 49 (2): 383–403.

Van der Waal, Jeroen, Peter Achterberg, Dick Houtman, Willem De Koster, and Katerina Manevska. 2010. "'Some Are More Equal Than Others': Economic Egalitarianism and Welfare Chauvinism in the Netherlands". *Journal of European Social Policy* 20 (4): 350–363.

Van der Waal, Jeroen, Willem De Koster, and Wim Van Oorschot. 2013. "Three Worlds of Welfare Chauvinism? How Welfare Regimes Affect Support for Distributing Welfare to Immigrants in Europe". *Journal of Comparative Policy Analysis* 15 (2): 164–181.

Wright, Matthew, and Tim Reeskens. 2013. "Of What Cloth Are the Ties That Bind? National Identity and Support for the Welfare State across 29 European Countries". *Journal of European Public Policy* 20 (10): 1443–1463.

APPENDIX

Table 8A.1 Descriptive information for all variables

Variable and operationalization	$\bar{x}$	s	n
Neoliberalism: Index of views that government should not reduce differences in income levels, large differences in income are acceptable to reward talents and efforts, and a fair society does not require small differences in standard of living; beliefs that social benefits place too much strain on economy, cost businesses too much in taxes, make people lazy, and make people less willing to care for each other; and views that most unemployed do not really try to find a job, and that many people manage to obtain benefits to which they are not entitled ($\alpha = 0.745$)	0.475	0.150	24,439
Xenophobia: Index of views that immigrants of same race, different race, and from poorer countries should not be admitted; beliefs that immigration is bad for the economy, undermines country's cultural life, and makes the country a worse place to live; and views that the government should not be generous judging applications for refugee status, that most refugee applicants are not in real fear of persecution, and that granted refugees should not be allowed to bring close family members ($\alpha = 0.886$)	0.434	0.194	24,450
Nationalism: Emotional attachment to country	0.775	0.214	28,291
Euroscepticism: Index of distrust in European Parliament, belief that European unification has gone too far, and lack of emotional attachment to Europe ($\alpha = 0.636$)	0.494	0.191	25,571
Authoritarianism: Index of beliefs in importance of living in secure and safe surroundings, doing what one is told and following rules, having a government that is strong and ensures safety, behaving properly, and following traditions and customs ($\alpha = 0.746$)	0.630	0.189	27,534
Social distrust: Index of views that you can't be too careful, most people try to take advantage of others, and most people look out for themselves ($\alpha = 0.759$)	0.436	0.181	28,181
Institutional distrust: Index of distrust in parliament, the legal system, politicians, and parties; and lack of satisfaction with state of economy, the national government, and the way democracy works in country ($\alpha = 0.913$)	0.519	0.196	26,510
Inefficacy: Index of no interest in politics; belief that the political system does not allow people a say in what government does or influence in politics; and lack of confidence in own ability to participate in politics ($\alpha = 0.713$)	0.627	0.192	27,426
Native: 0 = born abroad; 0.5 = second generation; 1 = born in country	0.849	0.332	28,240
Age: Age in years divided by 100	0.497	0.186	28,266
Male: Respondent identifies as male	0.486	0.500	28.368
Single: Not living with husband/wife/partner	0.407	0.491	28,234

172   Handbook on migration and welfare

Table 8A.1   (continued)

Variable and operationalization	$\bar{x}$	s	n
Rural residence: Low population density of region of residence, Eurostat data (0 => 500 inhabitants/km²; 0.25: 250–500; 0.5 = 100–250; 0.75 = 25–100; 1 = <25)	0.484	0.286	28,374
Isolated residence: Small immigrant population in region of residence, OECD data (0 => 20% foreign-born; 0.25 = 15–20%; 0.5 = 10–15%; 0.75 = 5–10%; 1 = <5%)	0.484	0.296	28,367
Low education: Education level according to ES-ISCED scheme, inverted	0.518	0.319	28,187
Low income: Household income in deciles, inverted	0.521	0.305	23,754
Concern about income: Finding it difficult to cope with household income	0.263	0.264	28,131
Benefit dependence: Main source of income is pension or other benefit	0.323	0.468	27,963
Religiosity: Index of level of religiosity, frequency of attendance of religious services, and frequency of praying ($\alpha = 0.848$)	0.337	0.299	22,643
Union: Current or former member of trade union	0.394	0.489	28,242

Table 8A.2   Party classifications

Country	Socialist/green	Center-left	Center-right	Anti-immigrant
Austria	Grüne	SPÖ	ÖVP, NEOS, Stronach	FPÖ, BZÖ
Belgium	Groen!, PvdA+, Ecolo, PTB	Open VLD, PS	CD&V, N-VA, CDH, MR	VB
Finland	VIHR, VAS	SFP, KESK, SDP	KOK, KD	PS
France	LO, FDG, EELV, other green	NC, PRG, PS, MODEM	UMP	FN, MPF
Germany	Linke, Grünen	SDP, Piraten	CDU/CSU, FDP	AfD, NPD
Iceland	VG	BF, FSF, S, Vidreisn, P	SSF	F
Ireland	PBP, GP, SF	LAB, SD	FF, FG	
Italy	SEL	PD, M5S	UDC, PdL, Destra	LN, FdI
Netherlands	SP, GL, PvdD	PvdA, D66, 50+	VVD, CDA, CU, SGP	PVV
Norway	Rødt, SV, MDG	A, V, SP	KRF, H	FRP
Portugal	BE, PCP-PEV, PAN	PS	PPD-PSD/CDS-PP	
Spain	Pod, ECP, Comp, PACMA	PSOE, ERC, CDC-PdeCat	PP, Cs, EAJ-PNV	
Sweden	MP, V, FI	C, S	FP, KD, M	SD
Switzerland	GPS	SP, GLP	FDP, CVP, BDP, EVP	SVP
United Kingdom	GP	LAB, LD, SNP, PC, SDLP	CON	UKIP

Welfare chauvinist or neoliberal opposition   173

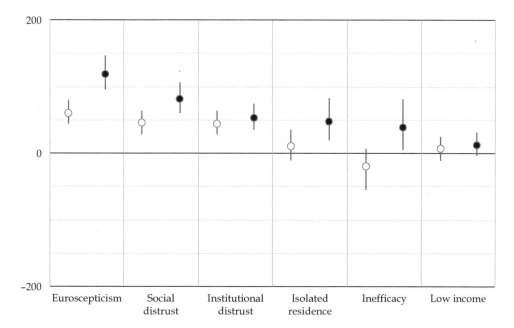

Note: Figure depicts predicted percentage change in probability of neoliberal opposition (open markers) and welfare chauvinism (closed markers) with a maximum increase in the value of the independent variable, with 95 percent confidence interval, while controlling for all other variables, country-fixed effects, and views on neoliberalism. For the variables Euroscepticism, social distrust, and institutional distrust, the figure depicts the predicted change in probability with an increase of half the maximum range. Estimates based on six different multinomial regression models in which the variable under study has been switched for (a) highly correlated variable(s) in the model in Table 8.2 (not shown, but can be made available upon request).

Figure 8A.1   Effects of variables that were omitted to avoid multicollinearity

174 *Handbook on migration and welfare*

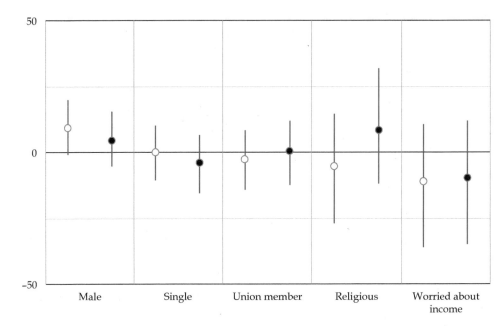

Note: Figure depicts predicted percentage change in probability of neoliberal opposition (open markers) and welfare chauvinism (closed markers) with a maximum increase in the value of the independent variable, with 95 percent confidence interval, while controlling for all other variables, country-fixed effects, and views on neoliberalism. Estimates based on multinomial regression model that adds these variables to the model in Table 8.2 (not shown, but can be made available upon request).

Figure 8A.2   Effects of variables that were omitted because of lack of explanatory power

9. Personal and contextual foundations of welfare chauvinism in Western Europe
Conrad Ziller and Romana Careja

INTRODUCTION

Europe has faced an increase in immigration during the past decades. This development has triggered public and political debate about the integration of immigrants, which includes immigrants' access to social security systems. At the same time, a classical anti-immigrant narrative is that immigrants are "free-riders" who receive social benefits without having contributed adequately. Welfare chauvinism in the context of immigration entertains this belief, and refers to the individual perception that welfare state access should remain the preserve of native-born citizens. As such, welfare chauvinism is—in its core—about how group-based social inequality is perceived and justified.

This chapter reviews personal and contextual foundations of welfare chauvinistic beliefs in immigrant-receiving societies in Western Europe. First, we focus on matters related to the conceptualization and measurement of welfare chauvinistic attitudes. Second, we review theoretical mechanisms and empirical evidence on individual-level factors that underlie welfare chauvinistic beliefs. This includes individuals' social status, perceived deprivation, as well as value-related orientations. Third, we examine contextual determinants referred to in the literature. In addition to the presence of immigrants and asylum seekers, which has been heightened as an influential factor in intergroup conflict approaches, we examine the role of economic, political and institutional factors. Fourth, we conduct an empirical analysis using two waves of the European Social Survey merged with contextual country-level information on economic, immigration-related and policy-related factors. The chapter concludes by referring to recent conceptual developments and methodological advances (e.g., longitudinal research and experiments), as well as open questions that should be addressed in future research on welfare chauvinism in immigrant-receiving societies.

Conceptual Matters

The term welfare chauvinism originates from studies aiming at accounting for the unorthodox position occupied by political parties that, in the market-state dimension, exert support for extensive welfare state measures (similar to left-leaning parties), but in the sociocultural dimension occupy conservative-authoritarian positions by claiming that the national culture should be the dominant one—a stance typically rooted in nativist arguments drawing on the notion of incompatibility between cultures. In a related vein, Andersen and Bjørklund (1990) analyzed emerging cleavages in the Nordic countries, and observed that voters of the so-called Progress Parties in Denmark and Norway supported redistribution (as they were likely to benefit directly from it), but at the same time favored excluding immigrants from state-provided welfare. The authors concluded "we think that 'welfare state chauvinism'—the welfare services should be restricted to 'our own'—is a more appropriate headline for support to the Progress parties than 'racism' or 'prejudice'" (p. 210). A few years later, Kitschelt and McGann (1995) elaborated a definition of welfare chauvinism as an ideological position according to which "the welfare state ... is a system of social protection for those who belong to the ethnically defined community and who have contributed to it" (p. 22). With some variations (van der Waal et al. 2010; De Koster et al. 2013; Jylhä et al. 2019; Goldschmidt and Rydgren 2018, for more complex definitions see Crepaz and Damron 2009), this definition underlies the vast majority of the empirical investigations of causes and effects of welfare chauvinism.

The relevance of this term has grown exponentially since it was first coined in 1990: a Google Scholar search (excluding citations and patents) finds that "welfare chauvinism" appeared in 18 instances between 1991 and 1995, in 53 between 1996 and 2000, in more than 100 between 2001 and 2005, in more than 200 between 2006 and 2010, in almost 800 between 2011 and 2015 and in more than 2,800 between 2016 and 2020. At the same time, the term "welfare chauvinism" has not been unanimously embraced. For example, Larsen (2020) considers that "welfare chauvinism" carries negative connotations, and therefore uses the term "welfare nationalism" instead.[1] Other authors describe the same phenomenon with terms like "welfare restrictiveness" (Degen et al. 2019), "exclusive solidarity" (Lefkofridi and Michel 2017) or "selective solidarity" (Koning 2013; Magni 2020).

Measurement of Welfare Chauvinistic Beliefs

Within the community of scholars studying "welfare chauvinistic attitudes," the approach of measurement follows two strategies by and large (for exceptions, see Crepaz and Damron 2009; Crepaz 2020; Häusermann and Kriesi 2015; van der Waal et al. 2010). The first one emphasizes the "exclusion" element of welfare chauvinism, thereby opting for a binary measure where agreement with statements that explicitly exclude immigrants from redistribution is considered "welfare chauvinism" (Heizmann et al. 2018; Mewes and Mau 2012; Hjorth 2016). The second is based on the argument that welfare chauvinism attitudes are a matter of degree: people often express agreement with a partial exclusion, and few people are in favor of excluding foreigners from redistribution altogether. To empirically investigate these degrees of welfare chauvinism, the European Social Survey includes an item measuring degrees of conditionality with regard to granting immigrants' social rights. This approach has been widely adopted in previous comparative studies (Kros and Coenders 2019; Eger and Breznau 2017; Mewes and Mau 2013; van der Waal et al. 2013; Reeskens and Van Oorschot 2012). Although the European Social Survey item formulation captures opinions about the *inclusion* of immigrants into the group of social rights recipients, many scholars used this scale in order to measure approval of degrees of *exclusion*. In any case, these strategies for measuring welfare chauvinism rely on the assumption that individuals' responses are driven by their preferences for excluding immigrants from an *existing* system of redistribution. In contrast, some authors opt to measure welfare chauvinism conjointly as support for redistribution and preferences for excluding immigrants (De Koster et al. 2013; Jylhä et al. 2019).

INDIVIDUAL-LEVEL FOUNDATIONS

In the following section, we systematically identify individual-level factors associated with welfare chauvinistic attitudes.

Economic Concerns and Relative Group Status as Determinants

The effect of economic factors on attitudes toward immigrants is explained in the vast majority of studies by realistic conflict (or ethnic competition) and related theories (Blumer 1958; Stephan and Renfro 2002). According to conflict theory, members of the ingroup are aware of the scarcity of certain resources, and construe members of the outgroup as competitors for these resources. However, this is true only for some of the members of the ingroup. In particular, individuals who objectively find themselves in precarious economic positions (e.g., welfare-dependent or unemployed), or who perceive themselves as being at risk (e.g., of unemployment or of losing welfare benefits) are more likely to see immigrants as competitors for the resources they themselves need, such as jobs or benefits (Kurer 2020). Ethnic competition theory is often complemented with insights from ethnic threat theory, according to which individuals identify with one group, and construe the interests of the ingroup as being in conflict with the interests of outgroups (Esses et al. 1998). When members of an ingroup perceive a certain level of threat to the group and its interests, they react by expressing negative prejudice against outgroups and their members. As Allport (1954) has argued, the presence of prejudice is a precondition for other acts directed toward members of outgroups, from verbal expressions through to denial of access to resources (up to violent acts).

Both theories have been used to explain the occurrence of welfare chauvinistic attitudes. As predicted by ethnic competition theory, individuals with a low socioeconomic position, who are unemployed and welfare-dependent, or have a low income, have all been found to express welfare chauvinistic attitudes. This indicates that perceived ethnic competition is a relevant underlying mechanism (Mewes and Mau 2012; Crepaz 2020; Heizmann et al. 2018; Reeskens and Van Oorschot 2012; Crepaz and Damron 2009; however, in a Dutch sample van der Waal et al. 2010 did not find a significant effect of weak economic positions of low-educated individuals). Moreover, it is not only objective economic conditions, but also subjective perceptions such as personal assessment of income, or own perception of being at risk, that are associated with welfare chauvinistic attitudes (Heizmann et al. 2018; Reeskens and Van Oorschot 2012). Mewes and Mau (2013) argue that welfare chauvinistic attitudes cannot be separated from broader phenomena such as globalization, which embeds individuals in processes that simultaneously enhance contact with foreigners, as well as exacerbating competition for scarce resources. The authors find that globalization moderates the effects of socioeconomic status in a nuanced manner: those with a relatively high socioeconomic status temper their welfare chauvinistic attitudes under the condition of prevalent social globalization (i.e., enhanced contact with immigrants), but increase them when faced with the effects of economic globalization (i.e., enhanced labor market competition).

While most of the studies cited use cross-sectional datasets (with the limitations of cross-sectional research designs), there are a handful of studies that implement more complex designs. Although sacrificing the breath of the study (as they include data from fewer countries), experimental and longitudinal research designs uncover the complex mechanisms that link individual objective and subjective economic conditions to welfare chauvinistic attitudes. For example, Hjorth's (2016) survey experiment (on a Swedish sample) found that while individual self-interest matters for welfare chauvinism, individuals' opinions about immigrants' access to benefits rely on more complex chains of factors: he found that both stereotypes and prejudices about beneficiaries as well as individuals' sensitivity to economic threat are mechanisms through which information about race and migrant status is translated into predispositions to limit foreigners' access to financial support (i.e., welfare chauvinism). More recently, Kros and Coenders (2019), using a four-wave panel in the United Kingdom and the Netherlands, found that the effect of subjective and objective individual economic risk on welfare chauvinism is carried by respondents' perception of ethnic threat, independent of their egalitarian economic views.

Another potential driver of anti-immigrant attitudes, more generally, is relative deprivation, a feeling triggered not by what one has, but by what one wants to have and perceives to be entitled to have. At the core of the theory of relative deprivation is the argument that, relatively independent of their objective situation, those who perceive themselves as worse off than others are likely to express negative emotions and attitudes (Runciman 1966; Smith et al. 2012). Deprivation at group level occurs when individuals conduct a negative comparison on behalf of their entire group against the position of another group, while individual relative deprivation is generated by negative comparisons between individuals and their peers. Both individual and group-based relative deprivation have been found to be associated with perceptions of ethnic threat (Meuleman et al. 2020) and anti-immigrant prejudice (Pettigrew et al. 2008; Yoxon et al. 2019a, 2019b). Although to the best of our knowledge, no study has so far explored the impact of relative deprivation on welfare chauvinistic attitudes, the study by Ferrera and Pellegata (2018) suggests that a positive impact is likely. The two authors found that labor market-chauvinistic attitudes, i.e., support for the exclusion of immigrants from labor market access, are affected by intergroup contact experiences, as well as by perceived relative deprivation.

Yet another category of studies embraces sociotropic explanations. Sociotropic concerns originating in both economic concerns and in cultural ones have been found to be associated with anti-immigrant attitudes (for an extensive overview, see Hainmueller and Hopkins 2014). Recently, Solodoch (2020) found that sociotropic concerns about economic and cultural implications of immigration are relevant drivers of immigration preferences, while ethnic prejudice as a motivational force only plays a moderate role. Gerber et al. (2017) show that concerns about fiscal burden for welfare states due to immigration predict an increase in opposition to immigration. In a related vein, Tzeng and Tsai (2020) find that individuals who are worried about welfare-related burdens rejected low-skilled immigration, but those concerned that immigrants would take away jobs disapproved of both low-skilled and high-skilled immigration. Although these factors are not at the center of studies on welfare chauvinistic attitudes, similar empirical relationships have been found with regard to such attitudes (Crepaz 2020; Kros and Coenders 2019).

Social Identity and Value Orientations

Apart from motives centered on economic threat, identity-related and cultural concerns of immigrants undermining the national cohesion and cultural homogeneity of receiving societies have been heightened as critical individual-level determinants of anti-immigrant attitudes. Given that negative intergroup relations potentially spur zero-sum perceptions and envious reactions when immigrants make economic progress and assimilate (Wilkins and Kaiser 2014; Ziller 2020), we may presume a similar mechanism to be in operation in the case of welfare chauvinistic views toward immigrants.

A number of authors have extended ethnic threat theory to argue that underlying perceptions and feelings originate not only in (egoistic or sociotropic) economic concerns, but also in concerns over one's own group's distinctiveness vis-à-vis an outgroup. According to social identity theory (Tajfel 1978; Tajfel and Turner 1979), it is common for individuals to identify with groups, and individuals differentiate between groups in such a way that ingroups are positively evaluated in comparison to outgroups. More importantly, however, from the perspective of attitude formation/expression, people tend to display a favorable bias toward members of the ingroup, and an unfavorable one toward members of outgroups, which facilitates a positive social identity. When national identification, which provides group boundaries and the blueprint for understanding and assessing outgroup behavior, is the basis for establishing social identity, then immigrants are the obvious "other" who is denigrated and rejected (Wimmer 2008).

The association between anti-immigrant attitudes and national identification has been repeatedly confirmed (Billiet et al. 2003; Pehrson et al. 2009; Kende et al. 2018), and more recently the distinction into distinct sentiments regarding national identification, nationalism and patriotism has resulted in more nuanced findings: anti-immigrant sentiments are associated with nationalism, but not with patriotism (Wagner et al. 2012; Raijman and Hochman 2011; Mummendey et al. 2001). Some studies have focused on the relationship between national identification and identified feelings of threat as a mediator that translates how national identification relates to rejection of immigrants or other negative outcomes (prejudice, derogation, bias) (Caricati 2018; Falomir-Pichastor and Frederic 2013). Relatedly, social disintegration theory incorporates the sociopolitical context in explaining attitudinal consequences of social identification. It states that—under conditions of rapid societal change and (perceived) disintegration—people's identification with an ingroup (as well as the devaluation of and discriminatory acts toward outgroups) becomes a remedy in order to cope with feelings of uncertainty (Anhut and Heitmeyer 2000).

Another critically relevant determinant of anti-immigrant attitudes is individual ideological positions and values. In particular, authoritarian predispositions have been repeatedly found to be associated with a large array of negative outgroup attitudes, including anti-immigrant attitudes (McFarland 2010; Yoxon et al. 2019a, 2019b; Cohrs and Stelzl 2010). Such an association is explained by the fact that immigration is seen as a threat to the core elements of an authoritarian worldview, i.e., maintenance of order, pre-eminence of group norms, cohesion and stability (Duckitt 2006). Individual values have been found to be connected to anti-immigrant attitudes in complex ways. In a series of studies, Davidov and colleagues found that conservative individuals are more adverse to immigration, while self-transcendent individuals are more supportive (Davidov and

Meuleman 2012). Similarly, universalism values appear to be associated with positive attitudes toward immigration, and conformity or tradition reinforce anti-immigration sentiments, while these effects are moderated by the level of cultural embeddedness and size of the immigrant group in the country (Davidov et al. 2014). Moreover, symbolic threat has been found to mediate the relationship between values and attitudes (Davidov et al. 2020).

From a somewhat different (yet related) perspective, social dominance theory (Sidanius and Pratto 1999) argues that individuals desire for their own group to occupy a superior or dominant position vis-à-vis other groups that are considered to be inferior. This in turn results in an expression of bias, prejudice and derogatory treatment toward members of outgroups. People who are high in social dominance orientation tend to perceive outgroups as potential competitors for social status. Negative attitudes toward immigrants have been found to be correlated to a higher social dominance orientation (Kuepper et al. 2010; Guimond et al. 2013; McFarland 2010; Danso et al. 2007; Duriez and Van Hiel 2002; Pratto et al. 1997).

Value-related factors have also been explored in relation to welfare chauvinism. In line with studies of anti-immigrant attitudes more generally, authoritarian views are associated with agreement with welfare chauvinistic positions (Mewes and Mau 2012; Crepaz 2020). Moreover, the effect of authoritarianism mitigates the impact of objective economic conditions, but not that of subjective ones (Mewes and Mau 2012). The positive effect of stereotypes (Hjorth 2016) and ethnocentric attitudes (Ford 2016) on welfare chauvinistic attitudes has been explained in light of individuals' perception of belonging to a group. As immigrants are a social group that strives toward upward mobility, it is plausible that people who score highly in social dominance orientation are particularly prone to limit immigrants' access to social rights, which are one of the facilitating factors of social mobility. Eger and Breznau (2017) directly test the social identity argument, and find that those who differentiate strongly between groups also display reduced support for a variety of redistribution-related issues, including limiting immigrants' access to social rights. Van der Waal and colleagues (2010) bring to the fore a classical argument according to which, more than education, a person's entire cultural capital has a liberalizing effect because it provides a sophisticated understanding of society and of social relations between groups. The authors focus on low-educated individuals (who consistently display welfare chauvinistic attitudes), and found for this group that it was not the low competences or the precarious economic position that transmitted the effect of education, but the limited cultural capital, and the cultural insecurity. Interestingly, studies that tested competing hypotheses originating in value theories or economic threat/conflict theories found that the latter are not supported when value-related factors are included in the analysis (see e.g., Mewes and Mau 2012; van der Waal et al. 2010; but see Hjorth 2016 and Ford 2016, who find support for both explanations).

CONTEXTUAL FOUNDATIONS

In addition to individual-level explanations of variations of welfare chauvinism, researchers have looked at the degree to which welfare chauvinistic attitudes vary across countries, and have examined to what extent these differences may be explained by specific economic, demographic and political country-level characteristics.

Economic Factors

Mapping theoretical arguments related to realistic group threat, scholars have argued that economic circumstances, especially resource stress such as labor market competition or an economic crisis, result in immigrants (and other minorities) being perceived as competitors (Kuntz et al. 2017; Hainmueller and Hiscox 2010; Quillian 1995). Similarly, economic downturns and high or increasing unemployment rates can be expected to fuel welfare chauvinism, while economic growth and low unemployment should mitigate it. Mewes and Mau (2012) find that greater wealth (measured as gross domestic product (GDP) per capita) negatively relates to welfare chauvinistic attitudes, while unemployment rates are positively associated, providing empirical evidence to arguments informed by realistic group conflict. However, not all the evidence points in the same direction, as other studies find no systematic association for country-specific wealth (Gorodzeisky and Semyonov 2009; Heizmann et al. 2018), unemployment rates (Eger and Breznau 2017) or sector-specific employment conditions (Mewes and Mau 2012). Moreover, van der Waal et al. (2013) find that in contexts of greater income inequality, immigrants are perceived to be less entitled to welfare benefits, compared to contexts in which there is less inequality.

Demographic Factors

In the 1990s, immigrants became increasingly portrayed in several Western European countries as being difficult to integrate and highly dependent on welfare, and public opinion turned increasingly negative. Some studies find that the presence of immigrants was associated with opposition to immigration (Bohman and Hjerm 2016), and with a variety of anti-immigrant attitudes (Schlueter and Scheepers 2010; see also Ceobanu and Escandell 2010), but other authors disagree. Hjerm (2007), for example, argues that neither the real nor the perceived size of immigrant groups matters for anti-immigrant attitudes, while Laurence and Bentley (2018) find that increased ethnic diversity in fact leads to a polarization of attitudes, which means an increase in both positive and negative sentiments.

Existing research has found a similarly ambiguous pattern with regard to welfare chauvinistic attitudes: while several studies find non-significant effects of proportions of immigrants (van der Waal et al. 2013; Reeskens and Van Oorschot 2012; Mewes and Mau 2012; Crepaz and Damron 2009), Eger and Breznau (2017) use proportions of immigrant groups as an indicator at both national and regional levels, and find negative effects only in the former case. This indicates that, in regions with a large proportion of foreigners, individuals articulate lower levels of welfare chauvinism (compared to regions with a small proportion of foreigners). Under an even stronger magnifying lens, combining contextual and experimental evidence, van der Meer and Reeskens (2020) find that ethnically diverse neighborhoods are linked to substantially higher levels of welfare chauvinism among residents. Although not directly measuring the impact of immigrant group size, Marx and Naumann's experiment—conducted at a time of peak immigration during the so-called refugee crisis in Germany—finds an increase in welfare chauvinistic attitudes across the entire political spectrum, and argues that the refugee crisis (resulting in increasing numbers of foreigners in Germany) has triggered a "general psychological disposition to respond to growing population heterogeneity with in-group favouritism" (Marx and Naumann 2018, p. 115).

Political and Institutional Factors

Welfare state regimes
In an early study on the role of welfare institutions, Crepaz and Damron (2009) argue (and empirically show) that the degree of decommodification—that is, the programmatic aspects of welfare states that reflect the degree to which social security is detached from market-based mechanisms—has a statistically significant negative effect on welfare chauvinism among the population. In other words, welfare systems that take responsibility in promoting social security as an element of public service provision facilitate solidarity among its citizens (or at least reduce perceptions of group-based competition for welfare services). With regard to welfare regimes, van der Waal and colleagues (2013) corroborate the earlier finding by Crepaz and Damron (2009) that social democratic welfare states are characterized by lower levels of welfare chauvinistic attitudes among their citizens. However, their more detailed analysis, focusing on the characteristics of the welfare systems, found that the varying levels of welfare chauvinism cannot be explained by differences in the selectivity of a welfare state (i.e., universal versus means-tested), or differences in employment protection policies. Instead, the variation in welfare chauvinism across welfare regimes is driven by the capacity of welfare regimes to mitigate income inequality.

Looking at welfare systems under the principles that govern their notions of redistribution such as need, equality and merit, Reeskens and Van Oorschot (2012) found that citizens who favor merit or equality-based redistribution did not significantly differ in their attitudes toward immigrants. However, they found that citizens who favor needs-based redistribution are more likely to exclude immigrants from welfare access. Most recently, Larsen (2020) finds that existing entitlement criteria for immigrants shape both how the public perceives these entitlement criteria as well as the preferences for which entitlement criteria are seen as appropriate. In other words, the prevalent institutional context of welfare state access shapes citizens' normative views on which groups should, and should not, profit from welfare state measures.

In addition to these studies focusing on broad principles of welfare state institutions, several empirical works have tested more specific dimensions: Mewes and Mau (2012) find a negative relationship between social spending and welfare chauvinism, while studies by Eger and Breznau (2017) or Reeskens and Van Oorschot (2012) find no conclusive evidence regarding the role of overall social spending. A potential reason for the divergent patterns might be rooted in sample characteristics such as different countries or time points included, as well as further variation in research designs such as the type and number of control variables included. In essence, it needs to be emphasized that most of the studies reviewed use cross-sectional designs that are prone to suffer from omitted variable bias (but see Heizmann et al. 2018). Longitudinal approaches have only limited utility for welfare regimes, as their characteristics hardly change over time. At the same time, social spending may change over time, but is generally conflated with further political characteristics such as incumbent government goals and party politics, as well as policy-related factors including immigrant integration policies and the provision of social rights for minority groups more generally. These characteristics may have normative effects on citizens and their readiness to demand that outgroups be excluded from welfare benefits. We thus review the role of policies and political parties in the next section.

The role of policies and political parties
Besides the role of welfare regimes and general approaches to social security systems, another relevant factor consists of policies and regulations (Pierson 1993). Koning (2020) shows substantial variations in social rights for immigrants across European countries, while many countries have made efforts to adapt their welfare systems with the specific aim of better accommodating immigrants. Numerous studies have identified that populist right-wing parties have been the main promoters of welfare chauvinistic policies (Lefkofridi and Michel 2017). Radical right-wing parties typically justify their positions in terms of protecting the welfare state from being exploited by non-natives (Careja et al. 2016; Keskinen 2016; Jørgensen and Thomsen 2016; Norocel 2016), while mainstream center-right parties are by no means immune from this political issue. They have even been found to adapt their positions on welfare and social policy by becoming more exclusionary in response to the positioning and electoral success of (populist) radical right-wing parties (Schumacher and Van Kersbergen 2016; Koning 2017).

In this context, a handful of studies find a link between policies and welfare chauvinistic attitudes. Häusermann and Kriesi (2015) argue that welfare chauvinism is part of a new electoral universalism–particularism cleavage, which is shaped by a series of transformations prompted by globalization-related processes. The authors find that economic preferences are a driving force for voters of various left-wing parties, but not for voters of right-wing populist parties who are motivated by cultural factors related to immigration. They argue that welfare chauvinism is a distribution-related issue that is clearly different from other distribution-related preferences, as it is motivated by both economic and cultural factors. Fernández (2019) argues that the rights which immigrants possess under different models of citizenship reflect different conceptualizations of community and "us" versus "them" distinctions. He finds that regulations related to citizenship play a role in shaping individuals' preferences concerning the scope of redistribution: pluralist incorporation regimes are associated with greater acceptance of immigrants being included in welfare redistribution.

EMPIRICAL EXAMPLE USING EUROPEAN SOCIAL SURVEY DATA

Empirical Setup

The aim of the following empirical exercise is to illustrate how personal and contextual determinants relate to welfare chauvinistic attitudes in Western European countries. To do so, we use two waves of the European Social Survey (2008 and 2016) which entail measures of welfare chauvinism. Similar to previous studies, we use an ordinal measure representing varying degrees of conditionality of permitting immigrants' social rights. Specifically, respondents were asked whether they approve of immigrants being entitled to receive welfare benefits upon arrival, after living in the receiving country for at least one year (whether they have worked or not), after at least one year of having worked and paid taxes, upon becoming citizens, or never. We build a scale with four answer categories as done in previous studies (Reeskens and Van Oorschot 2012) by collapsing the two categories referring to living in the receiving country into one category (recoded scale ranges from 1 to 4, where higher values reflect greater welfare chauvinism).

As relevant individual-level predictors, we include respondents' gender (dummy variable, 1 = female), age in years and education (ISCED-coded dummy variables, ranging from no formal education to tertiary education completed). As factors mapping economic relative deprivation, we include variables on employment status (dummy variables: employed, unemployed, housework/in education and retired/permanently sick), as well as coping on current income (four-point scale ranging from "very difficult" to "very comfortable"). As an indicator related to values centered on defending the status quo (including group-related arrangements), we employ an indicator of conservatism using items from Schwartz's basic human values (Schwartz 1992). This conservatism indicator refers to respondents' approval of three sub-scales: tradition (e.g., importance of "following traditions"), conformity (e.g., importance of "following rules") and security (e.g., importance of "living in safe surroundings"). Cronbach's alpha indicates a reliable scale of 0.73. Moreover, as we are interested in responses in the native population, we include only respondents who themselves and their parents were born in the survey country. It is noteworthy that the results reported below are substantially similar when including all respondents.

In addition to the individual-level factors, we also merge time-varying country-level information into the survey waves used. Per capita GDP, as well as unemployment rates in 2008 and 2016 (from the Eurostat database), serve as indicators of potential resource conflict. Proportions of immigrants in 2008 and 2016 (from the Eurostat database) are used to indicate a potential source of identity conflict and salience of immigration, which should also capture heterogeneous developments over time due to the so-called refugee crisis (Heizmann and Ziller 2020). To indicate differences in immigrant integration policies, we use data from the Migrant Integration Policy Index (MIPEX; Huddleston et al. 2015) in 2010 and 2015.[2] Moreover, we include social spending as a share of a country's GDP to indicate governments' overall welfare generosity (from the Eurostat database).

In terms of method, we use a multilevel framework, and incorporate a country-year random intercept in the empirical models (Schmidt-Catran and Fairbrother 2016). To account for common shifts in the outcome variable over time, we include a time variable (i.e., a time fixed effect). Moreover, we examine the robustness of the country-level estimates by including country fixed effects that absorb all cross-sectional variance and thus account for unobserved heterogeneity at country level. As this leaves us with variation over time at macro level only, we avoid potentially biased coefficient estimates due to omitted country-level variables, including historical legacies or institutional differences, which essentially represents a rigorous control strategy (Allison 2009). To facilitate the interpretation of the results, we use an identity link function as an estimation strategy (linear multilevel regression). Using an ordered logistic link function nonetheless leads to substantially similar conclusions. All continuous predictor variables have been linearly transformed to range between 0 and 1, which facilitates the interpretation and comparability of coefficient estimates in terms of effect sizes.

Empirical Results

Table 9.1 presents the results from multilevel regression results. Model 1 includes individual-level predictor variables. With reference to sociodemographic and socioeconomic background variables, we find that age positively relates to welfare chauvinistic

Table 9.1 Results from multilevel regression models (European Social Survey waves 2008 and 2016)

Dependent variable	(M1) Welfare chauvinism	(M2) Welfare chauvinism	(M3) Welfare chauvinism
Age	0.097**	0.097**	0.097**
	(0.028)	(0.028)	(0.028)
Female	−0.049**	−0.049**	−0.049**
	(0.008)	(0.008)	(0.008)
Education, ref.: less than lower secondary education (ISCED 0–1)			
Lower secondary education completed (ISCED 2)	−0.026	−0.026	−0.027
	(0.015)	(0.015)	(0.015)
Upper secondary education completed (ISCED 3)	−0.054**	−0.055**	−0.055**
	(0.014)	(0.014)	(0.014)
Post-secondary non-tertiary education completed (ISCED 4)	−0.090**	−0.090**	−0.091**
	(0.022)	(0.022)	(0.022)
Tertiary education completed (ISCED 5–6)	−0.215**	−0.215**	−0.216**
	(0.015)	(0.015)	(0.015)
Coping on income	−0.153**	−0.153**	−0.153**
	(0.017)	(0.017)	(0.017)
Employment status, ref.: employed	0.000	0.000	0.000
Unemployed			
	(0.020)	(0.020)	(0.020)
Housework/education	−0.065**	−0.065**	−0.066**
	(0.012)	(0.012)	(0.012)
Retired/sick	−0.034**	−0.034**	−0.034**
	(0.012)	(0.012)	(0.012)
Conservation values	0.414**	0.416**	0.415**
	(0.025)	(0.025)	(0.025)
Per capita GDP		−0.023	0.520
		(0.138)	(0.288)
Unemployment rate		−0.418**	0.113
		(0.134)	(0.133)
Proportion of immigrants		−0.367**	0.559*
		(0.131)	(0.245)
MIPEX integration policy		−0.320**	−0.324
		(0.085)	(0.215)
Social spending (% of GDP)		0.085	0.431
		(0.106)	(0.250)

Table 9.1 (continued)

Dependent variable	(M1)	(M2)	(M3)
	Welfare chauvinism	Welfare chauvinism	Welfare chauvinism
Constant	2.161**	2.475**	1.747**
	(0.048)	(0.125)	(0.260)
Time fixed effects	Yes	Yes	Yes
Country fixed effects	No	No	Yes
Random effects (std. dev.)			
Random intercept (country-year)	0.146**	0.099**	0.033**
	(0.021)	(0.014)	(0.006)
Residual	0.800**	0.800**	0.800**
	(0.003)	(0.003)	(0.003)
N respondents	41932	41932	41932
N country-years	26	26	26

Note: Countries included: Austria, Belgium, Finland, France, Germany, Ireland, the Netherlands, Norway, Portugal, Spain, Sweden, Switzerland and the United Kingdom; standard errors in parentheses; * $p < 0.05$, ** $p < 0.01$.

attitudes. With reference to the coefficient for age, comparing respondents with the lowest and highest ages is associated with an increase of 0.1 in welfare chauvinistic attitudes. Given a standard deviation of 0.8, the age effect is rather small. Being female is negatively and statistically significantly related to welfare chauvinism, but the association is negligible in terms of effect size. Estimates of educational levels show that having completed tertiary education compared to less than lower secondary education is negatively and significantly related to welfare chauvinistic attitudes. With reference to variables indicating occupational status and income, we find that people's perception of living comfortably on their current income (compared to having difficulties) is systematically related to lower welfare chauvinism. While being in an educational program or being retired is related to a slight decrease in welfare chauvinism, being unemployed yields no statistically significant association (given other included covariates on social status). Conservative values are strongly related to greater levels of welfare chauvinistic attitudes (0.4, which equals half a standard deviation of the outcome).

Model 2 additionally includes country-level covariates. As for economic factors, unemployment negatively and statistically significantly relates to welfare chauvinism, while wealth is not significantly related. Immigration is negatively (and significantly) associated with welfare chauvinism. At the same time, we find that permissive integration policies relate to lower levels of welfare chauvinism across countries. In contrast, social spending is not a significant macro-level predictor.[3] The individual-level estimates are virtually congruent to those obtained from Model 1. Nevertheless, we cannot rule out the possibility that unobserved heterogeneity drives the results found, especially for country-level predictor variables. We thus estimate a model (Model 3) with country fixed effects. From this model, we find that only proportions of immigrants as a macro-level factor are statistically significantly related to welfare chauvinism. In contrast to Model 2 based on cross-sectional variance, the effect is now positive, meaning that an increase in immigration over time relates to increasing levels of welfare chauvinism.[4] The relationship is substantially strong in terms of effect size. Moving from the country with the lowest level of immigration to that with the highest level is associated with an increase in the outcome variable by 0.6 (i.e., three-quarters of a standard deviation), which even exceeds the effect size of conservative values.

CONCLUDING REMARKS AND OUTLOOK

This review examined the role of individual-level and contextual determinants of welfare chauvinistic attitudes in Western Europe. Among the individual-level factors, we reviewed the literature focused on socioeconomic status, perceived relative deprivation and value-related determinants. Although personal economic status and sociotropic concerns about the fiscal consequences of immigration are prominently mentioned in public debate and numerous research articles, their effects are actually ambiguous. While there is only limited support for the role of individuals' economic circumstances and labor market positions, perceptions about relative group positioning appear to be more relevant (Smith et al. 2012), especially for people who are prone to thinking in terms of zero-sum competition (Esses et al. 1998; Ziller 2020). In a related vein, approaches that focus on individual differences in value orientations and personality traits have highlighted the role of preferences related to social hierarchy and dominance, conformity, tradition or openness toward outgroups, which in turn are relevant in the generation of welfare chauvinistic beliefs or support for minority social rights (Sidanius and Pratto 1999; Ziller and Berning 2019).

As for contextual determinants of welfare chauvinism, we reviewed economic, demographic and political factors. Economic conditions are relevant for citizens, as they represent cues about resource strains and developments related to labor markets. Citizens are typically quite aware of the broad economic developments in their country, which renders economic conditions as relevant contexts for the development of welfare chauvinistic attitudes on the part of native citizens. Notwithstanding their prominent role in comparative cross-national studies, their predictive capacity remains ambiguous, in terms of both direction and magnitude. Political and institutional factors critically shape resource distribution and access to welfare programs and other public services, which makes them a likely candidate for shaping public opinion related to welfare chauvinism. However, the reviewed studies on political and institutional conditions produced ambivalent findings. It is important at the same time to note that most studies rely on cross-sectional observational research designs. One reason for this is that the mentioned factors (e.g., welfare state regimes) are typically quite constant over time, which makes it difficult to implement experimental or longitudinal research designs. Nonetheless, this raises the question as to the extent to which the results are robust to unobserved heterogeneity. In addition to economic and political factors, we also included demographic factors related to immigration and ethnic diversity in our review, as they have become increasingly relevant, due not least to the so-called refugee crisis of 2014–16. Again, we find studies producing empirical associations that range from negative effects, through null findings, to positive effects.

Subsequent to the review of the literature, we conducted an empirical analysis using data from the European Social Survey (waves 4 and 8) from 13 Western European countries. In line with the current literature, we find that individuals' socioeconomic status and resource stress have limited explanatory capacity compared to value orientations related to conservative values (similar to findings of Mewes and Mau 2012; van der Waal et al. 2010). With regard to macro-level conditions, we find that unemployment rates, liberal integration policies and proportions of immigrants relate to lower levels of welfare chauvinism across countries. However, accounting for unobserved heterogeneity using country fixed effects leads to results featuring a positive link between (change in) immigration and (change in) welfare chauvinism, whereas economic and policy-related factors do not yield systematic associations under this rigorous empirical specification. Our finding corroborates evidence from a recent survey experiment (van der Meer and Reeskens 2020), showing that people who are confronted with ethnic diversity are less willing to support welfare measures for immigrants. However, it contrasts null results found by Heizmann et al. (2018), using proportions of asylum seekers as an indicator. A possible reason for the divergent results is that the authors compared Western and Eastern European countries, which were affected by the so-called refugee crisis to different degrees (Heizmann and Ziller 2020).

Another yet understudied line of research is to focus on meaningful interactions between contextual factors and individual attributes. For example, Sibley et al. (2013) find that individuals' value orientations have varying effects on opposition to immigration, depending on the economic or immigration-related conditions of the neighborhoods in which people live. With regard to welfare chauvinistic attitudes, individuals' economic or cultural characteristics might interact with threat-enhancing factors, whether these refer to economic, cultural or political contexts. In a similar vein, Citrin et al. (2014) find that people who oppose immigration become increasingly critical of the political system in countries that have adopted extensive multicultural policies.

In terms of methodology, our review shows that most empirical studies use comparative (cross-national) data. While most studies adequately account for non-dependence of observations using multilevel regression models (Schmidt-Catran and Fairbrother 2016), only a few address issues related to endogeneity and unobserved heterogeneity that could potentially bias coefficient estimates from regression analysis. Apart from longitudinal studies employing fixed effects approaches that are better able to account for unobserved heterogeneity from time-constant confounders, some studies employ experimental methods (e.g., Ford 2016; Hjorth 2016; van der Meer and Reeskens 2020). An important issue in this regard that calls for further attention in studies on welfare chauvinism (and public opinion research more generally) is the trade-off between external validity, referring to the real-world relevance of research findings (typically maximized by representative observational studies), and internal validity, referring to an unbiased identification of causal effects (typically maximized by laboratory experiments).

In common with most existing studies, this review focuses on established welfare states in Western European countries. An important avenue for future research is thus to focus on group-based inclusion and exclusion through social rights and social policies in countries other than those in Europe and North America. Moreover, several recent studies on political behavior have stressed that immediate living environments are a relevant factor in attitude formation, especially regarding intergroup relations (Enos 2017). At the same time, community contexts represent critical environments where national welfare policies are implemented and public service-related problems are resolved (or not) (Ziller and Goodman 2020). We thus suggest that future studies on welfare chauvinism would benefit from applying a more localized focus by taking the role of communities and neighborhoods into account.

NOTES

1. It is important to note that the term welfare nationalism has an ambiguous meaning in the literature. For example, Keskinen (2016) refers to welfare nationalism as the discourse which presents the welfare state as an integral part of nation and national identity.
2. We use the 2010 MIPEX data because the 2007 MIPEX wave has several missing values, and would additionally shrink the number of observations at the country level.
3. Due to non-trivial correlations between the macro-level predictors, we estimated supplementary models with only one macro-level predictor at a time. We find (marginal) statistically significant negative coefficient estimates for unemployment rates (B = –0.384, SE = 0.137, p = 0.005) and immigrant integration policy (B = –0.149, SE = 0.088, p = 0.092).
4. Empirical models with country fixed effects (based on Model 3) incorporating one macro-level predictor at a time return only immigration as a statistically significant coefficient estimate (B = 0.409, SE = 0.196, p = 0.037).

REFERENCES

Allison, Paul. 2009. *Fixed Effects Regression Models*. London: SAGE.
Allport, Gordon. 1954. *The Nature of Prejudice*. Boston, MA: Addison-Wesley.
Andersen, Jørgen, and Tor Bjørklund. 1990. "Structural changes and new cleavages: The progress parties in Denmark and Norway." *Acta Sociologica* 33 (3): 195–217.
Anhut, Reimund, and Wilhelm Heitmeyer. 2000. "Desintegration, Konflikt und Ethnisierung. Eine Problemanalyse und theoretische Rahmenkonzeption [Disintegration, conflict and ethnicisation: A problem analysis and theoretical frame]." In *Bedrohte Stadtgesellschaft*, eds. Wilhelm Heitmeyer and Reimund Anhut, 17–76. Cham: Springer.
Billiet, Jaak, Bart Maddens, and Roeland Beerten. 2003. "National identity and attitude towards foreigners in a multinational state: A replication." *Political Psychology* 24: 241–257.
Blumer, Herbert. 1958. "Race prejudice as a sense of group position." *Pacific Sociological Review* 1 (1): 3–7.
Bohman, Andrea, and Mikael Hjerm. 2016. "In the wake of radical right electoral success: A cross-country comparative study of anti-immigration attitudes over time." *Journal of Ethnic and Migration Studies* 42 (11): 1729–1747.
Careja, Romana, Christian Elmelund-Præstekær, Michael Baggesen Klitgaard, and Erik Gahner Larsen. 2016. "Direct and indirect welfare chauvinism as party strategies: An analysis of the Danish People's Party." *Scandinavian Political Studies* 39 (4): 435–457.
Caricati, Luca. 2018. "Perceived threat mediates the relationship between national identification and support for immigrant exclusion: A cross-national test of intergroup threat theory." *International Journal of Intercultural Relations* 55: 41–51.
Ceobanu, Alin, and Xavier Escandell. 2010. "Comparative analyses of public attitudes toward immigrants and immigration using multinational survey data: A review of theories and research." *Annual Review of Sociology* 36 (1): 309–332.
Citrin, Jack, Morris Levy, and Matthew Wright. 2014. "Multicultural policy and political support in European democracies." *Comparative Political Studies* 47 (11): 1531–1557.
Cohrs, Christopher, and Monika Stelzl. 2010. "How ideological attitudes predict host society members' attitudes toward immigrants: Exploring cross-national differences." *Journal of Social Issues* 66 (4): 673–694.
Crepaz, Markus. 2020. "Coveting uniformity in a diverse world: The authoritarian roots of welfare chauvinism in postmigration crisis Germany." *Social Science Quarterly* 101 (4): 1255–1270.
Crepaz, Markus, and Regan Damron. 2009. "Constructing tolerance: How the welfare state shapes attitudes about immigrants." *Comparative Political Studies* 42 (3): 437–463.

Danso, Henri, Alexandra Sedlovskaya, and Sumarga Suanda. 2007. "Perceptions of immigrants: Modifying the attitudes of individuals higher in social dominance orientation." *Personality and Social Psychology Bulletin* 33 (8): 1113–1123.

Davidov, Eldad, and Bart Meuleman. 2012. "Explaining attitudes towards immigration policies in European countries: The role of human values." *Journal of Ethnic and Migration Studies* 38 (5): 757–775.

Davidov, Eldad, Bart Meuleman, Shalom Schwartz, and Peter Schmidt. 2014. "Individual values, cultural embeddedness, and anti-immigration sentiments: Explaining differences in the effect of values on attitudes toward immigration across Europe." *KZfSS Kölner Zeitschrift für Soziologie und Sozialpsychologie* 66: 263–285.

Davidov, Eldad, Daniel Seddig, Anton Gorodzeisky, Rebeca Raijman, Peter Schmidt, and Moshe Semyonov. 2020. "Direct and indirect predictors of opposition to immigration in Europe: Individual values, cultural values, and symbolic threat." *Journal of Ethnic and Migration Studies* 46 (3): 553–573.

De Koster, Willem, Peter Achterberg, and Jeroen van der Waal. 2013. "The new right and the welfare state: The electoral relevance of welfare chauvinism and welfare populism in the Netherlands." *International Political Science Review* 34 (1): 3–20.

Degen, Daniel, Theresa Kuhn, and Wouter van der Brug. 2019. "Granting immigrants access to social benefits? How self-interest influences support for welfare state restrictiveness." *Journal of European Social Policy* 29 (2): 148–165.

Duckitt, John. 2006. "Differential effects of right wing authoritarianism and social dominance orientation on outgroup attitudes and their mediation by threat from and competitiveness to outgroups." *Personality and Social Psychology Bulletin* 32 (5): 684–696.

Duriez, Bart, and Alain Van Hiel. 2002. "The march of modern fascism: A comparison of social dominance orientation and authoritarianism." *Personality and Individual Differences* 32 (7): 1199–1213.

Eger, Maureen A., and Nate Breznau. 2017. "Immigration and the welfare state: A cross-regional analysis of European welfare attitudes." *International Journal of Comparative Sociology* 58 (5): 440–463.

Enos, Ryan D. 2017. *The Space between Us: Social Geography and Politics*. Cambridge: Cambridge University Press.

Esses, Victoria, Lynne Jackson, and Tamara Armstrong. 1998. "Intergroup competition and attitudes toward immigrants and immigration: An instrumental model of group conflict." *Social Issues* 54 (4): 699–724.

Falomir-Pichastor, Juan, and Natascha Frederic. 2013. "The dark side of heterogeneous ingroup identities: National identification, perceived threat, and prejudice against immigrants." *Journal of Experimental Social Psychology* 49 (1): 72–79.

Fernández, Eva. 2019. "Migration incorporation regimes and institutionalized forms of solidarity: Between unconditional institutional solidarity and welfare chauvinism." *American Behavioral Scientist* 63 (4): 506–522.

Ferrera, Maurizio, and Alessandro Pellegata. 2018. "Worker mobility under attack? Explaining labour market chauvinism in the EU." *Journal of European Public Policy* 25 (10): 1461–1480.

Ford, Robert. 2016. "Who should we help? An experimental test of discrimination in the British welfare state." *Political Studies* 64 (3): 630–650.

Gerber, Alan, Gregory Huber, Daniel Biggers, and David Hendry. 2017. "Self-interest, beliefs, and policy opinions: Understanding how economic beliefs affect immigration policy preferences." *Political Research Quarterly* 70 (1): 155–171.

Goldschmidt, Tina, and Jens Rydgren. 2018. "Social distance, immigrant integration, and welfare chauvinism in Sweden." Discussion Papers, Research Unit: Migration, Integration, Transnationalization SP VI 2018–102, WZB Berlin Social Science Center.

Gorodzeisky, Anastasia, and Moshe Semyonov. 2009. "Terms of exclusion: Public views towards admission and allocation of rights to immigrants in European countries." *Ethnic and Racial Studies* 32 (3): 401–423.

Guimond, Serge, Richard J. Crisp, Pierre de Oliviera, Rodolphe Kamiejski, Nour Kteily, Beate Kuepper, Richard N. Lalonde et al. 2013. "Diversity policy, social dominance, and intergroup relations: Predicting prejudice in changing social and political contexts." *Journal of Personality and Social Psychology* 104 (6): 941–958.

Hainmueller, Jens, and Michael J. Hiscox. 2010. "Attitudes toward highly-skilled and low-skilled immigration: Evidence from a survey experiment." *American Political Science Review* 104 (1): 61–84.

Hainmueller, Jens, and Daniel J. Hopkins. 2014. "Public attitudes toward immigration." *Annual Review of Political Science* 17 (1): 225–249.

Häusermann, Silja, and Hanspeter Kriesi. 2015. "What do voters want? Dimensions and configurations in individual-level preferences and party choice." In *The Politics of Advanced Capitalism*, eds. Pablo Beramendi, Silja Häusermann, Herbert Kitschelt, and Hanspeter Kriesi, 202–230. Cambridge: Cambridge University Press.

Heizmann, Boris, and Conrad Ziller. 2020. "Who is willing to share the burden? Attitudes towards the allocation of asylum seekers in comparative perspective." *Social Forces* 98 (3): 1026–1051.

Heizmann, Boris, Alexander Jedinger, and Anja Perry. 2018. "Welfare chauvinism, economic insecurity and the asylum seeker crisis." *Societies* 8 (3): 83.

Hjerm, Mikael. 2007. "Do numbers really count? Group threat theory revisited." *Journal of Ethnic and Migration Studies* 33 (8): 1253–1275.

Hjorth, Frederik. 2016. "Who benefits? Welfare chauvinism and national stereotypes." *European Union Politics* 17 (1): 3–24.

Huddleston, Thomas, Özge Bilgili, Anne-Linde Joki, and Zvezda Vankova. 2015. *Migrant Integration Policy Index* 2015. Barcelona and Brussels: CIDOB and MPG.

Jørgensen, Martin B., and Trine L. Thomsen. 2016. "Deservingness in the Danish context: Welfare chauvinism in times of crisis." *Critical Social Policy* 36 (3): 330–351.

Jylhä, Kirsti M., Jens Rydgren, and Pontus Strimling. 2019. "Radical right-wing voters from right and left: Comparing Sweden Democrat voters who previously voted for the Conservative Party or the Social Democratic Party." *Scandinavian Political Studies* 42 (3–4): 220–240.

Kende, Anna, Márton Hadarich, and Zolt Szabó. 2018. "Inglorious glorification and attachment: National and European identities as predictors of anti- and pro-immigrant attitudes." *British Journal of Social Psychology* 58 (3): 569–590.

Keskinen, Suvi. 2016. "From welfare nationalism to welfare chauvinism: Economic rhetoric, the welfare state and changing asylum policies in Finland." *Critical Social Policy* 36 (3): 352–370.

Kitschelt, Herbert, and Anthony J. McGann. 1995. *The Radical Right in Western Europe: A Comparative Analysis*. Ann Arbor, MI: University of Michigan Press.

Koning, Edward Anthony. 2013. *Selective Solidarity: The Politics of Immigrants' Social Rights in Western Welfare States*. PhD dissertation. Queen's University, Canada. http://hdl.handle.net/1974/7922.

Koning, Edward Anthony. 2017. "Selecting, disentitling, or investing? Exploring party and voter responses to immigrant welfare dependence in 15 West European welfare states." *Comparative European Politics* 15: 628–660.

Koning, Edward Anthony. 2020. "Accommodation and new hurdles: The increasing importance of politics for immigrants' access to social programmes in Western democracies." *Social Policy and Administration*. doi:10.1111/spol.12661.

Kros, Mathijs, and Marcel Coenders. 2019. "Explaining differences in welfare chauvinism between and within individuals over time: The role of subjective and objective economic risk, economic egalitarianism, and ethnic threat." *European Sociological Review* 35 (6): 860–873.

Kuepper, Beate, Carina Wolf, and Andreas Zick. 2010. "Social status and anti-immigrant attitudes in Europe: An examination from the perspective of social dominance theory." *International Journal of Conflict and Violence* 4 (2): 205–219.

Kuntz, Anabel, Eldad Davidov, and Moshe Semyonov. 2017. "The dynamic relations between economic conditions and anti-immigrant sentiment: A natural experiment in times of the European economic crisis." *International Journal of Comparative Sociology* 58 (5): 392–415.

Kurer, Thomas. 2020. "The declining middle: Occupational change, social status, and the populist right." *Comparative Political Studies* 53 (10–11): 1798–1835.

Larsen, Christian Albrekt. 2020. "The institutional logic of giving migrants access to social benefits and services." *Journal of European Social Policy* 30 (1): 48–62.

Laurence, James, and Lee Bentley. 2018. "Countervailing contact: Community ethnic diversity, anti-immigrant attitudes and mediating pathways of positive and negative inter-ethnic contact in European societies." *Social Science Research* 39 (2): 285–295.

Lefkofridi, Zoe, and Elie Michel. 2017. "The electoral politics of solidarity." In *The Strains of Commitment: The Political Sources of Solidarity in Diverse Societies*, eds. Keith Banting and Will Kymlicka, 583–605. Oxford: Oxford University Press.

Magni, Gabriele. 2020. "Economic inequality, immigrants and selective solidarity: From perceived lack of opportunity to in-group favoritism." *British Journal of Political Science*. doi:10.1017/S0007123420000046.

Marx, Paul, and Elias Naumann. 2018. "Do right-wing parties foster welfare chauvinistic attitudes? A longitudinal study of the 2015 'refugee crisis' in Germany." *Electoral Studies* 52 (April): 111–116.

McFarland, Sam. 2010. "Authoritarianism, social dominance, and other roots of generalized prejudice." *Political Psychology* 31 (3): 453–477.

Meuleman, Bart, Koen Abts, Peter Schmidt, Thomas F. Pettigrew, and Eldad Davidov. 2020. "Economic conditions, group relative deprivation and ethnic threat perceptions: A cross-national perspective." *Journal of Ethnic and Migration Studies* 46 (3): 593–611.

Mewes, Jan, and Steffen Mau. 2012. "Unraveling working-class welfare chauvinism." In *Contested Welfare States: Welfare Attitudes in Europe and Beyond*, ed. Stefan Svallfors, 119–157. Stanford, CA: Stanford University Press.

Mewes, Jan, and Steffen Mau. 2013. "Globalization, socio-economic status and welfare chauvinism: European perspectives on attitudes toward the exclusion of immigrants." *International Journal of Comparative Sociology* 54 (3): 228–245.

Mummendey, Amélie, Andreas Klink, and Rupert Brown. 2001. "Nationalism and patriotism: National identification and out-group rejection." *British Journal of Social Psychology* 40: 159–172.

Norocel, Ov Christian. 2016. "Populist radical right protectors of the folkhem: Welfare chauvinism in Sweden." *Critical Social Policy* 36 (3): 371–390.

Pehrson, Samuel, Vivian Vignoles, and Rupert Brown. 2009. "National identification and anti-immigrant prejudice: Individual and contextual effects of national definitions." *Social Psychology Quarterly* 72 (1): 24–38.

Pettigrew, Thomas, Oliver Christ, Ulrich Wagner, Roel Meertens, Rolf Van Dick, and Andreas Zick. 2008. "Relative deprivation and intergroup prejudice." *Journal of Social Issues* 64 (2): 385–401.

Pierson, Paul. 1993. "When effect becomes cause: Policy feedback and political change." *World Politics* 45 (4): 595–628.

Pratto, Felicia, Lisa Stallworth, and Jim Sidanius. 1997. "The gender gap: Differences in political attitudes and social dominance orientation." *British Journal of Social Psychology* 36: 49–68.

Quillian, Lincoln. 1995. "Prejudice as a response to perceived group threat: Population composition and anti-immigrant and racial prejudice in Europe." *American Sociological Review* 60 (4): 586–611.

Raijman, Rebeca, and Oshrat Hochman. 2011. "National attachments, economic competition, and social exclusion of non-ethnic migrants in Israel: A mixed-methods approach." *Quality and Quantity* 45: 1151–1174.

Reeskens, Tim, and Wim Van Oorschot. 2012. "Disentangling the 'new liberal dilemma': On the relation between general welfare redistribution preferences and welfare chauvinism." *International Journal of Comparative Sociology* 53 (2): 120–139.

Runciman, Walter G. 1966. *Relative Deprivation and Social Justice: A Study of Attitudes to Social Inequality in Twentieth-Century England*. Berkeley, CA: University of California Press.

Schlueter, Elmar, and Peer Scheepers. 2010. "The relationship between outgroup size and anti-outgroup attitudes: A theoretical synthesis and empirical test of group threat- and intergroup contact theory." *Social Science Research* 39 (2): 285–295.

Schmidt-Catran, Alexander, and Malcolm Fairbrother. 2016. "The random effects in multilevel models: Getting them wrong and getting them right." *European Sociological Review* 32 (1): 23–38.

Schumacher, Gijs, and Kees Van Kersbergen. 2016. "Do mainstream parties adapt to the welfare chauvinism of populist parties?" *Party Politics* 22 (3): 300–312.

Schwartz, Shalom. 1992. "Universals in the content and structure of values: Theoretical advances and empirical tests in 20 countries." In *Advances in Experimental Social Psychology, Vol. 25*, 5, ed. M.P. Zanna, 1–65. Cambridge, MA: Academic Press.

Sibley, Chris G., John Duckitt, Robin Bergh, Danny Osborne, Ryan Perry, Frank Asbrock, Andrew Robertson, Gavin Armstrong, Marc Stewart Wilson, and Fiona K. Barlow. 2013. "A dual process model of attitudes towards immigration: Person × residential area effects in a national sample." *Political Psychology* 34 (4): 553–572.

Sidanius, Jim, and Felicia Pratto. 1999. *Social Dominance: An Intergroup Theory of Social Hierarchy and Oppression*. New York: Cambridge University Press.

Smith, Heather, Thomas Pettigrew, Gina Pippin, and Silvana Bialosiewicz. 2012. "Relative deprivation: A theoretical and meta-analytic review." *Personality and Social Psychology Review* 16 (3): 203–232.

Solodoch, Omer. 2020. "Do sociotropic concerns mask prejudice? Experimental evidence on the sources of public opposition to immigration." *Political Studies*. doi:10.1177/0032321720946163.

Stephan, Walter, and Lausanne Renfro. 2002. "The role of threats in intergroup relations." In *From Prejudice to Intergroup Emotions*, eds. Diane M. Mackie and Eliot R. Smith, 191–208. New York: Psychology Press.

Tajfel, Henri (ed.). 1978. *Differentiation between Social Groups*. London: Academic Press.

Tajfel, Henri, and John Turner. 1979. "An integrative theory of intergroup conflict." In *The Social Psychology of Intergroup Relations*, eds. William G. Austin and Stephen Worchel, 33–47. Monterey, CA: Brooks/Cole.

Tzeng, Rueyling, and Ming-Chang Tsai. 2020. "Good for the common good: Sociotropic concern and double standards toward high- and low-skilled immigrants in six wealthy countries." *Social Indicators Research* 152: 473–493.

van der Meer, Tom, and Tim Reeskens. 2020. "Welfare chauvinism in the face of ethnic diversity: A vignette experiment across diverse and homogenous neighbourhoods on the perceived deservingness of native and foreign-born welfare claimants." *European Sociological Review*. doi:10.1093/esr/jcaa037.

van der Waal, Jeroen, Peter Achterberg, Dick Houtman, Willem de Koster, and Katerina Manevska. 2010. "'Some are more equal than others': Economic egalitarianism and welfare chauvinism in the Netherlands." *Journal of European Social Policy* 20 (4): 350–363.

van der Waal, Jeroen, Willem de Koster, and Wim Van Oorschot. 2013. "Three worlds of welfare chauvinism? How welfare regimes affect support for distributing welfare to immigrants in Europe." *Journal of Comparative Policy Analysis: Research and Practice* 15 (2): 164–181.

Wagner, Ulrich, Julia Becker, Oliver Christ, Thomas Pettigrew, and Peter Schmidt. 2012. "Longitudinal test of the relation between German nationalism, patriotism, and outgroup derogation." *European Sociological Review* 28 (3): 319–332.

Wilkins, Clara, and Cheryl Kaiser. 2014. "Racial progress as a threat to the status hierarchy: Implications for perceptions of anti-white bias." *Psychological Science* 25 (2): 439–446.

Wimmer, Andreas. 2008. "The making and unmaking of ethnic boundaries: A multilevel process theory." *American Journal of Sociology* 113 (4): 970–1022.

Yoxon, Barbara, Maria Grasso, Sotirios Karampampas, and Luke Temple. 2019a. "Prejudice and relative deprivation: The effects of self-referenced individual relative deprivation on generalized prejudice in European democracies." *European Societies* 21 (2): 280–302.

Yoxon, Barbara, Steven M. Van Hauwaert, and Johaness Kiess. 2019b. "Picking on immigrants: A cross-national analysis of individual-level relative deprivation and authoritarianism as predictors of anti-foreign prejudice." *Acta Politica* 54: 479–520.

Ziller, Conrad. 2020. "Established and excluded? Immigrants' economic progress, attitudes toward immigrants, and the conditioning role of egalitarianism and intergroup contact." *Political Studies*. doi:10.1177/0032321720953561.

Ziller, Conrad, and Carl C. Berning. (2019). "Personality traits and public support of minority rights." *Journal of Ethnic and Migration Studies*: 1–18.

Ziller, Conrad, and Sara W. Goodman (2020). "Local government efficiency and anti-immigrant violence." *Journal of Politics*, 82 (3): 895–907.

PART III

POLITICAL INSTITUTIONS AND POLICIES AS SHAPERS OF THE WELFARE-MIGRATION CONTEXT

10. Framing matters: Pathways between policies, immigrant integration, and native attitudes
Anita Manatschal

INTRODUCTION

Integration policy is a multidimensional policy field, comprising policies that regulate immigrants' integration in the socioeconomic, political, and cultural-religious realms of society. Policy measures can range, thus, from granting immigrants' access to state employment (as a teacher or police officer, for example), to allowing for non-citizen voting provisions, to authorizing religious minority rights (such as the right to Islamic burial), or, respectively, demanding cultural or linguistic adaptation (Koopmans et al. 2012; Manatschal et al. 2020; Boswell 2003; Rosenberger 2020). With the increasing interest in policies regulating cultural diversity and immigrant integration, a host of studies have started to assess policy outcomes—how these policies affect natives' and immigrants' attitudes and behavior. No matter whether these studies are based on neo-institutional premises (Pierson 2006; Schlicht-Schmälzle and Möller 2012), adhere to the "political opportunities structure" framework (Cinalli and Giugni 2011; Ireland 2006), or relate to policy feedback effects (Filindra and Manatschal 2020; Pierson 1993), they all start from the basic assumption that integration policies embody societal norms of inclusion or exclusion, which can influence natives' inclusive or exclusive attitudes toward immigrants, as well as immigrants' attitudes and behavior. Studies assessing policy effects capture natives' inclusive attitudes typically via their levels of social or political trust or different manifestations of tolerance, such as being supportive of granting immigrants access to social, political, or cultural rights, or pro-diversity beliefs more broadly (Weldon 2006; Kauff et al. 2013; Bloemraad and Wright 2014). Conversely, exclusive attitudes comprise prejudices against particular groups such as foreigners (xenophobia) or Muslims, which entail a rejection of others based merely on their place of origin or religious affiliation (Green et al. 2020; Guimond et al. 2013).

A large body of comparative and experimental evidence suggests that inclusive policies lead to higher levels of inclusive native attitudes, and, conversely, lower levels of exclusive attitudes toward immigrants. At the same time, we still find enough evidence of the exact opposite: that inclusive or multiculturalist policies coincide with more exclusive attitudes, or that the integration policy context does not make much difference at all. Besides this inconclusive evidence, existing research suffers from certain methodological limitations. To start with, observational studies are challenged by endogeneity issues, as they cannot provide a clear answer to the famous chicken-and-egg question of whether policy shapes attitudes, or whether attitudes translate into more inclusive or exclusive policies. While existing research suggests the causal arrow goes both ways, and that there is a mutually reinforcing relationship between policies and attitudes (Weldon 2006), experimental and quasi-experimental research designs can provide more convincing empirical evidence for causal effects of policies on attitudes (e.g. Morrison et al. 2010; Plaut et al. 2011). To date, however, there are hardly any experimental studies outside of laboratory settings to document how a real-world integration policy or policy change causes an immediate attitudinal change among the majority population. The paucity of natural experiments on this particular question may relate to the fact that reality is much more complex than a simple policy–attitudes change link would suggest.

Related to this point, studies scrutinizing integration policy outcomes on natives tend to blend out the side of immigrants, even though they are the primary target population of these policies. In spite of some mixed findings, a large body of research substantiates a link between more inclusive policies and immigrants' sense of belonging, naturalization (intentions and behavior), school and labor market integration, as well as their political and civic engagement (Bennour 2020; Cinalli and Giugni 2011; Koopmans 2010; Celeste et al. 2019; Manatschal and Stadelmann-Steffen 2014; Bloemraad 2006). Occasionally, even exclusive integration policies can trigger immigrant political engagement, e.g. through mobilization via threat (Filindra and Manatschal 2020). More successful integration in terms of psychological wellbeing, language skills, and labor market, civic, and political participation implies, in turn, lower dependency of immigrants on state supports such as social benefits.

The chapter brings these so far unconnected literatures on integration policy outcomes on native majority attitudes on the one hand, and on immigrant integration on the other hand, into dialog. It postulates that to fully understand how integration policies affect majority attitudes toward immigrants, we must also take into account the effect these policies yield on immigrant integration.

WHAT IS INTEGRATION POLICY, AND WHY SHOULD IT MATTER?

> Integration is a chaotic concept: a word used by many but understood differently by most. (Robinson 1998, 167)

Robinson's statement, although formulated more than 20 years ago, still has some validity today. In public and scholarly discourses, integration is frequently related to a diverse range of behavioral and attitudinal outcomes. In spite of the fact that public and political discourses conceive of integration as a mutual process involving immigrants and natives, integration is typically "measured" on immigrants only. If immigrants speak the host country's language, have a job, engage in the civic and political realm, and cultivate friendly and cooperative exchanges with the native population, meaning if they dispose of so-called *bridging social capital* (Nannestad et al. 2008), they are considered "well integrated" (Ager and Strang 2008; Harder et al. 2018).[1] Further indicators of immigrant integration include good mental and physical health as well as security, e.g. in terms of a stable legal status (Ager and Strang 2008). At the same time, a multiculturalist understanding of integration includes the maintenance of linguistic, cultural-religious, social, and emotional ties to the country of origin via contacts with co-ethnics—so-called *bonding social capital* (Nannestad et al. 2008). The complex and multifaceted meanings of integration must, and do, inform our understanding of integration policy as a multidimensional policy field. In line with the notion that immigrants need to find their place in the *market*, the *nation*, and the *state* (Entzinger 2000), many scholars identify three principal dimensions of integration policy (Manatschal et al. 2020; Koopmans et al. 2012; Boswell 2003): *socioeconomic* integration policies regulate aspects such as immigrants' access to the labor market or social benefits; *legal-political policies* govern immigrants' political rights, e.g. in terms of non-citizen voting rights or access to citizenship; and finally, *cultural-religious policies* address questions of cultural assimilation or adaptation (e.g. language acquisition) and diversity (e.g. religious minority rights), and are often also referred to as "multiculturalist policies" (Bloemraad and Wright 2014). Integration policies can thus be defined as policies regulating processes of immigrant integration in the socioeconomic, legal-political, and cultural-religious domains. Legal-political and socioeconomic policies can render access to social benefits or citizenship easy (inclusive) or difficult (exclusive). Cultural-religious policies, in turn, can demand a high degree of cultural assimilation (cultural monism) or be more permissive in terms of cultural or religious minority rights (cultural pluralism).

The multidimensional nature of integration policy implies that it cuts across policy areas that are normally dealt with in separate disciplines and literatures, such as political science, economics, or social psychology. Different disciplinary backgrounds notwithstanding, existing research postulates that integration policies trigger reactions in both natives and immigrants. These policies can influence individual affect, attitudes, and behavior among the native majority population—discussed in the following section—but even more so among immigrants themselves, who are the primary targets of these policies.

Integration Policy and Natives' Inclusive and Exclusive Attitudes

A host of studies investigate how integration policies affect the attitudes of native majority populations. Many of them test the central premise that more inclusive integration policies coincide with more inclusive, or less exclusive, attitudes toward immigrants. The assumption is that if immigrant integration policies express inclusive and permissive societal norms, these norms will also reflect in majority attitudes (e.g. Schlueter et al. 2013).

There are four major research strands on how integration policies relate to attitudes and behaviors of the majority population. The first deals largely with the relationship between policies and interpersonal trust. Only a few studies report a direct relationship between inclusive policies and higher levels of generalized trust (Reeskens 2010), with more research focusing on the conditional effects of integration policy. Qualifying the often-cited proposition that diversity hampers trust (Putnam 2007), Zimdars and Tampubolon (2012) show that more inclusive integration policies can counterbalance the potential negative effects of increasing diversity on trust. Accounting for attitudinal and behavioral aspects of social capital, Kesler and Bloemraad (2010) further observe that trust, civic engagement, and political participation are not negatively influenced by cultural diversity, nor by policies promoting individual equality and cultural recognition. Furthermore, analyses of integration policies at the subnational level bring the literature closer to individual realities and provide more nuanced findings. They suggest that the negative impact of immigrant presence on social trust is significantly reduced in regions with inclusive socioeconomic integration policies. However, inclusive civic-political rights and family reunification policies at the regional level seem to increase the negative effect of diversity on social trust (Gundelach and Manatschal 2017). Beyond interpersonal trust, studies have shown that multiculturalist policies coincide with higher levels of trust in political institutions and government support, especially among respondents with higher education levels (Hooghe and de Vroome 2015). Looking at the interplay of policies, national identity, and political trust, McLaren (2017) finds relatively high trust levels when both individual identity and immigrant incorporation policies are inclusive. While several studies suggest a link between more inclusive policies and higher trust, others point to more mixed results, and empirical evidence may still be "too thin to draw strong conclusions" (Bloemraad and Wright 2014, 315).

The second literature strand looks at the relationship between integration policies and another type of inclusive attitude, namely tolerance. Starting with the study by Wright et al. (2017) on religious tolerance in the United States (US) and Canada, their contextual comparison across different multicultural policy regimes lends credence to a fairly subdued role for policy and a much larger role for political culture. In contrast, Guimond et al. (2013) suggest that anti-Muslim prejudice is significantly reduced in multicultural policy contexts. This finding resonates with the study by Kauff et al. (2013), who find that more liberal migrant integration policies can increase pro-diversity beliefs among the population. In a similar vein, a comparative analysis of Western European countries observes that social and political tolerance toward ethnic minorities is highest in those countries with the most liberal and inclusive citizenship policies (Weldon 2006). Adding more nuance to this picture, Reeskens and van Oorschot (2017) show that inclusive opinions in the fields of political and civil rights coincide with increased tolerance toward newcomers. Conversely, they find a negative correlation between a strong commitment to social rights and tolerance, which, according to the authors, may help to understand the rise of welfare chauvinism (Kitschelt 1997; Crepaz 2008). The picture emerging from the tolerance literature is thus mixed. While some studies show that inclusive policies coincide with more tolerant attitudes, it would be too far-fetched to speak of a unanimous consensus on this question.

A third strand of research focuses on how integration policy shapes social identities and intergroup attitudes, such as natives' attitudes toward immigrant outgroups, or their perception of the national ingroup, e.g. their understanding of national identity (Tajfel and Turner 2004). Xenophobia—the fear of foreigners—represents one of the clearest exclusive attitudes toward immigrants. Triggered by feelings of cultural threat or competition over scarce resources (Ceobanu and Escandell 2010; Hainmueller and Hopkins 2014), xenophobia demarcates the "us" from the foreign "others" via exclusive and protectionist attitudes. With respect to the policy–intergroup attitudes link, several studies report a direct relationship, showing, for instance, that inclusive or permissive integration policies are associated with reduced feelings of perceived threat and more pro-diversity beliefs (Hooghe and de Vroome 2015; Schlueter et al. 2013; Kauff et al. 2013). According to Schlueter et al. (2013), this shows that integration policies can convey dominant group norms to which citizens conform, and that such policies can function as a political socialization mechanism. Beyond this, research examines indirect policy effects building on the prominent contact theory, which stipulates that contact with foreigners reduces intergroup prejudice and xenophobia (Pettigrew 2016), and increases trust (Uslaner 2011). Green et al. (2020) document such a moderating effect of integration policies on the contact–xenophobia link across 20 European countries. They show that the decreasing effect of natives' contact with immigrants on cultural threat perceptions is strongest in countries with inclusive integration policies.

The fourth literature analyzes multiculturalist policies and cultural diversity, revealing a more inconclusive picture. Morrison et al. (2010) demonstrate that, in the US context, White American respondents primed with multiculturalist messages show higher levels of threat to group values and higher levels of prejudice. Plaut et al. (2011) further document, via experimental studies among White Americans, that majority group members tend to associate multiculturalism with exclusion rather than inclusion—what they call the "What about me?" effect. Building on these critical approaches to multiculturalism, Citrin and colleagues (2014) reveal that strong multicultural policies magnify the degree to which hostility to immigration is negatively associated with political support across Europe. Relating this discussion to national identity, Wright's (2011) longitudinal cross-country study shows how respondents become much more exclusive in their understanding of national identity in the most politically multicultural countries, whereas their notions of national identity become more inclusive in countries with liberal citizenship regimes. Overall, these studies seem to support the popular argument of a "backlash" toward multiculturalist policies in public opinion (Bloemraad and Wright 2014; Vertovec and Wessendorf 2010). Conversely, Hooghe and de Vroome (2015) find no evidence for the backlash thesis in the context of Western Europe, and conclude that public concerns about multiculturalist policies are overestimated. Ward and Masgoret (2008) even show how multicultural ideology coincides with diminished threat perception and more positive attitudes toward immigrants in New Zealand.

Critique and the Missing Link

As the preceding section revealed, a host of studies analyze how integration policies, or specific aspects thereof, relate to natives' attitudes toward immigrants. Although many studies find a direct or indirect link between policies and trust, tolerance, or xenophobia in the majority population, the evidence on the nature of this relationship is mixed. While studies suggesting a positive link between inclusive policies and inclusive attitudes seem to prevail, we still find enough studies postulating the exact opposite, or suggesting that integration policies do not make much of a difference. It seems that, in and of themselves, integration policies do not convey strong enough group norms to which citizens simply conform. Rather, the framing of these policies in a given society plays an important role too (Hooghe and de Vroome 2015). As Plaut et al. (2011) argue, multiculturalism can be framed as a more exclusive or inclusive concept from the perspective of White majority members; if multiculturalism is also framed as an inclusive concept, it is associated with more positive majority attitudes. Relatedly, Guimond and colleagues (2013) suggest that the relationship between prejudice and support for multiculturalism much depends on the national context and on local norms associated with policies that support diversity. In other words, it is not enough to just look at the policy–attitudes link; we must also consider the larger societal or political context in which these policies operate.

Another challenge to these studies relates to the inherent endogeneity of policies and attitudes (Coleman 1990; Weldon 2006). Following the simple policy cycle heuristics (Jann and Wegrich 2007), each of the studies discussed above should ask whether integration policy really affects attitudes, or whether it is the other way around. The causal arrow could go either way, as documented by research analyzing how societal norms, in terms of aggregated attitudes, translate via policy inputs into policy outputs (Favell 2001; Butz and Kehrberg 2019; Crepaz 2008, 252; Manatschal 2012). While it seems most likely that the causal arrows do in fact go both ways, and that there is a reciprocal and mutually reinforcing relationship between policies and attitudes (Weldon 2006), the mechanisms through which policies affect majority attitudes remain obscure. From a methodological perspective, (quasi-)experimental studies outperform correlational research in providing convincing evidence that it is indeed the policy that affects attitudes, rather than the other way around. So far, however, experimental research has been based in laboratories and has largely tested the impact of policies on attitudes via hypothetical manipulations of societal norms (Morrison et al. 2010; Plaut et al. 2011). Natural experiments exploiting real-world policies or policy changes and their impact on majority attitudes remain scarce. One reason for this paucity of studies may relate to the fact that experiments adopt a too simplistic view on policy outcomes. Hypothetical experiments cannot fully capture the complex and multifaceted ways in which real-world policy outputs, in concert with particular societal and political contexts and discourses, shape majority attitudes.

More importantly, with the exception of research relating to contact theory (Pettigrew 2016; Green et al. 2020; Uslaner 2011), the studies discussed above completely neglect the side of immigrants, even though they are the actual target group of integration policies. It seems reasonable to assume that the impact of integration policy on natives' attitudes toward immigrants depends on whether immigrants themselves profit from a given integration policy, and whether this, in turn, alters their role and representation in society. It makes a difference whether immigrants are perceived as a needy and marginalized out-group or as successful colleagues at work. The remainder of this chapter will therefore try to shed light on this neglected perspective: how policies may indirectly affect the attitudes of the native majority population via their impact on immigrant integration. To elaborate on potential mechanisms, the following section first examines existing evidence on integration policy outcomes on immigrants.

Integration Policy and Immigrant Integration

Given that integration policies target immigrant inclusion in the three respective domains, it seems straightforward to assume that these policies affect immigrants' structural integration into schools and labor markets, their political and cultural inclusion, as well as their social and psychological integration into society (Condon et al. 2016; Manatschal and Stadelmann-Steffen 2014; Green and Staerklé 2013). But which policies are most effective? Are inclusive integration policies more "successful" in supporting and fostering immigrant inclusion than exclusive ones? And is it more beneficial for individual integration processes if policies make concessions toward cultural diversity—e.g. via bilingual education or religious minority rights—than if they demand strict cultural assimilation?

Starting with policy effects on labor market integration, large-N cross-national studies present mixed evidence on these policies' effectiveness. Using, for instance, policy data from the Migrant Integration Policy Index (MIPEX, see Huddleston et al. 2015), Aleksynska and Tritah (2013) report a positive association between MIPEX and labor market outcomes, whereas other studies find no significant correlation between integration policy and immigrants' unemployment propensity, labor force participation, or occupational class (Pichler 2011). Summarizing multilevel studies examining the impact of the MIPEX, Bilgili et al. (2015) further reveal that there is no systematic link between general integration policies and immigrants' individual labor market inclusion. Koopmans (2010) suggests, in turn, that assimilationist integration regimes outperform multiculturalist policies when it comes to immigrants' labor market inclusion. Besides the limitation that broad integration policy indices often represent too rough instruments to identify policy effects on very distinct groups (such as refugees or highly skilled immigrants), these studies can only detect correlations, not causation. Small-scale experimental or quasi-experimental policy evaluations can sidestep these shortcomings, allowing for a more precise identification of the causal effect of specific labor market integration policies on particular immigrant groups. Although the verdict on policy performance is once again mixed, and not all policies seem to work as intended, these studies reveal that inclusive programs that are closely linked to the labor market (e.g. specific types of active labor market policies), or procedural aspects related to specific groups (e.g. long waiting periods for asylum seekers) (Hainmueller et al. 2016), do affect immigrants' economic inclusion. As Hainmueller et al. (2019) show, even apparently unrelated integration policies, such as citizenship regulations, can catalyze immigrants' long-term economic integration.

Education scholars focus in turn on the cultural and political integration context of schools and educational curricula (Hansen and Wenning 2003; Dupriez and Dumay 2006; Fossati 2011). However, empirical evidence on the effect of integration policy on immigrant pupils' school inclusion is scarce, and studies using national integration policy indices find no relevant effects on immigrants' performance in school (Fossati 2011; Schlicht-Schmälzle and Möller 2012). Research on integration policies across the subnational units of Swiss cantons suggests, in turn, that inclusive cantonal integration policies significantly improve the school performance of students with an immigrant background relative to natives (Manatschal and Stadelmann-Steffen 2013). Refining the analysis all the way down to the level of individual schools, Celeste et al. (2019) document that multicultural school policies predict smaller achievement and belonging gaps between immigrant and native pupils in Belgium.

Turning to the effects of integration policy on immigrants' political attitudes and behavior, scholarly work can be aligned with the classical policy feedback literature (Pierson 1993). According to this theory, public policies can influence individuals' attitudes about governments and toward societal groups, or enhance or decrease rates of political participation of groups that are targeted by a specific policy (Condon et al. 2016; Mettler 2002; Pierson 1993). Supporting the argument of policy feedback effects on political engagement, inclusive integration or citizenship policies and practices have been shown to alter both the intention to naturalize and the likelihood of doing so (Bloemraad 2006; Bennour 2020; Hainmueller and Hangartner 2013). A more nuanced picture emerges from studies simultaneously analyzing different dimensions of integration policy. When combined with policies balancing the demand for cultural assimilation with concessions toward cultural diversity, integration policies facilitating immigrants' political or labor market inclusion are conducive to civic and political engagement (Cinalli and Giugni 2011; Manatschal and Stadelmann-Steffen 2014). Research further suggests that inclusive integration policies are perceived of as welcoming signals. Studies document that these policies can increase immigrants' attachment to the place or country of residence (Bennour and Manatschal 2019), generalized trust (Wright and Bloemraad 2012), psychological wellbeing (Pecoraro et al. 2019), and even governor approval ratings in the US context (Filindra and Manatschal 2020). It therefore seems to make an important difference whether the receiving policy context gives immigrants a "warm handshake" or shows them a "cold shoulder" (Reeskens and Wright 2014).

However, research on symbolic or psychological effects suggests that even restrictive policies can trigger immigrant engagement. Besides material effects, which explain political reactions as a response to impending material losses or desired gains, policies can act symbolically as signals of inclusion or exclusion (Bloemraad 2013). Symbolic or psychological policy effects are not restricted to the immigrant group targeted by the policy, but may spill over to their offspring and co-ethnics (Condon et al. 2016; Bloemraad et al. 2011). Filindra and Manatschal (2020) document such spillover effects in the US, showing that restrictive integration policy changes at the state level coincide with higher voter turnout among first- and second-generation immigrants, as well as Hispanics in general. The authors explain this finding with symbolic mobilization via the threat emanating from exclusive policies (Pantoja and Segura 2003; Zepeda-Millán 2017).

Summing up, the literature on integration policy outcomes on immigrants clearly suggests that these policies matter, and that they affect immigrants' socioeconomic, political, as well as cultural or psychological adaptation processes. Research observes that inclusive policies, in particular, coincide with better educational performance, labor market outcomes, higher political and civic engagement, and increased psychological wellbeing. At the same time, research suggests that even restrictive policy measures can trigger immigrant action in terms of heightened political engagement.

CONNECTING THE DOTS: THE INTERPLAY OF POLICIES, IMMIGRANT INTEGRATION, AND NATIVE ATTITUDES

Existing research documents how integration policies can affect both immigrant and native attitudes and behaviors. At the same time, these literatures clearly reveal that there is no simple link between policy and individual reactions. Some policies may be more effective than others in certain contexts, and depending on the outcome of interest, different levels of analysis may be more appropriate than others. Research focusing on the subnational level of regions documents for instance how regional integration policies "make regional citizens" (Manatschal et al. 2020), by altering for instance immigrants' political engagement (Filindra and Manatschal 2020), their national attachment to the host country (Bennour and Manatschal 2019), as well as their intention to naturalize (Bennour 2020). Regional or local policies may also be the more relevant analytic unit when interested in policy effects on interpersonal or intergroup attitudes such as trust or xenophobia (Gundelach and Manatschal 2017; Kesler and Bloemraad 2010). Existing research acknowledges further the relevance of the larger societal and political context for policy outcomes. They highlight, for instance, the relevance of the political framing of these policies, the larger societal context and predominant norms and discourses, as well as the sociodemographic context, pointing in particular to the important role of interpersonal contact with immigrants in reducing prejudice (Plaut et al. 2011; Uslaner 2011; Green et al. 2020; Pettigrew 2016).

Yet, given that these policies are designed to foster immigrant integration, what if policy effects on majority attitudes depend on how integration policies shape immigrant integration and, thus, their representation in society in the first place? What if policies unfold their effect on native attitudes primarily via the impact they yield on immigrant integration, given that improved inclusion also alters immigrants' role and representation in society? While it is up to future research to test this moderating or mediating expectation empirically, the remainder of this chapter will elaborate on possible mechanisms through which integration policy may alter majority attitudes via improved immigrant integration. I will focus on three possible and interrelated mechanisms through which this process may unfold: improved agency, increased visibility, and altered representation.

As documented in the preceding section, inclusive integration policies may improve immigrants' school performance and labor market integration, increasing thereby the chances that immigrants are self-sufficient and independent. This *increased agency* may imply a reduced welfare state dependency and reduced victimization of immigrants. Inclusive policies further coincide with higher political and civic engagement levels among immigrants, and an increased likelihood of naturalization. Symbolic policy effects can reinforce this process, given that more inclusive integration policies convey a stronger feeling of belonging for immigrants, which is conducive to psychological wellbeing. Multicultural policies, which give immigrants a sense of legitimate membership and standing in society, especially increase the likelihood that immigrants will feel they have a stake in society, further motivating them to actively engage in the civic and political realm (Bloemraad 2013). Research and common sense suggest that the relationship between individual integration domains is interdependent and mutually reinforcing (Ager and Strang 2008; Martén et al. 2019): social and cultural (e.g. language skills) integration likely benefits labor market integration and vice versa. Psychological wellbeing, in turn, is an important precondition for partaking in civic, political, or economic activities. The fact that inclusive integration policies foster immigrant integration in different domains makes these policies particularly powerful instruments for fostering immigrant agency.

However, as we have seen, exclusive policies can also foster immigrant agency, especially in the political realm. The example of immigrant political mobilization in the US in the late 1990s and early 2000s illustrates that exclusive legislation, especially toward undocumented migrants, can provoke massive political protests in the streets, translate to higher naturalization rates, shift political ideologies among immigrants, and increase formal political engagement levels (Voss and Bloemraad 2011; Pantoja et al. 2008; Bowler et al. 2006). Overall, both inclusive and exclusive policies regulating immigrant integration can thus drastically alter immigrant agency. This transformation from passive and potentially dependent to active and self-sufficient members of society is unlikely to go unnoticed by the majority population.

This is because increased agency also implies *higher visibility*, the second mechanism discussed here. Besides altering immigrants' visibility indirectly via increased agency, integration policies can also directly foster immigrant visibility. Examples include policies that facilitate or even promote immigrant representation in state institutions such as the teaching force, public administration, or the judiciary (Manatschal 2012). Inclusive integration policies and a non-discriminating political context can further encourage immigrants' political and civic engagement and representation via immigrant politicians (Dancygier et al. 2015; Cinalli and Giugni 2011). This increases the likelihood of encountering immigrants in the public realm, be it as teachers, police officers, bureaucrats, or politicians.

In addition, multicultural policies can significantly contribute to the visibility of ethnic diversity in a municipality or region. If a municipality provides Muslim cemeteries or minarets for its Muslim community, this may shape the self-perception of that community as being inclusive and diverse. In contrast to the often heated and highly symbolic debates around multiculturalism and cultural diversity dominating national political arenas (Bloemraad and Wright 2014; Vasta 2007), local integration policymaking is typically characterized by a more pragmatic and solution-oriented impetus (Manatschal et al. 2020; Caponio and Borkert 2010, 188–190; Scholten 2016). Inclusive cultural policies and lived diversity at the local level may thereby offset exclusive national narratives around cultural diversity.

As shown by the US immigrant marches of 2006, restrictive immigration and integration policies can also trigger immigrant political engagement, and contribute thereby to greater visibility and representation of immigrants' claims and interests (Pantoja et al. 2008). The successful framing of these struggles around American values around family and work was crucial as it brought to the public mind that immigrants, documented and undocumented, are part of US society (Bloemraad et al. 2011). From invisible non-citizens, who were often treated and seen as deportable criminals, the marches from 2006 rendered them visible as members of families and hard workers. By appealing to their Americanism and to their belonging in US society, the protesters found visibility in public opinion and in mainstream media coverage of the protests (Bloemraad et al. 2011).

This brings me to the third mechanism—*altered representation*—which is a consequence of both improved agency and increased visibility. As the preceding section showed, exclusive or restrictive integration policies can trigger immigrant political engagement and visibility. In the case of the US immigrant marches, immigrants' political claims not only helped to render their cause visible, but also gave it a human face. Apart from this notable example, existing research suggests that inclusive integration policies, in particular, can alter the representation of immigrants. By treating immigrants on a fair and equal basis, inclusive policies are expected to soften formerly salient differences between the national ingroup and the foreign outgroup, and to engender feelings of general inclusion (Gundelach and Manatschal 2017; Dinesen and Hooghe 2010; Kesler and Bloemraad 2010; Weldon 2006).

In the long run, these processes may also lead to a more inclusive "reconstruction of social identities" (Putnam 2007). For this process to unfold, immigrants must however be broadly and visibly perceived of as equal members of society. Through altering immigrants' agency and public visibility, integration policies may thus also reshape social identities. A stronger representation of immigrants in the public realm should, for instance, weaken the stereotypical perception of teachers, bureaucrats, judges, the police corps, or politicians as predominantly White and native, thereby diversifying the perception of what is "normal." Rendering the perception of immigrants as public actors more familiar and normal will not only soften the stark distinction between the foreign "them" and the known "us," it will also render immigrants more relatable, be it as co-workers, co-protesters, or fellow citizens. Feeling relatable, being able to identify with immigrants, and seeing immigrants as more similar to oneself should also increase the likelihood of entering into positive intergroup contact (Koopmans et al. 2019), which is, as we have seen, a particularly powerful instrument for reducing prejudice and xenophobia.

CONCLUSION

Motivated by the inconclusive evidence emerging from existing research, this chapter is a plea to pay closer attention to the indirect effects of integration policies on native attitudes via their impact on immigrant integration. If, as a result of certain integration policies, immigrants feel that they are more part of, and have more of a stake in, society, and are, as a consequence, less dependent and participate more in labor markets and civic organizations, such outcomes also affect natives' views of immigrants. The chapter showed how by facilitating—or impairing—immigrants' access to socioeconomic, civic-political, and cultural rights, integration policies foster immigrant agency and visibility, thereby altering also their representation in society. As a result, these policies have the potential to turn immigrants from passive and dependent strangers into familiar, relatable, and contributing active members of society. While existing research suggests that it is in particular inclusive integration policies that can support processes of immigrant integration, studies show that also exclusive policies can trigger reactions among immigrants. It seems thus that more important than whether a given policy has an inclusive or exclusive orientation is the fact that there is a policy at all, which can have feedback effects on immigrants.

The chapter argued that thanks to immigrants' increased agency, visibility, and representation due to these policies, natives should no longer see them primarily as the unknown "other" or as a potential burden to the welfare state, but as active and equal, or at least more similar, members of society. A decrease in exclusive sentiments such as xenophobia, and an increase in inclusive attitudes such as trust and tolerance, may result from this. At best, future studies examine the mechanisms theorized here empirically in seeking to account for the complexity of how integration policy affects majority attitudes via improved immigrant integration. At the very least, however, research should acknowledge that it is too short-sighted to simply blend out the effect these policies have on immigrants, toward whom they are directed in the first place, when analyzing how these policies may reshape majority attitudes.

NOTE

1. One might correctly object that bridging social capital between immigrants and natives describes a two-way process. However, the argument made here is that it counts only as an indicator for integration for immigrants, not for natives.

REFERENCES

Ager, Alastair, and Alison Strang. 2008. "Understanding Integration: A Conceptual Framework." *Journal of Refugee Studies* 21 (2): 166–191.
Aleksynska, Mariya, and Ahmed Tritah. 2013. "Occupation–Education Mismatch of Immigrant Workers in Europe: Context and Policies." *Economics of Education Review* 36: 229–244.
Bennour, Salomon. 2020. "Intention to Become a Citizen: Do Subnational Integration Policies Have an Influence? Empirical Evidence from Swiss Cantons." *Regional Studies* 54 (11): 1535–1545.
Bennour, Salomon, and Anita Manatschal. 2019. "Immigrants' Feelings of Attachment to Switzerland: Does the Cantonal Context Matter?" In *Migrants and Expats: The Swiss Migration and Mobility Nexus*, eds. Ilka Steiner and Philippe Wanner, 189–220. Cham: Springer Open.
Bilgili, Özge, Thomas Huddleston, and Anne-Linde Joki. 2015. *The Dynamics between Integration Policies and Outcomes: Synthesis of the Literature*. Barcelona Centre for International Affairs and the Migration Policy Group.
Bloemraad, Irene. 2006. "Becoming a Citizen in the United States and Canada: Structured Mobilization and Immigrant Political Incorporation." *Social Forces* 85 (2): 667–695.
Bloemraad, Irene. 2013. "'The Great Concern of Government': Public Policy as Material and Symbolic Resources." In *Outsiders No More? Models Of Immigrant Political Incorporation*, eds. Jennifer Hochschild, Jacqueline Chatiopadhyay, Claudine Gay, and Michael Jones-Correa, 195–208. Oxford: Oxford University Press.
Bloemraad, Irene, and Matthew Wright. 2014. "'Utter Failure' or Unity out of Diversity? Debating and Evaluating Policies of Multiculturalism." *International Migration Review* 48 (1): 292–334.
Bloemraad, Irene, Kim Voss, and Taeku Lee. 2011. "The Protests of 2006: What Were They, How Do We Understand Them, Where Do We Go?" In *Rallying for Immigrant Rights. The Fight for Inclusion in 21st Century America*, eds. Kim Voss and Irene Bloemraad, 3–43. Berkeley, CA: University of California Press.
Boswell, Christina. 2003. *European Migration in Flux: Changing Patterns of Inclusion and Exclusion*. Oxford: Blackwell.
Bowler, Shaun, Stephen P. Nicholson, and Gary M. Segura. 2006. "Earthquakes and Aftershocks: Race, Direct Democracy, and Partisan Change." *American Journal of Political Science* 50 (1): 146–159.
Butz, Adam M., and Jason E. Kehrberg. 2019. "Anti-Immigrant Sentiment and the Adoption of State Immigration Policy." *Policy Studies Journal* 47 (3): 605–623.
Caponio, Tiziana, and Maren Borkert. 2010. *The Local Dimension of Migration Policymaking*. Amsterdam: Amsterdam University Press.
Celeste, Laura, Gülseli Baysu, Loes Meeussen, and Judit Kende. 2019. "Can School Diversity Policies Reduce Belonging and Achievement Gaps between Minority and Majority Youth? Multiculturalism, Colorblindness, and Assimilationism Assessed." *Personality and Social Psychology Bulletin*. https://doi.org/10.1177/0146167219838577.
Ceobanu, Alin M., and Xavier Escandell. 2010. "Comparative Analyses of Public Attitudes toward Immigrants and Immigration Using Multinational Survey Data: A Review of Theories and Research." *Annual Review of Sociology* 36: 309–328.
Cinalli, Manlio, and Marco Giugni. 2011. "Institutional Opportunities, Discursive Opportunities and the Political Participation of Migrants in European Cities." In *Social Capital, Political Participation and Migration in Europe: Making Multicultural Democracy Work?*, eds. Laura Morales and Marco Giugni, 43–62. Houndmills: Palgrave.
Citrin, Jack, Morris Levy, and Matthew Wright. 2014. "Multicultural Policy and Political Support in European Democracies." *Comparative Political Studies* 47 (11): 1531–1557.
Coleman, James Samuel. 1990. *Foundations of Social Theory*. Cambridge, MA: Belknap Press of Harvard University Press.
Condon, Meghan, Alexandra Filindra, and Amber Wichowsky. 2016. "Immigrant Inclusion in the Safety Net: A Framework for Analysis and Effects on Educational Attainment." *Policy Studies Journal* 44 (4): 424–448.
Crepaz, Markus M.L. 2008. *Trust beyond Borders: Immigration, the Welfare State and Identity in Modern Societies*. Ann Arbor, MI: University of Michigan Press.
Dancygier, Rafaela, Karl-Oskar Lindgren, Sven Oskarsson, and Kare Vernby. 2015. "Why Are Immigrants Underrepresented in Politics? Evidence from Sweden." *American Political Science Review* 109 (4): 703–724.
Dinesen, Peter Thisted, and Marc Hooghe. 2010. "When in Rome, Do as the Romans Do: The Acculturation of Generalized Trust among Immigrants in Western Europe." *International Migration Review* 44 (3): 697–727.
Dupriez, Vincent, and Xavier Dumay. 2006. "Inequalities in School Systems: Effect of School Structure or of Society Structure?" *Comparative Education* 42 (2): 243–260.

Entzinger, Han. 2000. "The Dynamics of Integration Policies: A Multidimensional Model." In *Challenging Immigration and Ethnic Relations Politics: Comparative European Perspectives*, eds. Ruud Koopmans and Paul Statham, 97–118. Oxford: Oxford University Press.

Favell, Adrian. 2001. *Philosophies of Integration: Immigration and the Idea of Citizenship in France and Britain*. Basingstoke: Macmillan.

Filindra, Alexandra, and Anita Manatschal. 2020. "Coping with a Changing Integration Policy Context: American State Policies and Their Effects on Immigrant Political Engagement." *Regional Studies* 54 (11): 1546–1557.

Fossati, Flavia. 2011. "The Effect of Integration and Social Democratic Welfare States on Immigrants' Educational Attainment: A Multilevel Estimate." *Journal of European Social Policy* 21 (5): 391–412.

Green, Eva G.T., and Christian Staerklé. 2013. "Migration and Multiculturalism." In *The Oxford Handbook of Political Psychology*, eds. Leonie Huddy, David O. Sears, and Jack S. Levy, 852–889. Oxford: Oxford University Press.

Green, Eva G.T., Emilio Paolo Visintin, Oriane Sarrasin, and Miles Hewstone. 2020. "When Integration Policies Shape the Impact of Intergroup Contact on Threat Perceptions: A Multilevel Study across 20 European Countries." *Journal of Ethnic and Migration Studies* 46 (3): 631–648.

Guimond, Serge, Richard J. Crisp, Pierre De Oliveira, Rodolphe Kamiejski, Nour Kteily, Beate Kuepper, Richard N. Lalonde, Shana Levin, Felicia Pratto, Francine Tougas, Jim Sidanius, and Andreas Zick. 2013. "Diversity Policy, Social Dominance, and Intergroup Relations: Predicting Prejudice in Changing Social and Political Contexts." *Journal of Personality and Social Psychology* 104 (6): 941–958.

Gundelach, Birte, and Anita Manatschal. 2017. "Ethnic Diversity, Social Trust and the Moderating Role of Subnational Integration Policy." *Political Studies* 65 (2): 413–431.

Hainmueller, Jens, and Dominik Hangartner. 2013. "Who Gets a Swiss Passport? A Natural Experiment in Immigrant Discrimination." *American Political Science Review* 107 (1): 159–187.

Hainmueller, Jens, and Daniel J. Hopkins. 2014. "Public Attitudes toward Immigration." *Annual Review of Political Science* 17: 225–249.

Hainmueller, Jens, Dominik Hangartner, and Duncan Lawrence. 2016. "When Lives Are Put on Hold: Lengthy Asylum Processes Decrease Employment among Refugees." *Science Advances* 2 (8): e1600432.

Hainmueller, Jens, Dominik Hangartner, and Dalston Ward. 2019. "The Effect of Citizenship on the Long-Term Earnings of Marginalized Immigrants: Quasi-Experimental Evidence from Switzerland." *Science Advances* 5 (12): 1–8.

Hansen, Georg, and Norbert Wenning. 2003. *Schulpolitik für andere Ethnien in Deutschland. Zwischen Autonomie und Unterdrückung*. Münster: Waxmann.

Harder, Niklas, Lucila Figueroa, Rachel M. Gillum, Dominik Hangartner, David D. Laitin, and Jens Hainmueller. 2018. "Multidimensional Measure of Immigrant Integration." *Proceedings of the National Academy of Sciences* 115 (45): 11483–11488.

Hooghe, Marc, and Thomas de Vroome. 2015. "How Does the Majority Public React to Multiculturalist Policies? A Comparative Analysis of European Countries." *American Behavioral Scientist* 59 (6): 747–768.

Huddleston, Thomas, Özge Bilgili, Anne-Linde Joki, and Zvezda Vankova. 2015. *Migrant Integration Policy Index 2015*. Barcelona and Brussels: CIDOB and MPG.

Ireland, Patrick. 2006. "Institutions, Political Opportunity Structures, and the Shaping of Migration Policies in Western Europe." In *Dialogues on Migration Policy*, eds. Marco Giugni and Florence Passy, 137–155. Lanham, MD: Lexington Books.

Jann, Werner, and Kai Wegrich. 2007. "Theories of the Policy Cycle." In *Handbook of Public Policy Analysis: Theory, Politics, and Methods*, eds. Frank Fischer, Gerald J. Miller, and Mara S. Sidney, 43–62. Boca Raton, FL: CRC Press.

Kauff, Mathias, Frank Asbrock, Stefan Thörner, and Ulrich Wagner. 2013. "Side Effects of Multiculturalism: The Interaction Effect of a Multicultural Ideology and Authoritarianism on Prejudice and Diversity Beliefs." *Personality and Social Psychology Bulletin* 39 (3): 305–320.

Kesler, Christel, and Irene Bloemraad. 2010. "Does Immigration Erode Social Capital? The Conditional Effects of Immigration-Generated Diversity on Trust, Membership, and Participation across 19 Countries, 1981–2000." *Canadian Journal of Political Science* 43 (2): 319–347.

Kitschelt, Herbert. 1997. *The Radical Right in Western Europe: A Comparative Analysis*. Ann Arbor, MI: University of Michigan Press.

Koopmans, Ruud. 2010. "Tradeoffs between Equality and Difference: Immigrant Integration, Multiculturalism and the Welfare State in Cross-National Perspective." *Journal of Ethnic and Migration Studies* 36 (1): 1–26.

Koopmans, Ruud, Ines Michalowski, and Stine Waibel. 2012. "Citizenship Rights for Immigrants: National Political Processes and Cross-National Convergence in Western Europe, 1980–2008." *American Journal of Sociology* 117 (4): 1202–1245.

Koopmans, Ruud, Susanne Veit, and Ruta Yemane. 2019. "Taste or Statistics? A Correspondence Study of Ethnic, Racial and Religious Labour Market Discrimination in Germany." *Ethnic and Racial Studies* 42 (16): 233–252.

Manatschal, Anita. 2012. "Path Dependent or Dynamic? Cantonal Integration Policies between Regional Citizenship Traditions and Right Populist Party Politics." *Ethnic and Racial Studies* 35 (2): 281–297.

Manatschal, Anita, and Isabelle Stadelmann-Steffen. 2013. "Cantonal Variations of Integration Policy and Their Impact on Immigrant Educational Inequality." *Comparative European Politics* 11 (5): 671–695.

Manatschal, Anita, and Isabelle Stadelmann-Steffen. 2014. "Do Integration Policies Affect Immigrants' Voluntary Engagement? An Exploration at Switzerland's Subnational Level." *Journal of Ethnic and Migration Studies* 40 (3): 404–423.

Manatschal, Anita, Verena Wisthaler, and Christina Zuber. 2020. "Making Regional Citizens? The Political Drivers and Effects of Subnational Immigrant Integration Policies in Europe and North America." *Regional Studies* 54 (11): 1475–1485.

Martén, Linna, Jens Hainmueller, and Dominik Hangartner. 2019. "Ethnic Networks Can Foster the Economic Integration of Refugees." *Proceedings of the National Academy of Sciences* 116 (33): 16280–16285.

McLaren, Lauren. 2017. "Immigration, National Identity and Political Trust in European Democracies." *Journal of Ethnic and Migration Studies* 43 (3): 379–399.

Mettler, Suzanne. 2002. "Bringing the State Back in to Civic Engagement: Policy Feedback Effects of the G.I. Bill for World War II Veterans." *American Political Science Review* 96 (2): 351–365.

Morrison, Kimberly Rios, Victoria C. Plaut, and Oscar Ybarra. 2010. "Predicting Whether Multiculturalism Positively or Negatively Influences White Americans' Intergroup Attitudes: The Role of Ethnic Identification." *Personality and Social Psychology Bulletin* 36 (10): 1648–1661.

Nannestad, Peter, Gunnar Lind Haase Svendsen, and Gert Tinggaard Svendsen. 2008. "Bridge over Troubled Water? Migration and Social Capital." *Journal of Ethnic and Migration Studies* 34(4): 607–631.

Pantoja, Adrian D., and Gary Segura. 2003. "Fear and Loathing in California: Contextual Threat and Political Sophistication among Latino Voters." *Political Behavior* 25 (3): 265–286.

Pantoja, Adrian D., Cecilia Menjívar, and Lisa Magaña. 2008. "The Spring Marches of 2006. Latinos, Immigration, and Political Mobilization in the 21st Century." *American Behavioral Scientist* 52 (4): 499–506.

Pecoraro, Marco, Anita Manatschal, Eva G.T. Green, and Philippe Wanner. 2019. "Does Integration Policy Improve Labour Market, Sociocultural and Psychological Adaptation of Asylum-Related Immigrants? Evidence from Sri Lankans in Switzerland." *IRENE working paper 19-08*. https://ideas.repec.org/p/irn/wpaper/19-08.html.

Pettigrew, Thomas F. 2016. "In Pursuit of Three Theories: Authoritarianism, Relative Deprivation, and Intergroup Contact." *Annual Review of Psychology* 67 (1): 1–21.

Pichler, Florian. 2011. "Success on European Labor Markets: A Cross-National Comparison of Attainment between Immigrant and Majority Populations." *International Migration Review* 45 (4): 938–978.

Pierson, Paul. 1993. "When Effect Becomes Cause. Policy Feedback and Political Change." *World Politics* 45: 595–628.

Pierson, Paul. 2006. "Public Policies as Institutions." In *Rethinking Political Institutions: The Art of the State*, eds. Ian Shapiro, Stephen Skowronek, and Daniel Galvin, 114–131. New York: New York University Press.

Plaut, Victoria C., Flannery G. Garnet, Laura E. Buffardi, and Jeffrey Sanchez Burks. 2011. "'What about Me?' Perceptions of Exclusion and Whites' Reactions to Multiculturalism." *Journal of Personality and Social Psychology* 101 (2): 337–353.

Putnam, Robert David. 2007. "*E Pluribus Unum*: Diversity and Community in the Twenty-first Century: The 2006 Johann Skytte Prize Lecture." *Scandinavian Political Studies* 30(2): 137–174.

Reeskens, Tim. 2010. "Ethnic-Cultural Diversity, Migrant Integration Policies and Social Cohesion in Europe: Investigating the Conditional Effect of Ethnic-Cultural Diversity on Generalized Trust." Paper presented at the international conference "Migration: A World in Motion," February 18–20, Maastricht.

Reeskens, Tim, and W.J.H. van Oorschot. 2017. "Conceptions of Citizenship and Tolerance towards Immigrants: A Comparative Study of Public Opinion Data." In *The Strains of Commitment: The Political Sources of Solidarity in Diverse Societies*, eds. Keith Banting and Will Kymlicka, 177–198. Oxford: Oxford University Press.

Reeskens, Tim, and Matthew Wright. 2014. "Host-Country Patriotism among European Immigrants: A Comparative Study of Its Individual and Societal Roots." *Ethnic and Racial Studies* 37 (14): 2493–2511.

Robinson, Vaughan. 1998. "Defining and Measuring Succesfull Refugee Integration." ECRE International Conference on Integration of Refugees in Europe, Antwerp, November.

Rosenberger, Sieglinde. 2020. *Integration erwünscht? Österreichs Integrationspolitik zwischen Fördern, Fordern und Verhindern*. Vienna: Czernin Verlag.

Schlicht-Schmälzle, Raphaela, and Sabrina Möller. 2012. "Macro-Political Determinants of Educational Inequality between Migrants and Natives in Western Europe." *West European Politics* 35 (5): 1044–1074.

Schlueter, Elmar, Bart Meuleman, and Eldad Davidov. 2013. "Immigrant Integration Policies and Perceived Group Threat: A Multilevel Study of 27 Western and Eastern European Countries." *Social Science Research* 42 (3): 670–682.

Scholten, Peter. 2016. "Between National Models and Multi-Level Decoupling: The Pursuit of Multi-Level Governance in Dutch and UK Policies towards Migrant Incorporation." *Journal of International Migration and Integration* 17 (4): 973–994.

Tajfel, Henry, and John C. Turner. 2004. "The Social Identity Theory of Intergroup Behavior." In *Political Psychology: Key Readings*, eds. John T. Jost and Jim Sidanius, 276–293. New York: Psychology Press.

Uslaner, Eric M. 2011. "Trust, Diversity and Segregation in the United States and the United Kingdom." *Comparative Sociology* 10 (2): 221–247.

Vasta, Elie. 2007. "Accommodating Diversity: Why Current Critiques of Multiculturalism Miss the Point." *COMPAS Working Paper* 53.

Vertovec, Steven, and Susanne Wessendorf. 2010. *The Multiculturalism Backlash: European Discourses, Policies and Practices*. New York: Routledge.

Voss, Kim, and Irene Bloemraad. 2011. *Rallying for Immigrant Rights: The Fight for Inclusion in 21st Century America*. Berkeley, CA: University of California Press.

Ward, Colleen, and Anne-Marie Masgoret. 2008. "Attitudes toward Immigrants, Immigration, and Multiculturalism in New Zealand: A Social Psychological Analysis." *International Migration Review* 42 (1): 227–248.

Weldon, Steve A. 2006. "The Institutional Context of Tolerance for Ethnic Minorities: A Comparative Multilevel Analysis of Western Europe." *American Journal of Political Science* 50 (2): 331–349.

Wright, Matthew. 2011. "Policy Regimes and Normative Conceptions of Nationalism in Mass Public Opinion." *Comparative Political Studies* 44 (5): 598–624.

Wright, Matthew, and Irene Bloemraad. 2012. "Is There a Trade-Off between Multiculturalism and Socio-Political Integration? Policy Regimes and Immigrant Incorporation in Comparative Perspective." *Perspectives on Politics* 10 (1): 77–95.

Wright, Matthew, Richard Johnston, Jack Citrin, and Stuart Soroka. 2017. "Multiculturalism and Muslim Accomodation: Policy and Predisposition across Three Political Contexts." *Comparative Political Studies* 50 (1): 102–132.

Zepeda-Millán, Chris. 2017. *Latino Mass Mobilization: Immigration, Racialization, and Activism*. Cambridge: Cambridge University Press.

Zimdars, Anna, and Gindo Tampubolon. 2012. "Ethnic Diversity and European's Generalised Trust: How Inclusive Immigration Policy Can Aid a Positive Association." *Sociological Research Online* 17 (3). www.socresonline.org.uk/17/3/15.html.

11. The politics of multiculturalism and redistribution: Immigration, accommodation, and solidarity in diverse democracies
Keith Banting, Daniel Westlake, and Will Kymlicka

INTRODUCTION

For half a century, liberal-democratic nations have struggled to adapt to new waves of immigration and the ethno-racial diversity it brings in its wake. In the ensuing debates, few issues have provoked more controversy or have been more polarizing than the adoption of multiculturalism policies (MCPs) in response to contemporary diversity. Several heads of government have pronounced multiculturalism a failure. Critics blamed MCPs for cementing social divisions and weakening support for the welfare state, and proposed a different path for the future. Yet, as we shall see, MCPs have proven remarkably resilient. They are not dead or even in retreat. In the decade 2010–2020, the number of countries that adopted new MCPs or strengthened existing ones was much greater than the number of countries that abandoned policies they had adopted earlier.

This chapter explores this paradox. It first demonstrates that, despite the political storms, MCPs for immigrants have proven remarkably resilient, and explores the reasons for their persistence. The chapter then turns to one of the core criticisms of the multicultural approach, testing arguments that MCPs weaken support for the welfare state. We review existing studies of this question, and then present new updated evidence. Both sets of evidence find no support for the criticism. Indeed, the evidence points to a positive relationship between MCPs and public support for the redistributive state. We then extend the analysis to the new frontier of debate about the welfare state, examining whether MCPs have an impact on the extent of welfare chauvinism, the exclusion of immigrants from social programs.

The picture that emerges is of a deeply misunderstood policy domain. Despite the seemingly hostile political environments, multicultural policies have proven durable in most countries that adopted them. Moreover, the most biting criticism of the approach – that it weakens redistribution – is simply wrong. This chapter argues it is time to move on to a new research agenda grounded in the challenges before us, as opposed to relitigating anxieties from the past.

THE RISE AND RESILIENCE OF MULTICULTURALISM POLICIES

How should states respond to growing ethno-racial and religious diversity? The history of state–minority relations throughout most of the nineteenth and twentieth centuries was one of constant pressure for assimilation, combined with animosity towards, if not prohibition of, minority political mobilization. Starting in the 1960s, however, we see a shift towards a more multicultural approach to state–minority relations. The public expression and political mobilization of minority ethnic identities is less likely to be seen as an inherent threat to the state, but is accepted as a normal and legitimate part of a democratic society. Across the Western democracies, we see a trend towards adopting MCPs, which accommodate and support distinctive ethnic minorities, including immigrant minorities.

The essential feature of MCPs is that they go beyond the protection of the basic civil and political rights guaranteed to all individuals in a liberal-democratic state, to also extend some level of recognition, accommodation and support for minorities to express their distinct identities and practices. The rise of MCPs goes beyond the broader politics of civil rights and non-discrimination. Until the 1950s and 1960s, many Western states explicitly discriminated against certain racial or religious groups, denying them the right to immigrate or to become citizens, or subjecting them to discrimination in access to public education, housing or employment. This sort of explicit state-sanctioned discrimination has been repudiated, and most countries have adopted measures to tackle such discrimination. Multiculturalism, however, is not just about ensuring the non-discriminatory application of laws, but about changing the laws and regulations themselves to accommodate the distinctive needs and aspirations of minorities. We see a clear trend across the Western democracies towards the strengthening of both anti-discrimination and MCPs since the 1960s. By the early 2000s, many countries had adopted some elements of a multicultural approach to diversity.

Multiculturalism has proven more controversial than anti-discrimination measures. The first decade of the 2000s witnessed a pervasive backlash against the idea of multiculturalism in many countries, especially in Europe. Political leaders as diverse as Chancellor Angela Merkel of Germany, Prime Minister David Cameron of the United Kingdom and President Nicolas Sarkozy of France pronounced multiculturalism to be a failed strategy. Critics blamed multiculturalism for legitimating and increasing social segregation, and argued it should be rejected in favor of civic integration, which was presented as a completely different approach to diversity. Subsequent analysis demonstrated that, far from being in retreat, MCPs actually strengthened, even in Europe, during the first decade of the twenty-first century. Moreover, MCPs proved fully compatible with more liberal, voluntary forms of civic immigration programs, confirming the feasibility of a multicultural approach to integration in diverse societies (Banting and Kymlicka 2013; Vertovec and Wessendorf 2010; Modood 2007, 2012).

During the second decade of the twenty-first century, the battle lines over diversity shifted, taking on more ominous forms. In country after country, the political landscape was transformed by the upsurge of right-wing populism, including in the 2016 presidential election in the United States, the Brexit referendum in the United Kingdom and the rise of right-wing populist parties in many European countries. Many radical right movements harbored authoritarian instincts, putting democracy itself under strain, with populist leaders openly challenging many of the norms and procedures that underpin liberal-democratic governance (Levitsky and Ziblatt 2018). These populist parties were fueled in large part by ethnonationalism – the mobilization of an ethnically or racially exclusionary conception of the nation (Bonikowski 2017; Akkerman et al. 2014; Ivaldi 2018). Far-right leaders built their movements by appealing to historic conceptions of national identity, stoking a sense of cultural anxiety among their supporters about immigration, and pledging to save the nation by closing borders and protecting the historic people (Norris and Inglehart 2019). Controversy over Islamic practices, especially religious dress, have further roiled political debates.

At first glance, an era of rising right-wing nationalism and Islamophobia would also seem to be inhospitable terrain for multicultural approaches to diversity. The rhetoric of right-wing populists is often civilizational in tone, emphasizing fundamental incompatibilities between the historic nation and "others", a discourse that is intrinsically contrary to the ethos of multiculturalism. Of course, the rise of right-wing populism has triggered a strong counter-reaction, and in many countries mainstream economic and political elites mobilized to defend a more open and tolerant vision of the nation. Whereas the civic integration trend of the 2000s was embraced by both right and left, and endorsed by the European Union and the Council of Europe, right-wing populism remains a polarizing ideology, and is often viewed as a threat by mainstream elites. Nevertheless, it is striking that this counter-mobilization against right-wing populism has rarely been in the name of defending multiculturalism. Critics of right-wing populism often talk about anti-racism, civic nationalism and tolerance, but not multiculturalism. The Council of Europe has been actively promoting the idea of "interculturalism", which may sound close to multiculturalism, but which the Council insists is very different, since it is focused more on cohesion than on respect for difference (Council of Europe 2008).[1] So neither right-wing populists nor their critics defended multiculturalism, at least not under that label.

Despite this seemingly hostile terrain, MCPs have once again emerged from the second decade of the century relatively unscathed. Through all of these controversies, the resilience of MCPs stands out. For evidence, we turn to the Multiculturalism Policy Index, which has recently been updated to 2020.

Multiculturalism Policy Index

The MCP Index focuses exclusively on MCPs designed to recognize, accommodate and support the cultural differences of minority groups in 21 Western democracies. The Index is based on a range of public policies that are seen, by both critics and defenders, as emblematic of a multiculturalist turn. They all offer some degree of positive recognition, accommodation and support of minorities. The eight indicators used to build the MCP Index for immigrant minorities are:

1. constitutional, legislative or parliamentary affirmation of multiculturalism, at the central and/or regional and municipal levels;
2. the adoption of multiculturalism in the school curriculum;
3. the inclusion of ethnic representation/sensitivity in the mandate of public media or media licensing;
4. exemptions from dress codes, either by statute or by court cases;
5. allowing of dual citizenship;
6. the funding of ethnic group organizations to support cultural activities;
7. the funding of bilingual education or mother-tongue instruction;
8. affirmative action for disadvantaged immigrant groups.

These eight indicators capture the main ways in which states express multiculturalist commitments, which we earlier described as "recognition" (indicators 1–3), "accommodation" (indicators 4–5) and "support" (indicators 6–8). To build the Index, countries are scored on each indicator as 0 (no such policy), 0.5 (partial) or 1.0 (clear policy). The component scores are then aggregated, with equal weighting for each indicator, producing a country score ranging from 0 to 8 (for the empirical evidence supporting rankings, see Wallace 2021).

Table 11.1 presents the MCP Index summary scores for 1980, 1990, 2000, 2010 and 2020. Several patterns stand out. Comparing the scores for 2000 and 2010 confirms that, despite the rhetorical backlash against the idea of multiculturalism, actual MCPs grew stronger, not weaker in that decade. Actual reductions in MCPs were limited to a couple of countries. In similar fashion, comparing the scores for 2010 and 2020 demonstrates that, despite the rise of right-wing populism and Islamophobia, MCPs strengthened during the decade in eight countries, remained unchanged in nine countries and declined in only four countries. Moreover, changes – both strengthening and weakening – were small.

This resilience reappears when one focuses on sub-components of the Index that represent flashpoints in recent political debates: dual citizenship and exemptions from dress codes. (For details of all sub-components of the Index, see www.queensu.ca/mcp).

Table 11.1 The evolution of multiculturalism policies, 1980–2020

	Rankings from the Multiculturalism Policy Index				
	1980	1990	2000	2010	2020
Australia	5.5	8	8	8	8
Austria	0	0	1	1.5	1.5
Belgium	1	1.5	3.5	5.5	5.5
Canada	5	6.5	7.5	7.5	7
Denmark	0	0	0	0	1
Finland	0	0	1.5	6	7
France	1	2	2	2	1.5
Germany	0	0.5	2	2.5	3
Greece	0.5	0.5	0.5	2.5	2.5
Ireland	1	1	1.5	4	4.5
Italy	0	0	1.5	1.5	1.5
Japan	0	0	0	0	0
Netherlands	2.5	3	4	2	1
New Zealand	2.5	5	5	6.5	6.5
Norway	0	0	0	3.5	4.5
Portugal	0	1	3	3.5	3.5
Spain	0	1	1	3.5	3
Sweden	3	3.5	5	7	7
Switzerland	0	0	1	1	1
United Kingdom	2.5	5	5	5.5	6
United States	3.5	3	3	3	3.5

Source: www.queensu.ca/mcp/

Between 2010 and 2020, three countries – Denmark, Germany and Norway – moved to accept dual citizenship in whole or in part, and 18 countries maintained their position. In the case of exemptions from dress codes, two countries – New Zealand and the United States – strengthened their exemptions, and three countries – the Netherlands, Norway and Canada – weakened theirs. After a series of failed initiatives throughout the mid-2000s and early 2010s, the government of the Netherlands passed a ban on face coverings in 2018, prohibiting individuals from wearing religious veils, such as the niqab and burqa, in public buildings and on public transit. In the same year, the government of Norway voted to ban the burqa and niqab in daycares, schools and universities, suggesting that they represented a barrier to communication in educational settings. The Canadian case is complicated. The federal government remains committed to the multicultural approach, and its Multiculturalism Act continues to apply in federal areas of jurisdiction across the country, including in Quebec. However, the province of Quebec, home to about a quarter of the Canadian population, has adopted legislation prohibiting the wearing of all religious dress by provincial public servants and those employed in the wider public sector.

How can we explain this pattern? What does the literature say about the political origins and persistence of MCPs?

Political Origins

Several explanations have been put forward to explain the development of MCPs. One line of argument links multiculturalism to the spread of broader norms around the spread of human rights and acceptance of diversity that emerged after the Second World War (Triadafilopoulos 2012; Soysal 1994). Norm diffusion on its own, however, cannot explain variation in the extent and development of policies in different countries, and Triadafilopoulos (2012) demonstrates that norms interacted with different institutions and values in Canada and Germany to produce different policy outcomes.

The existing country studies point to unique politics in each of the early adopters of MCPs, although a common theme is that governments were responding to the arrival of immigrants who were culturally close. In Canada, explanations focus on the early lobbying by Eastern European ethnic groups (Kymlicka 2008), a state-led effort to develop a common multicultural identity in response to immigration and Quebec nationalism (Winter 2011), and the electoral incentives implicit in an ethnically diverse electorate and first-past-the-post electoral system (Triadafilopoulos 2012). In Australia, the adoption of multiculturalism is connected to the dismantling of the White Australia policy (Tavan 2004), early lobbying efforts by Eastern and Southern European immigrant associations (Lopez 2000) and electoral pressure from an increasingly diverse society (Van Krieken 2012). Swedish MCP has been connected to human rights norms and an extension of the positive rights model underpinning the Swedish welfare state (Borevi 2012), as well as to the lobbying of post-war refugees from the Baltic countries (Wickström 2015). This suggests that multiculturalism often emerges initially in response to culturally familiar forms of immigrant diversity. The issue then becomes what happens when culturally distant groups arrive: does multiculturalism stick even when the hard cases arise, or does it wilt?[2]

Cross-national work has also highlighted the importance of a more diverse electorate (Koopmans et al. 2012) and support from mainstream conservative parties as well as left parties (Westlake 2020) in the adoption of MCPs. By contrast, the emergence of far-right parties makes policy adoption less likely (Koopmans et al. 2012). While this work demonstrates the generalizability of some of the electoral and partisan factors that influence policy, there is much less work exploring other explanations that come out of the single and two-country comparative case analysis.

Persistence

How then do we explain the persistence of MCPs, which have outlasted the governments that put them in place? Institutionalist literature seems to offer insight here, pointing to the role of path dependency in explaining stability in public policies. One version of this approach describes a process of "punctuated equilibrium", in which a pattern of long continuity suddenly gives way to a sharp burst of radical change, which in turn locks in a new trajectory that persists for a long time. In Pempel's words, "path-dependent equilibrium is periodically ruptured by radical change, making for sudden bends in the path of history" (1998: 3; also Tuohy 1999). Many interpretations of the shift in Europe towards civic integration had this flavor, implying a radical transition from multiculturalism to civic integration. However, given the actual persistence of MCPs, a different institutionalist interpretation seems more relevant. This approach sees policies and institutions evolving through incremental adaptation (Thelen 2004). In this tradition, Hacker (2004) argues that much change takes place through drift, conversion and layering. Drift occurs when policy-makers choose not to alter programs in response to changing external circumstances, allowing them to settle into the ongoing policy architecture. Conversion occurs when existing policies and institutions are redirected to new purposes through often obscure administrative adjustments. Layering occurs when new governments simply work around existing programs, laying new policies on top of old policies (Schickler 2001). In this view, countries seldom eliminate the old when they establish the new. The more common pattern is for each generation to layer new programs, reflecting new concerns, over an existing program base.

This perspective is helpful in understanding the evolution of diversity policies in the first decade of the twenty-first century. In many countries, efforts to strengthen civic integration were layered over older programs recognizing and supporting diversity. The fact that the old and new policies were motivated by different concerns was no barrier to a layering process. As Freeman reminds us, "No state possesses a truly coherent incorporation regime ... Rather one finds sub-system frameworks that are weakly, if at all, coordinated" (Freeman 2004: 946). In particular, MCPs have proved compatible with liberal forms of civic integration that prevailed in many countries that had earlier adopted a multicultural approach to diversity. In these countries, the combination of MCPs and civic integration generated a strategy of multicultural integration, which have proved durable over time (Banting and Kymlicka 2013; Goodman 2010).

The persistence of MCPs in the current era of right-wing populism and Islamophobia is more puzzling. There is clearly a much deeper incompatibility between the "conflict of civilizations" discourse adopted by many populists and any meaningful conception of a multicultural society. And while there has been an important counter-mobilization against right-wing populism, it has rarely taken the form of defending multiculturalism. So why then have MCPs persisted, and indeed expanded?

Part of the explanation is that populists seem to have focused their political energy primarily on restricting or stopping the flow of immigrants, asylum seekers and refugees, rather than on how newcomers are treated once settled in a country. To be sure, controversy did swirl around multicultural accommodation of some cultural differences, with the hijab worn by Muslim women becoming a lightning rod for exclusionary impulses. However, many of these controversies occurred in countries or regions that never embraced a multicultural strategy, such as France and the province of Quebec in Canada. Elsewhere, contemporary politics has not prevented countries adopting full or partial exemptions from dress codes, or from maintaining accommodations adopted earlier. The populist attack on the admission of newcomers has not been matched by a similar attack on their accommodation once admitted.

In addition, while the critics of far-right populism did not explicitly defend multiculturalism, their call for "interculturalism" has proven compatible with multiculturalism. Despite the Council of Europe's claim that interculturalism is an alternative to multiculturalism, the evidence to date suggests that interculturalism initiatives have been layered on top of MCPs, not in place of them (Mansouri and Modood 2020), just as civic integration initiatives were layered on top of multiculturalism. While many of the pro-diversity initiatives in the 2010s in Europe were done in the name of interculturalism rather than multiculturalism, interculturalism can in fact take a more assimilationist or a more multiculturalist form. The evidence from the MCP Index suggests that the more accommodative sort of interculturalism has often been layered on top of multiculturalism (Wallace 2021).

MULTICULTURALISM AND REDISTRIBUTION: THE DEBATE

Is there a tension between MCPs and a robust redistributive state? Building and sustaining solidarity is an enduring challenge in all liberal-democratic societies, and the challenge seems even greater in ethnically and religiously diverse societies. Most interpretations see solidarity as a reflection of a shared sense of community that binds its members together in a distinctive set of obligations to each other (Marshall 1950/1963; Smith 2003). Anxiety about the impact of diversity on this sense of a common community has been a recurring theme in both scholarly and public debates. To some extent, this anxiety was a product of a coincidence of timing. The welfare state was under serious pressure in the 1980s and 1990s, when MCPs were also being introduced in many democracies. Most analysts of the welfare state focused on globalization and neoliberalism as the critical drivers of retrenchment and restructuring in social programs. However, some analysts added the adoption of MCPs to the list, and the fate of the welfare state quickly became the prime exhibit of the alleged folly of multiculturalism (Barry 2001; Wolfe and Klausen 1997; Hooker 2009). As we shall see in this section, however, two decades of empirical research offers no support for the fear.

Before jumping into the empirical studies, it is important to clarify a critical distinction. Throughout these debates, there has been a persistent failure to distinguish the argument about MCPs from the debate about the impact of immigration and ethno-racial diversity on the welfare state. Evidence of a tension between diversity and solidarity emerged first in studies of economic development in Africa and studies of the American experience of building social security programs in a country historically divided on racial lines. The debate expanded dramatically as scholars extrapolated from those contexts to suggest an inherent or universal tension between diversity and solidarity. In 1986, Gary Freeman predicted that immigration would lead to the "Americanization" of welfare politics in Europe (Freeman 1986). Almost three decades later, another influential account worried that "As Europe has become more diverse, Europeans have increasingly been susceptible to exactly the same form of racist, anti-welfare demagoguery that worked so well in the United States" (Alesina and Glaeser 2004: 180–181). A small industry quickly emerged to test the impact of diversity on various dimensions of social cohesion, including support for redistribution. One survey of 464 articles found that "there are nearly as many studies rejecting the negative effects of diversity as arguing for them" (Schaeffer 2014: 4; also Van der Meer and Tolsma 2014). Another review added that the effects, whether positive or negative, seem to be small (Stichnoth and Van der Straeten 2013). More recent reviews emphasize that the effects of diversity on redistribution are highly context dependent (Elsner and Concannon 2020; Reeskens 2020). Given the diversity of findings, it is not surprising that the debate continues, and is explored in several chapters in this volume.

The parallel debate relevant here focuses on the role of multiculturalism. Critics have argued that MCPs exacerbate any underlying trade-off between diversity and redistribution, by encouraging an identity politics that weakens or displaces support for the welfare state (Barry 2001). This concern has been labeled the "progressive's dilemma" (Goodhart 2004), which holds that contemporary democracies face a troubling trade-off between the accommodation of ethno-racial diversity on the one hand and support for redistribution on the other. Implicitly, one can have one but not both. Defenders of MCPs reply that such policies do not create distrust among groups, but rather can ease intercommunal tensions over time, and strengthen the sense of mutual respect, trust and support for redistribution. From their perspective, the ideal of a multicultural welfare state is not a utopian dream, but a realistic goal in contemporary democracies.

The critics point to three mechanisms through which MCPs are alleged to erode the welfare state (for greater detail, see Banting and Kymlicka 2006: 10–22).

- *The crowding-out effect*: According to this version of the argument, MCPs weaken pro-redistribution coalitions by diverting political energy from redistribution to recognition. People who would otherwise be fighting for greater economic redistribution are instead campaigning for recognition and accommodation of their cultural differences.
- *The corroding effect*: Here MCPs are held to institutionalize difference, thereby telling citizens that what divides them into ethnocultural groups is more important than what they have in common, and that citizens from other groups are not really part of "us". Over time, this institutionalization erodes trust and a sense of shared identity or shared fate among citizens, weakening popular support for redistribution.
- *The misdiagnosis effect*: This third line of argument holds that MCPs lead minorities to misdiagnose the conditions they face, encouraging them to believe that their problems are rooted primarily in cultural misrecognition rather than economic inequality and class. Over time, this makes pan-ethnic coalitions to support redistribution less likely.

Given the intensity of this debate, there has been surprisingly little research on the impact of MCPs on solidarity. The studies that do exist fall into two groups. The first group focuses on public attitudes, looking at the relationship between support for multiculturalism and support for redistribution among members of the public. The second set of studies shifts to the level of the state, looking at the relationship between the strength of MCPs and two forms of solidarity: first, the strength of public support for social programs; and second, the actual strength of the welfare state.

In most critiques of multiculturalism, the alleged negative effects of multiculturalism flow through the impact on public attitudes. The corroding and misdiagnosis arguments contend that public support for multicultural strategies weakens public support for redistribution. The implication is that at the individual level, support for multiculturalism and support for redistribution are in tension. Existing studies, however, find the opposite. A study of public attitudes in Denmark found that support for multiculturalism is positively associated with redistributive solidarity – indeed, more so than either national identity or liberal values (Breidahl et al. 2016). Similarly, an analysis of attitudes in the United States and Canada finds that "at the individual level, support for multiculturalism policies is positively correlated with support for redistribution" (Soroka et al. 2018: 282; also Johnston et al. 2017). Obviously, one needs to be cautious about attributing causality here. Perhaps views of multiculturalism influence views on redistribution but the reverse might also be true. Perhaps both orientations reflect some deeper common factor, such as an underlying progressive orientation to all forms of inequality. At a minimum, there is no evidence of an inherent tension between support for multiculturalism and support for redistribution. People can support different progressive causes at the same time.

The second set of studies moves to the state level, analyzing the impact of MCPs by comparing across countries that embraced the multicultural approach and countries that steadfastly resisted such a strategy. Most cross-national analyses of the effects of MCPs concentrate on other forms of social integration, such as interpersonal trust, perceived discrimination, citizenship acquisition, trust in political institutions, minority political participation and representation in political institutions, or national identity (for a summary, see Bloemraad 2017). However, a handful of studies focus directly on the impact of MCPs on redistributive solidarity, deploying multilevel analysis to tease out the effects. Once again, the studies offer little support to the critics of MCPs. Some studies simply conclude that there is no negative relationship between MCPs and redistributive solidarity (Brady and Finnigan 2014; Sumino 2014). Other studies, however, find a *positive* relationship between strong MCPs and public support for welfare. Perhaps the most thorough analysis comes from Markus Crepaz, who finds that countries with strong MCPs show statistically significant increased public support for the welfare state compared to those with weaker MCPs (Crepaz 2008). He concludes that MCPs "lower the cultural distance between members of the dominant society and minorities", and reinforce support for the redistributive state (Crepaz 2008: 198). More recently, Kwon and Curran (2016) come to similar conclusions.

The critique of multiculturalism also finds no support in studies that look at MCPs and the actual strength of the welfare state, as measured by the level of social spending and/or the impact of the social programs in reducing poverty and inequality. At this level, presumably all of the mechanisms cited by critics would be in play. However, the drivers of welfare state policies are complex, and strong relationships with multiculturalism would be surprising. An early study revealed no evidence of a negative relationship between MCPs and welfare state outcomes: countries that adopted such policies in the late twentieth century did not experience an erosion of their welfare states or even slower growth in social spending than countries that resisted such programs (Banting et al. 2006). This conclusion has been confirmed in subsequent studies (for example Crepaz 2008: 174–180; also Soroka et al. 2018: 274).

New Evidence

The 2020 update of the MCP Index provides another opportunity to analyze the impact of multiculturalism on redistribution. To investigate the possibility that the impact of MCPs is very slow acting, emerging over decades, we present a bivariate analysis of change in policy and change in social spending over the 1980–2020 period. We also investigate the impact over shorter periods, presenting multivariate regression analysis based on five-year periods. Throughout, we focus on social spending as a percentage of gross domestic product (GDP), a measure that spans the 1980–2020 period for which we also have MCP scores. In our analysis, we adopt an approach similar to that by Soroka et al. (2016), and the methodological choices and details for the multivariate analysis are discussed in the online appendix A (https://danielwestlakepolitics.wordpress.com/data/).

Figure 11.1 shows the bivariate relationship between policy change and change in social spending between 1980 and 2020 (or in the case of social spending the most recent year for which data from the Organisation for Economic Co-operation and Development is available). The figure shows no evidence that countries that adopted more MCPs over the 1980–2020 period reduced their social spending. Indeed, the figure shows a slightly positive (though not statistically significant) relationship between policy adoption and social spending. Notably, the only country to have dramatically reduced its level of MCPs over this period, the Netherlands, is also the country that has done the most to reduce its social spending.

A bivariate analysis does not account for how other variables might affect social spending. It also does not consider shorter-term effects of the adoption of MCPs on social spending. To account for this, we run time-series cross-section multivariate regression models. In these models, we test the impact of the MCP ranking at the beginning of each five-year period and the impact of change in the MCP ranking over the five-year period. Our unit of analysis is five-year periods between 1980 and 2020 (e.g. 2015–2020, 2010–2015, etc.). Following Soroka et al. (2016), controls are included for change in the foreign-born population, the left/right ideology of the government, the age distribution of the population and change in unemployment and inflation. We also include controls for previous social spending and a time trend. Finally, we run models with controls for the number of women in the labor force and union density. These controls are added separately because data were not available for all cases over all of the time periods we analyzed.

The first set of models in Table 11.2 shows little evidence of a relationship between the number of MCPs adopted over a four-year period and social spending.[3] One would expect to see a negative relationship if efforts to expand multiculturalism were crowding

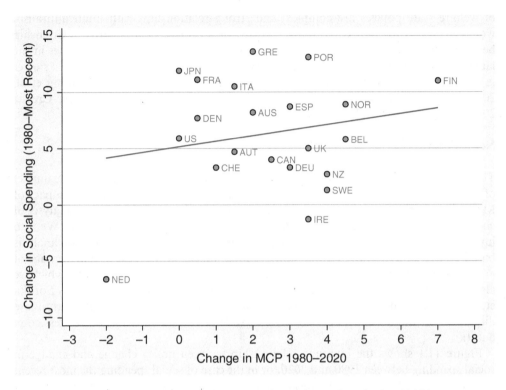

Figure 11.1 Change in multicultural policy and social spending (1980–2020)

out advocacy for welfare state expansion or leading minorities to focus on cultural recognition instead of the welfare state. Instead, there is a slightly positive, though not statistically significant, relationship between policy adoption and change in social spending. If multiculturalism were corroding support for the welfare state one would expect to see countries with more policies reducing welfare state spending. The second set of models in Table 11.2 shows a negative relationship between the number of policies at the beginning of a five-year period and change in social spending over that period. However, this relationship only holds when one does not include controls. When other factors that affect social spending are included in the model, this relationship turns positive (though not statistically significant).

In summary, analysis on the updated MCP Index once again shows no evidence of a conflict between MCPs and the welfare state either in the long term or in shorter periods. Absence of evidence of an effect is not necessarily evidence of the absence of an effect. However, the fact that repeated analyses have failed to find evidence of a negative relationship between MCPs and welfare spending should lead one to be skeptical of claims of a "progressives' dilemma" between supporting multiculturalism and supporting the welfare state.

Table 11.2 Impact of multiculturalism policies on social spending

	Change in MCP			MCP at start of 5-year period		
	Model 1	Model 2	Model 3	Model 1	Model 2	Model 3
Change in MCP	0.705* (0.386)	0.209 (0.226)	0.182 (0.265)			
MCP at start of 5-year period				−0.295** (0.113)	0.039 (0.196)	0.055 (0.171)
Change in foreign born %		0.133 (0.141)	−0.086 (0.172)		0.145 (0.134)	−0.082 (0.165)
Right cabinet % (lagged by one year)		0.000 (0.007)	0.000 (0.006)		0.001 (0.007)	0.000 (0.006)
Left cabinet % (lagged by one year)		0.001 (0.006)	−0.001 (0.006)		0.002 (0.006)	0.000 (0.006)
Change in under-15 population		0.338* (0.166)	0.238 (0.150)		0.342* (0.167)	0.229 (0.156)
Change in over-65 population		0.052 (0.285)	0.004 (0.225)		0.043 (0.282)	−0.006 (0.227)
Change in unemployment		0.346*** (0.081)	0.288*** (0.084)		0.348*** (0.082)	0.288*** (0.083)
Change in inflation		−0.041 (0.066)	−0.019 (0.058)		−0.045 (0.064)	−0.022 (0.056)
Previous social spending		−0.362*** (0.086)	−0.406*** (0.080)		−0.365*** (0.086)	−0.408*** (0.080)
Time trend		0.049 (0.024)	0.091*** (0.030)		0.046 (0.028)	0.089** (0.033)
Change in women in labor force			0.813*** (0.199)			0.836*** (0.194)
Change in union density			0.048 (0.046)			0.056 (0.044)

Table 11.2 (continued)

	Change in MCP			MCP at start of 5-year period		
	Model 1	Model 2	Model 3	Model 1	Model 2	Model 3
Constant	0.588	6.987	6.547	1.564	7.005	6.493
Within R^2	0.040	0.606	0.676	0.028	0.603	0.674
Between R^2	0.030	0.009	0.003	0.067	0.006	0.005
Overall R^2	0.039	0.336	0.305	0.022	0.324	0.292
Observations	166	166	149	166	166	149
Countries	21	21	20	21	21	20

Note: * $p < 0.1$, ** $p < 0.05$, *** $p < 0.01$; standard errors are in parentheses; models are time-series cross-section regression models with fixed effects and clustered standard errors by country; the dependent variable in all models is change in social spending as a percentage of GDP.

MULTICULTURALISM AND *INCLUSIVE* REDISTRIBUTION: THE NEW DEBATE

Controversy about multiculturalism and the welfare state has shifted. In the original debates, the question was whether growing diversity would erode the welfare state generally. In retrospect, the idea that immigration would lead citizens to withdraw their support from major social programs they value was a bit implausible. In most countries, citizens value major social programs, which provide them with an element of security in an insecure world and help them meet basic social needs such as health and education (Brooks and Manza 2007; Svallors 2003). The dominant response to immigrant diversity is public support for barriers that deny immigrants access to social benefits, a response now commonly referred to as welfare chauvinism. At its core, the message is simple: the welfare state is for "us" and immigrants are not "us".

There is a sizeable qualitative literature tracking the politics of immigrant exclusion in specific settings. An early harbinger arrived in the 1996 welfare reform in the United States, which excluded undocumented immigrants from any federal, state and local benefit and denied all non-citizens access to food stamps and supplemental security income (Weaver 2000). In the United Kingdom, reforms in 1996 and 1999 excluded temporary immigrants from non-contributory benefits and denied welfare to asylum seekers awaiting a decision on their application (Sales 2002). In Denmark, social assistance reform decreased the benefit level for recent immigrants (Andersen 2007), and the Netherlands limited the social rights of undocumented immigrants, asylum seekers and family immigrants (Minderhoud 1999). More recent studies have added a comparative dimension. Diane Sainsbury conducted detailed research on the social rights of immigrants in France, Denmark, Germany, Sweden, the United Kingdom and the United States (Sainsbury 2012); and Edward Koning has compared the social rights of immigrants in Canada, Sweden and the Netherlands (Koning 2019; also Banting and Koning 2017).

There is also considerable research on the drivers of welfare chauvinist attitudes held by the public, which is well summarized in Chapter 8 by Edward Koning in this *Handbook*. Not surprisingly, anti-immigrants' attitudes, whether rooted in a sense of ethnic threat or racism, are closely associated with support for excluding immigrants from social benefits. Traditional forms of national identity can also spill over into welfare chauvinism, reflecting a belief that newcomers are not full members of the nation. Socio-economic status matters: individuals with high levels of education, efficacy and income tend to be less welfare chauvinist than those on the margins of the economy who live with considerable income insecurity. Not surprisingly, immigrants perhaps themselves are less hostile to benefits for newcomers than the native born. Finally, politics also matters. Political parties, especially radical anti-immigrant parties, mobilize exclusionary attitudes and inject them directly into political debate (for references, see Koning in this *Handbook*).

To our knowledge, no study has analyzed whether MCPs induce countries to exclude immigrants from welfare benefits. Clearly, in responding to the idea of a "progressive's dilemma", it is no longer enough to demonstrate that multicultural strategies do not weaken the general strength of the redistributive state. We also need to analyze whether multiculturalism influences *inclusive* redistribution. Determined critics of multiculturalism might argue that by emphasizing immigrants' difference, multiculturalism impedes the recognition of immigrants as "one of us", and hence impedes their recognition as deserving recipients of solidarity. It is indeed a striking feature of public opinion across the Western democracies that immigrants are at the bottom of the "deservingness ladder". This is so ubiquitous that Van Oorschot calls it "a truly universal element in the popular welfare culture of present Western welfare states" (2006: 25). Does multiculturalism exacerbate the tendency to see immigrants as undeserving, or does it rather help to legitimate immigrant diversity, and thereby help immigrants move up the deservingness ladder?

New Evidence

Here we explore whether countries that have adopted MCPs are more or less prone to also adopt welfare chauvinism. We draw on the new Immigrant Exclusion from Social Programs Index (IESPI), developed by Edward Koning (2020). The IESPI provides a summary indicator of the extent to which the welfare systems of 19 democratic countries differentiate between immigrants and native-born citizens in granting access to social programs. This summary indicator is based on the examination of eight specific social programs, and is available for 1990, 2000, 2010 and 2015. Comparing the IESPI to the updated MCP Index suggests that countries with stronger MCPs also have more inclusionary welfare states, though there are plenty of outliers to this trend. Figure 11.2 shows

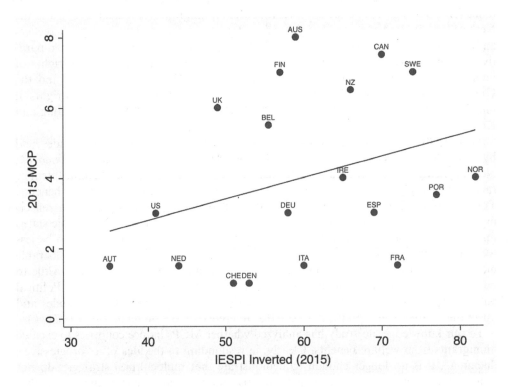

Figure 11.2 Multiculturalism policies compared to the Immigrant Exclusion from Social Programs Index

the relationship between a country's IESPI score in 2015 and its MCP score in the same year.[4] The IESPI score has been inverted so that higher scores for both the IESPI and the MCP represent pro-immigrant policy. The general trend is positive, although not statistically significant. Countries with higher inverted IESPI scores also tend to have stronger MCPs. There are, however, important outliers. France and Spain have welfare states that are relatively open to immigrants despite having few MCPs. In contrast, Australia, Finland and the United Kingdom have quite exclusionary welfare state policies given the strength of their MCPs.

A similar pattern emerges with respect to policy change. Figure 11.3 compares change in the IESPI (again inverted for ease of interpretation) with change in the MCP Index between 1990 and 2015 (the earliest and latest dates for which IESPI data are available). Countries that have made their welfare states less exclusionary also tend to be the countries that have adopted more MCPs. For example, New Zealand, Spain and Portugal made immigrant access to their welfare states easier as they adopted more MCPs. In contrast, the Netherlands and the United States have made their welfare states more exclusionary as they have either adopted no additional MCPs (United States) or removed existing MCP policies (Netherlands). There is, however, a great deal of variation in MCP adoption amongst countries that have done little to change the accessibility of their welfare state. For example, Finland and Norway have adopted several new MCPs while Austria and Denmark have adopted few to none.

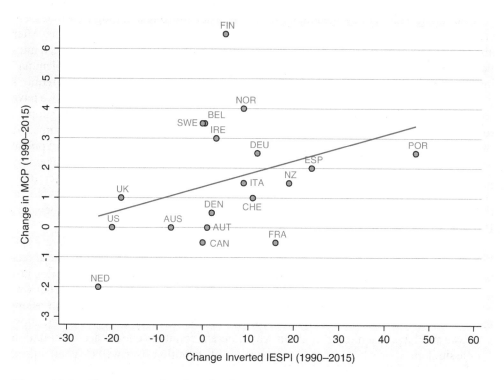

Figure 11.3 Change in multicultural policies and the Immigrant Exclusion from Social Programs Index (1990–2015)

This first look at the relationship between MCPs and exclusionary welfare policies suggests that countries with many MCPs are more likely to have inclusive welfare states. That relationship, however, is not strong. There are plenty of outliers that have strong MCPs without increasing the accessibility of their welfare states. This suggests plenty of avenues for further study of conditional factors that may influence the relationship between multiculturalism and welfare state accessibility.

CONCLUSIONS

Despite the dramatic politics of the last two decades, MCPs have proven remarkably resilient. The rhetorical backlash against the multicultural approach in the 2000s and the right-wing populism and Islamophobia in the 2010s have not changed the basic policy trajectory. MCPs have persisted, and even grown slowly across liberal democracies. In many countries, these policies have become part of the policy infrastructure, with new policies, driven by changing political concerns, being layered on top of multicultural policies adopted decades before. Often the political and policy rhetoric accompanying new policy layers has depicted them as representing a rejection of a multicultural philosophy. In practice, however, old and new have often proven highly compatible, holding out the possibility of a new hybrid – a multicultural form of integration. It is time to dig below the divergent discourses to explore the ways in which old and new are interacting.

In designing a new policy agenda, we should set aside the long-standing view that there is an inherent trade-off between multicultural accommodation and redistribution. After almost 20 years of analysis, there is simply no evidence of a general tension between multicultural policies and the welfare state. Insofar as talk about a "progressive's dilemma" implies a hydraulic relationship between the two – as if driving up redistribution requires driving down multiculturalism – it is an unhelpful starting point for analysis. As we have seen, at the individual level, support for multiculturalism is positively related to support for redistribution. People can support different progressive causes at the same time. At the level of state policies, there is a positive relationship between strong MCPs and public support for the welfare state. Moreover, the accumulated evidence, confirmed again by the updated analysis here, finds no evidence that countries that adopted a multicultural strategy have systematically greater difficulty in sustaining their welfare states. Nor is there a relationship between MCPs and the exclusion of immigrants from social benefits. It is time to lay the ghost of the progressive's dilemma to rest.

However, what is undoubtedly true is that immigrants' claims both to cultural recognition and to economic redistribution are precarious. Progress towards multicultural recognition is continually threatened by the reassertion of assimilationist frameworks, just as progress towards inclusive redistribution is threatened by projects of welfare chauvinism. Contra the "progressive's dilemma", we have no reason to believe that we can secure redistribution by abandoning recognition (or vice versa). However, once we set that ghost aside, we still have much to learn about why different countries choose accommodation over assimilation, or why they choose inclusive redistribution over welfare chauvinism, and how these choices interact over time.

In our view, further progress will require digging deeper into the status hierarchies that underpin conceptions of deservingness and membership and that impose membership penalties on immigrants and ethnic minorities, not just in access to social protection but also to full participation in the political process through which countries shape their future.[5] There is an exciting new research agenda ahead of us.

NOTES

1. Whether there really is a significant difference between multiculturalism and interculturalism is much debated in the literature. Some have argued that the Council of Europe exaggerates the contrast in order to avoid the political stigma attached to "the m word" (Modood 2017). That in itself is indicative of the hostile climate facing defenders of multiculturalism (Kymlicka 2016).
2. To press the point, one could argue that multiculturalism in the United Kingdom was first adopted primarily for (English-speaking, Christian) Caribbean immigrants, and in the Netherlands primarily for (Christian) Surinamese and Moluccans from former Dutch colonies – that is, for groups that were seen as sharing a certain kind of "civilizational" similarity.
3. To save space, only three models are presented here. For models that add control variables in smaller blocks see the online appendix B (https://danielwestlakepolitics.wordpress.com/data/).
4. The 2015 MCP data are from the annualized MCP data set developed by Daniel Westlake.
5. For some preliminary speculations on the link between multiculturalism, deservingness judgments and inclusive redistribution, see Banting et al. (2020).

REFERENCES

Akkerman, Anges, Cas Mudde and Andrej Zaslove. 2014. "How Populist Are the People? Measuring Populist Attitudes in Voters". *Comparative Political Studies* 47(9): 1324–1353.
Alesina, Alberto, and Edward Glaeser. 2004. *Fighting Poverty in the US and Europe: A World of Difference*. Oxford: Oxford University Press.
Andersen, J. G. 2007. "Restricting Access to Social Protection for Immigrants in the Danish Welfare State". *Benefits* 15: 257–269.
Banting, Keith, and Edward Koning. 2017. "Just Visiting? The Weakening of Social Protection in a Mobile World", in Anna Triandafyllidou, ed. *Multicultural Governance in a Mobile World*. Edinburgh: Edinburgh University Press.
Banting, Keith, and Will Kymlicka. 2006. "Introduction: Multiculturalism and the Welfare State: Setting the Context", in Keith Banting and Will Kymlicka, eds. *Multiculturalism and the Welfare State: Recognition and Redistribution in Contemporary Democracies*. Oxford: Oxford University Press.
Banting, Keith, and Will Kymlicka. 2013. "Is There Really a Retreat from Multiculturalism Policies? New Evidence from the Multiculturalism Policy Index". *Comparative European Politics* 11(5): 577–598.
Banting, Keith, Richard Johnston, Will Kymlicka and Stuart Soroka. 2006. "Do Multiculturalism Policies Erode the Welfare State? An Empirical Analysis", in Keith Banting and Will Kymlicka, eds. *Multiculturalism and the Welfare State: Recognition and Redistribution in Contemporary Democracies*. Oxford: Oxford University Press.
Banting, Keith, Will Kymlicka, Allison Harell and Rebecca Wallace. 2020. "Beyond National Identity: Liberal Nationalism, Shared Membership and Solidarity", in Gina Gustavsson and David Miller, eds. *Liberal Nationalism and its Critics: Normative and Empirical Questions*. Oxford: Oxford University Press.
Barry, Brian. 2001. *Culture and Equality: An Egalitarian Critique of Multiculturalism*. Cambridge, MA: Harvard University Press.
Bloemraad, Irene. 2017. "Solidarity and Conflict: Understanding the Causes and Consequences of Access to Citizenship, Civic Integration Policies, and Multiculturalism", in Keith Banting and Will Kymlicka, eds. *The Strains of Commitment: The Political Sources of Solidarity in Diverse Societies*. Oxford: Oxford University Press.
Bonikowski, Bart. 2017. "Ethno-nationalist Populism and the Mobilization of Collective Resentment". *British Journal of Sociology* 68: S181–S213.
Borevi, Karin. 2012. "Sweden: The Flagship of Multiculturalism", in Grete Brochmann and Anniken Hagelund, eds. *Immigration Policy and Scandinavian Welfare State 1945–2010*. New York: Palgrave.
Brady, David, and Ryan Finnigan. 2014. "Does Immigration Undermine Public Support for Social Policy". *American Sociological Review* 79(1): 17–42.

Breidahl, Karen, Nils Holtug and Kristian Kongshøj. 2016. "Do Shared Values Promote Social Cohesion? If So, Which? Evidence from Denmark". *European Political Science Review*.

Brooks, Clem, and Jeff Manza. 2007. *Why Welfare States Persist: The Importance of Public Opinion in Democracies*. Chicago, IL: University of Chicago Press.

Council of Europe, Committee of Ministers. 2008. *White Paper on Intercultural Dialogue*. Strasbourg: Council of Europe.

Crepaz, Markus. 2008. *Trust beyond Borders: Immigration, the Welfare State, and Identity in Modern Societies*. Ann Arbor, MI: University of Michigan Press.

Elsner, Benjamin, and Jeff Concannon. 2020. "Immigration and Redistribution". Working Paper 202024, School of Economics, University College, Dublin.

Freeman, Gary. 1986. "Migration and the Political Economy of the Welfare State". *Annals of the American Academy of Political and Social Science* 485: 51–63.

Freeman, Gary. 2004. "Immigrant Incorporation in Western Democracies". *International Migration Review* 38(3): 945–969.

Goodhart, David. 2004. "Too Diverse?" *Prospect*, February: 30–37.

Goodman, S. 2010. "Integration Requirements for Integration's Sake? Identifying, Categorizing and Comparing Civic Integration Policies". *Journal of Ethnic and Migration Studies* 36(5): 753–772.

Hacker, J. 2004. "Privatizing Risk without Privatizing the Welfare States: The Hidden Politics of Social Policy Retrenchment in the United States". *American Political Science Review* 98(2): 243–260.

Hooker, Juliet. 2009. *Race and the Politics of Solidarity*. Oxford: Oxford University Press.

Ivaldi, Gilles. 2018. "Populisme et choix électoral". *Revue française de science politique* 68(5): 847–872.

Johnston, Richard, Matthew Wright, Stuart Soroka and Jack Citrin. 2017. "Diversity and Solidarity: New Evidence from Canada and the US", in Keith Banting and Will Kymlicka, eds. *The Strains of Commitment: The Political Sources of Solidarity in Diverse Societies*. Oxford: Oxford University Press.

Koning, Edward. 2019. *Immigration and the Politics of Welfare Exclusion: Selective Solidarity in Western Democracies*. Toronto: University of Toronto Press.

Koning, Edward. 2020. "Accommodation and New Hurdles: The Increasing Importance of Politics for Immigrants' Access to Social Programmes in Western Democracies". *Social Policy and Administration*, DOI: 10.1111/spol.12661.

Koopmans, Ruud, Ines Michalowski and Strinnbe Waibel. 2012. "Citizenship Rights for Immigrants: National Political Processes and Cross-National Convergence in Western Europe: 1980–2008". *American Journal of Sociology* 117(4): 1202–1245.

Kwon, Ronald, and Michaela Curran. 2016. "Immigration and Support for Redistributive Social Policy: Does Multiculturalism Matter?" *International Journal of Comparative Sociology* 57(6): 375–400.

Kymlicka, Will. 2008. "Marketing Canadian Pluralism in the International Arena", in Linda White, Richard Simeon, Robert Vipond and Jennifer Wallner, eds. *The Comparative Turn in Canadian Political Science*. Vancouver: University of British Columbia Press.

Kymlicka, Will. 2016. "Defending Diversity in an Era of Populism: Multiculturalism and Interculturalism Compared", in Nasar Meer, ed. *Multiculturalism and Interculturalism: Debating the Dividing Lines*. Edinburgh: Edinburgh University Press.

Levitsky, Steven, and Daniel Ziblatt. 2018. *How Democracies Die*. New York: Broadway Books.

Lopez, Mark. 2000. *The Origins of Multiculturalism in Australian Politics 1945–1975*. Melbourne: Melbourne University Press.

Mansouri, Fethi, and Tariq Modood. 2020. "The Complementarity of Multiculturalism and Interculturalism: Theory Backed by Australian Evidence". *Ethnic and Racial Studies*: 1–20.

Marshall. T.H. 1950/1963. *Sociology at the Crossroads*. London: Heinemann.

Minderhoud, Paul. 1999. "Asylum Seekers and Access to Social Security: Recent Developments in the Netherlands, United Kingdom, Germany, and Belgium", in A. Bloch and C. Levy, eds. *Refugees, Citizenship, and Social Policy in Europe*. Houndmills: Macmillan.

Modood, T. 2007. *Multiculturalism: A Civic Idea*. Cambridge: Polity.

Modood, T. 2012. *Post-immigration "Difference" and Integration: The Case of Muslims in Western Europe*. London: British Academy.

Modood, T. 2017. "Must Interculturalists Misrepresent Multiculturalism?" *Comparative Migration Studies* 5(1): 1–17.

Norris, Pippa, and Ronald Inglehart. 2019. *Cultural Backlash: Trump, Brexit, and Authoritarian Populism*. New York: Cambridge University Press.

Pempel, T.J. 1998. *Regime Shift: Comparative Dynamics of the Japanese Political Economy*. Ithaca, NY: Cornell University Press.

Reeskens, Tim. 2020. "Migration and the Welfare State: Welfare Magnets and Welfare Chauvinism", in Nicolas Ellison and Tin Haux, eds. *Handbook on Society and Social Policy*. Cheltenham, UK and Northampton, MA, USA: Edward Elgar Publishing.

Sainsbury, Diane. 2012. *Welfare States and Immigrant Rights: The Politics of Inclusion and Exclusion.* Oxford: Oxford University Press.
Sales, Rosemary. 2002. "The Deserving and the Undeserving? Refugees, Asylum Seekers and Welfare in Britain". *Critical Social Policy* 22(3): 456–478.
Schaeffer, M. 2014. *Ethnic Diversity and Social Cohesion: Immigration, Ethnic Fractionalization and Potentials for Civic Action.* Farnham: Ashgate.
Schickler, E. 2001. *Disjointed Pluralism: Institutional Innovation and the Development of the U.S. Congress.* Princeton, NJ: Princeton University Press.
Smith, Rogers. 2003. *Stories of Peoplehood: The Politics and Morals of Political Membership.* New York: Cambridge University Press.
Soroka, Stuart, Richard Johnston, Anthony Kevins, Keith Banting and Will Kymlicka. 2016. "Migration and Welfare State Spending". *European Political Science Review* 8(2): 173–194.
Soroka, Stuart, Matthew Wright, Irene Bloemraad and Richard Johnston. 2018. "Multiculturalism Policy and Support for the Welfare State", in Elizabeth Goodyear-Grant, Richard Johnston, Will Kymlicka and John Myles, eds. *Federalism and the Welfare State in a Multicultural World.* Montreal: McGill-Queen's University Press.
Soysal, Yasemin. 1994. *The Limits of Citizenship: Migrants and Postnational Membership in Europe.* Chicago, IL: University of Chicago Press.
Stichnoth, H., and K. Van der Straeten. 2013. "Ethnic Diversity, Public Spending, and Individual Support for the Welfare State: A Review of the Empirical Literature". *Journal of Economic Surveys* 27(2): 364–389.
Sumino, Takanori. 2014. "Does Immigration Erode the Multicultural Welfare State? A Cross-National Multilevel Analysis in 19 OECD Member States". *Journal of Ethnic and Migration Studies* 40(3): 436–455.
Svallors, Stefan. 2003. "Welfare Regimes and Welfare Opinions: A Comparison of Eight Western Countries". *Social Indicators Research* 64: 495–520.
Tavan, Gwenda. 2004. "The Dismantling of the White Australia Policy: Elite Conspiracy or Will of the Australian People". *Australian Journal of Political Science* 39(1): 109–125.
Thelen, K. 2004. *How Institutions Evolve: The Political Economy of Skills in Germany, Britain, the United States, and Japan.* New York: Cambridge University Press.
Triadafilopoulos, Triadafilos. 2012. *Becoming Multicultural: Immigration and the Politics of Membership in Canada and Germany.* Vancouver: University of British Columbia Press.
Tuohy, C. 1999. *Accidental Logics: The Dynamics of Change in the Health Care Arena in the United States, Britain, and Canada.* New York: Oxford University Press.
Van der Meer, T., and J. Tolsma. 2014. "Ethnic Diversity and Its Supposed Detrimental Effects on Social Cohesion". *Annual Review of Sociology* 40: 459–478.
Van Krieken, Robert. 2012. "Between Assimilation and Multiculturalism: Models of Integration in Australia". *Patterns of Prejudice* 46(5): 500–517.
Van Oorschot, Wim. 2006. "Making the Difference in Social Europe: Deservingness Perceptions among Citizens of European Welfare States". *Journal of European Social Policy* 16(1): 23–42.
Vertovec, S., and S. Wessendorf. 2010. "Introduction: Assessing the Backlash against Multiculturalism in Europe", in S. Vertovec and S. Wessendorf, eds. *The Multiculturalism Backlash: European Discourses, Policies and Practices.* London: Routledge.
Wallace, Rebecca. 2021. *Multiculturalism Policy Index: Immigrant Minority Policies*, Third Edition. www.queensu.ca/mcp/.
Weaver, Kent. 2000. *Ending Welfare as We Know It.* Washington, DC: Brookings Institution.
Westlake, Daniel. 2020. "Following the Right: Left and Right Parties' Influence over Multiculturalism". *Canadian Journal of Political Science* 53(1): 171–188.
Wickström, Mats. 2015. "Comparative and Transnational Perspectives on the Introduction of Multiculturalism in Post-War Sweden". *Scandinavian Journal of History* 40(4): 512–534.
Winter, Elke. 2011. *Us, Them, and Others: Pluralism and National Identities in Diverse Societies.* Toronto: University of Toronto Press.
Wolfe, Alan, and Jyette Klausen. 1997. "Identity Politics and the Welfare State". *Social Philosophy and Policy* 14(2): 213–255.

12. The politicization of immigration and welfare: The progressive's dilemma, the rise of far-right parties, and challenges for the left
Maureen A. Eger and Joakim Kulin

INTRODUCTION

In recent decades, Western European countries have transitioned from countries of emigration to ones of immigration, like the United States (U.S.), and, in the process, have also become multiethnic. Much of this new diversity is due to European Union enlargement, but asylum seekers from war zones and politically unstable regions of the world make up an increasingly large proportion of immigrants in countries like Sweden and Germany. Given this unprecedented social change, there is concern that immigration-generated ethnic diversity will undermine support for the welfare state—the rationale being that diversity erodes trust, which then decreases solidarity, making popular support for a redistributive welfare state less likely (Banting and Kymlicka 2006). Some scholars call this theoretical tension between social solidarity and ethnic diversity—or between immigration and a redistributive welfare state—the "heterogeneity/redistribution trade-off" (Banting et al. 2006). Others have described this as a "progressive's dilemma" (Goodhart 2004; Banting 2010; Koopmans 2010) or a "new liberal dilemma" (Newton 2007; Kumlin and Rothstein 2010; Reeskens and van Oorschot 2012), because, if diversity undermines solidarity, progressive values and social democratic institutions are at risk. As argued by Goodhart (2004, 30):

> acts of sharing are more smoothly and generously negotiated if we can take for granted a limited set of common values and assumptions ... And therein lies one of the central dilemmas of political life in developed societies: sharing and solidarity can conflict with diversity. This is an especially acute dilemma for progressives who want plenty of both solidarity—high social cohesion and generous welfare paid out of a progressive tax system—and diversity—equal respect for a wide range of peoples, values and ways of life. The tension between the two values is a reminder that serious politics is about trade-offs. It also suggests that the left's recent love affair with diversity may come at the expense of the values and even the people that it once championed.

The terms progressive's dilemma and new liberal dilemma stem from a real concern among social progressives that diversity and solidarity are difficult to combine; yet, in empirical research, these terms commonly refer to the hypothesis that immigration undermines support for the welfare state (Reeskens and van Oorschot 2012; Brady and Finnigan 2014; Spies and Schmidt-Catran 2016) or that multiculturalism undercuts support for the welfare state (Koopmans 2010; Banting et al. 2006) or that ethnic diversity reduces social capital (Kumlin and Rothstein 2010). To be clear, no previous empirical research treats the progressive's dilemma as a meta-theory, and none of these studies have limited their analyses to self-identified progressives. Thus, our use of the term progressive's dilemma is consistent with its common usage in previous sociological research.

In this chapter, we design research to assess the relationship between immigration and welfare; however, we return to the basic premise underlying the progressive's dilemma—that immigration and welfare are not easily combined—instead of analyzing how immigration affects support for welfare. In a first step, we track the prominence of different configurations of attitudes towards redistribution and immigration over time (Kulin et al. 2016). In a second step, we assess the impact of these attitudes on voting for the far-right (nationalist parties), center-right (conservative and neoliberal parties), center-left (social democratic and green parties), and the far left (socialist parties). The existence of the progressive's dilemma should have political implications; yet, research on how immigration-welfare attitudes translate into support for political parties is scarce (cf. Finseraas 2012b). Considering the twenty-first-century decline of social democratic parties and rise of far-right parties with nationalist platforms that politicize immigration and welfare (Barker 2017; Eger and Valdez 2015, 2019; Rydgren 2012), research of this type is essential for understanding shifting electoral patterns over time.

In the sections that follow, we first review research on the progressive's dilemma. We then introduce our country cases: Sweden, Germany, and the U.S.—three major immigrant destinations that are also often regarded as the prototypical social democratic, conservative, and liberal welfare states. Next, we describe our data, methods, and results. Using pooled cross-sectional data from the European Social Survey (ESS) (2002–2018) and the American General Social Survey (GSS) (2004–2018), we find that attitudes consistent with the progressive's dilemma have long existed in these three countries. Results from multinomial logistic regression models reveal that anything but the most progressive attitudes make support for left parties unlikely, confirming the political significance of the dilemma. Nevertheless, the relative share of progressive attitudes is actually increasing in both Germany and the U.S. and, despite a small dip, remains strikingly large in Sweden. These trends suggest that the progressive's dilemma, while certainly a challenge for left-wing parties, is not insurmountable.

THE PROGRESSIVE'S DILEMMA

The progressive's dilemma is the theoretical tension between supporting a liberal immigration policy and a redistributive welfare state (Goodhart 2004). The logic is that immigration-generated ethnic diversity undermines the social trust, cohesion, and solidarity necessary to maintain the welfare state (Banting and Kymlicka 2006). Previous scholarship shows that ethnic and racial diversity pose challenges for interpersonal trust (Alesina and La Ferrara 2000; Uslaner 2002; Putnam 2007; Dinesen et al. 2020), empathy (Gutsell and Inzlicht 2010), reciprocity (Trivers 1971; Habyarimana et al. 2009), solidarity (Lipset and Marks 2000), and social cohesion (Koopmans and Schaeffer 2016). Thus, some view increasing immigration as a potential challenge for European welfare states and their political champions (Eger 2010a; Ford 2015).

However, evidence of the progressive's dilemma is somewhat mixed, arguably in part due to how it has been operationalized. Scholars have approached the question of whether immigration undermines the welfare state from three related yet distinct vantage points. The first wave of research in this area focuses on the relationship between *objective ethnic and racial diversity* and *welfare state expenditure*. These studies show that heterogeneity, measured at the U.S. state, county, or city level is inversely related to social expenditure and the provision of public goods (Hero 1998; Alesina et al. 1999). Cross-national studies also indicate a negative relationship between ethnic fractionalization and welfare effort (Alesina et al. 2001; Alesina and Glaeser 2004; Steele 2016) and welfare state growth (Soroka et al. 2006).

The second wave of studies on the progressive's dilemma investigates the relationship between *objective ethnic and racial diversity* and *welfare attitudes*. This body of research has produced mixed results, with cross-national studies yielding weak or no support for the hypothesis (Brady and Finnigan 2014; Heizmann et al. 2018; Hjerm and Schnabel 2012; Mau and Burkhardt 2009) and cross-regional analyses lending support to the notion that diversity and welfare are difficult to reconcile. Results from case studies of the U.S. find more opposition to welfare in states that are disproportionately Latino (Fox 2004) and African-American (Fullerton and Dixon 2009; Gilens 1999). Further, research shows that, in U.S. communities, support for welfare depends on the race of welfare recipients (Luttmer 2001) or nativity of those in poverty (Eger 2010b). Similarly, a study from Germany shows that natives are less supportive of unemployment policies in regions where the share of foreigners among the unemployed is high (Stichnoth 2012). Results from case studies of Sweden also find a negative relationship between support for social welfare and immigration measured at the county (Eger 2010a) and municipality level (Dahlberg et al. 2012). Finseraas (2012a) finds that support for redistribution is lower in sub-national regions in Europe where there is a higher concentration of ethnic minorities among the poor. This wave of research also includes analyses of welfare chauvinism, or the notion that immigrants should not have the same social rights or access to the welfare state as native-born citizens (Andersen and Bjørklund 1990; Kitschelt and McGann 1995). Some of these empirical studies find little evidence that immigration increases opposition to immigrants' social rights chauvinism (Eger and Breznau 2017; Mewes and Mau 2012; Reeskens and van Oorschot 2012) while others report findings more consistent with the dilemma (Eger et al. 2020; Marx and Naumann 2018).

One possible reason for these divergent results is that country-level indicators of immigration may not be as perceptible or meaningful for individuals as more local contexts (Eger and Breznau 2017). Other research that shows country-level measures of immigration are poor indicators of Europeans' perceptions of the diversity of their country (Herda 2010) and are not strongly associated with anti-immigrant sentiment (van Klingeren et al. 2015; Pottie-Sherman and Wilkes 2017). While these related studies may help explain why country case studies reveal negative relationships between sub-national measures of diversity and welfare attitudes while cross-national studies do not, we contend that such findings also highlight the need for more research that investigates *subjective* reactions to immigration.

There are relatively fewer studies that adopt the third approach to the progressive's dilemma by investigating the relationship between *subjective reactions to diversity* and *welfare attitudes*. Ford (2006) finds that prejudice has a significant, negative effect on whites' support for the British welfare state, while Goldschmidt (2015) shows that prejudice is negatively associated with Germans' support for government assistance for the unemployed. Multiple studies find that holding negative views or stereotypes of immigrants is associated with less supportive views of social welfare (Harell et al. 2016; Larsen 2011; Senik et al. 2009). Other research shows that the relationship between attitudes about immigrants and support for welfare depends on other individual and contextual factors (Breznau and Eger 2016; Burgoon and Rooduijn 2021).

Taking a somewhat literal approach to the progressive's dilemma, Kulin et al. (2016) argue that if diversity and solidarity are indeed difficult to reconcile, specific combinations of immigration-welfare attitudes should exist. They contend that attitudinal profiles where the probability of supporting *both* immigration and redistribution is low are indicative of the progressive's dilemma. Specifically these are attitudinal combinations where individuals either support immigration but not redistribution or support redistribution but not immigration. They claim that, even though the latter is not emphasized in previous research, opposing immigration while supporting redistribution is nevertheless indicative of the theoretical tension. Using ESS data from 2008, they examine attitudes towards redistribution, immigration, and immigrants' social rights across 24 countries. Their analyses reveal a number of attitudinal profiles with unique combinations of immigration-welfare attitudes. The two largest clusters, which constitute over half of the sample, provide evidence of the progressive's dilemma.

To our knowledge, only one study has investigated the relationship between the progressive's dilemma and support for political parties. Finseraas (2012b) examines the indirect effect of immigration attitudes on support for redistribution by analyzing support for left parties, which traditionally support redistributive policies. He finds that those who oppose immigration but support redistribution—what he calls "cross-cutting preferences"—are less likely to support a left party than those who support both redistribution and immigration. Finseraas also finds the degree to which these groups' voting behavior differs depends on how national political parties position themselves in regards to the immigration issue.

ANALYTICAL STRATEGY

In this chapter, we adopt the perspective that the progressive's dilemma is best understood as the notion that immigration and welfare are incompatible. Building on Kulin et al. (2016), we focus our analyses on different combinations of support for/opposition to redistribution and immigration. We characterize different configurations of these attitudes as either progressive, conservative, or mixed. Progressive attitudinal profiles are both pro-immigration and pro-redistribution, while conservative attitudinal profiles are anti-immigration and anti-redistribution. Mixed attitudinal combinations, or cross-cutting preferences (Finseraas 2012b), are either pro-immigration and anti-redistribution or anti-immigration and pro-redistribution. Drawing inspiration from Finseraas (2012b), we hypothesize that immigration-welfare attitudes have consequences for voting behavior, specifically that holding anything but the most progressive attitudes makes support for a left-wing party less likely.

With our research, we extend the work of these scholars in three ways. First, we adopt a comparative case study approach to explore how differences in welfare state regimes are related to the prominence of specific attitudinal profiles. We focus on three contemporary immigrant destinations—the U.S., Germany, and Sweden—that are also the prototypical liberal, conservative, and social democratic welfare states (Esping-Andersen 1990). Despite having similar levels of immigration, these countries differ in their approach to immigrant integration and social rights (Sainsbury 2006, 2012). Although immigrants have access to a more comprehensive welfare state in Germany than the U.S. (Sainsbury 2006), its emphasis on prior contributions (Goldschmidt 2015) makes it more exclusionary than Sweden, whose welfare policies are more comprehensive and inclusive towards immigrants (Sainsbury 2012). Federal assistance in the U.S. requires many years of residence and contributions to social security (Sainsbury 2006); however, states have the right to establish their own welfare programs and rules, which means political debates over immigrants' access to means-tested or universal benefits often happen at the state level (e.g., Jacobson 2009). Although our own empirical analyses do not permit formal tests of hypotheses related to these institutional differences, identifying similarities or differences in the progressive's dilemma in these three particular countries makes possible contributions to the comparative welfare state and immigration literatures.

Second, we also extend previous research on the progressive's dilemma (Kulin et al. 2016) by adding a longitudinal perspective, tracking the prominence of different attitudinal configurations over time. The past two decades have seen a global economic crisis (Laenen et al. 2020) and so-called European migration crisis, both of which increased the salience of welfare and immigration politics (Eger et al. 2020). Changes (or lack thereof) in the relative size of attitudinal profiles within countries speak not only to the national character of immigration-welfare attitudes but also their trajectory over time. Third, we provide a more nuanced analysis of the political implications of the progressive's dilemma by assessing the relationship between attitudes and voting for either a far-right (nationalist), center-right (conservative, neoliberal), or far-left (socialist) party compared to a center-left party (social democratic or green). In doing so, we help make sense of electoral trends, specifically increasing support for anti-immigration parties and declining support for the traditional champions of a redistributive welfare state.

DATA AND METHODS

The following analyses rely on two different attitudinal surveys. The first is the ESS, a cross-sectional survey covering over 30 nations in Europe between 2002 and 2018. All nine rounds have variables measuring individuals' attitudes towards immigrants and redistribution, voting behavior, as well as other attitudinal, behavioral, and demographic information. Much of the European research on welfare and immigration attitudes this century has relied on the ESS. Ns for our Swedish and German cross-sections are 11,929 and 15,794, respectively. We also use the GSS from the U.S. This nationally representative, cross-sectional survey has been administered since 1972 and is regarded as one of the best sources of attitudinal data in the U.S., though questions regarding immigration have not appeared until more recently. Our sub-sample includes 3,568 respondents from eight rounds between 2004 and 2018.

Immigration-Welfare Attitudes

Each round of the ESS contains a measure of *redistributive preferences*. Respondents are asked the extent to which they agree that the government should reduce differences in income levels. Possible responses are: 1 = agree strongly; 2 = agree; 3 = neither agree nor disagree; 4 = disagree; 5 = strongly disagree. We recode this variable to distinguish between individuals who support redistribution (agree and strongly agree) and those who do not articulate clear support. The GSS contains a similarly worded question about redistribution, asking respondents the extent to which they believe the government should reduce income differences between the rich and poor. Respondents are instructed to place themselves on a seven-point scale where 1 = the government should and 7 = the government should not. We recode this variable to distinguish between individuals who support redistribution (1–3) and those who do not (4–7).

Both surveys also contain questions about the *regulation of immigration*. In the ESS, respondents are asked how many of a particular type of immigrant should be allowed to immigrate to their country: immigrants of the same ethnic/racial group as the majority; immigrants of a different ethnic/racial group as the majority; and immigrants from poorer countries outside Europe. Possible responses are: 1 = many; 2 = some; 3 = few; 4 = none. These items are highly correlated (Cronbach's alpha = .92 and .87 for Swedish and German samples) and often combined in empirical research. From the row mean of these three items, we create a dichotomous variable to distinguish between respondents who articulate support for many or some immigrants, regardless of ethnic background or country of origin, and those who prefer little to no immigration. In the GSS, respondents are also asked their opinion about the number of immigrants allowed to enter the U.S. Respondents choose from 1 = increased a lot; 2 = increased a little; 3 = remain the same; 4 = reduced a lot; 5 = reduced a little. We recode this variable so that those who prefer a reduction in immigration are distinguished from those who either approve of current levels or favor increases.

Based on these two dichotomous measures of support for redistribution and immigration, we create four possible combinations of immigration-welfare attitudes: progressive (pro-immigration, pro-redistribution); conservative (anti-immigration, anti-redistribution); and two versions of mixed (supportive of either immigration or redistribution but not both).

Vote in Previous National Election

To investigate the political consequences of immigration-welfare attitudes, we create a categorical measure of partisan support. We are interested in being able to compare within and between countries, so our variable stems from parties' relative location in domestic political space, political coalitions, and membership in "party families" broadly defined. For Sweden, we categorize the nationalist Sweden Democrats (*Sverigedemokraterna*, SD) as far right. This party has only been included as a response category in the ESS since 2010 when the party had its electoral breakthrough. We categorize members of the self-described "Alliance"—Center Party (*Centerpartiet*, C), Liberals (*Folkpartiet*, FP), Christian Democrats (*Kristdemokraterna*, KD), and Moderates (*Moderaterna*, M)—as center-right. We categorize the Social Democratic

Party (*Sveriges Socialdemokratiska Arbetareparti*, S) and Green Party (*Miljöpartiet*, MP) as center-left and the socialist Left Party (*Vänsterpartiet*, V) and Feminist Initiative (Fi) as far left. Despite never having been in the national parliament, Fi has been a response option in the ESS since 2010.

Far-right parties in Germany are: the Republicans (*Die Republikaner*, REP), included in the ESS between 2002 and 2012; the National Democratic Party of Germany (*Nationaldemokratische Partei Deutschlands*, NPD) included between 2004 and 2018; and relative newcomer Alternative for Germany (*Alternative für Deutschland*, AfD) included between 2014 and 2018. Center-right parties are the Christian Democratic Union (*Christlich Demokratische Union Deutschlands*, CDU), Christian Social Union (*Christlich-Soziale Union*, CSU), and Free Democratic Party (*Freie Demokratische Partei*, FDP), and center-left parties are the Social Democrats (*Sozialdemokratische Partei Deutschlands*, SDP) and Alliance 90/The Greens (*Bündnis 90/Die Grünen*, GRÜNE). The German far left includes the Left Party (*Die Linke*), active since 2007, and the Party of Democratic Socialism (*Partei des Demokratischen Sozialismus*, PDS), active until 2007 when it merged with a less popular socialist party to form the Left.

For our U.S. sample, five presidential elections are implicated in our analysis: 2000, 2004, 2008, 2012, and 2016. With few exceptions, the U.S. operates a two-party system. Center-right presidential candidates were George Bush (2000, 2004), John McCain (2008), and Mitt Romney (2012), each running as the leader of the Republican Party (GOP). Center-left candidates were Al Gore (2000), John Kerry (2004), Barack Obama (2008, 2012), and Hillary Clinton (2016), who all ran as leaders of the Democratic Party (DEM). Although Donald Trump (2016) could be categorized as far right, he ran as the leader of the Republican Party (GOP), so he is categorized as such. Third-party candidate Ralph Nader has run for president numerous times and has been officially affiliated with a green party and nominated by various far-left parties over the years. He is included in the GSS as a possible answer for the 2000 and 2004 elections. For the U.S. analysis, we dichotomize our measure of political support into left-wing (DEM plus Nader) and right-wing (GOP).

Controls

We also include the following controls: age, sex, years of education, union membership, labor force status, and type/size of one's residential community. Due to missing data that are likely non-random, we do not include self-reported information on income; however, we control for subjective income (i.e., opinion of income). Importantly, both surveys ask about immigration status. To control for race/ethnicity, for the U.S. sample, we include a binary variable: white/non-white, and for the European samples, we add foreign background (i.e., being native-born with one or two foreign-born parents) to our measure of immigration status. Descriptive statistics are reported in Table 12.1.

Estimation Methods

To assess how different combinations of immigration-welfare attitudes translate into political support, we use multinomial logistic regression for the European samples. This type of regression model allows for the analysis of a dependent variable with more than

Table 12.1 Descriptive statistics

	Sweden					Germany					United States				
	N	Mean	SD	Min	Max	N	Mean	SD	Min	Max	N	Mean	SD	Min	Max
Vote in previous national election															
Far right	11929	0.03	0.18	0	1	15794	0.03	0.16	0	1					
Center right	11929	0.48	0.50	0	1	15794	0.43	0.50	0	1	3568	0.43	0.50	0	1
Center left	11929	0.41	0.49	0	1	15794	0.45	0.50	0	1	3568	0.57	0.50	0	1
Far left	11929	0.08	0.26	0	1	15794	0.09	0.29	0	1					
Immigration-welfare attitudes															
Progressive	11929	0.58	0.49	0	1	15794	0.40	0.49	0	1	3568	0.26	0.44	0	1
Conservative	11929	0.06	0.24	0	1	15794	0.13	0.34	0	1	3568	0.29	0.45	0	1
Mixed (pro-redist, anti-imm)	11929	0.10	0.30	0	1	15794	0.28	0.45	0	1	3568	0.20	0.40	0	1
Mixed (pro-imm, anti-redist)	11929	0.26	0.44	0	1	15794	0.19	0.39	0	1	3568	0.25	0.43	0	1
Controls															
Age (years)	11929	50.69	17.68	18	91	15794	52.11	16.52	17	91	3568	51.74	16.65	20	89
Female	11929	0.50	0.50	0	1	15794	0.48	0.50	0	1	3568	0.56	0.50	0	1
Immigration background	11929	0.24	0.59	0	2	15794	0.17	0.49	0	2	3568	0.07	0.25	0	1
Race/ethnicity											3568	0.22	0.41	0	1
Education (years)	11929	13.05	3.59	0	30	15794	14.12	3.38	1	30	3568	14.22	2.81	0	20
Subjective income	11929	3.53	0.68	1	4	15794	3.26	0.69	1	4	3568	2.96	0.93	1	5
Labor force status	11929	2.31	1.80	1	5	15794	2.70	1.91	1	5	3568	2.46	1.86	1	5
Union	11929	0.83	0.37	0	1	15794	0.42	0.49	0	1	3568	0.12	0.32	0	1
Residence	11929	3.09	1.18	1	5	15794	3.14	1.09	1	5	3568	6.88	2.68	1	10
ESS/GSS round	11929	4.89	2.59	1	9	15794	4.99	2.57	1	9	3568	5.66	2.23	2	9

Source: European Social Survey (ESS1-8e01; ESS9e01_2) and General Social Survey (GSS 1972-2018 Release 3, May 2020).

two categorical outcomes and is often used in analyses of political support in multiparty systems (e.g., de Koster et al. 2012). We rely on logistic regression for the U.S. sample.

RESULTS

Longitudinal Portrait of Immigration-Welfare Attitudes

Figure 12.1 illustrates the relative size of different attitudinal combinations of immigration-welfare attitudes in each country over time. Beginning at the top, social democratic Sweden stands out in two regards: first for its striking stability, and second for the large proportion with progressive attitudes. On average, 58 percent hold progressive attitudes, supporting both redistribution and immigration. This relatively large profile is evidence that the progressive's dilemma is not inevitable—that it is possible to combine support for diversity and equality. The next largest profile is characterized by pro-immigration but anti-redistribution attitudes. Approximately one quarter hold these attitudes. The smallest two attitudinal profiles are opposed to immigration but split on the issue of redistribution. On average, only 6 percent hold conservative attitudes (i.e., opposition to both).

Attitudes in Germany look different not only in terms of the size of the profiles but also in the degree to which those relative sizes change over time. In 2002, the sizes of these attitudinal profiles were fairly similar. The two largest groups, equivalent in size (29 percent), were characterized by support for redistribution but split on the issue of immigration. Twenty-three percent held pro-immigration but anti-redistribution attitudes and the smallest percentage (18 percent) held conservative attitudes. Over the next 16 years, attitudinal profiles consistent with the progressive's dilemma declined while progressive attitudinal profiles steadily increased in prominence. By 2018, 50 percent held progressive attitudes.

Although not as obvious as the Swedish trends, there is some stability in American attitudes over time. Between 2004 and 2014, the relative sizes of these attitudinal profiles are not too dissimilar though their relative ranking varies between GSS waves. Since 2014, however, there has been a noticeable change in the prominence of progressive attitudes and the decline of profiles consistent with the progressive's dilemma. By 2018, 34 percent support both immigration and redistribution. In summary, in each of these three countries, progressive attitudes are on the rise—despite objective increases in immigration in the 2010s and the politicization of immigration and welfare by SD and M in Sweden, AfD in Germany, and Trump in the U.S.

Voting Analyses

Next, we present models of voting behavior by country. Tables 12.2 and 12.3 report the relative risk ratios from multinomial logistic regression models of the Swedish and German data. These exponentiated coefficients indicate the probability of being in the outcome category (voting for either a far-right party, center-right party, or far-left party) compared to the reference category (voting for a center-left party). Relative risk ratios are typically interpreted like odds ratios from binary logistic regression. Values above 1

The politicization of immigration and welfare 239

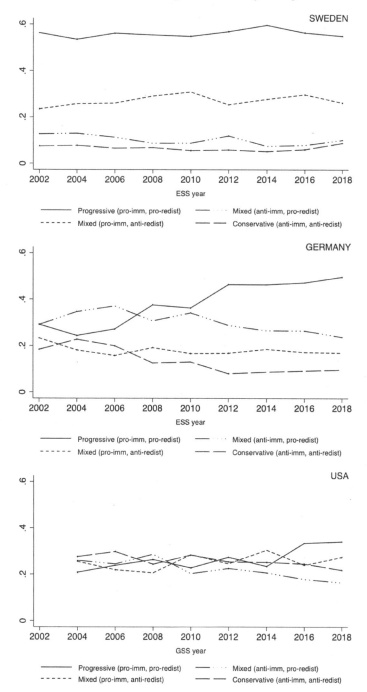

Source: European Social Survey (ESS1-8e01; ESS9e01_2) and General Social Survey (GSS 1972-2018 Release 3, May 2020).

Figure 12.1 Immigration-welfare attitudes, 2002–2018

Table 12.2 Multinomial logistic regression models of voting behavior (reference category = center-left party), Sweden

	Far-right party			Center-right party			Far-left party		
	(M1)	(M2)	(M3)	(M1)	(M2)	(M3)	(M1)	(M2)	(M3)
Immigration-welfare attitudes (ref = progressive)									
Conservative	15.998***		14.175***	4.415***		4.746***	0.416**		0.437**
	(2.576)		(2.535)	(0.425)		(0.475)	(0.114)		(0.121)
Mixed (pro-redist, anti-imm)	5.625***		6.177***	1.247**		1.397***	0.364***		0.482***
	(0.792)		(0.964)	(0.087)		(0.103)	(0.060)		(0.081)
Mixed (pro-imm, anti-redist)	3.172***		3.063***	4.302***		4.057***	0.396***		0.340***
	(0.460)		(0.467)	(0.213)		(0.210)	(0.052)		(0.045)
Controls									
Age (years)		0.986**	0.988**		1.010***	1.012***		0.982***	0.981***
		(0.004)	(0.005)		(0.002)	(0.002)		(0.003)	(0.003)
Female		0.411***	0.496***		0.843***	0.962		1.165*	1.091
		(0.048)	(0.060)		(0.034)	(0.041)		(0.086)	(0.081)
Immigration (ref = native-born, native-born parents)									
Native-born with one or two foreign-born parents		0.961	1.007		0.913	0.920		1.019	1.016
		(0.189)	(0.204)		(0.068)	(0.072)		(0.127)	(0.128)
Foreign-born		0.574**	0.475***		0.563***	0.512***		1.060	1.107
		(0.121)	(0.104)		(0.043)	(0.041)		(0.122)	(0.129)
Education (years)		0.844***	0.862***		1.099***	1.088***		1.116***	1.113***
		(0.017)	(0.018)		(0.007)	(0.008)		(0.013)	(0.013)
Subjective income		0.790**	0.845*		1.378***	1.316***		0.850**	0.853**
		(0.060)	(0.067)		(0.044)	(0.043)		(0.042)	(0.043)

	(M1)	(M2)	(M3)
Labor force status (ref = paid work)			
Education		0.532* (0.137)	0.533* (0.144)		0.756** (0.070)	0.750** (0.073)		1.082 (0.145)	1.105 (0.150)
Unemployed, looking		0.784 (0.260)	0.909 (0.306)		0.638** (0.087)	0.696* (0.099)		0.765 (0.165)	0.748 (0.162)
Unemployed, not looking		0.300 (0.347)	0.320 (0.368)		0.379*** (0.104)	0.367*** (0.105)		1.717 (0.494)	1.823* (0.534)
Not in labor force		0.955 (0.160)	0.897 (0.158)		1.088 (0.069)	1.110 (0.073)		1.194 (0.142)	1.188 (0.142)
Union		0.710* (0.108)	0.818 (0.130)		0.429*** (0.026)	0.487*** (0.030)		1.019 (0.111)	0.985 (0.109)
Residence (ref = farm or home in countryside)			
Country village		0.572** (0.106)	0.559** (0.109)		0.562*** (0.044)	0.572*** (0.047)		0.653** (0.098)	0.649** (0.098)
Town or small city		0.453*** (0.078)	0.420*** (0.075)		0.507*** (0.037)	0.490*** (0.037)		0.637*** (0.086)	0.642** (0.087)
Suburbs/outskirts of big city		0.504*** (0.094)	0.462*** (0.090)		0.611*** (0.047)	0.555*** (0.044)		0.734*** (0.104)	0.756 (0.108)
Big city		0.384*** (0.089)	0.343*** (0.083)		0.627*** (0.054)	0.579*** (0.052)		0.980 (0.145)	0.991 (0.148)
ESS round		1.841*** (0.059)	1.854*** (0.060)		0.982* (0.008)	0.985 (0.008)		1.042** (0.015)	1.038** (0.015)
Constant	0.036*** (0.003)	0.243** (0.116)	0.054*** (0.027)	0.714*** (0.019)	0.293*** (0.051)	0.185*** (0.034)	0.234*** (0.009)	0.170*** (0.050)	0.232*** (0.070)
Log pseudolikelihood	−11446.121	−11368.274	−10605.625
Pseudo R^2	0.0711	0.0763	0.1383
N	11,929	11,929	11,929

Note: Coefficients are relative risk ratios; standard errors in parentheses; *** p < 0.001, ** p < 0.01, * p < 0.05.

Source: European Social Survey (ESS1-8e01; ESS9e01_2).

Table 12.3 Multinomial logistic regression models of voting behavior (reference category = center-left party), Germany

	Far-right party			Center-right party			Far-left party		
	(M1)	(M2)	(M3)	(M1)	(M2)	(M3)	(M1)	(M2)	(M3)
Immigration-welfare attitudes (ref = progressive)									
Conservative	5.894***		10.444***	2.996***		3.070***	0.462***		0.566***
	(0.973)		(1.811)	(0.166)		(0.178)	(0.061)		(0.077)
Mixed (pro-redist, anti-imm)	5.808***		6.974***	1.854***		1.849***	1.502***		1.478***
	(0.809)		(1.023)	(0.081)		(0.085)	(0.095)		(0.101)
Mixed (pro-imm, anti-redist)	1.074		1.450	1.970***		2.065***	0.356***		0.416***
	(0.236)		(0.323)	(0.092)		(0.100)	(0.039)		(0.046)
Controls									
Age (years)		0.976***	0.974***		1.006***	1.006***		1.004	1.003
		(0.004)	(0.004)		(0.001)	(0.002)		(0.003)	(0.003)
Female		0.440***	0.433***		0.815***	0.836***		0.781***	0.758***
		(0.050)	(0.050)		(0.029)	(0.030)		(0.046)	(0.045)
Immigration (ref = native-born, native-born parents)									
Native-born with one or two foreign-born parents		0.642*	0.745		0.829**	0.866*		0.933	0.944
		(0.140)	(0.165)		(0.055)	(0.059)		(0.101)	(0.102)
Foreign-born		1.040	0.969		1.115	1.078		0.749	0.738*
		(0.227)	(0.214)		(0.088)	(0.087)		(0.115)	(0.114)
Education (years)		0.882***	0.923***		0.962***	0.970***		1.029**	1.045***
		(0.017)	(0.019)		(0.005)	(0.006)		(0.009)	(0.010)
Subjective income		0.622***	0.682***		1.130***	1.101***		0.643***	0.685***
		(0.046)	(0.052)		(0.031)	(0.031)		(0.027)	(0.029)

Labor force status (ref = paid work)						
Education		0.352**	0.467*	0.741**	0.798*	1.249	1.263
		(0.112)	(0.151)	(0.070)	(0.077)	(0.198)	(0.201)
Unemployed, looking		2.131**	2.005**	1.093	1.124	2.312***	2.119***
		(0.546)	(0.532)	(0.128)	(0.134)	(0.335)	(0.309)
Unemployed, not looking		3.452***	3.939***	0.869	0.901	1.891**	1.770*
		(1.144)	(1.335)	(0.167)	(0.176)	(0.444)	(0.418)
Not in labor force		1.167	1.177	1.061	1.087	1.198*	1.163
		(0.168)	(0.174)	(0.049)	(0.052)	(0.096)	(0.094)
Union		0.923	0.920	0.616***	0.640***	2.144***	2.046***
		(0.105)	(0.106)	(0.023)	(0.024)	(0.137)	(0.132)
Residence (ref = farm or home in countryside)							
Country village		0.823	0.800	0.750*	0.734*	1.032	1.012
		(0.276)	(0.275)	(0.095)	(0.094)	(0.267)	(0.263)
Town or small city		0.734	0.684	0.606***	0.585***	1.148	1.117
		(0.246)	(0.235)	(0.076)	(0.075)	(0.294)	(0.288)
Suburbs/outskirts of big city		0.636	0.643	0.523***	0.509***	1.054	1.043
		(0.226)	(0.234)	(0.068)	(0.068)	(0.278)	(0.276)
Big city		0.451*	0.489	0.379***	0.385***	1.284	1.268
		(0.162)	(0.180)	(0.049)	(0.051)	(0.333)	(0.331)
ESS round		1.515***	1.607***	1.031***	1.068***	1.077***	1.068***
		(0.039)	(0.042)	(0.007)	(0.008)	(0.013)	(0.013)
Constant	0.021***	0.863	0.084***	1.588*	0.811	0.184***	0.148***
	(0.003)	(0.438)	(0.046)	(0.287)	(0.152)	(0.061)	(0.050)
			0.617***		0.222***		
			(0.017)		(0.009)		

243

Table 12.3 (continued)

	(M1)	(M2)	(M3)
Log pseudolikelihood	−15827.995	−15527.557	−15041.967
Pseudo R^2	0.0335	0.0519	0.0815
N	15,794	15,794	15,794

Note: Coefficients are relative risk ratios; standard errors in parentheses; *** $p < 0.001$, ** $p < 0.01$, * $p < 0.05$.

Source: European Social Survey (ESS1-8e01; ESS9e01_2).

indicate a higher risk of voting for a specific type of party relative to the reference category, whereas values below 1 point to a lower risk. Table 12.4 reports the odd ratios from binary logistic models of the U.S. data. Values above 1 indicate that the odds of voting for a Republican Party presidential candidate are higher compared to candidates from the political left, and values below 1 indicate the likelihood is lower. Note that the key independent variable—immigration-welfare attitudes—is also categorical. Progressive attitudes are the reference category, and the relationship between any of the other attitudinal profiles and voting behavior is relative to holding progressive attitudes. Each table has three models: model 1 (M1) includes only immigration-welfare attitudes; model 2 (M2) includes only demographic controls; and model 3 (M3) is the full model.

Results from Sweden reflect a clear left–right divide, a pattern consistent with what one might expect in a social democratic welfare state. Holding anything but progressive attitudes reduces the likelihood of supporting a far-left party compared to the center left, while conservative and mixed attitudinal profiles greatly increase the risk of supporting either the nationalist SD or one of the four center-right "Alliance" parties compared to the center left. Supporting immigration but opposing redistribution doubles one's risk of voting for a center-right party. Moreover, results also clearly illustrate the particular challenge for social democratic parties, which have historically relied on working-class support (e.g., Rydgren 2002). One who supports redistribution but opposes immigration is more than six times more likely to vote for the SD than a center-left party, which in Sweden is dominated by the Social Democratic Party.

Like in Sweden, one who supports redistribution but opposes immigration in Germany is more than six times more likely to vote for the far right than the center left. However, in Germany, being pro-redistribution and anti-immigration compared to being supportive of both makes one more likely to vote for *any* party family—including the far left. This is a striking finding and a clear indication of the progressive's dilemma in Germany. Further, holding conservative attitudes compared to progressive attitudes increases the risk of voting for a far-right party compared to center-left ten-fold. These attitudes also make it three times more likely to vote for a center-right party. Supporting immigration but opposing redistribution doubles one's risk of voting for a center-right party. Both of these attitudinal profiles reduce the risk of supporting a far-left party.

Results from the U.S., reported in Table 12.4, are consistent with those from Sweden and Germany, despite having fewer party families. Holding conservative attitudes compared to progressive attitudes makes it almost 15 times more likely of voting for the Republican Party. The mixed attitudinal profiles are also strongly associated with increased odds of voting for the GOP. The fact that any attitudinal profile compared to progressive attitudes increases the odds of supporting the GOP is evidence of the progressive's dilemma and a clear challenge for the Democratic Party in the twenty-first century.

The inclusion of control variables did not substantively change the magnitude or significance of the immigration-welfare attitudes. However, there are some interesting findings worth reporting. The most consistent effect is gender: females are more likely to vote left wing. Also, subjective income, often used as an indicator of economic class, and years of education, often used as an indicator of liberal values, have consistent effects in Sweden and Germany even after including immigration-welfare attitudes. However, the effects of those variables disappear in the U.S. when attitudes are considered. The rural–urban divide is most obvious in Sweden, with more differences in vote based on where one lives.

246 *Handbook on migration and welfare*

Table 12.4 Logistic regression models of voting for Republican Party candidate (reference category = center-left or left candidate), United States

	Center-right party		
	(M1)	(M2)	(M3)
Immigration-welfare attitudes (ref = progressive)			
Conservative	14.389***		14.747***
	(1.952)		(2.112)
Mixed (pro-redist, anti-imm)	3.767***		3.950***
	(0.538)		(0.611)
Mixed (pro-imm, anti-redist)	7.268***		7.699***
	(0.993)		(1.103)
Controls			
Age (years)		1.003	0.998
		(0.003)	(0.003)
Female		0.754***	0.755**
		(0.064)	(0.071)
Immigration (ref = native-born)		1.336	1.941**
		(0.282)	(0.465)
Race/ethnicity (ref = white)		0.139***	0.126***
		(0.019)	(0.018)
Education (years)		0.952**	0.987
		(0.016)	(0.018)
Subjective income		1.218***	1.112
		(0.060)	(0.060)
Labor force status (ref = paid work)			
Education		0.711	0.734
		(0.240)	(0.278)
Unemployed, looking		0.550*	0.512**
		(0.136)	(0.128)
Unemployed, not looking		1.090	0.922
		(0.321)	(0.309)
Not in labor force		1.030	1.008
		(0.112)	(0.119)
Union		0.723*	0.792
		(0.095)	(0.114)
Residence (ref = open country)			
Smaller areas		0.773	0.796
		(0.287)	(0.288)
Town: pop 2500+		0.681	0.625
		(0.165)	(0.175)
City: pop 10,000–49,999		0.683	0.753
		(0.158)	(0.205)
Unincorporated, medium city		1.347	1.244
		(0.262)	(0.270)

Table 12.4 (continued)

	Center-right party		
	(M1)	(M2)	(M3)
Unincorporated, large city		1.088	1.000
		(0.205)	(0.216)
Suburb of medium city		1.011	1.000
		(0.186)	(0.208)
Suburb of large city		0.770	0.799
		(0.128)	(0.153)
City: pop 50,000–250,000		0.668*	0.691
		(0.117)	(0.135)
City: pop > 250,000		0.603**	0.554**
		(0.109)	(0.113)
GSS round		0.935***	0.953*
		(0.018)	(0.020)
Constant	0.162***	2.435**	0.421*
	(0.018)	(0.803)	(0.169)
	(M1)	(M2)	(M3)
Log pseudolikelihood	−2042.558	−2097.5534	−1802.6513
Pseudo R²	0.1454	0.1224	0.2457
N	3,568	3,568	3,568

Note: Coefficients are odds ratios; standard errors in parentheses; *** $p < 0.001$, ** $p < 0.01$, * $p < 0.05$.

Source: General Social Survey (GSS 1972–2018 Release 3, May 2020).

DISCUSSION

In this chapter, we examined the salience and political implications of the progressive's dilemma in Sweden, Germany, and the U.S. this century. Our analyses yield a number of novel findings with important theoretical and political implications. First, our results show that attitudes consistent with the progressive's dilemma are rather widespread in all three countries. On average, approximately 40 percent of Swedes, 60 percent of Germans, and 75 percent of Americans hold attitudes consistent with the notion that immigration and welfare are difficult to combine. Indeed, these are not minority views in Germany and in the U.S. Only in social democratic Sweden, where immigrants have nearly universal access to the welfare state, are the majority of attitudes consistently progressive.

Second, a large proportion of these attitudes reflect a profile not often examined but that is nevertheless indicative of the tension between diversity and equality: support for immigration and opposition to redistribution. Of the three non-progressive attitudinal configurations, this profile has been most salient in Sweden (62 percent), while only representative of 32 percent of Germans and 34 percent of Americans during this period. In Germany, the dominant non-progressive configuration has been pro-redistribution and anti-immigration (47 percent) and, in the U.S., opposition to both (39 percent). These cross-national differences show that, to the extent that there is a trade-off between immigration and welfare, it is not always redistribution that is preferred over immigration. In Sweden, it is immigration—which is consistent with the politics espoused by the center-right "Alliance" this century. In the U.S., conservative attitudes have been most dominant, though that profile is declining in prominence. These cross-national differences also suggest that differences in welfare state, immigration, and integration regimes matter for the magnitude of the progressive's dilemma.

However, some similarities exist. Despite attitudes consistent with the progressive's dilemma being widespread, a third finding is that progressive attitudes have increased in two countries while remaining relatively high in the third. The increase in the relative size of the attitudinal configuration that is supportive of both immigration and redistribution is most evident in Germany, with the steepest rise between 2004 and 2012 during center-right Christian Democratic Union leader Angel Merkel's first two terms as chancellor. Progressive attitudes have continued to increase in prominence since then, while anti-immigration/pro-redistribution attitudes have declined, despite Alternative for Germany's electoral breakthrough. In the U.S., the increase in progressive attitudes is more recent, coinciding with the candidacy, election, and presidency of the anti-immigrant figure Donald Trump. Although the increase in the prominence of progressive attitudes in both countries coincides with right-wing heads of state, Merkel's and Trump's stances on immigration could not be more different. Merkel's response to the 2015–2016 European crisis cannot be characterized as anything except pro-immigration, while Trump consistently used anti-immigrant rhetoric and politicized migration at the southern border during his presidency. Further, three of Merkel's four governing coalitions have included the center-left German Social Democratic Party. Trump, on the other hand, did not collaborate with the Democrats during his tenure. Recent debates about immigration in both of these countries have largely focused on crime and culture (Czymara and Schmidt-Catran 2017), though Trump claims immigrants are welfare dependent (Wegmann 2019) and AfD leadership argues that "a social welfare state and open borders do not go together" (Hansel 2017).

Sweden, in stark contrast, stands out for its stability in the relative share of progressive attitudes. Although the attitudinal profile's dominance has dipped slightly since 2014, given the extent to which immigration and its relationship to welfare has been politicized since 2014, it is actually somewhat surprising that progressive attitudes have not declined more. For most of the twenty-first century, immigration was not politically salient (Rydgren 2010), and, for the most part, ignored by mainstream parties (Odmalm 2011; Widfeldt 2014). Officially, all but one party represented in parliament between 2006 and 2014 was either an open proponent of immigration, pointing to the importance of accepting asylum seekers as well as the long-term benefits of immigration more generally, or actively avoided taking an anti-immigration stance.

In practice, though, the majority of parties' relative silence on the immigration issue has meant that one party has long dominated the discussion, arguably leaving voters skeptical of immigration with only one choice: SD. This party has consistently politicized immigration *and* welfare by attempting to mobilize voters based on the contention that immigration and welfare are incompatible. For example, in 2010, SD produced a controversial campaign video depicting women in burkas overtaking a Swedish pensioner in a queue to collect welfare benefits, while the state runs out of money in the background.[1] Moreover, the cover of its 2014 election manifesto explicitly pits immigration against welfare by indicating that SD prioritizes the latter.[2] During the so-called European migration crisis, SD argued that the Swedish welfare state could not afford more immigrants.

SD is not the only party during this time to politicize immigration and welfare. In the month prior to the 2014 election, Prime Minister Reinfeldt said in a televised speech that the costs of granting asylum to those fleeing Syria and Iraq would limit state spending on other social programs.[3] Moreover, by urging the Swedish people to "open their hearts" to the large number of current and expected refugees (SVT 2014), Reinfeldt's comments indicated what his government (the center-right Alliance) and conservative party prioritized: more immigration over (raising taxes to fund more) social programs. While this stance differs fundamentally from SD's position, which is to strengthen the welfare state by dramatically reducing immigration to Sweden (Rydgren 2010; Nordensvard and Ketola 2015; Widfeldt 2014; Eger and Valdez 2015), both the center right and far right have made the case that immigration and welfare are not to be combined. Despite this, progressive attitudes have remained quite high, which may speak to the effect of social democratic institutions on attitudes towards immigrants (Crepaz and Damron 2009; Larsen 2019).

Nevertheless, as our voting analyses show, there are clear political implications of the progressive's dilemma. In all three countries, attitudes consistent with the progressive's dilemma make supporting center-right and far-right parties much more likely than supporting a center-left party. Put simply, anything but the most progressive attitudes makes support for left-wing parties unlikely. Results from Sweden imply that some of the most progressive voters support the far left. However, in Germany being pro-redistribution but anti-immigration also increases the likelihood of voting for a far-left party compared to the center left, demonstrating differences in the scope of the progressive's dilemma between these two European countries. Given these analyses and taking into consideration the recent electoral success of anti-immigrant parties and candidates, AfD, SD, and Trump, the stakes for center-left, predominately social democratic parties could not be more evident.

CONCLUSION

This research contributes to the growing literature on immigration and the welfare state. We use the conceptual framework of the progressive's dilemma, or the notion that there is a trade-off between diversity and solidarity, and analyze the relationships among attitudes towards welfare, immigration, and the intersection of the two. By focusing on subjective reactions to immigration versus objective measures of the foreign-born population, we more precisely capture the theoretical relationship proposed in previous scholarly work. In doing so, we find evidence that progressive views regarding redistribution are not necessarily compatible with progressive attitudes towards immigration. Our analyses also indicate that attitudes about immigration present a challenge for the political left—the champions of social equality, redistributive justice, and the welfare state.

The prevalence of attitudinal profiles indicative of the progressive's dilemma and their relationship to voting behavior lend credence to the existential concern among social progressives that diversity and solidarity are difficult to combine. When faced with a situation where immigration and welfare are pitted against each other, our results imply that center-left parties are the most likely to lose voters. This finding is consistent with the tendency of left-wing government actors to seek to protect their working-class base by limiting social protection for immigrants (Schmitt and Teney 2019). Yet, we contend that future electoral results and ultimately social policies (Koning 2020) will have much to do with the left's ability not only to build solidarity across class divisions (Schall 2016) but also across ethnic and racial lines.

ACKNOWLEDGMENTS

The authors owe special gratitude to Jens Rydgren for the use of Swedish survey data that allowed for initial tests of our hypothesis. The authors also thank Keith Banting, Henning Finseraas, Mikael Hjerm, Eric Kaufmann, Staffan Kumlin, Stefan Svallfors, and Sarah Valdez for their critical comments on our analytical strategy and preliminary analyses of the Swedish case. Earlier drafts based on the Swedish case were presented at the 2016 American Sociological Association and 2016 American Political Science annual meetings as well as research seminars at the Institute for Analytical Sociology at Linköping University, Department of Sociology at Stockholm University, Department of Sociology at Umeå University, School of Social Sciences at Södertörn University, and the "Citizens in Changing Welfare States: Pressures, Frames, and Feedback Workshop" in the Department of Political Science at the University of Gothenburg.

This research was supported by the Marianne and Marcus Wallenberg Foundation (MMW 2014.0019), the Swedish Foundation for Humanities and Social Sciences (RJ P14-0775:1), and the Swedish Research Council for Health, Working Life and Welfare (FORTE 2011-00205 and 2016-07177).

NOTES

1. The video was banned from public television but can be viewed on YouTube: www.youtube.com/watch?v=eeRqAR6rzYQ.
2. The cover of SD's official 2014 election manifesto reads "*Vi väljer välfärd! Sverigedemokraterna väljer välfärd framför oansvarig massinvandring*" which means "We choose welfare! The Sweden Democrats choose welfare before irresponsible mass immigration."
3. "Today I ask of the Swedish people to have patience with what is coming, to open their hearts to very vulnerable people from different parts of the world ... When great numbers, when a lot of people, seek refuge in a short period of time, then that creates tensions in Swedish society. Because many more are coming than what we initially planned for, and that leads to discussions back home in Sweden about what this will cost. And I can already tell you that there will be considerable costs associated with the people that have already come and those that will arrive in the coming years. They are so considerable that it will put restrictions on the scope of public finance. And I will be completely frank and open about this. Therefore, I am saying, we are promising not nearly anything during this election, because there is no room for it. And I am astonished, I will say, by the promises that I hear others make and I wonder what basis they have to claim that these possibilities exist. Today, I will flat out say that they do not exist" (Swedish Prime Minister Fredrik Reinfeldt, Press Conference, Stockholm, August 16, 2014; authors' translation).

REFERENCES

Alesina, Alberto, and Edward L. Glaeser. 2004. *Fighting Poverty in the U.S. and Europe: A World of Difference*. Oxford: Oxford University Press.

Alesina, Alberto, and Eliana La Ferrara. 2000. "Participation in Heterogeneous Communities." *Quarterly Journal of Economics* 115(3): 847–904.

Alesina, Alberto, Reza Baqir, and William Easterly. 1999. "Public Goods and Ethnic Divisions." *Quarterly Journal of Economics* 114(4): 1243–1284.

Alesina, Alberto, Edward L. Glaeser, and Bruce Sacerdote. 2001. "Why Doesn't the US Have a European-Style Welfare System?" *Brookings Papers on Economic Activity* October: 187–248.

Andersen, Jørgen Goul, and Tor Bjørklund. 1990. "Structural Changes and New Cleavages: The Progress Parties in Denmark and Norway." *Acta Sociologica* 33(3): 195–217.

Banting, Keith. 2010. "Is There a Progressive's Dilemma in Canada? Immigration, Multiculturalism and the Welfare State." *Canadian Journal of Political Science* 43(4): 797–820.

Banting, Keith, and Will Kymlicka, eds. 2006. *Multiculturalism and the Welfare State: Recognition and Redistribution in Contemporary Democracies*. Oxford: Oxford University Press.

Banting, Keith, Richard Johnston, Will Kymlicka, and Stuart Soroka. 2006. "Do Multiculturalism Policies Erode the Welfare State? An Empirical Analysis." In *Multiculturalism and the Welfare State: Recognition and Redistribution in Contemporary Democracies*, eds. Keith Banting and Will Kymlicka, 49–91. Oxford: Oxford University Press.

Barker, Vanessa. 2017. "Nordic Vagabonds: The Roma and the Logic of Benevolent Violence in the Swedish Welfare State." *European Journal of Criminology* 14(1): 120–139.

Brady, David, and Ryan Finnigan. 2014. "Does Immigration Undermine Public Support for Social Policy?" *American Sociological Review* 79(1): 17–42.

Breznau, Nate, and Maureen A. Eger. 2016. "Immigrant Presence, Group Boundaries, and Support for the Welfare State in Western European Societies." *Acta Sociologica* 59(3): 195–214.

Burgoon, Brian, and Matthijs Rooduijn. 2021. "'Immigrationization' of Welfare Politics? Anti-Immigration and Welfare Attitudes in Context." *West European Politics* 44(2): 177–203.

Crepaz, Markus M.L., and Regan Damron. 2009. "Constructing Tolerance: How the Welfare State Shapes Attitudes about Immigrants." *Comparative Political Studies* 42(3): 437–463.

Czymara, Christian S., and Alexander W. Schmidt-Catran. 2017. "Refugees Unwelcome? Changes in the Public Acceptance of Immigrants and Refugees in Germany in the Course of Europe's 'Immigration Crisis'" *European Sociological Review* 33(6): 735–751.

Dahlberg, Matz, Karin Edmark, and Helene Lundqvist. 2012. "Ethnic Diversity and Preferences for Redistribution." *Journal of Political Economy* 120(1): 41–76.

de Koster, Willem, Peter Achterberg, and Jeroen van der Waal. 2012. "The New Right and the Welfare State: The Electoral Relevance of Welfare Chauvinism and Welfare Populism in the Netherlands." *International Political Science Review* 34(1): 3–20.

Dinesen, Peter Thisted, Merlin Schaeffer, and Kim Mannemar Sønderskov. 2020. "Ethnic Diversity and Social Trust: A Narrative and Meta-Analytical Review." *Annual Review of Political Science* 23(1): 441–465.

Eger, Maureen A. 2010a. "Even in Sweden: The Effect of Immigration on Support for Welfare State Spending." *European Sociological Review* 26(2): 203–217.

Eger, Maureen A. 2010b. *Ethnic Heterogeneity and the Limits of Altruism*. PhD Dissertation, Department of Sociology, University of Washington.

Eger, Maureen A., and Nate Breznau. 2017. "Immigration and the Welfare State: A Cross-Regional Analysis of European Welfare Attitudes." *International Journal of Comparative Sociology* 58(5): 440–463.

Eger, Maureen A., and Sarah Valdez. 2015. "Neo-Nationalism in Western Europe." *European Sociological Review* 31(1): 115–130.

Eger, Maureen A., and Sarah Valdez. 2019. "From Radical Right to Neo-Nationalist." *European Political Science* 18(3): 379–399.

Eger, Maureen A., Christian Albrekt Larsen, and Jan Mewes. 2020. "Welfare Nationalism before and after the 'Migration Crisis.'" In *Welfare State Legitimacy in Times of Crisis and Austerity: Between Change and Continuity*, eds. Tijs Laenen, Bart Meuleman, and Wim van Oorschot, 177–198. Cheltenham, UK and Northampton, MA, USA: Edward Elgar Publishing.

Esping-Andersen, Gøsta. 1990. *The Three Worlds of Welfare Capitalism*. Princeton, NJ: Princeton University Press.

European Social Survey Cumulative File, ESS 1-8. 2018. Data file edition 1.0. NSD: Norwegian Centre for Research Data, Norway, Data Archive and Distributor of ESS Data for ESS ERIC. doi:10.21338/NSD-ESS-CUMULATIVE.

European Social Survey Round 9 Data. 2018. Data file edition 2.0. NSD: Norwegian Centre for Research Data, Norway, Data Archive and distributor of ESS data for ESS ERIC. doi:10.21338/NSD-ESS9-2018.

Finseraas, Henning. 2012a. "Poverty, Ethnic Minorities among the Poor, and Preferences for Redistribution in European Regions." *Journal of European Social Policy* 22(2): 164–180.

Finseraas, Henning. 2012b. "Anti-Immigration Attitudes, Support for Redistribution and Party Choice in Europe." In *Changing Social Equality: The Nordic Welfare Model in the 21st Century*, eds. Jon Kvist, Johan Fritzell, Bjørn Hvinden, and Olli Kangas, 23–44. Bristol: Policy Press.

Ford, Robert. 2006. "Prejudice and White Majority Welfare Attitudes in the UK." *Journal of Elections, Public Opinion and Parties* 16(2): 141–156.

Ford, Robert. 2015. "Who Should We Help? An Experimental Test of Discrimination in the British Welfare State." *Political Studies*. doi: 10.1111/1467-9248.12194.

Fox, Cybelle. 2004. "The Changing Color of Welfare? How Whites' Attitudes toward Latinos Influence Support for Welfare." *American Journal of Sociology* 110(3): 580–625.

Fullerton, Andrew S., and Jeffrey C. Dixon. 2009. "Racialization, Asymmetry and the Context of Welfare Attitudes in the American States." *Journal of Political and Military Sociology* 37(1): 95–120.

Gilens, Martin. 1999. *Why Americans Hate Welfare*. Chicago, IL: University of Chicago Press.

Goldschmidt, Tina. 2015. "Anti-Immigrant Sentiment and Majority Support for Three Types of Welfare: The Case of Germany." *European Societies* 17(5): 620–652.

Goodhart, David. 2004. "Too Diverse?" *Prospect* February: 30–37.

Gutsell, Jennifer N., and Michael Inzlicht. 2010. "Empathy Constrained: Prejudice Predicts Reduced Mental Simulation of Actions during Observation of Outgroups." *Journal of Experimental Social Psychology* 46: 841–845.

Habyarimana, James, Macartan Humphreys, Dan Posner, and Jeremy Weinstein. 2009. *Coethnicity: Diversity and the Dilemmas of Collective Action*. New York: Russell Sage Foundation.

Hansel, Frank-Christian. 2017. "A Social Welfare State and Open Borders Do Not Go Together: AfD." *CNBC*, Video, September 25. www.cnbc.com/video/2017/09/25/a-social-welfare-state-and-open-borders-do-not-go-together-afd.html.

Harell, Allison, Stuart Soroka, and Shanto Iyengar. 2016. "Race, Prejudice and Attitudes toward Redistribution: A Comparative Experimental Approach." *European Journal of Political Research* 55(4): 723–744.

Heizmann, Boris, Alexander Jedinger, and Anja Perry. 2018. "Welfare Chauvinism, Economic Insecurity and the Asylum Seeker 'Crisis.'" *Societies* 8(3): 1–17.

Herda, Daniel. 2010. "How Many Immigrants? Foreign-Born Population Innumeracy in Europe." *Public Opinion Quarterly* 74(4): 674–695.

Hero, Rodney E. 1998. *Faces of Inequality: Social Diversity in American Politics*. New York: Oxford University Press.

Hjerm, Mikael, and Annette Schnabel. 2012. "How Much Heterogeneity Can the Welfare State Endure? The Influence of Heterogeneity on Attitudes to the Welfare State." *Nations and Nationalism* 18(2): 346–369.

Jacobson, Robin Dale. 2009. *The New Nativism: Proposition 187 and the Debate over Immigration*. Twin Cities, MI: University of Minnesota Press.

Kitschelt, Herbert, and Anthony J. McGann. 1995. *The Radical Right in Western Europe: A Comparative Analysis*. Ann Arbor, MI: University of Michigan Press.

Koning, Edward. 2020. "Accommodation and New Hurdles: The Increasing Importance of Politics for Immigrants' Access to Social Programmes in Western Democracies." *Social Policy and Administration*. https://doi.org/10.1111/spol.12661.

Koopmans, Ruud. 2010. "Trade-Offs between Equality and Difference: Immigrant Integration, Multiculturalism and the Welfare State in Cross-National Perspective." *Journal of Ethnic and Migration Studies* 36(1): 1–26.

Koopmans, Ruud, and Merlin Schaeffer. 2016. "Statistical and Perceived Diversity and Their Impacts on Neighborhood Social Cohesion in Germany, France and the Netherlands." *Social Indicators Research* 125(3): 853–883.

Kulin, Joakim, Maureen A. Eger, and Mikael Hjerm. 2016. "Immigration or Welfare? The Progressive's Dilemma Revisited." *Socius: Sociological Research for a Dynamic World* 2: 1–15.

Kumlin, Staffan, and Bo Rothstein. 2010. "Questioning the New Liberal Dilemma: Immigrants, Social Networks and Institutional Fairness." *Comparative Politics* 43(1): 63–80.

Laenen, Tijs, Bart Meuleman, and Wim van Oorschot, eds. 2020. *Welfare State Legitimacy in Times of Crisis and Austerity: Between Change and Continuity*. Cheltenham, UK and Northampton, MA, USA: Edward Elgar Publishing.

Larsen, Christian Albrekt. 2011. "Ethnic Heterogeneity and Public Support for Welfare: Is the American Experience Replicated in Britain, Sweden and Denmark?" *Scandinavian Political Studies* 34(4): 332–353.

Larsen, Christian Albrekt. 2019. "The Institutional Logic of Giving Migrants Access to Social Benefits and Services." *Journal of European Social Policy* 30(1): 48–62.

Lipset, Seymour Martin, and Gary Marks. 2000. *It Didn't Happen Here: Why Socialism Failed in the United States*. New York: W.W. Norton and Company.

Luttmer, Erzo F.P. 2001. "Group Loyalty and the Taste for Redistribution." *Journal of Political Economy* 109(3): 500–528.

Marx, Paul, and Elias Naumann. 2018. "Do Right-Wing Parties Foster Welfare Chauvinistic Attitudes? A Longitudinal Study of the 2015 'Refugee Crisis' in Germany." *Electoral Studies* 52: 111–116.

Mau, Steffen, and Christoph Burkhardt. 2009. "Migration and Welfare State Solidarity in Western Europe." *Journal of European Social Policy* 19(3): 213–229.

Mewes, Jan, and Steffen Mau. 2012. "Welfare Chauvinism, Class, and Economic Uncertainty." In *Contested Welfare States: Welfare Attitudes in Europe and Beyond*, ed. Stefan Svallfors, 119–157. Stanford, CA: Stanford University Press.

Newton, Kenneth. 2007. "The New Liberal Dilemma: Social Trust in Mixed Societies." Paper Presented at the ECPR Workshop on Social Capital, the State, and Diversity. Helsinki, May 7–12. http://ecpr.eu/Filestore/PaperProposal/2bf67b79-61a2-42fd-b98c-e58385ced442.pdf.

Nordensvard, Johan, and Markus Ketola. 2015. "Nationalist Reframing of the Finnish and Swedish Welfare States: The Nexus of Nationalism and Social Policy in Far-Right Populist Parties." *Social Policy and Administration* 49(3): 356–375.

Odmalm, Pontus. 2011. "Political Parties and 'the Immigration Issue': Issue Ownership in Swedish Parliamentary Elections 1991–2010." *West European Politics* 34(5): 1070–1091.

Pottie-Sherman, Yolanda, and Rima Wilkes. 2017. "Does Size Really Matter? On the Relationship between Immigrant Group Size and Anti-Immigrant Prejudice." *International Migration Review* 51(1): 218–250.

Putnam, Robert. 2007. "*E Pluribus Unum*: Diversity and Community in the Twenty-First Century, The 2006 Johan Skytte Prize Lecture." *Scandinavian Political Studies* 30(2): 137–174.

Reeskens, Tim, and Wim van Oorschot. 2012. "Disentangling the 'New Liberal Dilemma': On the Relation between General Welfare Redistribution Preferences and Welfare Chauvinism." *International Journal of Comparative Sociology* 53(2): 120–139.

Rydgren, Jens. 2002. "Radical Right Populism in Sweden: Still a Failure, But for How Long?" *Scandinavian Political Studies* 25(1): 27–56.

Rydgren, Jens. 2010. "Radical Right-Wing Populism in Denmark and Sweden: Explaining Party System Change and Stability." *SAIS Review of International Affairs* 30(1): 57–71.

Rydgren, Jens, ed. 2012. *Class Politics and the Radical Right*. New York: Routledge.

Sainsbury, Diane. 2006. "Immigrants' Social Rights in Comparative Perspective: Welfare Regimes, Forms in Immigration and Immigration Policy Regimes." *Journal of European Social Policy* 16(3): 229–244.

Sainsbury, Diane. 2012. *Welfare States and Immigrant Rights: The Politics of Inclusion and Exclusion*. Oxford: Oxford University Press.

Schall, Carly Elizabeth. 2016. *The Rise and Fall of the Miraculous Welfare Machine: Immigration and Social Democracy in Twentieth-Century Sweden*. Ithaca, NY: Cornell University Press.

Schmitt, Carina, and Céline Teney. 2019. "Access to General Social Protection for Immigrants in Advanced Democracies." *Journal of European Social Policy* 29(1): 44–55.

Senik, Claudia, Holger Stichnoth, and Karine Van der Straeten. 2009. "Immigration and Natives' Attitudes towards the Welfare State: Evidence from the European Social Survey." *Social Indicators Research* 91(3): 345–370.

Soroka, Stuart, Keith Banting, and Richard Johnston. 2006. "Immigration and Redistribution in a Global Era." In *Globalization and Egalitarian Redistribution*, eds. Pranab K. Bardhan, Michael Wallerstein, and Samuel Bowles, 261–288. Princeton NJ: Princeton University Press and Russell Sage Foundation.

Spies, Dennis, and Alexander Schmidt-Catran. 2016. "Migration, Migrant Integration and Support for Social Spending: The Case of Switzerland." *Journal of European Social Policy* 26(1): 32–47.

Steele, Liza G. 2016. "Ethnic Diversity and Support for Redistributive Social Policies." *Social Forces* 94(4): 1439–1481.

Stichnoth, Holger. 2012. "Does Immigration Weaken Natives' Support for the Unemployed? Evidence from Germany." *Public Choice* 151(3): 631–654.

SVT. 2014. "Reinfeldts vädjan till svenska folket." www.svt.se/nyheter/val2014/reinfeldts-vadjan-till-svenska-folket.

Trivers, Robert L. 1971. "The Evolution of Reciprocal Altruism." *Quarterly Review of Biology* 46: 35–57.

Uslaner, Eric M. 2002. *The Moral Foundations of Trust*. Cambridge: Cambridge University Press.

van Klingeren, Marijn, Hajo G. Boomgaarden, Rens Vliegenthart, and Claes H. de Vreese. 2015. "Real World Is Not Enough: The Media as an Additional Source of Negative Attitudes toward Immigration, Comparing Denmark and the Netherlands." *European Sociological Review* 31(3): 268–283.

Wegmann, Phillip. 2019. "Trump to Bill Sponsors for Immigrants' Welfare Benefits." *Real Clear Politics*, May 23. www.realclearpolitics.com/articles/2019/05/23/trump_to_bill_sponsors_for_immigrants_welfare_benefits.html.

Widfeldt, Anders. 2014. *Extreme Right Parties in Scandinavia*. London: Routledge.

13. Inclusive solidarity? The social democratic dilemma: Between EU rules and supporters' preferences

Zoe Lefkofridi and Susanne Rhein

INTRODUCTION

Since the 1980s, European party systems have been witnessing high degrees of electoral volatility, voters' de-alignment and re-alignment. Mainstream, moderate social democratic parties (SDPs) that made up part of government coalitions in the post-Second World War era have been experiencing decline. Already at the end of the 1990s, scholars talked about the uncertain future of SDPs due to the "social democratic dilemma": this lies in the fact that to govern in a globalized, advanced market capitalist system, SDPs are under pressure to abandon major economic policy ideals (Thomson 2000). Interestingly, however, the decline of SDPs' electoral shares has not benefited the radical left, which has most consistently opposed (globalized) market capitalism, but the radical right (RR).

In parallel to the shrinking of SDPs' electoral shares, populist radical right parties (PRRPs) have not only thrived electorally, but they have even become partners in the formation of cabinets at national and local levels (e.g. Austria, Denmark, and the Netherlands). Be they in government or opposition, PRRPs have substantial effects on European party politics and policies (e.g. Van Spanje 2010; Bale 2003; Minkeberg 2001; Röth et al. 2018).

PRRPs are characterized as "populist" because they portray electoral politics as a battle between the corrupt elite and the good and pure people (populus) (Mudde 2004). In the populists' Manichean world, hostility is directed specifically towards SDPs and Christian Democratic/Conservative parties, which typically constitute the "establishment" in many European countries. PRRPs' proposal for "radical" change consists of returning to an idealized past of traditional value-driven lifestyle, law and order, "nativism" and less immigration (Lefkofridi and Casado-Asensio 2013). While the positions of these parties on sociocultural issues have been clearly and consistently "right", their stance on socioeconomic issues is not as straightforward. Traditionally, they have been supporting little state involvement in the economy – thus occupying a "right-wing" position on the socioeconomic axis of political competition. In recent years, however, the situation seems to have changed (Lefkofridi and Michel 2017). They tried to place the issue of SDPs within their most successful (anti-immigration) frame, what has been termed "exclusive solidarity" (Lefkofridi and Michel 2017).

By promoting a welfare state for "blood and soil" nationhood (Banting and Kymlicka 2017), PRRPs have emerged as SDPs' key competitors: though initially these parties appealed to the working class on the issue of immigration, they now compete over these voters with SDPs on the issue of welfare, which they frame in exclusive terms (exclusive solidarity, welfare chauvinism) (Lefkofridi and Michel 2017). This poses a major challenge to SDPs: while immigration is an issue typically owned by PRRPs, redistribution is an issue owned by SDPs. How are SDPs likely to respond and why?

In pursuit of this question, we advance this debate by contextualizing the social democratic dilemma in a broader theory of office-seeking party behavior within the European Union (EU) (Lefkofridi and Nezi 2019; Lefkofridi 2020). More specifically, we argue that the behavior of office-seeking SDPs depends upon the room of maneuver available to them, which, in turn, is shaped by their institutional context *and* by the policy preferences of their supporters on key dimensions of political conflict.

The remainder of this chapter is structured as follows. Approaching the SD dilemma as a dilemma between responsiveness and responsibility (Mair 2013; Lefkofridi and Nezi 2019), we theorize the conditions under which SDPs can present a coherent argument against the PRRP challenge of exclusive solidarity. We derive working hypotheses about variation at the macro (context) and micro levels (supporters). We then elaborate on the research design that we employ to empirically examine whether SDPs face varied pressures for responsibility across institutional contexts, with a focus on EU membership; and whether SDPs face united or divided supporters on key lines of political conflict: redistribution – an issue typically owned by SDPs; and immigration – an issue typically owned by the challengers, PRRPs. We present our results, which we critically discuss in our conclusion.

ARE SOCIAL DEMOCRATS TRAPPED IN A DILEMMA BETWEEN RESPONSIVENESS AND RESPONSIBILITY?

We argue that the "social democratic dilemma" is an instance of what the late Peter Mair (2009) called the "dilemma between Responsiveness and Responsibility" (RR dilemma). On the one hand, political parties represent, which presupposes listening to and voicing citizens' opinions in the policy-making process (*responsiveness*). On the other hand, parties govern, and they are expected to do so in a prudent and consistent manner, following accepted procedural norms and practices (*responsibility*); this means that the way they govern honors agreements they or their predecessors have signed (e.g. international agreements, EU treaties). Both the social democratic and the RR dilemma concern parties that are willing and able to seek office, since parties remaining outside the government can evade policy compromises and thus can cater to unrealistic demands (Lefkofridi and Nezi 2019).

Mair argued that, in the contemporary multilevel institutional setting of global governance, there is a tension between these two basic functions of political parties, which would, eventually, lead to the bifurcation of party systems: a group of "mainstream" or "core" parties would offer the choice of government (but not citizens' expression and representation) and a second group of parties, which would constitute the new opposition, would express and represent the citizens. Though Mair's prediction about the bifurcation of party systems is contested – especially since challengers do enter into government or support governments from the outside (Kriesi 2014) – his framework about the tension between the governing and responsive functions of parties remains very useful. Mair's (2013) framework was inspired by developments within the EU, and the Memoranda of

Understanding signed by countries in financial trouble, but it is applicable to all policy areas where international agreements restrain governments.

Recently, Lefkofridi and Nezi (2019) developed Mair's framework to accommodate variation. More specifically, they theorized potential sources of variation in how parties experience the RR dilemma (degrees of tension) and, consequently, how they manage it (strategies). In the case of the EU, the degree of integration varies across policy areas, so EU constraints (responsibility) also vary and so does their capacity to respond to voters' preferences (responsiveness). Whether there is a dilemma or not, and how parties are expected to respond, depends upon (a) the policy content of "responsibility" *and* its degree of congruence with the party's policy goal and (b) voters' preferences on this issue (Lefkofridi and Nezi 2019). With this in mind, we now turn to the situations facing SDP parties and their challengers coming from the right.

Varied Pressures for Responsibility

Negative economic integration weakens institutions of social market economies within the EU due to competitive pressures and deregulatory effects. As a consequence, these processes impede domestic welfare states. Because negative economic integration is the predominant form of integration in the EU, autonomy of member states over welfare policies is constrained by EU rules (Scharpf 1997, 2010). Beckfield (2006) argues and empirically demonstrates that European integration drives welfare state retrenchment in market-oriented regional polities as states adopt liberal policies in a context of fiscal austerity. As all office-seeking parties became more constrained in economic policy making *because of* European integration, center-left parties came closer to the positions of center-right parties on socioeconomic issues (see Dorussen and Nanou 2006). This has negative consequences especially for SDP parties (e.g. Damhuis and Karremans 2017; Karremans and Damhuis 2020), because they have historically been the prime advocates of the welfare state and are considered to "own" the issue of redistribution.

SDPs emerged when the political competition was mainly structured by a division between labor and capital. This means that citizens initially formed their alliance with SDPs based on the socioeconomic dimension (Häusermann et al. 2012; Hooghe and Marks 2018; Beramendi et al. 2015). SDPs represented labor, and typically mobilized the working class, which has preferences for redistributive policies and holds traditional values. The constraints originating from EU rules, however, increasingly restricted parties' possibilities to pursue redistributive policies when in government (Scharpf 1997). Therefore, European economic integration limits SDPs' capacity for responsiveness towards (parts of) their main constituency on the socioeconomic dimension (Häusermann et al. 2012; Lefkofridi and Michel 2017; Oesch and Rennwald 2018). In other words, EU membership puts their major policy goal (expansion of the welfare state) under pressure. How are SDPs likely to respond in this situation?

To answer this question, we first draw on the salience theory of party competition, which posits that parties *selectively* emphasize topics where they feel they have a *good reputation*, while deemphasizing those that may be electorally costly and put them at a disadvantage against their competitors (Sjöblom 1985; Budge and Farlie 1983; Petrocik 1996; Meguid 2008; Bélanger and Meguid 2008). In this way, parties seek to prime their "own issues" salience in the decisional calculus of voters. Parties' tendency to focus on the issues of electoral advantage is relatively path-dependent given the role of parties' institutional and organizational legacies in determining their policy package (Marks and Wilson 2000). Within a certain historical context, the argument goes, political actors favor a specific policy direction, and each party identifies a set of policy issues that they "own" (Van der Brug 2004). To illustrate, all around Europe RRPs own the issue of immigration, SDPs own the issue of redistribution, and the Greens own the issue of the environment.

While focusing on the issue that gives them advantages, strategic parties are likely to obfuscate the offer on issues that present them with high risks, for example, by deemphasizing it. The EU constrains the room of policy maneuver and generates electoral costs related to the issue that SDPs own. In other words, their (historical) issue ownership is challenged by EU membership: SDPs within the EU are more constrained on redistribution compared to those outside it. It follows that in an effort to minimize electoral costs SDPs within the EU are under pressure to deemphasize welfare state expansion. Based on this argument, we hypothesize that:

Hypothesis 1: *Constraints posed by EU membership motivate SDPs to deemphasize the issue they own: redistribution*

If this hypothesis holds, however, it means that that SDPs leave space for other parties to politicize this issue on their own terms. In other words, SDPs' pact with neoliberalism (e.g. Third Way) not only leads to a gradual "shifting" of their representative role (from working to middle class) but also to the gradual loss of ownership of the redistribution issue (and workers' protection against globalization forces).

Where the "owners" of redistribution are unable to address the issue properly due to the constraints they face, parts of their electorates get disappointed and challengers see opportunities in attracting those disenchanted social segments by reframing the issue as their own. Where issue ownership is "less clear among the party's competitors" (De Sio and Weber 2014, 882), there is more potential to win new voters. For this purpose, PRRPs increased their emphasis on redistribution over time, and they framed it in an anti-immigrant, exclusionary way (Lefkofridi and Michel 2017).

The anti-immigration frame is the issue on which PRRPs have a reputation of consistent opposition to migration and multiculturalism. Also, EU member states retain a significant degree of control on immigration issues. Competences are thus shared between EU and national levels: EU membership does imply some common rules in migration policy but EU member states do not yet speak with one voice, as the refugee crisis that started in the summer of 2015 manifests. Studies show that, especially with regard to asylum policies, member states still hold sufficient control and there has only been limited convergence in this policy field (Toshkov and de Haan 2013). Reasons for this are: weak monitoring, a lack of harmonization, low solidarity and the absence of a central EU institution that oversees implementation of those policies. The problem is observed for both asylum policies and immigration policies that address immigrants from EU third countries. In sum, migration is an area where European integration is not as developed as in economic policy. Thus, parties have a lot more room for maneuver with regard to what they propose with regard to migration policy than with regard to economic policy.

Besides the EU institutional context, parties' emphasis and position on major issues is determined also by their supporters' preferences (Häusermann et al. 2012). Here, we will focus on the two-dimensional policy space that resulted from structural transformation of society in the last decades (Beramendi et al. 2015; Hooghe and Marks 2018; Kriesi et al. 2006). This space encompasses socioeconomic (e.g. taxation and redistribution) and sociocultural (e.g. immigration and multiculturalism) issues (Kriesi et al. 2008). To be sure, divergent policy orientations may exist *within* the group of party supporters (Lefkofridi and Nezi 2019). For instance, voters from different social classes may perceive a policy issue, e.g. redistribution, from different perspectives, and have different or diverging policy preferences. This makes it more difficult for parties to construct a coherent argument against their opponents. The question, then, is where SDP and PRRP supporters stand on redistribution and immigration over time, and whether their preferences are coherent, thus expressing a clear message to parties. In the next section, we develop our argument further to address the second part of the RR dilemma: parties' capacity to respond to voters' (changing) policy preferences.

Varied Pressures for Responsiveness

The social structures of society changed with the transition from industrial to post-industrial times, and a new cleavage emerged between modernization winners and losers (Kriesi et al. 2006; Hooghe and Marks 2018): those who can engage and benefit from these processes and those who cannot. In Europe, the traditional socioeconomic cleavage between the left and the right has been shifting into a new cleavage between integration (openness to globalization) and demarcation (protection from globalization) (Kriesi et al. 2012). Liberalization and economic competition brought about by globalization and European integration has been especially harmful for the poorer strata: as the working class lacks the resources (e.g. education, trade unions at the global level) to survive in a global market, its jobs, wages and welfare benefits are endangered.

The initial response of RRPs to globalization and European integration was to pursue a rightist path on both economic and cultural dimensions of political conflict. In a seminal piece, Kitschelt and McGann (1995) argued that the winning formula for RRPs was the combination of neoliberal views on socioeconomic issues and authoritarian views on sociocultural issues. While on the economic dimension they advocated free market economy, PRRPs capitalized on the cultural threats of globalization (e.g. on how immigration threatens national identity and way of life). On sociocultural issues PRRPs have consistently held traditional-conservative positions (Hooghe and Marks 2018; Beramendi et al. 2015; Oesch and Rennwald 2018). As SDPs and Conservative or Christian-Democratic Parties (CCDs) that alternated in government were converging on economic matters, RRPs seized the opportunity to shift voters' focus on the cultural dimension of political conflict (Kitschelt and McGann 1995): they emphasized tradition, cultural heritage, law and order as well as a negative perception of immigration.

Through their advocacy of authoritarian and nationalistic imageries of society, PRRPs did not only render sociocultural issues, and especially immigration, highly salient but they have even shifted entire party systems towards their preferred positions on these issues (e.g. Lefkofridi and Horvath 2012; Van Spanje 2010). Under the pressure of competition from RRPs, CCDs shifted to the right, and immigration policies got more restrictive. Hence, even when not in government, RRPs proved successful in achieving their policy goals concerning immigration.

Their supporters aligned with RR parties on the basis of their sociocultural preferences (Lefkofridi and Casado-Asensio 2013); but supporters also include the working class, which typically favors redistribution. This suggests that PRRPs supporters' preferences should not be homogeneous on the issue of redistribution. This would be reflected in inconsistent PRRP positioning on this issue, such as right-wing positions (but also moderate or even left-leaning ones) (Afonso 2015; Lefkofridi and Michel 2017; Röth et al. 2018). Satisfying diverse socioeconomic preferences is not easy, however. If their supporters have diverse preferences on redistribution (left-leaning working class versus right-leaning small-business owners), parties can lower the tension by connecting it to an issue that unites their supporters (immigration) (De Sio and Weber 2014; Lefkofridi and Nezi 2019) and allows them to compete with SDPs over those voters that simultaneously favor redistribution and oppose immigration (Lefkofridi et al. 2014).

When support for redistribution becomes linked to voters' attitudes to immigration, however, the discourse on redistribution shifts towards a discussion about who deserves welfare/whether immigrants are deserving of welfare or not. This brings SDP to a difficult situation. To compete with PRRPs' *exclusionary* vision of redistribution, they must propose an alternative policy package. To oppose exclusive solidarity (Lefkofridi and Michel 2017), one can either argue in favor of inclusive solidarity, or against solidarity of all kinds. As advocating the dismantling of the welfare state would go against the SDPs' historical roots and foundational ideology, it would be a suicidal move. In essence, SDPs are under pressure to defend redistribution for all citizens, even those with migration backgrounds. This option would represent a "responsible" stance for intra-EU migration since the common legal framework entails the free movement of labor and services: this implies that EU citizens working in a different member state other than that of origin shall be treated equally – and this includes equal access to the welfare state. Whether SDPs can gain electorally from such a strategy, however, depends upon what voters want. We expect their supporters to have diverse preferences; if this is the case, SDPs lack a united basis that enables them to capitalize on the defense of inclusive solidarity against the PRRPs' exclusive version of redistribution.

In sum, the following hypotheses regarding diversity within the supporters of SDPs and PRRPs will guide our empirical investigation:

Hypothesis 2a: *SDP supporters are likely to be divided on the sociocultural dimension*

and

Hypothesis 2b: *PRRP supporters are likely be divided on the socioeconomic dimension.*

RESEARCH DESIGN

To evaluate our hypotheses empirically, we rely on a comparative design that employs mixed (quantitative and qualitative) methods. We elaborate on our case selection and the operationalization of our key theoretical concepts.

Case Selection

The empirical examination of the hypotheses introduced in this chapter necessitates comparative methodology. Since Hypothesis 1 addresses a causal relationship, and Hypothesis 2 is of a descriptive nature, they require different approaches to case selection.

To evaluate Hypothesis 1, we select the Austrian and Swiss cases following the logic of a most similar system design. Austria and Switzerland are similar on certain factors: first, both countries are characterized by a party system in which similar party families are represented and SDPs as well as PRRPs have been successful (Parline 2019a, 2019b). Second, the Austrian and Swiss PRRPs and SDP depict similar types of party leadership (Heinisch and Mazzoleni 2016; SP 2019; SPÖ 2019). Third, the countries are situated in close geographic proximity. The countries differ in the central contextual factor, which is EU membership. Whereas Austria has been an official EU member since 1995, Switzerland is not. This means that by examining those two cases and their SDPs we can draw conclusions about the impact of EU membership and its possible restrictions.

With regard to Hypothesis 2, the Austrian Social Democratic Party (Sozialdemokratische Partei Österreich (SPÖ)) and the Swiss Social Democratic Party (Sozialdemokratische Partei der Schweiz (SP)) remain at the heart of our analysis. However, to gain insights into whether our results are generalizable beyond the Austrian and Swiss cases, we examine SDPs and their voters in three additional countries that differ with regard to their welfare state, EU and European Monetary Union (EMU) memberships as well as the electoral system. Our evaluation of Hypothesis 2 thus adopts a most different system design. This selection of countries aspires at robust and generalizable results and at generating not a static but a dynamic picture of European parties and supporters (over time). The selected cases' variation across these criteria is displayed in Table 13.1.

Data, Operationalization and Measurement

In this section, we explain the operationalization of our central concepts (independent and dependent variables). The independent variable of Hypothesis 1 is EU membership and the dependent variable is the emphasis SDPs place on welfare. To examine whether EU membership impacts the salience of welfare issues on the SDPs' agenda requires variation with regard to EU membership. We investigate an EU member (Austria) and a

Table 13.1 Variables by country according to Esping-Andersen's (1990) Decommodification Index, EU (2020a), EU (2020b) and IDEA (2021)

Country	Welfare state	EU member	EMU member	Electoral system
Austria	Social-democratic	Yes	Yes	Proportional representation
Switzerland	Conservative	No	No	Proportional representation
Italy	Conservative	Yes	Yes	Mixed/proportional representation
Denmark	Social-democratic	Yes	No	Proportional representation
United Kingdom	Liberal	Yes	No	Plurality

non-EU member (Switzerland) longitudinally. In detail, we measure the extent to which Austrian and Swiss SDPs mention the welfare state in their electoral manifestos over a timeframe of almost half a century: from 1970 to 2018. This timeframe can offer clear answers about whether the behavior of the post-accession SPÖ differs compared to the pre-EU accession SPÖ and to see whether the SPÖ differs from the Swiss SP (outside the EU). In essence, in the case selection we study the salience of welfare issues in SDPs' manifestos not only between countries (EU/non-EU member) but also over time (pre-/post-accession).

We measure this with the help of two variables coded by the Comparative Manifesto Project (Volkens et al. 2020), which capture the salience of welfare state expansion and welfare state limitation by assessing how often parties mention issues related to those in their manifestos. The two variables we use are called *Welfare State Expansion* and *Welfare State Limitations*. The variable *Welfare State Expansion* measures the frequency of positive mentions of the introduction or development of new or already established public social services and social security schemes. The *Welfare State Limitation* variable on the other hand accounts for the extent to which parties elaborate on social subsidiary principles in their manifesto.

Hypothesis 2 requires information on parties' (SDPs and PRRPs) supporters and their preferences on socioeconomic and sociocultural issues. We use the mean position and the dispersion of each economic and cultural preference of voters. The ideal measure to capture the dispersion of preferences is the standard deviation since it measures the average deviation of values from the mean. We examine two-year intervals from 2002 until 2018 for all five selected countries (Table 13.1). We rely on data from the European Social Survey (ESS). Although data for some parties and years of observation were not available, we are able to compare the preference position and deviation of SDP and PRRP voters over a long period of time The ESS allows us to identify the supporters of each party by asking respondents for which parties they voted in the last election (ESS 2018, 2016b, 2014, 2012, 2010, 2008, 2006, 2004, 2002).[1] If a respondent answers this question by naming a SDP, s/he will be classified as SDP partisan. The same logic applies to PRRPs.[2]

We estimate the possible divide of party supporters by combining partisanship and policy preferences and calculating the standard division for both partisan groups' preferences. To capture the policy preferences of partisans we use two questions from the ESS, which are suitable to determine their positions on the socioeconomic and sociocultural dimensions. The question that is most suitable to capture an individual's position on the socioeconomic dimension asks whether an individual thinks that "the government should take measures to reduce income inequality" (ESS 2016b). Individuals can state how much they approve with a measure like that on a five-point scale. The higher the scale the more a respondent disagrees with the statement.

For the sociocultural dimension, we use a question that measures position on immigration, which reads as follows: "Is [country] made a worse or a better place to live by people coming to live here from other countries?" (ESS 2016b). Respondents can answer this question on a scale from 0 to 10. We code the variable in a way that a higher score indicates a more negative perspective on immigration. As the variable that captures the socioeconomic dimension is measured on a five-point scale, we rescaled this variable to make both dimensions comparable.[3]

Inclusive solidarity? 263

EMPIRICAL RESULTS

We begin the presentation of our findings with the salience of welfare state expansion and limitation for SDPs in Switzerland and Austria, i.e. the SP and the SPÖ, respectively (Hypothesis 1). After having established the differences between those two parties, we then continue by demonstrating the extent to which there exists a divide among SDP and PRRP supporters on the socioeconomic and sociocultural dimensions. In this way, we look at both sides of the dilemma (responsibility versus responsiveness). While we examine five different countries, the analysis mainly focuses on the differences between SDPs and PRRP parties and their supporters in Switzerland and Austria. The remaining cases serve the purpose of showing whether results for the "supporter divide hypothesis" are generalizable beyond the Alps.

On Responsibility: EU Constraints and the Salience of the Welfare State in SDP Manifestos

We argued that because EU rules constrain SDPs on the socioeconomic dimension, SDPs within the EU will be more likely than those outside it to downplay the issue they own (Hypothesis 1). Applied to our selected cases this suggests that in Austria (EU member state), the respective SDP, SPÖ, cannot be as vocal about the issue of welfare state expansion after the country joined the EU compared to the SDP in the non-EU country (Swiss SDP: SP). In the empirical world, salience of both the Austrian SPÖ and the Swiss SP should be similar up to Austria's EU accession in 1995. After Austria's accession this similarity should fade, and welfare state expansion should be less salient in Austria than in Switzerland. The opposite should hold for welfare state limitations: if at all mentioned, they should be more salient in the SPÖ's manifesto compared to the SP's manifesto.

Figure 13.1 shows our results for the Swiss SP and the Austrian SPÖ's salience on welfare state expansion and limitation in their respective electoral manifestos (in percent) from 1970 to 2018. The upper graphs describe the Swiss SP's welfare policy salience (left graph: limitation; right graph: expansion), whereas the lower graphs concern the Austrian SPÖ (left graph: limitation; right graph: expansion). Put simply, the two graphs on the left-hand side depict the extent to which a SDP vocalizes welfare state limitations, whereas the two graphs on the right-hand side of Figure 13.1 do the same for SDPs' mentions of welfare state expansion.

What we see in Figure 13.1 is that until 1995, which is the year of Austria's EU accession, the data show a similar – though not identical – development of the salience of welfare state expansion in both SDPs' manifestos. The Austrian SPÖ even scores clearly higher in salience values than the SP in four of the six elections (or seven in the Austrian case) taking place from 1970 to 1995 in these countries. After 1995, however, this changes as predicted in our theoretical argument. While the development of emphasis on welfare state expansion salience follows similar patterns for the Austrian and Swiss SDPs, the salience is much more pronounced in the Swiss case. For the SP, the salience of welfare expansion in its manifesto is generally higher than for the elections that took place after the mid-1990s (with the exception of the election in 1975 when it is also high). This means that we can generally report a decisive upward trend for the salience of welfare state expansion in the SP manifesto. The same cannot be said for the SPÖ, which following

264 *Handbook on migration and welfare*

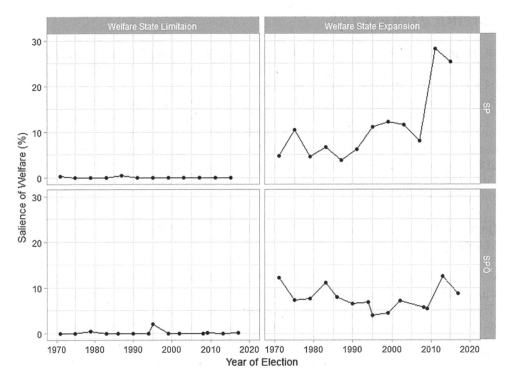

Figure 13.1 The salience of welfare state policy (limitation/expansion) in the Swiss SP and the Austrian SPÖ manifestos from 1970 to 2018

Austria's accession to the EU does not mention welfare state expansions as frequently as before 1995 in their manifestos; in the most recent elections, the SPÖ has increased references to welfare state expansion. Yet, in comparison with its Swiss counterpart, these scores are low (in support of Hypothesis 1).

After having presented our results for the salience of welfare state expansion in both the SP and the SPÖ manifestos before and after 1995, we also shortly address the salience of welfare limitations in those manifestos. While our general expectation is that none of these parties should emphasize this kind of issue due to their very nature as SDPs, there is still one remarkable exception to this: the manifesto of the SPÖ in 1995, which is the year of Austria's EU accession. Even if we recognize that the graph does not show a substantial increase, it is still a piece of evidence showing that the EU accession destabilized the Austrian SDP. In sum, the salience of issues dealing with welfare state limitation is consistently low in both parties' manifestos during the period of investigation, apart from SPÖ in 1995.

Taking into account all information portrayed in Figure 13.1, our data support the argument about EU membership restraining SDPs: the Austrian SPÖ responds, as expected, with deemphasizing the issue it owns. This is manifest in less frequent mentions of *Welfare State Expansion* in the Austrian SDP manifestos relative to its Swiss counterpart that is not as exposed to European integration. When parties depoliticize their key issue, however, they also make space for PRRPs to shape the debate in their interest. Faced with welfare policy proposals about exclusive solidarity from the right (Lefkofridi and Michel 2017), SDPs are under pressure to present an alternative. One such possibility is to propagate inclusive solidarity, that is defending redistribution for all citizens, even those with a migration background. This would constitute a "responsible" policy stance especially for intra-EU migration. SDPs' response to the PRRP exclusionary proposals, however, depends upon conditions at the voter level: the (lack of) coherence of voter preferences on sociocultural and socioeconomic issues, to which we now turn.

On Responsiveness: What Do SDP and PRRP Supporters Want on Redistribution and Immigration?

Given our findings about the impact of contextual conditions (varied pressures for responsibility, Hypothesis 1), we now turn to the examination of conditions at the voter level (varied pressures for responsiveness). Hypothesis 2 specifically concerns the divide among SDP and PRRP voters on sociocultural (H2a) and socioeconomic (H2b) issues. Here, we focus our discussion on Switzerland and Austria, but we are interested in whether our arguments can be generalized beyond these two cases; hence, our figures demonstrate findings for five countries in total: Austria (Figures 13.2 and 13.5); Switzerland (Figures 13.3 and 13.6); Italy, Denmark and the United Kingdom (UK) (Figures 13.4 and 13.7).

All figures in this section are structured identically: the left side of each graph shows the mean preferences of supporters (indicated by dots) for the sociocultural dimension and the right side of the graph shows mean preferences on the socioeconomic dimension from 2002 to 2018. On the issue of immigration (left) a higher score indicates support for immigration. On the issue of welfare (right) a higher value signifies disapproval of government measures to reduce income inequality, whereas lower scores imply support for such measures. The whiskers connected to the dots indicate the standard deviation and therefore the degree of division of SDP supporters on both topics. If the graphs do not indicate mean preferences for a given year this means that there were no data available for those years.

Figure 13.2 depicts SDP supporters' preferences in Austria, a case for which data in the year 2012 are missing. Nevertheless, it seems like the mean preferences of SPÖ supporters are quite constant over the years. On the left: the general position of SPÖ supporters on immigration seems to be rather neutral as all scores vary between the values 1.5 and 2 which are located at the center of the scale. The standard deviation for this sociocultural issue again is always close to the value 1. The Austrian case therefore does not support our Hypothesis 2a: supporters are not divided. That said, their position is unclear, because they are not pushing the Austrian SDP towards a specific direction, neither in favor nor against immigration. Its supporters' preferences motivate this party to stand still, rather than take a clear position on the matter.

On the contrary, SPÖ supporters have a clear left-wing position on government measures to reduce inequality, which is typically the goal of redistributive policies. Over the observational frame the preferences of SPÖ voters for welfare state expansion usually approximate a value of 1. This implies that the SPÖ supporters on average are pro-welfare state. The standard deviation for their position on welfare state expansion also

266 *Handbook on migration and welfare*

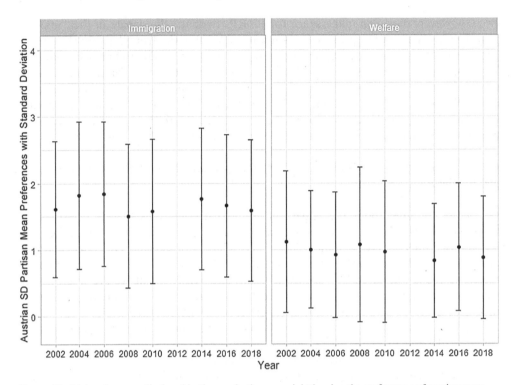

Note: The higher the score displayed in the graph, the more right leaning the preferences of partisans are. Immigration preferences – question: "Is [country] made a worse or a better place to live by people coming to live here from other countries?" (0 = Better place to live; 4 = Worse place to live). Welfare preferences – question: "The government should take measures to reduce differences in income levels" (0 = Agree strongly; 4 = Disagree strongly).

Figure 13.2   Mean preferences of Austrian SDP supporters (dots) and standard deviation (whiskers) from 2002 to 2018 on both immigration and welfare

averagely approximates 1. Whether this is high or low needs to be evaluated in relation to our results for SDP supporters in other countries and on other issues (see below).

Note that the dispersion of the SPÖ supporters on both socioeconomic and sociocultural issues is similar. Combining the clearly left-leaning position on redistribution with the neutral/undecided position on immigration SPÖ supporters send a message to their party that is difficult to translate in policy within the EU. The electoral ground for an argument in favor of inclusive solidarity is neither fertile nor hostile.

Figure 13.3 shows voter preferences in non-EU member Switzerland focusing on the SDP electorate in this country. The mean preferences of the SP supporters are rather constant and similar to the Austrian case regarding the socioeconomic dimension (right side of the graph): Swiss SP supporters also seem to generally support welfare state expansions. While the mean values depicted here are a little bit higher than in Austria the mean welfare preferences of the SP supporters are also approximating the value 1.[4] The standard deviation from the mean preference on redistribution of SD supporters in Switzerland is again very similar to the Austrian case.

Inclusive solidarity? 267

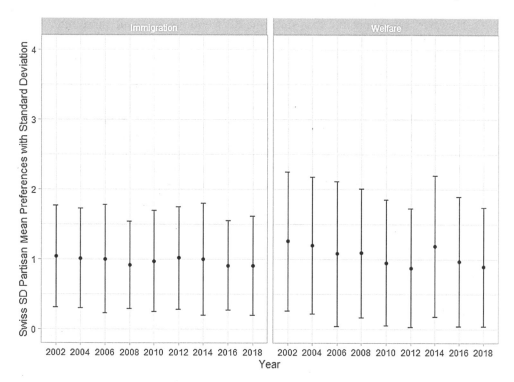

Note: The higher the score displayed in the graph, the more right leaning the preferences of partisans are. Immigration preferences – question: "Is [country] made a worse or a better place to live by people coming to live here from other countries?" (0 = Better place to live; 4 = Worse place to live). Welfare preferences – question: "The government should take measures to reduce differences in income levels" (0 = Agree strongly; 4 = Disagree strongly).

Figure 13.3 Mean preferences of Swiss SDP supporters (dots) and standard deviation (whiskers) from 2002 to 2018 on both immigration and welfare

The mean immigration preferences of Swiss SDP supporters (left side of the graph) seem more positive and clearer compared to the Austrian ones.[5] The reported standard deviation of Swiss SDP supporters' immigration preferences is also slightly but not substantially smaller compared to their division on the socioeconomic dimension. Once again, we do not find evidence in favor of the claim that SDP supporters are divided on the sociocultural dimension.

While neither the Austrian (Figure 13.2) nor the Swiss case (Figure 13.3) support Hypothesis 2a, they enable us to draw useful conclusions for the SDP dilemma against the background of Hypothesis 1. The focus hereby is on the mean preferences of the Austrian SPÖ and the Swiss SP supporters. The two parties' supporters have indistinguishable positions on welfare state expansion according to our results. This is an important conclusion because it implies that the higher salience of welfare state expansion in the SP manifestos after 1995 cannot be explained by a higher demand of their electorate compared to Austrian SPÖ supporters. If it were only for the preferences of their party supporters, the SP would be equally vocal about welfare state expansion compared to the

268 *Handbook on migration and welfare*

SPÖ. However, this is not the case since the SP mentions this issue more often. The analysis therefore demonstrates how EU membership matters for the salience of welfare state issues in SDP manifestos.

Since the claim that SDP supporters should be less divided on economic issues compared to cultural ones is quite established in the literature (see Beramendi et al. 2015; Häusermann et al. 2012; Oesch and Rennwald 2018), we also analyze parties in three additional countries to see whether our findings are generalizable. Figure 13.4 presents the results for the Italian, Danish and British SDP supporters. Italian and Danish SDP supporters complement the picture of constant preferences painted by Austrian and Swiss SDP supporters. Moreover, the standard deviations of the preferences from SDP supporters in these countries are similar for both welfare and immigration preferences, which

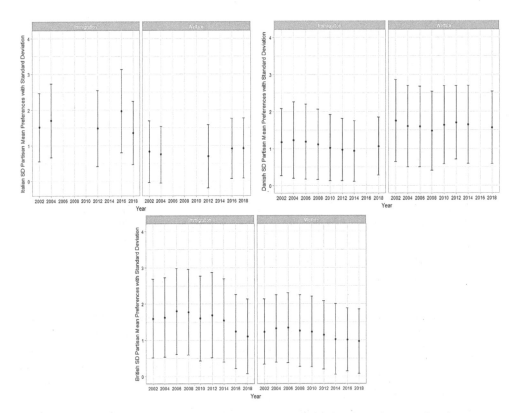

Note: The higher the score displayed in the graph, the more right leaning the preferences of partisans are. Immigration preferences – question: "Is [country] made a worse or a better place to live by people coming to live here from other countries?" (0 = Better place to live; 4 = Worse place to live). Welfare preferences – question: "The government should take measures to reduce differences in income levels" (0 = Agree strongly; 4 = Disagree strongly).

Figure 13.4 *Results for Italy (upper left), Denmark (upper right) and the United Kingdom (lower) with regard to mean preferences of SDP supporters (dots) and standard deviation (whiskers) from 2002 to 2018 on both immigration and welfare*

Inclusive solidarity? 269

means that the divide of the SDP supporters is here also similar for both the socioeconomic and the sociocultural dimensions. This indicates that our findings (against Hypothesis 2a) can indeed be generalized beyond our two main cases (Austria and Switzerland). The British SDP supporters are the only ones that follow the logic proposed by Hypothesis 2a. Here the standard deviation and hence the division of the SDP electorate is indeed higher on the issue of immigration, i.e. the sociocultural dimension. That said, the difference between the standard deviation of British SDP supporters' immigration and welfare preferences is small.

All in all, our findings do not show a stronger division of SDP supporters on the sociocultural dimension in any country, except for the UK. While the data do not support Hypothesis 2a, it is important to note that SDP supporters occupy neutral positions: across countries, there is no strong message in favor of immigration. This means that linking redistribution with immigration in a frame of inclusive solidarity would not be profitable for SDPs. Having manifested the conditions that discourage SDPs from presenting a coherent argument on sociocultural issues (due to supporters' lukewarm preferences on immigration) and on socioeconomic issues (due to constraints by European integration), we now turn to the situation faced by their challengers from the right.

Our last hypothesis (2b) expects PRRP supporters to be more divided on the socioeconomic rather than on the sociocultural dimension. The descriptive analysis we perform to examine this claim closely reflects our approach for investigating the SDP supporter divide. Figures 13.5–13.7 resemble the structure used to visualize the results for the SDP supporters.

Figure 13.5 shows the mean preferences of Austrian PRRP supporters as well as their degree of division (standard deviation). Their preferences on redistribution (right side) are less stable over time compared to Austrian SDP supporters (Figure 13.2). PRRP supporters in Austria were less in favor of welfare state expansion from 2002 to 2010; but still all values approximate a mean preference of 1.5. Only in 2010 the mean welfare preferences of 2 indicates a more neutral position on welfare issues. From 2014 onwards the average position of PRRP supporters even approaches the value 1. In 2014 the mean value is even smaller than 1.[6] On redistribution, the division among voters supporting PRRPs in Austria according to standard deviation is higher than 1 from 2002 to 2010. It is smaller than 1 from 2014 to 2018 except for 2016 where it is slightly higher. While PRRP supporters are similarly supportive towards welfare state expansion as SD supporters, their mean preferences on immigration are more negative varying in-between a value of 2 and 3. The divide of supporters (standard deviation) is smaller for immigration preferences with all values being close to 1 in the period between 2002 and 2010. All observations after that show a similar pattern of division on both immigration and welfare issues. This means the results for Austrian PRRP supporters provide evidence for Hypothesis 2b as the divide of RR supporters is moderately higher on the socioeconomic dimension during the period from 2002 to 2010.

Figure 13.6 presents our findings for Swiss PRRP supporters, which are again quite stable over time. The mean preferences on welfare (right side of the graph) vary between values of 1.5 and 2. This implies that Swiss PRRP supporters are *less* supportive of welfare state expansion compared to Swiss SDP supporters but generally approach a more neutral position on this issue.[7] The standard deviation of PRRP supporters' welfare

270 *Handbook on migration and welfare*

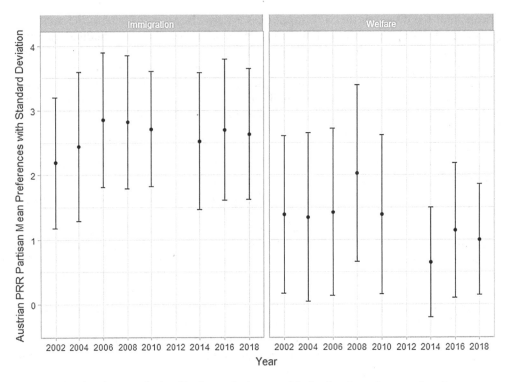

Note: The higher the score displayed in the graph, the more right leaning the preferences of partisans are. Immigration preferences – question: "Is [country] made a worse or a better place to live by people coming to live here from other countries?" (0 = Better place to live; 4 = Worse place to live). Welfare preferences – question: "The government should take measures to reduce differences in income levels" (0 = Agree strongly; 4 = Disagree strongly).

Figure 13.5 Mean preferences of Austrian PRRP supporters (dots) and standard deviation (whiskers) from 2002 to 2018 on both immigration and welfare

preferences on average approximates a value of 1. Regarding immigration (left side of the graph), the Swiss PRRP electorate is more positive compared to the Austrian PRRP but again the observed difference is not significant. Mean values ranging between 1.5 and 2 imply that supporters of the Swiss PRRP seem to be rather neutral on the issue of immigration and even show a slightly positive outlook on foreigners. Additionally, the PRRP supporters are mostly slightly less divided on the issue of immigration relative to welfare state issues. For this reason, the preference formation of the Swiss PRRP electorate also lends reluctant support to the claim that the divide of PRRP supporters is higher on the socioeconomic dimension (Hypothesis 2b).

To check the generalizability of our findings beyond the Austrian and the Swiss cases, we performed the same analysis for Italian, Danish and British PRRP supporters (Figure 13.7). In the Italian case, the PRRP supporters' divide is quite similar on both the sociocultural and the socioeconomic dimensions. Danish PRRP supporters display a smaller standard deviation regarding their immigration preferences compared to their welfare preferences until 2012. Only in 2014 is the division of their supporters slightly higher

Inclusive solidarity? 271

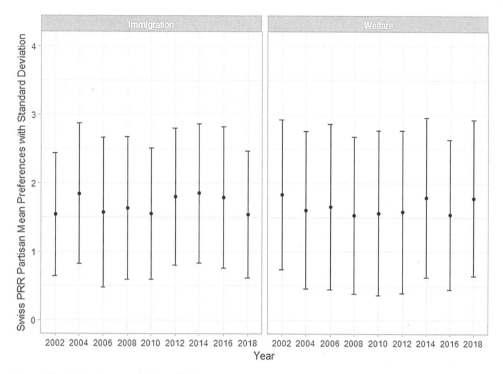

Note: The higher the score displayed in the graph, the more right leaning the preferences of partisans are. Immigration preferences – question: "Is [country] made a worse or a better place to live by people coming to live here from other countries?" (0 = Better place to live; 4 = Worse place to live). Welfare preferences – question: "The government should take measures to reduce differences in income levels" (0 = Agree strongly; 4 = Disagree strongly).

Figure 13.6 Mean preferences of Swiss PRRP supporters (dots) and standard deviation (whiskers) from 2002 to 2018 on both immigration and welfare

concerning redistribution. The results for the UK show clearly that British PRRP supporters are less divided on the sociocultural dimension in 2006. From 2014 to 2018 the standard deviation is smaller for the mean preferences of PRRP supporters on welfare compared with immigration.

To summarize, our findings show a slightly bigger divide of the PRRP electorate on socioeconomic issues relative to sociocultural issues for Austrian, Danish and British PRRP supporters during the earlier years of our observational frame. In later years, however, the divide of these voters on the socioeconomic dimension decreases. As a consequence, it becomes either similar to or even smaller than the PRRP supporters' divide on the issue of immigration. In the Swiss case, PRRP supporters were generally less divided on the issue of immigration. Considering this, the results lend moderate support to Hypothesis 2b but also show that its logic is not generally applicable. While in earlier years PRRP supporters are generally more split regarding distribution compared to immigration, in later years the picture changes. This implies that redistribution constitutes a less and less divisive issue within the supporters of PRRPs.

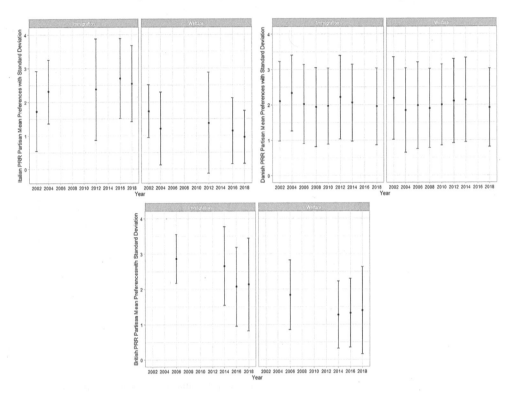

Note: The higher the score displayed in the graph, the more right leaning the preferences of partisans are. Immigration preferences – question: "Is [country] made a worse or a better place to live by people coming to live here from other countries?" (0 = Better place to live; 4 = Worse place to live). Welfare preferences – question: "The government should take measures to reduce differences in income levels" (0 = Agree strongly; 4 = Disagree strongly).

Figure 13.7 Results for Italy (upper left) Denmark (upper right) and the UK (lower) with regard to mean preferences of PRRP supporters (dots) and standard deviation (whiskers) from 2002 to 2018 on both immigration and welfare

CONCLUSION

Our chapter is a narrative of SDP decline and PRRP rise that synthesizes existing knowledge and goes beyond it. We theorize the dilemma faced by SDP parties as one between Responsibility (what rules say) and Responsiveness (what voters want) and embed it in the broader theory of competitive party behavior. We focus on SDPs' emphasis on the issue they own, to illustrate how responsibility constrains SDP in EU member states compared to non-EU member states; we examined a case that has a partnership with the EU, Switzerland, and observed a big difference between the levels of salience of welfare state expansion within and outside the EU. This difference became even more striking when we examined the Austrian and Swiss SDP supporters, and saw that they equally favored redistribution.

As SDPs refrained from voicing redistribution, PRRPs seized the opportunity. However, given its diverse supporters (e.g. working class and small-business owners), their preferences on welfare were expected to be diverse. To produce a coherent frame given these inconsistencies, PRRP linked redistribution to immigration. Our analysis shows that the diversity within PRRP supporters on the socioeconomic dimension decreases over time. Can SDPs articulate a coherent response to this nativist, anti-immigrant concept of welfare?

When looking within national electorates, SDP supporters display coherence on both issues; however, on immigration their stances send a halfhearted message. While PRRPs frame redistribution in an anti-immigrant way and unite their supporters, SDPs see few reasons to defend the rights of migrants to the welfare state, which is constrained by the EU. Yet, if inclusive solidarity cannot be pursued at the national level, then it could and should be pursued at the EU level. This means that to regain ownership on the issue and compete over redistribution on their "own" terms, SDPs need to come up with transnational policy proposals for redistribution that challenge the definition of redistributive solidarity in nativist, anti-immigrant terms. Millions of EU citizens,[8] who are living and working in different member states other than their country of origin, are likely to have preferences for such transnational policies (see Lefkofridi 2020). To address these voters, SDPs in the EU should work much more closely together than they currently do. Political integration, especially at the party level, has been very hard to achieve – not least because politicians are products of local and national politics. For social democracy, however, this – difficult yet possible – path may be the only alternative to decay.

NOTES

1. An alternative measure would be party identification. However, fewer and fewer people truly identify with specific parties (Dalton 2013); hence, analyzing only those respondents that state that they identify with a party reduces the already low number of observations available to us in certain cases even more. Since we need to aggregate party supporters' responses in order to estimate mean positions and standard deviations the low numbers of observations available to us might bias the results of our analysis.
2. We gathered the information about the ideological background of a party from Appendix 3 of the respective ESS round (2016a).
3. We do that by merging the categories 2–4 and 6–8 since we assume that those categories are most likely to substitute the intermediate category on a five-point scale. The logic behind that is that those categories express moderate agreement or disagreement with immigration. Categories 0 and 1, as well as 9 and 10, are also merged to make up the outside categories of the scale (express more radical preferences).
4. We perform a t-test that compares the mean preferences of Austrian SDP supporters and Swiss SDP supporters over the years to test whether those differences are statistically significant. The results of a t-test show that the differences on welfare preferences in the Austrian and Swiss cases are not statistically significant.
5. The t-test shows that there is no statistically significant difference when comparing their mean preferences on immigration.
6. A t-test confirms that this means that Austrian PRRP supporters have similarly positive preferences towards welfare expansion compared to Austrian SDP supporters. The differences between the means of both samples are not statistically significant.
7. A t-test shows, however, that the observed difference between Swiss PRRP and SDP supporters is not statistically significant.
8. On the basis of the free movement of labor, EU citizens can seek jobs in different member states, which results in increasing mobility within the EU territory: in 2017 about 17 million (4 percent of the EU's working population) lived in a country other than their member state of origin, while an additional 1.4 million constitute cross-border workers (European Commission 2018).

REFERENCES

Afonso, Alexandre. 2015. "Choosing whom to betray: Populist right-wing parties, welfare state reforms and the trade-off between office and votes". *European Political Science Review* 7(2): 271–292.
Bale, Tim. 2003. "Cinderella and her ugly sisters: The mainstream and extreme right in Europe's bipolarising party systems". *West European Politics* 26(3): 67–90.
Banting, Keith, and Will Kymlicka. 2017. *The Strains of Commitment: The Political Sources of Solidarity in Diverse Societies*. Oxford: Oxford University Press.
Beckfield, Jason. 2006. "European integration and income inequality". *American Sociological Review* 71(6): 964–985.
Bélanger, Éric, and Bonnie Meguid. 2008. "Issue salience, issue ownership, and issue-based vote choice". *Electoral Studies* 27(3): 477–491.
Beramendi, Pablo, Silja Häusermann, Herbert Kitschelt, and Hanspeter Kriesi. 2015. "Introduction: The politics of advanced capitalism". In *The Politics of Advanced Capitalism*, eds Pablo Beramendi, Silja Häusermann, Herbert Kitschelt, and Hanspeter Kriesi, 1–64. New York: Cambridge University Press.
Budge, Ian, and Dennis Farlie. 1983. *Explaining and Predicting Elections: Issue Effects and Party Strategies in Twenty-Three Democracies*. London: Allen and Unwin.
Dalton, Russell J. 2013. *Citizen Politics: Public Opinion and Political Parties in Advanced Industrial Democracies*. Thousand Oaks, CA: Cq Press.
Damhuis, Koen, and Johannes Karremans. 2017. "Responsive to whom? A comparison of the Mitterrand and Hollande presidencies". *West European Politics* 40(6): 1267–1287.
De Sio, Lorenzo, and Till Weber. 2014. "Issue yield: A model of party strategy in multidimensional space". *American Political Science Review* 108(4): 870–885.
Dorussen, Han, and Kyriaki Nanou. 2006. "European integration, intergovernmental bargaining, and convergence of party programmes". *European Union Politics* 7(2): 235–256.
Esping-Andersen, G. 1990. *The Three Worlds of Welfare Capitalism*. Princeton, NJ: Princeton University Press.
ESS. 2002. *ESS Round 1 Source Questionnaire*. London: ESS ERIC Headquarters c/o City University London.
ESS. 2004. *ESS Round 2 Source Questionnaire*. London: ESS ERIC Headquarters c/o City University London.
ESS. 2006. *ESS Round 3 Source Questionnaire*. London: ESS ERIC Headquarters c/o City University London.
ESS. 2008. *ESS Round 4 Source Questionnaire*. London: ESS ERIC Headquarters c/o City University London.
ESS. 2010. *ESS Round 5 Source Questionnaire*. London: ESS ERIC Headquarters c/o City University London.
ESS. 2012. *ESS Round 6 Source Questionnaire*. London: ESS ERIC Headquarters c/o City University London.
ESS. 2014. *ESS Round 7 Source Questionnaire*. London: ESS ERIC Headquarters c/o City University London.
ESS. 2016a. "Appendix 3". European Social Survey, www.europeansocialsurvey.org/docs/round8/survey/ESS8_appendix_a3_e02_1.pdf.
ESS. 2016b. *ESS Round 8 Source Questionnaire*. London: ESS ERIC Headquarters c/o City University London.
ESS. 2018. *ESS Round 9 Source Questionnaire*. London: ESS ERIC Headquarters c/o City University London.
EU. 2020a. "Die 28 Mitgliedstaaten der EU". https://europa.eu/european-union/about-eu/countries_de#eurol%C3%A4nder.
EU. 2020b. "Österreich". https://europa.eu/european-union/about-eu/countries/member-countries/austria_de.
European Commission. 2018. "2018 Annual Report on intra-EU Labour Mobility". Directorate-General for Employment, Social Affairs and Inclusion Directorate D – Labour Mobility Unit D/1 – Free Movement of Workers, EURES.
Häusermann, Silja, Georg Picot, and Dominik Geering. 2012. "Review article: Rethinking party politics and the welfare state: Recent advances in the literature". *British Journal of Political Science* 43(1): 221–240.
Heinisch, Reinhard, and Oscar Mazzoleni. 2016. *Understanding Populist Party Organisation*. London: Palgrave Macmillan.
Hooghe, Liesbet, and Gary Marks. 2018. "Cleavage theory meets Europe's crises: Lipset, Rokkan, and the transnational cleavage". *Journal of European Public Policy* 25(1): 109–135.
IDEA. 2021. "Electoral systems for national legislature – Europe". www.idea.int/data-tools/continent-view/Europe/44.
Karremans, Johannes, and Koen Damhuis. 2020. "The changing face of responsibility: A cross-time comparison of French social democratic governments". *Party Politics* 26(3): 305–316.
Kitschelt, Herbert, and Anthony J. McGann. 1995. *The Radical Right in Western Europe: A Comparative Analysis*. Ann Arbor, MI: University of Michigan Press.
Kriesi, H. 2014. "The populist challenge". *West European Politics* 37(2): 361–378.
Kriesi, H., E. Grande, R. Lachat, M. Dolezal, S. Bornschier, and T. Frey. 2006. "Globalization and the transformation of the national political space: Six European countries compared". *European Journal of Political Research* 45(6): 921–956.

Kriesi, Hanspeter, Edgar Grande, Romain Lachat, Martin Dolezal, Simon Bornschier, and Timotheus Frey. 2008. *West European Politics in the Age of Globalization*. Cambridge: Cambridge University Press.

Kriesi, Hanspeter, Edgar Grande, Martin Dolezal, Marc Helbling, Dominic Höglinger, Sven Hutter, and Bruno Wüest. 2012. *Political Conflict in Western Europe*. Cambridge: Cambridge University Press.

Lefkofridi, Zoe. 2020. "Competition in the European arena: How the rules of the game help nationalists gain". *Politics and Governance* 8(1): 41–49.

Lefkofridi, Zoe, and Juan Casado-Asensio. 2013. "European vox radicis: Representation and policy congruence on the extremes". *Comparative European Politics* 11(1): 93–118.

Lefkofridi, Zoe, and Ken Horvath. 2012. "Migration issues and representation in European liberal democracies". *Representation* 48(1): 29–46.

Lefkofridi, Zoe, and Elie Michel. 2017. "The electoral politics of solidarity: The welfare agendas of radical right parties". In *The Strains of Commitment: The Political Sources of Solidarity in Diverse Societies*, eds Keith Banting and Will Kymlicka, 233–267. Oxford: Oxford University Press.

Lefkofridi, Zoe, and Roula Nezi. 2019. "Responsibility versus responsiveness ... to whom? A theory of party behavior". *Party Politics* 26(3): 1–13.

Lefkofridi, Zoe, Markus Wagner, and Johanna E. Willmann. 2014. "Left-authoritarians and policy representation in Western Europe: Electoral choice across ideological dimensions". *West European Politics* 37(1): 65–90.

Mair, Peter. 2009. "Representative versus Responsible Government". MPIfG Working Paper 09/8, Keulen: Max-Planck-Institut für Gesellschaftsforschung.

Mair, Peter. 2013. *Ruling the Void: The Hollowing of Western Democracy*. London: Verso.

Marks, Gary, and Carole J. Wilson. 2000. "The past in the present: A cleavage theory of party response to European integration". *British Journal of Political Science* 30(3): 433–459.

Meguid, Bonnie. 2008. *Party Competition between Unequals: Strategies and Electoral Fortunes in Western Europe*. Cambridge: Cambridge University Press.

Minkenberg, Michael. 2001. "The radical right in public office: Agenda-setting and policy effects". *West European Politics* 24(4): 1–21.

Mudde, Cas. 2004. "The populist zeitgeist". *Government and Opposition* 39(4): 541–563.

Oesch, Daniel, and Line Rennwald. 2018. "Electoral competition in Europe's new tripolar political space: Class voting for the left, centre-right and radical right". *European Journal of Political Research* 57(4): 783–807.

Parline. 2019a. "Switzerland". http://archive.ipu.org/parline-e/reports/2305.htm.

Parline. 2019b. "Austria". http://archive.ipu.org/parline-e/reports/2017.htm.

Petrocik, John R. 1996. "Issue ownership in presidential elections, with a 1980 case study". *American Journal of Political Science* 40(3): 825–850.

Röth, Leonce, Alexandre Afonso, and Dennis C. Spies. 2018. "The impact of populist radical right parties on socio-economic policies". *European Political Science Review* 10(3): 325–350.

Scharpf, Fritz W. 1997. "Economic integration, democracy and the welfare state". *Journal of European Public Policy* 4(1): 18–36.

Scharpf, Fritz W. 2010. "The asymmetry of European Integration, or why the EU cannot be a social market economy?". *Socio-Economic Review* 8(2): 211–250.

Sjöblom, Gunnar. 1983. "Political change and political accountability: A propositional inventory of causes and effects". In *Western European Party Systems: Continuity and Change*, eds Hans Daadler and Peter Mair, 369–403. London: SAGE.

SP (2019). Organisation. [Online] https://www.sp-ps.ch/de/partei/organisation (accessed 15.12.2019).

SPÖ (2019). Aufbau der Partei. [Online] https://www.spoe.at/das-sind-wir/aufbau-der-partei/ (accessed 15.12.2019).

Thomson, Stuart. 2000. *The Social Democratic Dilemma: Ideology, Governance and Globalization*. Berlin: Springer.

Toshkov, Dimiter, and Laura de Haan. 2013. "The Europeanization of asylum policy: An assessment of the EU impact on asylum applications and recognitions rates". *Journal of European Public Policy* 20(5): 661–683.

Van der Brug, Wouter. 2004. "Issue ownership and party choice". *Electoral Studies* 23(2): 209–233.

Van Spanje, Joost. 2010. "Contagious parties: Anti-immigration parties and their impact on other parties' immigration stances in contemporary Western Europe". *Party Politics* 16(5): 563–586.

Volkens, Andrea, Tobias Burst, Werner Krause, Pola Lehmann, Theres Matthieß, Nicolas Merz, Sven Regel, Bernhard Weßels, and Lisa Zehnter. 2020. *The Manifesto Data Collection. Manifesto Project (MRG/CMP/MARPOR)*. Version 2020b. Berlin: Wissenschaftszentrum Berlin für Sozialforschung. https://doi.org/10.25522/manifesto.mpds.2020b.

14. Institutional sources of trust resilience in diverse societies: The mitigating role of inclusive and egalitarian welfare state institutions
Elif Naz Kayran and Melanie Kolbe

INTRODUCTION

In this chapter, we ask what are the institutional sources of trust resilience in diverse industrialized democracies? More specifically, we investigate whether equal treatment of immigrants by welfare state institutions can mitigate the long-debated corrosive impact of diversity on trust. Defined broadly as the personal understanding that others in the society "will not deliberately or knowingly do us harm, if they can avoid it, and will look after our interests" (Delhey and Newton 2005, 313), generalized trust refers to individualistic beliefs about the whole society rather than feelings about a specific group (Uslaner 2002). Importantly, this individual trait is at the core of how pro-social behavioral outcomes and attitudes, such as social solidarity, are formed. Therefore, generalized trust is central to reinforcing social cohesion at times of increasing social, economic, and political turmoil in the last decades. Yet, ongoing debates surrounding the tension between this foundational element of social cohesion and growing racial diversity due to immigration are far from resolved.

While some studies have revealed a negative link between trust and diversity (Putnam 2007; Alesina and La Ferrara 2002), others have contested such results because the evidence is sensitive to measurement choices and case selection (Sonderskov and Dinesen 2014; Hooghe et al. 2009; Delhey and Newton 2005; Dinesen et al. 2020). Crucially, several authors have pointed to a serious lack of theoretical clarity as to why ethnic heterogeneity should weaken trust (Nannestad 2008; Van der Meer and Tolsma 2014). Considering this wide range of contestation in the field, *if anything*, extant literature confirms the difficulty in understanding this complicated relationship. Nonetheless, academics and policymakers alike require an answer to whether such continuing demographic trends of increasing diversity will have detrimental consequences for the social fabric in advanced democracies. Understanding how generalized trust can be preserved thus emerges as a valuable and timely research agenda. Therefore, in this chapter we intend to contribute to this rich debate by providing an overview of the previous work that studied this contentious link between diversity and trust and identify several areas that deserve further inquiry. Next, considering this review, we develop and evaluate an original argument adding to existing evidence.

The research gap we concentrate on concerns whether there are institutional sources of trust resilience in diverse societies that can explain cross-country variation in the presumed negative impact of immigration on generalized trust. While much of the earlier work has been concerned with testing and demonstrating whether higher diversity indeed predicts lower trust, little has been understood about factors that may mitigate this link. Moreover, socio-economic institutions, namely welfare state arrangements, have often been studied as dependent variables influenced by immigration and diversity but are rarely seen as mitigators themselves. Instead, here, we turn to the welfare institutions to grasp the extent to which and through what mechanisms such policies can mitigate the link between diversity and trust – an otherwise understudied topic in the literature.

Our appraisal of the institutional theories of generalized trust informs the novel argument and empirical analysis we conduct in this chapter. We thereby move the debates further by going beyond testing multiculturalism effects and welfare state norms separately. We contend that the extent to which welfare institutions treat immigrants non-discriminately, relative to their treatment of citizens, may have a mediating role in absorbing the negative impact of diversity/immigration on trust. To test our theoretical argument and hypotheses, we conduct an original analysis of 17 European countries from 2002 to 2018 using the European Social Survey (ESS) and a new cross-national comparative indicator of immigrant exclusion index that systematically quantifies relative treatment differences between citizens and immigrants in the context of social benefits (Koning 2020). We indeed find that higher ethnic diversity and negative attitudes towards such diversity are correlated with lower trust. When looking at the environmental effect of exposure to foreigners, we do not find a mitigating effect of institutions. However, we see a remarkably robust conditioning effect suggesting that the link between anti-diversity attitudes and mistrust is weaker in contexts where welfare institutions treat immigrants more equally.

A CRISIS OF TRUST IN DIVERSE SOCIETIES?

Since Putnam's (2007) *E Pluribus Unum* address on the corrosive effects of racial diversity on generalized trust, civic engagement, and public participation, the topic of how diversity influences social cohesion has developed into a small cottage industry. While prior work has already demonstrated a negative impact of ethnic diversity on trust in the United States and Canada (Alesina and La Ferrara 2002; Soroka et al. 2006), since Putnam's contentious study, many have further tested whether demographic heterogeneity and diversity influences trust among citizens (Bjornskov 2007; Van der Meer and Tolsma 2014; Dinesen and Sonderskov 2015). Despite a wealth of empirical evidence, these past research efforts seem to have led to mixed results. Notably, the *hunkering-down* effect put forward by Putnam "connecting more racially populated neighborhoods with lower social trust" has received criticism on the grounds of the ambiguity of the mechanisms as to why such a decline is observed and the generalizability of the effect beyond the North American context (Marschall and Stolle 2004; Hooghe et al. 2009). Most recently, a comprehensive meta-analysis of 87 studies investigating the link between diversity and trust document that despite considerable variation on effect sizes between studies, there is a negative relationship between higher demographic diversity and generalized trust (Dinesen et al. 2020). Even though we are currently far from a consensus on the mechanisms leading to trust decline due to diversity, two inter-related logics have been suggested: one concentrates on the contextual effects while the other emphasizes subjective attitudes towards diversity perceptions.

The first explanation takes stock of the social psychology theoretical frameworks of group conflict theory and social theory (Tajfel 1982; Jackson 1993; Olzak 1995). This logic operates as "mere exposure" to people of different ethnic backgrounds (mostly in residential areas), leading to weaker trust (Sonderskov and Dinesen 2014). The mechanism considers how the size of the ethnic out-groups can generate a feeling of threat amongst majority group members over "scarce material or immaterial resources such as jobs, housing, power, safety, morality, and identity" (Van der Meer and Tolsma 2014, 463). Therefore, this environmental exposure to newcomers and ethnically dissimilar or culturally distant groups leads to socio-tropic anxiety and fears about personal well-being explaining the eventual *hunkering down* and withdrawal from collective and social life (Putnam 2007). Importantly, such a retreat and subsequent distrust is attributed to not just distrust of out-groups but spills over to a general decline in "*both* in-group and out-group solidarity – that is, both bonding *and* bridging social capital" (Putnam 2007, 144).

Second, the corrosive effects of diversity on social cohesion have also been studied with a focus on the subjective attitudinal dynamics at the micro level, which is to say how diversity is perceived among native residents of host societies (Emmenegger and Klemmensen 2013; Finseraas 2008). For instance, scholars seem to agree that citizens view foreigners as less likely to respect the rules and norms of the host society, engage more in cheating behavior, and disproportionately use the scarce material resources of the country (Reeskens and van Oorschot 2012; Reeskens and Van der Meer 2019; Kymlicka 2015). This mechanism differs from the "mere exposure" logic, which relies on the effect of the presence and size of out-groups. It instead emphasizes how the downward impact of diversity on trust is due to the negative views that citizens hold towards immigrants as detrimental to trust regardless of the objective presence of ethnic diversity. Such subjective attitudes lead to anomie among individuals, where citizens no longer exhibit feelings of shared societal norms and moral values (Van der Meer and Tolsma 2014, 464). This, in turn, translates into feelings of disunity and distrust among diverse and multicultural societies (Alesina and Glaeser 2004; Alesina and La Ferrara 2002).

Overall, earlier work paints a rather pessimistic picture of the sustainability of social cohesion and trust, mainly due to the rise of immigration-induced diversity in the last two decades. Yet, there are several reasons why this clear conception of the link between diversity and trust may be problematic. As well documented by meta-reviews of the field, evidence supporting this claim is relatively weak and mixed at best (Van der Meer and Tolsma 2014; Dinesen et al. 2020). A substantive portion of earlier work reported no evidence of such a relationship with negligible effect sizes (Hooghe et al. 2009; Portes and Vickstrom 2011). This is especially concerning when many of these earlier works have focused on cross-sectional evidence or single-case studies without paying attention to how trust and diversity interact over time in different contexts. It means that while being adequate in explaining individual differences in certain places, such research designs are ill-fitted to support arguments that assume a reactive decline of trust because of rising immigration.

Most recently, studies with a careful focus on causality that use longitudinal panel evidence from Dutch, Swiss, and Danish cases demonstrate that trust is indeed malleable and time-variant (Seifert 2018; Sonderskov and Dinesen 2014). On the surface, this seems to add credence to the argument that such a trait could be reactively changing due to rising diversity in the last decades. Yet, the dynamics of diversity and trust seem to be mitigated by how citizens engage with existing socio-economic and political institutions (Kesler and Bloemraad 2010; Seifert 2018). Moreover, this link is also influenced by native citizens' interaction frequency and the quality of contact they have with these groups (Stolle 2002; Stolle et al. 2013; Dinesen and Sonderskov 2015). Overall, evidence points to critical mitigators of a relationship between diversity and trust that is mostly missing in earlier work.

Finally, despite such a demonstrable influence of institutions, there has been a surprising lack of attention when thinking of these environmental factors as potential backstops for preserving trust. This is surprising because it has become a commonplace observation in recent years that the trust erosion argument has not been observed equally strongly in many European welfare states (Rothstein 2017; Crepaz 2008; Crepaz and Damron 2009). Chief factors suggested on this front have been welfare state institutions and integration policies managing the ethnic relations offsetting this crisis of trust in the face of ethnic diversity (Kesler and Bloemraad 2010; Gundelach and Manatschal 2017). This means that it is time for a turn in the field, moving away from merely looking at testing whether higher diversity predicts (lower) trust to testing what kind of policy and institutional factors may be influential in shaping this complex link.

STATE OF THE LITERATURE OF THE INSTITUTIONAL SOURCES OF TRUST

Despite the relatively scant attention paid to institutions' conditioning role on the relationship between diversity and trust, there is a rich literature focusing on how trust and state institutions are linked. To grasp why such contextual factors may play a role when mitigating social cohesion in diversity conditions, we turn to the literature on the institutional sources of generalized trust. We cluster such institutional effects in two broad groups focusing on regulatory and governing institutions on the one hand and institutions managing the socio-economic and cultural dimensions on the other. Regulatory institutions mean bureaucratic offices and actors, such as the police, the military, and the judicial system. In contrast, examples of governing institutions include the national government, political parties, parliaments, and politicians. Regarding socio-economic institutions, we primarily focus on welfare state programs and concentrate on multiculturalism and integration policies when looking at diversity-managing cultural institutions.

Regulatory and Governing Institutions

Good governance and fair treatment of the regulatory and governing institutions in a country are robust and positive predictors of higher generalized trust (Zak and Knack 2001; Knight 2001; Uslaner 2002). For instance, studies document that governance and democratic deficits such as revolutionary coups, civic unrest, and the presence of a dominant shadow economy negatively correlate with trust, whereas contract enforceability, quality of democracy, and the rule of law relate positively (Beugelsdijk 2006). Such a relationship between better practices among regulatory and governing branches and higher trust holds both when such contextual effects are measured using objective national-level indicators and when studies use micro-level survey items capturing citizens' perceptions towards these institutions subjectively (Johnston et al. 2017). Illustrating the latter, distrust and negative views of such institutions are some of the most reliable predictors of lower generalized trust (Seifert 2018). Even though institutions' conditional effects are not well understood when it comes to the negative impact of diversity on trust, looking at this strong correlation's mechanisms could be highly informative.

Most notably, studies seem to point to the idea that institutions reduce fears and anxieties over potential negative consequences of corruption, opportunistic strategies, and unpredictable behavior, which makes individuals' experience and lives orderly and unpredictable (Rothstein and Uslaner 2005; Rothstein and Stolle 2008). If there is stronger confidence in the way policies are governed fairly and equally, such confidence translates into higher social trust concerning members of the society as well (Rothstein 2017, 320–321). This means that the negative impact of increasing demographic heterogeneity on trust may look vastly different depending on whether regulatory and governing institutions in a country uphold the principles of fairness, transparency, and good governance – and are perceived as such by citizens.

Socio-economic and Cultural Institutions: Welfare States and Diversity-Managing Policies

The crux of understanding how welfare state institutions relate to trust lies in recognizing the strong negative link between inequality and social cohesion. Income and wealth inequalities reduce the sense of shared fate and collective action in a society (Delhey and Newton 2005). An uneven distribution of economic resources fosters individualistic and self-interested views leading to alienation from collective actions and trust in others (Rothstein and Uslaner 2005). In this respect, welfare state institutions come into play by mitigating, governing, and dampening the economic inequality in societies caused by markets (Pontusson 2005). Ultimately, if strong welfare state institutions can keep economic disparities and the effects of market volatilities on people's lives in check, this builds trust and solidarity (Kumlin and Rothstein 2005; Kymlicka 2015). While there are debates concerning the causal arrow between welfare institutions and higher trust (Hooghe and Stolle 2003; Uslaner 2002; Alesina and Glaeser 2004), evidence has shown a robust correlation between universal welfare states that can socialize market risks and higher trust (Banting and Kymlicka 2017; Rothstein 1998; Crepaz 2008).

Regardless of what came first, an essential consideration for answering whether welfare institutions can build resilience against the corrosive effect of diversity is related to the divide between universal welfare states and other regimes. It has long been observed that universal welfare states, such as in the cases of Norway, Sweden, Finland, and Denmark, not only exhibit higher levels of trust but also have been able to preserve relatively more substantial generalized trust levels despite increasing ethnic diversity due to immigration (Rothstein and Uslaner 2005). Rothstein and Stolle make sense of this resilience of trust in universal welfare states by drawing a connection between welfare functions and the societal norms of "impartiality, fairness and efficiency" that they instill (2008). This link, from a more operational logic, suggests lower perceptions of cheating, arbitrariness, and discrimination among citizens regarding their views about public institutions (Rothstein 2001). Such opinions are stronger where universal welfare state regimes apply a strict rule of equal treatment and non-particularistic functioning of socio-economic institutions.

Due to a strong sense of egalitarianism and non-discretion, universal welfare regimes have been able to beget and preserve higher trust among citizens, even in higher diversity conditions (Rothstein and Uslaner 2005).

Next, we focus on how diversity-managing institutions (i.e., integration policy and multiculturalism) impact trust (Kesler and Bloemraad 2010; Crepaz 2008). Two findings stand out in this field. First, policy contexts that foster better integration of ethnic minorities and immigrants lead to higher trust. For instance, less segregated distribution of ethnic groups across the territory of the host country seems to alleviate the negative impact of diversity on trust. This is explained by the fact that non-segregation reduces the chances of disproportionate exposure to demographic heterogeneity by majority group members (Uslaner 2012). Moreover, an even distribution of diversity increases the chances of more frequent (and more positive) inter-ethnic contact opportunities (Van der Meer and Tolsma 2014). Likewise, inclusive integration policies mitigate real and perceived differences between ethnic groups, fostering social cohesion in diverse societies (Bloemraad and Wright 2014). Policies ameliorating immigrants' employability and laws against non-equal treatment lessen the perceived cultural and social distances, dampening the erosion of trust (Gundelach and Manatschal 2017). While there is evidence supporting this proposition concerning the impact of socio-economic and cultural policies separately (Zimdars and Tampubolon 2012; Lupo 2010), very few studies have so far concentrated on the precise logic of equal treatment of institutions when looking at its mitigating effect on the relationship between diversity and generalized trust (Kesler and Bloemraad 2010). Importantly, due in significant part to a comparative dearth of data, no study has systematically studied either the direct or the conditioning effect of whether treating immigrants as equal – relative to citizens – can dampen the perceived socio-cultural proximities and subsequent lower trust in host societies.

Finally, there is a demonstrable positive link between multiculturalism policies – as opposed to assimilationist strategies and cultural policy regimes paying little attention to the recognition and rights of minorities – and more social cohesion, trust, and solidarity (Banting and Kymlicka 2006). Crepaz explains the trust-constructive role of such multiculturalism efforts by their leveling, signaling, and destigmatizing effects on society, altering both the natives' subjective perceptions towards diversity and the immigrants' objective position in the communities simultaneously (2008). Multicultural policies giving voice, affirmative action, and an equal footing to immigrants and minorities in the host societies reduce the opportunity gaps between immigrants and citizens (Crepaz 2008, 257). These strengthen immigrants' position in the host society as equal community members, removing the stigma often predicated on them. Based on these logics, cultural policies that can position minorities and racial groups as equal members of society may develop some resilience against diversity's trust-eroding effects.

ARGUMENT: EQUAL TREATMENT PRACTICES IN INSTITUTIONS DAMPEN THE NEGATIVE EFFECT OF DIVERSITY ON TRUST

Our theoretical framework brings together two emerging claims from the extant literature: so far, we have discussed the evidence concerning the trust-building role of universal welfare institutions on the one hand and the social distance-removing function of liberal and inclusive diversity-managing policies on the other. Given such insights, our novel argument in this chapter focuses on how the non-discriminatory treatment of immigrants and minorities by institutions can strengthen trust in diverse societies. To the best of our knowledge, existing work has not yet systematically studied whether equal treatment of immigrants in the domain of socio-economic policies can mitigate the impact of diversity on generalized trust. These institutional characteristics may influence trust as a direct and/or conditional effect.

Starting with the direct impact, our first proposition centers on environmental channels of norm diffusion and policy feedback effects of existing governing structures on social cohesion and solidarity (Sainsbury 2012; Reeskens and van Oorschot 2012; Larsen 2008). This argument is still on familiar ground as earlier studies of welfare chauvinism have already demonstrated higher levels of nativist reaction to immigrant inclusion to social benefits in liberal and conservative regimes when compared to universalistic social-democratic welfare states (van der Waal et al. 2013). Welfare regimes that are universal, i.e., treating people equally, and more decommodifying, i.e., decoupling individuals from the effects of market volatility, boost social solidarity and trust (Crepaz and Damron 2009; Crepaz 2008). Likewise, we suggest that the extent to which immigrants are treated more closely to how citizens are treated by welfare institutions may have the potential to protect trust in diverse societies by removing the stigma and negatively connoted out-group categorizations predicated upon immigrants. The more socio-economic institutions treat immigrants as equal members of the community, giving them the same chances of access to the country's public resources, the less such ethnic groups will be perceived as distant. This leads us to formulate our first hypothesis as follows.

Hypothesis 1: Socio-economic institutions that treat immigrants and citizens equally enhance generalized trust.

In this direct conception of policy effects, welfare state institutions' structure and operation are defined as exogenous external factors related to building trust by reducing social distance and enhancing shared fates. Admittedly, this is less informative concerning a resilience-building role of preserving trust when faced with diversity due to increasing immigration. Moreover, Bloemraad suggests, for instance, that the well-documented solidarity and trust-building role of multiculturalism policies' effect on social cohesion is not so applicable outside of a few exceptional cases such as the Canadian context (2017). The author contends that such a direct impact of institutions on individual-level traits – such as trust – are context specific and highly dependent on the origins and development processes of national welfare and cultural institutions. Thus, a direct impact of institutions on social cohesion at the individual level may be unobservable and difficult to assess in comparative research designs.

With these considerations in mind, we take a substantively different approach from focusing only on the direct relationship between institutions and trust and instead turn to how non-discriminatory welfare institutions shape trust by mitigating the negative (i.e., hunkering-down) effect of diversity. Building on the previous mechanisms identifying how diversity weakens social cohesion, we study institutions' conditioning effect on generalized trust in two ways. The first channel of why diversity weakens trust emphasizes residential exposure and proximity to ethnic diversity focusing on the numbers and the share of out-groups (Putnam 2007; Van der Meer and Tolsma 2014; Alesina and La Ferrara 2002). Consequently, economic or culturally rooted grievances lead people to retreat from collective life resulting in social isolation and subsequent lower trust amongst members of the society. The second channel attributed a more significant role to subjective rather than objective exposure to diversity (Reeskens and Van der Meer 2019; Emmenegger and Klemmensen 2013). Regardless of whether individuals are objectively exposed to demographic heterogeneity in the host country, negative attitudes towards diversity and the unfamiliarity with newcomers lessen citizens' sense of shared community leading to lower trust. Yet, here, we add that both mechanisms may be influenced by how state institutions treat diverse groups. Thus, the corrosive effect of diversity or anti-diversity sentiments may not be critical in every country context.

Focusing on Denmark, Germany, and the Netherlands, Larsen empirically demonstrates that social programs that visibly show a solidaristic treatment towards immigrants have a robust positive correlation with a higher willingness among citizens of sharing economic resources with immigrants (Larsen 2020). Having equal categories when thinking of access to welfare benefit and public resources is vital because "selective benefits can lock societies into an unending conversation about deservingness, while universal benefits seem to dampen discussion of the legitimacy of diverse groups of recipients" (Banting and Kymlicka 2017, 28). Thus, the way welfare institutions treat immigrants has a non-negligible influence on the way immigrants' position in society is understood by the majority group members. If citizens see that immigrant residents are treated as equal and given recognition concerning their social policy needs by the political structures and institutional regimes, this can convey their similarity, familiarity, and belonging to the nation. This could, then, dampen the effect of exposure and skepticism towards such groups on inter-personal trust by mitigating such *hunkering-down* mechanisms. This leads us to formulate the following hypothesis:

Hypothesis 2a: *Socio-economic institutions that treat immigrants and citizens equally dampen the contextual effect of diversity on generalized trust.*

Next, even if visible minorities and cultural distance may result in potentially insurmountable differences in how diversity is perceived by citizens (Reeskens and Van der Meer 2019). Yet, removing at least the economic categorizations and the stigmatizing discriminatory treatment of immigrants can nevertheless have a role in preserving the collective sense of shared fates and trust in diverse societies. This can attenuate how attitudes towards these out-groups influence generalized trust in the society. Therefore, the framework we develop here leads also to the following testable hypothesis concerning the conditioning effect of immigrant-inclusive and non-discriminatory welfare institutions on the negative relationship between attitudes towards diversity and generalized trust.

Hypothesis 2b: *Socio-economic institutions that treat immigrants and citizens equally dampen the effect of attitudes towards diversity on generalized trust.*

EMPIRICAL ANALYSIS: THE MITIGATING ROLE OF INSTITUTIONAL EQUALITY ON POLITICAL TRUST AND DIVERSITY IN 17 EUROPEAN COUNTRIES

The purpose of our analysis is to examine how varying immigrant inclusion and non-discriminatory treatment by national institutions mitigate the effect of diversity on trust. Considering the wealth of evidence from North America, we concentrate on the European region, where diversity exists not just because of racial cleavages between minority and majority populations but has been a contentious phenomenon due to increasing immigration rates (Hooghe et al. 2009). To test our hypotheses, we use data from the ESS, which contains several question items of generalized trust precisely fit for the analysis we aim to conduct here, concentrating on a sample of citizens in each respective country. ESS is a cross-sectional survey project implemented in nine waves, covering a temporal period of about two decades from 2002 to 2018. We use all available ESS waves from 17 West European countries with similar democratic and socio-economic institutional contexts and with comparable historical experiences with diversity.[1]

Measurement of Variables and Descriptive Results

By and large, survey indicators of solidarity, trust, social capital, civic participation, and various other pro-social attitudes and behavior are strongly correlated. Despite this, here, we precisely focus on the concept of generalized trust, considering the measurement-sensitive results in earlier work (Kesler and Bloemraad 2010; Van der Meer and Tolsma 2014). Therefore, we measure our dependent variable using a three-item index scale well established in previous work on the topic as a reliable cross-cultural indicator of generalized trust (Reeskens and Hooghe 2008). Our dependent variable is composed of the questions on whether respondents think that "most people can be trusted", "most people try to take advantage of you or try to be fair", and "most of the time people are helpful or look out for themselves". We scale our index to vary from 0 to 10, where higher values indicate more trust (Cronbach's *alpha* reported is 0.7595).

To measure our key independent variables, we also collect national-level data on diversity, institutions, and other theoretically relevant factors. We capture the effect of diversity in two ways following our hypotheses 2a and 2b. First, we measure ethnic heterogeneity at the contextual level with data from the Organisation for Economic Co-operation and Development (OECD) on the stock of foreigners as a share of the population at the national level. While non-specific when it comes to the characteristics of the foreign population itself, this measure is a comprehensive indicator of diversity amongst societies. Over the scope of our analysis, immigration has been a vital component of European societies' demographic fabric. The average of diversity is about 8 percent in our sample. Notably, even many of the countries that do not characterize themselves as traditional immigration societies, such as Germany and the Netherlands, reach well above 10 percent (or higher) shares of foreigners in the 2002 to 2018 period (see Figure 14.1).[2] Moreover, average trust in these European societies seems to be relatively time-constant (or slow-moving), displaying only minor variation over this period. Merely looking at this national-level aggregated relationship between trust and diversity demonstrates no direct correlation between these factors. As Figure 14.1 displays, the diversity differences are not strikingly or

Institutional sources of trust resilience in diverse societies 285

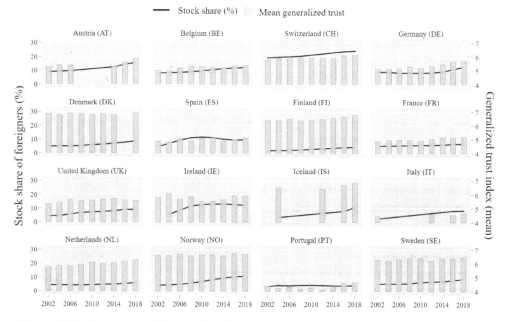

Figure 14.1   Diversity and generalized trust in Europe

systematically different between countries on the higher end of the average trust, such as the Netherlands, Norway, Sweden, or Finland, compared to those at the lower end, such as Italy, Portugal, and Spain.

Next, we suggested a second way in which diversity may impact trust through a mechanism at the individual level. To measure how citizens perceive the impact of diversity on their society, we create a three-item index available across all ESS waves. The question items we use allow us to have information on the diversity attitudes concerning immigrants' effect on the country's cultural, economic, and general well-being. We scale our index to vary from 0 to 10, where higher values indicate more skeptical views about diversity (Cronbach's *alpha* reported is 0.8510). As expected, countries with higher trust are at the lower end of these anti-immigration attitudes, such as Finland, Sweden, and Switzerland. Likewise, countries at the lower end of the generalized trust index, such as Italy and Portugal, rank the highest when looking at skepticism about diversity effects.

To measure our conceptualization of equal immigrant treatment in welfare institutions, we use a new indicator developed by Edward Anthony Koning entitled "Immigrant Exclusion from Social Programs Index (IESPI)", which is uniquely fit for our analysis here (see Figure 14.2). There have been several systematic comparative accounts aimed at quantifying generosity of immigrant integration policy and social rights access on the one hand (Solano and Huddleston 2020; Helbling et al. 2017), and universality of social programs at large on the other (Scruggs et al. 2017; Nelson et al. 2020). However, the IESPI is the first study systematically documenting the relative treatment of immigrants versus natives comparatively across many cases over time. Therefore, it is ideal for

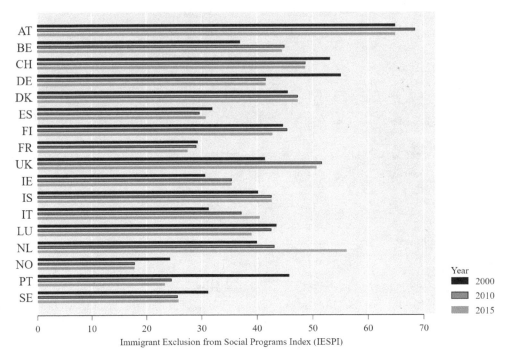

Figure 14.2 Immigrant exclusion from social institutions in Europe

capturing discrimination regardless of the absolute levels of socio-economic or diversity policy designs.

The IESPI uses the framework developed by Koning (2019), focusing on the criteria for differentiation in treatment between citizens and immigrants. The stringency of such conditionalities put upon immigrants is indicated by concentrating on residence status, duration, location of immigrants' residence, integration success criteria, and whether these benefits are exclusively available to only a particular group of the population (Koning 2020, 6). The index includes differentiation in seven core programs: tax-paid benefits, contributory pension benefits, public health care, contributory unemployment benefits, housing benefits, social assistance, and active labor market benefits. For more details about the methodology of the index's composition and coding, see Koning's article introducing and describing the IESPI data (2020).

Overall, the aggregated IESPI comprises 25 indicators for four time points (1990, 2000, 2010, 2015). Given our temporal focus, we use the most recent three data points in IESPI matched to relevant ESS rounds respecting time ordering.[3] Higher values on the index mean that the country's social institutions exclude immigrants relatively more strongly, indicating more discriminatory treatment. Figure 14.2 displays that with the notable exceptions of the Netherlands and the United Kingdom, which have grown markedly more exclusive compared to 2000, other cases either have remained relatively stable or became more inclusive over time. We also see stronger relative inclusiveness in traditional universal welfare states such as Sweden, Finland, and Norway. In contrast, the opposite holds in the corporatist welfare states of Europe, such as Austria and Germany, hinting at an institutional path dependency when it comes to the universality logic in welfare and socio-economic institutions and diversity management.

Since we combine nine waves of ESS data at the individual level with country-level variables, we end up with a large dataset with a hierarchical structure, where individuals are nested within countries each year (Hox 2010). Therefore, we use three-level linear mixed-effects models to avoid anti-conservative bias and reduce potential inconsistency in our coefficient estimations (Schmidt-Catran and Fairbrother 2016). To better isolate the direct and the conditional effects of equal treatment in institutions and diversity on trust, we control for several theoretically relevant potential confounders at both levels of analysis. At the macro level, informed by earlier contextual predictors of trust, we control for economic inequality (using the Gini index), unemployment rate (in share percentage of the workforce), and economic growth (real gross domestic product growth from the previous year) in our models (Armingeon et al. 2020).

At the individual level, we add an indicator of the life satisfaction of respondents in our equation. We also add satisfaction with government and democratic institutions of the country to control for respondents' perceptions and engagement with these governing and regulatory institutions at the micro level. Next, we account for the socio-economic status differences. We include respondents' subjective well-being measured by their reflections on their household income and their objective employment status. We add a series of socio-demographic factors such as age, gender, education, religiosity, and whether the respondent has an immigration background themselves to our models. Finally, given that urban areas display lower trust than rural areas, we add a categorical variable capturing the respondents' residential area characteristics.

Findings

Does diversity harm trust? Table 14.1 presents the results from four linear mixed-effects models to answer this question. Model 1 is fully specified except for the equal treatment in the social programs (IESPI) variable, while Model 2 adds this factor. Models 3 and 4 test our conditional hypotheses interacting diversity and diversity attitudes with the IESPI, respectively. Table 14.1 provides evidence in line with a negative relationship between demographic heterogeneity and trust in European societies. In both Models 1 and 2, our contextual diversity measure of foreigners' stock share is negatively correlated with higher generalized trust. This negative relationship is corroborated by the attitudinal mechanism as well. Across the board, skepticism about the effects of diversity predicts lower generalized trust. These findings do not come as a surprise considering existing evidence (Dinesen et al. 2020). Our results show that diversity has a robust and direct dampening effect on trust, using both environmental and attitudinal measures.

When looking at other covariates at the micro and macro levels, our results align with previous work and find that personal, political, and institutional satisfaction correlate positively with higher trust (Hooghe et al. 2009; Nannestad 2008). Compared to those individuals with a more secure economic status, those who perceive their well-being as more uncomfortable and those facing more economic difficulty have lower trust levels. Concerning demographic and civic factors, being a woman and being older, living in rural

Table 14.1 *Diversity, unequal treatment, and generalized trust: direct and indirect effects*

	Model 1	Model 2	Model 3	Model 4
Stock share of immigrants (%)	−0.013**	−0.013*	0.022	−0.013*
	(0.005)	(0.005)	(0.035)	(0.005)
Anti-immigration attitudes	−0.182***	−0.182***	−0.182***	−0.136***
	(0.002)	(0.002)	(0.002)	(0.006)
Immigrant Exclusion index (IESPI)		−0.001	0.006	0.004
		(0.003)	(0.007)	(0.003)
Stock share of immigrants*IESPI			−0.001	
			(0.001)	
Anti-immigration attitudes*IESPI				−0.001***
				(0.000)
Individual-level control variables				
Life satisfaction	0.136***	0.136***	0.136***	0.136***
	(0.002)	(0.002)	(0.002)	(0.002)
Government satisfaction	0.062***	0.062***	0.062***	0.062***
	(0.002)	(0.002)	(0.002)	(0.002)
Democratic satisfaction	0.090***	0.090***	0.090***	0.090***
	(0.002)	(0.002)	(0.002)	(0.002)
Economic well-being (ref: living comfortably on present income)				
Coping on present income	−0.112***	−0.112***	−0.112***	−0.112***
	(0.008)	(0.008)	(0.008)	(0.008)
Difficult on present income	−0.208***	−0.208***	−0.208***	−0.208***
	(0.012)	(0.012)	(0.012)	(0.012)
Very difficult on present income	−0.320***	−0.320***	−0.320***	−0.320***
	(0.020)	(0.020)	(0.020)	(0.020)
Age	0.007***	0.007***	0.007***	0.007***
	(0.000)	(0.000)	(0.000)	(0.000)
Female	0.111***	0.111***	0.111***	0.111***
	(0.007)	(0.007)	(0.007)	(0.007)
Education	0.024***	0.024***	0.024***	0.024***
	(0.001)	(0.001)	(0.001)	(0.001)
Religiosity	0.010***	0.010***	0.010***	0.010***
	(0.001)	(0.001)	(0.001)	(0.001)
Born in the country	0.362***	0.362***	0.362***	0.362***
	(0.014)	(0.014)	(0.014)	(0.014)
Employment status (ref: employee)				
Self-employed	−0.079***	−0.079***	−0.079***	−0.080***
	(0.013)	(0.013)	(0.013)	(0.013)
In training	0.062***	0.062***	0.062***	0.061***
	(0.014)	(0.014)	(0.014)	(0.014)
Retired	−0.052***	−0.052***	−0.052***	−0.052***
	(0.012)	(0.012)	(0.012)	(0.012)
Unemployed	−0.032*	−0.032*	−0.032*	−0.032*
	(0.016)	(0.016)	(0.016)	(0.016)

Table 14.1 (continued)

	Model 1	Model 2	Model 3	Model 4
Other employment status	−0.084***	−0.084***	−0.084***	−0.085***
	(0.011)	(0.011)	(0.011)	(0.011)
Residential areas (ref: big city)				
Suburbs or outskirts of big city	−0.022	−0.022	−0.022	−0.021
	(0.012)	(0.012)	(0.012)	(0.012)
Town or small city	0.025*	0.025*	0.025*	0.025*
	(0.010)	(0.010)	(0.010)	(0.010)
Country village	0.105***	0.105***	0.105***	0.106***
	(0.011)	(0.011)	(0.011)	(0.011)
Farm/home in countryside	0.165***	0.165***	0.165***	0.165***
	(0.015)	(0.015)	(0.015)	(0.015)
Country-level control variables				
Economic growth	0.008	0.007	0.007	0.008
	(0.015)	(0.015)	(0.015)	(0.015)
Income inequality (Gini)	−0.076***	−0.076***	−0.074***	−0.076***
	(0.010)	(0.010)	(0.010)	(0.010)
Unemployment rate (%)	−0.019*	−0.020*	−0.022*	−0.020*
	(0.008)	(0.009)	(0.009)	(0.009)
BIC	740226.7	740275.5	740286.7	740228.1
N observations	204,724	204,724	204,724	204,724
N groups: country	17	17	17	17
N groups: year	9	9	9	9
Intercept (constant)	6.288	6.320	5.998	6.110
	(0.284)	(0.300)	(0.434)	(0.301)
Country intercept variance	0.107	0.107	0.106	0.107
	(0.014)	(0.014)	(0.013)	(0.014)
Year intercept variance	0.000	0.000	0.000	0.000
	(0.000)	(0.000)	(0.000)	(0.000)

Note: Standard errors in parentheses; *** $p < 0.001$, ** $p < 0.01$, * $p < 0.05$.

areas, having more education, frequent attendance to religious events, and not having an immigration background correlate with higher trust. As expected, at the country level, higher levels of inequality and unemployment rate correlate with lower trust across all our models.

Let us now turn to the question concerning not just the link between diversity and trust, but whether institutional inclusion and non-discrimination towards immigrants has discernible effects. First, we wanted to test the following proposition as formulated in Hypothesis 1: do socio-economic institutions that are more exclusive have a negative relationship with trust? In Table 14.1, we added the direct effect of the IESPI variable to our equation in Model 2. We found that micro-level differences of trust are not predicted by this institutional factor at $p < 0.05$. This result means that some of the earlier concerns vocalized by Bloemraad may have been right (2017). Yet, this does not mean that institutions have no role in mitigating the relationship between diversity and trust.

If our second set of hypotheses concerning the conditioning effect of equal treatment can be supported, our models should return statistically significant results for our interaction terms between the share of immigrants at the national level and IESPI (see Model 3) and between attitudes towards immigration and IESPI (see Model 4). This is partially what we find in Table 14.1. While the interaction coefficient estimated in Model 3 tests Hypothesis 2a, Model 4 introduces the interaction term to test Hypothesis 2b. Looking at Table 14.1, there seems to be no impact of institutions on dampening the environmental exposure to diversity on trust, revealing no evidence for Hypothesis 2a. However, when looking at the negative effect of skepticism towards diversity, IESPI seems to mitigate how such attitudes relate to trust. More precisely, on the IESPI, going from contexts that treat immigrants more equally to those that treat them more discriminatorily seems to strengthen the negative impact anti-diversity attitudes have on trust. This means that diversity attitudes of people living in countries where welfare institutions treat immigrants more equally have less of an impact on influencing the generalized trust attitudes they hold. This can, thus, beget stronger resilience of trust in such contexts. To facilitate the interpretation of these interaction results, Figure 14.3 presents the marginal effects of diversity (3a) and diversity attitudes (3b) across various levels of immigrant exclusion in social institutions.

The visualization of the impact of ethnic heterogeneity in Figure 14.3a demonstrates once again that this negative link between diversity and trust does not change as a function of institutional treatment and characteristics (at the $p < 0.05$ level). It should nevertheless be noted that the negative effect of higher heterogeneity is larger in size at higher values of the IESPI variable. Turning to the plot in Figure 14.3b, we can now observe the dampening effect of inclusivity on the corrosive impact of anti-diversity attitudes on trust. This seems to be exactly in line with what scholars such as Crepaz (2008), Banting and Kymlicka (2006, 2017), and Larsen (2020, 2008) have documented. Wherever immigrants are treated more equally to natives and questions of deservingness and access are put to rest, skepticism about these out-groups have a lesser impact on social cohesion in a society. Focusing on inter-personal generalized trust, our findings are clearly in line with these arguments in the literature.

We would also like to address several issues about our empirical results that require further discussion. The first is concerned with our model specification. In our fully specified equations, we include the IESPI variable indicative of the relative treatment differences between citizens and immigrants. One objection could be that our omission of the absolute level of socio-economic programs in our models can bias our estimations. Without considering the baseline of social policy in each country, these relative differences may indicate more generous provisions in inclusive societies. To account for this, we replicate our models by adding *total social expenditure* as the share percentage of each country's gross domestic product in our estimations. Second, checking for the issue of confounding more broadly, while we excluded a modeling strategy that introduced country and year fixed effects because we are theoretically interested in between-country differences and not within-country changes, we ensure that period effects do not alter our findings. Thus, we replicate our results by adding a *year dummy* in the models.

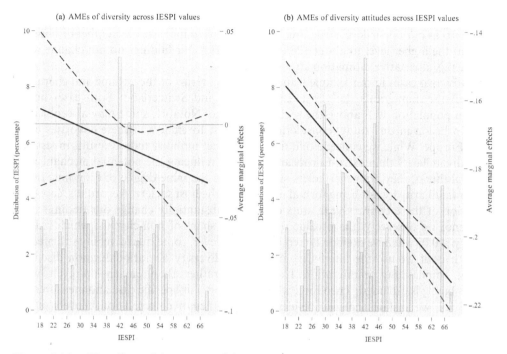

Figure 14.3 The effect of diversity and diversity attitudes on trust as immigrant exclusion from institutions changes, 95 percent confidence intervals

Moreover, while we already include substantively influential subjective factors such as satisfaction with the democratic institutions and government in our models, we check the sensitivity of our results with the inclusion of theoretically relevant correlates of generalized trust such as *trust in the parliament, the legal system, the police, politicians, and satisfaction with the economy and the education and health systems* of the country. Overall, our results are remarkably robust to these changes in the model specification at micro and macro levels.

Third, we alternate our measure of diversity captured at the national level. Our primary operationalization indicates the share of diversity based on citizenship, i.e., *foreigners*. We have chosen to use this measure because of its wider availability and cross-national comparability, considering the different registry rules in various countries regarding citizens with an immigration background. Nevertheless, our results do not change using an alternative measure of diversity focusing instead on differences based on immigration background, i.e., *foreign-born residents*. We also report the same findings when using the *inflow* of immigration each year instead of the stock share of foreigners as a measure of ethnic diversity at the national level.

Next, while our country-level observations are on the lower end of what is needed for multi-level estimations (Maas and Hox 2005), we have opted to use a three-level structure better suited for our data to avoid bias in our coefficients. Yet, this small number increases the risk of Type 2 errors for our country-level and cross-level interaction terms testing hypotheses 2a and 2b, respectively. To check the sensitivity of our results against this, we replicate our estimations using two-level mixed-effects models where we consider *country-year units* as our upper-level structure. This allows us to increase the number of observations at the higher level to about 128 country-years.[4] Our findings do not change when we use this alternative estimation strategy.

Lastly, two cases in our sample stand out both in terms of the volume and characteristics of the immigrants they host: Luxembourg and Switzerland. Both cases host a foreign population well above the regional average. Notably, some may also object to their inclusion in this study, considering that most foreigners in these countries come from Europe. While we concede that intra-European mobility indeed results in less cultural dissimilarity than extra-European migration reducing the potential mechanism of cultural threat, they are nevertheless susceptible to the same degree of economic threat and unfamiliarity by not being formal members of the host society. Regardless, case-wise exclusion of these country-year units does not substantially change our findings. One difference we observe is the p-value of the stock share of non-citizens, which reaches below $p < 0.05$ when we exclude Luxembourg. However, contextual diversity still predicts lower trust if we use the alternative contextual diversity operationalization discussed above, emphasizing immigration background rather than citizenship even when Luxembourg is excluded. Therefore, while we report this specific case and measurement sensitivity, we sustain that our results confirm a negative correlation between ethnic diversity and weaker generalized trust.

CONCLUSION

What have we learnt so far about the complicated relationship between institutions, trust, and diversity? Our goal in this contribution was to map the extant work on the link between diversity and trust to better understand the sources of disparity in existing evidence and to develop and test an original argument concerning whether welfare institutions have a mitigating role in the cross-country variation in the strength of this link. Based on our review of the literature on diversity and trust on the one hand and the institutional sources of trust in diverse societies on the other, we draw the following conclusions.

First, the negative relationship between diversity and social cohesion is indeed sensitive to methodological and conceptual choices. Yet, if we consider only the specific link between the effect of ethnic diversity, defined broadly at the national level, and generalized trust, there seems to be evidence confirming a negative impact. *Second*, such exposure to living with ethnically diverse groups and lower trust seem to operate through the environmental effects of the presence of heterogeneity in line with the expectations of group conflict theory and, all things considered, through the subjective attitudes and skepticism towards out-group members. *Third*, this negative relationship between trust and diversity is not uniform when looking at different countries. The relationship seems to be shaped by several institutional and inter-personal contact-related mitigators. However, these types of conditioning effects have received relatively little attention so far. *Fourth*, when concentrating on the institutional factors, a principle of equal treatment in socio-economic institutions and cultural policies fostering recognition and integration of migrant communities seems to have the potential of building the resilience of trust in diverse societies. Building on extant work, then, we assessed whether equal treatment of immigrants by welfare institutions mitigates the negative impact of diversity on trust, adding to this ample literature.

Our empirical findings echoed the most recent meta-analysis results conducted by Dinesen et al. (2020). By and large, our analyses of 17 European societies over the last two decades confirmed that higher shares of immigrant populations predict lower generalized trust levels. Taking stock of the literatures on welfare chauvinism, multiculturalism, and the political economy of immigration, we argued and empirically demonstrated that countries that allow equal access of immigrants to public resources dampen the adverse effect of anti-diversity attitudes on trust. We also showed that negative attitudes towards such diversity are a remarkably robust correlate of distrust. Empirically, we used a new measure of relative treatment of social policy towards immigrants and natives, adding to the policy factors that are shown to mitigate and opening new potential avenues of research for the sustainability of immigration and social cohesion in Europe. In line with previous studies, higher education, economic security, political and institutional trust and satisfaction, being older, religiosity, and living in non-urban contexts predict higher trust. At the country level, we also corroborate the negative impact of economic inequality.

Our results have three important implications concerning the sustainability of trust in increasingly diverse societies and future research on the topic. Perhaps the most critical weakness in earlier work seems also to be the least discussed. Studies, so far, have mostly focused on testing whether diversity predicts lower trust using a myriad of complex measurement strategies to capture this contentious link. Yet, efforts instead should be more focused on elucidating through which mechanisms we should expect to observe the trust decline. Here, reviewing previous work carefully, we propose to look at not just the national context but the micro-level reflections subjectively. This is a crucial step considering that the extent to which racial tensions become a potential problem for trust and, more broadly, social cohesion varies temporally and is not equally strong everywhere.

Next, understanding the mitigators and mediators of the relationship between diversity and trust warrants further research. While our study and several notable earlier works have taken the first steps, we need more research exploring the role of policy when it comes to facing increasing contextual diversity and citizens' resentments towards such diversity. Fruitful research areas to explore could be to look at other equalizing policies such as non-discrimination laws and labor market organizing policies such as wage bargaining or the role of unions. Lastly, including this present analysis, most of what we know about the effect of diversity on trust comes from cross-sectional comparative studies. However, implicitly, the core of Putnam's hunkering-down argument, and its later variants, implies a dynamic relationship. Considering the developments in the availability of high-quality longitudinal data from household and population surveys and registers, future research should focus on evaluating this reactive relationship over time to answer whether an increase in diversity is followed by a decline in trust – and under which conditions.

NOTES

1. The countries included in the analysis are Austria, Belgium, Denmark, Finland, France, Germany, Iceland, Ireland, Italy, Luxembourg, the Netherlands, Norway, Portugal, Spain, Sweden, Switzerland, and the United Kingdom.
2. Wherever bar graphs are missing for a given year, this indicates that the country was not in the ESS wave that year. In addition to the 16 cases shown in Figure 14.1, our analysis includes Luxembourg which is only present in the 2002 and 2004 waves.
3. The IESPI values from 2000 are matched with the ESS waves from 2002, 2004, 2006, and 2008; values from 2010 are matched with the 2010, 2012, and 2014 waves; and 2015 values are matched with waves from 2016 and 2018. Alternative ways of matching the IESPI values to survey waves are inconsequential to the results.
4. Our country-year observations do not amount to a multiplication of nine years and 17 countries because not all countries are surveyed in every wave of the ESS.

REFERENCES

Alesina, A., and E.L. Glaeser. 2004. *Fighting Poverty in the US and Europe: A World of Difference*. Oxford: Oxford University Press.
Alesina, A., and E. La Ferrara. 2002. "Who Trusts Others?". *Journal of Public Economics* 85 (2): 207–34.
Armingeon, K., V. Wenger, F. Wiedemeier, C. Isler, L. Knöpfel, D. Weisstanner, and S. Engler. 2020. "Comparative Political Data Set 1960–2018". University of Berne.
Banting, K., and W. Kymlicka. 2006. *Multiculturalism and the Welfare State Recognition and Redistribution in Contemporary Democracies*. Oxford: Oxford University Press.
Banting, K., and W. Kymlicka. 2017. "Introduction: The Political Sources of Solidarity in Diverse Societies". In *The Strains of Commitment: The Political Sources of Solidarity in Diverse Societies*, ed. K. Banting and W. Kymlicka. Oxford: Oxford University Press.
Beugelsdijk, S. 2006. "A Note on the Theory and Measurement of Trust in Explaining Differences in Economic Growth". *Cambridge Journal of Economics* 30: 371–85.
Bjornskov, C. 2007. "Determinants of Generalized Trust: A Cross-Country Comparison". *Public Choice* 130: 1–21.
Bloemraad, I. 2017. "Solidarity and Conflict: Understanding the Causes and Consequences of Access to Citizenship, Civic Integration Policies, and Multiculturalism". In *The Strains of Commitment: The Political Sources of Solidarity in Diverse Societies*, ed. K. Banting and W. Kymlicka. Oxford: Oxford University Press.
Bloemraad, I., and M. Wright. 2014. "'Utter Failure' or Unity out of Diversity? Debating and Evaluating Policies of Multiculturalism". *International Migration Review* 48 (1): 292–334.
Crepaz, M. 2008. *Trust beyond Borders: Immigration, Identity and the Welfare State in Modern Societies*. Ann Arbor, MI: University of Michigan Press.
Crepaz, M., and R. Damron. 2009. "Constructing Tolerance: How the Welfare State Shapes Attitudes about Immigrants". *Comparative Political Studies* 42 (3): 437–63.
Delhey, J., and K. Newton. 2005. "Predicting Cross-National Levels of Social Trust: Global Pattern or Nordic Exceptionalism?" *European Sociological Review* 21 (4): 311–27.
Dinesen, P.T., and K.M. Sonderskov. 2015. "Ethnic Diversity and Social Trust: Evidence from the Micro-Context". *American Sociological Review* 80 (3): 550–73.
Dinesen, P.T., M. Schaeffer, and K.M. Sonderskov. 2020. "Ethnic Diversity and Social Trust: A Narrative and Meta-Analytical Review". *Annual Review of Political Science* 23: 441–65.
Emmenegger, P., and R. Klemmensen. 2013. "What Motivates You? The Relationship between Preferences for Redistribution and Attitudes toward Immigration". *Comparative Politics* 45 (2): 227–46.
ESS. 2020. "European Social Survey Rounds 1–9". Norwegian Centre for Research Data.
Finseraas, H. 2008. "Immigration and Preferences for Redistribution: An Empirical Analysis of European Survey Data". *Comparative European Politics* 6 (4): 407–31.
Gundelach, B., and A. Manatschal. 2017. "Ethnic Diversity, Social Trust and the Moderating Role of Subnational Integration Policy". *Political Studies* 65 (2): 413–31.
Helbling, M., L. Bjerre, F. Römer, and M. Zobel. 2017. "Measuring Immigration Policies: The IMPIC Database". *European Political Science* 16 (1): 79–98.
Hooghe, M., and D. Stolle, eds. 2003. *Generating Social Capital: Civil Society and Institutions in a Comparative Perspective*. New York: Palgrave Macmillan.

Hooghe, M., T. Reeskens, D. Stolle, and A. Trappers. 2009. "Ethnic Diversity and Generalized Trust in Europe: A Cross-National Multilevel Study". *Comparative Political Studies* 42 (2): 198–223.

Hox, J. 2010. *Multilevel Analysis: Techniques and* Applications, 2nd ed. New York: Routledge.

Jackson, J.W. 1993. "Realistic Group Conflict Theory: A Review and Evaluation of the Theoretical and Empirical Literature". *The Psychological Record* 43 (3): 395–413.

Johnston, R., M. Wright, S. Soroka, and J. Citrin. 2017. "Diversity and Solidarity: New Evidence from Canada and the US". In *The Strains of Commitment: The Political Sources of Solidarity in Diverse Societies*, ed. K. Banting and W. Kymlicka. Oxford: Oxford University Press.

Kesler, C., and I. Bloemraad. 2010. "Does Immigration Erode Social Capital? The Conditional Effects of Immigration-Generated Diversity on Trust, Membership, and Participation across 19 Countries, 1981–2000". *Canadian Journal of Political Science* 43 (2): 319–47.

Knight, J. 2001. "Social Norms and the Rule of Law: Fostering Trust in a Socially Diverse Society". In *Trust in Society*, ed. K.S. Cook. New York: Russell Sage.

Koning, E.A. 2019. *Immigration and the Politics of Welfare Exclusion: Selective Solidarity in Western Democracies*. Toronto: Toronto University Press.

Koning, E.A. 2020. "Accommodation and New Hurdles: The Increasing Importance of Politics for Immigrants' Access to Social Programmes in Western Democracies". *Social Policy and Administration*. DOI: 10.1111/spol.12661.

Kumlin, S., and B. Rothstein. 2005. "Making and Breaking Social Capital: The Impact of Welfare-State Institutions". *Comparative Political Studies* 38 (4): 339–65.

Kymlicka, W. 2015. "Solidarity in Diverse Societies: Beyond Neoliberal Multiculturalism and Welfare Chauvinism". *Comparative Migration Studies* 3 (17): 1–19.

Larsen, C.A. 2008. "The Institutional Logic of Welfare Attitudes: How Welfare Regimes Influence Public Support". *Comparative Political Studies* 41 (2): 145–68.

Larsen, C.A. 2020. "The Institutional Logic of Giving Migrants Access to Social Benefits and Services". *Journal of European Social Policy* 30 (1): 48–62.

Lupo, G. 2010. "Is Immigration Detrimental for Social Trust in the European Union? A Three-Level Model of Cultural Heterogeneity and Citizenship Regime as Social Capital Predictors". *International Journal of Social Inquiry* 3 (1): 67–96.

Maas, C.J.M., and J. Hox. 2005. "Sufficient Sample Sizes for Multilevel Modeling". *Methodology* 1 (3): 86–92.

Marschall, M.J., and D. Stolle. 2004. "Race and the City: Neighborhood Context and the Development of Generalized Trust". *Political Behavior* 26: 125–53.

Nannestad, P. 2008. "What Have We Learned about Generalized Trust, if Anything?" *Annual Review of Political Science* 11 (1): 413–36.

Nelson, K., D. Fredriksson, T. Korpi, W. Korpi, J. Palme, and O. Sjöberg. 2020. "The Social Policy Indicators (SPIN) Database". *International Journal of Social Welfare*. https://doi.org/10.1111/ijsw.12418.

Olzak, S. 1995. *The Dynamics of Ethnic Competition and Conflict*. Stanford, CA: Stanford University Press.

Pontusson, J. 2005. *Inequality and Prosperity: Social Europe vs. Liberal America*. Ithaca, NY: Cornell University Press.

Portes, A., and E. Vickstrom. 2011. "Diversity, Social Capital, and Cohesion". *Annual Review of Sociology* 37: 461–79.

Putnam, R. 2007. "*E Pluribus Unum*: Diversity and Community in the Twenty-First Century: The 2006 Johan Skytte Prize Lecture". *Scandinavian Political Studies* 30 (2): 137–74.

Reeskens, T., and M. Hooghe. 2008. "Cross-Cultural Measurement Equivalence of Generalized Trust: Evidence from the European Social Survey". *Social Indicators Research* 85: 515–32.

Reeskens, T., and T. van der Meer. 2019. "The Inevitable Deservingness Gap: A Study into the Insurmountable Immigrant Penalty in Perceived Welfare Deservingness". *Journal of European Social Policy* 29 (2): 166–81.

Reeskens, T., and W. van Oorschot. 2012. "Disentangling the 'New Liberal Dilemma': On the Relation between General Welfare Redistribution Preferences and Welfare Chauvinism". *International Journal of Comparative Sociology* 53 (2): 120–39.

Rothstein, B. 1998. *Just Institutions Matter: The Moral and Political Logic of the Universal Welfare State*. Cambridge: Cambridge University Press.

Rothstein, B. 2001. "Social Capital in the Social Democratic Welfare State". *Politics and Society* 29 (2): 207–41.

Rothstein, B. 2017. "Solidarity, Diversity, and the Quality of Government". In *The Strains of Commitment: The Political Sources of Solidarity in Diverse* Societies, ed. K. Banting and W. Kymlicka. Oxford: Oxford University Press.

Rothstein, B., and D. Stolle. 2008. "The State and Social Capital: An Institutional Theory of Generalized Trust". *Comparative Politics* 40 (4): 441–59.

Rothstein, B., and E. Uslaner. 2005. "All for All: Equality, Corruption and Social Trust". *World Politics* 58 (3): 41–73.

Sainsbury, D. 2012. *Welfare States and Immigrant Rights: The Politics of Inclusion and Exclusion*. Oxford: Oxford University Press.
Schmidt-Catran, A.W., and M. Fairbrother. 2016. "The Random Effects in Multilevel Models: Getting Them Wrong and Getting Them Right". *European Sociological Review* 32 (1): 23–8.
Scruggs, L., D. Jahn, and K. Kuitto. 2017. "Comparative Welfare Entitlements Dataset 2. Version 2017–09". University of Connecticut and University of Greifswald.
Seifert, N. 2018. "Yet Another Case of Nordic Exceptionalism? Extending Existing Evidence for a Causal Relationship between Institutional and Social Trust to the Netherlands and Switzerland". *Social Indicators Research* 136: 539–55.
Solano, G., and T. Huddleston. 2020. "MIPEX: Migrant Integration Policy Index".
Sonderskov, K. M., and P. T. Dinesen. 2014. "Danish Exceptionalism: Explaining the Unique Increase in Social Trust over the Past 30 Years". *European Sociological Review* 30 (6): 782–95.
Soroka, S., R. Johnston, and K. Banting. 2006. "Ethnicity, Trust and the Welfare State". In *Social Capital, Diversity and the Welfare State*, ed. F. Kay and R. Johnston. Vancouver: University of British Columbia Press.
Stolle, D. 2002. "Trusting Strangers: The Concept of Generalized Trust in Perspective". *Österreichische Zeitschrift für Politikwissenschaft* 31 (4): 397–412.
Stolle, D., S. Petermann, K. Schmid, K. Schönwälder, M. Hewstone, S. Vertovec, T. Schmitt, and J. Heywood. 2013. "Immigration-Related Diversity and Trust in German Cities: The Role of Intergroup Contact". *Journal of Elections, Public Opinion and Parties* 23: 279–98.
Tajfel, H. 1982. "Social Psychology of Intergroup Relations". *Annual Review of Psychology* 33: 1–39.
Uslaner, E. 2002. *The Moral Foundations of Trust*. Cambridge: Cambridge University Press.
Uslaner, E. 2012. *Segregation and Mistrust: Diversity, Isolation, and Social Cohesion*. Cambridge: Cambridge University Press.
van der Meer, T., and J. Tolsma. 2014. "Ethnic Diversity and Its Supposed Detrimental Effects on Social Cohesion". *Annual Review of Sociology* 40: 459–78.
van der Waal, J., W. de Koster, and W. van Oorschot. 2013. "Three Worlds of Welfare Chauvinism? How Welfare Regimes Affect Support for Distributing Welfare to Immigrants in Europe". *Journal of Comparative Policy Analysis: Research and Practice* 15 (2): 164–81.
Zak, P., and S. Knack. 2001. "Trust and Growth". *Economic Journal* 111: 295–321.
Zimdars, A., and G. Tampubolon. 2012. "Ethnic Diversity and European's Generalised Trust: How Inclusive Immigration Policy Can Aid a Positive Association". *Sociological Research Online* 17 (3): 1–11.

15. Inequality, immigration, and welfare regimes: Untangling the connections
Christel Kesler

INTRODUCTION

Over recent decades, scholars and pundits have raised numerous questions about the interconnections between redistributive social policy and immigration. Perhaps the most hotly debated question concerns whether and how immigration-generated diversity alters public support for the welfare state. Related debates look further "upstream" in the policymaking process (e.g., at general measures of social solidarity or social capital) or "downstream" (e.g., at fiscal support for the welfare state or the character of actual welfare programs). Consensus has largely been elusive on all of these questions, and as a consequence, more recent research has turned to the question of why results seem to vary so much.

Comparative welfare state scholars have long examined welfare regimes as stratifying institutions that structure social citizenship and socioeconomic inequalities. Contemporary scholarship on these issues owes a particular debt to pivotal scholarly interventions in the 1990s by scholars such as Esping-Andersen (1990), who emphasized the central role of the organization of welfare states for decommodification, and Orloff (1993), who highlighted the gendered nature of this decommodification concept, and the role that welfare states can play in supporting access to labor markets in the first place for predominantly female caregivers. This chapter will focus on how the socioeconomic inequalities that grow out of different political-economic arrangements may help us to understand the considerable variation in the relationship between immigration and public support for the welfare state. The analysis considers two particular kinds of inequalities: overall economic inequalities that have been the focus of considerable research in the welfare state literature, as well as inequalities related to how successfully immigrants are incorporated into the labor markets of their host societies.

The chapter begins with a review of existing literature underscoring the lack of consensus about the question of whether immigration-generated diversity undermines public support for the welfare state. The discussion then continues with a review of literature concerning why welfare regimes and different forms of inequality may be critical to understanding variation in how publics respond to immigration-generated diversity. Next, after describing data sources and variables, analyses of macro-level data illustrate variation across welfare regimes in socioeconomic inequalities, including immigrant/native-born unemployment inequalities. The last section of the chapter turns to a multivariate analysis of how these inequalities condition the relationship between immigrant population size and welfare state support across different welfare regimes.

IMMIGRATION-GENERATED DIVERSITY AND SUPPORT FOR THE WELFARE STATE

Goodhart (2004) popularized the term "progressive dilemma" to refer to the purported tension between the two progressive values of economic solidarity (embodied in a generous and redistributive welfare state) and cultural diversity (increasing in advanced democracies because of immigration). Alesina and Glaeser's (2004) influential book addressing why the United States has a less generous and redistributive welfare state than other advanced democracies attributes a major role to racial and ethnic fractionalization, though their suggestions about the role of contemporary migration remain, like Goodhart's, highly speculative. "We shall see," they write at the end of that volume, "whether the generous European welfare state can really survive in a heterogeneous society" (Alesina and Glaeser 2004, 181).

Many scholars, in a plethora of papers and books, have taken up the challenge to test these claims over the last decade and a half. Because the "progressive dilemma" is often framed in terms of more general sentiments of solidarity, scholars interested in the effects of immigration on the welfare state often look "upstream" from actual policymaking, at the large and growing body of work about the effects of diversity on social cohesion, social capital, and social trust. One of the most influential works on this topic was authored by Putnam (2007) and examines how ethnic diversity at the census tract level affects social trust, altruism, and civic participation in the United States. He uncovers a pattern of what he calls "hunkering down," in which diversity appears to reduce these measures of trust and engagement. A number of existing reviews attempt to synthesize and make sense of the veritable mountain of sometimes conflicting findings that have emerged within the literature on this topic (Dinesen et al. 2020; Koopmans 2013; van der Meer and Tolsma 2014; Portes and Vickstrom 2011). Portes and Vickstrom (2011) argue that the most important form of social cohesion in advanced democracies is closer to the Durkheimian ideal of organic solidarity based on heterogeneity than to the communitarianism lauded by Putnam (2007) and others. "No developed nation in North America or Western Europe has been seriously challenged by mass migration," Portes and Vickstrom (2011, 474) argue, and "the core institutions of these societies have remained intact." While this review is compelling, the events of the last decade, and in particular the rise of populist nationalism in numerous countries around the world, may yet challenge this rather optimistic conclusion regarding the resilience of "core institutions" including the welfare state. Koopmans's (2013, 163) review addresses the relationship between immigration and social trust in a relatively brief section of a larger review of the literature on multiculturalism policies, concluding that "the tension between diversity and solidarity may be real" but is not significantly altered by how societies formally recognize and accommodate diversity. Van der Meer and Tolsma's (2014) review, which, very usefully, takes the form of a meta-analysis, shows that there are consistent negative effects of diversity for measures of neighborhood cohesion only (e.g., trust in and contact with neighbors); these effects rarely "spill over" to less narrowly geographically bounded pro-social behavior. Finally and most recently, Dinesen et al.'s (2020) review, which includes a meta-analysis alongside a narrative review of existing literature, concludes similarly that the effect of ethnic diversity on trust is most pronounced when diversity is measured at the local, neighborhood level, and when the trust target is also more localized (e.g., neighbors).

If we extend the discussion about the effects of immigration on the welfare state beyond these trust and cohesion measures that are "upstream" from policymaking, there are still a number of key dimensions that vary in existing studies. First and perhaps most obviously, the precise outcome of relevant studies varies considerably. Some studies focus, as will this chapter, on public opinion about the welfare state (e.g., Brady and Finnigan 2014; Breznau and Eger 2016; Schmidt-Catran and Spies 2016) and others focus on actual welfare spending or welfare programs (e.g., Fox et al. 2013; Gaston and Rajaguru 2013; Soroka et al. 2016). In either type of study, there is often a further distinction between overall support (attitudinal or fiscal) for the welfare state and issues of "welfare chauvinism," or immigrant access to benefits. This chapter maintains a focus on the broader issue of overall welfare state support.

Studies also vary with respect to how "immigration" is operationalized, with relatively systematic variation by whether a study is explicitly cross-nationally comparative. Single-country studies, and especially those with a focus on the United States, have generally greater levels of nuance, with specification of immigrants by ethnicity (Brown 2013; Fox 2012) and a more careful disentangling of ethnic or racial diversity from immigration or immigration-generated diversity per se (Hero 2010). Cross-national studies more often look at either the total stock or total recent inflow of immigrants, sometimes with distinctions by citizenship status or broad category of origin, such as European Union versus "other" in European studies (Mau and Burkhardt 2009). There are at least two reasons for the lower level of specificity in cross-national studies. First, there is a lack of comparable data across countries that would permit the same level of nuance as in single-country studies. Second and more substantively, significant ethnic and racial diversity is a newer social phenomenon in non-settler societies that comprise much of the universe of advanced democracies, and indicators of immigration are highly correlated with other kinds of indicators of racial or ethnic diversity in many countries (Dinesen et al. 2020).

Another important dimension for existing studies of the relationship between diversity and the welfare state, as highlighted above with respect to trust and social cohesion studies, is the geographic unit of analysis. The geographic unit of analysis, like the choice of diversity measure, often coincides with whether a study is cross-nationally comparative. Cross-national studies generally focus on immigration to the country as a whole, whereas single-country studies include measures of immigration at the state or local level. More recently, however, a few studies have emerged that are able to capture sub-national-level variation and also include cross-national comparisons (e.g., Eger and Breznau 2017; Koopmans and Schaeffer 2016).

One further issue that helps to explain variation in existing studies of the relationship between immigration and the welfare state is contextual factors. Consensus about the shape of the general effect of immigration on the welfare state may be elusive precisely because contextual factors are so critical. This point informs the approach in this chapter. Though there are numerous types of contextual factors that may be important, this chapter focuses on the role of socioeconomic inequalities, including those that are in part generated by the welfare state itself. An approach focusing on the conditional effects of immigration or immigration-generated diversity on the welfare state has an important advantage: it underscores the agency of immigration host countries in shaping the ways in which their populations respond to immigration. Though the policy levers to control immigration itself have been found to be of questionable importance, especially in advanced democracies (de Haas et al. 2019; Massey et al. 2016), policies that control other kinds of conditions within receiving countries may well be more tractable in a policy sense.

DIFFERENT WELFARE REGIMES, DIFFERENT RESPONSES TO IMMIGRATION?

In various ways, the welfare state itself may condition responses to diversity and then feed back to public support for or spending on the welfare state. As existing literature shows, established welfare states are, in general, relatively resistant to retrenchment, in part because they have strong constituencies supportive of existing programs (Brooks and Manza 2008; Pierson 1994). Therefore, the historical timing of the advent of large-scale immigrant and ethnic diversity is important to consider. Even if diversity undermines the development of a solidaristic welfare state, as the literature on race and the early United States welfare state tends to conclude (though see Fox 2010), the implications for the contemporary effects of immigration on welfare states should be examined in their own right (Crepaz 2008). Related to this, the continued role of longstanding racial diversity should be distinguished from the role of diversity generated by contemporary immigration (Fox 2012; Fox et al. 2013; Hero 2010).

One specific way in which the welfare state itself may condition responses to diversity is through its effects on economic inequality. Strong and redistributive social policy, as exhibited to greater and lesser degrees by advanced welfare states, reduces economic inequality and insecurity. Inequality and insecurity may affect how majority populations feel about immigrant newcomers and demographic or social change more generally. Numerous scholars have highlighted that it is diversity combined with economic inequality that may most negatively affect social cohesion, attitudes toward immigrants, and welfare state support (Heizmann 2015; Kesler and Bloemraad 2010; van der Meer and Tolsma 2014; Nagayoshi and Hjerm 2015; Portes and Vickstrom 2011). Thus, it may be the case that welfare state institutions that effectively reduce economic inequality and generate economic security are more robust in the face of immigration. The first hypothesis follows from this proposition.

Hypothesis 1: *Immigration will have a less negative impact on welfare state support in more economically equal societies than in less economically equal societies.*

On the other hand, public opinion may be sensitive to what Hero and Levy (2016) have labeled the "racial structure of economic inequality" (see also An et al. 2018; Hero and Levy 2018). The idea here is that inequality may have more pernicious effects on welfare policy and public goods provision when redistribution flows across racial boundaries; the necessity of interracial redistribution will be highest in the context of large existing racial inequalities. In a cross-national framework comparing different kinds of welfare states, majority populations may be particularly resentful of immigrants and eager to retrench the welfare state in contexts where the immigrant population is growing, where immigrants have access to generous and decommodifying benefits that they are not perceived to have earned, and where, at least initially, labor market integration may proceed more slowly. Therefore, a robust analysis of the interconnections among welfare state support, immigration, and inequality must consider the potentially different ways in which immigrants are incorporated into their host societies.

Some research has carefully compared whether welfare policies are accessible to different kinds of immigrants in a cross-national framework (e.g., Sainsbury 2012). However, even within welfare states that are highly decommodifying for immigrants and therefore ensure a reasonable standard of living independent of the labor market, employment may be a socially and symbolically important form of integration, especially in the eyes of native-born observers. Therefore, focusing on actual socioeconomic inequalities between immigrants and their native-born counterparts is important, but existing comparisons across welfare regime types often remain speculative. For example, Alba and Foner (2015) consider "political economy" (a broad term including both welfare state and labor market institutions) as a potential explanation for cross-national differences in the incorporation of immigrants and their children, but they do not find convincing evidence. This is in part a "small-N" problem (Lieberson 1991), common in many if not most cross-nationally comparative studies. Most studies of immigrant incorporation are only able to include a small number of host countries, and these countries differ from one another in many important ways. Nonetheless, some studies have made headway for specific socioeconomic outcomes, carefully reasoning about how various dimensions of the welfare state (e.g., decommodification, active labor market programs, work/family policies) might affect observed patterns of inequality (Kesler 2015, 2018; Kogan 2006; Koopmans 2010; Morissens and Sainsbury 2005; Quillian et al. 2019). One intriguing pattern that begins to emerge from this literature is that the social democratic welfare regime type that has been famously successful at reducing inequalities by class and gender is arguably less successful at reducing inequalities between immigrant and native-born populations, especially in terms of labor market integration.

The question then becomes whether different levels of immigrant incorporation affect the ways in which the public responds to immigration. Finseraas (2008) draws out implications of immigrants' incorporation in Nordic countries, where benefits are more universal, and Continental European countries, where benefits are more likely to follow a social insurance model, and finds evidence for the idea that the presence of universal benefits increases the potential for immigration to undermine welfare state support. Recently, papers by Burgoon and colleagues (Burgoon 2014; Burgoon and Rooduijn 2021) have also highlighted for European countries how poor integration of immigrants into the labor market and immigrants' disproportionate use of welfare can lower the public's willingness to support the welfare state. Hypothesis 2 follows the same line of reasoning and attempts to replicate the finding of these existing studies for a wider range of countries, including those outside of Europe. This may be especially informative, as the liberal welfare regime type is composed primarily of non-European settler societies, which have typically been somewhat more effective at integrating immigrants into their labor markets (Heath and Cheung 2007).

Hypothesis 2: Immigration will have a less negative impact on welfare state support in societies where immigrants are well integrated into the labor market than in societies where immigrants are poorly integrated into the labor market.

If immigrant labor market integration affects public support for the welfare state, it should do so more when the immigrant population grows, and also when overall labor market conditions worsen. Existing literature (De Jong et al. 2017; Finseraas et al. 2016; Quillian 1995) shows that both immigrant population size and labor market conditions affect anti-immigrant sentiments, and we might expect the same to be true for welfare state support. With welfare state support, we would expect an interaction of these two factors: if a country has extremely low unemployment, the composition of the unemployed population should matter less than in a context where unemployment is more widespread and visible. If unemployment rises and immigrants are well integrated into the labor market, there may actually be growing support for the protection of the welfare state, whereas if unemployment rises and immigrants are poorly integrated into the labor market, welfare state support may decrease. The third and final hypothesis articulates this logic.

Hypothesis 3: Poor labor market integration of immigrants will have a more negative impact on welfare state support in societies with poorer overall labor market conditions.

I turn now to the background information for the analysis that will examine the evidence for these various hypotheses.

DATA, VARIABLES, AND METHODS

Data used in the remainder of this chapter are drawn from four different sources. Macro-level data come from the World Bank's World Development Indicators Database (2020), from the Organisation for Economic Co-operation and Development's OECD.Stat Database (2020), and from the Luxembourg Income Study's Key Figures (2020). Individual-level data come from the International Social Survey Program (ISSP) Role of Government modules (ISSP Research Group 2008a, 2008b, 2018). For a few initial figures, I use the 1990, 1996, 2006, and 2016 waves of ISSP data for all Western European countries, plus Australia, Canada, Israel, New Zealand, and the United States, resulting in 69,119 individuals within 20 countries and 54 country-years. In the main analyses, due to unavailability of a key macro-level predictor, I exclude the 1990 ISSP wave, reducing the sample to 57,730 individuals within 20 countries and 46 country-years. Data from all sources are merged by country and year.

The primary outcome derives from a set of ISSP questions concerning opinions about government responsibility in seven different realms, including providing jobs, providing healthcare, providing for the elderly, providing for the unemployed, providing for the poor, reducing income differences between the rich and poor, and providing financial help to students. The variables are all ordinal and on the same four-point scale, with answers ranging from the government "definitely should not be" responsible to the government "definitely should be" responsible. I create a scale that indicates the mean level of all seven standardized items for each respondent (alpha = 0.82), but I also include two appendix tables that look separately at the seven items.

All analyses include a limited set of individual-level demographic and socioeconomic controls from the ISSP. Included controls are available for all countries and years in the analysis. These are age (range 15–97), gender (male, female), highest educational level (lower secondary or less, upper secondary, tertiary), and employment status (employee, self-employed, unemployed, other).

Because of the limited number of macro-level cases, any given model must use macro-level predictors selectively. The analysis begins with a look at some straightforward bivariate relationships among a number of relevant macro-level variables. These include total public social spending (OECD), the overall unemployment rate (World Bank), income inequality as measured by the Gini coefficient (LIS), total foreign-born stock (World Bank), and the ratio of the foreign-born unemployment rate to the native-born unemployment rate (OECD). Overall unemployment is available for all years in the analysis with the exception of 1990; 1991 values are used here instead. Gini coefficients are available at regular intervals from LIS, but not every year; they are therefore interpolated between estimates and matched to the closest available year at the beginning or end of the series, as necessary. For two countries (Portugal and New Zealand), Gini coefficients are available from the OECD but not from LIS, so I use the OECD figures. Total public social spending and foreign-born stock are available every five years through 2015 and are interpolated as necessary and carried forward to 2016 from 2015. The ratio of the foreign-born unemployment rate to the native-born unemployment rate is available every year from 2000 only. The analyses that include this variable exclude the 1990 ISSP wave, as noted above, and use 2000 values of the variable for the 1996 ISSP wave.

Welfare regimes are defined in the now fairly conventional way, following Esping-Andersen's (1990) "three worlds" approach. Social democratic regimes in the analysis include Denmark, Finland, Iceland, Norway, and Sweden. Conservative regimes include Belgium, France, Germany, Israel, Italy, the Netherlands, Portugal, and Spain. Liberal regimes include Australia, Canada, Ireland, New Zealand, Switzerland, the United Kingdom, and the United States.

Given the very limited number of countries and country-years, the analysis rests not on formal multilevel models, which demand a relatively large number of macro-level cases, but instead on standard regression models, with robust standard errors clustered by both country and year, according to the method outlined in Cameron et al. (2012). See Moller et al. (2003) for a discussion of the appropriateness of this methodological choice in the context of a cross-nationally comparative analysis using unbalanced panel data as I have here.

WELFARE REGIMES AND INEQUALITY: MORE AND LESS FAMILIAR PATTERNS

I begin with some illustrations of familiar and less familiar patterns across welfare regime types, as displayed in Table 15.1. One place to start is with simple measures of public spending, economic performance, and economic inequality. Though the welfare state literature has generally moved away from purely quantitative measures of social spending, and has instead emphasized qualitative differences in the decommodifying nature of social benefits, it is nonetheless still the case that welfare regime types differ in their average levels of public social spending.

Table 15.1 Selected characteristics of different welfare regime types

Variable	Social democratic Mean	s.d.	Conservative Mean	s.d.	Liberal Mean	s.d.	Overall Mean	s.d.
*Public social spending (% GDP)	24.8	4.3	22.7	4.9	16.8	2.0	20.6	5.1
*Unemployment (%)	6.0	2.1	10.0	4.6	6.6	2.9	7.7	3.8
*Gini coefficient (%)	24.4	1.1	30.8	3.6	32.7	2.4	30.2	4.2
*Foreign-born stock (%)	9.4	4.1	13.8	9.8	16.7	7.2	14.0	8.1
*Ratio, foreign-born:native-born unemployment	2.2	0.5	1.5	0.6	1.3	0.5	1.6	0.7
*Mean, welfare state support scale	0.06	0.13	0.15	0.21	−0.19	0.26	−0.02	0.27

Note: The unit of analysis is country-year (n = 54 for most variables, n = 46 for the foreign-born:native-born unemployment indicator); * p < .05 for test of differences in means across welfare regime types.

Source: World Bank, OECD, LIS, and ISSP.

For the countries and years in this analysis, social democratic regimes post the highest level of public social spending (24.8 percent of gross domestic product (GDP) on average), with the lowest level of spending in liberal regimes (16.8 percent of GDP on average) and conservative regimes in an intermediate position (22.7 percent of GDP on average). This masks substantial intra-type variation, however, especially within the social democratic and conservative regime types.

In terms of economic performance, there are some similarities and some differences across regime types. Across these countries and years, there are no significant differences in GDP per capita growth, one conventional measure of economic performance, across regime types (not shown here); all regime types have average GDP growth in the range of 2–3 percent. However, an indicator of economic performance that is perhaps more directly relevant for public opinion about the welfare state is the unemployment rate, which I use in the multivariate analyses below. In terms of unemployment rates, the conservative regime type stands out, with higher average unemployment (10.0 percent) than liberal (6.6 percent) or social democratic (6.0 percent) countries, but also the highest variability in unemployment rates.

Two measures of inequality that have often been examined in the context of welfare regime variation are general income inequality and relative poverty. Though they are conceptually distinct, they are extremely closely correlated with each other for this sample of countries (not shown here), and I choose to use the more general measure, the Gini coefficient, here. We see a quite familiar pattern. Social democratic regimes are the most successful in maintaining low income inequality, with an average Gini coefficient of 24.4 for these country-years, compared to 30.8 in conservative regimes and 32.7 in liberal regimes, and there is also relatively little variability in income inequality within the social democratic regime type.

If we turn to measures related to immigration, patterns across welfare regimes are perhaps somewhat less familiar. A look at the relative size of the immigrant population across welfare regimes reveals that the liberal regime type, which includes all of the Anglo immigrant-receiving settler societies, has larger immigrant populations, 16.7 percent of the population on average. Social democratic and conservative regimes have fewer immigrants relative to their population size (13.8 and 9.4 percent, respectively). Again, however, as with all of the figures, these averages mask substantial variation across countries within regime types.

Turning finally to the other main form of inequality that will be a focus in the analysis below, inequality between immigrants and the native-born population, we also see a less well-known pattern across welfare regimes. If social democratic regimes have been quite successful at keeping overall income inequality low, their levels of immigrant/native-born inequality are extreme in the opposite direction. The ratio of immigrant to native-born unemployment rates is, on average, 2.2 in social democratic regimes, compared to 1.5 in conservative regimes and 1.3 in liberal regimes. Immigrant unemployment is obviously higher, on average, than native-born unemployment in all three regime types, but the problem is especially pronounced in social democratic countries, with immigrant unemployment rates more than twice as high as native-born unemployment rates.

Table 15.2 provides more detail on the two immigration-related characteristics, giving figures for individual countries (averaged across country-years, if more than one

Table 15.2 Selected immigration-related characteristics of countries

	Foreign-born stock (%)	Ratio, foreign-born:native-born unemployment
Netherlands	10.7	2.9
Sweden	13.5	2.7
Belgium	12.3	2.5
Norway	8.2	2.4
Switzerland	25.1	2.3
Finland	4.8	2.1
Denmark	9.2	2.0
France	11.2	1.8
Germany	11.2	1.7
Great Britain	9.3	1.4
Ireland	9.2	1.4
Iceland	11.4	1.4
Spain	8.6	1.3
Portugal	7.3	1.2
Canada	18.0	1.2
Italy	2.9	1.1
New Zealand	20.0	1.1
Australia	24.7	1.1
United States	12.0	0.9
Israel	30.6	0.7
Overall	14.0	1.6

Note: Figures are averaged across country-years (n = 54 for foreign-born stock, n = 46 for the foreign-born: native-born unemployment indicator), if more than one country-year of data is available for the given country.

Source: World Bank and OECD.

country-year of data is available for the given country). Countries are sorted according to the measure of immigrant/native-born unemployment inequality, so as to clearly highlight the variation in this. In line with the regime type figures given above, we see most of the social democratic countries near the top of the table, with among the highest levels of immigrant/native-born inequality. An exception is Iceland, which has a more intermediate position. The liberal settler societies (the United States, Australia, New Zealand, and Canada) are near the bottom of the table, with relatively low levels of immigrant/native-born inequality. However, liberal countries in Europe that are not settler societies are in more intermediate (the United Kingdom, Ireland) or even high (Switzerland) positions on the list. The group of conservative welfare states is spread most widely across the range of the immigrant/native-born inequality measure, with more familial regimes such as Israel and the Southern European countries having relatively low levels of this kind of inequality, while countries such as the Netherlands and Belgium are at the top of the list. In other words, though there are some patterns by welfare regime type, the correspondence is not perfect.

The modelling strategy is necessarily selective in terms of the macro-level variables just discussed, given the relatively small macro-level sample size, and it is therefore especially important and informative to examine how macro-level variables are intercorrelated. Table 15.3 shows these correlations. A number of high correlations stand out. First, it is clear that public spending is strongly negatively correlated ($r = -0.6$) with income inequality; this is unsurprising.

Another, more intriguing pattern is that it seems that societies may in practice face a certain kind of tradeoff between overall economic inequality and unemployment inequality between immigrant and native-born workers. The correlation between these two kinds of measures of inequality is strong and negative ($r = -0.8$). Figure 15.1 gives a more detailed look at the relationship between income inequality, as measured by the Gini coefficient, and the ratio of immigrant to native-born unemployment. Belgium, the Netherlands, and, in the most recent ISSP wave, Sweden appear to have the most extreme levels of immigrant/native-born inequality, even given their relatively low levels of income inequality, whereas Iceland is the most outlying observation in the other direction, with a lower level of immigrant/native-born inequality than one would expect at its relatively low level of income inequality. Therefore, within both the social democratic and conservative regime types, there is some useful variation in terms of disentangling the influence of these two macro-level variables.

It follows unsurprisingly from all of the previous that, though a higher level of public social spending is negatively associated with income inequality, it is positively associated ($r = 0.5$) with unemployment inequality between immigrant and native-born workers. This means that, if Hypotheses 1 and 2 both find support, they may in practice have countervailing effects: if income inequality and immigrant/native-born inequality both create the conditions for more negative public reactions to immigration in terms of welfare state support, these two effects could often cancel each other out. It remains to be seen how these patterns of inequality play out in terms of support for the welfare state.

Table 15.3 Pairwise correlations among selected country-year characteristics

	Public social spending (% GDP)	Unemployment (%)	Gini coefficient (%)	Foreign-born stock (%)	Ratio, foreign-born:native-born unemployment	Mean welfare state support scale
Public social spending (% GDP)	1.0					
Unemployment (%)	0.1	1.0				
Gini coefficient (%)	−0.6*	0.2	1.0			
Foreign-born stock (%)	−0.4*	−0.2	0.2+	1.0		
Ratio, foreign-born:native-born unemployment	0.5*	−0.2	−0.8*	−0.2	1.0	
Mean, welfare state support scale	0.3+	0.5*	0.0	−0.4*	0.0	1.0

Note: The unit of analysis is country-year (n = 54 for most correlations, n = 46 for correlations with the foreign-born:native-born unemployment indicator); * p < .05, + p < .10.

Source: World Bank, OECD, LIS, and ISSP.

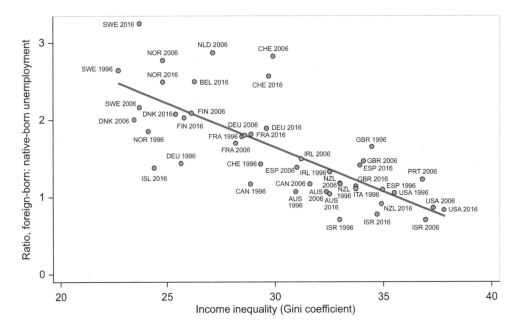

Note: n = 46; r = 0.8.

Source: OECD and LIS.

Figure 15.1 Relationship between income inequality and foreign-born/native-born unemployment inequality

PUBLIC SUPPORT FOR THE WELFARE STATE ACROSS WELFARE REGIME TYPES

I begin the analysis of public support for the welfare state with a further look at simple bivariate statistics at the level of country-years. As noted above, the outcome measure is a scale indicating the mean level of seven standardized attitudinal items.

In line with arguments that stronger public support for the welfare state undergirds higher welfare state spending, there is indeed a positive association (r = 0.3) between total public social spending and the average level of public support for the welfare state across countries and years. Note that there is no way in this simple setup to disentangle the direction of causality, though realistically, there are likely to be recursive feedback effects, such that over time, public support may lead to increased spending, which then may also feed back into greater support. Interestingly, across welfare regime types, it is actually conservative regimes that post the highest average level of support for the welfare state (0.15), followed by social democratic regimes (0.06) and then liberal regimes (−0.19), despite the fact that above, we observed the highest level of social spending in the social democratic regimes.

There is some initial support here in these raw figures for the assertion that immigration leads to less public support for the welfare state, as the correlation between the size of the

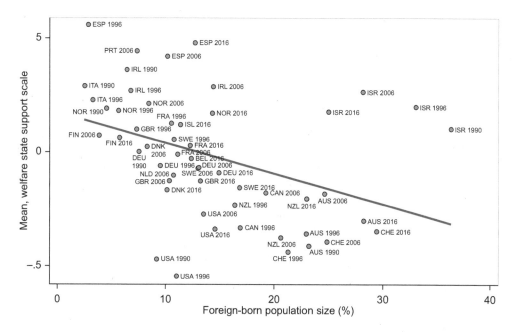

Note: n = 54, r = –0.4.

Source: OECD and ISSP.

Figure 15.2 Relationship between welfare state support and foreign-born population size

immigrant population as a percentage of the total population and the welfare state support scale is –0.4. Figure 15.2 shows this correlation in more detail.

The United States is a notable outlier in this relationship, as it – perhaps not surprisingly – has lower levels of support for the welfare state than one would expect given the size of its foreign-born population, though interestingly this outlier status is more pronounced in earlier years than in more recent years. Israel, Spain, and Portugal are outliers in the opposite direction: they have a higher level of welfare state support than one would expect, given the size of their foreign-born populations.

The other macro-level variable that is quite highly correlated with public support for the welfare state is unemployment (r = 0.5). It is worth noting here that the general strength of this relationship holds even when excluding the original opinion item that pertains specifically to welfare state support for the unemployed. The strength of the relationship between unemployment and welfare state support is driven in part by the extremely high values of both variables in Spain, though the correlation remains strong (r = 0.4) and significant even when excluding Spain.

Interestingly, there is essentially no correlation between general economic inequality as measured by the Gini coefficient and support for the welfare state. Neither is immigrant/native-born unemployment inequality correlated with support for the welfare state. Nevertheless, the hypotheses above pertain not to a direct effect of inequality on welfare state support, but instead, to interaction effects between these indicators of inequality and the size of the immigrant population. I turn now to more complex models that allow these propositions to be tested.

The models in Table 15.4 test the key hypotheses outlined above. Model 1 is a baseline model and includes main effects only. Model 2 introduces interaction effects between foreign-born stock and the two key measures of inequality, the Gini coefficient and the ratio of foreign-born to native-born unemployment. Model 3 adds an additional interaction between overall unemployment and the ratio of foreign-born to native-born unemployment, to examine the idea that the effect of immigrant labor market integration will depend on overall labor market conditions. Using the insights gained from Models 1 to 3, Models 4 to 6 turn to comparisons across welfare regime types. Model 4 looks at overall differences in the effect of foreign-born stock across regime types, net of basic sociodemographic controls. Model 5 is similar to Model 3, but substitutes welfare regime type for the inequality measures (Gini coefficient and ratio of foreign-born to native-born unemployment), on the logic that these inequality characteristics are quite strongly associated with welfare regime type. Finally, Model 6 attempts to disentangle the role of welfare regime type from the role of immigrant/native-born unemployment inequality. Note that, because of the inclusion of the immigrant/native-born unemployment inequality measure in some of the models in Table 15.4, all models are run on the restricted set of 46 country-years for which this variable is available.

The effects of the basic demographic controls are consistent across all six models. Age has no significant effect on welfare state support, whereas women are consistently and significantly more supportive of government responsibility for welfare programs. Respondents in disadvantaged socioeconomic situations (e.g., those with lower levels of education or who are currently unemployed) are most supportive of the welfare state, while those who are self-employed are least supportive of it. Employees and those in "other" employment situations (this is primarily those who are out of the labor force) have intermediate levels of support for the welfare state.

There is no indication in baseline Model 1 of a significant effect, either positive or negative, of foreign-born stock. That is, an increase in the relative size of the immigrant population has no effect one way or the other on support for the welfare state. This is consistent with previous work that has seen little overall effect of immigration in the aggregate country-level picture. Indeed, the only macro-level characteristic that seems to affect welfare state support in an overall significant way is the unemployment rate. Increases in unemployment increase support for the welfare state, which is logically consistent with the positive individual-level effect of being unemployed.

Model 2 addresses Hypotheses 1 and 2 by examining interaction effects between the foreign-born stock variable and the two inequality measures. Overall income inequality as measured by the Gini coefficient does not appear to interact with the foreign-born stock variable at all. So not only is there no significant main effect of income inequality on support for the welfare state, but income inequality also appears to make little difference in shaping whether the public responds to immigration by altering their support for the welfare state. There is, in other words, no support here for Hypothesis 1. However, the interaction between foreign-born stock and the ratio of foreign-born to native-born unemployment is negative and statistically significant, lending support to Hypothesis 2. In contexts of lower unemployment inequality between immigrants and the native born, there is an insignificant and even slightly positive effect of foreign-born stock on welfare

Table 15.4 Models predicting welfare state support

	Model 1	Model 2	Model 3	Model 4	Model 5	Model 6
Age	−0.001	−0.001	−0.001	−0.001	0.000	0.000
Female	0.113*	0.114*	0.114*	0.121*	0.118*	0.117*
Upper secondary education	−0.160*	−0.168*	−0.180*	−0.155*	−0.152*	−0.156*
Tertiary education	−0.226*	−0.236*	−0.247*	−0.237*	−0.225*	−0.227*
Self-employed	−0.111*	−0.109*	−0.113*	−0.093*	−0.106*	−0.112*
Unemployed	0.225*	0.223*	0.223*	0.275*	0.226*	0.225*
Other employment status	0.088*	0.082*	0.075*	0.095*	0.077*	0.073*
2006	0.206*	0.168*	0.174*	0.039*	0.134*	0.142*
2016	0.181*	0.164*	0.211*	0.006	0.093*	0.133*
Foreign-born stock (%)	−0.009	0.007	0.022		−0.013	−0.001
Unemployment (%)	0.034*	0.034*	0.094*		−0.027*	0.048
Gini coefficient (%)	−0.010	0.000	0.000			
Ratio, foreign-born:native-born unemployment	−0.082	0.252	0.552*			0.160
Foreign-born stock × Gini coefficient		0.000	0.000			
Foreign-born stock × foreign-born:native-born unemployment		−0.017*	−0.019*			−0.003
Unemployment × foreign-born:native-born unemployment			−0.046*			−0.031*
Conservative welfare regime				0.079	−0.589*	−0.216
Liberal welfare regime				−0.297*	−0.537*	−0.300
Conservative welfare regime × foreign-born stock					0.018*	0.005
Liberal welfare regime × foreign-born stock					0.002	−0.007
Conservative welfare regime × unemployment					0.059*	0.018
Liberal welfare regime × unemployment					0.059*	0.023
Constant	0.239	−0.516*	−0.905*	0.107*	0.314*	−0.131

Note: Excluded categories are male, lower secondary education or less, employee, 1996, and social democratic welfare regime; standard errors are adjusted for clustering by country and year; * p < .05.

Source: World Bank, OECD, LIS, and ISSP.

state support. In contexts of higher immigrant/native-born inequality, on the other hand, the effect of foreign-born stock is considerably more negative.

Model 3 shows similar patterns in terms of effects relevant to Hypotheses 1 and 2, and further allows us to consider Hypothesis 3, by including an interaction effect between the immigrant/native-born unemployment inequality measure and the overall unemployment rate. Figure 15.3 illustrates how immigrant/native-born unemployment inequality affects

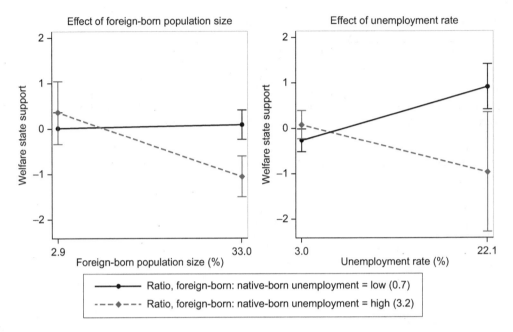

Note: Marginal effects are based on Model 3 in Table 15.4; confidence intervals are at the 95 percent level.

Source: World Bank, OECD, LIS, and ISSP.

Figure 15.3 Marginal effects of immigrant/native-born unemployment inequality on welfare state support

welfare state support via its interaction with the foreign-born stock measure and the unemployment measure. The marginal effects in this figure are plotted with 95 percent confidence intervals and are calculated from Model 3. The values of predictors used for these calculations capture the full range of these variables in the data. We see that, when immigrant/native-born unemployment inequality is low, the foreign-born stock effect is negligible and the effect of unemployment is positive. However, if immigrant/native-born unemployment inequality is high, the effects of both foreign-born population size and the unemployment rate grow more negative. In other words, if immigrants are poorly integrated into host-country labor markets, then a larger immigrant population and a higher unemployment rate can be detrimental to welfare state support. The reverse way of thinking about these interaction effects is to examine the effect of the immigrant/native-born unemployment inequality measure in different contexts. If there is little immigration or little unemployment, this form of inequality does not statistically matter for welfare state support. If either foreign-born population size is large or unemployment is high, then the immigrant/native-born inequality measure has a statistically significant impact on welfare state support. In sum, there is support for both Hypothesis 2 and Hypothesis 3 in Model 3.

Models 4 to 6 in Table 15.4 turn to variation across welfare regime types. Model 4 provides an overall look at how welfare state support varies across regime type, net of the demographic and socioeconomic controls. This overall variation across regime type is displayed in the first graph of Figure 15.4. In line with earlier findings in Table 15.1, we see the highest levels of welfare state support in conservative regimes, followed closely by social democratic regimes, and with liberal regimes having significantly lower levels of welfare state support.

Model 5 takes into account the ways in which the indicators of inequality (Gini coefficient and immigrant/native-born unemployment inequality) are associated with welfare state regime type. Recall from the descriptive results in Table 15.1 that social democratic regimes are distinctive in terms of both low levels of income inequality and high levels of immigrant/native-born unemployment inequality, whereas liberal regimes have exactly the opposite pattern (higher levels of income inequality and lower levels of immigrant/native-born inequality). Conservative regimes have, on average, intermediate values on both measures. Given the interaction effects we observed in Model 3 and Figure 15.3, it would generally follow that countries with high immigrant/native-born inequality, such as social democratic regimes, would experience more negative/less positive effects of a larger immigrant population and more negative/less positive effects of higher unemployment.

That is exactly the pattern we see in Model 5. The second and third graphs of Figure 15.4 display average margins, with 95 percent confidence intervals, calculated from Model 5. We see that, when the foreign-born population size and unemployment rate are set to low values (the lowest values actually occurring in the data), social democratic regimes display levels of welfare state support that are statistically higher than conservative regimes, and higher than but statistically indistinguishable from liberal regimes. If we turn instead to the picture in the final graph of Figure 15.4, where the foreign-born population size and the unemployment rate are set to high values, social democratic regimes instead have levels of welfare state support that are lower than in conservative countries and lower but statistically indistinguishable from levels in liberal countries. In short, characteristic features of social democratic regimes interact with immigrant population size and unemployment, such that if these variables have low values, welfare state support is relatively high in social democratic regimes. However, if these variables have high values, welfare state support is relatively low in social democratic regimes.

The final model in Table 15.4, Model 6, includes interaction effects that enable us to see whether these differences across welfare regimes can be attributed to differing levels of immigrant/native-born unemployment inequality. Indeed, the inclusion of the interaction between this inequality measure and unemployment, which remains significant in this final model, appears to explain the variation by welfare regime type observed in Model 5 and Figure 15.4. In this final model, the main effects of welfare regime type and the interactions of welfare regime type with foreign-born stock and with unemployment are no longer statistically significant. This suggests that the different effects of foreign-born stock and unemployment in different welfare regime types can be explained by systematically different levels of immigrant/native-born unemployment inequality.

DISCUSSION

The analysis laid out in this chapter provides additional evidence to support a growing body of literature showing that immigration's effect on public support for the welfare state is highly conditional on other characteristics of the contexts in which that growing

314 *Handbook on migration and welfare*

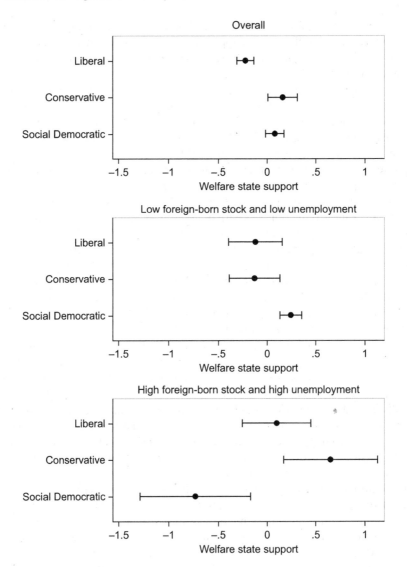

Note: Marginal effects are based on Models 4 and 5 in Table 15.4; confidence intervals are at the 95 percent level.

Source: World Bank, OECD, LIS, and ISSP.

Figure 15.4   Welfare state support, by regime type

diversity unfolds. The characteristics that were the focus of this chapter are those that tap various dimensions of socioeconomic inequality. Though overall income inequality as measured by the Gini coefficient appears to play little role in shaping responses to immigration, another form of inequality more proximal to immigration itself – the level of integration of immigrants into their host-country labor markets – does matter.

Countries in which immigrant labor market integration has been particularly challenging, and in which immigrant/native-born unemployment inequality is high, experience particular risks in terms of immigration undermining public support for the welfare state. Labor market integration of immigrants has been a more pronounced problem in the social democratic welfare states than in other kinds of countries, though a handful of other countries such as the Netherlands and Belgium have also experienced quite severe levels of immigrant/native-born unemployment inequality. In such countries, as the immigrant population becomes larger, and as immigrant/native-born unemployment inequality therefore presumably becomes more salient, public welfare state support declines. Similarly, if overall unemployment goes up in such countries, which presumably also increases the salience of immigrant/native-born unemployment inequality, again public support for the welfare state declines.

It is important to point out, however, that it is not a large immigrant population which is a problem per se in terms of undermining support for the welfare state. In contexts where immigrant labor market integration proceeds rather more smoothly, we observe no negative effects of immigrant population size. Similarly, higher unemployment by itself tends to increase rather than decrease support for the welfare state, because respondents probably perceive certain risks to their own ability to secure welfare in the market in the context of high unemployment. But combined with higher immigrant/native-born unemployment inequality, higher levels of unemployment actually undermine welfare state support.

As with all country-level analyses of the issues that are the focus of this chapter, there are shortcomings that should be addressed in future research. Countries vary in so many ways, and though the findings from this analysis are intriguing and suggestive, they should be triangulated with other forms of evidence. Evidence from different surveys could further elucidate the mechanisms through which immigrant/native-born inequality produces the patterns that we observe in the analysis here. For instance, it would be interesting to know whether immigrant/native-born inequality changes people's perceptions of the actual level of immigration or unemployment. This could be examined with existing datasets that ask about such perceptions. In addition to survey data, experimental evidence from vignettes that manipulate the key variables (e.g., Koopmans and Veit 2014) could prove more conclusive than observational data such as that used in this chapter. Finally, qualitative research that delves more deeply into people's beliefs about inequality, immigration, social solidarity, and welfare state support would also be a welcome addition to what has remained, at least in the cross-national literature, largely the realm of quantitatively oriented social scientists.

One primary take-away from the chapter is that an important and, to some readers, somewhat unfamiliar characteristic of the most generous welfare states, including the social democratic regimes but also countries such as Belgium and the Netherlands, is higher levels of immigrant/native-born inequality in the labor market. Furthermore, this characteristic conditions how the public responds, in terms of their support for the welfare state, to both growing immigration and changing economic circumstances. These generous welfare states have historically been effective at maintaining relatively low levels of overall economic inequality. Going forward, these countries will need to devote further attention to their growing immigrant populations and to the particularly severe challenges immigrant newcomers often face in accessing stable employment, which even in countries with high levels of decommodification remains an important indicator of integration. If these countries fail to address immigrant integration challenges, they risk public support for the policies that have made this welfare state model distinctive.

The upshot of these findings, however, is that there is not one single inevitable consequence of growing immigration on public support for the welfare state. Immigrant/native-born inequalities in the labor market certainly present policy challenges, but these inequalities are arguably more tractable from a policy perspective than immigration itself. Host countries would be well advised to focus on policies of immigrant integration. Such policies would benefit immigrants and would also have positive consequences for overall welfare state support.

REFERENCES

Alba, Richard, and Nancy Foner. 2015. *Strangers No More: Immigration and the Challenges of Integration in North America and Western Europe*. Princeton, NJ: Princeton University Press.

Alesina, Alberto, and Edward Glaeser. 2004. *Fighting Poverty in the US and Europe: A World of Difference*. Oxford: Oxford University Press.

An, Brian, Morris Levy, and Rodney Hero. 2018. "It's Not Just Welfare: Racial Inequality and the Local Provision of Public Goods in the United States." *Urban Affairs Review* 54(5): 833–65.

Brady, David, and Ryan Finnigan. 2014. "Does Immigration Undermine Public Support for Social Policy?" *American Sociological Review* 79(1): 17–42.

Breznau, Nate, and Maureen A. Eger. 2016. "Immigrant Presence, Group Boundaries, and Support for the Welfare State in Western European Societies." *Acta Sociologica* 59(3): 195–214.

Brooks, Clem, and Jeff Manza. 2008. *Why Welfare States Persist: The Importance of Public Opinion in Democracies*. Chicago, IL: University of Chicago Press.

Brown, Hana E. 2013. "Race, Legality, and the Social Policy Consequences of Anti-Immigration Mobilization." *American Sociological Review* 78(2): 290–314.

Burgoon, Brian. 2014. "Immigration, Integration, and Support for Redistribution in Europe." *World Politics* 66(3): 365–405.

Burgoon, Brian, and Matthijs Rooduijn. 2021. "'Immigrationization' of Welfare Politics? Anti-Immigration and Welfare Attitudes in Context." *West European Politics* 44(2): 177–203.

Cameron, A. Colin, Jonah B. Gelbach, and Douglas L. Miller. 2012. "Robust Inference with Multiway Clustering." *Journal of Business and Economic Statistics* 29(2): 238–49.

Crepaz, Markus M.L. 2008. *Trust beyond Borders: Immigration, the Welfare State, and Identity in Modern Societies*. Ann Arbor, MI: University of Michigan Press.

de Haas, Hein, Mathias Czaika, Marie-Laurence Flahaux, Edo Mahendra, Katharina Natter, Simona Vezzoli, and María Villares-Varela. 2019. "International Migration: Trends, Determinants, and Policy Effects." *Population and Development Review* 45(4): 885–922.

De Jong, Gordon F., Deborah Graefe, Chris Galvan, and Stephanie Howe Hasanali. 2017. "Unemployment and Immigrant Receptivity Climate in Established and Newly Emerging Destination Areas." *Population Research and Policy Review* 36(2): 157–80.

Dinesen, Peter Thisted, Merlin Schaeffer, and Kim Mannemar Sønderskov. 2020. "Ethnic Diversity and Social Trust: A Narrative and Meta-Analytical Review." *Annual Review of Political Science* 23(1): 441–65.

Eger, Maureen A., and Nate Breznau. 2017. "Immigration and the Welfare State: A Cross-Regional Analysis of European Welfare Attitudes." *International Journal of Comparative Sociology* 58(5): 440–63.

Esping-Andersen, Gosta. 1990. *The Three Worlds of Welfare Capitalism*. Princeton, NJ: Princeton University Press.

Finseraas, Henning. 2008. "Immigration and Preferences for Redistribution: An Empirical Analysis of European Survey Data." *Comparative European Politics* 6(4): 407–31.

Finseraas, Henning, Axel West Pedersen, and Ann-Helén Bay. 2016. "When the Going Gets Tough: The Differential Impact of National Unemployment on the Perceived Threats of Immigration." *Political Studies* 64(1): 60–73.

Fox, Cybelle. 2010. "Three Worlds of Relief: Race, Immigration, and Public and Private Social Welfare Spending in American Cities, 1929." *American Journal of Sociology* 116(2): 453–502.

Fox, Cybelle. 2012. *Three Worlds of Relief: Race, Immigration, and the American Welfare State from the Progressive Era to the New Deal*. Princeton, NJ: Princeton University Press.

Fox, Cybelle, Irene Bloemraad, and Christel Kesler. 2013. "Immigration and Redistributive Social Policy." In *Immigration, Poverty, and Socioeconomic Inequality*, eds. David Card and Steven Raphael. New York: Russell Sage Foundation, 381–420.

Gaston, Noel, and Gulasekaran Rajaguru. 2013. "International Migration and the Welfare State Revisited." *European Journal of Political Economy* 29: 90–101.

Goodhart, David. 2004. "Too Diverse? Is Britain Becoming Too Diverse to Sustain the Mutual Obligations That Underpin a Good Society and a Generous Welfare State?" *Prospect*, February 20.

Heath, Anthony, and Sin Yi Cheung. 2007. *Unequal Chances: Ethnic Minorities in Western Labour Markets*. Oxford: Oxford University Press.

Heizmann, Boris. 2015. "Social Policy and Perceived Immigrant Labor Market Competition in Europe: Is Prevention Better Than Cure?" *Social Forces* 93(4): 1655–85.

Hero, Rodney E. 2010. "Immigration and Social Policy in the United States." *Annual Review of Political Science* 13(1): 445–68.

Hero, Rodney E., and Morris E. Levy. 2016. "The Racial Structure of Economic Inequality in the United States: Understanding Change and Continuity in an Era of 'Great Divergence.'" *Social Science Quarterly* 97(3): 491–505.

Hero, Rodney E., and Morris E. Levy. 2018. "The Racial Structure of Inequality: Consequences for Welfare Policy in the United States." *Social Science Quarterly* 99(2): 459–72.

ISSP Research Group. 2008a. *International Social Survey Programme: Role of Government I–IV – ISSP 1985–1990–1996–2006*. Cologne: GESIS Data Archive. https://doi.org/10.4232/1.4747.

ISSP Research Group. 2008b. *International Social Survey Programme: Role of Government IV – ISSP 2006*. Cologne: GESIS Data Archive. https://doi.org/10.4232/1.4700.

ISSP Research Group. 2018. *International Social Survey Programme: Role of Government V – ISSP 2016*. Cologne: GESIS Data Archive. https://doi.org/10.4232/1.13052.

Kesler, Christel. 2015. "Welfare States and Immigrant Poverty: Germany, Sweden, and the United Kingdom in Comparative Perspective." *Acta Sociologica* 58(1): 39–61.

Kesler, Christel. 2018. "Gender Norms, Work–Family Policies, and Labor Force Participation among Immigrant and Native-Born Women in Western Europe." *Socius* 4: 1–16.

Kesler, Christel, and Irene Bloemraad. 2010. "Does Immigration Erode Social Capital? The Conditional Effects of Immigration-Generated Diversity on Trust, Membership, and Participation across 19 Countries, 1981–2000." *Canadian Journal of Political Science/Revue canadienne de science politique* 43(2): 319–47.

Kogan, Irena. 2006. "Labor Markets and Economic Incorporation among Recent Immigrants in Europe." *Social Forces* 85(2): 697–721.

Koopmans, Ruud. 2010. "Trade-Offs between Equality and Difference: Immigrant Integration, Multiculturalism and the Welfare State in Cross-National Perspective." *Journal of Ethnic and Migration Studies* 36(1): 1–26.

Koopmans, Ruud. 2013. "Multiculturalism and Immigration: A Contested Field in Cross-National Comparison." *Annual Review of Sociology* 39: 147–69.

Koopmans, Ruud, and Merlin Schaeffer. 2016. "Statistical and Perceived Diversity and Their Impacts on Neighborhood Social Cohesion in Germany, France and the Netherlands." *Social Indicators Research* 125(3): 853–83.

Koopmans, Ruud, and Susanne Veit. 2014. "Ethnic Diversity, Trust, and the Mediating Role of Positive and Negative Interethnic Contact: A Priming Experiment." *Social Science Research* 47: 91–107.

Lieberson, Stanley. 1991. "Small N's and Big Conclusions: An Examination of the Reasoning in Comparative Studies Based on a Small Number of Cases." *Social Forces* 70(2): 307–20.

Luxembourg Income Study. 2020. *LIS Inequality and Poverty Key Figures*. Luxembourg: LIS. www.lisdatacenter.org.

Massey, Douglas S., Jorge Durand, and Karen A. Pren. 2016. "Why Border Enforcement Backfired." *American Journal of Sociology* 121(5): 1557–600.

Mau, Steffen, and Christoph Burkhardt. 2009. "Migration and Welfare State Solidarity in Western Europe." *Journal of European Social Policy* 19(3): 213–29.

Moller, Stephanie, David Bradley, Evelyne Huber, Françoise Nielsen, and John D. Stephens. 2003. "Determinants of Relative Poverty in Advanced Capitalist Democracies." *American Sociological Review* 68(1): 22–51.

Morissens, Ann, and Diane Sainsbury. 2005. "Migrants' Social Rights, Ethnicity and Welfare Regimes." *Journal of Social Policy* 34(4): 637–60.

Nagayoshi, Kikuko, and Mikael Hjerm. 2015. "Anti-Immigration Attitudes in Different Welfare States: Do Types of Labor Market Policies Matter?" *International Journal of Comparative Sociology* 56(2): 141–62.

Organisation for Economic Co-operation and Development. 2020. *OECD.Stat*. https://stats.oecd.org/.

Orloff, Ann Shola. 1993. "Gender and the Social Rights of Citizenship: The Comparative Analysis of Gender Relations and Welfare States." *American Sociological Review* 58(3): 303–28.

Pierson, Paul. 1994. *Dismantling the Welfare State? Reagan, Thatcher and the Politics of Retrenchment.* Cambridge: Cambridge University Press.

Portes, Alejandro, and Erik Vickstrom. 2011. "Diversity, Social Capital, and Cohesion." *Annual Review of Sociology* 37: 461–79.

Putnam, Robert D. 2007. "*E Pluribus Unum*: Diversity and Community in the Twenty-First Century: The 2006 Johan Skytte Prize Lecture." *Scandinavian Political Studies* 30(2): 137–74.

Quillian, Lincoln. 1995. "Prejudice as a Response to Perceived Group Threat: Population Composition and Anti-Immigrant and Racial Prejudice in Europe." *American Sociological Review* 60(4): 586–611.

Quillian, Lincoln, Anthony Heath, Devah Pager, Arnfinn H. Midtbøen, Fenella Fleishmann, and Ole Hexel. 2019. "Do Some Countries Discriminate More Than Others? Evidence from 97 Field Experiments of Racial Discrimination in Hiring." *Sociological Science* 6: 467–96.

Sainsbury, Diane. 2012. *Welfare States and Immigrant Rights: The Politics of Inclusion and Exclusion.* Oxford: Oxford University Press.

Schmidt-Catran, Alexander W., and Dennis C. Spies. 2016. "Immigration and Welfare Support in Germany." *American Sociological Review* 81(2): 242–61.

Soroka, Stuart N., Richard Johnston, Anthony Kevins, Keith Banting, and Will Kymlicka. 2016. "Migration and Welfare State Spending." *European Political Science Review* 8(2): 173–94.

van der Meer, Tom, and Jochem Tolsma. 2014. "Ethnic Diversity and Its Effects on Social Cohesion." *Annual Review of Sociology* 40(1): 459–78.

World Bank. 2020. *World Development Indicators.* https://databank.worldbank.org/source/world-development-indicators.

APPENDIX

Table 15.A.1 Replications of Model 3 in Table 15.4, using separate welfare state support items

	Jobs	Healthcare	Elderly	Unemployed	Poor	Income differences	Students
Age	−0.004*	0.000	0.002*	0.000	0.000	−0.001	−0.002
Female	0.156*	0.061*	0.088*	0.074*	0.116*	0.101*	0.039*
Upper secondary education	−0.339*	−0.067*	−0.087*	−0.123*	−0.265*	−0.131*	−0.050*
Tertiary education	−0.511*	−0.093*	−0.160*	−0.097*	−0.385*	−0.159*	−0.057*
Self-employed	−0.159*	−0.040*	−0.036*	−0.102*	−0.220*	−0.070*	−0.046*
Unemployed	0.261*	0.062*	0.058*	0.355*	0.241*	0.205*	0.117*
Other employment status	0.098*	0.014	−0.005	0.093*	0.060*	0.076*	0.100*
2006	−0.027	0.145*	0.127*	0.059	0.209*	0.197*	0.180*
2016	0.026	0.201*	0.176*	0.055	0.342*	0.193*	0.110*
Foreign-born stock (%)	0.003	0.043	0.012	−0.016	0.05.	0.029	−0.005
Unemployment (%)	0.124*	0.058*	0.055*	0.092*	0.086*	0.063*	0.045*
Gini coefficient (%)	−0.008	0.000	−0.006	−0.022	0.007	0.014	0.012
Ratio, foreign-born:native-born unemployment	0.837*	0.511*	0.408*	0.356*	0.595*	0.315*	0.029
Foreign-born stock × Gini coefficient	0.001	−0.001	0.000	0.000	−0.001	0.000	0.000
Foreign-born stock × foreign-born:native-born unemployment	−0.021*	−0.022*	−0.016*	−0.006	−0.021*	−0.017	−0.001
Unemployment × foreign-born:native-born unemployment	−0.063*	−0.041*	−0.033*	−0.043	−0.039*	−0.022	−0.012
Constant	1.926	2.936*	3.088*	2.974*	1.658*	2.049*	2.739*

Note: Excluded categories are male, lower secondary education or less, employee, and 1996; standard errors are adjusted for clustering by country and year; * $p < .05$.

Source: World Bank, OECD, LIS, and ISSP.

Table 15.A.2 Replications of Model 6 in Table 15.4, using separate welfare state support items

	Jobs	Healthcare	Elderly	Unemployed	Poor	Income differences	Students
Age	-0.003*	0.000	0.002*	0.001	0.001	-0.001	-0.002*
Female	0.163*	0.060*	0.087*	0.074*	0.121*	0.104*	0.043*
Upper secondary education	-0.292*	-0.068*	-0.082*	-0.111*	-0.230*	-0.106*	-0.03
Tertiary education	-0.463*	-0.102*	-0.163*	-0.088*	-0.345*	-0.136*	-0.033
Self-employed	-0.156*	-0.043*	-0.038*	-0.105*	-0.217*	-0.068*	-0.042*
Unemployed	0.260*	0.066*	0.063*	0.358*	0.240*	0.206*	0.115*
Other employment status	0.093*	0.016	-0.003	0.093*	0.057*	0.074*	0.096*
2006	-0.129*	0.144*	0.126*	0.01	0.136*	0.204*	0.183*
2016	-0.109*	0.171*	0.127*	-0.055	0.239*	0.169*	0.106*
Foreign-born stock (%)	0.000	0.029*	0.016	-0.033*	-0.008	0.000	-0.028*
Unemployment (%)	0.057	0.034	0.017	0.035	0.058	0.055	0.016
Ratio, foreign-born:native-born unemployment	0.418	0.392*	0.134	-0.118	0.184	0.01	-0.178
Foreign-born stock x foreign-born:native-born unemployment	-0.004	-0.018*	-0.007	0.012*	-0.001	-0.001	0.01
Unemployment x foreign-born:native-born unemployment	-0.048*	-0.030*	-0.018	-0.018	-0.03	-0.021	-0.009
Conservative welfare regime	-0.102	-0.058	-0.198	-0.515	-0.107	0.001	-0.188
Liberal welfare regime	-0.154	-0.269	-0.243	-0.766*	-0.167	0.038	-0.036
Conservative welfare regime x foreign-born stock	0.013	-0.017*	-0.012	0.015	0.018	0.003	0.022*
Liberal welfare regime x foreign-born stock	-0.002	-0.011	-0.017*	0.011	0.003	-0.015	0.004
Conservative welfare regime x unemployment	0.025	0.011	0.019	0.016	0.000	0.000	0.021*
Liberal welfare regime x unemployment	-0.009	0.033	0.032	0.03	-0.011	0.01	0.017
Constant	2.618*	3.138*	3.412*	3.462*	2.690*	2.894*	3.548*

Note: Excluded categories are male, lower secondary education or less, employee, 1996, and social democratic welfare regime; standard errors are adjusted for clustering by country and year; * p < .05 .

Source: World Bank, OECD, LIS, and ISSP.

16. Welfare states and migration policy: The main challenges for scholarship
Frida Boräng, Sara Kalm, and Johannes Lindvall

In the last two decades, there has been a surge in research among social scientists, and among historians, on the relationship between the development of the welfare state and the development of migration policy. The scholarly literature on this topic has grown not only in volume and scope, but also in theoretical and methodological sophistication. In the first part of our chapter, we review this growing literature, paying especially close attention to how scholars have understood and interpreted the relationship between the welfare state and migration policy—how they co-evolve, and how they can be combined. In the second part of the chapter, we discuss three central problems that scholars have confronted in this literature.

The first problem concerns the distinctions among different types of migration policy. We argue that since the differences among labor migration policy, asylum and refugee policy, and immigrant policy are great—both historically and today—it is not meaningful to analyze the relationship between social policy and migration policy in general terms; analyses must be specific to different forms of policy.

The second problem concerns the scope of most empirical research of welfare states and migration policy. We argue that since the welfare state has co-evolved with migration policy ever since the late nineteenth and early twentieth centuries, it is difficult to understand the relationship between the two without analyzing that relationship in an historical context.

The third problem concerns how to make causal claims about the relationship between the welfare state and migration policy. Some scholars treat the welfare state as an outcome to be explained and migration policy as the cause (Alesina and Glaeser 2004; Spies 2018); others do the opposite, suggesting that the welfare state shapes migration policy (see for example Banting 2000). We argue that precisely because the welfare state and migration policy have co-evolved, these sorts of claims are often difficult to sustain, for welfare state policy and migration policy are closely related and typically emerge from the same underlying political process.

Throughout our review, we note that there are fundamentally different expectations in the literature concerning the compatibility of generous welfare state policies and generous migration policies.

Those who argue that large migration is incompatible with generous social policies tend to focus on the relatively high costs of benefits and services in generous welfare states (see for example Freeman 1986). Expensive benefits and services, it is argued, cannot exist in combination with a substantial inflow of migrants that are able to enjoy them. Something must go. Depending on the specific version of the argument, it will either be benefits and services (welfare retrenchment), the inflow of migrants (more restrictive admission policies), or the ability of migrants to enjoy benefits and services (more restrictive welfare access for migrants).

But there are also those who argue that generous welfare states and open migration policies can co-exist (see for example Crepaz 2008). In fact, according to one view, the very size of a large, generous welfare state makes it easier to include more people without enhancing distributional conflict (Boräng 2018; Römer 2017). Scholars within this strand of research tend to highlight that welfare state policies matter not only for individuals' incentive structures but also for norms and values, making it easier to include outsiders (Esping-Andersen 1990).

The chapters in Parts I and II of this volume offer more detailed accounts of what we know about topics such as welfare chauvinism and migration as a threat to the welfare state, and the chapters in Part III offer a wealth of detail on various political responses to migration. In this chapter, we put these scholarly and political debates in context by examining the long-run co-evolution of the welfare state and migration policy and by drawing lessons that are relevant for understanding current political conflicts.

EXPLAINING THE WELFARE STATE

This section reviews the scholarly debate on the viability of the welfare state in a context of migration and increasing social diversity. We concentrate on the debate within political science and to some extent also sociology. It is important to keep in mind, however, that this debate is closely related to a debate among economists about the impact of migration on public finances. Some scholars argue that migrants burden the welfare state since they often require economic assistance, at least initially. According to one line of reasoning, generous welfare states can even function as "welfare magnets" (Borjas 1999) that attract low-skilled and unskilled migrants, which exacerbates this effect. On the other side of this debate, we find those who regard the economic gains from migration as greater than the costs (see for example Battisti et al. 2018). The aging of the populations of many advanced welfare states is likely to result in financial challenges, and according to some scholars, these challenges can at least in part be solved through immigration (for a summary of this debate, see Nannestad 2007).

In the political science literature, which is our main concern here, there are two main positions, to which scholars arrive via different arguments: on the one hand, there are those who regard migration as a threat to the welfare state; on the other hand, there are those who regard migration as compatible with the welfare state.

The New Progressive's Dilemma: Migration as a Threat to the Welfare State

Early research on migration and the welfare state contended that open migration policies—or ethnic heterogeneity—make it difficult for an encompassing welfare state to develop or survive. Gary Freeman (1986, 61) stated more than 30 years ago that "From the perspective of the politics of the welfare state ... there can be no doubt that migration has been little short of a disaster" since "it has contributed to the erosion of the political consensus on which the welfare state rests." This idea has been picked up in more recent debates, and it is now often labeled "the diversity-versus-solidarity thesis" or "the new progressive dilemma" (Pearce 2004). The basic contention is that the relationship between migration and welfare is fraught with conflict and that they are ultimately incompatible. The assumption that undergirds the new progressive dilemma is that of a necessary trade-off between ethnic heterogeneity and redistribution (Goodhart 2004; Kymlicka and Banting 2006). The problem is not so much immigration as such but the ethnic diversity that it brings about. The populations of Western welfare states, it is argued, are unwilling to pay for the welfare of ethnically and culturally distant others. Over time, these critical attitudes will translate into retrenchment, and the welfare state itself will become untenable. The basis of this argument is often found in social psychology, where Henri Tajfel and others have observed that people are more willing to allocate resources to members of their own ingroup than to members of outgroups (Tajfel 1974). Outgroups, it is argued, are often defined by ethnic or cultural markers: "To put it bluntly—most of us prefer our own kind," as Goodhart (2004) puts it.

Loyalty to—and therefore welfare solidarity with—one's own racial or ethnic group is thus an important mechanism that connects ethnic diversity with welfare retrenchment. For example, Luttmer (2001) showed that in the United States, support for welfare spending increased with the share of local recipients from one's own racial group. Another mechanism is social capital, the idea being that diversity lowers trust, which, in turn, lowers support for redistribution (Putnam 2007). A third mechanism is that conflicts over immigration tend to reduce support for parties that are in favor of a large welfare state, notably mainstream parties on the left (Kitschelt 1995). A fourth mechanism is that ethnic heterogeneity makes it more difficult to "forge a common class-based identity" (Alesina and Glaeser 2004, 134).

Freeman (1986, 51) argued that immigration has led to the "Americanization of European welfare politics." Indeed, the United States case has had great impact on the new progressive dilemma scholarship, with scholars anticipating an Americanization of European social policy, with shrinking welfare states as a long-term consequence. The work of Alesina and Glaeser (2004) has been immensely influential and therefore merits special attention. They argue that ethnic fractionalization, resulting from slavery as well as immigration, is one of the main reasons why the United States has not developed a European-style welfare state. But Alesina and Glaeser do not claim that ethnic diversity *in itself* explains this outcome, something that is often forgotten in the debate that has followed. A crucial intervening variable has been that poor people in the United States—that is, the most likely recipients of welfare benefits—have disproportionately belonged to ethnic and racial minorities. In addition, politicians have made strategic use of racialized poverty to delegitimize the welfare state.

At the end of their book, Alesina and Glaeser argue that the same factors are now present in Europe: large-scale immigration has resulted in ethnic heterogeneity, ethnic minorities are disproportionately poor, and there is no shortage of right-wing populist politicians in Europe who try to politicize this fact. They therefore contend that "Europe's new immigrant-based heterogeneity may ... push the continent toward more American levels of redistribution" (Alesina and Glaeser 2004, 175).

This prediction has spurred a surge in empirical research. So far, however, the results are inconclusive. Starting with the micro-level link, the new progressive dilemma thesis holds that increased ethnic diversity will lead to less support for redistribution among the native population. Spies (2018) argues that large-scale immigration has indeed made people less supportive of redistribution and finds that those who oppose migration also tend to oppose welfare spending. Brady and Finnigan (2014), on the other hand, find very little support for the generic new progressive dilemma thesis and therefore conclude that other factors must be more important when explaining declining support for the welfare state. In fact, they observe that surges in immigration have sometimes led to *increased* support for the welfare state. The reason, they hypothesize, is that natives' perceptions of threats to their own employment and subsistence are intensified in such periods, which leads people to turn to the welfare state for support. Similarly, Burgoon et al. (2012) question the idea that immigration will reduce support for the welfare state.

After having concluded that "the fear that the welfare state might lose its support when the share of migrants increases seems to be exaggerated," Mau and Burkhardt (2009, 225) explain this finding with certain characteristics of the welfare state itself. People's reaction to immigration is mediated by the welfare regime in which they live. More precisely, it matters to public opinion whether "inclusion is institutionally organized and whether social benefit schemes have been constructed in such a way that they reinforce or lessen conflicts over redistribution" (Mau and Burkhardt 2009, 226).

This brings us to the specific strand of the literature that emphasizes how welfare states, and in particular mature welfare states, can deflect many potential threats to their survival.

The Resilience of Mature Welfare States

The merits of the new progressive's dilemma literature's assumptions at the micro level have been questioned, as described above. There are also those who question the assumptions at a macro level, arguing that the new progressive dilemma scenario has not panned out as expected in European social policy (Baldwin and Huber 2010; Kymlicka and Banting 2006; Soroka et al. 2016). Dennis C. Spies (2018) is one scholar who makes this sort of argument. As mentioned earlier, he argues that large-scale immigration has made people less supportive of redistribution, and he finds that those who oppose migration also tend to oppose welfare spending. The puzzle, to him, is that these negative public attitudes have so far not been translated into policy. There are two main reasons for this, he argues. One concerns the role of parties as intermediaries between public opinion and welfare policies. European mainstream parties—left and right—do not want to alienate immigrant voters by championing cuts in welfare spending. In addition, right-wing populist parties, which have emerged and gained success by channeling negative attitudes toward immigrants, are themselves on average not anti-welfare, reflecting the heterogeneous welfare policy views of their supporters. The second reason is that European welfare institutions have a different structure than welfare institutions in the United States. Spies observes that, in both regions, not all programs are equally criticized, even among the welfare skeptics. He finds that it is mainly "means tested, ungenerous, tax-financed, and flat-rate programs"—which target the poor—that lose support when diversity increases (Spies 2018, 92). Programs that are more comprehensive and universal fare better: reaching the middle class, they are less likely to be retrenched. In the advanced welfare states of Europe, more welfare programs are of the latter type, which accounts for their resilience, in Spies's view.

These results are in line with Soroka et al. (2016). Although they find that, over time, increases in migration are associated with smaller welfare spending increases, the effect is uneven across programs. Again, universal programs are found to be more resilient when diversity increases than targeted programs are. Soroka et al. go on to suggest that this might be the case also at the level of welfare regimes, leading them to ask whether "universal systems resist or accommodate immigration pressure better than conservative or liberal regimes" (Soroka et al. 2016, 188). Taylor-Gooby (2005) similarly finds that "left politics" tempers the "Americanization" of European social policy.

A key point in this literature is that the early United States experience may not be relevant for understanding contemporary Europe, where mature welfare state institutions are already in place. This point is most clearly formulated by Crepaz (2008, 9):

> The central thesis of this book is that extrapolating from the American experience is problematic for the following reason: the primordial challenge to the European welfare state is unfolding at a time when it has *reached maturity*, as opposed to the American experience in which diversity hampered the development of a more comprehensive welfare state *from the beginning*.

Although he argues against the "primordial" argument, Crepaz (2008) also makes the point that the causal arrow could go in both directions: welfare states may shape how societies respond to international migration. This brings us to the part of the migration-welfare state literature that treats policies toward migrants as the outcome to be explained and the welfare state as the cause.

EXPLAINING MIGRATION POLICY

The idea that the welfare state may itself shape the response to international migration is often influenced by comparative welfare state research, not least by the notion of welfare "regimes." Such regimes come in different varieties. In his classical study of the welfare state, Esping-Andersen (1990) distinguished between the "liberal," the "conservative," and the "social democratic" welfare regime. Korpi and Palme (1998) instead distinguish between "targeted," "basic security," "corporatist," or "encompassing" welfare state models, whereas Rothstein (1998) concentrates on the distinction between selective and universal systems (Rothstein 1998). While different scholars stress somewhat different organizational characteristics, they are all in various ways concerned with the extent of the state's commitment to protecting the well-being of individuals.

We can distinguish between two different views concerning the compatibility of generous welfare policies and open migration policies also when we start from the welfare state and imagine how it might shape immigration and immigration policy. These two views can be called the "closing-the-doors-to-the-welfare-state approach" and the "normative power-of-welfare-states approach."

The Closing-the-Doors-to-the-Welfare-State Approach

Those who argue that open migration policies are incompatible with generous social policies tend to focus on the high cost of benefits and services in generous welfare states—costs that citizens are willing to bear only when recipients are fellow nationals. The specific qualities of the welfare state people live in are—in other words—expected to have different implications for people's calculations of costs and benefits for various policies. In this sense, the ideas that we refer to as the "closing-the-doors-to the-welfare-state approach" are similar to the ideas behind the new progressive dilemma approach. In this case, however, the way out of the dilemma is assumed to be generous welfare policies toward natives in combination with restrictive policies toward migrants.

Indeed, many scholars expect that increased diversity will not lead so much to withdrawal of support for the welfare state as to support for restrictive policies toward migrants. Similarly, it is expected that political leaders who wish to expand or preserve the welfare state will react to international migration not with welfare retrenchment, but with policies that exclude migrants from the welfare state. Such policies can either exclude migrants internally—by restricting the access of resident migrants to government services, a response often captured by the term "welfare chauvinism" and defined by the idea that "welfare services should be restricted to 'our own'" (Andersen and Bjørklund 1990, 212)—or already at the border, limiting migrants' access to the welfare state through strict admission policies (Banting 2000; Razin et al. 2011).

The idea that the response in public opinion will be welfare chauvinism rather than reduced support for the welfare state *in toto* is in line with findings by Brady and Finnigan (2014). While they do not find a negative effect of diversity on support for the welfare state, they find some evidence for the welfare chauvinism hypothesis: diversity does not lead to dwindling overall support for the welfare state, but it does reduce the willingness to share benefits with outsiders (Brady and Finnigan 2014). Another study, by contrast, found that during the refugee crisis in 2015, high numbers of asylum seekers were associated with less rather than more welfare chauvinism among host populations in Europe. The authors attribute this somewhat surprising finding to charitableness toward refugees (Heizmann et al. 2018). This interpretation is in line with the results in Van Der Meer and Reeskens (2020). They test the general idea that diversity is associated with welfare chauvinism through a vignette experiment conducted in areas in the Netherlands with varying degrees of diversity. They find that ethnic diversity is indeed associated with more welfare chauvinism—but only toward labor migrants, not political refugees (Van Der Meer and Reeskens 2020).

When it comes to policy responses, the idea that generous welfare states will react to international migration by restricting access to welfare services for migrants has been labeled the "dualization hypothesis," which posits that there will be a negative association between overall welfare generosity and immigrants' access to welfare benefits (Römer 2017, 174).

But there are also those who argue that generous welfare states will respond to international migration with restrictive *admission* policies. Restricting access to welfare for resident migrants is, according to Banting (2000, 24), the expected policy choice of states with liberal welfare regimes. Not only do these states have weaker social commitments; since they are immigrant societies, they have been more reluctant to protect the welfare state by closing the borders. In contrast, the logic of encompassing welfare states makes it hard to exclude resident migrants from benefits and services. Therefore, external border control and strict admission policies will be the primary policy choice. In a similar vein, Hollifield (2000, 110) suggests that one of the preferred strategies for immigrant control in strong welfare states is external border control. The strong welfare state will thus function as a "double-edged sword" since "it may facilitate immigrant incorporation, but it can also function as an efficient mechanism for immigration control."

The empirical evidence to support these claims is so far limited. Vadlamannati (2020) studies the relationship between refugee inflows and electoral support for populist-right parties. While this is not an indicator of policy, it is certainly an indicator of demand for restrictive policies toward migrants (most likely in terms of both internal and external exclusion). He finds that in societies with high levels of social spending, inflows of refugees are positively associated with electoral support for populist-right parties, suggesting that high levels of social protection might fuel welfare chauvinism in these societies.

The Normative-Power-of-Welfare-States Approach

There are several studies disputing the idea that generous welfare states will be associated with more restrictive policies vis-à-vis migrants. Indeed, some scholars expect generous welfare states to be associated with more *inclusive* rather than more exclusive policies.

As discussed above, those who see generous welfare policies and open migration policies as incompatible tend to focus on how the type of welfare state impacts on the relative costs and benefits of various policies, an impact that can be expected to be quite immediate. The strand of literature that holds the view that generous welfare states are compatible with open policies toward migrants instead tends to argue that welfare state institutions can have much more profound effects. The basis of this argument is institutional theory which underlines that institutions do not merely reflect societal norms, but also contribute to shaping them. Welfare state policies do not only shape individuals' incentive structures: they also have the power to shape norms and values. In the words of Esping-Andersen (1990, 55), "The organizational features of the welfare state help determine the articulation of social solidarity." In particular, encompassing welfare states with strong universal traits have been argued to blur the line between *us* (the tax-paying majority) and *them* (the welfare recipients), making issues of redistribution less divisive, and promoting egalitarian norms. In contrast, systems where means-testing is a central part tend to bring issues of cheating and fraud to the forefront, and to classify recipients as "deserving" or "undeserving" (Crepaz and Damron 2009; Rothstein 1998).

Transferring these arguments to the field of migration, scholars have argued that rather than evoking a restrictive response to migration in what is seen as a zero-sum game about public resources—where gains for migrants equal losses for natives—encompassing welfare states can make the distinction between us and them less clear also in the context of international migration and ethnic diversity. It is also pointed out that higher levels of trust are found in more encompassing welfare states (Freitag and Bühlmann 2009) which, it is argued, promotes more welcoming attitudes toward migrants. Moreover, the simple fact that encompassing welfare states protect individuals from market risks is expected to reduce the extent to which immigration induces feelings of economic competition and threat among the native population (Crepaz 2008).

Indeed, public opinion analyses show that welfare chauvinism is lower in social-democratic welfare regimes while citizens in liberal or conservative welfare states are more reluctant to distribute welfare services to immigrants (Van Der Waal et al. 2013). Similarly, tolerance for migrants is higher in the more generous welfare states, leading

Crepaz and Damron (2009, 437) to conclude that "contemporary welfare states have a similar capacity to bridge ethnic divisions as their 19th-century incarnations."

The expectations about the inclusive effect of welfare state institutions are, at the policy level, manifested in the expectation that immigrants will, quite contrary to what the "dualization hypothesis" suggests, have *more* access to welfare benefits in generous welfare states—an expectation Römer (2017, 174) labels the "generosity hypothesis." In the end, the generosity hypothesis is the one that receives empirical support in her study. The results are thus similar to those of Sainsbury (2006, 2012) who finds that immigrants enjoy more entitlements, and are less likely to be poor, in comprehensive welfare states.

Boräng (2015, 2018) relies on similar arguments about the norm-shaping potential of welfare state institutions, but applies them to admission policy. She finds that welfare state generosity is associated with more open policies toward forced migrants (refugees and asylum seekers) and argues that norms of social solidarity and trust prevail in comprehensive welfare states.

MOVING FORWARD

In this section, we discuss three points that we believe need to be addressed in the literature on the welfare state and migration. The first concerns the distinctions among different types of migration. The second concerns the scope of empirical research and the related lack of attention to shifting patterns over time. The third concerns the nature of the causal claims that are made in the empirical literature about these topics.

Types of Migration

More needs to be done to distinguish, theoretically and empirically, between different types of migration, since the welfare state can be expected to relate to different types of migration in different ways.

First, different types of migration policy have very different purposes. Asylum and refugee policies were developed in a context of international cooperation, with the explicit goal of assisting individuals in need of protection. They first and foremost assign *rights* to individuals and *responsibilities* to states. In contrast, the main purpose of labor migration policies is to achieve economic benefits for the receiving country. Unless specific bilateral or multilateral agreements have been made for that purpose, states are under no obligation to accept labor migrants.

The different beneficiaries of labor migration policy on the one hand and asylum and refugee policy on the other lead to even sharper differences between the predictions of those who see migration as compatible with the welfare state, and those who do not.

For those, like for example Freeman (1986), who argue that migration constitutes a financial threat to the welfare state (either by increasing costs or by reducing taxpayers' willingness to contribute), the clash between migration and the welfare state should be far greater for asylum and refugee migration than for labor migration. Asylum seekers and refugees tend to be dependent on the welfare state at least initially, for several reasons: many do not belong to the working-age population, and even when they do, asylum seekers are often not allowed to take up employment. Moreover, when it comes to accepted refugees it is harder to exclude this group from the welfare state internally, since the Geneva Convention has accorded refugees the same rights as nationals when it comes to social security (Sainsbury 2006: 230).

People who are admitted as labor immigrants, on the other hand, tend to either have a job offer upon arrival, or have skills that are in demand in the labor market. These migrants are not expected to be a burden on the welfare state. Indeed, Freeman (1986) argues that whether migration will be a threat or not depends in part on the type of migration. From this perspective, guest workers—who tend to be young, employed taxpayers, and who can be more easily excluded from the welfare state—are beneficial for the fiscal survival of the welfare state, whereas more permanent migration—including family and refugee migration—is more of a threat.

One implication should therefore be that those who expect a negative relationship between the generosity of social policy and the openness of migration policy should expect this to be the case especially for asylum and refugee policy, and less so for labor migration policy.

This stands in sharp contrast to accounts that build on the norm-shaping qualities of institutions. They instead argue that precisely because asylum and refugee policies are about the protection of individuals rather than economic gain for the receiving country, norms about solidarity can take precedence over economic interests (Boräng 2015). The norms generated by generous welfare states can therefore lead to more open policies, especially for forced migration.

There are some empirical results to support this idea. On public attitudes, the vignette experiment by Van Der Meer and Reeskens (2020) shows that ethnic diversity is associated with less welfare solidarity with labor migrants—but not so with political refugees. On admission policy, Boräng (2018) finds a positive association between welfare generosity and the admission of forced migrants, but not labor migrants.

Apart from having different policy goals, labor immigration policies, unlike asylum or refugee policies, are strongly tied to interests in the labor market more generally. Generous welfare states typically co-exist with labor market institutions that have been shown to discourage—and offer alternatives to—large-scale labor migration, including centralized wage bargaining and the inclusion of trade unions in the policy process (Boräng 2018; Boräng and Cerna 2019). We could therefore expect a negative relationship between the welfare state and the admission of labor migrants—but this negative relationship may well result from the specific type of labor market institutions that tend to go along with a generous welfare state, rather than the welfare state as such.

The importance of distinguishing between different types of migration when analyzing the relationship between the welfare state and migration policy is illustrated in Figure 16.1. This figure, which is based on data on welfare state programs from Korpi and Palme (2008) and data on immigration policies from Peters (2015, 2017), Shin (2019), and our own work, shows that the relationship between the generosity of the welfare state (defined here as the average replacement rate in social insurance times the average coverage rate) and the orientation of immigration policy varies greatly between policies concerning the admission of labor migrants and policies concerning asylum seekers and refugees. Each point in these scatterplots is a country-year between 1930 and 2010, representing one of

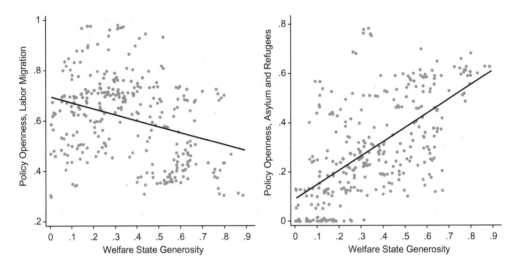

Note: The figure distinguishes between the admission of labor migrants and policies vis-à-vis refugees and asylum seekers. Welfare state generosity is defined as the average replacement rate times the average coverage of social insurance programs, using data from Korpi and Palme (2008).

Source: For immigration policy: Peters (2015, 2017), Shin (2019), Kalm and Lindvall (2019), and authors' own data collection.

Figure 16.1   Welfare state generosity and immigration policy, 1930–2010

18 countries (Australia, Austria, Belgium, Canada, Denmark, Finland, France, Germany, Ireland, Italy, Japan, the Netherlands, New Zealand, Norway, Sweden, Switzerland, the United Kingdom, and the United States).

The figure shows that whereas there is a *negative* relationship between welfare state generosity and the openness of labor migration policies (a relationship that would be stronger if the first two decades after the Second World War were excluded), there is a *positive* relationship between welfare state generosity and the openness of asylum and refugee policies.

Empirical Scope

The second problem we observe is that most studies have only been concerned with a fairly brief historical period, usually a decade or two from the post-1945 era. But the modern, social insurance-based welfare state is almost 150 years old. During the period between the late nineteenth century and today, both migration policies and welfare state policies have changed greatly; they have also varied greatly among countries. An important problem when studies of the relationship between welfare regimes and migration policy take on a short-term view is that this causes them to take either migration policy traditions or welfare regimes for granted. Therefore, most studies cannot really differentiate between the argument that migration policy has implications for the type of welfare state that will develop, and the argument that welfare state type has implications for migration policy.

Moreover, accounts that assume a mature welfare state—in which social programs are institutionalized enough to shape societal norms—cannot be used to address the relationship between migration policy and social policy when the modern welfare state was neither mature nor advanced. This is an important omission since the questions of migration policy and social policy have both been at policy-makers' agendas for a long time, and often at the same time.

Both a short time span and lack of attention to different types of migration would be less of a problem if all forms of immigration policy had developed in the same manner over time. As shown in Figure 16.2, however, this is clearly not the case. When it comes to the admission of labor migrants and the rights of resident migrants, immigration policies became increasingly restrictive from the second half of the nineteenth century until the Second World War (a period during which specific asylum and refugee policies only existed in a few countries). In the next phase—essentially the *trente glorieuses* after the Second World War—*all* forms of immigration policy became increasingly open. Then, from the late 1960s onward, policies concerning the rights of migrants and policies vis-à-vis refugees and asylum seekers became even more open, albeit at a much slower rate from the 1980s onward, but policies concerning labor migration became much more restrictive in the early 1970s and have continued to become slightly stricter since then.

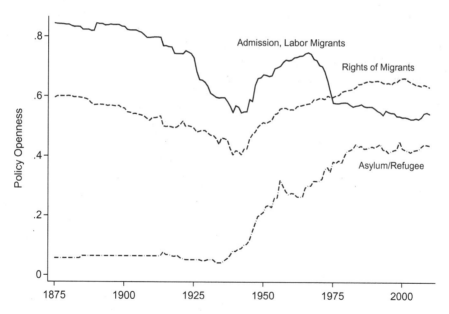

Note: The figure distinguishes between the admission of labor migrants, the rights enjoyed by resident migrants, and policies vis-à-vis refugees and asylum seekers.

Source: Peters (2015, 2017), Shin (2019), Kalm and Lindvall (2019), and authors' own data collection.

Figure 16.2 Average immigration policy openness, 1875–2010

The Problem of Causality

The third problem we observe, which is related to the second, is the widespread assumption that it is possible to distinguish between the welfare state and migration policy in such a way that it is meaningful to speak of a causal effect of one on the other. This point applies equally to "pessimistic" and "optimistic" views concerning the welfare state and migration policy. The modern welfare state and modern immigration policy emerged around the same time (Kalm and Lindvall 2019). This means that they have been subject to the same structural conditions. More importantly, it means that they are mutually dependent to such an extent that it typically becomes difficult to disentangle them and say that one has "caused" the other. Indeed, there are many historical examples of how important migration policy decisions and important welfare policy decisions have been made more or less simultaneously. Yet, few studies are open to the possibility that the relationship is non-causal, with both welfare policy and migration policy emerging from the same underlying social, economic, and political conditions.

The most influential theory of causality in contemporary social science is the counterfactual theory of causality, which is also known as the potential outcomes framework for causal inference (see, for example, Imbens and Rubin 2015, chapter 1). According to this view, the causal effect of an event or action—or "treatment," using medical terminology—is defined as the difference between the state of the world after the event or action and what the world *would have been like* if the event or action had not occurred. Put simply, if it were not for the cause, things would have turned out differently.

Under this theory, someone who makes a causal claim needs to identify precisely the action or event that produced the alleged causal effects, and the action or event must be defined in such a way that it might have occurred where it did not and might not have occurred where it did. In other words, it must be meaningful to think of the treatment as alterable or "manipulable." Only once these things have been made clear is it possible to proceed to the difficult methodological and practical question of how one might use empirical evidence to make *inferences* about the causal effect. The causal effect is in principle unobservable, since it is defined as the difference between what is and what might have been, but it can be estimated through various different empirical research designs and methods, ranging from experiments all the way through comparative case-study methods for observational data (cf. Przeworski and Teune 1970). However, those research designs and methods are not possible to evaluate if one does not begin by specifying clearly what the treatment is, and by thinking clearly about whether the counterfactual claim that is implicit in a causal argument makes sense: that is, whether it is meaningful to conceive of a counterfactual world in which units that are "treated" at time t—that is units where the action or event occurred—were *not* treated at time t, but were otherwise identical, pre-treatment, in all other important respects.

What does this discussion imply for the relationship between the welfare state and immigration policy? The point we wish to make here is that an important problem with many of the causal claims that scholars make about the "effects" of the welfare state on immigration policy (or vice versa) is that it is not clear what the treatment is supposed to be, which means that it is unclear what causal effect is being estimated. Take the idea that having a universal welfare state leads to more generous immigration policies. "The welfare state," in this case, is not a well-defined treatment, for two reasons.

First of all, the label "the welfare state" could apply to many different treatments, and it is important to know which one we're talking about. Are we interested in what happens to immigration policy in the next few years after the adoption and implementation of major changes in welfare state programs in a modern democracy (such as the consequences of a policy that reduces the generosity of social insurances)? Or are we interested in the differences between the migration policies countries pursue today and the policies they would have pursued if previous generations had built a different type of welfare state than the one they actually built (that is, the "legacy effects" of historical political decisions)? Those are two very different types of questions (not two ways of getting at the same thing), and they are therefore best answered using different research designs and methods. And those are just two examples among many of how one might interpret the phrase "the welfare state matters for migration policy."

Second, regardless of how the action or event of "changing welfare policies" is defined, it only makes sense to describe the relationship between "the welfare state" and migration policy as a causal one if it is possible to separate the treatment (changing welfare policies) from the outcome (changing migration policies). More often than not, it is not possible to do so. Those decisions are typically taken by the same agents (the government, the legislature, the bureaucracy) and emerge from the same underlying political process. It is therefore not always clear that the decision to change welfare policies can be thought of as a distinct action or event that results in a subsequent, distinct migration policy change. There are circumstances in which it might be meaningful to think of social policy and migration policy as distinct in this way—perhaps because the welfare state change is a result of events that are beyond the control of the decision makers, such as an economic crisis that forces the government to make cuts, or because a country's welfare state policies are "locked in" through a process of path dependence—but if that is the case, explaining why it is meaningful to make this separation in the particular case at hand is a very important task for a scholar who wishes to make a causal claim.

There is certainly room for causal claims also in this field, but we believe that they are warranted in particular when it is possible to define the causal relationship in a very precise way. To a larger extent than today, such analyses may concern local effects and more specific aspects of the relationship between migration policy and the welfare state.

In other cases we believe that it is often more promising to think of both social policies and immigration policies as outcomes of an underlying political process, and to look further back in the causal chain for the economic, social, and political events or actions that influence both of them, and that we can plausibly argue are exogenous to the underlying political process from which both types of policies emerge. The counterfactual question "What sort of immigration policy would the government of country i have pursued at time $t+1$ if it hadn't decided to change social policies at time t (or even time $t+1$)" often makes little sense, at least as a *causal* question, but the counterfactual question "What combination of social policies and immigration policies would the government of country i have pursued at time $t+1$ if [a distinct economic, social, or political event] had not occurred at time t" often does make sense.

CONCLUSION

This chapter has reviewed the scholarly literature on the relationship between the development of the welfare state and the development of migration policy. While examining how scholars have understood this relationship, we noted that there are fundamentally different views not only regarding the direction of the relationship (when the relationship is interpreted as causal), but also concerning the possibility of combining generous welfare state policies with open migration policies.

Following this review, we discussed three problems that we believe deserve more attention. The first problem concerns the distinctions among different types of migration policy. We argued that it is often not meaningful to analyze the relationship between social policy and migration policy in general terms; analyses must be specific to different forms of policy. We illustrated this point with historical data over social policy and different types of migration policy, showing that welfare state generosity is typically negatively related to labor migration policy, but positively related to asylum and refugee policy.

The second problem concerns the scope of most empirical research in the field. Most studies deal with a rather short time period, with the consequence that either the migration policy regime or the welfare regime often is taken as a given. We argue that since the welfare state has co-evolved with migration policy ever since the late nineteenth and early twentieth centuries, it is more fruitful to analyze that relationship in a dynamic, historical context.

The third problem concerns how to make causal claims about the relationship between the welfare state and migration policy. Since the welfare state and migration policy have co-evolved over time—and are shaped by the same underlying political process—broad causal claims about this relationship are often difficult to sustain, and we argued for more theoretical and empirical precision when causal claims are made.

Neither of these objections is meant to suggest that it is not meaningful to analyze the relationship between the welfare state and immigration policy. Indeed, the whole reason we are writing this chapter is that we believe that relationship is exceptionally important. We also believe that in addressing the problems we observe lie many opportunities to make important contributions to an already rich field.

To take a few examples: paying more attention to types of migration might spur scholars to discuss more explicitly how policy frames contribute to shaping a policy area. Are, for example, "rational" or "norm-based" responses more likely in a specific situation? Expanding the time frame of empirical studies could invite a discussion about whether the described processes can be expected to unfold in the short or in the long term. And more attention to the challenges in making causal claims might spur theoretical refinement and methodological development in the field.

Finally, it should be noted that our critique of some of the causal claims in the literature is not to question the value of the studies that make such claims. But their value sometimes does not lie primarily in the causal claims as such, but rather in the descriptive accounts of how the welfare state and migration policy have co-evolved, and which combinations of welfare state policy and migration policy have been more common (and when and where). There is sometimes a tendency to undervalue descriptive accounts, which we think is unfortunate: such accounts have contributed greatly to our understanding of various social phenomena, including the relationship between migration policy and the welfare state.

REFERENCES

Alesina, Alberto and Edward Glaeser. 2004. *Fighting Poverty in the US and Europe*. Oxford: Oxford University Press.
Andersen, Jørgen Goul and Tor Bjørklund. 1990. "Structural Changes and New Cleavages: The Progress Parties in Denmark and Norway." *Acta Sociologica* 33 (3): 195–217.
Baldwin, Kate and John D. Huber. 2010. "Economic versus Cultural Differences: Forms of Ethnic Diversity and Public Goods Provision." *American Political Science Review* 104 (4): 644–662.
Banting, Keith G. 2000. "Looking in Three Directions: Migration and the European Welfare State in Comparative Perspective." In *Immigration and Welfare: Challenging the Borders of the Welfare State*, edited by Michael Bommes and Andrew Geddes. London: Routledge, 13–33.
Battisti, Michele, Gabriel Felbermayr, Giovanni Peri, and Panu Poutvaara. 2018. "Immigration, Search and Redistribution: A Quantitative Assessment of Native Welfare." *Journal of the European Economic Association* 16 (4): 1137–1188.
Boräng, Frida. 2015. "Large-Scale Solidarity? Effects of Welfare State Institutions on the Admission of Forced Migrants." *European Journal of Political Research* 54 (2): 216–231.
Boräng, Frida. 2018. *National Institutions—International Migration*. London: Rowman and Littlefield.
Boräng, Frida and Lucie Cerna. 2019. "Constrained Politics: Labour Market Actors, Political Parties and Swedish Labour Immigration Policy." *Government and Opposition* 54 (1): 121–144.
Borjas, George J. 1999. "Immigration and Welfare Magnets." *Journal of Labor Economics* 17 (4): 607–637.
Brady, David and Ryan Finnigan. 2014. "Does Immigration Undermine Public Support for Social Policy?" *American Sociological Review* 79 (1): 17–42.
Burgoon, Brian, Ferry Koster, and Marcel van Egmond. 2012. "Support for Redistribution and the Paradox of Immigration." *Journal of European Social Policy* 22 (3): 288–304.
Crepaz, Markus M.L. 2008. *Trust beyond Borders: Immigration, the Welfare State, and Identity in Modern Societies*. Ann Arbor, MI: University of Michigan Press.
Crepaz, Markus M.L. and Regan Damron. 2009. "Constructing Tolerance: How the Welfare State Shapes Attitudes about Immigrants." *Comparative Political Studies* 42 (3): 437–463.
Esping-Andersen, Gøsta. 1990. *The Three Worlds of Welfare Capitalism*. Princeton, NJ: Princeton University Press.
Freeman, Gary P. 1986. "Migration and the Political Economy of the Welfare State." *Annals of the American Academy of Political and Social Science* 485: 51–63.
Freitag, Markus and Marc Bühlmann. 2009. "Crafting Trust: The Role of Political Institutions in a Comparative Perspective." *Comparative Political Studies* 42 (12): 1537–1566.
Goodhart, David. 2004. "Too Diverse?" *Prospect Magazine* 95: 30–37.
Heizmann, Boris, Alexander Jedinger, and Anja Perry. 2018. "Welfare Chauvinism, Economic Insecurity and the Asylum Seeker 'Crisis.'" *Societies* 8 (3): 83.
Hollifield, James F. 2000. "Immigration and the Politics of Rights: The French Case in Comparative Perspective." In *Immigration and Welfare: Challenging the Borders of the Welfare State*, edited by Michael Bommes and Andrew Geddes. London: Routledge, 108–131.
Imbens, Guido W. and Donald B. Rubin. 2015. *Causal Inference for Statistics, Social, and Biomedical Sciences: An Introduction*. Cambridge: Cambridge University Press.
Kalm, Sara and Johannes Lindvall. 2019. "Immigration Policy and the Modern Welfare State, 1880–1920." *Journal of European Social Policy* 29 (4): 463–477.
Kitschelt, Herbert. 1995. *The Radical Right in Western Europe*. Ann Arbor, MI: University of Michigan Press.
Korpi, Walter and Joakim Palme. 1998. "The Paradox of Redistribution and Strategies of Equality." *American Sociological Review* 63: 661–687.
Korpi, Walter and Joakim Palme. 2008. *The Social Citizenship Indicator Program (SCIP)*. Swedish Institute for Social Research.
Kymlicka, Will and Keith Banting. 2006. "Immigration, Multiculturalism, and the Welfare State." *Ethics and International Affairs* 20 (3): 281–304.
Luttmer, Erzo F.P. 2001. "Group Loyalty and the Taste for Redistribution." *Journal of Political Economy* 109 (3): 500–528.
Mau, Steffen and Christoph Burkhardt. 2009. "Migration and Welfare State Solidarity in Western Europe." *Journal of European Social Policy* 19 (3): 213–229.

Nannestad, Peter. 2007. "Immigration and Welfare States: A Survey of 15 Years of Research." *European Journal of Political Economy* 23 (2): 512–532.
Pearce, Nicholas. 2004. "Diversity versus Solidarity: A New Progressive Dilemma?" *Renewal* 12 (3): 79–87.
Peters, Margaret E. 2015. "Open Trade, Closed Borders." *World Politics* 67 (1): 114–154.
Peters, Margaret E. 2017. *Trading Barriers*. Princeton, NJ: Princeton University Press.
Przeworski, Adam and Henry Teune. 1970. *The Logic of Comparative Social Inquiry*. New York: John Wiley & Sons.
Putnam, Robert D. 2007. "*E Pluribus Unum*: Diversity and Community in the Twenty-First Century." *Scandinavian Political Studies* 30 (2): 137–174.
Razin, Assaf, Efraim Sadka, and Benjarong Suwankiri. 2011. *Migration and the Welfare State*. Cambridge, MA: MIT Press.
Römer, Friederike. 2017. "Generous to All or 'Insiders Only'? The Relationship between Welfare State Generosity and Immigrant Welfare Rights." *Journal of European Social Policy* 27 (2): 173–196.
Rothstein, Bo. 1998. *Just Institutions Matter*. Cambridge: Cambridge University Press.
Sainsbury, Diane. 2006. "Immigrants' Social Rights in Comparative Perspective: Welfare Regimes, Forms in Immigration and Immigration Policy Regimes." *Journal of European Social Policy* 16 (3): 229–244.
Sainsbury, Diane. 2012. *Welfare States and Immigrant Rights*. Oxford: Oxford University Press.
Shin, Adrian J. 2019. "Primary Resources, Secondary Labor: Natural Resources and Immigration Policy." *International Studies Quarterly* 63 (4): 805–818.
Soroka, Stuart N., Richard Johnston, Anthony Kevins, Keith Banting, and Will Kymlicka. 2016. "Migration and Welfare State Spending." *European Political Science Review* 8 (2): 173–194.
Spies, Dennis C. 2018. *Immigration and Welfare State Retrenchment*. Oxford: Oxford University Press.
Tajfel, Henri. 1974. "Social Identity and Intergroup Behaviour." *Social Science Information* 13 (2): 65–93.
Taylor-Gooby, Peter. 2005. "Is the Future American? Or, Can Left Politics Preserve European Welfare States from Erosion through Growing 'Racial' Diversity?" *Journal of Social Policy* 34 (4): 661–672.
Vadlamannati, Krishna Chaitanya. 2020. "Welfare Chauvinism? Refugee Flows and Electoral Support for Populist-Right Parties in Industrial Democracies." *Social Science Quarterly* 101 (4): 1600–1626.
Van Der Meer, Tom and Tim Reeskens. 2020. "Welfare Chauvinism in the Face of Ethnic Diversity: A Vignette Experiment across Diverse and Homogenous Neighbourhoods on the Perceived Deservingness of Native and Foreign-Born Welfare Claimants." *European Sociological Review* 37 (1): 89–103.
Van Der Waal, Jeroen, Willem De Koster, and Wim Van Oorschot. 2013. "Three Worlds of Welfare Chauvinism? How Welfare Regimes Affect Support for Distributing Welfare to Immigrants in Europe." *Journal of Comparative Policy Analysis: Research and Practice* 15 (2): 164–181.

PART IV

POLITICAL CULTURE, MIGRATION, AND REDISTRIBUTION

17. What explains opposition to immigration: Economic anxiety, cultural threat, or both?
Hanna Kleider

INTRODUCTION

With immigration into western countries having grown rapidly in the 1990s and 2000s, it has now become one of the most incendiary issues in today's political debates, pitching an increasingly hostile share of the population against those who continue to defend open borders and the freedom of movement. The backlash against immigration might put pressure on governments to implement more restrictive immigration policies, but it could also affect other policy areas. For instance, a growing strand of research argues that immigration will lead to cutbacks in social policy since it is likely to undermine people's willingness to engage in solidarity and to invest in public goods (Mau and Burkhardt 2009; Alesina and Glaeser 2004).

Given the size and vigor of this public backlash, the impact of immigration might, however, be even more fundamental. As Hainmueller and Hopkins have pointed out: "immigration is thus an issue with the potential to emerge suddenly and to destabilize existing political alignments" (Hainmueller and Hopkins 2014, 232). The recent electoral successes of the radical right in Europe might perhaps be the most obvious fallout of public opposition to immigration. Studies on radical right parties in the Netherlands (Coffé et al. 2007) and Austria (Halla et al. 2017) find that opposition to immigration has been one of the most important drivers of their recent electoral gains. Other scholars do, however, caution against single-issue explanations for a larger political phenomenon like the rise of the radical right (Rooduijn 2020). Immigration, as part of a broader breakdown of national borders, has also been thought to change the very nature of political contestation itself. Contestation over social issues, including immigration, is thought to soon eclipse contestation over economic issues in importance (Hooghe and Marks 2018; Kriesi et al. 2006). The issue of immigration seems to have played an important role in at least two decisive votes, the 2016 Trump vote and the 2016 British referendum to leave the European Union (EU) (Mutz 2018; Schaffner et al. 2018).

The potential impact of immigration on the very fabric of modern social and political life is reflected in the extensive academic attention it has received. There is now an immense literature on the underpinnings of attitudes towards immigrants, spanning a large number of disciplines, including social psychology, sociology, and political science.

This literature has contrasting viewpoints on whether opposition to immigration is caused by cultural threat or economic anxiety. Some claim that people's opposition to immigration is primarily driven by economic anxiety, in particular by concerns that immigration will negatively impact earnings and employment opportunities (Malhotra et al. 2013; Hanson 2007; Scheve and Slaughter 2001). Others believe that economic considerations are largely irrelevant and that the perception of cultural threat is the primary cause of anti-immigrant attitudes (Hainmueller and Hiscox 2010; Brader et al. 2008; Citrin et al. 1997). The jury is still out, but there seems to be solid empirical evidence supporting the effect of cultural considerations, while evidence on the effect of economic considerations is mixed.

The usefulness of viewing the analysis of attitudes towards immigration as a horse race between these two influences is, however, questionable (Malhotra et al. 2013). It presumes that we can isolate the influence of one cause on a relatively complex process of attitude formation. Even assuming for a moment that the current effects of economic anxiety and cultural threat could be easily compartmentalized, it is not clear whether the effect of either factor would be independent of an individual's psychological predispositions. Rather than focusing on the dichotomy of cultural versus economic explanations, a third option would, therefore, be to shift the analysis towards examining how the two influences relate and interact. For instance, cultural predispositions might help explain whether the experience of economic hardship triggers anti-immigrant attitudes. Or vice versa, the experience of economic hardship might trigger perceptions of cultural threat.

The real drivers of anti-immigrant attitudes might also be a different set of factors altogether. A possible culprit that has not yet received sufficient attention is the framing of immigration by mass media and political parties (Hainmueller and Hopkins 2014). Indeed, the coverage of the immigration issue by mass media and political parties has the potential to condition the influence of all other individual-level drivers of opposition to immigration.

This contribution will proceed as follows: I will begin by reviewing economic and cultural explanations of opposition to immigration. Drawing on research in social psychology, I will then develop several hypotheses on how both influences might interact. Given the scarcity of empirical research on these interactions, this section will primarily be an exercise in theory generation. The contribution will end with a review of alternative explanations for anti-immigrant attitudes. The aim of this contribution is to provide a review of the existing literature and a toolset for critically evaluating existing studies, while also pointing towards future lines of inquiry.

ECONOMIC CONSIDERATIONS

Economic explanations of anti-immigrant sentiments tend to highlight voters' labor market concerns (Mayda 2006; Scheve and Slaughter 2001). These explanations argue that individuals are substantially more opposed to immigration the more they perceive incoming immigrants as harming their earnings prospects or employment opportunities (Mayda 2006; Scheve and Slaughter 2001). Empirical evidence in support of the labor market competition hypothesis has mostly relied on the finding that lower-skilled individuals – where educational attainment is used as a proxy for skills – are those more opposed to immigration (Mayda 2006; Kessler 2001; Scheve and Slaughter 2001).

There are several reasons for challenging the interpretation of evidence used to support the labor market competition hypothesis (Malhotra et al. 2013). First, most basic economic accounts would have us expect that low-skilled workers perceive a greater threat to their wages and employment from low-skilled workers, while highly skilled workers perceive a greater threat from highly skilled immigrants (Borjas 2003). Nevertheless, studies have consistently shown that both the high-skilled and low-skilled workers strongly prefer high-skilled immigrants (Hainmueller and Hiscox 2007, 2010).

Second, most studies in support of the labor market competition hypothesis have relied on educational attainment as a proxy for skills (Mayda 2006; Kessler 2001; Scheve and Slaughter 2001). Education is, however, also correlated with cultural tolerance and cosmopolitanism, which makes it a problematic proxy for skills (Hainmueller and Hiscox 2007, 2010; Chandler and Tsai 2001). In other words, low levels of education might be associated with anti-immigrant sentiment because they are associated with a culturally closed predisposition, not because they capture low levels of skill and an increased threat from low-skilled immigrants. Furthermore, individuals with the same educational level may possess very different skills, which also makes educational attainment an inaccurate proxy for skills (Malhotra et al. 2013). More recent studies have therefore focused on the economic sector in which a respondent is employed as a predictor of labor market threat (Dancygier and Donnelly 2012; Malhotra et al. 2013). They find that respondents working in industries with a higher share of immigrant labor are indeed more opposed to immigration but conclude that this type of labor market competition is not very prevalent in the population, which might help explain the null findings of previous studies (Malhotra et al. 2013).

Creating a downward pressure on earnings and employment prospects is, however, not the only way in which immigration might induce economic concerns. An alternative strand of the literature emphasizes fiscal concerns, in particular concerns about immigrants' reliance on social welfare programs (Citrin et al. 2007; Hanson 2007; Hanson et al. 2005; Harell et al. 2012). By this view, voters' opposition to immigration is grounded in the anticipated effect on taxes, which entails an increased use of social services by immigrants. The fiscal argument squares well with the observation that both high-skilled and lower-skilled natives prefer high-skilled immigration. It suggests that concerns about the employability of immigrants and the expected fiscal burden outweigh concerns about labor market competition (Bansak et al. 2016). Studies on the fiscal aspect of immigration also suggest that opposition to low-skilled immigration will be particularly strong in communities where it is easier for immigrants to gain access to social services (Facchini and Mayda 2009; Hanson 2007). Yet, the fact that people with higher incomes – those who also bear a higher tax burden – are invariably more likely to favor immigration casts doubt on this interpretation (Tingley 2012; Hainmueller and Hiscox 2010). It seems to be the case that poorer native citizens, rather than richer citizens, are most concerned about immigrants' reliance on social welfare. This might suggest that concerns about an overcrowding of publicly provided services are more relevant than concerns about rising taxes (Hainmueller and Hiscox 2010).

While empirical evidence for economic explanations based on self-interest narrowly construed is mixed, explanations focusing on voters' sociotropic economic concerns have fared rather well (Citrin et al. 1997; Mansfield and Mutz 2009). Voters who are pessimistic about national economic performance are much more likely to harbor anti-immigrant attitudes than those who have a more optimistic outlook (Hainmueller and Hopkins 2014; Goldstein and Peters 2014; Mansfield and Mutz 2009; Citrin et al. 1997). Concerns about the national economy do not, however, necessarily reflect personal economic vulnerability (Goldstein and Peters 2014). Indeed, these concerns are often not even tied to objective indicators of national economic performance. In other words, while these studies suggest that economic factors might play a role in the form of sociotropic concerns about the state of the national economy, they clearly reject economic self-interest as a relevant source of anti-immigrant sentiment. Furthermore, assessments of national economic performance are often extremely biased and tend to be strongly influenced by partisan considerations. This makes it difficult to establish that a respondent's assessment of the economy is truly exogenous to her cultural considerations and her views on immigration in particular (Goldstein and Peters 2014).

CULTURAL CONSIDERATIONS

While there is mixed empirical evidence in support of explanations based on economic self-interest, cultural explanations seem to have fared much better. Cultural explanations tend to focus on the group-specific underpinnings of attitudes towards immigration. They overwhelmingly tend to draw on insights from the analysis of intergroup relations in social psychology. An influential strand of research in social psychology subsumed under the term social identity theory suggests that people have a tendency to divide the world into two distinct categories: "we's" and "they's" (Gaertner and Dovidio 2000; Brewer 1979; Tajfel and Turner 1979; Tajfel 1969). They automatically categorize everybody in their social environment into ingroups – that is, groups to which they belong – and outgroups. In doing so, they tend to overemphasize similarities within the group and differences between groups. This tendency to categorize is believed to derive from an inherent desire to belong and a need for positive distinctiveness (Brewer 1991).

Experiments in social psychology have consistently shown that once people feel part of an ingroup they tend to harbor fewer negative evaluations of members of the group and become more forgiving in their explanations for the behaviors of ingroup relative to outgroup members (Gaertner and Dovidio 2000). They are also more likely to show prosocial behavior to members of their ingroup and to invest in public goods while at the same time deemphasizing competition and conflict (De Cremer and Van Vugt 1999; Kramer and Brewer 1984). This has led researchers to explore the link between ethnically homogeneous groups and support for social policy (Burgoon 2014; Mau and Burkhardt 2009; Brady and Finnigan 2013; Crepaz and Damron 2009).

In contrast to earlier theories about group relations that assumed outright hostility and aggression, social identity theory is more about ingroup favoritism than outgroup derogation (Brewer 1979; Wenzel and Mummendey 1996). Nevertheless, it acknowledges that the distortions and evaluative biases that reflect favorably on the ingroup and, consequently, on the self can become problematic if generalized to character traits (Tajfel and Turner 1979). For instance, studies have shown that positive behaviors and successful outcomes are more likely to be attributed to character traits of ingroup members, whereas negative outcomes are more likely to be ascribed to the personalities of outgroup members (Hewstone 1989; Pettigrew 1979). These cognitive biases help to perpetuate social biases that create stereotypes and prejudices. A prejudice is understood as "an antipathy based on faulty and inflexible generalization" (Allport 1954, 1). A prejudice generally involves both negative feelings and beliefs towards another group and provides a foundation for generating hostility and conflict.

This raises questions about the ultimate source of these negative attitudes. Two potential sources have been identified by the social psychology literature: realistic threat and symbolic threat. On the one hand, prejudices might result from a realistic intergroup threat, such as competition over resources (Stephan et al. 2000; Bobo 1983). The resource-stress explanation, which predates social identity theory, is in many ways reminiscent of explanations that highlight sociotropic economic concerns, in that both prioritize the material interest of a social group over individual self-interest. An example of realistic threat explanations frequently used to explain opposition to immigration is the so-called minority threat theory (Quillian 1995; Wang 2012; Meuleman et al. 2009; Semyonov et al. 2006). It suggests that threat is triggered by the fear and suspicion that the minority group will seek to undermine the dominant group's privilege and advantage (Blumer 1958).

On the other hand, the source of threat could be symbolic in nature and result from the perception of cultural encroachment. This explanation is more in line with social identity theory. Simply put, the sheer presence of a distinctive outgroup might lead to intergroup antagonism (Harell et al. 2012; Leong 2008, Sniderman et al. 2004; Tajfel and Turner 1979). There is increasing evidence that symbolic threat might be sufficient to generate opposition to immigration. Studies suggest that any foreign influence is opposed regardless of the immigrant group's economic impact. Research by Sniderman et al. on immigrants in the Netherlands, for instance, shows that the perception that immigrants did not fit in well with Dutch culture was much more influential than economic cues. As Sniderman and co-authors have pointedly argued: "not fitting in culturally evokes significantly more opposition to immigration than not fitting in economically" (2004, 43).

What it is about culturally distinct outgroups that is perceived to be threatening is still subject to debate. Research by Schildkraut suggests that language is perhaps the most visible marker (Schildkraut 2005). Immigrants not speaking the host society's language are often thought of as violating a central norm. Which aspects of immigrant populations are perceived to be culturally threatening might, however, also depend on people's conceptions of what it means to be a member of a national community (Hainmueller and Hopkins 2014). For instance, civic conceptions of national community and national boundaries might be more easily accommodated than ethnic conceptions of national community (Wright et al. 2012; Hainmueller and Hopkins 2014).

However, regardless of whether the threat is realistic or symbolic, empirical studies have shown that threat perceptions depend on the degree of ingroup social identification. The more an individual identified with the ingroup, the higher the perceived threat from the outgroup (Gaertner and Dovidio 2000).

While there is increasing support for cultural explanations of anti-immigrant sentiments, most studies still use educational attainment as the main explanatory variable, this time, however, as a proxy of cultural openness (Hainmueller and Hiscox 2007, 2010). While education attainment is certainly associated with tolerance and less racial prejudice, it is not synonymous with cultural tolerance (Burns and Gimpel 2000). It captures economic standing but also a respondent's ability to answer survey questions. Research suggests that better-educated people might not necessarily be more culturally tolerant, but simply better trained to avoid sounding racist when answering survey questions (Burns and Gimpel 2000; Jackman and Muha 1984).

More importantly, perhaps, cultural explanations of anti-immigrant sentiments fall short in explaining change in anti-immigrant attitudes over time. Most assume that cultural predispositions form during pre-adult socialization and rarely change over the life course. This makes it difficult to explain changes in attitudes towards immigration which do however occur from time to time, especially in times of economic crisis (Kleider and Stoeckel 2018).

ARE ECONOMIC ANXIETY AND CULTURAL THREAT TRULY SEPARABLE INFLUENCES?

Existing scholarship on attitudes towards immigration has tended to examine the relative influence of economic anxiety and cultural threat. Only very few studies treat both influences as complementary or interlinked (see Kuk 2019; Mutz 2018). It is possible that the effect of economic anxiety and cultural threat is additive. For instance, cultural predispositions formed in early childhood might predict people's baseline attitudes towards immigration, whereas economic shocks could explain deviations from the baseline (Kleider and Stoeckel 2018). Their joint effect could also be interactive. That is, cultural predispositions might condition the impact of economic anxiety on anti-immigrant attitudes, or vice versa economic anxiety might trigger the effect of cultural threat. Existing studies have, however, mostly treated economic anxiety and cultural factors as separate explanations (Kuk 2019). This siloed approach to analyzing the processes of attitude formation presumes that an individual's experience of economic anxiety is clearly separable from the experience of cultural threat. This presumption might create a false dichotomy (Kuk 2019). Drawing on insights from social psychology, I will now suggest several potential ways in which the two influences could interact.

Cultural Predispositions Condition the Effect of Economic Shocks: The Role of Responsibility Attributions

Proponents of economic self-interest explanations argue that opposition to immigration can be traced back to immigration's effect on earnings and job security. However, this view presumes that individuals who experience increased job insecurity attribute responsibility for this experience to immigrants rather than to other factors, such as their own ability or the state of the economy. Simply put, while the loss of a job might have directly visible effects on wellbeing, it does not always have an obvious cause. Individuals first have to make the connection between their economic hardship and increased immigration for it to lead to greater anti-immigrant attitudes. In other words, they have to attribute responsibility, which acts as the "psychological adhesive" that connects events to actors (Schlenker et al. 1994).

A vast psychological literature suggests that attributing responsibility for an event to a specific actor is not always straightforward, particularly when responsibilities are diffuse, and events are complicated (Schlenker et al. 1994). For instance, studies on economic voting show that governments are not always penalized for bad economic performance. For voters to penalize incumbent governments, they must first believe that the government produced these results and that it is the government's job to fix them (Rudolph 2003; Peffley and Williams 1985; Peffley 1984).

Research on the formation of responsibility attributions suggests that they are often biased by predispositions and prior beliefs (Hobolt and Tilley 2014). In the case of attributing responsibility for bad economic performance to incumbent governments, for instance, we know that a voter's prior political beliefs, in particular their partisanship, bias responsibility judgments (De Vries et al. 2018; Rudolph 2003; Bartels 2000; Lewis-Beck 1997; Rahn 1993; Campbell et al. 1960). Research by Rudolph on responsibility attribution in the United States shows that partisan voters will typically attribute responsibility for improved economic perceptions to institutions controlled by their own party and responsibility for worsened economic perceptions to institutions controlled by the opposition party (Rudolph 2003).

However, partisanship is not the only perceptual bias influencing responsibility attributions. Hobolt and Tilley show that when it comes to forming opinions about EU-level policies partisanship is not a decisive factor (Hobolt and Tilley 2014). They identify voters' predispositions towards the EU, in particular, whether they have an exclusive national identity, as the most important perceptual bias influencing responsibility attributions (Hooghe and Marks 2005, 2009). Individuals with an exclusive national identity who are negatively predisposed towards the EU will be more likely to attribute responsibility to the EU when things go badly, whereas voters who are positively predisposed towards the EU are more likely to blame negative outcomes on their national government. As Hobolt and Tilley point out: "Partisanship and EU support are not identical types of predispositions, but they may well act in a similar way" (Hobolt and Tilley 2014: 801). As a general rule, responsibility judgments seem to be influenced by the same "group-serving attribution biases" discussed by the literature on social identity theory; just that different group identities are decisive in different situations (Fiske and Taylor 2007; Hewstone 1989; Pettigrew 1979).

It is therefore plausible that the attribution of responsibility for an economic shock, like the loss of a job, is also subject to group-serving biases with racial or national identities being the relevant group identities. People who identify strongly with their ingroup and are negatively predisposed towards immigrants might be more likely to attribute the responsibility for losing a job to increasing immigration, whereas individuals with a weaker national or racial identity who are less negatively predisposed towards immigrants might blame it on the economic situation or their own personal failure. This would mean that economic anxiety and cultural threat perceptions are not clearly separable. Economic anxiety is only likely to increase anti-immigrant sentiments among those individuals who strongly identify with their national or racial ingroup and who are likely to attribute responsibility for economic hardship to the immigrant outgroup, but not among individuals who do not strongly identify with their national or racial social group. This would also mean that there is significant individual-level heterogeneity in the way economic anxiety is linked to anti-immigrant attitudes, which could explain why existing large-N studies that focus on the average effect of economic anxiety have not found strong empirical support.

Economic Hardship Activates Perceptions of Cultural Threat

While cultural predispositions might influence the effect of economic shocks on anti-immigrant sentiments, the reverse could also be true: the experience of an economic shock might influence the effect of cultural predispositions. For instance, the experience of economic distress could activate an individual's identification with the ingroup and prejudice towards the outgroup, which would result in more intense anti-immigrant attitudes (Kuk 2019; Burns and Gimpel 2000). Although we often think of cultural predispositions as relatively stable across the life course after being formed during pre-adult socialization it might well be the case that they can be updated when an individual's economic circumstances change (Kuk 2019).

One potential pathway through which the experience of economic distress could influence cultural predispositions is the need for higher self-esteem. The experience of an economic shock, such as the loss of a job, is likely to have a pervasive effect on an individual's self-esteem. It often goes hand in hand with having problems paying the bills or providing children with a good education. Financially insecure individuals might, therefore, be motivated to identify with their social group in an attempt to make up for self-esteem losses. Numerous studies show that identification with a social group, including with one's nation, is an important source of self-esteem (Rubin and Hewstone 1998; Tajfel and Turner 1979). Strengthening self-esteem by identifying with the ingroup might, however, come at the expense of greater outgroup bias (Branscombe and Wann 1994; Hewstone et al. 2002). This could take the form of stressing the hierarchy of their group and identifying the negative aspects of outgroups.

The psychological mechanism via self-esteem is similar to dynamics based on group hierarchies discussed in the literature, which argue that individuals' sense of where they belong in the social hierarchy might be overturned if they experience economic hardship (Sidanius and Pratto 2001). As they want to preserve their position in the hierarchy, they emphasize a social hierarchy, which stresses the superiority of their social group relative to other minority groups.

To sum up, developing stronger anti-immigrant attitudes could be a compensatory mechanism to make up for a self-image harmed by economic insecurity. Interestingly, this would suggest that economic threat can activate opposition to immigration regardless of whether immigrants are the source of this economic threat. The motivation for opposition to immigration is psychological rather than instrumental. Very few studies have subjected this mechanism to empirical tests, with some notable exceptions (see Kuk 2019). Using survey experiments, Kuk, for instance, shows that respondents primed with economic anxiety showed a higher level of racial resentment and ethnocentrism. He also shows that areas in the United States with higher local economic disruption show a higher level of racial resentment (Kuk 2019).

FUTURE QUESTIONS

To date, there has been very little empirical testing of the potential interactive effects between economic anxiety and cultural threat. With much of the literature on anti-immigrant attitudes still focusing on the relative influence of economic versus cultural considerations, it might be time to move towards a more nuanced evaluation of how the two influences interact. This might also need to entail a methodological shift towards methods more apt at detecting mechanisms rather than correlations, a change already called for by previous reviews (e.g. Hainmueller and Hopkins 2014).

It is, however, also possible that the literature's focus on economic anxiety and cultural threat is not justified. In other words, anti-immigrant attitudes could be caused by a different combination of factors. Education seems to be a particularly interesting candidate. It appears to be an important variable in both economic explanations – as a proxy for skill – and in cultural explanations as a proxy for cultural openness and cosmopolitanism. It is one of the few variables that is consistently associated with anti-immigrant attitudes in different empirical studies. Yet, while these studies find that education, in particular college education, is associated with lower concerns about immigration, we know very little about what it is about education that leads individuals to be less opposed to immigrants (Chandler and Tsai 2001; Espenshade and Calhoun 1993). It might be the case that education inherently immunizes individuals against anti-immigrant sentiments, but its effect could also be due to strong selection effects with pre-adult dispositions predicting both: educational attainment and attitudes towards immigration (Kunst et al. 2020).

Religiosity has also been discussed as a potential predictor of attitudes towards immigration, but it appears to be a double-edged sword. It has been associated with both more negative attitudes towards immigrants and more compassionate feelings. More recent studies have tried to shed light on this apparent contradiction. They find that religiosity increases opposition to immigrants who are dissimilar in religion or ethnicity, but it leads to welcoming attitudes to immigrants who share the same religion (Bloom et al. 2015).

This relates to research which examines whether attitudes towards immigrants might be different for distinct immigrant groups. Some studies find that attitudes towards immigrants are relatively undifferentiated, with individuals who portray negative attitudes towards one immigrant group also being likely to portray negative attitudes towards other groups (Sniderman et al. 2000). Other studies, however, argue that natives reject some immigrant populations more than others (Hainmueller and Hangartner 2013; Ford 2011; Lee and Fiske 2006). Hainmueller and Hangartner, for instance, show that Swiss voters are much more likely to reject immigrants from Turkey and Yugoslavia than those from elsewhere in Europe. Interestingly, antipathy towards those two groups grew sharply in the 1990s, as the Swiss People's Party began to mobilize voters on this issue (Hainmueller and Hangartner 2013).

This raises questions about the importance of contextual factors, in particular about the role of political parties and the mass media and their portrayal of different immigrant groups. Studies on the role of political parties that examines how their political cues on immigration interact with voters' partisanship and prior political ideology are, however, few and far between (Tichenor 2002; Messina 1989). Indeed, previous reviews have already called for a more serious analysis of political context (see Hainmueller and Hopkins 2014).

Research on media framing effects, by contrast, seems to be more developed. How the media portray immigrants – and in particular which immigrant groups they portray – has a strong influence on attitudes towards immigration. They construct both the dominant group's identity but also the perception of minority threat. Research, for instance, suggests that media coverage of Latinx immigrants changed drastically in 1994 when

California passed legislation prohibiting undocumented immigrants from using non-emergency healthcare and other public services. Since then, American news media has come to emphasize Latino immigration. This emphasis, in turn, is reflected in Americans' immigration attitudes (Valentino et al. 2013).

Media do not necessarily change beliefs, but they might simply trigger important emotions like anxiety (Brader et al. 2008). This can start a vicious cycle in which anxious citizens disproportionately seek out more threatening information, which further raises anxiety levels (Gadarian and Albertson 2014). For instance, even liberals' support for restrictive immigration policies grows when immigration is framed as a national security threat (Lahav and Courtemanche 2012).

This suggests that the effect of variables like economic hardship, cultural predispositions, education, or religiosity might not be independent of how immigrants are framed in the national discourse. In other words, media and political entrepreneurs might trigger the effect of individual-level characteristics. When the issue of immigration is made salient and politicized, economic and cultural factors might be associated with more opposition to immigration, but there is no such relationship at other times (Hainmueller and Hopkins 2014). Seeing that the information environment might not be static across time, nor similar for all individuals within a country at a given point in time, media and elite discourse might explain important dynamics in an otherwise static framework.

REFERENCES

Alesina, A. and Glaeser, E.L. (2004) *Fighting Poverty in the US and Europe: A World of Difference*. Oxford: Oxford University Press.
Allport, G.W. (1954). *The Nature of Prejudice*. Cambridge, MA: Addison-Wesley.
Bansak, K., Hainmueller, J., and Hangartner, D. (2016). How economic, humanitarian, and religious concerns shape European attitudes toward asylum seekers. *Science*, 354(6309), 217–222.
Bartels, Larry M. (2000). Partisanship and voting behavior, 1952–1996. *American Journal of Political Science*, 44(1), 35–50.
Bloom, P.B.N., Arikan, G., and Courtemanche, M. (2015). Religious social identity, religious belief, and anti-immigration sentiment. *American Political Science Review*, 109(2), 203–221.
Blumer, H. (1958). Race prejudice as a sense of group position. *Pacific Sociological Review*, 1(1), 3–7.
Bobo, L. (1983). Whites' opposition to busing: Symbolic racism or realistic group conflict? *Journal of Personality and Social Psychology*, 45(6), 1196–1210.
Borjas, G.J. (2003). The labor demand curve is downward sloping: Reexamining the impact of immigration on the labor market. *Quarterly Journal of Economics*, 118(4), 1335–1374.
Brader, T., Valentino, N.A., and Suhay, E. (2008). What triggers public opposition to immigration? Anxiety, group cues, and immigration threat. *American Journal of Political Science*, 52(4), 959–978.
Brady, D. and Finnigan, R. (2013). Does immigration undermine public support for social policy? *American Sociological Review*, 79, 17–42.
Branscombe, N.R. and Wann, D.L. (1994). Collective self-esteem consequences of outgroup derogation when a valued social identity is on trial. *European Journal of Social Psychology*, 24(6), 641–657.
Brewer, M.B. (1979). Ingroup bias in the minimal intergroup situation: A cognitive-motivational analysis. *Psychological Bulletin*, 86(2), 307–324.
Brewer, M.B. (1991). The social self: On being the same and different at the same time. *Personality and Social Psychology Bulletin*, 17, 475–482.
Burgoon, B. (2014). Immigration, integration, and support for redistribution in Europe. *World Politics*, 66(3), 365–405.
Burns, P. and Gimpel, J.G. (2000). Economic insecurity, prejudicial stereotypes, and public opinion on immigration policy. *Political Science Quarterly*, 115(2), 201–225.
Campbell, A., Converse, P., Miller, W., and Stokes, D.E. (1960). *The American Voter*. Chicago, IL: University of Chicago Press.

Chandler, C.R. and Tsai, Y.M. (2001). Social factors influencing immigration attitudes: An analysis of data from the General Social Survey. *The Social Science Journal*, 38(2), 177–188.

Citrin, J., Green, D.P., Muste, C., and Wong, C. (1997). Public opinion toward immigration reform: The role of economic motivations. *Journal of Politics*, 59(3), 858–881.

Citrin, J., Lerman, A., Murakami, M., and Pearson, K. (2007). Testing Huntington: Is Hispanic immigration a threat to American identity? *Perspectives on Politics*, 5(1), 31–48.

Coffé, H., Heyndels, B., and Vermeir, J. (2007). Fertile grounds for extreme right-wing parties: Explaining the Vlaams Blok's electoral success, *Electoral Studies*, 26(1), 142–155.

Crepaz, M.M.L. and Damron, R. (2009). Constructing tolerance: How the welfare state shapes attitudes about immigrants. *Comparative Political Studies*, 42(3), 437–463.

Dancygier, R.M. and Donnelly, M.J. (2012). Sectoral economies, economic contexts, and attitudes toward immigration. *Journal of Politics*, 75(1), 17–35.

De Cremer, D. and Van Vugt, M. (1999). Social identification effects in social dilemmas: A transformation of motives. *European Journal of Social Psychology*, 29(7), 871–893.

De Vries, C.E., Hobolt, S.B., and Tilley, J. (2018). Facing up to the facts: What causes economic perceptions? *Electoral Studies*, 51, 115–122.

Espenshade, T.J. and Calhoun, C.A. (1993). An analysis of public opinion toward undocumented immigration. *Population Research and Policy Review*, 12(3), 189–224.

Facchini, G. and Mayda, A.M. (2009). Does the welfare state affect individual attitudes toward immigrants? Evidence across countries. *Review of Economics and Statistics*, 91(2), 295–314.

Fiske, S.T. and Taylor, S.E. (2007). *Social Cognition: From Brains to Culture*. New York: McGraw-Hill.

Ford, R. (2011). Acceptable and unacceptable immigrants: How opposition to immigration in Britain is affected by migrants' region of origin. *Journal of Ethnic and Migration Studies*, 37(7), 1017–1037.

Gadarian, S.K. and Albertson, B. (2014). Anxiety, immigration, and the search for information. *Political Psychology*, 35(2), 133–164.

Gaertner, S.L. and Dovidio, J.F. (2000). *Reducing Intergroup Bias: The Common Ingroup Identity Model. Essays in Social Psychology*. Hove: Psychology Press.

Goldstein, J.L. and Peters, M.E. (2014). Nativism or economic threat: Attitudes toward immigrants during the great recession. *International Interactions*, 40(3), 376–401.

Hainmueller, J. and Hangartner, D. (2013). Who gets a Swiss passport? A natural experiment in immigrant discrimination. *American Political Science Review*, 107(1), 159–187.

Hainmueller, J. and Hiscox, M.J. (2007). Educated preferences: Explaining attitudes toward immigration in Europe. *International Organization*, 61(2), 399–442.

Hainmueller, J. and Hiscox, M.J. (2010). Attitudes toward highly skilled and low-skilled immigration: Evidence from a survey experiment. *American Political Science Review*, 104(1), 61–84.

Hainmueller, J. and Hopkins, D.J. (2014). Public attitudes toward immigration. *Annual Review of Political Science*, 17, 225–249.

Halla, M., Wagner, A.F., and Zweimüller, J. (2017). Immigration and voting for the far right. *Journal of the European Economic Association*, 15(6), 1341–1385.

Hanson, G.H. (2007). *The Economic Logic of Illegal Immigration*. New York: Council on Foreign Relations.

Hanson, G.H., Scheve, K., and Slaughter, M.J. (2005). Individual preferences over high-skilled immigration in the United States. Mimeo, University of California, San Diego.

Harell, A., Soroka, S., Iyengar, S., and Valentino, N. (2012). The impact of economic and cultural cues on support for immigration in Canada and the United States. *Canadian Journal of Political Science/Revue canadienne de science politique*, 45(3), 499–530.

Hewstone, M. (1989). *Causal Attribution: From Cognitive Processes to Collective Beliefs*. Oxford: Blackwell.

Hewstone, M., Rubin, M., and Willis, H. (2002). Intergroup bias. *Annual Review of Psychology*, 53(1), 575–604.

Hobolt, S.B. and Tilley, J. (2014). Who's in charge? How voters attribute responsibility in the European Union. *Comparative Political Studies*, 47(6), 795–819.

Hooghe, L. and Marks, G. (2005). Community, calculation and cues. *European Union Politics*, 6(4), 421–445.

Hooghe, L. and Marks, G. (2009). A postfunctionalist theory of European integration: From permissive consensus to constraining dissensus. *British Journal of Political Science*, 39(1), 1–23.

Hooghe, L. and Marks, G. (2018). Cleavage theory meets Europe's crises: Lipset, Rokkan, and the transnational cleavage. *Journal of European Public Policy*, 25(1), 109–135.

Jackman, M.R. and Muha, M.J. (1984). Education and intergroup attitudes: Moral enlightenment, superficial democratic commitment, or ideological refinement? *American Sociological Review*, 49(6), 751–769.

Kessler, A. (2001). Immigration, economic insecurity, and the "ambivalent" American public. *UC San Diego Working Paper*.

Kleider, H. and Stoeckel, F. (2018). Economic insecurity and attitudes towards immigrants: Evidence from a panel study. Paper presented at the American Political Science Association.

Kramer, R.M. and Brewer, M.B. (1984). Effects of group identity on resource utilization in a simulated commons dilemma. *Journal of Personality and Social Psychology*, 46, 1044–1057.

Kriesi, H., Grande, E., Lachat, R., Dolezal, M., Bornschier, S., and Frey, T. (2006). Globalization and the transformation of the national political space: Six European countries compared. *European Journal of Political Research*, 45(6), 921–956.

Kuk, J. (2019). The effects of economic distress on racial attitudes. Paper presented at the Toronto Political Behaviour Workshop. Munk School of Global Affairs and Public Policy, University of Toronto.

Kunst, S., Kuhn, T., and van de Werfhorst, H.G. (2020). Does education decrease Euroscepticism? A regression discontinuity design using compulsory schooling reforms in four European countries. *European Union Politics*, 21(1), 24–42.

Lahav, G. and Courtemanche, M. (2012). The ideological effects of framing threat on immigration and civil liberties. *Political Behavior*, 34(3), 477–505.

Lee, T.L. and Fiske, S.T. (2006). Not an outgroup, not yet an ingroup: Immigrants in the stereotype content model. *International Journal of Intercultural Relations*, 30(6), 751–768.

Leong, C.H. (2008). A multilevel research framework for the analyses of attitudes toward immigrants. *International Journal of Intercultural Relations*, 32(2), 115–129.

Lewis-Beck, M.S. (1997). Who's the chef? Economic voting under a dual executive. *European Journal of Political Research*, 31(3), 315–326.

Malhotra, N., Margalit, Y., and Mo, C.H. (2013). Economic explanations for opposition to immigration: Distinguishing between prevalence and conditional impact. *American Journal of Political Science*, 57(2), 391–410.

Mansfield, E.D. and Mutz, D.C. (2009). Support for free trade: Self-interest, sociotropic politics, and outgroup anxiety. *International Organization*, 63(3), 425–457.

Mau, S. and Burkhardt, C. (2009). Migration and welfare state solidarity in Western Europe. *Journal of European Social Policy*, 19(3), 213–229.

Mayda, A.M. (2006). Who is against immigration? A cross-country investigation of individual attitudes toward immigrants. *Review of Economics and Statistics*, 88(3), 510–530.

Messina, A.M. (1989). *Race and Party Competition in Britain*. Oxford: Clarendon.

Meuleman, B., Davidov, E., and Billiet, J. (2009). Changing attitudes toward immigration in Europe, 2002–2007: A dynamic group conflict theory approach. *Social Science Research*, 38(2), 352–365.

Mutz, D.C. (2018). Status threat, not economic hardship, explains the 2016 presidential vote. *Proceedings of the National Academy of Sciences*, 115(19), E4330–E4339.

Peffley, M. (1984). The voter as juror: Attributing responsibility for economic problems. *Political Behavior*, 6(3), 275–294.

Peffley, M. and Williams, J.T. (1985). Attributing presidential responsibility for national economic problems. *American Politics Quarterly*, 13(4), 393–425.

Pettigrew, T.F. (1979). The ultimate attribution error: Extending Allport's cognitive analysis of prejudice. *Personality and Social Psychology Bulletin*, 5(4), 461–476.

Quillian, L. (1995). Prejudice as a response to perceived group threat: Population composition and anti-immigrant and racial prejudice in Europe. *American Sociological Review*, 60(4), 586–611.

Rahn, W.M. (1993). The role of partisan stereotypes in information processing about political candidates. *American Journal of Political Science*, 37(2), 472–496.

Rooduijn, M. (2020). Immigration attitudes have barely changed – so why is far right on rise? *The Guardian*, March 2.

Rubin, M. and Hewstone, M. (1998). Social identity theory's self-esteem hypothesis: A review and some suggestions for clarification. *Personality and Social Psychology Review*, 2(1), 40–62.

Rudolph, T.J. (2003). Who's responsible for the economy? The formation and consequences of responsibility attributions. *American Journal of Political Science*, 47(4), 698–713.

Schaffner, B.F., MacWilliams, M., and Nteta, T. (2018). Understanding white polarization in the 2016 vote for president: The sobering role of racism and sexism. *Political Science Quarterly*, 133(1), 9–34.

Scheve, K.F. and Slaughter, M.J. (2001). Labor market competition and individual preferences over immigration policy. *Review of Economics and Statistics*, 83(1), 133–145.

Schildkraut, D.J. (2005). *Press One for English: Language Policy, Public Opinion, and American Identity*. Princeton, NJ: Princeton University Press.

Schlenker, B.R., Britt, T.W., Pennington, J., Murphy, R., and Doherty, K. (1994). The triangle model of responsibility. *Psychological Review*, 101(4), 632–652.

Semyonov, M., Raijman, R., and Gorodzeisky, A. (2006). The rise of anti-foreigner sentiment in European societies, 1988–2000. *American Sociological Review*, 71(3), 426–449.

Sidanius, J. and Pratto, F. (2001). *Social Dominance: An Intergroup Theory of Social Hierarchy and Oppression*. Cambridge: Cambridge University Press.

Sniderman, P.M., Peri, P., de Figueiredo, R.J.P., and Piazza, T. (2000). *The Outsider: Prejudice and Politics in Italy*. Princeton, NJ: Princeton University Press.

Sniderman, P.M., Hagendoorn, L., and Prior, M. (2004). Predisposing factors and situational triggers: Exclusionary reactions to immigrant minorities. *American Political Science Review*, 98(1), 35–49.

Stephan, W.G., Diaz-Loving, R., and Duran, A. (2000). Integrated threat theory and intercultural attitudes: Mexico and the United States. *Journal of Cross-Cultural Psychology*, 31(2), 240–249.

Tajfel, H. (1969). Cognitive aspects of prejudice. *Journal of Social Issues*, 25(4), 79–97.

Tajfel, H. and Turner, J.C. (1979). An integrative theory of intergroup conflict. In *Social Psychology of Intergroup Relations*, eds. W.G. Austin and S. Worchel, 33–47. Monterey, CA: Brooks/Cole.

Tichenor, D. (2002). *Dividing Lines: The Politics of Immigration Control in America*. Princeton, NJ: Princeton University Press.

Tingley, D. (2012). Public finance and immigration preferences: A lost connection? *Polity*, 45(1), 4–33.

Valentino, N.A., Brader, T., and Jardina, A.E. (2013). Immigration opposition among U.S. whites: General ethnocentrism or media priming of attitudes about Latinos? *Political Psychology*, 34(2), 149–166.

Wang, X. (2012). Undocumented immigrants as perceived criminal threat: A test of the minority threat perspective. *Criminology*, 50(3), 743–776.

Wenzel, M. and Mummendey, A. (1996). Positive-negative asymmetry of social discrimination: A normative analysis of differential evaluations of ingroup and outgroup on positive and negative attributes. *British Journal of Social Psychology*, 35(4), 493–507.

Wright, M., Citrin, J., and Wand, J. (2012). Alternative measures of American national identity: Implications for the civic-ethnic distinction. *Political Psychology*, 33(4), 469–482.

18. Economic resentment or cultural malaise: What accounts for nativist sentiments in contemporary liberal democracies?
Hans-Georg Betz

Recent electoral trends in advanced liberal capitalist democracies have once again shown to what degree the challenges posed by international migration have the potential to decisively influence ballot-box outcomes. Take, for instance, the upsurge in support for the AfD in the most recent federal election in Germany and subsequent regional elections in the eastern part of the country. Given Germany's history, the fact that a party that unabashedly promotes a blatantly *völkisch* agenda is now represented in the German *Bundestag* is arguably the most dramatic manifestation of the mobilizational force of anti-migrant sentiments if it is successfully exploited by nativist political entrepreneurs. Germany is hardly an exceptional case. Even in the Nordic countries, once heralded as beacons of tolerance and social progressivism, anti-immigrant sentiments rule the day. Denmark, for instance, has become a "model" for how to deter refugees from applying for asylum in the country – a model eagerly studied by various, including left-wing, parties throughout Western Europe. And in Sweden, the populist radical right has established itself as a major political force, exploiting widespread popular unease with the country's traditional openness to international migration. In both countries, the politics of exclusion has been justified primarily in terms of safeguarding the future of the countries' comprehensive welfare state.[1] The result is emblematic of a new wave of nativism, which in recent years has spread across most affluent Western capitalist societies.

Nativism is informed by the notion that the material and cultural claims of the "native-born" should be accorded absolute priority over those new to the community – and this solely on the grounds that the former are natives. More often than not nativism is informed by notions of infrahumanization, i.e., "a form of dehumanization in which one's in-group is considered fully human while out-groups are denied some of the key attributes that constitute humanity" (Banton et al. 2020, 158). It reflects a "subtle denial of the humanity of out-groups which is then expressed in the differential treatment of out-group members (relative to in-group members)" (Banton et al. 2020, 159; see also Vaes et al. 2003). Politically, it involves a variety of measures in favor of the "indigenous" population designed to defend, maintain, and revive the cherished heritage of their culture. The ensuing rhetoric is not necessarily limited to "organic justifications of culture"; it also, and often primarily, includes an appeal to civic conceptions of culture that are foundational to Western civilization (Halikiopoulou 2019, 37).

At the same time, however, the nativist discourse fundamentally challenges, if not outright rejects, the progressive extension of "moral boundaries" – i.e., the "distinction between those entities that are deemed worthy of moral consideration and those that are not" – which has been one of the central characteristics of modern societies (Crimston et al. 2016, 636). Instead, it advocates a narrow conception of solidarity on the grounds that only such a conception will sustain solidarity in an age of rampant individualization (De Beer and Koster 2009). Politically, the nativist doctrine holds that governments have as their primary duty the promotion and protection of the well-being and welfare of its own citizens, more often than not defined in narrow ethnic terms. The nativist doctrine also demands that governments actively demonstrate a "reasonable partiality towards compatriots" – particularly with regard to job opportunities and social benefits (Miller 2005).

As will be demonstrated throughout the discussion that follows, nativism derives much of its mobilizing force and appeal from its ability to evoke a wide range of diffuse emotions and exploit them for political gain. To be sure, nativism is nothing new. It boasts a long genealogy that in Europe extends all the way to the Middle Ages. Politically, however, it was not until the first half of nineteenth-century America with the arrival of the first wave of mass immigration that it became a salient issue. The new arrivals provoked an often violent backlash among the "native-born" population, informed by widespread anxiety and resentment, fear and hatred. The resurgence of nativist sentiments today is reminiscent of these earlier episodes, even if the structural conditions have fundamentally changed. Today globalization, rapid technological change, a dramatic rise in inequality, and profound sociocultural transformations provoke a panoply of emotions that feed into nativist sentiments, particularly among those who feel victimized and powerless.

NATIVIST NARRATIVES ACROSS TIME AND SPACE

Nineteenth-century American nativism already displayed all the features that make it paradigmatic for understanding contemporary anti-immigrant sentiments. And it provides a first tentative answer to the central question that informs this chapter: are anti-immigrant sentiments primarily a reflection of economic anxieties or are they primarily a manifestation of cultural threat perceptions? The answer is relatively clear-cut – they are both. This, too, is nothing new. As Yotam Margalit noted, popular attitudes towards various aspects of globalization – and here particularly migration – "fuse both economic and social-cultural concerns." Negative sentiments towards migrants are largely informed by "individuals' cultural values and beliefs, not just by fears about the fiscal and labor market consequences of immigration" (Margalit 2012, 487). In short, non-economic factors are just as important to explain episodes of popular backlash against international migration as are purely economic ones. By the same token, economic anxieties continue to play a significant role in engendering and fueling anti-immigrant sentiments, particularly among those social groups most negatively affected by the twin challenges of globalization and incipient technological change.

Political parties that have been exploiting these sentiments are keenly aware of the two dimensions underlying present-day nativism. And, in fact, virtually all of them mobilize popular anti-migrant affects along both dimensions – arguably best encapsulated in the Flemish populist radical right's classical slogan "*Eigen volk eerst*" (our people [in terms of ethnic entity] first), recently "updated" as "*Eerst onze mensen*" (first our people [in terms of human beings]).[2] The slogan's reference to the "people" is not only with regard to an absolute entitlement to a privileged position with respect to social and political rights; it also establishes "the own people" as carriers of a particular idiosyncratic culture, which migrants are expected to adopt and absorb in a process of assimilation if they want to stay in the country. As the Flemish radical populist right blatantly put it: *aanpassen of terugkeren* (assimilate or go back).

Remarkably enough, in support of their exclusionary positions, more often than not these parties almost instinctively advance arguments that have been at the core of the academic debate on the socioeconomic and sociocultural effect of mass immigration for the past decades. Central to this debate are the questions of whether or not growing ethnic diversity fatally undermines solidarity and whether or not it poses a threat to national identity. These are hardly new concerns. As early as 1978, Margaret Thatcher charged that the British "people are really rather afraid that this country might be rather swamped by people with a different culture" and that this might lead them to "react and be rather hostile to those coming in."[3] Thatcher's anti-immigrant rhetoric proved highly seductive, winning the Tories the 1979 election. In response, some on the left developed a new agenda, which put the focus on "the communal virtues of locality and solidarity" – a potentially dangerous proposition. For, as David Goodhart (who later on would popularize the notion of the "progressive's dilemma") charged at the time, "left communitarianism" could "easily mutate into a nativism in which solidarity across ethnic divisions can be dismissed as yet another fad imposed by metropolitan liberals on once homogeneous working-class communities."[4] Goodhart was right. This is what has happened throughout advanced liberal democracies, more often than not actively promoted by radical right-wing populist parties.

THE ORIGINS OF NATIVISM

The origins of (politically relevant) nativism lie in early nineteenth-century America. Starting in the 1830s, the new republic was confronted with a first major wave of mass immigration. The vast majority of immigrants arrived from Ireland, fleeing poverty and starvation. Others were from the southern parts of Germany. Most of the new arrivals were Catholics. A large majority of them settled in the large cities of the north east.

There the newcomers were met with suspicion and open hostility. They quickly provoked a vicious response on the part of large segments of the native-born population. At times, most infamously during the Philadelphia "bible riot" of 1844, anger and resentment escalated into open violence involving the destruction of private property and loss of human life. Several factors accounted for the explosion of public anti-immigrant hostility. There was the fear of job competition and competition for scarce public services; there were religious and cultural prejudices; and, last but not least, there was blatant racism, directed against Europeans deemed belonging to an inferior race. Although all of these factors played a significant role in fueling nativist sentiments, none was more important than the question of cultural identity.

The United States was founded as a Protestant country; and the Protestant majority was intent on defending the new country's Anglo-Saxon Protestant cultural heritage against the "popish" threat. American nativist organizations – most famously the "Know Nothings" – held that it was Anglo-Saxon Protestantism that undergirded the essential moral and intellectual qualities, which were indispensable for democratic citizenship and a precondition for self-government. This is what distinguished American identity, grounded in the centuries' old association between "Christianity and liberty, liberty and Protestantism, and Protestantism and English identity" (Farrelly 2017, 21). It was this identity which made American culture supposedly superior, particularly with respect to Europe. Immigrants from Catholic countries, such as Ireland, not only threatened to debase the foundation of American culture and values, such as republican virtue, but also posed a fundamental threat to the very essence of American democracy, which was based on the independence of mind, impervious to manipulation by an ecclesiastical hierarchy.

Nativists also charged that European countries were "dumping" paupers and criminals onto American shores leaving their charge to the new country. Particularly in the big cities, public authorities complained that they were being overburdened by the costs of having to care for immigrant paupers. It was American workers, New York City nativists claimed, who paid the bill "for the support of foreign-born inmates of the city institutions"; it was American workers whose "high rents for tenement rooms really paid for the upkeep of immigrant paupers and criminals" (Ernst 1948, 173). At the same time, American workers were increasingly pressured by the acceleration of industrial development. Technological progress together with the expansion of industrial capitalism led to the devaluation of traditional skills, the breakdown of the traditional crafts system and, with it, the erosion of the position of urban artisans, leaving them to the vicissitudes of the wage labor market (Ernst 1948, 175). The psychological impact on them was dramatic, "provoking bitterness and resentment" which, in turn, led to the search for "effective countermeasures for restoring their former economic and social status" (Lane 1987, 23). Not being able to impede and reverse technological innovation, urban laborers directed their frustration, apprehension and anger against immigrants, blaming them for the deterioration of their situation and, in the process, fueling the flames of nativism (Huston 1989, 371).

Even after the collapse of the Know Nothings on the eve of the Civil War, nativism continued to flare up again and again throughout the nineteenth century. As late as 1883, a cartoon that appeared in *Harpers Weekly* fueled the flames of American nativism, depicting a British steamship full of Irish paupers, "shipped by the British government" and bound for Boston Harbor.[5] At that time, however, American nativism was no longer only directed against the Irish, but against a range of "aliens" – most notably the Chinese. Again, the reason was a combination of economic and cultural issues. Economically, in the West, once the Gold Rush and the railroad boom had come to an end, the Chinese increasingly threatened job opportunities for women in domestic service and increasingly also in manufacturing where they worked for low wages (Boswell 1986, 362). Culturally, the Chinese were portrayed as deviants, as threats to established social norms, with prostitution, gambling and crammed living conditions cited as major evidence of deviance from the American norm (Fong and Markham 1991, 483). In the decades that followed, nativists found a new target – the growing influx of immigrants from southern Italy. Italians met open hostility, for economic, religious and cultural reasons. Cartoons depicted Italian immigrants as knife- and pistol-wielding rats, reflecting a widely shared view that Italian immigrants were little short of criminal "scum" dumped onto American shores and fundamentally incapable of understanding America's republican virtues and institutions (Botein 1979, 276–278).[6]

The range of public responses to mass immigration in the nineteenth-century United States provides a striking illustration of the complexity of the sentiments that migration tends to provoke. To be sure, throughout the period, anti-immigrant sentiments were to a significant extent informed by a strong belief in the existence of racialized hierarchies, with the Irish, Italians, and particularly Asians being considered of inferior stock. In fact, the "racial status" of Asians, most prominently Japanese, Indians, and Chinese, became "a matter of great controversy" which would remain unresolved for decades to come (Tehranian 2000, 826). Eventually, Catholics, the Irish and Italian immigrants, did manage to be accepted as Americans – at least as long as they demonstrated "evidence of whiteness in their character, religious practices and beliefs, class orientation, language, ability to intermarry, and a host of other traits that had nothing to do with intrinsic racial grouping" (Tehranian 2000, 821). By contrast, the Chinese, and Asians in general, were for a long time excluded, on the grounds of their limited "assimilability" – i.e., their limited potential "to assimilate within mainstream Anglo-American culture" (Tehranian 2000, 820). As the Supreme Court – in a well-known naturalization case – would put it, this had nothing to do with notions of "racial superiority or inferiority"; rather, it merely reflected a recognition of "racial difference" – a difference which was "of such character and extent that the great body of our people instinctively recognize it and reject the thought of assimilation" (Tehranian 2000, 823, fn. 36).

At the same time, anti-immigrant sentiments were fueled by very real material concerns, anxieties and *ressentiments*. Take, for instance, the case of the considerable number of women who joined the nativist movement. A substantial proportion of them were working women, such as factory hands and seamstresses. They joined the movement out of "'self-defense' to combat the influx of cheap European workers," which would invariably lead to the elimination of job opportunities for native-born female labor (Hales 1979, 122). Anxiety and resentment, however, were not only provoked by mass immigration and its presumed impact on labor markets and rudimentary social services; they were also, and perhaps even more so, triggered by the experience of profound macro-structural changes, such as industrialization and urbanization, perceived as being outside and beyond the purview of individual control.

For today's observers, early nineteenth-century American nativism might appear like ancient history, quaint and, perhaps, amusing, but largely irrelevant. Yet the parallels to the current situation are striking, both in terms of the structural conditions that gave rise to early nineteenth-century nativist mobilization and with respect to the sentiments and nativist rhetoric they provoked. The 1840s and 1850s were a period of wide-reaching socioeconomic change, which had a particularly momentous impact on urban workshops. The rapid expansion of manufacturing thwarted the prospects of traditionally trained mechanics and other craftsmen to advance the career ladder and eventually become masters of their trade and thus attain a respected social position. At the time, among those fallen victims of these developments their plight engendered a range of emotions – powerlessness, anger, and resentment, which, perhaps not entirely surprisingly, erupted into nativist frenzy.

Today, the twin processes of globalization and the acceleration of the pace of technological innovation pose an even more fundamental sociopolitical challenge. Automation – i.e., the substitution of robots for human labor – artificial intelligence and big data threaten a growing number of working people with obsolescence, rendering them "structurally irrelevant from the perspective of the profit-making programs of global capitalism," as workers, consumers or both (Castells 2009, 33). In the process, the sense of purpose, "meaningfulness" and worth inherent in traditional working-class life has all but evaporated, more often than not with traumatic consequences.[7]

At the same time, the dynamics released by the "space–time compression" central to the current phase of globalization pose a profound sociocultural challenge, particularly with respect to the question of identity. John Tomlinson has convincingly argued that globalization, rather than destroying identities, in fact amplifies "the identity positions" which it tends to generate and produce – even in those societies where identity was of little concern before the most recent onslaught of globalization (Tomlinson 2003, 271). In a later piece, Tomlinson has elaborated on what he means by identity positions. Two are most relevant for the discussion which follows: on the one hand, there is what Tomlinson characterizes as the "'benign' form of universalism" grounded in notions of "human mutuality" and a sense of "global solidarity." This is the "cosmopolitan" vision. On the other hand, there is the defense of the "integrity of local context and practices, cultural autonomy, cultural identity and 'sovereignty,'" in short, the right to particularity, idiosyncrasy and difference. This is the parochial/communitarian position. In Tomlinson's view, both the support for universal human rights and for cultural difference represent "strong rational principles" providing "good reasons to stand beside both." Yet more often than not they pull "in different directions" giving rise to cultural conflicts, which, in turn, spawn a new – cosmopolitan versus parochial – sociopolitical cleavage (Tomlinson 2012, 363).

It is within these parameters that the public response to the upturn in migratory flows during the past several decades has to be seen. As was the case in early nineteenth-century United States, the most recent upsurge in mass migration – or at least its anticipation for the future – has provoked both economic and cultural anxieties and resentment in receiving countries. These worries are heightened and magnified by apprehension in the face of accelerated technological innovation – both with regard to immediate/intermediate job security and particularly to the precarious prospects of future generations.

WHY CULTURE TRUMPS ECONOMICS TODAY

In an influential article Daniel Oesch maintained more than a decade ago that in contemporary advanced capitalist democracies "questions of community and identity" are "clearly more important than economic grievances" (Oesch 2008, 349). A study of 21 European countries, based on the 2002 European Social Survey, found that economic considerations regarding wages and taxes did matter, but "compositional amenities" (common and shared culture and traditions, religion and language) considerably more (Card et al. 2009). There are a number of potential explanations for why this might be so. On the most abstract level, there is the fact that over the past several decades, international finance has increasingly curtailed the ability of sovereign states to pursue autonomous fiscal policies. In response, left-wing political parties have largely abandoned promoting the materialistic interest of the traditional working class, instead adopting "identity politics" in favor of sexual and ethnic minorities. This, in turn, has opened up space for radical right-wing populist parties to advance a novel combination of nativist and identity politics. The former centers upon demands that "our people" come first, particularly with respect to social benefits; the latter around the trope of the allegedly discriminated white, heterosexual majority. In the process, a nativist reconceptualization of identity has steadily been gaining ground.

Leon Wieseltier, writing for the *Washington Post* in 2016, makes the case. Noting that the left had wondered for ages "why people in economic distress do not vote according to their economic interests," he charged that the answer "should have been obvious long ago: People in adversity turn not to economics but to culture. They are fortified not by policy but by identity according to their economic interests." Once "the direness of their circumstances appears to imperil their identity, they affirm it by asserting it ferociously against others."[8]

More recently, Dani Rodrik has advanced a more nuanced argument. Rodrik interprets contemporary populism primarily as a backlash against globalization and its disruptive impact on large numbers of citizens in advanced liberal capitalist and developing countries alike. He contends that "even when the underlying shock is fundamentally economic the political manifestations can be cultural and nativist. What may look like a racist or xenophobic backlash may have its roots in economic anxieties and dislocations" (Rodrik 2018, 25). In fact, more often than not, it is difficult, if not outright impossible, to disentangle the two and cleanly separate them from each other.

Radical right-wing populist parties have not only been well aware of this fact but have also been quite astute to exploit its mobilizational potential. A paradigmatic example is an election spot produced by the Sverigedemokraterna in the run-up to the country's 2010 parliamentary election. Swedish television refused to air the spot charging that it promoted "racial hatred." In the age of social media, the refusal was irritating for the radical right, but hardly a big deal. The spot was put on YouTube where it reached a broad audience.[9] It showed a race between a frail elderly Swedish woman, desperately holding onto her rollator, and several women in burqas pushing baby carriages. The party's message was clear: Sweden's political establishment had no qualms about pitting vulnerable native-born Swedish pensioners against presumably fit, young and, above all, culturally alien migrants – with both sides competing for limited and presumably dwindling resources.

A few years later, Arlie Hochschild, the author of an acclaimed study of Tea Party supporters in Louisiana, made almost identical observations (Hochschild 2016). Choosing the metaphor of a "pilgrimage facing the top of the hill" to characterize the "American Dream," Hochschild referred to the resentment of white (male) Americans who had worked hard to attain the goal (i.e., the American Dream), only to see their efforts cruelly thwarted by "line-cutters" – blacks, women, immigrants – all of them being given preference. Marginalized as a result of dwindling job opportunities and plummeting wages, their privileged position threatened by demographic change, their cultural values grounded in conservative Christianity mocked and dismissed, they have become archetypical "strangers from the predominant values in their own country, left behind by progressive tides of cultural change which they do not share" (Ingelhart and Norris 2016, 5). To add insult to injury, when they (i.e., white, lower-class Americans from the "heartland") dare to complain, "someone more educated, living in a coastal city, turns around and says that they are uneducated, racist, homophobic, sexist rednecks" (cited in Blättler 2017, 585). In response, they support political entrepreneurs who are adamantly opposed to policies that would directly benefit ordinary people (such as universal health care and the rigorous enforcement of environmental protection regulations).

358   *Handbook on migration and welfare*

The two examples come from very different parts of the advanced capitalist world. In fact, for many Americans, Sweden represents a socialist dystopia, diametrically opposed to everything the United States purportedly stands for. (The opposite is presumably true for Swedes.) And yet, the diagnosis of what has gone wrong is remarkably similar on the two sides of the Atlantic. A campaign poster produced by a regional section of the Swiss populist right (Swiss People's Party, SVP) in 2003 provides a striking illustration of the material side of the nativist coin. The content of the poster provoked considerable critique in the Swiss media, primarily because of its racist connotations. As a result, it was withdrawn – but not until the media had already published small facsimile copies that exposed a wider audience to its content.

The poster charged that ordinary Swiss citizens were increasingly asked to pay for, and agree to, a range of projects and policies – from close relations with the European Union to the generous acquisition of Swiss citizenship – none of which Swiss citizens wanted. In order to drive home the point, the authors came up with a striking image accompanied by an equally striking caption: over the image of a grumpily looking man featuring a caricature of a black face – including a ring through the nose – the caption read "We Swiss are increasingly the negroes."[10] Christoph Blocher, the party's billionaire strongman, refused to distance himself from the content of the poster, charging instead that it expressed the feelings of many Swiss that their interests were no longer accorded priority, that they were losing out, particularly compared to immigrants.[11]

These three examples illustrate to what degree, on the question of transnational migration, material/economic concerns and culturally grounded resentment are closely intertwined – and not necessarily the way one might expect. The economic/material part is relatively straightforward. These concerns stem largely from fears about labor market competition and, arguably most importantly, about competition for diminishing social benefits. The cultural aspect of anti-immigrant sentiments is more complex. Most directly, it involves the question of cultural "compatibility" which has always been central to nativism. In contemporary Western liberal democracies, cultural compatibility centers primarily upon the question of the place of Islam in overwhelmingly secular societies.

More important for the future of Western liberal societies, however, it involves a culture clash between two fundamentally different socionormative conceptualizations that pit the proponents of universalistic, libertarian values against those defending parochial, particularistic ones (Häusermann and Kriesi 2012). The result is the emergence of a potentially new political cleavage encompassing various dimensions closely linked to globalization (Zürn and de Wilde 2016; de Wilde et al. 2019; Ford and Jennings 2020). A central dimension of this new cleavage is the urban/rural divide. In a recent paper, Will Wilkinson from the Niskanen Center points out that urbanization (i.e., the growing concentration of large parts of the population in cities) is at the root of special sorting dynamics that divide societies along a number of attributes, such as education, ethnicity, personality and value dispositions with important implications for both economic fortunes and cultural values (Wilkinson 2019). Dani Rodrik summarizes the core of the argument:

> [Urbanization] creates thriving, multicultural, high-density areas where socially liberal values predominate. And it leaves behind rural areas and smaller urban centers that are increasingly uniform in terms of social conservatism and aversion to diversity. This process, moreover, is

self-reinforcing: economic success in large cities validates urban values, while self-selection in migration out of lagging regions increases polarization further. In Europe and the U.S. alike, homogenous, socially conservative areas constitute the basis of support for nativist populists.[12]

As was the case of early nineteenth-century mass immigration to the United States, the vast majority of today's migrants to advanced capitalist countries end up in metropolitan areas. As the 2015 *World Migration Report* put it, in today's world, migration "is essentially an urban affair" (International Organization for Migration 2015, 2). In Australia, for instance, according to official data from 2016, roughly two-thirds of skilled migrants settled in the country's major cities, most prominently Sydney and Melbourne. Sajeda Tuli says the reason is simple: "The big cities offer diverse opportunities, similar jobs to advance their careers and a lifestyle for them and their families"; "Migrants want to live in the big cities, just like the rest of us."[13]

More often than not, metropolitan areas are home to some of the most competitive and innovative firms there are, which, in turn, benefit from the spatial clustering of other innovative firms. At the same time, big cities boast large concentrations of knowledge-industry workers, both native-born and immigrants attracted by these firms. Knowledge workers tend to be, on average, younger, better educated, highly skilled, relatively affluent and mobile. This presumably makes them more likely to be open-minded with respect to ethnic, cultural and sexual diversity, tolerant and cosmopolitan (Warf 2015). Furthermore, contact theory suggests that close contact with strangers on a daily basis tends to create a sense of familiarity with diversity, reducing prejudices and promoting integration (Pettigrew et al. 2011).

The emergence of "global cities" such as Paris, London, New York and Melbourne has important cultural repercussions – most importantly, for the sake of this chapter, with respect to identity. Some years ago, the prominent German sociologist Ulrich Beck noted that "an increasing number of people nowadays trade internationally, work internationally, love internationally, marry internationally, do research internationally, and their children are growing up and are being educated internationally." This has resulted in the partial "de-territorialization" of national identity, i.e., allowing the sense of belongingness to escape from the narrow confines of the nation state (Beck 2002, 31). At the same time, the erosion of national identity in the wake of accelerated globalization has provoked a powerful political backlash aimed at defending and protecting a country's national identity. The result has been a new line of polarization, between a "'progressive,' open, self-reflexive sense of place and a 'regressive,' closed, parochial sense of place." As Marco Antonsich has empirically shown, the two dispositions depend to a large extent on whether or not an individual feels "threatened or not by globalization" (Antonsich 2009, 292).

A prime example of these developments is Switzerland, particularly given the country's distinct form of direct democracy. The analysis of recent referenda and popular initiatives shows that over the past several decades, urban centers and rural periphery have increasingly drifted apart. Take, for instance, the anti-minaret initiative from 2009. The initiative was rejected by relatively large majorities in the major metropolitan cities (Basel, Berne, Zurich and Geneva), while finding relatively large support in rural areas, particularly in the German-speaking parts of the country. Shin Koseki has argued that what accounts for these differences is primarily the degree to which local populations are connected to global networks (Koseki 2018, 25). Given Switzerland's relatively small size and its dependence on international trade, most Swiss are, in one way or another, exposed to the rest of the world and therefore relatively open to the world. In fact, Switzerland is largely considered the most globalized country in the world.[14] And yet, the urban/rural cleavage has not only persisted but grown stronger in recent decades, largely as a result of divergent values: "postmodern affinities" here, clinging to age-old traditions there.[15] The urban/rural gap has been particularly pronounced with regard to migration-related issues, pitting the (urban) proponents of international openness against its (more rural) opponents. The resulting polarization was to a large degree the result of a profoundly changing urban population structure, engendered by the influx of better-educated, more affluent, cosmopolitan people, attracted by a metropolitan life-style and ethnic diversity (Hermann 2014, 32–33).

Politically, the cleavage has been reflected in the dramatic upsurge of the SVP. Starting in the 1990s the party progressively increased its share of the vote from around 11 percent of the vote in 1997 to almost 30 percent of the vote in 2007. In the process the SVP pulled ahead of its main competitors and conquered the center stage of Swiss politics. In subsequent elections, the party lost some ground, but remained the largest of the major parties. Most importantly, the SVP managed to hold on to its support among lower-class constituencies. In fact, in 2016, leading Swiss newspapers characterized the SVP as "the new workers' party."[16]

Hardly surprising, the SVP has consistently and quite adamantly opposed Switzerland's seeking membership in the European Union as well as the official, hitherto relatively liberal, policy on immigration – on both economic and cultural grounds. On the one hand, the party mobilized welfare-chauvinist sentiments against "asylum tourism" and the abuse of the Swiss welfare state by "welfare-scrounging" migrants;[17] on the other hand it mobilized popular *ressentiments* against the country's growing Muslim community, stating that it would do whatever necessary to prevent official/legal recognition of Islam.[18]

In its campaigns, the party has quite deliberately appealed to the country's "rural tradition connected to Swiss national identity" to bolster its nativist/xenophobic agenda (Ströbele 2017, 261). A poster from 2019, for instance, depicted a typical Swiss chalet surrounded by trees, complete with a pole flying the Swiss flag and the caption – or rather the challenge – "Attached to your home?"[19] In other words, anyone who cared about preserving Swiss traditions and the Swiss way of life had only one choice – to vote for the SVP. In reality, of course, the SVP's conjuring up of a rural idyll has little to do with reality – a reality dominated by urban sprawl, strip malls and commercial outlets that have turned a growing part of the country into an ugly concrete nightmare. It is exemplary of a new politics of nostalgia, which seeks to turn back the clock. Ironically enough, nostalgia has a particular affinity to Switzerland. It was coined by the Swiss physician Johannes Hofer in 1688 combining two Greek words – *nostos* (homecoming) and *algos* (pain) to make sense of a psychological affliction particularly affecting Swiss soldiers during the Thirty Years War who were "reportedly so susceptible to nostalgia when they heard a particular Swiss milking song, Khue-Reyen, that its playing was punishable by death."[20]

During the past few years, the politics of nostalgia has become a hallmark of radical right-wing populist mobilization against immigration throughout advanced capitalist countries. In Australia, for instance, Pauline Hanson has owed her return to the country's political limelight (getting herself elected to the country's Senate in 2016 after two decades in the political wilderness) to a large degree to her ability to evoke a time when there were "jobs for everyone." This was a time when Australia was "a prosperous nation" which still had industries and manufacturing. Hanson succeeded because she managed to promote herself as the "voice of any number of wistful Australians whose distant youth is tucked away in happy, if inaccurate, memory, and who can't understand or who actually fear what has happened to the nation that gave spring to that golden period."[21]

Economic concerns, however, are only half of the equation. Her success was also owed to her ability to appeal to cultural anxieties. Largely adopting the rhetoric of the Western European radical right, she promoted herself as the lone voice warning of the threat posed by migrants from Muslim countries. Charging that Australia was being "swamped by Muslims who bear a culture and ideology that is incompatible with our own," she warned that Australians might eventually be forced to live under sharia law if there was no radical change in the country's immigration laws.[22]

THE EMOTIONAL UNDERPINNINGS OF NATIVIST SENTIMENTS

The current literature on both immigration and the radical populist right abounds with references to emotions, most prominently anger and anxiety, rage and indignation, resentment and nostalgia. To a large extent, emotions have served as ad hoc explanations for why individuals feel the way they do and/or vote the way they do. More often than not, emotions have been taken for granted, "as given" – without much regard to the mechanisms and links that lead one (emotions) to the other (nativist mobilization). This is hardly surprising. For too long, emotions were relegated to the realm of the irrational. It is only in recent decades that emotions have been accepted as worthy of serious analysis by social science.

For the purpose of this chapter, the focus is on emotions as triggering mechanisms of nativist mobilization. Four emotions appear to be pivotal: fear, anger, resentment and shame. Each of these emotions is central to contemporary nativist mobilization. Take, for instance, Ruth Wodak's masterful study of *The Politics of Fear*. In the introduction Wodak cites an observation by David Altheide, author of *Creating Fear*, which states that in contemporary society, "fear has emerged as a framework for developing identities and for engaging in social life" (Wodak 2015, 5). The same holds true for resentment. Katherine Cramer, in her analysis of the state of mind in rural Wisconsin and its impact on the 2016 presidential election, provides a vivid illustration of the role of resentment in contemporary politics. Looking back at her encounter with ordinary Wisconsinites she notes their "basic concern" that "people like them, in places like theirs, were overlooked and disrespected. They were doing what they perceived good Americans ought to do to have the good life. And the good life seemed to be passing them by."[23]

Then there is anger. Guy Standing, author of the influential *The Precariat: The New Dangerous Class* (2011), has characterized the present as the "age of anger" – in response to the dramatic increase in inequality and social injustice. As Standing puts it, for millions of workers in advanced capitalist countries, the old notion that work is the best route out of poverty has become "a sick joke."[24] George Marcus et al. have argued that it is anger, not fear or anxiety, which is most conducive to nativist mobilization. Anger, they note, "has long been apparent in the reactions to various progressive projects, such as continued population movement from rural areas to urban, increasing cosmopolitan patterns ... acceptance of previously disparaged groups (such as single women, women in the workplace, gay marriage, atheists, and more)." From this they conclude that anger "springs from the sense that core values and core habits of thought and action are under attack" (Marcus et al. 2019, 131). Robert Wuthnow has shown to what degree the eruption of anger and fury in rural America skewed the 2016 election in favor of Donald Trump. Much of that anger, he argues, stemmed from "Washington's seeming lack of empathy for such small-town norms as personal responsibility, frugality, cooperation, and common sense" (https://press.princeton.edu/books/hardcover/9780691177663/the-left-behind).

SHAME, HUMILIATION AND NATIVIST MOBILIZATION

Thomas Scheff has argued that shame, together with pride, constitutes the most powerful of social emotions, "the master emotion of everyday life" (Scheff 2003). Shame can be experienced both individually and collectively, resulting from, among other things, humiliation, embarrassment and particularly from feelings of failure, inferiority and rejection (Scheff 2000, 97). The arguably most important and well-established aspect of shame is the fact that shame tends to trigger anger and aggression (for an overview of the literature, see Elison et al. 2014). This suggests that shame plays a major role in paving the ground for mobilizing anger and resentment both against migrants and those in power seen as giving preference to migrants while ignoring the suffering of the "native-born" – victimized by large-scale structural changes beyond their control.

By now, the narrative is well known: at one time in the not so distant past, those who worked hard were able to advance, make a better living, for themselves and their children, resulting in a sense of pride, based on accomplishment. Today, this can no longer be taken for granted. Globalization and rapid technological change have resulted in stagnating wages, growing inequality and an overall sense of insecurity. The result is individual humiliation, a sense of having failed, and/or worse, of having become "structurally irrelevant." Even working hard no longer serves as a guarantee against being "left behind." At the same time, those who are seen as knowing how to manipulate the system – ranging from corporations to migrants and refugees – receive government "handouts."

The result is a combination of shame (over no longer being able to meet social expectations) and resentment (over the perception of no longer counting as an individual and/or voter), which turns into outrage and anger, directed against those above and those below. Arlene Stein, in her review of Arlie Russell Hochschild's *Strangers in Their Own Land: Anger and Mourning on the American Right*, recounts how in the mid-1990s a single mother expressed her resentment against "those who used food stamps to buy avocadoes. 'I can't afford avocadoes,' she said, 'but they're buying them like there's no tomorrow'" (Stein 2017, 508). Similar charges could be heard in the aftermath of the 2015/2016 "refugee crisis." For instance, in Germany, ordinary citizens complained that refugees would get "everything" and immediately, while needy German citizens "had to fight for every cent." In the eastern part of the country, resentment has been brewing for decades.

It largely stems from the "feeling" that east Germans are treated as if they were "second-class citizens." Resentment finally exploded in support for the radical right-wing populist AfD in the national and regional elections. In the aftermath of the refugee crisis, popular resentment reached a new high, culminating in the seemingly absurd demand that the federal government should "first integrate us" (i.e., eastern German native-born citizens) rather than worrying about how to integrate refugees.[25] Refugees were resented for having smart phones (which some east Germans claimed they could not afford) and if not, that "the state" was handing them out to them for free, a benefit east Germans did not enjoy.[26]

CONCLUDING THOUGHTS

International migration shapes up to be one of this century's most important sociopolitical issues. The combination of large and growing inequality with regard to standards of living and the acceleration of the impact of adverse conditions linked to global warming is likely to increase migration pressures. In the affluent capitalist societies of the global north, these pressures have provoked, and are likely to continue to provoke, a strong, visceral response, largely immune to "rational reasoning." Whether or not, and to what degree, popular opposition to policies that appear to favor immigration are motivated by economic or cultural concerns is largely settled. It is both. This, however, is hardly essential for developing reasonable migration policies that have a chance to find support among a majority of the electorate. Reality is that today, political competition with respect to major issues in advanced liberal democracies is largely driven by emotions. More often than not, these emotions are not primarily triggered by concerns about migration. Yet, for the reasons outlined in this chapter, they have a direct impact on sentiments towards migration. A reasonable immigration policy not only has to take these emotions seriously, but has to devise policies designed to assuage them.

NOTES

1. Óscar García Agustín and Martin Bak Jørgensen, Danes First, Welfare Last, *Jacobin*, January 31, 2019, available online at www.jacobinmag.com/2019/01/denmark-social-democrats-immigration-welfare.
2. Rik Arnoudt, Vlaams Belang recycleert "Eigen volk eerst" tot "Eerst onze mensen," *vrtNWS*, August 21, 2018, available online at www.vrt.be/vrtnws/nl/2018/08/21/vlaams-belang-recycleert-eigen-volk-eerst-tot-eerst-onze-mens/.
3. TV Interview for Granada *World in Action* ("rather swamped"), Margaret Thatcher Foundation, January 27, 1978, available online at www.margaretthatcher.org/document/103485.
4. David Edgar, In the decade since Oldham, the only thing to be swamped is the BNP, *The Guardian*, May 11, 2011, available online at www.theguardian.com/commentisfree/2011/may/11/decade-since-oldham-bnp-swamped.
5. www.harpweek.com/09Cartoon/BrowseByDateCartoon.asp?Month=April&Date=28.
6. A vivid account of Italian immigration can be found on the website of the Italian American Museum of Los Angeles, available online at https://artsandculture.google.com/exhibit/dago-italian-american-museum-of-los-angeles/3AJigyt4JBtlIw?hl=en.
7. Nicholas Kristof and Sheryl WuDunn, Who killed the Knapp family? Across America, working-class people – including many of our friends – are dying of despair. And we're still blaming the wrong people, *New York Times*, January 9, 2020, available online at www.nytimes.com/2020/01/09/opinion/sunday/deaths-despair-poverty.html.

8. Leon Wieseltier, How voters' personal suffering overtook reason – and brought us Donald Trump, *Washington Post*, June 22, 2016.
9. www.youtube.com/watch?v=XkRRdth8AHc.
10. www.politikforen.net/showthread.php?171747-Rassismus-in-der-Schweiz!
11. Interview Blocher with Robert Treichel, *Profil*, October 23, 2003, available online at www.blocher.ch/en/2003/10/27/ich-bin-so-wie-ich-bin/.
12. Dani Rodrik, What's driving right-wing populism? It's both economic insecurity and the culture wars, *MarketWatch*, July 16, 2019, available online at www.marketwatch.com/story/whats-driving-populism-its-both-economic-insecurity-and-the-culture-wars-2019-07-10/.
13. Sajeda Tuli, Migrants want to live in the big cities, just like the rest of us, *The Conversation*, April 1, 2019, available online at https://theconversation.com/migrants-want-to-live-in-the-big-cities-just-like-the-rest-of-us-113911.
14. Switzerland remains the most globalized country in the world, KOF Swiss Economic Institute, December 4, 2020, available online at https://kof.ethz.ch/en/news-and-events/news/kof-bulletin/kof-bulletin/2020/12/Switzerland-remains-the-most-globalised-country%20in-the-world.html.
15. Samuel Jaberg, Stadt-Land, der Graben, der die Schweiz entzweit, *swissinfo*, October 21, 2012, available online at www.swissinfo.ch/ger/politik/politischer-konflikt_stadt-land--der-graben--der-die-schweiz-entzweit/33717334.
16. Die SVP ist die neue Arbeiterpartei, *Tagesanzeiger*, February 8, 2016, available online at www.google.com/search?q=svp+arbeiterpartei&oq=svp+arbeiterpartei&aqs=chrome..69i57.4087j1j4&sourceid=chrome&ie=UTF-8.
17. Christoph Mörgeli, Was bedeutet Opposition? November 23, 2003, available online at www.svp.ch/news/artikel/referate/was-bedeutet-opposition/.
18. Delegierte verabschieden Forderungskatalog, 'Null Toleranz gegenüber radikalem Islam in der Schweiz,' October 28, 2017, available online at www.svp.ch/news/artikel/medienmitteilungen/delegierte-verabschieden-forderungskatalog-null-toleranz-gegenueber-radikalem-islam-in-der-schweiz-2/.
19. www.facebook.com/SVPch/photos/a.180156395461646/1811680688975867/?type=3&theater.
20. Julie Beck, When nostalgia was a disease, *The Atlantic*, August 14, 2013, available online at www.theatlantic.com/health/archive/2013/08/when-nostalgia-was-a-disease/278648/.
21. Tony Wright, Federal election 2016: Pauline Hanson mixes nostalgia with hate and dresses it as patriotism, *Sydney Morning Herald*, July 4, 2016, available online at www.smh.com.au/politics/federal/federal-election-2016-pauline-hanson-mixes-nostalgia-with-hate-and-dresses-it-as-patriotism-20160704-gpy9dx.html.
22. Jane Norman, Pauline Hanson calls for Muslim immigration ban in maiden speech to Senate, *ABC*, September 14, 2016, available online at www.abc.net.au/news/2016-09-14/one-nation-senator-pauline-hanson-makes-first-speech-to-senate/7845150.
23. Katherine J. Cramer, For years, I've been watching anti-elite fury build in Wisconsin. Then came Trump, *Vox*, November 16, 2016, available online at www.vox.com/the-big-idea/2016/11/16/13645116/rural-resentment-elites-trump.
24. Guy Standing, The 5 biggest lies of global capitalism, World Economic Forum, December 12, 2016, available online at www.weforum.org/agenda/2016/12/lies-of-global-capitalism-guy-standing/.
25. Die Sorgen der Männer im Osten – "Integriert doch erst mal uns," *Die Welt*, September 26, 2017, available online at www.welt.de/politik/deutschland/article169032071/Die-Sorgen-der-Maenner-im-Osten-Integriert-doch-erst-mal-uns.html.
26. Christoph Drösser, Bekommt jeder Flüchtling vom Staat ein Smartphone? *Die Zeit*, December 26, 2018, available online at www.zeit.de/2019/01/staatliche-leistungen-fluechtlinge-smartphones-stimmts.

REFERENCES

Antonsich, Marco. 2009. "National Identities in the Age of Globalisation: The Case of Western Europe." *National Identities* 11 (3): 281–299.
Banton, Olivia, Keon West and Ellie Kinney. 2020. "The Surprising Politics of Anti-Immigrant Prejudice: How Political Conservatism Moderates the Effect of Immigrant Race and Religion on Infrahumanization Judgements." *British Journal of Social Psychology* 59 (1): 157–170.
Beck, Ulrich. 2002. "The Cosmopolitan Society and Its Enemies." *Theory, Culture and Society* 19 (1–2): 11–44.
Blättler, Andreas C. 2017. "Inclusive Klassenpolitik als Antwort auf eine Arbeiterbewegung von rechts." *Berliner Journal für Soziologie* 27 (3/4): 579–593.

Boswell, Terry E. 1986. "A Split Labor Market Analysis of Discrimination against Chinese Immigrants, 1850–1882," *American Sociological Review* 51 (3): 352–371.

Botein, Barbara. 1979. "The Hennessy Case: An Episode in Anti-Italian Nativism." *Louisiana History* 20 (3): 261–279.

Card, David, Christian Dustmann and Ian Preston. 2009. "Immigration, Wages, and Compositional Amenities." NBER Working Paper 15521, available online at http://davidcard.berkeley.edu/papers/wimmig%20wages.pdf.

Castells, Manuel. 2009. *Communication Power*. New York: Oxford University Press.

Crimston, Daniel, Paul G. Bain, Matthew J. Hornsey and Brock Bastian. 2016. "Moral Expansiveness: Examining Variability in the Extension of the Moral World." *Journal of Personality and Social Psychology* 111 (4): 636–653.

De Beer, Paul, and Ferry Koster. 2009. *Sticking Together or Falling Apart? Solidarity in an Era of Individualization and Globalization*. Amsterdam: Amsterdam University Press.

de Wilde, Pieter, Ruud Koopmans, Wolfgang Merkel, Oliver Strijbis and Michael Zürn, eds. 2019. *The Struggle over Borders: Cosmopolitanism and Communitarianism*. Cambridge: Cambridge University Press.

Elison, Jeff, Carlo Garofalo and Patrizia Velotti. 2014. "Shame and Aggression: Theoretical Considerations." *Aggression and Violent Behavior* 19 (4): 447–453.

Ernst, Robert. 1948. "Economic Nativism in New York City during the 1840s." *New York History* 29 (April): 170–186.

Farrelly, Maura Jane. 2017. *Anti-Catholicism in America, 1620–1860*. New York: Cambridge University Press.

Fong, Eric, and William T. Markham. 1991. "Immigration, Ethnicity, and Conflict: The California Chinese, 1849–1882." *Sociological Inquiry* 61 (4): 471–490.

Ford, Robert, and Will Jennings. 2020. "The Changing Cleavage Politics of Western Europe." *Annual Review of Political Science* 23 (1): 295–314.

Hales, Jean Gould. 1979. "'Co-laborers in the Cause': Women in the Ante-bellum Nativist Movement." *Civil War History* 25 (2): 119–138.

Halikiopoulou, Daphne. 2019. "Right-Wing Populism as a Nationalist Vision of Legitimating Collective Choice: A Supply-Side Perspective." *The International Spectator* 54 (2): 35–49.

Häusermann, Silja, and Hanspeter Kriesi. 2012. "What Do Voters Want? Dimensions and Configurations in Individual-Level Preferences and Party Choice." In *The Politics of Advanced Capitalism*, eds. Pablo Beramendi, Silja Häusermann, Herbert Kitschelt and Hanspeter Kriesi. Cambridge: Cambridge University Press, 202–230.

Hermann, Michael. 2014. "Politgeografische Studie zur Masseneinwanderungsinitiative." Forschungsstelle sotomo am Geographischen Institut UZH, available online at https://sotomo.ch/site/wp-content/uploads/2017/08/Politgeografische_Studie_MEI.pdf.

Hochschild, Arlie Russell. 2016. *Strangers in Their Own Land: Anger and Mourning on the American Right*. New York: New Press.

Huston, James L. 1989. "Economic Change and Political Realignment in Antebellum Pennsylvania." *Pennsylvania Magazine of History and Biography* 113 (3): 347–395.

Inglehart, Ronald, and Pippa Norris. 2016. "Trump, Brexit, and the Rise of Populism: Economic Have-Nots and Cultural Backlash." HKS Working Paper No. RWP16-026, available online at https://papers.ssrn.com/sol3/papers.cfm?abstract_id=2818659.

International Organization for Migration. 2015. *World Migration Report 2015: Migrants and Cities: New Partnerships to Manage Mobility*. Geneva: International Organization for Migration.

Koseki, Shin Alexandre. 2018. "The Geographic Evolution of Political Cleavages in Switzerland: A Network Approach to Assessing Levels and Dynamics of Polarization between Local Populations." *PLoS ONE* 13 (11): e0208227.

Lane, A.T. 1987. *Solidarity or Survival? American Labor and European Immigrants, 1830–1924*. Westport, CT: Greenwood Press.

Marcus, George E., Nicholas A. Valentino, Pavlos Vasilopoulos and Martial Foucault. 2019. "Applying the Theory of Affective Intelligence to Support for Authoritarian Policies and Parties." *Advances in Political Psychology* 40 (Suppl. 1): 109–139.

Margalit, Yotam. 2012. "Lost in Globalization: International Economic Integration and the Sources of Popular Discontent." *International Studies Quarterly* 56 (3): 484–500.

Miller, David. 2005. "Reasonable Partiality towards Compatriots." *Ethical Theory and Moral Practice* 8 (1/2): 63–81.

Oesch, Daniel. 2008. "Explaining Workers' Support for Right-Wing Populist Parties in Western Europe: Evidence from Austria, Belgium, France, Norway, and Switzerland." *International Political Science Review* 29 (3): 349–373.

Pettigrew, Thomas F., Linda R. Tropp, Ulrich Wagner and Oliver Christ. 2011. "Recent Advances in Intergroup Contact Theory." *International Journal of Intercultural Relations* 35 (3): 271–280.

Rodrik, Dani. 2018. "Populism and the Economics of Globalization." *Journal of International Business Policy* 1 (1/2): 12–33.
Scheff, Thomas J. 2000. "Shame and the Social Bond: A Sociological Theory." *Sociological Theory* 18 (1): 84–99.
Scheff, Thomas, J. 2003. "Shame in Self and Society." *Symbolic Interaction* 26 (2): 239–262.
Standing, Guy. 2011. *The Precariat: The New Dangerous Class*. London: Bloomsbury.
Stein, Arlene. 2017. "Rage against the State." *Contemporary Sociology* 46 (5): 507–510.
Ströbele, Maarit Felicitas. 2017. *What Does Suburbia Vote for? Changed Settlement Patterns and Political Preferences in Three European Countries*. Baden-Baden: Nomos.
Tehranian, John. 2000. "Performing Whiteness: Naturalization Litigation and the Construction of Racial Identity in America." *Yale Law Journal* 109 (4): 817–848.
Tomlinson, John. 2003. "Globalization and Cultural Identity." In *The Global Transformations Reader: An Introduction to the Globalization Debate*, eds. Anthony G. McGrew and David Held. Cambridge: Polity Press, 269–277.
Tomlinson, John. 2012. "Cultural Globalization." In *The Blackwell Companion to Globalization*, ed. George Ritzer. Malden, MA: Blackwell, 352–366.
Tuli, Sajeda C., and Richard Hu. 2018. "Knowledge Economy and Migrant Knowledge Workers in the Global City: A Case Study of Melbourne, Australia." *Australian Planner* 55 (2): 126–144.
Vaes, Jeroen, Maria Paola Paladino, Luigi Castelli, Jacques-Philippe Leyens and Anna Giovanazzi. 2003. "On the Behavioral Consequences of Infrahumanization: The Implicit Role of Uniquely Human Emotions in Intergroup Relations." *Journal of Personality and Social Psychology* 85 (6): 1016–1034.
Warf, Barney. 2015. "Global Cities, Cosmopolitanism, and Geographies of Tolerance." *Urban Geography* 36 (6): 927–946.
Wilkinson, Will. 2019. "The Density Divide: Urbanization, Polarization, and Populist Backlash." Niskanen Center Research Paper, June, available online at www.niskanencenter.org/wp-content/uploads/2019/09/Wilkinson-Density-Divide-Final.pdf.
Wodak, Ruth. 2015. *The Politics of Fear: What Right-Wing Populist Discourses Mean*. London: Sage.
Wuthnow, Robert. 2018. *The Left Behind: Decline and Rage in Rural America*, Princeton, NJ: Princeton University Press.
Zürn, Michael, and Pieter de Wilde. 2016. "Debating Gloobalization: Cosmopolitanism and Communitarianism as Political Ideologies." *Journal of Political Ideologies* 211 (3): 260–301.

19. Does contact with strangers matter?
Eric M. Uslaner

I spoke to a stranger at Heathrow Airport in the first week of September 1981. Twenty months later we were married and are close to celebrating our 40th anniversary. I rarely speak to strangers, especially not at airports, and I had no intention of continuing the conversation. I simply mentioned that I had been to Heathrow Airport twice before and each time the flight was delayed – the subject of this talk. We began talking and found that we had mutual interests and were heading to the same place. We sat together on the plane. She arranged for me to get a discount at the Athens hotel where her brother-in-law was the assistant manager. We then met up in Rhodes and wrote letters to each other during my year in Jerusalem, ultimately meeting in Paris on my way home, and we talked on the phone. On my next visit we became engaged.

Thirteen years earlier I spoke to another stranger in the lounge for the graduate student dormitory at Indiana University. I asked him if I could read a section of his newspaper, which was the *New York Times*. He readily gave me a section and I asked him if he was from New York and he said yes, from a suburb. I was from nearby New Jersey and found out that we were both studying political science. Over the course of many years our paths crossed in different ways and he ultimately left academia and became an attorney in the Washington area and we reconnected. Fifty-two years later he is still my best friend and my wife and I live less than 30 minutes from him and his wife.

Malcolm Gladwell (2019, 236–237) argues that "talking to strangers" is essential: we have no choice but to talk to strangers, especially in our modern, borderless world. We aren't living in villages anymore. Yet most interactions with strangers are not as consequential as mine were. They are routine and do not have larger consequences. We speak to a stranger on the street, we give our seats to strangers on buses or planes, we give people directions. But we never see them again. So most interactions have no effect on either our personal lives or our views more generally. They do not shape our personal friendships nor even our views toward other groups. And especially they do not shape our trust in groups we do not know, either specifically or generally. And these meetings are constrained by whether the interactions are likely to occur (where we live) or how positive the meetings are.

Routine interventions are not related to attitudes toward your own group or to other groups. But more frequent interactions may lead to greater tolerance, but not to trust. Such meetings are more common when people live among people like themselves. But regardless, the outcome, following Christa et al. (2013), will depend upon whether the interactions are positive or negative.

HOW AND WHY CONTACT MATTERS

Gladwell's argument stems from contact theory. This argument, which Pettigrew and Tropp (2006, 751–752) trace back to the 1940s and especially to the summary by

Williams (1947), is the claim that exposure to people of different backgrounds leads to less prejudice. When you meet people who are different from yourself, you are more likely to hold positive attitudes toward them. We find this in the line from the chimney sweep in the movie *Mary Poppins*: "Good luck will rub off when I shakes [sic] hands with you." This presumes positive interactions. When the meetings are negative, "conflict theory" holds that interactions among people of different backgrounds produce hostility. Key (1949, 666) argued that Southern whites in the United States were most likely to support racist candidates for office in areas with large populations of African-Americans. Simply interacting with people will not shape people's attitudes toward others. Too much depends upon the nature of interactions and the context.

Superficial meetings can reinforce negative stereotypes; "[o]nly the type of contact that leads people to do things together is likely to result in changed attitudes" (Allport, 1958, 252, 267). Allport formulated conditions of "optimal contact": equal status between the groups, common goals, cooperation between the groups; and a supportive institutional and cultural environment (Allport, 1958, 263, 267; Pettigrew, 1998, 66).

Christa et al. (2013) summarize a large body of research demonstrating that contact alone (regardless of the context) will lead to a reduction in prejudice – but interactions must be "sustained, positive contact between members of the two previously antipathetic groups."

In a meta-analysis of 513 studies of contact theory, Pettigrew and Tropp (2006, 760) found that any contact was likely to reduce prejudice (cf. Dixon et al., 2005, 2007), but that optimal contact had considerably greater effects. See also Williams et al. (1964, 185–190), Ihlanfeldt and Scafaldi (2002, 633), Dixon (2006, 2194–2195). McClelland and Linnander (2006, 107–108) find that whites develop more favorable attitudes about minorities only if they know and feel close to a minority group member. Simply interacting with others of different backgrounds is not sufficient to lead to either positive or negative attitudes toward their groups.

To increase tolerance toward other groups, you need to interact with them on an equal basis. One needs to meet with people regularly and have them as friends to increase tolerance. Infrequent meetings have no effect on tolerance. But if you do have a large number of friends from different groups, you will be more tolerant of their group (see below).

Most of the time we do not interact with people of different groups on an equal basis. Allport (1958, 18) argued:

> Thus, most of the business of life can go on with less effort if we stick together with our own kind. Foreigners are a strain. So too are people of a higher or lower social economic class ... We don't play bridge with the janitor. Why? Perhaps he prefers poker ... It's not that we have class prejudice, but only that we find comfort and ease in our own class.

You are most likely to interact with people of different backgrounds on an equal basis if you live in a positive environment. Context is critical – and the most important context is the nature of your community. Residential segregation leads to isolation, "exaggerate[s] the degree of difference between groups," and makes the outgroup "seem larger and more menacing than it is" (Allport, 1958, 18–19, 256). Contacts in segregated communities are most likely to be "frozen into superordinate–subordinate relationships" – exactly the opposite of what is essential for the optimal conditions to be met (Allport, 1958, 251). You may regularly see people who clean your house or your office, but this does not fulfill Allport's condition of equal status.

Williams et al. (1964, 185) argue from surveys conducted in Elmira, New York between 1949 and 1956:

> It is not the sheer fact that interaction occurs, but rather the type of interaction most commonly experienced between the members of two groupings that are culturally identified as different, which will change stereotypes and reduce prejudice. If the interaction occurs only rarely in highly formalized and restricted roles, no important changes are to be expected. If contact is frequent but occurs only in restricted roles that necessarily elicit traits similar to those already incorporated into stereotypes (for example, as in the case of domestic servants or money lenders), interaction will reinforce stereotypes and will contribute to simplicity and definiteness of the stereotyped conceptions. If contact is frequent, occurs in widely differing situations, and involves many diverse roles, old stereotypes may tend to be modified in the direction of greater complexity and flexibility.

Yet, at least for whites "The more intimate the level of interaction, the lower the prejudice. Prejudice is almost nonexistent among the majority group with regard to those minority individuals with whom one interacts on a close social basis." This dynamic does not hold as strongly for blacks, because of different socioeconomic backgrounds. For blacks who do have close white friends and socialize with them, there are more positive views of other people (Williams et al., 1964, 185, 189–190; see also Pettigrew, 1997 for studies in France, the Netherlands, Great Britain, and West Germany).

Stetler (1961) in a survey, equally divided between African-Americans and whites, found that the most frequent contact for whites of minorities is at work (47 percent) compared to 20 percent for friends or neighbors and 18 percent in organizations. For blacks, 56 percent is at work, 42 percent for friends or neighbors, and 32 percent in school. But most people's friendship networks are with people just like themselves (McPherson et al., 2001). In Germany, using data from Markus Crepaz (see below), only 16 percent of respondents said that they had friends of a different race or mixed with people of other backgrounds frequently.

Integrated neighborhoods "remove barriers to effective communication" (Allport, 1958, 261) and may lead to more contact with people of different backgrounds, especially among young people (Phinney et al., 2006, 94; Quillian and Campbell, 2003, 560). Forbes (1997, 144, 150) goes further, arguing that "[t]he more frequent and the more intimate the contacts among individuals belonging to different tribes or nations, the more these groups come to resemble each other culturally or linguistically ... Different languages, religions, customs, laws, and moralities – in short, different cultures – impede economic integration, with all its benefits ... Isolation and subordination, not gore and destruction, seem to be the main themes in linguistic conflict." Stetler (1961, 41) found positive effects for tolerance scores for whites with any type of contact. The largest impact is for people who work together (59 percent positive, 39 percent negative), followed by people who have friends or neighbors of other groups (32/17), and then for parents of children who go to the same schools (23/12) (Williams et al., 1964).

There is considerable support for the Allport argument and, ironically, some of it came even before he refined contact theory. Deutsch and Collins (1951) conducted a survey of people living in public housing in New York City and Newark, two of which were integrated and two segregated. "Neighborly contacts" between whites and blacks were almost non-existent in segregated projects but did occur in integrated units.

WHERE ONE LIVES MATTERS

When one lives in integrated neighborhoods, there will be more opportunities to overcome prejudice. In the Deutsch–Collins analysis, both whites and African-Americans became less hostile to each other, regardless of their levels of education, ideology, or religion (Deutsch and Collins, 1951, 57, 86, 97). A similar design in cities in the Northeast in 1951 also found that white women living in integrated housing projects had far more contact with African-Americans. They were also more likely to back integrated housing than those people living in segregated housing, and said that their views of blacks had improved (Wilner et al., 1955, 86, 92, 99).

Anglos living in integrated neighborhoods have more favorable attitudes toward Latinos (Rocha and Espino, 2009). There is also evidence (see below) that more intimate contact with people of different backgrounds – approximating Allport's optimal conditions – leads to more favorable attitudes toward outgroups (McClelland and Linnander, 2006, 108; McKenzie, 1948), especially if that contact occurs in more diverse and integrated neighborhoods (Dixon, 2006, 2194–2195; Stein et al., 2000, 298–299; Valentova and Berzosa, 2010, 29; Wagner et al., 2006, 386). Where people have many friends of different groups, there will be fewer ethnic tensions.

Contact can be negative as well as positive. When people interact only with members of their own group, there will be a greater likelihood of tensions among groups. This is especially likely when people live in segregated neighborhoods.

Segregated neighborhoods isolate people and make them less likely to interact with people of different backgrounds. McPherson et al. (2001, 429–432) argue that the greatest reason why there is so little interaction among parents of different backgrounds is that "[w]e are more likely to have contact with those who are closer to us in geographic location than those who are distant. Tracking within schools assures that children of similar backgrounds, abilities, and achievement levels are grouped into the same classes, where homophilous ties can form." And their workplaces are also composed of people of the same background.

Blalock (1982, 111) adds: "It is difficult ... to imagine how groups can socialize their members to prefer insulation without, at the same time, instilling in them a basic fear and distrust of outsiders, including other minorities. This is all the more true if there has been a previous history of mutually hostile contact." Hamilton et al. (1984, 105) also argue that when whites move into integrated neighborhoods, they became more tolerant of minorities (from a survey in New Haven in 1972).

Interactions with strangers – casual meetings, giving directions, giving up a seat on a bus or an airplane – don't shape attitudes toward other groups. Frequent meetings do so – especially when we feel comfortable entertaining strangers at home. Most people do have casual meetings with others frequently although they are not at ease interacting with strangers. These routine meetings are sporadic – people who give directions are only slightly more likely to give up their seats or to carry something for someone.

Gladwell (2019, 55) argues "We have a default to truth: our operating assumption is that the people we are dealing with are honest." But for routine interactions we do not need to make moral judgments about other people. We can accept directions from people, even give up our seats to them without judging their characters. Even my two major events – talking to the young woman who became my wife and the young man who became my best friend – had no initial moral judgment. Nor did they change my view of the rest of the world. Not even bad events would change your world view. I ask people whether their view of human nature would change if someone came up to them and hit them in the face. And they say no. Not even traumatic events such as disasters lead people to change their view of other people. We blame governments, not our fellow citizens, for bad outcomes of disasters such as earthquakes or even snowstorms (Uslaner, 2016).

There is a hierarchy of outcomes that stems from contact. At the lowest end are simple interactions that do not lead to different evaluations of anyone. If we meet people of different backgrounds often, then one of three possibilities may occur. First, nothing may change in terms of your reactions to others. Second, you may become more tolerant of others as the cases of integrated housing show. Frequent positive interactions may lead to greater tolerance of others and a reduction in ethnic tensions (see below). Third, many negative meetings could produce intolerance and greater ethnic tensions. Meetings that include only one's own group (such as in clubs or houses of worship) might lead to less tolerance and reflect lower outgroup trust. This suggests that the notion of talking to strangers is itself ambiguous. We can meet complete strangers on the street but if we come into contact with them in clubs or religious institutions, we immediately have something in common with them. They may look different – be of another race (or for clubs another religion) – but we do have common interests. So when I have colleagues of a different race, religion, or even nationality, they are seemingly "different" from me but we have much in common and may even work together (although clearly when we first met we were strangers to each other). So it is not surprising that Putnam (2000) sees bowling leagues, choral societies, and birders as creating social ties – they have at least some key things in common before they even met.

Yet none of these interactions are likely to increase or decrease trust. Trust is formed early in life. Trust is more than simple tolerance (this discussion is expanded in Uslaner, 2002, chs 1, 3, 4, 5, 6). Tolerating people means that you can live with them. Trusting others means accepting others as part of your "moral community," as equal to yourself. Strangers may look different from us, they may have different ideologies or religions. But we believe that there is an underlying commonality of values. So it is not quite so risky to place faith in others. If we share a common fate, it is unlikely that these strangers will try to exploit our positive attitudes. The idea of trust is based upon the Golden Rule: treat others as you would have them treat you – not as they treat you. So it does not depend upon reciprocity and others do not need to tolerate you for you to accept them. Here is where Gladwell's argument holds: we must presume that others are trustworthy and act accordingly.

There is a form of trust that does depend upon experience: it is what I call "strategic" trust: do you trust me to repay a loan or to paint your house? But generalized trust does *not* depend upon experience and, even if you find contrary experience, you are likely to dismiss it as an aberration. Generalized trust is unconditional. Yet Gladwell's argument is about conversations in daily life. We only need to presume honesty for tolerance or especially for trust and that is a different and far more consequential decision.

We have pictures of trusters as people who are joiners (Lane, 1959; Putnam, 2000; Rosenberg, 1956). In a few instances this is true, but mostly it is not. Trust solves bigger problems than getting people to hang out with people like themselves. It connects us to people we don't hang out with. And that is why it helps us to solve larger problems, such as helping those who have less, both in the private and public spheres, and in getting government to work better.

If we believe that we are connected to people who are different from ourselves and have a moral responsibility for their fate, we see that trust is a fundamentally egalitarian ideal. When we take others' moral claims seriously, we are treating them as our equals. A belief in hierarchy is inimical to moralistic trust. A culture of trust depends upon the idea that things will get better for those who have less and that it is in our power to make the world better.

It does not depend upon contacts as adults. Group membership has no effect on faith in others. It does depend upon how many friends of a different race or group you have as a child – when you are more impressionable (Uslaner, 2002, 163). But since most children go to schools in segregated neighborhoods, they may not be able to develop ties across racial divides early on. Segregation is strongly related to both trust and inequality. People who don't trust others of different backgrounds will not want to live among them and this will reinforce mistrust.

Segregation rests upon inequality and reinforces it. And inequality is the strongest determinant of trust – over time and across countries (Uslaner, 2002, chs 4, 6; 2012b).

As the level of economic inequality has grown over time, Americans have become more pessimistic about their future, less connected to people of different backgrounds, and more convinced that political leaders only respond to the wealthy – and these effects are far more pronounced for those at the bottom of the economic ladder. Yet, increasing disparities in wealth do not make people less optimistic about their own economic fate.

In the United States, people are 25–30 percent more likely to disagree that the lot of the average person is getting worse and that it is not fair to bring a child into the world when the income shares of the bottom four quintiles are at their highest level. They are about as likely to agree with these claims as the income shares of the top quintile and top 5 percent are at their peak. These questions were only asked from 1973 to 1994. Even as the income shifts were somewhat small, the public reacted strongly. By 1994 almost 70 percent of Americans said that the lot of the average person was getting worse and almost half believed that it was unfair to bring a child into the world. And patterns of trust are very strongly related to trends in inequality – over time in the United States and across nations.

While trust has declined in the United States, there is no evidence that informal social connections have become either more or less frequent over time. People are just as willing to give up their seats, carry someone's bags, or give directions over the past decade. And tolerance seems to be increasing (even if polarized). More Americans said that they are close to blacks in 2016 than they were in 1996 and that Africans are intelligent compared to 1990 (from the General Social Survey (GSS)). And while there is a big partisan divide, Americans have generally become more supportive of increased immigration (National Immigration Forum, 2019). So trust, tolerance, and social interactions do not necessarily move together.

Since trust is more demanding than "mere" prejudice reduction, so will be the conditions of boosting this stable value that doesn't change much over one's lifetime. Here context matters, as I shall argue and support. You learn trust early in life – from your parents – and it is not shaped by adult experiences but rather remains stable (Uslaner, 2002, chs 3–5). So where people live is determined by their level of trust (Uslaner, 2012a), but people may have friends of different backgrounds even if they do not trust people in general: you may look at a person who is different and say that he or she is not typical of his/her group. But this will not lead to greater trust in their group or of people in general.

People are more likely to have friends outside their own group if they trust people generally. And they will also find these connections more enjoyable. But these connections depend upon trusting others – they do not lead to greater faith in others. Most people trust others of a different religion or nationality as well as their neighbors but not people they meet for the first time (from a German survey). Yet none of these measures of trust in specific people is strongly related to generalized trust (although there are moderate relationships between generalized trust and faith in different groups).

I will examine these issues with several data sets to be described below.

THE DATA SOURCES

The data sets I will use come from the GSS (n.d.) in the United States, Putnam's Social Capital Community Benchmark Survey (Putnam, n.d.), data gathered in the United Kingdom by James Laurence and Miles Hewstone, and German data provided by Markus Crepaz. The data from Markus Crepaz come from data collected in Germany at the end of January 2019 using the Qualtrics online survey platform with 1,764 responses. The data from Laurence and Hewstone come from an IPSOS MORI survey, "Managing Cultural Diversity" (2010) at the University of Oxford, with 1,666 interviews (provided by Laurence). This is a two-stage random location quota sample, conducted using face-to-face interviews, resulting in 868 white British respondents and a booster sample of 798 non-white British individuals. The contextual-level data are taken from the 2011 UK Census (apart from contextual-level crime data which are taken from the 2010 English Indices of Deprivation compiled by the Department for Communities and Local Government (DCLG, 2011)).

My examination is based upon simple descriptive statistics and correlations. I focus on how the contexts shape social contexts, tolerance, and trust. For social contacts, I examine routine interactions such as casual meetings including giving your seat to someone, giving directions, allowing a stranger to go ahead of you in a line, carrying someone's packages, and hosting a stranger in your home (from the GSS) in the United States. I also examine a variety of both positive and negative forms of socializing for both ingroups and outgroups from Putnam's Social Capital Community Benchmark Survey in the United States, the Laurence/Hewstone survey in the United Kingdom, and the Crepaz survey in Germany. And finally I examine the roots of both trust and tolerance in all three countries – arguing that routine interactions and socialization have only modest correlations with trust or tolerance. Where there are greater tensions (ethnic, religious, or class based) among groups, socializing tends to be greater among ingroups than with outgroups. In segregated areas, there is also less contact with outgroups (which is to be expected since people don't have the opportunity to interact with groups that don't live among them; see Uslaner, 2012a). Yet, contrary to Putnam (2007), a more diverse population will lead to greater interaction with outgroups. There is no evidence, however, that living in a rural area makes people either more or less likely to have routine interactions with people or that living in a large city isolates people (Riesman et al., 1950). For the GSS data, the only form of socializing that is related to the urban–rural distinction is giving up your seat to someone, which is more common in urban areas (not surprising since there is more mass transportation there). And none of these forms of interactions varies over time. Nor are other forms of socializing, such as spending time with relatives or even at a bar (from the GSS). And neither these activities nor Putnam's most famous social organization, choral societies, lead to greater trust in others (see Uslaner, 2002, ch. 2).

Most people interact with others of their same ethnicity and religion. In 2013 three-quarters of whites and two-thirds of African-Americans have social networks made up entirely of people of their own background. Eighty percent of evangelicals and two-thirds of white mainline Protestants and African-American Protestants also have friendship networks comprised of people like themselves. These are the most segregated groups in the American population. Hispanics, who are less segregated, have the most diverse networks (Cox et al., 2016; see Uslaner, 2012a, 75–76). Yet for all groups, the share of friends of different backgrounds is only weakly related to how much people trust others of those backgrounds (Uslaner, 2012a, 33).

In 1997 the (then named) Pew Center for the People and the Press conducted a large survey of trust in the Philadelphia area, asking people whom they trusted and about a large number of social interactions. At the individual level, there were only slight correlations between various forms of trust (overall generalized trust and even faith in outgroups and respecting or admiring them) and social contacts (see Table 19.1). Neither diversity nor tensions by class or ethnicity led to a negative view of outgroups. There were also only minimal relationships with whether one met with ingroup members frequently, how close they were to people in their groups, whether they volunteered in their churches or schools, or even discussed personal news with them. The only modest relationships I found were for generalized trust and the belief that fewer Muslims immigrate to the United States and that one would be bothered if a Muslim married into your family. Overall, there was little relationship between trust and interactions with people of different backgrounds. With the exception of trusting one's boss and co-workers, there was also little relationship among ingroup trust and generalized faith in others (see Table 19.1).

For the United Kingdom (see Table 19.2), most forms of routine interactions are not related to trust. They include "mixing" or meeting with people of the same or different groups, including socializing with other non-Muslims (with simple correlations for trust below +−.20). However, there are strong correlations for mixing with Muslims, meeting with outgroups, and especially enjoying meeting with outgroups ($r = .392, .394,$ and $.496$). Trusting people are also far more likely to have positive feelings (as measured by thermometer scores, $r = -.360$) and to trust outgroups ($r = -.377$). At the individual level, there is no correlation between any of these measures and segregation, largely because people sort themselves into where they live by their levels of trust (Uslaner, 2012a) – so there is no further impact of segregation on socializing or even attitudes at the individual level. However, people are more likely to meet with outgroups and especially to mix with them and to enjoy the meetings in more diverse communities ($r = .200, .292, .292,$

Does contact with strangers matter? 375

Table 19.1 *Pearson correlations (Pew Philadelphia Survey)*

Variable	Trust	Trust neighbor	Trust boss	Trust co-workers	Trust church	Trust club	Trust in shop	Trust meet downtown
Trust neighbor	.201							
Trust boss	−.497	.235						
Trust co-workers	−.529	.300	.360					
Trust church	.134	.294	.185	.306		.296	.267	
Trust club	.180	.358	.223	.290				
Trust where shop	.251	.354	.214	.292	.267	.296	.285	
Trust meet downtown	.329	−.344	−.245	−.277	−.204	−.253	−.402	
Mingle adult education	−.094	.168	−.091	−.108	−.104	−.079	−.074	−.072
Mingle workout	.016	−.049	.040	.008	−.014	−.079	−.074	−.0134
Mingle church	−.001	−.056	−.012	−.008	−.050	−.065	−.048	−.035
Mingle sports	−.023	−.035	−.034	.080	.061	−.139	−.047	−.021
Close to workout group	.033	−.051	.031	.127	−.006	.037	−.001	−.001
Close to sports participants	.014	−.103	−.031	.066	.138	.026	.057	.079
Close to people playing cards	.029	−.045	−.033	.062	−.001	.006	−.044	−.029
Volunteer church	066	−.108	.044	.004	.097	.064	.066	.030
Volunteer school	.067	−.015	.016	.006	.007	.025	.001	.045
Volunteer children program	−.020	.010	.002	.051	.002	.036	−.024	.003
Share news friends	−.001	−.017	−.050	.026	.009	−.002	−.035	−.040
Share news co-workers	.016	.008	.044	−.019	−.017	.032	−.006	.227

and .377). They are especially more likely to mix with Muslims but not to mix with close-knit groups (r = .400 and −.394) in heterogeneous communities – simply because there are more opportunities to interact with people of different backgrounds. They are also more likely to enjoy such meetings (r = .263). Finally, religious and ethnic tensions are associated with less trust in both the United Kingdom and the United States (see also Table 19.2), but they do not effect social interactions with people of different backgrounds since people may have friends of different backgrounds and see them as exceptions to tensions among groups in both countries.

There is a similar pattern in the German data from Crepaz. Trust is not related to most forms of social interaction (see Table 19.3). You may have friends or contacts of a different race or background but this is not related to trust. While there is a slight correlation (r = .239) between trusting different nationalities and how often you mix with them, there is a stronger relationship among measures of contact with different outgroups (r = .618). Friendship and even contacts with outgroups are unrelated to either generalized trust or evaluations of outgroups or even to support for the anti-immigration AfD party. The AfD supporters are distinguished by their identification with German identity and opposition to multiculturalism and more immigration, but not with patterns of interaction

376 *Handbook on migration and welfare*

Table 19.2 Pearson correlations: Social Capital Community Benchmark Survey

Variable	Trust	Trust neighbor	Trust boss	Trust co-workers	Trust church	Trust club	Trust in shop	Trust meet downtown
Trust neighbor	.201							
Trust boss	−.497	.235						
Trust co-workers	−.529	.300	.360					
Trust church	.134	.294	.185	.306		.296	.267	
Trust club	.180	.358	.223	.290				
Trust where shop	.251	.354	.214	.292	.267	.296	.285	
Trust meet downtown	.329	−.344	−.245	−.277	−.204	−.253	−.402	
Mingle adult education	−.094	.168	−.091	−.108	−.104	−.079	−.074	−.072
Mingle workout	.016	−.049	.040	.008	−.014	−.079	−.074	−.0134
Mingle church	−.001	−.056	−.012	−.008	−.050	−.065	−.048	−.035
Mingle sports	−.023	−.035	−.034	.080	.061	−.139	−.047	−.021
Close to workout group	.033	−.051	.031	.127	−.006	.037	−.001	−.001
Close to sports participants	.014	−.103	−.031	.066	.138	.026	.057	.079
Close to people playing cards	.029	−.045	−.033	.062	−.001	.006	−.044	−.029
Volunteer church	.066	−.108	.044	.004	.097	.064	.066	.030
Volunteer school	.067	−.015	.016	.006	.007	.025	.001	.045
Volunteer children program	−.020	.010	.002	.051	.002	.036	−.024	.003
Share news friends	−.001	−.017	−.050	.026	.009	−.002	−.035	−.040
Share news co-workers	.016	.008	.044	−.019	−.017	.032	−.006	.227

Variable	Trust	Segregation	Diversity	Religious tensions	Ethnic tensions	Class tensions
Trust		.042	−.051	.187	.197	.081
Segregation				−.060	−.026	.022
Diversity				−.078	−.019	−.005
Trust outgroups	−.377	−.017	.113	−.140	−.124	−.047
Outgroups fair	.204	.052	−.055	.158	.160	.088
Outgroups courteous	.151	−.024	−.095	−.031	−.026	.013
Thermometer outgroups	.146	−.039	.081	.085	.080	.007
Admire outgroups	.190	−.044	.037	.103	.068	−.024
Respect outgroups	.105	−.068	.142	.087	.086	.036

Negative feelings outgroups

Outgroups make anxious	−.090	−.003	−.031	−.142	−.154	−.114
Outgroups make nervous						

Table 19.2 (continued)

Variable	Trust	Segregation	Diversity	Religious tensions	Ethnic tensions	Class tensions
Outgroups to be courteous	.151	−.024	.110	.142	.101	.020
Outgroups different values	−.115	−.008	−.078	−.130	−.140	−.098
Bothered by outgroup problems	−.158	.061	−.007	−.090	−.095	−.047
Outgroups should maintain traditions	.045	−.057	.066	.012	−.021	−.005
No pity outgroup problems	.123	.008	.026	.090	.053	−.019
Ingroups maintain traditions	.044	−.057	.066	.047	.056	−.009
Bother Muslim neighbor	−.154	.041	−.125	−.121	−.137	−.036
Bother more Muslims United Kingdom	−.183	.046	−.173	−.165	−.154	−.081
Bother marry Muslim	−.158	.061	−.007	−.090	−.095	−.047

Table 19.3a Pearson correlations: Social Capital Community Benchmark Survey

	Trust	Segregation	Diversity	Religious tensions	Ethnic tensions	Class tensions
Socializing outgroups						
Family % outgroups	.049	−.132	.164	−.067	−.027	−.033
Mix socially outgroups	.070	.018	.070	−.047	−.035	−.009
OK to mix socially	−.125	.064	−.136	.073	−.084	.015
Outgroup neighbors	.007	−.209	.263	−.135	−.130	−.165
Outgroup friends	.082	−.128	.145	−.027	−.028	−.087
Mix with Muslims	.084	−.147	.368	.007	.020	−.024
Outgroup friends	.019	−.141	.222	−.051	−.055	−.097
Meet outgroup friends	.051	−.112	.197	−.054	−.050	−.121
Work with outgroups	.020	−.146	.278	−.031	−.011	−.043
Enjoy outgroup friends	−.157	−.002	−.108	−.038	−.063	−.048
Socializing ingroups						
Help neighbors	−.161	−.035	.036	−.145	−.200	−.124
Join youth group	.026	.023	−.017	−.069	−.088	−.070
Mix non-Muslims	−.039	−.038	.046	−.033	.009	−.136
Close-knit neighbors	−.107	−.070	.017	−.092	−.129	−.101
Routine interactions						
Brief encounters outgroups	.037	−.155	.171	−.085	−.078	−.090

Table 19.3b   Pearson correlations: Crepaz (2019) data

Variable	Trust	Trust another religion	Trust different nationality	Sees self part German nation	Trust people meet first time	How often mix outgroup
Trust another religion	.263	.335	.002	−.209	−.133	.108
Trust different nationality	.335	.615		−.010	−.268	.350
Part German nation	.002	−.082	−.010		−.001	−.022
Trust meet first time	.031	.303	.350	−.001		−.070
Often mix with outgroup	−.133	−.131	−.185	−.022	.070	
Trust property other race	.108	.180	.239	.071	.045	−.365
Workers different race	.056	.082	.119	.021	−.187	.305
Number friends different race	.011	.152	.026	.081		.305
Contact different race	.108	.180	.239	.071	.046	.618

with either ingroups or outgroups. Yet, German respondents who have strong ingroup networks do not have extensive contacts with outgroups. So these attitudes tend to reflect social networks but not necessarily their outlook on society more generally.

REPRISE

Talking to strangers is a broad term encompassing a wide range of interactions. Most are routine, such as giving directions, surrendering your seat, or talking to people where you shop. These events have no consequences. They are brief and neither positive or negative. Some interactions are with people we know or with whom we have something in common. These include meeting people at our houses of worship, at our clubs, and sometimes in our neighborhoods – so it is likely that we will have positive interactions and even that we will trust them from surveys in the United States (from both surveys and in Germany). Most people do not trust people they meet for the first time since they may be total strangers and of different backgrounds. Everyone we meet for the first time is a stranger, but few become our close friends or our spouses (such as happened to me).

When these interactions are positive, we may become tolerant of the groups they represent. But we will not meet people of different groups often if we live in segregated areas. In such places we are likely to burrow into our subgroups – as Putnam (2007) claimed we do in diverse areas. And we will avoid people from outgroups. But in integrated areas, we are more likely to have positive interactions with people of different backgrounds. In such places there will be fewer ethnic or religious tensions so we will be more likely to meet strangers and enjoy those interactions.

What matters is not just whom we meet but also what we choose to talk about. We avoid conversations about controversial political topics except with people we already know – and our social networks are comprised of people who largely agree with us (Cox et al., 2016).

We choose our social networks by how similar people are to us. And increasingly we have become more tribal – socially and especially politically. Iyengar and Westwood

(2015, 690–691) argue: "Americans increasingly dislike people and groups on the other side of the political divide and face no social repercussions for the open expression of these attitudes." Given a hypothetical election, people will select candidates of their same background (race, religion) rather than of different traits.

We are willing to have discussions on topics that are not political with outsiders, but our tastes in all manner of things vary by our background. Even our tastes in beer, music, pastimes, movies, and television programs vary with our partisanship: Democrats prefer microbreweries, foreign cars, and ethnic restaurants, while Republicans prefer full lager beers, domestic cars, and fast food restaurants (Hetherington and Weiler, 2018, 113–115), And this especially shapes our discussion networks and choice of both dating partners and ultimately whom we choose to marry.

There is an irony in these findings at least for the United States. The country is becoming more diverse and segregation (even by race) is declining (Economist, 2018; Frey, 2015). Yet we are becoming more polarized – and segregated – in our political life, our political discussions, and in our social networks (Bishop and Cushing, 2008). So even as our society is becoming more diverse and less segregated, we are less likely to interact with strangers with different backgrounds. And this is not likely to be reversed since school segregation is increasing (Economist, 2018). So our contacts with people of different backgrounds may actually be less consequential.

We seek out partners with the same political views as our own and avoid romantic relationships with people who don't agree with us. Our partners do not convert to our views over time, but rather we seek out partners who already agree with us (Iyengar et al., 2018; Jennings et al., 2009; Rogers, 2019).

The biggest problem is that polarization has been increasing over time and trust has been falling. So we are less likely to seek out discussion partners or mates who disagree with us because such situations make us uncomfortable. In this sense, Putnam is correct: we are more likely to burrow into our communities and not to interact with people who are different from ourselves. Yet he is wrong in a more fundamental way: when we isolate ourselves we are less likely to live in diverse communities.

REFERENCES

Allport, Gordon W. 1958 (1954). *The Nature of Prejudice*. Garden City, NY: Doubleday Anchor.
Bishop, Bill and Robert G. Cushing. 2008. *The Big Sort: Why the Clustering of Like-Minded America Is Tearing Us Apart*. New York: Houghton Mifflin.
Blalock, Hubert M., Jr. 1982. *Race and Ethnic Relations*. Englewood Cliffs, NJ: Prentice Hall.
Christa, Oliver, Katharina Schmid, Simon Lolliot, Hermann Swart, Dietlind Stolle, Nicole Tausch, Ananthi Al Ramiah, Ulrich Wagner, Steven Vertovec, and Miles Hewstone. 2013. "Contextual Effect of Positive Intergroup Contact on Outgroup Prejudice," *PNAS*, accessed August 14, 2014 at www.pnas.org/cgi/doi/10.1073/pnas.1320901111.
Cox, Daniel, Juhem Navarro-Rivera, and Robert P. Jones. 2016. "Race, Religion, and Political Affiliation of Americans' Core Social Networks," accessed September 1, 2021 at www.prri.org/research/poll-race-religion-politics-americans-social-networks/.
DCLG. 2011. *The English Indices of Deprivation 2010*. London: Department for Communities and Local Government.
Deutsch, Morton and Mary Evans Collins. 1951. *Interracial Housing: A Psychological Evaluation of a Social Experiment*. Minneapolis, MN: University of Minnesota Press.
Dixon, Jeffrey C. 2006. "The Ties That Bind and Those That Don't: Toward Reconciling Group Threat and Contact Theories of Prejudice," *Social Forces*, 84: 2179–2204.

Dixon, John, Kevin Durrheim, and Colin Troedoux. 2005. "Beyond the Optimal Contact Strategy: A Reality Check for the Contact Hypothesis," *American Psychologist*, 60: 697–711.

Dixon, John, Kevin Durrheim, and Colin Troedoux. 2007. "Intergroup Contact and Attitudes toward the Principle and Practice of Racial Equality," *Psychoiogical Science*, 18: 867–882.

Economist. 2018. "Segregation in America," accessed February 24, 2020 at www.economist.com/graphic-detail/2018/04/04/segregation-in-america.

Forbes, Hugh Donald. 1997. *Ethnic Conflict: Commerce, Culture, and the Contact Hypothesis*. New Haven, CT: Yale University Press.

Frey, William H. 2015. "Census Shows Modest Declines in Black-White Segregation," accessed February 24, 2020 at www.brookings.edu/blog/the-enue/2015/12/08/census-shows-modest-declines-in-black-white-segregation/.

General Social Survey. n.d., accessed February 20, 2020 at https://gss.norc.org/.

Gladwell, Malcolm. 2019. *Talking to Strangers*. New York: Little Brown.

Hamilton, David L., Sandra Carpenter, and George D. Bishop. 1984. "Desegregation in Suburban Neighborhoods." In Norman Miller and Marilyn B. Brewer, eds, *Groups in Contact: The Psychology of Desegregation*. Orlando, FL: Academic Press, 97–105.

Hetherington, Marc and Jonathan Weiler. 2018. *Prius or Pickup?* Boston, MA: Houghton Mifflin.

Ihlanfeldt, Keith R. and Benjamin P. Scafaldi. 2002. "The Neighbourhood Contact Hypothesis: Evidence from the Multicity Study of Urban Inequality," *Urban Studies*, 39: 619–641.

Iyengar, Shanto and Sean Westwood. 2015. "Fear and Loathing across Party Lines: New Evidence on Group Polarization," *American Journal of Political Science*, 59: 690–707.

Iyengar, Shanto, Tobias Konitzer, and Kent Tedin. 2018. "The Home as a Political Fortress; Family Agreement in an Era of Polarization," *Journal of Politics*, 80: 1326–1338.

Jennings, M. Kent, Laura Stoker, and Jake Bowers. 2009. "Politics across Generations: Family Transmission Reexamined," *Journal of Politics*, 71: 782–799.

Key, V.O., Jr. 1949. *Southern Politics in State and Nation*. New York: Vintage Books.

Lane, Robert E. 1959. *Political Life*. Glencoe, IL: The Free Press.

McClelland, Katherine and Erika Linnander. 2006. "The Role of Contact and Information in Racial Attitude Change among White College Students," *Sociological Inquiry*, 76: 81–115.

McKenzie, Barbara. 1948. "The Importance of Contact in Determining Attitudes toward Negroes," *Journal of Abnormal Social Psychology*, 43: 417–441.

McPherson, Miller, Lynn Smith-Lovin, and James M. Cook. 2001. "Birds of a Feather: Homophily in Social Networks," *Annual Review of Sociology*, 27: 416–444.

National Immigration Forum. 2019. "Polling Update: American Attitudes on Immigration Steady, but Showing More Partisan Divides," *National Immigration Forum*, April 17.

Pettigrew, Thomas. 1997. "Generalized Intergroup Contact Effects on Prejudice," *Personality and Social Psychology*, 23: 173–185.

Pettigrew, Thomas. 1998. "InterGroup Contact Theory," *Annual Review of Psychology*, 49: 65–85.

Pettigrew, Thomas F. and Linda R. Tropp. 2006. "A Meta-Analytic Test of Intergroup Contact Theory," *Journal of Personality and Social Psychology*, 90: 751–783.

Phinney, Jean S., John W. Berry, Paul Vedder, and Karmela Liebkind. 2006. "The Acculturation Experience: Behaviors of Immigrant Youth." In John W. Berry, Jean S. Phinney, David L. Sam, and Paul Vedder, eds, *Immigrant Youth in Cultural Transition*, 17–43. Mahwah, NJ: Lawrence Erlbaum Associates.

Putnam, Robert, D. 2000. *Bowling Alone*. New York: Simon and Schuster.

Putnam, Robert, D. 2007. "'*E Pluribus Unum*': Diversity and Community in the Twenty-First Century," *Scandinavian Political Studies*, 30: 137–174.

Putnam, Robert, D. n.d. "Social Capital Community Benchmark Survey," accessed January 20 2010 at www.ksg.harvard.edu/saguaro/communitysurvey/index.html.

Quillian, Lincoln and Mary E. Campbell. 2003. "Beyond Black and White: The Present and Future of Multiracial Friendship Segregation," *American Sociological Review*, 68: 540–566.

Riesman, David, Nathan Glazer, and Reuel Denney. 1950. *The Lonely Crowd*. New Haven, CT: Yale University Press.

Rocha, Rene R. and Rodlpho Espino. 2009. "Racial Threat, Residential Segregation, and the Policy Attitudes of Anglos," accessed September 1, 2021 at https://asu.pure.elsevier.com/en/publications/racial-threat-residential-segregation-and-the-policy-attitudes-of.

Rogers, Katie. 2019. "Young, Conservative and Working for Trump? The Dating Pool Is Small," *New York Times*, accessed February 16, 2020 at www.nytimes.com/2020/02/17/us/politics/dating-trump.html.

Rosenberg, Morris. 1956. "Misanthropy and Political Ideology," *American Sociological Review*, 21: 680–696.

Stein, Robert M., Stephanie Shirley Post, and Allison L. Rinden. 2000. "Reconciling Context and Contact Effects on Racial Attitudes," *Political Research Quarterly*, https://journals.sagepub.com/doi/10.1177/106591290005300204.

Stetler, Henry G. 1961. *Attitudes toward Racial Integration in Connecticut*. Hartford, CT: Connecticut Commission on Civil Rights.

Uslaner, E.M. 2002. *The Moral Foundations of Trust*. New York: Cambridge University Press.

Uslaner, E.M. 2012a. *Segregation and Mistrust: Diversity, Isolation, and Social Cohesion*. New York: Cambridge University Press.

Uslaner, E.M. 2012b. "Income Inequality in the United States Fuels Pessimism and Threatens Social Cohesion," Working Paper for the Center for American Progress, December 5, accessed December 5, 2012 at www.americanprogress.org/issues/economy/report/2012/12/05/46871/income-inequality-in-the-united-states-fuels-pessimism-and-threatens-social-cohesion.

Uslaner, E.M. 2016. "Disasters, Trust, and Social Cohesion," *Ritsumeikan Studies in Language and Culture*, 28: 183–191.

Valentova, Narue and Guyamarmina Berzosa. 2010. "Attitudes toward Immigrants in Luxembourg: Do Contacts Matter," accessed September 1, 2021 at https://liser.elsevierpure.com/en/publications/attitudes-toward-immigrants-in-luxembourg-do-contacts-matter-2.

Wagner, Ulrich, Oliver Christ, Thomas F. Pettigrew, Jost Stellacher, and Carina Wolf. 2006. "Prejudice and Minority Proportion: Contact Instead of Threat Effects," *Social Psychology Quarterly*, 69: 380–390.

Williams, Robin M., Jr. 1947. *The Reduction of Intergroup Tensions*. New York: Social Science Research Council.

Williams, Robin M., Jr. in collaboration with John P. Dean and Edward A. Suchman. 1964. *Strangers Next Door: Ethnic Relations in American Communities*. Englewood Cliffs, NJ: Prentice Hall.

Wilner, Daniel M., Rosabelle Price Walkley, and Stuart W. Cook. 1955. *Human Relations in Interracial Housing: A Study of the Contact Hypothesis*. New York: Russell and Russell.

20. A world to win at work? An integrated approach to meaningful interethnic contact

Katerina Manevska, Roderick Sluiter, and Agnes Akkerman

INTRODUCTION

Interethnic contact is often put forward as one of the most important tools in striving for harmonious interethnic relations (Al Ramiah and Hewstone 2013; Pettigrew and Tropp 2011). This is because interethnic contact reduces prejudices towards outgroup members, and since more ethnic diversity means more opportunities for interethnic contact (Blau 1977; Huijts et al. 2014; Wagner et al. 2006), ethnic diversity should be related to less ethnic prejudice. However, despite increased globalization and ethnic diversity, interethnic relations in Western societies do not seem to have improved, especially not considering the ongoing support for nationalist and anti-immigrant political parties in these societies. This calls into question why increased ethnic diversity has not brought forth the harmonizing effects as expected by contact theory.

A general assumption within contact theory is that whether interethnic contact is capable of reducing ethnic prejudice depends on the type of interethnic contact. Only meaningful interethnic contact, i.e., intimate contact such as interethnic friendship, is thought to contribute to prejudice reduction, while contact situations that are not meaningful, most notably superficial contacts, are thought to reaffirm pre-existing prejudice (e.g., Hewstone 2015). As such, whether ethnically diverse societies will have more harmonious interethnic relations depends upon the type of interethnic contact that prevails in these societies. The most common type of interethnic contact in ethnically diverse societies is arguably superficial in nature (Thomsen and Rafiqi 2018). Thus, the finding that ethnic diversity is not related to more ethnic tolerance implies that ethnic diversity does not lead to the meaningful kind of interethnic contact that derogates prejudices towards members of other ethnic groups.

In this line of reasoning, meaningful contact is defined as contact that, as a consequence of the objective characteristics of the contact situation, reduces ethnic prejudice. Traditionally, four conditions have been put forth as important in this respect: equal status, cooperation, shared goals, and institutional support (Allport 1979 [1954]). Numerous studies have addressed and further refined these conditions (see Dixon et al. 2005 for an overview), but in more recent years these are seen as mostly facilitating conditions, whereas the condition of giving room for meaningful exchange, in which empathy for the outgroup can be formed, was put forth as an essential condition for prejudice-reducing contact (cf. Pettigrew 1998). This essential condition for meaningful contact is mostly found in intimate contact, such as interethnic friendship. The ultimate consequence of this argument is that some authors discard other types of interethnic contact in favor of focusing solely on interethnic friendship in their study (e.g., McLaren 2003), others argue that only studies focused on meaningful contact, defined as being beneficial for reducing prejudice, can be considered as truly testing contact theory (cf. Hewstone 2015, 431).

This special focus on meaningful contact within contact theory research may be understood from the tradition's commitment to work on improving interethnic relations (cf. Connolly 2000; Dixon et al. 2005; Torre 2010). Given the somewhat tautological nature of the definition of meaningful contact as contact that reduces ethnic prejudice, we doubt that this rather narrow focus on meaningful contact will really bring forth the theoretical development that the research field, as well as the current state of interethnic relations in ethnically diverse societies, need. In this chapter, we argue for a different approach to studying meaningful contact, which integrates both the perspective of objective situational characteristics of contact and the subjective, personal interpretations of contact.

The core argument for adding the subjective, personal dimension for studying meaningful contact is that, like in any social situation, people's pre-existing values are important for how they interpret interethnic contact (Asbrock et al. 2013; Manevska et al. 2018; Pettigrew 1998, 77; West et al. 2017; West and Greenland 2016). As such, an integrated approach to meaningful contact considers both characteristics of the contact situation that contribute to meaningful exchange, and the interpretation of contact according to the pre-existing prejudice of the people who experience interethnic contact. Furthermore, given that these pre-existing values are also related to the extent to which people are likely to engage in interethnic contact (Hodson et al. 2009, see also Altemeyer 1998; Hodson 2008; Pettigrew 1998), it is important to focus on types of contact that are difficult to avoid, such that the population under study will differ in terms of their pre-existing prejudice.

The workplace is one of the prime contexts to empirically study such an integrated approach to meaningful contact. This is because the workplace makes interethnic contact difficult to avoid and heavily relies upon structures of interdependency and cooperation, and often stimulates the creation of shared identities in order to work towards a common goal. As such, workplace interethnic contact likely contains many of the optimal contact conditions as discussed by Allport (1979 [1954]). Furthermore, the fact that interethnic contact is difficult to avoid at work makes it more likely that we will be able to study how it affects ethnic tolerance among people with different levels of pre-existing prejudice.

The research question that we address here is twofold: first, we study to what extent workplace interethnic contact affects ethnic tolerance. Second, we study to what extent people who differ in terms of their pre-existing prejudice also differ in the way in which workplace interethnic contact affects their levels of ethnic tolerance. Empirically, we study these questions using three-wave panel data from the Netherlands (N = 3,191), which is representative for the Dutch labor force aged between 15 and 67. These data include unique information on interethnic contacts at the workplace as well as outside work, which also enables us to zoom in on individuals who do not have interethnic ties outside work. Combining the answers to both of our research questions will give us a better idea of the way in which workplace interethnic contact affects ethnic tolerance, not only as a situational characteristic, but also as conditional on people's subjective interpretation.

AN INTEGRATED APPROACH TO STUDYING MEANINGFUL CONTACT

The Problematic Focus on Intimate Contact

A general assumption in contact theory is that only contact that is prolonged in nature, offers the possibility of empathizing with outgroup members and their concerns, and in which enduring relationships can be built, should be considered meaningful contact. Meaningful is here used in the sense of "offering the opportunity for prejudice reduction" and a clear distinction is made between meaningful contact on one hand and other forms of contact on the other. A central premise in this line of thought is that characteristics of the contact situation, so objective or situational conditions, determine to what extent contact is meaningful. Such an interest in the characteristics of the contact situation has been present from the very beginning of this research tradition, where Allport already coined the "optimal conditions" for interethnic contact (Allport 1979 [1954]).

Numerous studies to date have identified a great variety of relevant contact conditions, such as equal status contact (e.g., Robinson and Preston 1976), the possibility of cooperation (e.g., Kuchenbrandt et al. 2013), and contact in which group membership is salient (e.g., Voci and Hewstone 2003). In addition, in recent years, more and more emphasis has been put on distinguishing "positive," i.e., pleasant, contact from "negative" contact (Barlow et al. 2012; Graf and Paolini 2017; Laurence and Bentley 2018). Despite all these different conditions that are considered important for the potential that interethnic contact has to reduce ethnic prejudice, "intimacy," in the sense that the contact facilitates the formation of empathy and concern for the other, is still considered the most important condition (Pettigrew and Tropp 2008, 923).

From this perspective, it is not surprising that intimate contacts, most notably interethnic friendship, have been propagated as the most important form of meaningful interethnic contact. Numerous studies have indeed reported a rather strong and negative correlation between interethnic friendship and interethnic prejudice (Aberson et al. 2004; Levin et al. 2003; McLaren 2003; see Pettigrew and Tropp 2011 for an overview). This consistent finding is therefore often presented as the most important and convincing evidence that interethnic contact is capable of reducing ethnic prejudice. As such, interethnic friendship is effectively seen as the "holy grail" of meaningful interethnic contact.

However, in recent years, this focus on interethnic friendship has also been problematized: rather than reducing ethnic prejudice, interethnic friendship is likely a product of relatively low ethnic prejudice, in the sense that people who are already low on prejudice are likely to select interethnic friendship, while highly prejudiced people are more likely to avoid interethnic friendship (Eisnecker 2019; Manevska et al. 2018). The problem of self-selection is of course well known in social sciences, and often addressed in the context of contact theory (Aberson et al. 2004; Dixon 2006; McLaren 2003; Sigelman and Welch 1993), especially concerning intimate contacts (De Souza Briggs 2007; Eisnecker 2019). Furthermore, some empirical evidence exists that people who are relatively more prejudiced indeed avoid interethnic contact when possible (cf. Manevska et al. 2018). However, despite this theoretical and empirical evidence that interethnic friendship *requires* low ethnic prejudice rather than reducing it, interethnic friendship is still seen as the example *par excellence* of meaningful interethnic contact.

This special focus on interethnic friendship seems somewhat paradoxical: while meaningful contact is conceptualized as being able to reduce prejudice, the kind of interethnic contact that is seen as most meaningful actually seems to *require* rather than reduce low prejudice. We argue that one of the reasons why this contradiction has not resulted in systematic theoretical consequences for the approach to meaningful contact is, at least partly, due to the previously described focus on objective characteristics of the contact situation. And with it, the failure to pay due attention to the importance of personal conditions, and hence differences between social groups, in the way in which interethnic contact is experienced and interpreted.

An Integrated Approach to Studying Meaningful Contact

The idea that personal conditions should be included in studying how interethnic contact influences ethnic prejudice, although relatively underdeveloped compared to the bulk of the contact literature, has actually already been present in Allport's seminal work as well. Allport (1979 [1954]) argued that "contact, as a situational variable, cannot always overcome the personal variable in prejudice. This is true whenever the inner strain within the person is too tense, too insistent, to permit him to profit from the structure of the outer situation" (Allport 1979 [1954], 280–1). What Allport suggests here is that it is important to consider both the objective conditions of the contact situation and the personal, subjective, interpretation of contact: not in all cases can the objective conditions of contact mitigate prejudice.

The latter is actually common knowledge in theorizing on the effect of superficial interethnic contact on ethnic prejudice. A general assumption regarding the link between superficial contact and ethnic prejudice is that it does not reduce ethnic prejudice, but rather reaffirms pre-existing ideas about ethnic minorities (Allport 1979 [1954], 263–4; Dinesen and Sønderskov 2015; Manevska 2014). However, because superficial contact is not considered meaningful contact in the context of contact theory, the theoretical implications of this claim, being that subjective interpretations of contact experiences are important, seem to have failed to work through more generally in contact theory research. Instead, the idea that superficial interethnic contact does not "work" for prejudice reduction is fully attributed to the characteristics of the contact situation itself, namely the superficial nature of the contact.

Of course, we do not mean to argue that objective characteristics of interethnic contact are unimportant. Friendship, as a type of contact, undeniably offers the possibility to build empathy, is inducive to perspective taking, and stimulates the development of an interest for the other. We can thus see how interethnic friendship offers a space for meaningful exchange. Similarly, it is possible to identify certain social conventions of politeness that are more or less generally shared, so that following them is generally experienced as positive and pleasant. Yet, in intergroup contact situations ethnic background may for some be a strong enough trigger to disturb this process, while for others it is not. As such, it is unlikely that the same intergroup contact is interpreted the same way by every person. What meaningful contact is thus cannot be defined by looking at the nature of contact alone. We need to take an integrated approach to studying meaningful contact, by combining a focus on the contact situation itself on one hand and the interpretation of this situation based on pre-existing values on the other.

THE ROLE OF WORKPLACE INTERETHNIC CONTACT AND WORKPLACE SOCIAL RESOURCES

The Importance of the Workplace

To study meaningful interethnic contact from an integrated perspective, focusing on both objective and subjective characteristics, it is important to ensure that the type of interethnic contact studied complies with two criteria: providing room for meaningful exchange, and being present among a population that differs in levels of ethnic prejudice. The latter is important because, as we have seen with intimate contact such as interethnic friendship, failing to do so makes it difficult to assess whether contact actually reduces ethnic prejudice or whether it requires low ethnic prejudice to begin with. The focus on "room for meaningful exchange," which we define somewhat loosely as entailing either/or the optimal conditions coined by Allport (1979 [1954]), the potential to form empathy and concern for the others' interest, and the potential of building enduring interethnic ties, is important because we are interested in interethnic contact that has the potential to reduce and, hence, change ethnic prejudice, rather than reaffirming what is already there.

Taking these two criteria into account, an important candidate to study meaningful contact from an integrated perspective is workplace interethnic contact. This type of contact is less frequently studied (cf. Kokkonen et al. 2015), at least compared to the large amount of studies on other types of interethnic contact, most notably intimate contact. Nevertheless, the work context has been repeatedly suggested as one of the building blocks for ethnic tolerance (De Souza Briggs 2007; Eisnecker 2019; Estlund 2005; Kokkonen et al. 2015; McPherson et al. 2001). In general, the workplace is seen as an important place for political socialization (Greenberg et al. 1996; Pateman 1970; Peterson 1992). Not only do people spend many hours at work, the workplace is also known to be the place where most interactions outside of people's intimate circle take place. While contacts within the intimate circle tend to be rather homogeneous, diverse workplaces hold the potential to foster diverse contacts. As such, the workplace is seen as an importance social space for "cross-cutting discourses" (Mutz and Mondak 2006) and might therefore be an important source of interethnic contact.

The formation of interethnic contact at work is facilitated by the very structure of the workplace. Contacts are difficult to avoid and often form a necessary part of work. Ethnically diverse workplaces thus create repeated patterns of interethnic contact, even among those who might normally avoid interethnic contact (cf. Paolini et al. 2018). Furthermore, the structure of the workplace, focused as it is on striving for the organization's goals and purposes, stimulates cooperation. Workplaces also rely on structures of interdependence and collective identity (cf. De Souza Briggs 2007; Goldschmidt et al. 2017). As such, the workplace does indeed fulfil the two criteria that we suggested for studying meaningful contact from an integrated perspective: it has the potential to reach also highly prejudiced people, and thus be present among a population with different levels of ethnic prejudice. Moreover, it has the potential to foster meaningful exchange.

Relatively few empirical studies are available that explore the relationship between workplace interethnic contact and ethnic prejudice. Some of the few large-scale empirical studies found that having interethnic colleagues is associated with social trust (Kokkonen et al. 2014), positive interethnic relations outside work (Kokkonen et al. 2015), and reduced anti-foreigner sentiments (Sønderskov and Thomsen 2015). However, most of these studies are based on information about *having* interethnic coworkers, and thus merely consider ethnic diversity at work in itself, which does not really capture the contact or exchange that ethnically diverse workplaces might bring about. Furthermore, differences in interpretation according to people's pre-existing prejudice are seldom addressed. Kokkonen et al. (2015) do hint at this by hypothesizing a positive effect of workplace ethnic diversity on interethnic friendship, which should be stronger for lower-educated people and people with lower income (Kokkonen et al. 2015, 289). However, this is an indirect approach to the matter for two reasons: it does not directly address interethnic contact, and it does not directly address pre-existing ethnic prejudice. Thus, we still know little about how and for whom interethnic experience at work translates into ethnic tolerance.

Two Types of Workplace Interethnic Ties: Contact and Resources

So far, we have argued that the workplace contributes to the formation of interethnic contact. However, the workplace is also known for the formation of social capital (Helliwell and Huang 2010; Putnam 2000; Thommes and Akkerman 2018). Through cooperation at work, working together on the completion of tasks, workers get a sense of whom they can rely on whenever there is a problem to be solved or a specific goal to be achieved. Based on these experiences as well as on regular face-to-face communication, workers get a sense of whom they can trust (cf. McClurg 2003; Ostrom 2003; Thommes and Akkerman 2018). Such experiences with support and trust are necessary to gain access to social resources (Podolny and Baron 1997). These social resources can differ widely in nature, ranging from giving advice on how to address a problem at work, to helping with practical problems (e.g., purchasing groceries in cases of sickness). In ethnically diverse workplaces, such social resources can be formed interethnically, for example native Dutch workers who gain access to the resources of a Turkish or Moroccan coworker.

Based on this idea that the workplace not only produces opportunities for interethnic contact but also for building (or destroying) social capital, we distinguish between two types of interethnic ties at work that may influence ethnic tolerance: workplace interethnic contact and workplace interethnic social resources. With workplace interethnic contact, we refer to the common way of conceptualizing interethnic contact: namely a form of personal interaction with an ethnic outgroup coworker, which can be face to face but also through phone, email, and the like. In addition to workplace interethnic contact, we also look into the role of workplace interethnic social resources, such as having an outgroup coworker who you can easily approach for advice when having a problem at work, or with whom you can discuss politics. From here on, we use "interethnic ties" as the overarching term to indicate both interethnic contact and interethnic resources.

First, considering workplace interethnic contact, the general argument is that interethnic contact at work provides the opportunity to acquire more knowledge about ethnic outgroup coworkers, which results in greater understanding of and more empathy for ethnic outgroup coworkers (McLaren 2003; Pettigrew and Tropp 2008, 2011). Support for this line of reasoning can be found in early works on the effect of interethnic contact, such as findings based on research in the army (MacKenzie 1948; Singer 1948) and among seamen (Brophy 1946), as well as in a meta-analysis of interethnic contact research (Pettigrew and Tropp 2006, 765, table 12). Because contact theory assumes that interethnic contacts in one domain are generalized towards the evaluation of the total ethnic group, the empathy for ethnic outgroup coworkers formed through workplace interethnic contact may generalize into more positive ideas about the ethnic outgroup in general and hence more ethnic tolerance.

Following this line of reasoning, we hypothesize:

Hypothesis 1: The more workplace interethnic contact natives have, the higher their level of ethnic tolerance.

Second, focusing on the role of workplace interethnic resources, we argue that the formation of social resources represents a social tie based on trust and reciprocity. Here, trust represents the feeling of being able to count on the other, while reciprocity, almost by necessity, brings along a care for the other's interest (Onyx and Bullen 2000). This can be better understood by considering that the social obligations that follow from a reciprocity-based tie do not need to be repaid in the exact same way as the access to resources that shaped the tie in the first place. Instead, repayment of these social obligations may well be intangible, for example in the sense of being loyal to a person and to the person's interests (cf. Portes 1998, 7). As such, when a tie of trust and reciprocity is formed between worker and coworker, this is likely to foster the worker's general care for the interests of the coworker. If this tie is interethnic, then, through a process of generalization following a similar logic as in contact theory, this general care for the interest of the ethnic outgroup coworker might be generalized into general care for members of that same ethnic outgroup. This general care for the ethnic outgroup is then likely to entail more ethnic tolerance.

We thus hypothesize:

Hypothesis 2: The more workplace interethnic social resources natives have, the higher their level of ethnic tolerance.

THE EFFECT OF WORKPLACE INTERETHNIC TIES AMONG PEOPLE WHO DIFFER IN TERMS OF ETHNIC PREJUDICE AND INTERETHNIC TIES OUTSIDE WORK

So far, we have only considered workplace interethnic contact and workplace interethnic resources from the potentially prejudice-reducing perspective that these two types of interethnic ties entail in terms of their objective characteristics. In this next step we add the personal, subjective perspective, by considering a combination of pre-existing levels of prejudice and interethnic ties outside work as a moderator for the way in which workplace interethnic contact and workplace interethnic resources affect ethnic tolerance. We distinguish four ideal-typical groups: (1) people who are low on ethnic prejudice and who have interethnic ties outside work; (2) people who are low on ethnic prejudice and do not have outside work interethnic ties; (3) people who are high on ethnic prejudice and who have outside work interethnic ties; and (4) people who are high on ethnic prejudice and do not have outside work interethnic ties.

Distinguishing between these four groups of people will provide insight in two important aspects of the relationship between workplace interethnic ties and ethnic tolerance: whether the interpretation of workplace interethnic ties in terms of ethnic tolerance differs between the four groups; and whether workplace interethnic ties can provide an alternative route to ethnic tolerance for those people who do not have interethnic ties outside work. The latter is of course especially interesting to consider for the group of people that combines high prejudice with no interethnic ties outside work, since this is the group of people that is thought especially likely to avoid interethnic contact on one hand, but might potentially have more to gain on the other *if* interethnic contact can actually reduce ethnic prejudice among highly prejudiced people.

To be able to formulate expectations on how workplace interethnic ties affect each of these four groups, two lines of thought are available in the literature. First, it is argued that interethnic contact will be especially important for people who are high on prejudice. This is because highly prejudiced people have relatively more to "gain" from this contact. There are some studies that substantiate this line of reasoning (Hodson 2011; Kokkonen et al. 2015; Rydgren et al. 2013). Following this line of reasoning, those high on pre-existing prejudice should have the most to gain from meaningful interethnic exchange at work. This might be especially true for the group of people who combine high pre-existing prejudice with no interethnic ties outside work, because they have no alternative source of interethnic ties.

We thus hypothesize:

Hypothesis 3:   The positive effect of workplace interethnic contact and workplace interethnic resources will be stronger for people high on ethnic prejudice, especially when they do not have interethnic ties outside work.

Second, it can also be argued that workplace interethnic contact and workplace interethnic social resources will work less strongly for workers high on pre-existing prejudice, because it will be more difficult for them to be affected by interethnic contact and resources at work. This argument stems from the basic theoretical idea already discussed above that, like any other social situation, people will interpret interethnic experiences according to their pre-existing prejudice. If this is true, it is more likely that workplace interethnic contact and workplace interethnic resources result in more ethnic tolerance for those already relatively low on pre-existing prejudice, than for those relatively high on ethnic prejudice. Several theoretical mechanisms have been associated with this basic theoretical idea, such as motivated reasoning (Homola and Tavits 2018; Kunda 1990) and cultural moderation (Manevska 2014). We do not directly see how having or not having interethnic ties outside work would have a play in this line of reasoning, as such we do not expect a difference along these lines in this case.

We therefore hypothesize:

Hypothesis 4:   The positive effect of workplace interethnic contact and workplace interethnic resources will be stronger for people low on pre-existing prejudice, compared to people high on pre-existing prejudice.

DATA AND METHODS

Data

To test our hypotheses, we use the Work and Politics Panel Study (Akkerman et al. 2017, 2018, 2020). This is a three-wave panel survey conducted among a representative sample of the Dutch labor force (N = 7,599). The data collection was performed by Kantar Public, using the TNS NIPObase. The TNS NIPObase online panel comprises about 235,000 respondents from 145,000 households in the Netherlands. Recruiting of panel members is executed using random sampling. This way, each member of society has a chance to be selected into the panel. In total 12,013 respondents from the Dutch labor force, aged between 15 and 67 years and representative in terms of gender, region, and level of education, were selected and invited to participate in the first wave of the panel study in July to September 2017. A total of 7,599 respondents completed the full questionnaire in the first wave, which amounts to an initial response rate of 64 percent. Of the initial respondents, a total of 6,008 completed the second wave of the study; these data were collected from October to early November 2018. The third wave, then, was collected from March to May 2020 and had 4,855 participants.

We selected respondents who participated in the three waves and who were, at the moment of each interview, employed in an organization. Our analyses include employees with a permanent or temporary contract, solo self-employed individuals who work within an organization, people who work as a volunteer within an organization, and people who work as trainees within an organization. For our analyses we only selected Dutch natives, who were born in the Netherlands and whose parents were both born in the Netherlands, and focus on their interethnic relations with Turkish and Moroccan individuals, which currently is the largest ethnic minority group in the Netherlands. Thus, we solely focus on the perspective of the native majority, which ensures clearer interpretations of our findings. The total number of respondents in our analyses amounts to 3,191 Dutch workers in organizations.

These unique data enable us to move beyond mere measurements of interethnic exposure (i.e., *having* interethnic coworkers), to specifically measuring interethnic contact and interethnic social resources. Moreover, since we have this information both at work and outside work, we can specifically zoom in on people who do not have interethnic ties outside work and compare them with people who do have such ties outside work.

Measurements

We measured our dependent variable as the political dimension of ethnic tolerance (cf. Thomsen 2012), namely *support for immigrant entitlements*. To measure this, we asked respondents to indicate whether Turkish/Moroccan people should be allowed to do the following: (1) come and live in the Netherlands; (2) vote in local elections; (3) vote in national elections; (4) run as a candidate in elections; (5) claim the same labor rights as native Dutch individuals; and (6) claim the same welfare benefits as native Dutch individuals. Respondents indicated for each of the six items whether Turkish/Moroccan people should be entitled to it (1 = yes, 0 = no). We expected that these items would form an ordinal sequence, ranging from entitlements that more natives are willing to extend to immigrants (such as labor rights, and the right to come and live in the country), to entitlements that more natives find difficult to share, most notably political entitlements. We performed Mokken scale analysis on the six items to test to what extent these reflect such an underlying ordinal latent variable. All indicators were well above the common thresholds indicating a strong Mokken scale (H = 0.83; H_i ranges from 0.78 to 0.87; and H_{ij} scores are 0.72 and above). Therefore, we concluded that the six items indeed form an ordinal underlying variable that measures support for entitlements for Turks and Moroccans in the Netherlands, which can be captured in a sum scale. We thus calculated a sum score for which higher scores indicate a preference for more entitlements for Turks and Moroccans in the Netherlands.

We measured *ethnic diversity* in the workplace by asking respondents for a rough estimate of the percentage of workers within their organization with a Turkish/Moroccan background. This means that we measured perceived rather than observed ethnic diversity in the organization. While this is not ideal, we did aim to reduce potential bias in this measurement by using a two-step approach. First, we asked respondents how many people work in their organization, which primes respondents to think in terms of actual numbers. Second, immediately after the question about the size of the organization, we asked respondents to indicate how many people of different ethnic groups, including Dutch natives, are in their organization. We offered the following answer categories per ethnic group: none; almost none; about a quarter; about half; about three quarters; and almost everyone, which should stimulate rationalized, i.e., mathematical, rather than emotional responses to this question. Examining the frequencies of the categories for Turkish/Moroccan coworkers showed that "about three quarters" and "almost everyone" were only rarely mentioned. Therefore, we recoded this variable into four categories: 0 = none; 1 = almost none; 2 = about a quarter; 3 = about half or more.

Workplace interethnic contact, which here refers to contact between native Dutch colleagues and their Turkish and/or Moroccan coworkers, was measured by asking how often respondents have contact with coworkers. We emphasized that this concerns both face-to-face contact and other types of contact, such as by phone or through email. Our measurement of workplace interethnic contact is tailored to the work context. It is, hence, not intended to mimic measurements of interethnic contact used in other types of research. Also, it measures contact frequency rather than contact quality. The answer categories ranged from 0 to 5, with the following categories: (0) no contact; (1) less than once a year; (2) once or several times a year; (3) monthly; (4) weekly; and (5) (almost) daily. We transposed these answer categories such that they measure the number of contact experiences per year, given a five-day workweek (no contact = 0, less than once a year = 0.5, once or several times a year = 2, monthly = 12, weekly = 52, and (almost) daily = 208).

We also measured *workplace interethnic social resources*. We asked whether respondents had Turkish and/or Moroccan coworkers whom they could easily approach, e.g., whose name they know, with whom they sometimes talk, or whom they think they can ask for help, for each of the following five issues: (1) addressing or solving a source of discontent at work; (2) discussing politics; (3) borrowing 100 euros; (4) purchasing some groceries in case the respondent is sick; and (5) helping with transport, e.g., when the respondent is sick or the car is broken. For each of these items, respondents indicated whether they do (= 1) or do not (= 0) have access to the social resource. We calculated the variable interethnic resources at work as the sum of the scores on the five items. A higher score on the variable indicates more interethnic resources.

We control for several background characteristics, namely sex (female as reference category), *age* (15 = 0), level of *education* in three categories (low, middle, and high), and *occupation type* using a shortened version of the EGP class scheme (distinguishing among higher professionals, lower professionals, routine non-manual employees, self-employed/farmers, and workers). Furthermore, we control for the *size of the organization* (measured in seven categories, ranging from less than 11 employees to more than 500 employees) as well as the average number of *hours worked per week*. Here, we manually set the maximum number of hours per week to 40, reflecting a full-time working week. Furthermore, we control for *interethnic contact outside work* and *interethnic social resources outside work*. Both variables are measured in the same way as their workplace equivalent. We explicitly specified that respondents should not include coworkers in their reports of contacts and social resources outside work. Instead, respondents were asked to think of family, friends, and acquaintances. Finally, we include dummies for the wave of the panel study to account for changes over time. We present the overall descriptive statistics and the descriptive statistics per wave in Table 20.1.

RESULTS

Given the panel structure of our data, with three observations for each respondent, we make use of hierarchical models with respondent observations nested within respondents to test our hypotheses. We test the first two hypotheses, on workplace interethnic ties and ethnic tolerance, using multilevel regression models. For the third and fourth hypotheses we are interested in developments *within* respondents over time, which we want to compare between four groups based on time invariant characteristics (having or not having interethnic ties outside work and being high or low on prejudice in wave 1). Therefore, we analyze our data using fixed effects panel regression and test whether the way in which interethnic ties at work affect support for immigrant entitlements over time differs between the four pre-defined groups. Both testing whether the unique errors are correlated with the regressors (Hausman specification test) and a test for overidentifying restrictions ('xtoverid') confirmed that fixed effects (rather than random effects) models are appropriate for our analyses. Since this technique focuses on differences within respondents over time, we excluded sex as a control variable, as this is time invariant.

In Table 20.2 we test our first two hypotheses, which concern the overall effects of workplace interethnic contact and workplace interethnic resources on support for immigrant entitlements. We start with a model including ethnic diversity of the workplace, workplace interethnic contact, and the control variables. In the next model, we replace workplace interethnic contact with workplace interethnic social resources. In Model 3, we include both measures for interethnic ties at the workplace simultaneously, along with ethnic diversity at the workplace and the set of control variables.

Our first hypothesis read that workplace interethnic contact is positively related to support for immigrant entitlements. When we turn to the first model, we see that this hypothesis is not supported in our analysis. We do not find a significant effect for workplace interethnic contact on support for immigrant entitlements ($b = 0.00$, $p =$ ns). In

Table 20.1 Descriptive statistics

	Overall (N = 9,573)			Wave 1 (N = 3,191)		Wave 2 (N = 3,191)		Wave 3 (N = 3,191)	
	Mean/%	SD	Range	Mean/%	SD	Mean/%	SD	Mean/%	SD
Support for immigrant entitlements	3.23	2.56	0–6	3.07	2.57	3.14	2.57	3.46	2.52
Ethnic diversity									
none	34%		0–1	36%		36%		31%	
almost none	46%		0–1	44%		45%		47%	
about a quarter	19%		0–1	18%		18%		21%	
half or more	1%		0–1	1%		1%		2%	
Workplace interethnic ties									
Interethnic contact	49.21	81.94	0–208	48.77	81.84	43.52	78.22	55.35	85.20
Interethnic social resources	0.61	1.28	0–5	0.58	1.27	0.48	1.18	0.76	1.38
Control variables									
Sex (female = ref.)	54%		0–1	54%		54%		54%	
Age (0 = 15 years)	27.88	12.30	0–55	26.73	12.27	27.73	12.27	29.18	12.26
Level of education									
lower	8%		0–1	8%		8%		8%	
middle	47%		0–1	47%		47%		47%	
higher	45%		0–1	45%		45%		46%	
Occupation type									
higher professionals	21%		0–1	20%		21%		21%	
lower professionals	33%		0–1	33%		33%		33%	
routine non-manual	23%		0–1	23%		23%		23%	
self-employed/farmers	4%		0–1	4%		4%		4%	
workers	19%		0–1	19%		19%		19%	
Size of the organization									
1 to 10 employees	13%		0–1	13%		13%		12%	
11 to 25 employees	9%		0–1	9%		9%		8%	

Table 20.1 (continued)

	Overall (N = 9,573)			Wave 1 (N = 3,191)		Wave 2 (N = 3,191)		Wave 3 (N = 3,191)	
	Mean/%	SD	Range	Mean/%	SD	Mean/%	SD	Mean/%	SD
26 to 50 employees	10%		0–1	9%		9%		10%	
51 to 100 employees	9%		0–1	9%		9%		9%	
101 to 250 employees	11%		0–1	11%		11%		12%	
251 to 500 employees	11%		0–1	11%		11%		11%	
more than 500 employees	38%		0–1	37%		38%		38%	
Hours worked per week	32.02	9.29	0–40	31.82	9.73	32.02	9.31	32.23	8.81
Interethnic ties outside work									
Interethnic contact	8.81	32.43	0–208	8.98	31.90	8.38	31.30	9.07	34.04
Interethnic social resources	0.39	1.10	0–5	0.38	1.09	0.30	0.97	0.48	1.22

Table 20.2 Outcomes of multilevel regression analyses on support for immigrant entitlements (Ni = 9,573; Nj = 3,191)

	Model 1 b	Model 1 s.e.	Model 2 b	Model 2 s.e.	Model 3 b	Model 3 s.e.
Ethnic diversity (none = ref.)						
almost none	0.13	0.07	0.08	0.07	0.09	0.07
about a quarter	0.19*	0.09	0.12	0.09	0.13	0.09
half or more	−0.14	0.20	−0.22	0.20	−0.22	0.20
Workplace interethnic contact	0.00	0.00			0.00	0.00
Workplace interethnic social resources			0.10***	0.02	0.10***	0.02
Control variables						
Sex (female = ref.)	−0.25**	0.08	−0.25**	0.08	−0.25**	0.08
Age (0 = 15 years)	0.01**	0.00	0.01**	0.00	0.01**	0.00
Level of education (higher = ref.)						
lower	−1.62***	0.15	−1.59***	0.14	−1.59***	0.14
middle	−1.13***	0.08	−1.12***	0.08	−1.11***	0.08
Occupation type (workers = ref.)						
higher professionals	0.28*	0.12	0.27*	0.12	0.27*	0.12
lower professionals	0.30**	0.10	0.28**	0.10	0.28**	0.10
routine non-manual	0.26*	0.11	0.25*	0.11	0.25*	0.11
self-employed/farmers	0.11	0.20	0.11	0.20	0.11	0.20
Size of the organization (1 to 10 = ref.)						
11 to 25 employees	−0.02	0.11	−0.02	0.11	−0.02	0.11
26 to 50 employees	−0.06	0.12	−0.06	0.12	−0.06	0.12
51 to 100 employees	0.00	0.12	0.00	0.12	0.00	0.12
101 to 250 employees	−0.11	0.12	−0.12	0.12	−0.12	0.12
251 to 500 employees	−0.06	0.12	−0.04	0.12	−0.04	0.12
more than 500 employees	0.01	0.11	0.01	0.11	0.01	0.11
Hours worked per week	0.00	0.00	0.00	0.00	0.00	0.00
Interethnic contact outside work	0.00	0.00	0.00	0.00	0.00	0.00
Interethnic social resources outside work	0.17***	0.02	0.13***	0.02	0.13***	0.02
Wave 2 dummy	0.08	0.04	0.08*	0.04	0.08*	0.04
Wave 3 dummy	0.33***	0.04	0.32***	0.04	0.32***	0.04
Intercept	3.44***	0.17	3.45***	0.17	3.44***	0.17
Random effects						
Between	1.77	0.03	1.76	0.03	1.76	0.03
Within	1.66	0.01	1.66	0.01	1.66	0.01
Log likelihood	−20,787.28		−20,774.91		−20,774.90	

Note: * $p < 0.05$, ** $p < 0.01$, *** $p < 0.001$; two-tailed test.

Model 2, we do find a positive significant effect of workplace interethnic resources on support for immigrant entitlements (b = 0.10; $p < 0.001$). This supportive evidence for Hypothesis 2 is reconfirmed in Model 3, where both workplace interethnic contact and workplace interethnic resources are included: workplace interethnic contact still has no effect on support for immigrant entitlements, while workplace interethnic resources still has a positive and significant effect (b = 0.10; $p < 0.001$). As such, these findings indicate that workplace interethnic ties can contribute to ethnic tolerance, however, this is only true for workplace interethnic resources.

Next, we distinguish between four groups of workers to test the next two hypotheses. This distinction is based on whether or not respondents had interethnic ties, i.e., interethnic contact and/or interethnic resources, outside the workplace at the time of wave 1, and on their level of ethnic prejudice during the first wave. To account for the level of ethnic prejudice, we asked respondents the extent to which they agreed (1 = completely disagree, 5 = completely agree) with the following statements: (1) It is better if only members of the same people get married to each other; (2) It would be best if every people also had its own state; (3) You can only feel secure if your own people is in the majority; and (4) It is possible for different ethnic groups to cooperate, but never to create full trust. These statements were retrieved from Weiss (2003) and Sekulić et al. (2006). Factor analysis indicated that the four items measure the same latent construct, and the Cronbach's alpha of .85 indicates that the items result in a reliable scale. To account for ethnic prejudice, we computed a mean over the four items for each respondent. Respondents with scores below or on average are considered as having low ethnic prejudice, while respondents with above average scores are considered as having high ethnic prejudice. Unfortunately, the ethnic prejudice measurement instrument was not included in each wave of the survey, making it impossible to include the instrument as an independent variable in our models.

The four groups then result from combining the two dichotomies. Hence, we examine workers who, at the time of wave 1, had interethnic ties outside the workplace and had low levels of prejudice against ethnic minorities, workers who had interethnic ties outside the workplace but also had high levels of ethnic minorities, workers who did not have interethnic ties and had low levels of prejudice against ethnic minorities, and workers who did not have interethnic ties outside the workplace and had high levels of prejudice against ethnic minorities.

Applying fixed effects panel data analyses on the four groups of respondents, we test whether workplace interethnic contact and workplace interethnic social resources are more strongly and positively related to support for immigrant entitlements for workers high on ethnic prejudice, especially those *without* interethnic ties outside work in wave 1 (Hypothesis 3) or whether, on the contrary, workplace interethnic contact and workplace interethnic resources works more strongly for people low on ethnic prejudice in wave 1, compared to those high on pre-existing prejudice in wave 1 (Hypothesis 4).

As a first, and purely descriptive step, we look at the average level of support for immigrant entitlements per wave for each of these four groups in Figure 20.1. Three things stand out from this figure: first, the two groups representing people high on pre-existing prejudice in wave 1 score consistently lower on support for immigrant entitlements than those low on pre-existing prejudice in wave 1. Second, within the groups of people that are either high or low on pre-existing prejudice, people who do have outside work interethnic ties in wave 1 score consistently higher on support for immigrant entitlements

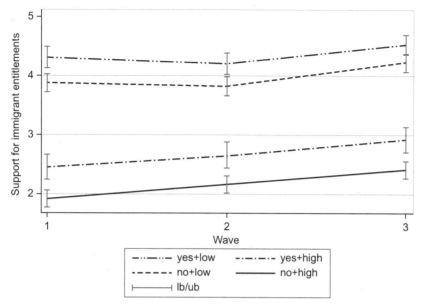

Figure 20.1 *Support for immigrant entitlements per wave for four groups of workers, based on having outside work interethnic ties (yes/no) and pre-existing prejudice (low/high) in wave 1*

than those who do not have outside work interethnic ties in wave 1. This difference seems to be somewhat larger for those high on pre-existing prejudice in wave 1. Third, for all four groups the average support for immigrant entitlements seems to increase over time, although this, again, is more pronounced for the two groups that represent people high on prejudice in wave 1.

We test the differences between the four groups of respondents in Table 20.3. Since separate models do not lead to different conclusions, we add workplace interethnic contact and workplace interethnic resources in the same model. The results from this analysis show that interethnic ties at the workplace seem to affect the ethnic tolerance of specific groups under study. Workplace interethnic contact is only significantly and positively related to support for immigrant entitlements among those respondents who already have interethnic ties outside work and low levels of ethnic prejudice (b = 0.00, $p < 0.05$). Workplace interethnic resources are positively related to support for immigrant entitlements for those who already have interethnic ties outside work and low levels of ethnic prejudice (b = 0.08, $p < 0.05$), and for those who did not have such ties while having high levels of ethnic prejudice (b = 0.10, $p < 0.05$). The effects of workplace interethnic ties for the two other groups are insignificant. Hypothesis 3 read that workplace interethnic ties are more important for increasing support for immigrant entitlements for those groups high on pre-existing prejudice, especially when combined with no outside work ties. This hypothesis seems to be supported by our results, although only for workplace interethnic social resources. Hypothesis 4 read that workplace interethnic ties would be more important for increasing support for immigrant entitlements for those groups that

Table 20.3 Outcomes of fixed effect panel regression analyses on support for immigrant entitlements, stratified for people with and without interethnic ties outside work, and with low and high levels of prejudice

	Yes/Low $N_i = 1,905$, $N_j = 635$		Yes/High $N_i = 1,518$, $N_j = 506$		No/Low $N_i = 2,871$, $N_j = 957$		No/High $N_i = 3,279$, $N_j = 1,093$	
	b	s.e.	b	s.e.	b	s.e.	b	s.e.
Ethnic diversity (none = ref.)								
almost none	−0.10	0.22	−0.14	0.22	−0.13	0.16	−0.01	0.14
about a quarter	0.20	0.27	−0.29	0.27	0.22	0.22	−0.15	0.20
half or more	−0.49	0.54	0.13	0.46	−1.12	0.75	0.01	0.37
Workplace interethnic contact	0.00*	0.00	0.00	0.00	0.00	0.00	0.00	0.00
Workplace interethnic soc. resources	0.08*	0.04	0.01	0.06	−0.04	0.04	0.10*	0.05
Control variables								
Age (0 = 15 years)	−0.20	0.16	−0.20	0.19	0.01	0.13	−0.13	0.12
Level of education (higher = ref.)								
lower	−0.03	2.15	0.41	0.96	0.70	1.17	−0.16	0.89
middle	−0.46*	0.64	−0.63	0.70	0.26	0.53	−1.65*	0.65
Occupation type (workers = ref.)								
higher professionals	−1.39*	0.64	0.04	0.60	0.61	0.50	−0.48	0.49
lower professionals	−1.42*	0.61	0.08	0.55	0.50	0.46	0.01	0.42
routine non-manual	−1.64*	0.64	0.25	0.57	0.67	0.44	−0.04	0.43
self-employed/farmers	−3.07*	1.32	2.25*	1.02	0.19	0.99	−0.79	0.88
Size of the organization (1–10 = ref.)								
11 to 25 employees	−0.19	0.37	0.05	0.35	−0.15	0.25	0.34	0.22
26 to 50 employees	−0.29	0.39	0.18	0.37	0.05	0.29	0.28	0.23
51 to 100 employees	0.05	0.40	−0.07	0.37	0.02	0.30	0.17	0.25
101 to 250 employees	−0.38	0.39	−0.17	0.38	0.00	0.30	−0.06	0.25
251 to 500 employees	0.03	0.39	−0.16	0.39	0.19	0.30	−0.09	0.26
more than 500 employees	−0.10	0.37	−0.20	0.35	0.02	0.28	0.13	0.24

Hours worked per week	0.03**	0.01	0.00	0.01	−0.01	0.01	−0.01	0.01
Interethnic contact outside work	0.00	0.00	0.00	0.00	0.00	0.00	0.00	0.00
Interethn. soc. resources outside work	0.02	0.04	0.12*	0.05	0.03	0.06	0.10	0.07
Wave 2 dummy	0.11	0.19	0.43	0.22	−0.07	0.15	0.34**	0.14
Wave 3 dummy	0.70	0.41	0.94*	0.48	0.32	0.34	0.76**	0.31
Intercept	10.48*	4.40	7.66	4.97	3.39	3.49	6.64	3.40
sigma_u	3.08		3.46		2.04		2.66	
sigma_e	1.62		1.73		1.66		1.62	
rho	0.78		0.80		0.60		0.73	
R² within	4%		4%		2%		4%	

399

are low on pre-existing prejudice. We did not expect a difference here between low prejudice groups with or without outside work interethnic ties. Our results partially support this hypothesis: both workplace interethnic contact and workplace interethnic resources are associated with more support for immigrant entitlements, but only for respondents low on pre-existing prejudice with outside work interethnic ties in wave 1.

These results underline the importance of considering differences in how interethnic ties contribute to support for immigrant entitlements differently for different groups of people. Whereas based on the analyses in Table 20.2 we would be inclined to conclude that workplace interethnic resources, contribute to support for immigrant entitlements, from the analyses in Table 20.3 we conclude that the extent to which this is true depends on personal, subjective characteristics. Table 20.3 also provides interesting information on the time effect that we could already visually deduce from Figure 20.1: only for the groups high on pre-existing prejudice does support for immigrant entitlements increase over time. For respondents high on pre-existing prejudice with outside work ties in wave 1 this is only significant for wave 3 ($b = 0.94$, $p < 0.05$), while for the group high on pre-existing prejudice without outside work ties in wave 1 this is significant both for wave 2 ($b = 0.34$, $p < 0.01$) and wave 3 ($b = 0.76$, $p < 0.01$). We did not anticipate this effect of time, which does not seem to be a general period effect in the sense that it affects all four groups over time. Future research will need to delve into this to understand what exactly is going on there.

CONCLUSION AND DISCUSSION

In this chapter we developed an integrated approach to studying meaningful interethnic contact, combining a focus on objective characteristics of the contact situation with a focus on the subjective interpretation thereof taking into account people's pre-existing values. We study this in the context of workplace interethnic ties using a unique, tailor-made three-wave panel survey containing information on 3,191 Dutch workers in the Netherlands. Based on our analyses we conclude that experiences with ethnic diversity at work, most prominently workplace interethnic social resources, contribute to more ethnic tolerance, which we measured as support for immigrant entitlements. This underlines the importance of considering the workplace as a source for ethnic tolerance. Furthermore, it indicates reciprocity as an important additional mechanism for understanding ethnic tolerance. From a perspective of objective conditions, workplace interethnic resources would be considered a meaningful form of interethnic contact.

However, this picture becomes more nuanced when looking at the results of our analyses of changes over time within respondents in four different groups, based on respectively high or low pre-existing prejudice and having or not having interethnic ties outside work in wave 1. Looking at the results for these groups, workplace interethnic ties seem to mostly affect ethnic tolerance for the "extremes" within these four groups: both for those low on prejudice who already had outside work ties and for those high on prejudice without previous interethnic ties outside work did workplace interethnic ties (for the latter group only the resources) result in more ethnic tolerance. This supports the idea that the same objective conditions of contact work differently for different groups of people according to their pre-existing values (Asbrock et al. 2013; Manevska et al. 2018;

West et al. 2017; West and Greenland 2016). Our findings also suggest that, to some extent, both hypothesized mechanisms seemed to be at work simultaneously (Hypothesis 3 and Hypothesis 4). These mechanisms are theoretically opposite, but can be present simultaneously because they seem to work for different groups.

Of course, there are several limitations to our study. First, we considered interethnic contact and interethnic resources separately and did not, theoretically or empirically, reflect upon the possible interdependencies between these two forms of interethnic ties, because it would add an additional layer of complexity to our, already rather complex, theoretical and empirical design. Nevertheless, such interdependencies might be present and it would be wise to address these in future research. Second, even though our study has an advantage over many cross-sectional studies in the sense that we can study the effect of interethnic ties on ethnic tolerance longitudinally, we still have information that only spans a three-year period. This means that, by necessity, we can only capture relatively short-term effects, and while our empirical design helps to account for endogeneity, this is still difficult to fully exclude, especially taking into account that the starting point of our first wave does not capture the starting point for people's experiences with interethnic contact. Third, other than the size of the organization we did not consider organizational characteristics that might also affect the nature of workplace interethnic contact. We suggest that future research addresses workplace characteristics that measure the extent to which the workplace indeed promotes cooperation, working towards a common goal, and the creation of a shared identity. As such, more research is needed to conclude just how much tolerance there is to win at work, and for which groups. We would additionally like to note that the groups considered should not only be based on pre-existing prejudice and interethnic ties outside work. While clearly important based on our results, other characteristics of workers, such as embeddedness and position in the organization, might be important as well to get a better and more nuanced understanding of how interethnic contact and interethnic resources at the workplace are formed and how these affect ethnic tolerance.

Despite these limitations we believe our study underlines the importance of considering workplace interethnic contact as an important form of meaningful interethnic contact, especially for highly prejudiced people without alternative interethnic ties. Furthermore, we believe our study shows how important it is to take into account both characteristics of the contact situation and personal characteristics when looking to understand the relationship between interethnic contact and ethnic tolerance and, hence, take an integrated approach to studying meaningful interethnic contact. This has wider implications, both for studying other types of contact, such as "positive" and "negative" contact, and for theorizing on the potential to reach harmonious interethnic relations in ethnically diverse societies. Both an integrated perspective on meaningful contact as well as the workplace context should have center stage in this future research agenda.

REFERENCES

Aberson, Christopher L., Carl Shoemaker, and Christina Tomolillo. 2004. "Implicit Bias and Contact: The Role of Interethnic Friendships." *Journal of Social Psychology* 144(3): 335–47.

Akkerman, Agnes, Katerina Manevska, Roderick Sluiter, and Antonia Stanojevic. 2017. *Work and Politics Panel Survey 2017*. Nijmegen: Radboud University.

Akkerman, Agnes, Bram Geurkink, Katerina Manevska, Roderick Sluiter, and Antonia Stanojevic. 2018. *Work and Politics Panel Survey 2018*. Nijmegen: Radboud University.

Akkerman, Agnes, Bram Geurkink, Katerina Manevska, Roderick Sluiter, Arjuna Snoep, and Antonia Stanojevic. 2020. *Work and Politics Panel Survey 2020*. Nijmegen: Radboud University.

Al Ramiah, Ananthi and Miles Hewstone. 2013. "Intergroup Contact as a Tool for Reducing, Resolving, and Preventing Intergroup Conflict: Evidence, Limitations, and Potential." *American Psychologist* 68(7): 527–42.

Allport, Gordon W. 1979 [1954]. *The Nature of Prejudice*. New York: Basic Books.

Altemeyer, Bob. 1998. "The Other 'Authoritarian Personality.'" *Advances in Experimental Social Psychology* 30: 47–91.

Asbrock, Frank, Lisa Gutenbrunner, and Ulrich Wagner. 2013. "Unwilling But Not Unaffected: Imagined Contact Effects for Authoritarians and Social Dominators." *European Journal of Social Psychology* 43: 404–12.

Barlow, Fiona K., Stefania Paolini, Anne Pedersen, Matthew J. Hornsey, Helena R.M. Radke, Jake Harwood, Mark Rubin, and Chris G. Sibley. 2012. "The Contact Caveat: Negative Contact Predicts Increased Prejudice More Than Positive Contact Predicts Reduced Prejudice." *Personality and Social Psychology Bulletin* 38(12): 1629–43.

Blau, Peter M. 1977. "A Macrosociological Theory of Social Structure." *American Journal of Sociology* 83(1): 26–54.

Brophy, Ira N. 1946. "The Luxury of Anti-Negro Prejudice." *Public Opinion Quarterly* 9: 456–466.

Connolly, Paul. 2000. "What Now for the Contact Hypothesis? Towards a New Research Agenda." *Race Ethnicity and Education* 3(2): 169–93.

De Souza Briggs, Xavier. 2007. "'Some of my best friends are …': Interracial Friendships, Class, and Segregation in America." *City and Community* 6(4): 263–90.

Dinesen, Peter T. and Kim M. Sønderskov. 2015. "Ethnic Diversity and Social Trust: Evidence from the Micro-Context." *American Sociological Review* 80(3): 550–73.

Dixon, Jeffrey C. 2006. "The Ties That Bind and Those That Don't: Toward Reconciling Group Threat and Contact Theories of Prejudice." *Social Forces* 84(4): 2179–204.

Dixon, John, Kevin Durrheim, and Colin Tredoux. 2005. "Beyond the Optimal Contact Strategy: A Reality Check for the Contact Hypothesis." *American Psychologist* 60(7): 697–711.

Eisnecker, Philipp S. 2019. "Non-Migrants' Interethnic Relationships with Migrants: The Role of the Residential Area, the Workplace, and Attitudes toward Migrants from a Longitudinal Perspective." *Journal of Ethnic and Migration Studies* 45(5): 804–24.

Estlund, Cynthia. 2005. "Working Together: Crossing Color Lines at Work." *Labor History* 46(1): 79–98.

Goldschmidt, Tina M., Martin Hällsten, and Jens Rydgren. 2017. "Are They Hunkering Down? Revisiting the Relationship between Exposure to Ethnic Diversity, Intergroup Contact, and Group Trust." *Working Paper Series*, Department of Sociology, Stockholm University.

Graf, Sylvie and Stefania Paolini. 2017. "Investigating Positive and Negative Intergroup Contact." In *Intergroup Contact Theory: Recent Developments and Future Directions*, eds. Loris Vezzali and Sofia Stathi, 92–113. Abingdon, UK: Routledge.

Greenberg, Edward S., Leon Grunberg, and Kelley Daniel. 1996. "Industrial Work and Political Participation: Beyond 'Simple Spillover.'" *Political Research Quarterly* 49(2): 305–30.

Helliwell, John F. and Haifang Huang. 2010. "How's the Job? Well-Being and Social Capital in the Workplace." *ILR Review* 63(2): 205–27.

Hewstone, Miles. 2015. "Consequences of Diversity for Social Cohesion and Prejudice: The Missing Dimension of Intergroup Contact." *Journal of Social Issues* 71(2): 417–38.

Hodson, Gordon. 2008. "Interracial Prison Contact: The Pros for (Social Dominant) Cons." *British Journal of Social Psychology* 47: 325–51.

Hodson, Gordon. 2011. "Do Ideologically Intolerant People Benefit from Intergroup Contact?" *Current Directions in Psychological Science* 20(3): 154–9.

Hodson, Gordon, Hannah Harry, and Andrea Mitchell. 2009. "Independent Benefits of Contact and Friendship on Attitudes toward Homosexuals among Authoritarians and Highly Identified Heterosexuals." *European Journal of Social Psychology* 39(4): 509–25.

Homola, Jonathan, and Margit Tavits. 2018. "Contact Reduces Immigration-Related Fears for Leftist But Not for Rightist Voters." *Comparative Political Studies* 51(13): 1789–820.

Huijts, Tim, Roderick Sluiter, Peer Scheepers, and Gerbert Kraaykamp. 2014. "Ethnic Diversity and Personal Contacts at Work and at School in the Netherlands: A Comparison of Natives and Ethnic Minorities." *Journal of International Migration and Integration* 15(2): 277–98.

Kokkonen, Andrej, Peter Esaiasson, and Mikael Gilljam. 2014. "Migration-Based Ethnic Diversity and Social Trust: A Multilevel Analysis of How Country, Neighbourhood and Workplace Diversity Affects Social Trust in 22 Countries." *Scandinavian Political Studies* 37(3): 263–300.

Kokkonen, Andrej, Peter Esaiasson, and Mikael Gilljam. 2015. "Diverse Workplaces and Interethnic Friendship Formation: A Multilevel Comparison across 21 OECD Countries." *Journal of Ethnic and Migration Studies* 41(2): 284–305.

Kuchenbrandt, Dieta, Friederike Eyssel, and Sarah K. Seidel. 2013. "Cooperation Makes It Happen: Imagined Intergroup Cooperation Enhances the Positive Effects of Imagined Contact." *Group Processes and Intergroup Relations* 16(5): 635–47.

Kunda, Ziva. 1990. "The Case for Motivated Reasoning." *Psychological Bulletin* 108: 480–98.

Laurence, James and Lee Bentley. 2018. "Countervailing Contact: Community Ethnic Diversity, Anti-Immigrant Attitudes and Mediating Pathways of Positive and Negative Inter-Ethnic Contact in European Societies." *Social Science Research* 69: 83–110.

Levin, Shana, Colette van Laar, and Jim Sidanius. 2003. "The Effects of Ingroup and Outgroup Friendship on Ethnic Attitudes in College: A Longitudinal Study." *Group Processes and Intergroup Relations* 6(1): 76–92.

MacKenzie, Barbara K. 1948. "The Importance of Contact in Determining Attitudes toward Negroes." *Journal of Abnormal and Social Psychology* 43: 417–41.

Manevska, Katerina. 2014. *Beyond the Ethnic Divide: Toward a Cultural-Sociological Understanding of Ethnocentrism*. Rotterdam: Erasmus University Rotterdam, PhD Thesis.

Manevska, Katerina, Peter Achterberg, and Dick Houtman. 2018. "Why There Is Less Supportive Evidence for Contact Theory Than They Say There Is: A Quantitative Cultural-Sociological Critique." *American Journal of Cultural Sociology* 6(2): 296–321.

McClurg, Scott D. 2003. "Social Networks and Political Participation: The Role of Social Interaction in Explaining Political Participation." *Political Research Quarterly* 56(4): 449–64.

McLaren, Lauren M. 2003. "Anti-Immigrant Prejudice in Europe: Contact, Threat Perception, and Preferences for the Exclusion of Migrants." *Social Forces* 81(3): 909–36.

McPherson, Miller, Lynn Smith-Lovin, and James M. Cook. 2001. "Birds of a Feather: Homophily in Social Networks." *Annual Review of Sociology* 27: 415–44.

Mutz, Diana C. and Jeffery J. Mondak. 2006. "The Workplace as a Context for Cross-Cutting Political Discourse." *Journal of Politics* 68(1): 140–55.

Onyx, Jenny and Paul Bullen. 2000. "Measuring Social Capital in Five Communities." *Journal of Applied Behavioral Science* 36(1): 23–42.

Ostrom, Elinor. 2003. "Toward a Behavioral Theory Linking, Trust, Reciprocity, and Reputation." In *Trust and Reciprocity: Interdisciplinary Lessons for Experimental Research*, eds. Elinor Ostrom and James Walker, 19–79. New York: Russell Sage Foundation.

Paolini, Stefania, Jake Harwood, Miles Hewstone, and David L. Neumann. 2018. "Seeking and Avoiding Intergroup Contact: Future Frontiers of Research on Building Social Integration." *Social and Personality Psychology Compass* 12(12): e12422.

Pateman, Carole. 1970. *Participation and Democratic Theory*. Oxford: Oxford University Press.

Peterson, Steven A. 1992. "Workplace Politicization and Its Political Spillovers: A Research Note." *Economic and Industrial Democracy* 13(4): 511–24.

Pettigrew, Thomas F. 1998. "Intergroup Contact Theory." *Annual Review of Psychology* 49: 65–85.

Pettigrew, Thomas F. and Linda R. Tropp. 2006. "A Meta-analytic Test of Intergroup Contact Theory." *Journal of Personality and Social Psychology* 90(5): 751–83.

Pettigrew, Thomas F. and Linda R. Tropp. 2008. "How Does Intergroup Contact Reduce Prejudice? Meta-analytic Test of Three Mediators." *European Journal of Social Psychology* 38: 922–34.

Pettigrew, Thomas F. and Linda R. Tropp. 2011. *When Groups Meet: The Dynamics of Intergroup Contact*. New York: Psychology Press.

Podolny, Joel M. and James N. Baron. 1997. "Resources and Relationships: Social Networks and Mobility in the Workplace." *American Sociological Review* 62(5): 673–93.

Portes, Alejandro. 1998. "Social Capital: Its Origins and Applications in Modern Sociology." *Annual Review of Sociology* 24(1): 1–24.

Putnam, Robert D. 2000. *Bowling Alone: The Collapse and Revival of American Community*. New York: Simon and Schuster.

Robinson, Jr, Jerry W. and James D. Preston. 1976. "Equal-Status Contact and Modification of Racial Prejudice: A Re-examination of the Contact Hypothesis." *Social Forces* 54(4): 911–24.

Rydgren, Jens, Dana Sofi, and Martin Hällsten. 2013. "Interethnic friendship, trust, and tolerance: Findings from two north Iraqi cities." *American Journal of Sociology* 118(6): 1650–94.

Sekulić, Duško, Garth Massey, and Randy Hodson. 2006. "Ethnic Intolerance and Ethnic Conflict in the Dissolution of Yugoslavia." *Ethnic and Racial Studies* 29(5): 797–827.

Sigelman, Lee and Susan Welch. 1993. "The Contact Hypothesis Revisited: Black–White Interaction and Positive Racial Attitudes." *Social Forces* 71(3): 781–95.

Singer, Henry A. 1948. "The Veteran and Race Relations." *Journal of Educational Sociology* 21: 397–408.

Sønderskov, Kim M. and Jens P.F. Thomsen. 2015. "Contextualizing Intergroup Contact: Do Political Party Cues Enhance Contact Effects?" *Social Psychology Quarterly* 78(1): 49–76.

Thommes, Kirsten and Agnes Akkerman. 2018. "Clean Up Your Network: How a Strike Changed the Social Networks of a Working Team." *Team Performance Management: An International Journal* 24(1/2): 43–63.

Thomsen, Jens P.F. 2012. "How Does Intergroup Contact Generate Ethnic Tolerance? The Contact Hypothesis in a Scandinavian Context." *Scandinavian Political Studies* 35(2): 159–78.

Thomsen, Jens P.F. and Arzoo Rafiqi. 2018. "When Does Superficial Intergroup Contact Reduce Anti-Foreigner Sentiment? Negative Contact as an Essential Condition." *International Journal of Comparative Sociology* 59(1): 25–43.

Torre, Maria E. 2010. *The History and Enactments of Contact in Social Psychology*. New York: Graduate Center of the City University of New York.

Voci, Alberto and Miles Hewstone. 2003. "Intergroup Contact and Prejudice toward Immigrants in Italy: The Mediational Role of Anxiety and the Moderational Role of Group Salience." *Group Processes and Intergroup Relations* 6(1): 37–54.

Wagner, Ulrich, Oliver Christ, Thomas F. Pettigrew, Jost Stellmacher, and Carina Wolf. 2006. "Prejudice and Minority Proportion: Contact Instead of Threat Effects." *Social Psychology Quarterly* 69(4): 380–90.

Weiss, Hilde. 2003. "A Cross-National Comparison of Nationalism in Austria, the Czech and Slovak Republics, Hungary, and Poland." *Political Psychology* 24(2): 377–401.

West, Keon and Katy Greenland. 2016. "Beware of 'Reducing Prejudice': Imagined Contact May Backfire if Applied with a Prevention Focus." *Journal of Applied Social Psychology* 46(10): 583–92.

West, Keon, Victoria Hotchin and Chantelle Wood. 2017. "Imagined Contact Can Be More Effective for Participants with Stronger Initial Prejudices." *Journal of Applied Social Psychology* 47: 282–92.

21. Constructing national identity and generalized trust in diverse democracies
Patti Tamara Lenard

Large-scale immigration has been accused of causing many ills, including declining support for a broad range of welfare state policies (Eger and Breznau 2017).[1] The decline in support is often described as mediated by *trust*. Fleshed out, the accusation proposes that before large-scale migration, democratic states were trusting states: citizens trusted each other and, furthermore, extended their trust to their political representatives. As a result, trusting citizens were willing to support institutionally organized welfare state policies. Why is trust essential? Welfare state policies, so the explanation goes, rely on citizens *trusting* that only those in need will take advantage of them, and that when they themselves are in need, such policies will be available to them. This generalized trust stems from a shared set of norms, values and practices, sometimes referred to as a shared public culture, that allows citizens to predict how others will behave and what choices they will make. Where it is widespread, citizens are willing to participate in the political institutions that regulate their shared lives. Large-scale immigration is said to disrupt this process: migrants travel with their own norms, values and practices that are unfamiliar to the citizens of a host country. Allegedly, their arrival thereby renders the basis on which trust is extended and reciprocated less able to do its work. As a result, trust declines, especially among citizens, and correspondingly so does their willingness to support welfare state policies, especially inclusive ones. This chapter evaluates this claim, and makes the two following arguments. First, the bulk of the evidence suggests that while increased diversity can strain trust relations, in most cases, diversity *alone* is not responsible for driving down levels of trust in a democratic state, but rather that there are conditions under which diversity travels with other trust-dampening factors. Second, there are multiple levers available to states that aim to protect against the conditions that dampen trust, and more importantly the conditions that lead many to connect diversity with difficulties in extending trust. One underappreciated lever is the state's capacity to shape the content of its national identity.

In the first part of the chapter, the empirical evidence proposing and rejecting the claim that immigration-related diversity causes a decline in the trust that is central to welfare state policy support is assessed. It begins with an assessment of what in particular is said to decline in response to immigration-related diversity. It then considers the evidence suggesting that diversity in general generates a decline in trust, and correspondingly that this decline translates into declining support for welfare state policies. This analysis proceeds by highlighting three dimensions of disagreement among scholarship in this area: whether it is in fact true that diversity drives down trust, and if so, what kind of diversity might be such a driver; whether other factors instead of diversity, or in combination with diversity, are in fact responsible for driving down trust, and whether, if diversity does have a negative influence on levels of trust, it matters for the support of welfare state policies. The second part of the chapter begins with an account of the macro-level policies, including income-equality policies and multicultural policies which are said to sometimes exacerbate, and other times to improve levels of trust, and if so, by what mechanism. It then argues that, absent from these discussions, is any consideration of whether the content of *national identity* is relevant to explaining levels of trust in increasingly diverse societies. So, I will argue in this section of the chapter that an identity must have *content* in order to build and sustain trust among members of a state, but that only some content is able to do so; as readers will see, the argument I offer fits neatly into the constructivism literature, suggesting that nations and national identity are made and remade by their members, and thus that they can reasonably be treated (in the case I am considering here) revisable to be more inclusive of the diversity that travels with new migrants. I will articulate this content in some detail.

MEASURING TRUST AND RELATED CONCEPTS

In the scholarship that assesses the connections among citizens' attitudes, how they shift in response to diversity and whether they matter for welfare state support, many concepts are deployed to explain what specifically must be sustained. These include cooperation, social capital, solidarity, social or cultural cohesion and civic mindedness – all of which either have trust at their core, or are intimately connected to the willingness to extend trust to others. To take just some examples, by way of illustration: collective mindedness is described as "social trust, civic engagement and political participation" (Kesler and Bloemraad 2010, 319); solidarity is described as "people's expressed concern with the living conditions" of others (Oorschot 2008, 3) or as "the sense of community and common identity ... and feelings of trust in fellow citizens" (Banting et al. 2011, 38); social capital is described as "social networks and the associated norms of reciprocity and trustworthiness" (Putnam 2007, 137) or as "the link between trust, interaction, belonging, and participation across groups" (Mata and Pendakur 2014, 330). These illustrative examples suggest that, whatever cluster concept is deployed by scholars focused on assessing the impacts of increasing ethno-cultural diversity, *trust* plays a central role.

The central role for trust, whatever the larger analytic concept with which scholars work, is manifest in the widespread use of surveys that ask either the general trust question ("Generally speaking, would you say that most people can be trusted or that you can't be too careful dealing with people?"), or variations that focus on the conditions under which particular others can or would be trusted. Scholars, for example, ask respondents to think about *particular* others, and then to consider whether they can be trusted, or whether they can be expected to respond in cooperative ways to requests to make sacrifices in cases of emergency (Banting et al. 2011, 43). Here is one example of such a question, "If public officials asked everyone to conserve water or electricity because of some emergency, how likely is it that people in your community would cooperate?" (Abascal and Baldassarri 2015, 737–8). This focus on particular others is, additionally, manifest in measures of "group-based" trust. Researchers attempt to identify cases in which trust is extended to fellow group members, however such individuals are identified, but not to those who are considered to be outsiders, including but not limited to immigrants (Schmid et al. 2014, 666). Typically, it is understood that generalized trust, across and between members of diverse groups, rather than particularized in-group trust, is key to supporting widespread collaboration in multiple ways, including with respect to the sustaining of inclusive welfare policies.

IMMIGRATION AND TRUST

The claim that immigration drives down trust has, to many, an initial plausibility. Newcomers travel with unfamiliar religions, ethnicities, cultures, and practices, for example, and if it is true that trust is easier to extend to those who are *known* then it may well be more difficult to extend under these circumstances. What extending trust *is* is assessing the likelihood that one's trust will be rewarded – it is rendering oneself vulnerable to others, who can make choices to reward or disappoint our trust. In other words, trust is a *risk*, and extending it involves making a probability assessment with respect to whether it will be reciprocated. This is a descriptive rather than a normative claim: normatively, it may be preferable to believe that trust is easy to extend, even to those whose way of life seems difficult to make sense of. Descriptively there is evidence that extending trust is more difficult when people perceive those whom they are asked to trust to be different in fundamental ways (for an elaboration of the latter two claims, see Lenard 2012). So, it may just be that the presence of *difference* that travels with migration renders trust more difficult to extend.

Does empirical evidence suggest that trust declines as diversity increases? Notice first that while diversity itself may dampen trust, the focus of many scholars' research, whose work I examine in detail below, is not on the relationship between diversity per se and trust, but rather on whether *increases* in perceived diversity, usually caused by immigration, translate first into dampened trust and, correspondingly, dampened enthusiasm for sustaining robust and open welfare state policies. The hypothesis that such a connection exists finds theoretical grounding in arguments defending a "right to cultural continuity," rather than a right to slowing or stopping immigration. These arguments emphasize that host countries value being able to *control* the pace of change that inevitably travels with migration, so that whatever is understood to be essential to a state's defining culture is protected from rapid and unwanted changes (Miller 2005; Scheffler 2007).

One well-known account of the relationship between diversity and trust is Robert Putnam's, whose study of levels of social capital in diverse communities in the United States (US) suggests that the more diverse a community is, the less trusting it is (Putnam 2007, 148). He suggests that all of the standard markers of "social capital" – as he understands it, "social networks and the associated norms of reciprocity and trustworthiness" (Putnam 2007, 137) – decline in heterogeneous communities. A study of Canadian neighborhoods finds the same result. Scholars asked residents of a range of communities whether, if they lost their wallet, they believed it would be returned to them if it was found by others who occupy various roles in their community, including police officers and grocery store clerks. They find that "the larger the presence of visible minorities in the neighborhood, the less trusting is the majority" (Banting et al. 2011, 43). Conversely, among ethnic minorities, who report lower levels of trust than do members of the majority, trust *rises* as does ethnic diversity in their neighborhoods.

Assessments of the relation between ethnic heterogeneity and levels of trust in Western Europe do not demonstrate the same trend, however. A neighborhood study conducted in diverse communities in England reports no significant decline in trust as a result of the presence of diversity; on the contrary, they propose that as a result of increased opportunities for contact, residents correspondingly (and as the contact hypothesis proposes) generally report increased trust (Schmid et al. 2014, 671). The finding that trust correlates well with levels of diversity is replicated in assessments of data taken from a host of European-wide surveys. An analysis of the European Values Survey (1999/2000) demonstrates that European countries with more diversity demonstrate more solidarity towards immigrants, assessed using responses to the question, "To what extent do you feel concerned about the living conditions of immigrants in your country?" (Oorschot 2008). Similarly, using the 2002–2003 European Social Survey, Hooghe et al. suggest that there is no statistical correlation between diversity and generalized trust in a population (Hooghe et al. 2009, 218). Some countries are "outliers," for example, in Italy, an increase in the number of foreign labor migrants appears correlated with declines in generalized trust (Hooghe et al. 2009, 213). In Switzerland, also, neighborhoods characterized by large numbers of non-citizens demonstrate a corresponding reduction in generalized trust (Hooghe et al. 2009, 211).

In other words, in some situations the presence of diversity – in particular in the form of increased migration – can decrease levels of trust among a citizenry. Not everyone agrees, however. Critiques of Putnam's initial thesis, suggesting that diversity dampens trust relations, abound, and one central criticism resists the claim that it is diversity per se that generates distrust, arguing instead that certain connected characteristics are better understood as responsible for generating distrust. One such study proposes that it is the presence not of diversity, but rather of "ethnoracial, residential and economic differences" that dampens trust (Abascal and Baldassarri 2015, 734). That is, when differences in ethnic or racial groups, including immigrant groups, *track* differences in material well-being, then distrust can rise.

This kind of conclusion, that where economic factors travel with diversity, trust is at risk, is consistent with additional observations that complicate the simple claim that diversity drives down trust. For one thing, it is well observed that indicators of economic well-being track trust, across ethnic and racial groups: wealthier and more educated citizens are more likely to report high levels of trust than comparatively less wealthy and less educated citizens, regardless of their status as minority or majority. Stable employment predicts higher trust; unemployment predicts lower trust (Abascal and Baldassarri 2015, 750). These trends are also evident among states; rates of recorded trust are higher among wealthier nations than among poorer nations (Hooghe et al. 2009); additionally, states characterized by economic inequality report lower levels of trust than do those in which there is greater economic equality.

So, trust is lower among those who are less well-off, in general, but also trust is generally lower in communities and states with significant economic inequalities among residents: economic instability and economic inequality both dampen trust (Uslaner 2004; Lenard 2010). Often, those who are most economically unstable are minorities, and correspondingly live in relatively poorer neighborhoods, and so in many countries, the most ethnically and racially diverse neighborhoods are also those that are poorest; in these cases, trust is lower than in comparatively homogeneous neighborhoods (Abascal and Baldassarri 2015, 751; Uslaner 2010).

TRUST, IMMIGRATION AND SUPPORT FOR THE WELFARE STATE

The worry that there is a connection between diversity and support for welfare state policies is typically attributed to early work conducted by Alesina and Glaeser, which makes the claim that in US states with high levels of diversity, there is correspondingly lower support for welfare state policies (Alesina and Glaeser 2004). They offer a range of explanations for this view, focusing in particular on a combination of the facts that the US is a highly diverse country and that, additionally, minorities are more likely to live in poverty. So, where citizens largely believe that certain racial or ethnic groups will be the beneficiaries of welfare policies, support for them declines (Hero and Preuhs 2007, 500). This sort of explanation finds empirical support in studies of "racial threat," according to which diversity is believed (for example in some American communities) to threaten "white, middle-class values and institutions," in such a way that as diversity increases there is a "decline in support for programs that have become racialized and immigrationalized" (Hawes and McCrea 2018, 356).

In their work, Alesina and Glaeser distinguish between patterns of welfare support in the US and European countries, the latter of which are historically characterized by both a greater degree of ethnic and racial homogeneity and more extensive welfare state policies. What happens, though, when relatively homogenous countries begin to experience in-migration, especially in large numbers? Some research suggests that a similar trend is emerging, with an explanation that goes like this: where newcomers migrate, especially if they migrate from global south countries, they will require substantial support from the welfare state in order to subsist. This worry often has an insidious component, in public discourse, that such migrants *intend* to migrate to take advantage of the welfare state system, rather than to integrate as best they can into a functional economy. These services are for those who *deserve* access to them; newcomers who *choose* to take advantage of these services rather than integrate into a new economy as efficiently as possible are not among those who deserve them (Zhu and Xu 2015, 477). The consequences of excluding immigrants from the many rights and benefits available in a host state is that, in many cases, they do remain (relatively) poor; just as in the US, this allows for the emergence of the public perception that welfare policies would be taken advantage of (and allegedly depleted) by poor immigrants, were they permitted to benefit from them.

The worry is that where immigration is responsible for increases in diversity, support for welfare state policies goes down, and additionally that this support is driven down further when it comes to be perceived that those who benefit from these policies are minorities, including but not limited to newcomers. This fear can be characterized as what David Goodhart has called the "progressive's dilemma": so-called progressives welcome both generous welfare policies and immigration, but perhaps evidence suggests that declining support for welfare policies travels *with* immigration, requiring progressives to choose between two of their values (Goodhart 2004).

Some evidence suggests that Canada does not (yet) suffer from this dilemma. For example, Banting argues that public opinion in Canada does not demonstrate a widespread fear of newcomers misusing the welfare state system upon arrival (Banting 2010). Banting's explanation for the widespread support of immigration, alongside generous access for newcomers to social assistance, highlights a range of facts – including Canada's generally effective immigration incorporation strategies and its careful selection of migrants for admission – that will be examined in the next section of the chapter. There are Canadians who believe that migrants are overly dependent on welfare state policies; but, says Banting, these same Canadians are generally among those who are critical of welfare state policies to begin with (Banting 2010, 804). Data in the US suggest the same trend as does the Canadian data: attitudes towards immigration and generous welfare state policies travel together (Garand et al. 2017). Among Americans who support migration (and who feel positively about migrants, including irregular migrants), there is also widespread support for state assistance policies (Garand et al. 2017, 146). Likewise, among high-trusting Americans, there is widespread willingness to include immigrants in these state assistance policies (Butz and Kehrberg 2015, 276).

Similarly, using data collected via the European Values Survey (1999/2000), Uunk and Oorschot assessed the connection between solidarity towards immigrants and commitment to welfare state policies (Uunk and Oorschot 2007). They found that communities with larger numbers of immigrants were also those that supported welfare policies: they argue, as a result, that "more welfare spending attracts more immigrants *and* more immigrants make people more solidaristic towards immigrants" (Uunk and Oorschot 2007, 233). In their view, in other words, immigration has a *positive* effect on attitudes towards welfare policies. As well, using data collected via the European Social Survey (2002/2003), Mau and Burkhardt in general find only a weak connection between increasing numbers of migrants and low or declining support for welfare policies (Mau and Burkhardt 2009). The aggregate data may seem to suggest that "the more fractionalized a country is," the lower the support for extending "equal rights to foreigners"; but, they say, this is largely driven by data from three "outlier" countries where the connection is strong, namely Belgium, Luxembourg and Switzerland (Mau and Burkhardt 2009, 219).

There are two additional trends worth noting in the data that complicate the easy conclusion that the so-called progressive's dilemma can be dispensed with. First, some evidence finds that while it is true that where communities are characterized by high levels of trust, there is also widespread support for extending welfare state benefits to immigrants, there is also evidence that although there is a positive correlation between high levels of in-migration to specific states and ease of gaining access to welfare state benefits, the quality of those benefits may be comparatively lower (Butz and Kehrberg 2015, 276). That is, although immigrant-welcoming states permit newcomers to gain access to welfare state services, the services to which they gain access are less robust than those offered in states that do not, comparatively, welcome large numbers of migrants (Hero and Preuhs 2007, 508). This evidence suggests that whereas there may not be a progressive's dilemma *per se* (progressives need not choose, in other words, between immigration and welfare state policy support), there is nevertheless a delicate balance to be found between levels of immigration and access to welfare state policies: while high rates of immigration does not reduce support for welfare state policies in general, perhaps it reduces support for a relatively more generous welfare policy package. Notice that welfare state policies can be generous in multiple ways: (1) they can be open to all or nearly all residents of a territorial jurisdiction (as opposed to only citizens, or citizens and long-term residents); (2) they can include many benefits programs (as opposed to few); and (3) they can be open to citizens regardless of their levels of wealth (or they can be means-tested). The choices states make differ along all of these dimensions. The evidence considered above suggests that communities welcoming an influx of migrants may be generous along the first dimension, but perhaps not along the second and third.

Second, research that measured social capital against "immigrant group size" suggests that participation in the various markers of social capital predicts support for welfare policies if and only if the immigrant population is small. Where the immigrant population grows, however, residents with high social capital measures are *less* supportive of welfare state policies (Hawes and McCrea 2018, 356); the explanation seems to be that, under conditions of increasing diversity, those who measure high on social capital indices direct their energies towards "in-group" activities. The trust that is thereby manifest is extended narrowly rather than broadly. So, again, support for welfare state policies in general does not decline in response to diversity; rather, support for inclusive and generous welfare state policies declines.

STATE LEVERS AVAILABLE TO PROTECT GENERALIZED TRUST IN A DIVERSE POPULATION

The evidence reviewed above suggests that increasing diversity alone does not explain attitudes towards welfare policies in general, and more particularly, that to the extent that diversity dampens welfare policies, it does so only in some contexts. Although some evidence reported above does suggest that "greater changes in diversity are linked to smaller increases in spending" (Banting et al. 2011, 40), there is nothing "inevitable" about this decline; rather, the response to diversity in general, and increases in in-migration in particular, is often shaped by the existing national context (Kesler and Bloemraad 2010, 320). As a result, state-level governments have multiple levers available to them to render immigration less threatening to a population, thereby protecting generalized trust among a population, along with public support for redistributive policies.

In one cluster of cases, the explanation stems largely from the interaction between diversity and economic status; that is, where those who are poorest are also ethnic or racial minorities, the *combined* effect is to dampen trust relations among all citizens. So, it stands to reason that one major set of levers that states possess to erase the connection between diversity and dampened trust are those that focus on reducing inequalities in general, i.e., by expanding the set of state assistance policies that are available to citizens and by expanding access to them. This latter point highlights that where state assistance policies are available expansively, the opportunity for the emergence of the public perception that those most in need are minorities is smaller (independently of whether this is true as a matter of fact). The latter is a tricky thing: as noted just above, in states where there are widespread positive views towards immigrants, there is also widespread support for the view that immigrants should be able to access social assistance on par with non-immigrant citizens. But, these positive views may stem from an earlier view that, in general, immigrants are not likely to be a burden on the welfare state: this suggests that work must be done by states to avoid the emergence of the perception that immigrants do pose such a burden. They must work to ensure that welfare state policies do not become "racialized or immigrationalized" in ways that reduce the widespread support on which they rely (Hawes and McCrea 2018, 356; Garand et al. 2017).

A second set of levers available to states are those collected under the label "multicultural policies." This label captures a broad range of policies that aim largely at supporting the integration of ethnic and cultural minorities into the larger economic and political spheres of society, by providing exemptions and accommodations in relation to rules, regulations and practices that otherwise render integration challenging (Kymlicka 1996). Classic examples include uniform requirement modifications and the translation of key documents or state-level media into minority languages (for example, and perhaps especially, including voting ballots). Multiculturalism has recently experienced a kind of backlash, among scholars and activists who propose that such policies serve to segregate rather than integrate minorities, who are (because of multicultural policies) permitted to pursue whatever ways of life they had pursued "at home," rather than commit themselves to the new ways of life that characterize their new home country (e.g., Vertovec and Wessendorf 2010). This hypothesis is controversial, and to the extent that there is evidence in favor of it, most scholars propose that this evidence in fact shows that where states render integration difficult, ethnic and cultural minorities correspondingly are forced into segregation. In other words, the relevant factor, in explaining cultural and ethnic segregation, is not the desire of newcomers to persist in ways of life that characterize the homes they have left behind, but rather their felt exclusion from the larger economic, political and social spheres of society, that is uncomfortable with or dismissive of the contributions that newcomers would otherwise make. On the contrary, say many scholars, there is evidence that where the policy context of a welcoming society is explicitly multicultural, and so where public institutions encourage minority participation, the supposed "negative effects of immigration on trust and engagement are mitigated or even reversed" (Kesler and Bloemraad 2010, 321; Arneil and Macdonald 2010).

To summarize: there are typically understood to be the two main macro-level policies available to states that are keen to welcome migrants without experiencing a corresponding decline in the trust that translates into support for welfare state policies. First, such states can adopt or protect policies that do relatively more to redistribute wealth from those who are most well-off to those who are least well-off. Second, they can adopt policies that facilitate rather than hamper the integration of newcomers into the public institutions that define the state broadly to include political, economic and social spaces. These policies can in principle be disconnected: states can pursue income-equalizing policies or multicultural policies. Yet, some evidence suggests that there can be a connection between them, in the sense that where citizens feel favorably towards immigrants, this feeling manifests in providing open access to them to partake in the benefits offered by income-equalizing policies, especially in the form of welfare state policies. The connection between income-equality and multicultural policies suggests that at least in some cases the so-called progressive's dilemma is, in one of its manifestations, not much of a dilemma. The set of people who are solidaristic, in general, with respect to migrants, manifest their solidarity in the form of commitment to open access to welfare state policies for migrants. This connection is not necessary, however, nor is it straightforward as the evidence considered in the earlier section suggested. What the connection in some cases suggests is that there is a need for an explanation of cases where openness towards migration travels with a willingness to include migrants in welfare state policies: one important explanation comes in the form of the "national identity" hypothesis.

Applied to the question of "levers" available to state-level governments, in cases where they may aim to generate the conditions under which increased diversity will not dampen trust, the national identity hypothesis suggests that where a state's national identity is at least in part defined by a commitment to welfare state redistribution, trust will not decline under conditions of increased rates of immigration. This hypothesis is most robustly developed by Canadian researchers, who aim to explain why it is that, at least comparatively speaking, there is no clear connection between immigration and dampened trust. For example, according to Banting et al., it is Canada's national identity that "protects the welfare state from toxic effects of cultural suspicion" (Banting et al. 2011, 46). In particular, among surveyed Canadians, those who identify strongly *as Canadian* report both higher levels of tolerance for immigration and support for welfare state policies, including health care in particular. Moreover, Banting and his colleagues classify countries in the Organisation for Economic Co-operation and Development according to whether they are strongly or weakly multicultural, to find that those that are strongly multicultural were also more likely in the period studied (between 1980 and 2000) to increase their commitment to redistributive spending, suggesting that these policies may help to mitigate any pressures that increased diversity can put on commitments to redistributive welfare policies (Banting et al. 2011, 42). Reeskens and Oorschot (2017) report a similar story, examining trends in 23 countries using the data taken from the 2012 European Social Survey: they find that those citizens who believe their state has done a good job at implementing and protecting civil, political and social rights also report feeling relatively more positively towards immigrants (Reeskens and Oorschot 2017, 191). They propose that the best way to understand the connection is through citizens' "aspirations about citizenship, as well as perceptions about its actual realization" (Reeskens and Oorschot 2017, 178). Specifically, they suggest that where citizens trust in their government to protect a wide range of rights for all citizens, they are more likely to extend that trust to those who are recent arrivals as well. A more detailed examination of Denmark and Sweden offers additional evidence that national identities can serve to interrupt the ways in which increased diversity might otherwise dampen trust. According to one interpretation, Sweden's robust welfare system has historically been understood in integrative terms: "in Sweden, the predominant idea is to regard the welfare state more as a promoter of integration, and less as an outcome of a pre-existing social and cultural homogeneity" (Borevi 2017, 378).

Later scholarship by Johnston and his colleagues complicates the findings suggested in the data above, to show that there are certainly cases where strength of national identity travels with high levels of trust, commitment to redistributive policies and openness to newcomers, but (and this is crucial) that the connection is not automatic. In some contexts, the strength of one's reported national identity travels with the opposite, i.e., decreased support for redistributive policies and immigration (Johnston et al. 2017). Their data suggest two possibilities, which may both be true. One possibility is that much will hinge on how national identity is measured, since it may well be that some measures of national identity will predict high levels of commitment to redistribution, or openness to outsiders, whereas others will not. Another possibility is that it is not simply national identity that matters for predicting welcoming and inclusive attitudes towards newcomers, but it may be that the *content* of this identity matters as well. David Miller and Sundas Ali have shown, first, that national identity is measured in multiple ways – for example in terms of national pride and national attachment, as well as in terms of how critical members are of their nation – and that among those whose national identity is defined by inclusivity and a comfort with critiquing the nation, its identity and its policies, most are also committed to redistributive policies (Miller and Ali 2014).

Follow-up work extends this analysis to examine the connection between trust, in general and towards newcomers, and national identity (Lenard and Miller 2018; Gustavsson and Stendahl 2020). One survey of the literature suggests that it is reasonable to conclude that the content of a national identity is at least partly predictive of whether it will support large-scale immigration by extending trust to newcomers. In particular, it demonstrates that where citizens describe their nation-state's identity in comparatively "civic" terms, with respect to a commitment to its institutions and to collaborating in a political project together, both products of relatively high levels of trust, they are also more likely to welcome newcomers to their state. Additional work suggests that the strength of one's attachment to a national identity correlates positively with a willingness to extend trust, and in particular that where individuals believe that their identity is superior to others, they are less likely to extend trust to those they perceive to be different (Gustavsson and Stendahl 2020). These observations have led to attempts to outline the content of an identity that would be most likely to generate trust within a diverse, even increasingly so, community, a challenge which I took up to argue that, for a national identity to build trust, it must possess some content – that is, it is not adequate to propose, as some civic nationalists have done, that all that is needed is commitment to a shared set of institutions that are adequately liberal and democratic. What is needed is an answer to what political theorists sometimes call the "particularity" problem, that is, an explanation for why people are more committed to this or that liberal, democratic state in particular, rather than any of them in general. One answer is that each state is defined by a national identity that shapes the particular operation and structure of their society, even where it is foundationally governed by democratic and liberal institutions.

Of course, the history of nation-states tells us that many defining features of past (and present) nation-states are exclusive in ways that are difficult for newcomers to penetrate; where nations self-define with reference to shared religion, or race, or ancestry, newcomers often cannot meet the criteria needed to be identified as an insider. The willingness to exclude newcomers who do not share the relevant criteria is problematic, and any liberal political theorist can see this clearly. But what is less clear is, what sort of content is available for national identities that is *both* able to generate trust among citizens *and* be adequately inclusive. One answer highlights the cultural content that can be mobilized to construct a distinctive but not exclusive national identity: this content highlights shared political conversations; shared current and historical icons in various domains including the arts, science and athletics; meaningful spaces including national parks and museums; meaningful moments in time, which may be historical but can also be present, and can be short-lived; shared cultural "tics," like common expressions and so on. What these features share is that they are adoptable by newcomers without their having to give up values that they hold dear, and they do not rest on possessing traits or characteristics that cannot be adopted by those who do not already possess them (Lenard 2019; Gustavsson 2019). The key point, then, is that the possession of a robust national identity, which may well generate generalized trust, is not a guarantee that this trust will extend to immigrants; content matters. In what follows, the chapter turns to an account of when and how a national identity can be shaped in ways that will make it more likely to generate inclusive trust.

NATIONAL IDENTITY AS A MACRO-LEVEL LEVER

As described above, two levers are usually considered as especially important in supporting trust among a citizenry and driving attitudes that support welcoming newcomers in general and into the welfare state system in particular. These are levers that focus on the adoption of redistributive policies and multicultural policies. In their best versions, both policies generate the conditions under which trust can thrive, in particular by encouraging or preparing the grounds for effective integration of newcomers into economic, social and political spheres of society. In the case of multicultural policies, they build the foundation for trust among newcomers by highlighting the accommodations a host state is willing to make in order to support their integration; and, they build the foundation of trust among host society members by signaling that the goal is *integration* of newcomers (Besco and Tolley 2019). In the case of inclusive welfare state policies, the foundation of trust is created among newcomers by signaling that the default stance of their new state is inclusion; and they sustain trust among host society members by protecting against the perception that newcomers are resource drains on the welfare state (because, since they are entitled to welfare state assistance on an equal basis, the perception that "only" immigrants use these resources, or that they use them in greater quantity, has difficulty emerging).

This final section of the chapter considers "national identity" as a third possible lever available for states in their attempts to ensure that increased diversity via immigration undermines neither trust nor support for welfare state policies. This account is meant to be different from the one pressed by Banting and his colleagues (2011), and by Borevi (2017), which proposes that it just *is* a key dimension of some states' existing identity that they welcome newcomers with trusting attitudes in general, and into the welfare state in particular. My account is meant to explain how and where a state that is keen to protect levels of trust and the robustness of a welfare state, in the face of increasing diversity, can shape and inform an inclusive national identity. The argument I offer in what follows is therefore firmly in the "constructivist" tradition of nationalism. Constructivists reject the idea that there is something inherent or essential to national groups, and instead takes seriously the role that individuals and institutions can play in *constructing* the boundaries of the group and the identity that its members share (Goode and Stroup 2015; Wallace Goodman 2019, 381). Recognizing that individuals, and the institutions they are a part of, can shift the content of a national identity and therefore the boundaries of the relevant group in an inclusive direction is key to what I will articulate next.

The challenge, it is worth noting, is that in order for "national identity" to be included among the available levers, it must be that those at the top levels of government wish it to be so. The suggestion here is *not* that central governments are the exclusive source of a nation's identity; on the contrary, the sources of this content are varied, as indicated above. The suggestion is that central governments are in a unique space to shape their states' national identity in various ways, in specific directions, if they aim to do so. If the objective is to pave the way for generalized trust towards newcomers and among citizens and newcomers, then they have at least four major ways to do so: via public pronouncements and declarations; via the shaping of naturalization requirements; via educational curricula; and via the construction/reconstruction of national symbols, including museums, the selection of whose image is honored on coins and bills and so on. Each of these will be considered in turn.

Public pronouncements and declarations from high-ranking government actors can have a profound impact on how citizens understand the content of their national identity. It is not that such actors have a monopoly on what defines a people, but with their perceived authority, they can use the microphones they are offered to make claims about how a people thinks of itself, or how it will react. Think of statements around whether a population will rise up against additional constraints on their freedom imposed as part of a collective effort to slow the spread of viruses, or whether they should act solidaristically in support of their most vulnerable members. Or think of conventions like concluding the American State of the Union Address with "May God bless America," which conveys to Americans that they are a faithful people in the Christian tradition. National authorities speak on behalf of a people and about them, in public spaces, and the ways in which they do so can shape the ways in which individual members think of themselves and what it means to be a part of (or excluded from) the relevant community. In the case at hand, high-ranking government officials can use this space to explain how a citizenry can be expected to welcome migrants, or that its citizenry recognizes the contributions migrants make to its society and so on. No such statement will be perfectly true, but they can press a population into adopting the attitude that such statements describe. Such statements have the secondary effect of communicating to newcomers that it is expected that they will be welcomed as fellow members of a society, because they are understood to be valuable contributors to it. These statements contribute to the foundation of trust that can be built between citizens and immigrants.

A second space in which national identity shaping transpires is via naturalization requirements, that is, via the requirements that newcomers must fulfill in order to be recognized as full and equal members of a society. The development of the requirements is a project carried out by insiders, and asks them to confront what it means to be a part of their community, and to assess what requirements newcomers must meet. They can vary from extended residency, to competence in language, to the completion of citizenship tests, to the public taking of citizenship oaths. All of these requirements are developed from an understanding of how a nation-state understands itself; and they give cues to newcomers about whether they will be welcomed and on what terms. The requirements for example signal whether newcomers can enter as they are, with their religious and cultural commitments, which can be rendered compatible with the requirements they are asked to undertake as members, or whether they will be asked to shed them as a condition of full membership. In so doing, they tell newcomers whether trust is being extended to them pre-emptively, or whether they will have to prove themselves as worthy of trust.

Educational curricula are a third space in which national identity can be shaped. Students are exposed over the course of their education to a version of a state's history, in courses and via history books. Their sense of their state is additionally shaped by the literature they are asked to read and evaluate, and by the public celebrations they are asked to acknowledge as worthy of recognition. So, students are told a *story* about what their nation is and what its values are, as they travel through primary and secondary education. Notice, as well, that for newcomers who arrive with young children, schools operate as a major integrating institution: newly arrived students learn the same story as all other students about what a nation stands for. The impact of selecting curricular material that emphasizes diversity or homogeneity is profound: do students learn that fellow students hail from different cultures and traditions, or do they learn that there is one dominant culture and tradition? This sort of choice can influence whether schools can integrate well: students are taught over the course of their education *how* to welcome newcomers, in their classrooms, in collaborative projects, on the recess playgrounds and so on. Because an educational curriculum is determined by authorities operating at the state level, its material guides and shapes how newcomer students are welcomed and can support the development or undermining of trust between children of diverse backgrounds.

Finally, a nation-state often has the authority to shape the content and design of key markers, including museums, money, flags and so on. All of these markers are national identity markers – they are symbols of a state that are widely seen and used. So, the choices that are made with respect to what museums should display, or who should be honored on money, are choices that themselves can serve to underpin or undermine trust, again by signaling whether a state sees the diversity of contributions made by immigrant citizens as worthy of highlighting *as* symbols.

The capacity of a state to shape a national identity faces constraints, however, and these constraints may partially explain why some attempts to shape identities fail (where others are successful). One such arguably failed attempt transpired in the Canadian context, when the Conservative Government (2006–15) attempted to reformulate the material on which Canadian identity was founded, by emphasizing its military victories and its connection to the British Royal Family. But, it turned out, these markers were not so attractive to Canadians who largely remained committed to a more benign view of Canadians as peacekeepers and rejected the idea that they should be understood as in some way subservient to the United Kingdom (Lenard 2018). So, central authorities do not have absolute license to shape identities as they prefer; on the contrary, they will face significant constraints from those they represent. In the case at hand, moreover, the use of a national identity as a lever to generate and support trust among citizens and newcomers with diverse backgrounds, for many reasons including to sustain support for welfare state policies, is one that such leaders must themselves support and see value in promoting. As the waves of support for anti-immigration parties suggest, it cannot be assumed that national leaders are themselves persuaded of the importance of using their levers to protect and promote trust among citizens and newcomers.

CONCLUSION

This chapter has intended to offer two distinct contributions. First, the chapter has aimed at making sense of the vast scholarship that has been conducted examining whether increases in diversity dampen trust relations, and correspondingly, support for the welfare state. This assessment of current scholarship suggested that there is at least some evidence that increases in diversity dampen generalized trust, but that the connection is not a necessary one. It suggested, as a whole, that there are national contexts, and associated policy choices, that can support or hinder the development of trust relations of the kind that are key to supporting a public's commitment to redistributive welfare state policies.

Second, two particular levers have been identified by scholars as key to supporting trust among a citizenry as immigration increases: open and inclusive welfare state policies and a vast array of multicultural policies. Operating together, they signal that newcomers are *welcome* and that efforts are made to support their integration into a range of major political, economic and social institutions. The chapter added national identity shaping as a third available lever which, if done well, can join these other policies in supporting the development and sustaining of trust relations among diverse citizenries. As articulated in the final section of the chapter, attempts to shape national identity in the "right" direction are not unconstrained; on the contrary, they can face resistance from citizens who may not be captured by the content of the identity that is offered to them. Moreover, such attempts to shape national identity in ways that render trust among diverse citizens more likely must be understood as valuable by those who exercise the relevant levers, and that too is not guaranteed. Nevertheless, the chapter has suggested, it is worth treating the shaping of national identity as a real and important contributor to the options states have, if its goal is to support and nurture trust relations, in particular (but not only) to secure ongoing support for welfare state policies.

NOTE

1. I acknowledge the superb research assistance of Madeleine Berry in the preparation of this chapter.

REFERENCES

Abascal, Maria, and Delia Baldassarri. 2015. "Love Thy Neighbor? Ethnoracial Diversity and Trust Reexamined." *American Journal of Sociology* 121 (3): 722–82.

Alesina, Alberto, and Edward Glaeser. 2004. *Fighting Poverty in the US and Europe: A World of Difference.* Oxford: Oxford University Press.

Arneil, Barbara, and Fiona Macdonald. 2010. "Multiculturalism in the Social Sphere." In *The Ashgate Research Companion to Multiclturalism*, edited by Duncan Ivison, 95–117. Aldershot: Ashgate.

Banting, Keith. 2010. "Is There a Progressive's Dilemma in Canada? Immigration, Multiculturalism and the Welfare State: Presidential Address to the Canadian Political Science Association, Montreal, June 2, 2010." *Canadian Journal of Political Science/Revue Canadienne de Science Politique* 43 (4): 797–820.

Banting, Keith, Richard Johnston, Will Kymlicka and Stuart Soroka. 2011. "Are Diversity and Solidarity Incompatible? Canada in Comparative Context." *Inroads: The Canadian Journal of Opinion* 28: 36–48.

Besco, Randy, and Erin Tolley. 2019. "Does Everyone Cheer? The Politics of Immigration and Multiculturalism in Canada." In *Federalism and the Welfare State in a Multicultural World*, edited by Elizabeth Goodyear-Grant, Richard Johnston, Will Kymlicka and John Myles, 291–318. Montreal: McGill-Queen's University Press.

Borevi, Karin. 2017. "Diversity and Solidarity in Denmark and Sweden." In *The Political Sources of Solidarity in Diverse Societies*, edited by Keith Banting and Will Kymlicka, 364–88. Oxford: Oxford University Press.

Butz, Adam M., and Jason E. Kehrberg. 2015. "Social Distrust and Immigrant Access to Welfare Programs in the American States." *Politics and Policy* 43 (2): 256–86.

Eger, Maureen A., and Nate Breznau. 2017. "Immigration and the Welfare State: A Cross-Regional Analysis of European Welfare Attitudes." *International Journal of Comparative Sociology* 58 (5): 440–63.

Garand, James C., Ping Xu and Belinda C. Davis. 2017. "Immigration Attitudes and Support for the Welfare State in the American Mass Public." *American Journal of Political Science* 61 (1): 146–62.

Goode, J. Paul, and David R. Stroup. 2015. "Everyday Nationalism: Constructivism for the Masses." *Social Science Quarterly* 96 (3): 717–39.

Goodhart, David. 2004. "Too Diverse?" *Prospect Magazine*, February.

Gustavsson, Gina. 2019. "Svenskhet Är Mer Än En Invandringsfråga." *Kvartal*, September 15. https://kvartal.se/artiklar/svenskhet-ar-mer-an-en-invandringsfraga/.

Gustavsson, Gina, and Ludwig Stendahl. 2020. "National Identity: A Blessing or a Curse? The Divergent Links from National Attachment, Pride, and Chauvinism to Social and Political Trust." *European Political Science Review*. https://doi.org/10.1017/S1755773920000211.

Hawes, Daniel P., and Austin Michael McCrea. 2018. "Give Us Your Tired, Your Poor and We Might Buy Them Dinner: Social Capital, Immigration, and Welfare Generosity in the American States." *Political Research Quarterly* 71 (2): 347–60.

Hero, Rodney E., and Robert R. Preuhs. 2007. "Immigration and the Evolving American Welfare State: Examining Policies in the US States." *American Journal of Political Science* 51 (3): 498–517.

Hooghe, Marc, Tim Reeskens, Dietlind Stolle and Ann Trappers. 2009. "Ethnic Diversity and Generalized Trust in Europe: A Cross-National Multilevel Study." *Comparative Political Studies* 42 (2): 198–223.

Johnston, Richard, Matthew Wright, Stuart Soroka and Jack Citrin. 2017. "Diversity and Solidarity: New Evidence from Canada and the US." In *The Strains of Commitment: The Political Sources of Solidarity in Diverse Societies*, edited by Keith Banting and Will Kymlicka, 152–76. Oxford: Oxford University Press.

Kesler, Christel, and Irene Bloemraad. 2010. "Does Immigration Erode Social Capital? The Conditional Effects of Immigration-Generated Diversity on Trust, Membership, and Participation across 19 Countries, 1981–2000." *Canadian Journal of Political Science* 43 (2): 319–47.

Kymlicka, Will. 1996. *Multicultural Citizenship: A Liberal Theory of Minority Rights*. Oxford: Oxford University Press.

Lenard, Patti Tamara. 2010. "Rebuilding Trust in an Era of Widening Inequality." *Journal of Social Philosophy* 41 (1): 73–91.

Lenard, Patti Tamara. 2012. *Trust, Democracy and Multicultural Challenges*. University Park, PA: Penn State University Press.

Lenard, Patti Tamara. 2018. "Wither the Canadian Model? Evaluating the New Canadian Nationalism (2006–2015)." In *Diversity and Contestations over Nationalism in Europe and Canada*, edited by John Erik Fossum, Riva Kastoryano, and Birte Siim, 211–36. London: Palgrave Macmillan.

Lenard, Patti Tamara. 2019. "Inclusive Identities: The Foundation of Trust in Multicultural Communities." In *Liberal Nationalism and Its Critics*, edited by Gina Gustavsson and David Miller, 155–71. Oxford: Oxford University Press.

Lenard, Patti Tamara, and David Miller. 2018. "Trust and National Identity." In *Oxford Handbook of Social and Political Trust*, edited by Eric Uslaner, 57–74. Oxford: Oxford University Press.

Mata, Fernando, and Ravi Pendakur. 2014. "Social Capital, Diversity and Giving or Receiving Help among Neighbours." *Social Indicators Research* 118 (1): 329–47.

Mau, Steffen, and Christoph Burkhardt. 2009. "Migration and Welfare State Solidarity in Western Europe." *Journal of European Social Policy* 19 (3): 213–29.

Miller, David. 2005. "Immigration: The Case for Limits." In *Contemporary Debates in Applied Ethics*, edited by Andrew Cohen and Christopher Wellman, 193–207. Malden, MA: Blackwell.

Miller, David, and Sundas Ali. 2014. "Testing the National Identity Argument." *European Political Science Review* 6 (2): 237–59.

Oorschot, Wim van. 2008. "Solidarity towards Immigrants in European Welfare States." *International Journal of Social Welfare* 17 (1): 3–14.

Putnam, Robert D. 2007. "*E Pluribus Unum*: Diversity and Community in the Twenty-First Century: The 2006 Johan Skytte Prize Lecture." *Scandinavian Political Studies* 30 (2): 137–74.

Reeskens, Tim, and W.J.H. Oorschot. 2017. "Conceptions of Citizenship and Tolerance towards Immigrants." In *The Strains of Commitment: The Political Sources of Solidarity in Diverse Societies*, 178–98. Oxford: Oxford University Press.

Scheffler, Samuel. 2007. "Immigration and the Significance of Culture." *Philosophy and Public Affairs* 35 (2): 93–125.

Schmid, Katharina, Ananthi Al Ramiah and Miles Hewstone. 2014. "Neighborhood Ethnic Diversity and Trust: The Role of Intergroup Contact and Perceived Threat." *Psychological Science* 25 (3): 665–74.

Uslaner, Eric. 2004. "Divided Citizens: How Inequality Undermines Trust in America." *Demos: A Network for Ideas and Action*. www.demos-org.

Uslaner, Eric. 2010. "Segregation, Mistrust and Minorities." *Ethnicities* 10 (4): 415–34.

Uunk, W.G.J., and W.J.H. Oorschot. 2007. "Multi-Level Determinants of the Public's Informal Solidarity towards Immigrants in European Welfare States." In *Social Justice, Legitimacy and the Welfare State*, edited by S. Mau and B. Veghte, 217–38. Aldershot: Ashgate.

Vertovec, Steven, and Susanne Wessendorf, eds. 2010. *The Multicultural Backlash: European Discourses, Policies, Practices*. London: Routledge.

Wallace Goodman, Sarah. 2019. "Liberal Democracy, National Identity Boundaries, and Populist Entry Points." *Critical Review* 31 (3–4): 377–88.

Zhu, Ling, and Ping Xu. 2015. "The Politics of Welfare Exclusion: Immigration and Disparity in Medicaid Coverage." *Policy Studies Journal* 43 (4): 456–83.

22. Critically different or similarly critical? The roots of welfare state criticism among ethnic minority and majority citizens in Belgium
Arno Van Hootegem, Koen Abts, and Bart Meuleman

INTRODUCTION

The question how societies are able to organize solidarity between individuals and groups is one of the core themes that has led to the formation of the social sciences as a separate discipline. From the classics, we know that rational self-interests, shared moral codes and a sense of group belonging play a crucial role in the willingness to build and sustain solidarity relationships. Increasing migration movements challenge these foundations of solidarity. According to the notion of the "New Liberal Dilemma," for instance, there is an irreconcilable trade-off between multiculturalism and strong levels of trust, social cohesion, solidarity and support for the welfare state (Kumlin and Rothstein 2010; Reeskens and van Oorschot 2012). Increased ethnic diversity rooted in migration introduces a new social question: How is diversity transforming the capacity of contemporary Western societies to organize solidarity (Banting and Kymlicka 2017; Crepaz 2008)?

In order to shed light on this all-encompassing question, this chapter necessarily selects a particular vantage point. First, we provide insight into citizens' beliefs and opinions regarding redistributive solidarity by analysing popular support for institutional arrangements that redistribute towards vulnerable target populations (as opposed to civic and democratic solidarity; cf. Banting and Kymlicka 2017, 4). Yet, rather than analysing generic attitudinal dimensions (such as support for government intervention), we focus on moral, economic and social criticisms of the welfare state (Ervasti 2012; van Oorschot 2010; van Oorschot et al. 2012). This approach shifts the focal point from opinions on how redistribution *should* be to evaluations on how the welfare state actually *is* performing. The reason is that critical views on welfare performance are at the very heart of contemporary debates on institutional fairness. Citizens agree to a large extent on the range, degree and goals of the welfare state (Roller 1995; Roosma et al. 2013; Sihvo and Uusitalo 1995; Svallfors 2012), but evaluations of actual welfare state performance are more contentious and more strongly divided according to social and ideological characteristics (Achterberg et al. 2011; van Oorschot and Meuleman 2012). While we do not investigate institutional arrangements, citizens' evaluations of institutional fairness play a key role in the obstruction or facilitation of solidarity (Kumlin and Rothstein 2010) and are an important aspect of bridging social capital (Habibov et al. 2018).

Second, in order to study the role of increasing ethnic diversity, we compare the prevalence and roots of welfare criticism between majority and ethnic minority populations (Kremer 2016; Reeskens and van Oorschot 2015; Schmidt-Catran and Careja 2017). As social exclusion, anomie and distrust can erode solidarity when shared social experiences or norms are lacking (Laurence and Bentley 2016; van der Meer and Tolsma 2014), examining attitudinal differences across ethnic groups helps to understand solidarity in multicultural societies. Moreover, as outgroups are evaluated on the basis of their congruency with ingroup norms and similar belief systems are perceived as an important prerequisite for the development of trust and cooperation, comparing these attitudes may provide additional insight into the formation of social solidarity in contemporary Western societies (Delhey and Newton 2005; Laurence and Bentley 2016). Rather than lumping together individuals with very diverse migration backgrounds, we focus on ethnic communities that already have a longer presence in the "host country" – i.e., Belgians of Turkish and Moroccan descent (for a similar approach, see Galle et al. 2019; Lubbers et al. 2018; Renema et al. 2020). Because of their dual position, these "established outsiders" (Elias and Scotson 1965) are particularly relevant to understand the nexus between diversity and solidarity. These minority members are often second- or third-generation migrants and many of them have the legal status of national citizen, which makes them formal members of the circle of national solidarity that are entitled to social protection. Yet at the same time, they often still remain outsiders compared to native-born citizens. Although being national citizens in many ways well integrated into European life, these ethnic minorities often occupy disadvantaged socio-economic positions, are more likely to rely on resources of the welfare state (Corluy and Verbist 2010; Sainsbury 2012) and have quite distinct experiences in terms of relative deprivation, discrimination and exclusion (Alanya et al. 2017; Kalmijn and Kraaykamp 2018; Messing and Ságvári 2020).

Comparing ethnic minority groups – with a distinct socio-economic profile, social experiences and cultural outlook – to majority citizens allows us to uncover how migration-related diversity transforms the sources of redistributive solidarity. Concretely, this chapter sets out to answer the following research questions: (1) are majority and minority group members comparable in terms of economic, moral and social criticisms of the welfare state? and (2) do the strands of welfare criticism have similar roots among majority and minority group members? To answer these research questions, we investigate the role of social-structural variables, resentful experiences and ideological preferences. Empirically, we apply multigroup structural equation modelling (SEM) to data of the Belgian National Election Study 2014 (BNES) and the Belgian Ethnic Minorities Election Study 2014 (BEMES; conducted among members of the Turkish and Moroccan community in Belgium).

THREE STRANDS OF WELFARE CRITICISM: EVALUATIONS OF ECONOMIC, MORAL AND SOCIAL CONSEQUENCES

In times of increasing welfare restructuring, scepticism about the negative effects of welfare distribution has not only been the subject of political debate, but has also resonated among the general public (Ervasti 1998). Broadly speaking, critical public opinions about the welfare state tend to crystallize in three different forms, namely economic, moral and social criticism (McCluskey 2003; Murray 1984; van Oorschot 2010; van Oorschot et al. 2012). First, the economic line of welfare criticism portrays the welfare state as too costly and bureaucratic. This type of reasoning sees the welfare state as a threat to the competitive position of companies, because it increases the cost of labour considerably (Ervasti 1998; Lindbeck 1995). Second, from a moral perspective the social security system is blamed for creating a dependency culture and undermining the work ethic by providing overly generous benefits (Likki and Staerklé 2015; Murray 1984). An allegedly oversized welfare state is believed to disincentivize taking responsibility for one's own income by misbalancing rights and responsibilities (Dwyer 2000; Ervasti 1998, 289). Third, the social strand of welfare criticism voices frustration that the welfare state is unable to live up to the promise of fair outcomes and justly targeted redistribution. According to this argument, the welfare state has failed in abolishing inequalities and tackling social problems.

These economic, moral and social strands of criticism are at the very heart of public debates on welfare reform and institutional fairness. Opinions that welfare systems have negative economic and moral side effects, and are unable to fulfil their social promise, constitute core elements in popular evaluations of welfare state legitimacy (Roosma et al. 2013; van Oorschot and Meuleman 2012) and are an integral part of welfare populism (De Koster et al. 2013; Van Hootegem et al. 2021).

Various empirical studies have evidenced that the three forms of welfare criticism resonate among substantial shares of European populations (Bryson 1997; Ervasti 2012; Gidengil et al. 2003; Sihvo and Uusitalo 1995; van Oorschot 2010) and are quite stable over time (Meuleman and Delespaul 2020). However, we know next to nothing about welfare-critical views among ethnic minority group members in Western societies. An exception is the study of van Oorschot (2010), which demonstrates that Dutch citizens who have at least one parent born in another country express similar levels of economic and social criticism, but voice more moral criticism than those without a migration background. Furthermore, Blomberg et al. (2012) conclude that, compared to other high-risk groups, immigrants in Europe are generally less critical about the social performance of the welfare state. These scattered findings suggest that ethnic minority group members might differ in their welfare views relative to the majority population. Long-term-residing ethnic minorities often acquire a status of legal citizenship and strongly identify with their host country, but simultaneously face persisting exclusion and discrimination. As a result, they are both in and out of the national circle of solidarity. This peculiar position as "established outsiders" might inspire their views on the welfare state and its institutional performance. Insight in such differences can enhance our understanding of how the legitimacy of redistributive arrangements transforms when societies become increasingly multicultural. Furthermore, it allows us to answer whether minority and majority group members hold similar social norms that are grounded on shared social experiences, which are key in establishing trust, cohesion and solidarity across ethnic communities (Delhey and Newton 2005; Laurence and Bentley 2016; van der Meer and Tolsma 2014). Before turning to empirical analyses, we start with a theoretical reflection on the origins of welfare criticism among minority and majority group members.

THE ROOTS OF WELFARE CRITICISM AMONG MAJORITY AND ETHNIC MINORITY GROUP MEMBERS

Deprived Social Positions: Self-Interest or Resentful Experiences?

In the welfare attitudes literature, the link between socio-economic positions and policy preferences is often theorized from the perspective of self-interest theory. According to this rational choice-based perspective, individuals' predispositions towards welfare and redistribution stem from cost–benefit calculations trying to maximize utility: if persons have a rational interest in social protection, they will develop a positive attitude towards it (Kangas 1997; Svallfors 2004). Self-interest mechanisms imply that social groups that benefit from the welfare state – for instance persons with a lower education degree or income, occupational classes with high unemployment risk and welfare beneficiaries – will be less critical of its performance. However, empirical research overwhelmingly contradicts these self-interest-based predictions. Individuals occupying lower socio-economic positions are – paradoxically enough – the ones voicing the strongest economic, moral and social criticism on the welfare state (Ervasti 2012; Van Hootegem et al. 2021; van Oorschot 2010; van Oorschot et al. 2012).

An alternative theoretical account links welfare state criticism not to individual interests, but to social experiences of resentment (Abts and Kochuyt 2013; Achterberg et al. 2011; De Koster et al. 2013; Derks 2006). This strand of research starts from the observation that processes of modernization and globalization have created tensions between the so-called "winners" and "losers," of which the latter feel structurally disadvantaged, distrustful and insecure (Betz 1994; Kriesi et al. 2006). Resentful experiences gain meaning in a discourse that blames the welfare state for breaking the social contract by granting resources to undeserving and unproductive groups (such as the elite and welfare scroungers), while disregarding the well-being of hard-working citizens (Abts and Achterberg 2021; De Koster et al. 2013; Derks 2006). Three dimensions of resentment are of particular interest in unravelling how welfare state criticism takes shape: group relative deprivation, economic insecurity and social distrust. First, group relative deprivation encompasses the feeling that one's group is unfairly disadvantaged in comparison to other groups (Smith et al. 2012). When the (welfare) state is held accountable for these perceived injustices, relative group deprivation can spur economic, moral and social welfare criticism. Second, economic insecurity refers to the fear of losing established living standards and the position within the hierarchy of economic prestige (Castel 2003). Feelings of economic insecurity can become consolidated in an authoritarian-populist discourse that emphasizes strong conformity to group norms and voices criticism on the arrangements of the welfare state (Inglehart and Norris 2017; Mughan et al. 2003; Rehm et al. 2012; Wroe 2016). Third, social distrust – that is, the general belief that others have bad intentions and are guided by self-interest (Baier 1994; Govier 1997) – is embedded in a more general cult of resentment that portrays institutions as tolerating abuse and social inequality (Daenekindt et al. 2018; Roosma et al. 2014). Summarizing, the framework of resentment argues that a number of resentful experiences lead the lower socio-economic classes to be more critical of the welfare state (Abts and Kochuyt 2013; Van Hootegem et al. 2021).

What do the self-interest and resentment mechanisms imply for the welfare criticism among ethnic minorities in particular? Ethnic minority groups are often confronted with a vulnerable socio-economic status and face a higher risk of being dependent on social welfare (Boeri et al. 2002; Heath et al. 2008). Because of their position as established outsiders, minority group members have, on average, a stronger rational interest in generous welfare schemes compared to the majority population. According to self-interest theory, minorities could therefore be expected to voice less criticism on the welfare state. Of course, minority groups harbour substantial variation in socio-economic positions as well. Previous research has shown that social-structural characteristics that are linked to self-interest (such as income, education or occupational class) have similar effects on welfare attitudes among minority and majority groups (Lubbers et al. 2018; Reeskens and van Oorschot 2015).

The resentful experiences of minority group members have a clearly distinct character. Feelings of discrimination, relative deprivation, economic insecurity and social distrust are strongly prevalent among minorities and can result in feelings of anger, fear and dissatisfaction (Grant 2008; Klandermans et al. 2008). However, these feelings of resentment are less pitted against others that are considered undeserving of welfare support (Baysu and Swyngedouw 2020). After all, in the social imagination of many majority group members, it is precisely minorities who figure as undeserving Others, because of a lack of identification and reciprocity (van Oorschot 2000). This distinct nature of resentment among minorities could have different consequences. On the one hand, the moralizing line of criticism – of which minorities are often a direct target themselves – is less likely to resonate among ethnic minority members. On the other hand, their feelings of resentment might fuel strong economic and social forms of welfare criticism. From a resentment-driven, anti-institutionalist perspective, ethnic minority members may hold the welfare state accountable for being wasteful, not providing security and insufficiently improving living conditions of the established outsiders. Perceptions of being discriminated against (which tie in closely with resentment) indeed shape minorities' welfare preferences. When they feel treated unfairly by the government or social system (Galle et al. 2019; van Dijk et al. 2010), this can spill over into hostile sentiments towards the political domain generally and the welfare state specifically. Grievances and breaches in norms of distributive justice have indeed been shown to be a pre-eminent basis of political protest and scepticism towards the welfare state among minorities (Fersch and Breidahl 2018; van Stekelenburg 2013). Moreover, as ethnic minorities generally experience stronger discrimination and exclusion (Alanya et al. 2017; Messing and Ságvári 2020), we expect resentment to have a stronger influence on welfare state criticism among this group.

Ideological Dispositions: Economic and Cultural Preferences

Besides being driven by structural positions and social experiences, citizens' preferences regarding welfare and redistribution are embedded in a set of broader values and norms (Feldman and Zaller 1992; Jaeger 2008). The three forms of welfare criticism are connected to particular ideological preferences, as demonstrated by empirical research (Van Hootegem et al. 2021; van Oorschot 2010; van Oorschot et al. 2012). Generally, criticism is more outspoken among individuals who identify as politically right-wing (Sihvo and Uusitalo 1995). However, going beyond catch-all left–right divides that have often been used, it is relevant to distinguish cultural from economic ideological leanings (van Oorschot et al. 2012). While the economic dimension is built upon the opposition between egalitarianism and laissez-faire, the cultural dimension is grounded in the cleavage between authoritarianism and libertarianism (Achterberg and Houtman 2009). A negative relationship is expected between egalitarianism and the three forms of criticism, as welfare state criticism is embedded in an anti-egalitarian and neoliberal political discourse that blames the welfare state for disregarding market efficiency (Ervasti 1998; McCluskey 2003). Authoritarianism, in contrast, operationalizes the cultural ideological dimension and emphasizes obedience to authorities and leaders, intolerance towards non-conforming individuals and conventionalism in conformity to norms (Stellmacher and Petzel 2005). An authoritarian disposition is closely connected to a neoconservative ideological paradigm that criticizes the welfare state for encouraging passivity and deviant behaviour by providing overly generous state support instead of sanctioning non-conforming individuals (Likki and Staerklé 2015; Murray 1984). As a result, we anticipate a positive relationship between authoritarian dispositions and welfare criticism – especially the moral strand.

Because of their different socio-economic positions and cultural background, ethnic minority groups can have a distinct profile with respect to the economic and cultural dimension of ideology. Available research shows that ethnic minorities generally score similarly or higher on economic progressiveness, while simultaneously being more culturally conservative (Dancygier 2017). Schmidt-Catran and Careja (2017), as well as Dancygier and Saunders (2006), demonstrate that migrants support the reduction of income differentials to a similar extent as the native population. Especially when minorities are or become national citizens, their views on welfare distribution start to converge with the attitudes of the majority population (Kolbe and Crepaz 2016). Culturally, however, ethnic minorities are more conservative on topics like marriage, sexuality and gender equality (Diehl et al. 2009; Kalmijn and Kraaykamp 2018). In addition, research from the United States demonstrated that ethnic minorities generally report higher levels of authoritarianism than native citizens (Henry 2011). Similarly, European scholars evidenced that individuals with a migration background adhere more strongly to conservative values, such as traditionalism and conformism (Röder and Mühlau 2012). In terms of the levels of welfare state criticism, it is unclear whether the ideological position of minorities would lead them to foster analogous or more negative evaluations of welfare performance. On the one hand, the relatively similar support for redistribution predicts comparable levels of welfare state criticism (Chauvet et al. 2016; Dancygier and Saunders 2006; Schmidt-Catran and Careja 2017). On the other hand, the more culturally conservative opinions among minorities might lead to higher levels of welfare state criticism (Diehl et al. 2009; Kalmijn and Kraaykamp 2018).

How these ideological profiles feed into welfare criticism among minorities is largely unknown. A few studies indicate that left–right placement shapes the redistribution preferences of ethnic minorities (Galle et al. 2019; Lubbers et al. 2018) and even appears to operate similarly as for the majority (Reeskens and van Oorschot 2015). With regard to the cultural and economic dimensions, it seems most plausible that ideological positions generally have a weaker impact among minorities. As they show larger value plurality, are socialized simultaneously in different belief systems and use the institutions in their country of origin as a frame of reference (Pels and De Haan 2007; Röder and Mühlau 2012), minorities might less strongly internalize the typical right-wing, conservative and neoliberal paradigms criticizing European welfare states. Moreover, the combination of progressive economic ideas with more culturally conservative attitudinal patterns might indicate lower levels of "ideological constraint" or "value coherence" among ethnic minorities (Achterberg and Houtman 2009). As minorities' perceptions of the consequences of the welfare state might thus be less embedded in a single and delineated set of normative beliefs, ideological dispositions are expected to have a larger influence for native citizens than for ethnic minorities.

DATA AND METHOD

Dataset

We analyse data from BEMES and BNES (Abts et al. 2015; Swyngedouw et al. 2015). BEMES specifically targets Belgian voters of Turkish and Moroccan descent, randomly selected from the population registers of Antwerp and Liège (sample size: 878; response rate: 34.9 per cent). BNES is a survey among a probability-based sample of the general population of Belgian citizens entitled to vote in the federal election of 2014 (sample size: 1901; response rate: 47.5 per cent). Because we focus on the comparison between Turkish and Moroccan minorities and the majority population, we omit respondents with a migration background from the BNES database (i.e., respondents whose mother or father were not Belgian citizens at birth), resulting in a final sample size of 1593 for BNES. To adjust for non-response bias, weights are applied according to age, gender, city of residence and ethnic background for BEMES, and according to age, gender and education for BNES. Both surveys were collected by means of Computer Assisted Personal Interviewing and about two-thirds of both questionnaires were fully harmonized (e.g., social-structural variables, ideological indicators, experiences of resentment, a series of welfare attitudes and various political opinions). All included indicators used in this analysis are identical in both surveys.

Indicators

Dependent variables
We measure economic, moral and social criticism on the welfare state by means of three five-point Likert scale items (disagree strongly–agree strongly) each. The three items on economic criticism probe whether respondents think that the welfare state costs too much relative to what it yields, harms the economy and should leave more tasks to the free market. Moral criticism is measured by three items that ask whether the welfare state makes people irresponsible and lazy, is too much of a hammock that people become dependent on and causes people to no longer take care of themselves. Social criticism is operationalized through three reverse-worded items asking whether the welfare state is the best system to guarantee the welfare of all, makes sure that widespread poverty is prevented and guarantees that everyone has access to good health care (see Table 22.1 for question wording and descriptive statistics).

Independent variables
A first set of independent variables concerns three dimensions of resentment, namely group relative deprivation, social distrust and economic insecurity. Group relative deprivation is measured by three items asking whether respondents feel that people like them always to have to wait longer to get something from the government, are systematically disadvantaged and are always the first victims of an economic crisis. Two items for social distrust ask to what extent respondents agree that it is hard to know who to trust and that one cannot be too careful when dealing with other people. Economic insecurity is operationalized by three items probing whether individuals feel that their financial worries will increase in the following years, that their social status will be hard to maintain and that

Table 22.1 Question wordings, factor loadings and percentages of respondents agreeing for the items of welfare criticism

	Ethnic minority				Majority			
	Eco.	Moral	Social	% agree	Eco.	Moral	Social	% agree
The costs of the welfare state are too high compared to its benefits	0.54			46.0	0.60			37.5
The responsibilities of the welfare state should be left to the free market	0.48			14.4	0.53			10.1
The welfare state is detrimental to businesses and places strain on the economy	0.64			30.4	0.68			27.6
The welfare state makes people lazy and irresponsible		0.57		29.6		0.69		31.3
The welfare state is a social hammock that makes people overly dependent		0.65		39.2		0.76		40.3
The welfare state makes people less willing to look after themselves		0.62		24.8		0.72		26.3
Our welfare state is the best system to guarantee the well-being of everyone (reversed)			0.55	10.8			0.59	10.5
The welfare state prevents widespread poverty and misery (reversed)			0.62	14.7			0.63	14.4
The welfare state guarantees equal access to good health care for everyone (reversed)			0.61	5.9			0.60	7.4
Correlation moral criticism	0.77	1			0.83	1		
Correlation social criticism	0.09	−0.08	1		0.34	0.17	1	
Latent means	0.03	−0.14*	−0.14*		0	0	0	

Note: * significant difference in latent means.

their children will have more economic difficulties. Multigroup Confirmatory Factor Analysis (CFA) confirms the general validity of the scales as well as their comparability between the majority and minority citizens. A scalar equivalence model shows good fit with the data (Chi-square = 225.235; df = 47; RMSEA = 0.055; CFI = 0.951; TLI = 0.942; SRMR = 0.074) and indicates that all factor loadings are sufficiently strong (see Tables 22A.1 and 22A.2).

Second, to compare the role of ideology, we study the impact of left–right placement, authoritarianism and egalitarianism. Left–right placement is measured by a single item on an 11-point scale (0 = left; 10 = right). Authoritarianism is operationalized by three items asking whether respondents agree that most problems would be solved if society gets rid of immoral people, that obedience and respect for authority are important virtues and that laws should become stricter. The instrument for egalitarianism consists of three items probing whether class differences should become smaller, income differences should remain the same and the government should intervene to limit inequality. Also here, a multigroup CFA points out that a scalar equivalence model fits the data well (Chi-square = 82.963; df = 26; RMSEA = 0.042; CFI = 0.945; TLI = 0.936; SRMR = 0.045) and that all items load strongly on their respective factors (see Tables 22A.1 and 22A.3).

Third, we include educational attainment, occupational class and welfare dependency as social-structural characteristics. Educational degree is divided into lower secondary education or less, higher secondary education and tertiary education. Occupational status consists of five classes based on the EGP-scheme: service class, white-collar workers, blue-collar workers, self-employed and economically inactive (including students) (Ganzeboom and Treiman 1996). Welfare dependency is measured by asking respondents whether they or a household member received a welfare benefit, such as income support, unemployment benefit or a work disability allowance, in the last two years. As controls, we also include age, gender and region (Dutch-speaking versus French-speaking). Table 22A.4 displays descriptive statistics for these characteristics in the minority and the majority sample, which shows that on average the majority sample is older, more highly educated and less welfare dependent than the Turkish and Moroccan minority sample.

Statistical Modelling

To compare the impact of structural characteristics, resentful experiences and ideological preferences on welfare criticism across minority and majority groups, we apply stepwise multigroup SEM. After assessing the dimensional structure of welfare criticism by means of CFA, a first SEM estimates the impact of social-structural characteristics per group. The second adds the indicators of resentment and ideology. All analyses are conducted in Mplus version 8.4 (Muthén and Muthén 2017). The parameter estimates are not standardized, as only unstandardized coefficients are comparable across groups when variances are not restricted to be equal.

RESULTS

The Dimensionality and Level of Welfare Criticism among Majority and Minority Citizens

As a first step, we test whether the three forms of welfare criticism can be distinguished as separate and comparable dimensions in the minority and majority samples. In particular, we assess measurement invariance of the three scales by using multigroup CFA (Davidov et al. 2014). A three-factor model implying scalar invariance (i.e., equal item intercepts and factor loadings across groups) fits the data adequately (Chi-square = 144.863; df = 60; RMSEA = 0.034; CFI =0.962; TLI = 0.954; SRMR = 0.043). In both groups, all items load sufficiently strong on the dimensions they are purported to measure (see Table 22.1). Not only can the three forms of welfare criticism be distinguished in the attitudinal structure of minority and majority members, the items also function similarly in both groups, which guarantees full score comparability for the latent variables (which is an important prerequisite for making valid comparisons).

Looking at the percentages of respondents agreeing with each of the items (see Table 22.1), we see that in both groups economic and moral forms of criticism are more frequently expressed than social criticism. At the item level, the most outspoken differences are found for economic criticism. Among the minority group, agreement with the items on economic criticism is a couple of percentage points higher than in the majority group. The largest difference is found for the item stating that the costs of the welfare state are too high, with 46 per cent of the minority respondents agreeing versus 38 per cent of the majority respondents. With respect to the items on social and moral criticism, the percentage agreeing is either similar across groups or slightly lower among minorities. However, comparisons of latent variable means (taking the whole answer distribution into account), reveal that minorities score significantly lower on moral and social criticism, while no significant differences exist between groups with respect to economic criticism. Rather than one group being more or less critical across the board, we observe an intricate pattern of dimension-specific differences. It is also noteworthy that the three forms of criticism are more strongly correlated among the majority.

When comparing means and percentages across groups one should not forget that the minority and majority samples differ substantially in their social-structural composition (see Table 22A.4 for more details). This makes it difficult to attribute the observed differences to a particular factor or cause. One possible explanation could be that the lower moral and social criticism of ethnic minorities reveals self-interest mechanisms, while lending little support to the ideas that experiences of discrimination or a culturally more conservative outlook of minorities lead to more negative attitudes towards welfare performance (Alanya et al. 2017; Kalmijn and Kraaykamp 2018). That minorities do not score lower on economic criticism might be in part related to the increased likelihood of immigrants to engage in entrepreneurial activities (Levie 2007), which fosters concerns for the competitive positions of businesses. Moreover, as individuals with a migration background use their country of origin as a frame of reference in evaluating institutions (Röder and Mühlau 2012), they might perceive taxes and costs of the Belgian welfare state to be relatively large. However, to gain more insight into the different mechanisms shaping criticism among both groups, we need more detailed explanatory models that take into account structural positions, resentful experiences and ideological preferences.

Explanatory Models: Comparing the Role of the Social Structure, Resentment and Ideology

Table 22.2 displays the results of stepwise multigroup SEMs explaining the three strands of welfare criticism among minority and majority respondents. In a first step, the effects of social-structural characteristics are estimated. A second model additionally includes indicators of resentment and the ideological dimensions.

Social-structural variables
The coefficients of the social-structural variables (see Model 1 in Table 22.2) reveal interesting similarities and differences between the minority and majority group. In both groups alike, benefit recipients express less moral criticism and the higher educated voice less economic criticism. While the lower levels of moral criticism among those on benefit could be interpreted in terms of self-interest theory, the more positive economic

Table 22.2 *Unstandardized effects of the social structure, ideology and resentment on welfare criticism for the ethnic minority and majority group*

	Model 1 minorities (N = 851)			Model 2 minorities (N = 878)		
	Eco.	Moral	Social	Eco.	Moral	Social
Gender						
Woman (ref.)						
Man	−0.064	−0.008	0.128*	−0.018	0.002	0.106
Age	0.001	0.000	−0.011***	0.003	0.000	−0.010***
Education						
Lower (secondary)	0.012	0.031	0.034	−0.049	−0.023	0.071
Higher secondary (ref.)						
Tertiary	−0.227**	−0.109	−0.137*	−0.220**	−0.078	−0.141*
Occupation						
Blue collar (ref.)						
Service class	−0.149	−0.101	0.081	0.008	−0.047	0.111
White collar	−0.283**	−0.250*	−0.037	−0.120	−0.193*	−0.003
Self-employed	0.209	0.230	0.150	0.146	0.127	0.131
Inactive	−0.103	0.003	−0.111	0.020	0.047	−0.092
Welfare dependency						
No benefit (ref.)						
Benefit	−0.073	−0.183**	0.069	−0.055	−0.137*	0.057
Region						
French-speaking (ref.)						
Dutch-speaking	−0.015	−0.193**	−0.120	−0.046	−0.280***	−0.076
Relative deprivation				0.223***	0.088	0.129*
Economic insecurity				0.026	−0.048	0.030
Social distrust				0.010	0.031	−0.025
Authoritarianism				0.378*	0.298*	−0.187
Egalitarianism				−0.112	−0.221*	−0.166*
Left–right placement				0.018	0.050***	0.011
R^2	0.081	0.068	0.128	0.326	0.237	0.195
ΔR^2	0.081	0.068	0.128	0.245	0.169	0.067

	Model 1 majority (N = 1582)			Model 2 majority (N = 1593)		
	Eco.	Moral	Social	Eco.	Moral	Social
Gender						
Woman (ref.)						
Man	−0.002	0.084*	−0.012	0.005	0.108**	−0.003
Age	0.001	0.002	−0.005***	−0.001	−0.001	−0.005***
Education						
Lower (secondary)	0.071	0.020	0.031	0.012	−0.021	−0.020

Table 22.2 (continued)

	Model 1 majority (N = 1582)			Model 2 majority (N = 1593)		
	Eco.	Moral	Social	Eco.	Moral	Social
Higher secondary (ref.)						
Tertiary	–0.125**	–0.124**	–0.045	0.064	0.115*	0.026
Occupation						
Blue collar (ref.)						
Service class	–0.134*	–0.027	–0.014	–0.054	0.108	0.010
White collar	–0.041	–0.018	0.056	0.014	0.069	0.078
Self-employed	0.189**	0.171*	0.056	0.074	0.062	0.017
Inactive	0.023	0.008	–0.092	0.101	0.137	–0.050
Welfare dependency						
No benefit (ref.)						
Benefit	–0.047	–0.119*	0.017	0.001	–0.028	–0.003
Region						
French-speaking (ref.)						
Dutch-speaking	–0.291***	–0.382***	–0.041	–0.229***	–0.287***	–0.007
Relative deprivation				0.216***	0.098*	0.181***
Economic insecurity				0.023	0.023	0.010
Social distrust				–0.017	–0.017	0.026
Authoritarianism				0.309***	0.600***	–0.074
Egalitarianism				–0.346***	–0.388***	–0.131**
Left–right placement				0.034***	0.021*	0.013
R^2	0.130	0.107	0.044	0.422	0.384	0.145
ΔR^2	0.130	0.107	0.044	0.292	0.277	0.101

Note: * $p \leq 0.05$; ** $p \leq 0.01$; *** $p \leq 0.001$; Fit model 1: Chi-square = 388.387; df = 183; RMSEA = 0.030; CFI = 0.932; TLI = 0.907; SRMR = 0.036; Fit model 2: Chi-square = 1638.142; df = 772; RMSEA = 0.030; CFI = 0.921; TLI = 0.897; SRMR = 0.039.

evaluations of the higher educated contradict this approach. Regarding occupational class, the effects are more group specific. Among the minorities, white-collar workers are substantially less economically and morally critical than blue-collar workers. In the majority group, blue- and white-collar employees demonstrate very similar levels of welfare criticism. Here, the service class takes a more distinct position with lower levels of economic criticism. In both groups, the highest levels of welfare criticism are found among the self-employed (although the effect is insignificant in the minority group, potentially due to the smaller sample size). The observed differences in the relationships with occupational class could be related to the different labour market situation of both groups, as even for similar jobs, minority and majority group members have profoundly unequal positions, access and mobility in the labour market (Vandezande et al. 2010).

Regarding the control variables, we find in both groups that Dutch-speaking respondents score lower on economic and moral criticism, while age has a negative impact on social criticism. The age gradient is larger among minorities, possibly reflecting a generational divide within the Turkish and Moroccan communities. This finding is in line with the study by Reeskens and van Oorschot (2015), which shows that first-generation immigrants are considerably more likely to support government involvement than their children. The impact of gender is different per group: while men score higher on moral criticism among the majority group, they have higher scores on social criticism among the minorities.

The explained variances also paint a slightly different picture with regard to the explanatory power of the social structure. The social-structural variables in Model 1 explain more variance of economic and moral criticism for the majority group (the R-squared equals 13 versus 8 per cent and 11 versus 7 per cent, respectively). Social criticism, on the contrary, is more strongly rooted in social positions among the minorities (13 versus 4 per cent explained variance). The reason is that we observe age-related and educational gradients among the minority group that are not present among the majority. However, despite some minor differences, we can conclude that these findings are in line with our expectation that the social positions of both groups play a rather modest and similar role in both samples.

Resentful experiences
Model 2 estimates the effects of three dimensions of resentment on the various forms of welfare criticism. A first noteworthy finding is that feelings of group relative deprivation stand out as a predictor of welfare criticism. Among the majority group, relative deprivation contributes significantly to all three forms of welfare criticism, but especially the effects on economic and social criticism are strong. In the minority sample we find a similar pattern, but the effects are a bit weaker and the effect on moral criticism is not significant. Thus, there is strong support for the hypothesis that relative deprivation contributes to critical views on welfare (Van Hootegem et al. 2021). However, unexpectedly, the effect of relative deprivation is not stronger among the minorities, although they report stronger experiences of exclusion and discrimination (Alanya et al. 2017; Messing and Ságvári 2020). A possible explanation can be sought in the specific configuration of intergroup positions in welfare debates. Among the majority, a sense of deprivation is projected onto various undeserving outgroups that "unrightfully" receive welfare support, including immigrants. Yet for the minority, deprivation is particularly perceived relative to the majority (Baysu and Swyngedouw 2020), and hence less straightforwardly captured in a welfare-critical discourse. Economic insecurity and social distrust, in contrast, are not related to welfare criticism in both groups. The absence of a relationship with economic insecurity can be sought in the fact that this concept reflects uncertainty about the personal economic status rather than in comparison to other groups (as group relative deprivation does).

Ideological preferences
Model 2 also includes authoritarianism, egalitarianism and left–right placement as predictors. The impact of these ideological dimensions differs in important ways between the two groups. First, although authoritarianism significantly increases economic and moral

criticism for both groups, the impact of authoritarianism on moral criticism is much more decisive in the majority sample (0.60 versus 0.30). This illustrates that this form of welfare criticism is among majority citizens very strongly embedded in a paradigm that criticizes the social security system for providing resources to non-conforming individuals (Likki and Staerklé 2015; Murray 1984; Staerklé et al. 2012). This pattern is less outspoken among minority members. Second, the relationship between criticism and egalitarian preferences is more outspoken among majority group members as well. In the majority group, egalitarianism strongly suppresses moral and economic criticism and has a smaller negative relationship with social criticism. In the minority group, a significant relationship with economic criticism is absent, and a weaker negative coefficient for moral criticism is found. The welfare criticism of majority members seems to be more strongly embedded in a neoliberal critique that blames the welfare state for pursuing equality at the cost of efficiency (Ervasti 1998; McCluskey 2003). Third, left–right placement also functions differently for both samples. Self-identification with the political right is only linked to moral criticism among ethnic minorities, but to both economic and moral criticism among the majority group. These results are in line with our expectation that the welfare state criticism of minority citizens is less strongly ideologically rooted than the negative views of majority group members.

The proportions of explained variance also reflect that certain forms of welfare criticism have a stronger ideological basis among majority members. In this group, the R-squared value of Model 2 equals 42.2 per cent for economic criticism and 38.4 per cent for the moral variant. Among the minorities, this is considerably lower at 32.6 and 23.7 per cent, respectively. Although roughly the same ideological preferences shape the welfare state in both groups, the criticism of the majority is more strongly patterned along right-wing, authoritarian and anti-egalitarian ideas.

The introduction of resentful experiences and ideological preferences in Model 2 brings about some changes in the regression coefficients of the social-structural variables. Most notably, among the majority population the negative effect of education disappears in the case of economic criticism and even becomes positive for moral criticism. When we control for their lower levels of resentment and more progressive worldview, precisely the higher educated express most moral criticism, which is in line with their self-interest. In addition, those who are dependent on welfare benefits do not report lower criticism for the majority and men do not score significantly higher on social criticism among minorities after controlling for the dimensions of resentment and ideology. Moreover, the relationships with occupational class disappear among the majority when controlling for resentment and ideology. This applies to a lesser extent for the minority members, where welfare criticism is less ideology-driven in the first place.

CONCLUSION AND DISCUSSION

This aim of this study was to provide insight into the connection between redistributive solidarity and ethnic diversity. By comparing different types of criticism on the welfare state among both established ethnic minorities and majority group members, we tried to determine whether these populations share welfare-related beliefs and experiences, which is considered to be relevant for establishing solidarity and cohesion across ethnic communities (Delhey and Newton 2005; Laurence and Bentley 2016; van der Meer and Tolsma 2014). Focusing on evaluations of institutional outcomes is particularly relevant, as these beliefs influence the willingness to help others and are an important component of bridging social trust (Habibov et al. 2018). Besides comparing levels of welfare state criticism, our study investigated whether the genesis of these criticisms was similar or critically different for both groups. Starting from the observation that ethnic minorities occupy an "established outsider" position, which combines legal citizenship status with persisting exclusion, this chapter set out to determine whether their distinct position also implies that different interests, ideas and experiences shape their criticism on redistributive institutions. While the social structure was anticipated to function similarly for both groups, experiences of resentment were expected to have a stronger influence among ethnic minorities, as they generally experience stronger discrimination and exclusion (Alanya et al. 2017; Messing and Ságvári 2020). Ideology, in contrast, was suggested to have a stronger impact among the majority, as minorities might be less strongly socialized into typical ideological discourses that criticize the welfare state.

Our results indicated, to begin with, that minorities score considerably lower on moral and social criticism, but simultaneously report similar levels of economic criticism. The more positive moral and social evaluations might be particularly related to the differential position that minorities occupy in the welfare domain, as their higher likelihood of becoming welfare dependent increases their material interests in redistribution (Boeri et al. 2002; Galle et al. 2019). Although the diverging interests of minority and majority citizens in welfare state distribution might in part explain the difference in levels of welfare state criticism, social positions are similarly related to welfare evaluations among both groups. Overall, in line with our expectations, the social structure has an equivalent yet modest influence among both groups, pointing towards the rather limited explanatory power of self-interest theory. In addition, while we expected the experiences of group relative deprivation, economic insecurity and social distrust would have a stronger influence among minorities, this turned out not to be the case. However, as expected, the ideological dimensions of egalitarianism, authoritarianism and left–right placement had a substantially stronger and more consistent impact among the majority group. Especially the relationships with egalitarianism and authoritarianism were much more outspoken, which reveals that majority members' criticisms on the welfare state are more clearly embedded in conservative and liberal paradigms that hold the welfare state accountable for disregarding market efficiency and stimulating deviance and passivity (Ervasti 1998; Likki and Staerklé 2015; McCluskey 2003; Staerklé et al. 2012).

The large degree of similarity between ethnic minorities and majority group members might in part be related to the composition of our sample, that contains only members of the Turkish and Moroccan community that have a Belgian nationality. As Kolbe and Crepaz (2016) demonstrate, individuals with a migration background that are or become national citizens generally hold more similar opinions to native citizens on welfare support and redistribution than minorities not yet naturalized. Not only do minorities who are legal citizens generally perceive a higher stake in the well-being of the country and participate to a larger extent in the political and economic domain, they also appear to more strongly identify with the majority group and to adopt similar norms (Kolbe and Crepaz 2016; Reeskens and van Oorschot 2015). The similar levels of economic criticism of ethnic minorities in our sample might for instance be related to their obligation to pay taxes, and equal interest in the fair and efficient allocation of scarce welfare resources. As a result, future research would benefit from replicating these findings among a more diverse group of minorities that also includes migrants who have not yet become naturalized citizens.

However, despite the finding that overall relatively similar positions, beliefs and experiences shape welfare state criticism among ethnic minorities and the majority, the strength of these mechanisms and the level of criticism differed somewhat across groups. The observed differences do not suggest that there is necessarily an unbridgeable divide between ethnic groups; yet they reflect the particular position of minorities as established outsiders, their distinct experiences with welfare state institutions and specific views on certain socio-economic and cultural issues (Baysu and Swyngedouw 2020; Galle et al. 2019).

REFERENCES

Abts, Koen, and Peter Achterberg. 2021. "The Roots and Electoral Consequences of Welfare Populism." In *Leading Social Policy Analysis from the Front: Essays in Honour of Wim van Oorschot*, eds. Tijs Laenen, Bart Meuleman, Adeline Otto, Femke Roosma and Wim Van Lancker, 301–18. Leuven: KU Leuven.

Abts, Koen, and Thierry Kochuyt. 2013. "De Vreemde Bedreiging van de Verzorgingsstaat." *Tijdschrift voor Sociologie* 34(3): 227–49.

Abts, Koen, Marc Swyngedouw, Bart Meuleman, Sharon Baute, Jolien Galle and Chris Gaasendam. 2015. *Belgian National Elections Study 2014: Codebook: Questions and Frequency Tables*. Leuven: ISPO-KU Leuven and CLEO-Université de Liège.

Achterberg, Peter, and Dick Houtman. 2009. "Ideologically Illogical? Why Do the Lower-Educated Dutch Display so Little Value Coherence?" *Social Forces* 87(3): 1649–70.

Achterberg, Peter, Dick Houtman and Anton Derks. 2011. "Two of a Kind? An Empirical Investigation of Anti-Welfarism and Economic Egalitarianism." *Public Opinion Quarterly* 75(4): 748–60.

Alanya, Ahu, Marc Swyngedouw, Veronique Vandezande and Karen Phalet. 2017. "Close Encounters: Minority and Majority Perceptions of Discrimination and Intergroup Relations in Antwerp, Belgium." *International Migration Review* 51(1): 191–217.

Baier, Annette. 1994. *Moral Prejudices: Essays on Ethics*. Cambridge, MA: Harvard University Press.

Banting, Keith, and Will Kymlicka. 2017. *The Strains of Commitment: The Political Sources of Solidarity in Diverse Societies*. Oxford: Oxford University Press.

Baysu, Gülseli, and Marc Swyngedouw. 2020. "What Determines Voting Behaviors of Muslim Minorities in Europe: Muslim Identity or Left–Right Ideology?" *Political Psychology* 41(5): 837–60.

Betz, Hans-Georg. 1994. *Radical Right-Wing Populism in Western Europe*. Basingstoke: Macmillan.

Blomberg, Helena, Johanna Kallio, Olli Kangas, Christian Kroll and Mikko Niemelä. 2012. "Attitudes among High-Risk Groups." In *Contested Welfare States: Welfare Attitudes in Europe and Beyond*, ed. Stefan Svallfors, 58–80. Stanford, CA: Stanford University Press.

Boeri, Tito, Gordon Hanson and Barry McCormick. 2002. *Immigration Policy and the Welfare System: A Report for the Fondazione Rodolfo Debenedetti*. Oxford: Oxford University Press.

Bryson, Caroline. 1997. "Benefit Claimants: Villains or Victims?" In *British Social Attitudes: The 14th Report*, eds. Roger Jowell, John Curtis, Alison Park, Lindsay Brook, Katarina Thomson and Caroline Bryson, 73–88. Aldershot: Ashgate.

Castel, Robert. 2003. *L'insécurité Sociale: Qu'est-Ce Qu'être Protégé*. Paris: Seuil.

Chauvet, Lisa, Flore Gubert and Sandrine Mesplé-Somps. 2016. "Do Migrants Adopt New Political Attitudes from Abroad? Evidence Using a Multi-Sited Exit-Poll Survey during the 2013 Malian Elections." *Comparative Migration Studies* 4(1): 19.

Corluy, Vincent, and Gerlinde Verbist. 2010. *Inkomen En Diversiteit: Onderzoek Naar de Inkomenspositie van Migranten in België*. Antwerpen: Centrum voor Sociaal Beleid Herman Deleeck.

Crepaz, Markus M.L. 2008. *Trust beyond Borders: Immigration, the Welfare State, and Identity in Modern Societies*. Ann Arbor, MI: University of Michigan Press.

Daenekindt, Stijn, Jeroen van der Waal and Willem de Koster. 2018. "Social Mobility and Political Distrust: Cults of Gratitude and Resentment?" *Acta Politica* 53(2): 269–82.

Dancygier, Rafaela. 2017. *Dilemmas of Inclusion: Muslims in European Politics*. Princeton, NJ: Princeton University Press.

Dancygier, Rafaela, and Elizabeth N. Saunders. 2006. "A New Electorate? Comparing Preferences and Partisanship between Immigrants and Natives." *American Journal of Political Science* 50(4): 962–81.

Davidov, Eldad, Bart Meuleman, Jan Cieciuch, Peter Schmidt and Jaak Billiet. 2014. "Measurement Equivalence in Cross-National Research." *Annual Review of Sociology* 40(1): 55–75.

De Koster, Willem, Peter Achterberg and Jeroen Van der Waal. 2013. "The New Right and the Welfare State: The Electoral Relevance of Welfare Chauvinism and Welfare Populism in the Netherlands." *International Political Science Review* 34(1): 3–20.

Delhey, Jan, and Kenneth Newton. 2005. "Predicting Cross-National Levels of Social Trust: Global Pattern or Nordic Exceptionalism?" *European Sociological Review* 21(4): 311–27.

Derks, Anton. 2006. "Populism and the Ambivalence of Egalitarianism: How Do the Underprivileged Reconcile a Right Wing Party Preference with Their Socio-Economic Attitudes?" *World Political Science* 2(3): 175–200.

Diehl, Claudia, Matthias Koenig and Kerstin Ruckdeschel. 2009. "Religiosity and Gender Equality: Comparing Natives and Muslim Migrants in Germany." *Ethnic and Racial Studies* 32(2): 278–301.

Dwyer, Peter. 2000. *Welfare Rights and Responsibilities: Contesting Social Citizenship*. Bristol: Policy Press.

Elias, Norbert, and John L. Scotson. 1965. *The Established and the Outsiders: A Sociological Enquiry into Community Problems*. London: Cass.

Ervasti, Heikki J. 1998. "Civil Criticism and the Welfare State." *Scandinavian Journal of Social Welfare* 7(4): 288–99.

Ervasti, Heikki J. 2012. "Who Hates the Welfare State? Criticism of the Welfare State in Europe." In *The Future of the Welfare State*, eds. Heikki Ervasti, Jørgen Goul Andersen, Torben Fridberg and Kristen Ringdal, 231–48. Cheltenham, UK and Northampton, MA, USA: Edward Elgar Publishing.

Feldman, Stanley, and John Zaller. 1992. "The Political Culture of Ambivalence: Ideological Responses to the Welfare State." *American Journal of Political Science* 36(1): 268–307.

Fersch, Barbara, and Karen N. Breidahl. 2018. "Building, Breaking, Overriding …? Migrants and Institutional Trust in the Danish Welfare State." *International Journal of Sociology and Social Policy* 38(7/8): 592–606.

Galle, Jolien, Koen Abts, Marc Swyngedouw and Bart Meuleman. 2019. "Attitudes of Turkish and Moroccan Belgians toward Redistribution and Government Responsibility: The Role of Perceived Discrimination, Generation, and Religious Involvement." *International Migration Review* 54(2): 423–46.

Ganzeboom, Harry B.G., and Donald J. Treiman. 1996. "Internationally Comparable Measures of Occupational Status for the 1988 International Standard Classification of Occupations." *Social Science Research* 25(3): 201–39.

Gidengil, Elisabeth, André Blais, Richard Nadeau and Neil Nevitte. 2003. "Women to the Left? Gender Differences in Political Beliefs and Policy Preferences." In *Gender and Elections in Canada*, eds. Manon Tremblay and Linda Trimble, 140–59. New York: Oxford University Press.

Govier, Trudy. 1997. *Social Trust and Human Communities*. Montreal: McGill-Queen's University Press.

Grant, Peter R. 2008. "The Protest Intentions of Skilled Immigrants with Credentialing Problems: A Test of a Model Integrating Relative Deprivation Theory with Social Identity Theory." *British Psychological Society* 47: 687–705.

Habibov, Nazim, Alex Cheung and Alena Auchynnikava. 2018. "Does Institutional Trust Increase Willingness to Pay More Taxes to Support the Welfare State?" *Sociological Spectrum* 38(1): 51–68.

Heath, Anthony F., Catherine Rothon and Elina Kilpi. 2008. "The Second Generation in Western Europe: Education, Unemployment, and Occupational Attainment." *Annual Review of Sociology* 34: 211–35.

Henry, P.J. 2011. "The Role of Stigma in Understanding Ethnicity Differences in Authoritarianism." *Political Psychology* 32(3): 419–38.

Inglehart, Ronald, and Pippa Norris. 2017. "Trump and the Populist Authoritarian Parties: The Silent Revolution in Reverse." *Perspectives on Politics* 15(2): 443–54.

Jaeger, Mads Meier. 2008. "Does Left–Right Orientation Have a Causal Effect on Support for Redistribution? Causal Analysis with Cross-Sectional Data Using Instrumental Variables." *International Journal of Public Opinion Research* 20(3): 363–74.

Kalmijn, Matthijs, and Gerbert Kraaykamp. 2018. "Determinants of Cultural Assimilation in the Second Generation: A Longitudinal Analysis of Values about Marriage and Sexuality among Moroccan and Turkish Migrants." *Journal of Ethnic and Migration Studies* 44(5): 697–717.

Kangas, Olli E. 1997. "Self-Interest and the Common Good: The Impact of Norms, Selfishness and Context in Social Policy Opinions." *Journal of Socio-Economics* 26(5): 475–94.

Klandermans, Bert, Jojanneke Van der Toorn and Jacquelien Van Stekelenburg. 2008. "Embeddedness and Identity: How Immigrants Turn Grievances into Action." *American Sociological Review* 73: 992–1012.

Kolbe, Melanie, and Markus M.L. Crepaz. 2016. "The Power of Citizenship: How Immigrant Incorporation Affects Attitudes towards Social Benefits." *Comparative Politics* 49(1): 105–23.

Kremer, Monique. 2016. "Earned Citizenship: Labour Migrants' Views on the Welfare State." *Journal of Social Policy* 45(3): 395–415.

Kriesi, Hanspeter, Edgar Grande, Romain Lachat, Martin Dolezal, Simon Bornschier and Timotheos Frey. 2006. "Globalization and the Transformation of the National Political Space: Six European Countries Compared." *European Journal of Political Research* 45(6): 921–56.

Kumlin, Staffan, and Bo Rothstein. 2010. "Questioning the New Liberal Dilemma: Immigrants, Social Networks, and Institutional Fairness." *Comparative Politics* 43(1): 63–80.

Laurence, James, and Lee Bentley. 2016. "Does Ethnic Diversity Have a Negative Effect on Attitudes towards the Community? A Longitudinal Analysis of the Causal Claims within the Ethnic Diversity and Social Cohesion Debate." *European Sociological Review* 32(1): 54–67.

Levie, Jonathan. 2007. "Immigration, In-Migration, Ethnicity and Entrepreneurship in the United Kingdom." *Small Business Economics* 28: 143–69.

Likki, Tiina, and Christian Staerklé. 2015. "Welfare Support in Europe: Interplay of Dependency Culture Beliefs and Meritocratic Contexts." *International Journal of Public Opinion Research* 27(1): 138–53.

Lindbeck, Assar. 1995. "Hazardous Welfare-State Dynamics." *American Economic Review* 85(2): 9–15.

Lubbers, Marcel, Claudia Diehl, Theresa Kuhn and Christian Albrekt Larsen. 2018. "Migrants' Support for Welfare State Spending in Denmark, Germany, and the Netherlands." *Social Policy and Administration* 52: 895–913.

McCluskey, Martha T. 2003. "Efficiency and Social Citizenship: Challenging the Neoliberal Attack on the Welfare State." *Indiana Law Journal* 78: 783–876.

Messing, Vera, and Bence Ságvári. 2020. *From Landing to Arrival: The Subtle Integration of Immigrants across Western Europe*. Budapest: Friedrich-Ebert-Stiftung.

Meuleman, Bart, and Sam Delespaul. 2020. "Welfare Criticism in Times of Economic Crisis: Perceptions of Moral, Economic and Social Consequences of the Welfare State, 2008–2016." In *Welfare State Legitimacy in Times of Crisis and Austerity*, eds. Tijs Laenen, Bart Meuleman, and Wim van Oorschot, 24–45. Cheltenham, UK and Northampton, MA, USA: Edward Elgar Publishing.

Mughan, Anthony, Clive Bean and Ian McAllister. 2003. "Economic Globalization, Job Insecurity and the Populist Reaction." *Electoral Studies* 22(4): 617–33.

Murray, Charles. 1984. *Losing Ground: American Social Policy, 1950–1980*. New York: Basic Books.

Muthén, Linda K., and Bengt Muthén. 2017. *Mplus User's Guide: Eighth Edition*. Los Angeles: Muthén and Muthén.

Pels, Trees, and Mariëtte De Haan. 2007. "Socialization Practices of Moroccan Families after Migration: A Reconstruction in an 'Acculturative Arena.'" *YOUNG* 15(1): 71–89.

Reeskens, Tim, and Wim van Oorschot. 2012. "Disentangling the 'New Liberal Dilemma': On the Relation between General Welfare Redistribution Preferences and Welfare Chauvinism." *International Journal of Comparative Sociology* 53(2): 120–39.

Reeskens, Tim, and Wim van Oorschot. 2015. "Immigrants' Attitudes towards Welfare Redistribution: An Exploration of Role of Government Preferences among Immigrants and Natives across 18 European Welfare States." *European Sociological Review* 31(4): 433–45.

Rehm, Philipp, Jacob S. Hacker and Mark Schlesinger. 2012. "Insecure Alliances: Risk, Inequality, and Support for the Welfare State." *American Political Science Review* 106(2): 386–406.

Renema, Jeanette A.J., Roza Meuleman and Marcel Lubbers. 2020. "Immigrants' Support for Welfare Spending and the Role of Perceived and Preferred Group's Access to Welfare: A Comparative Study among 10 Immigrant Groups in the Netherlands." *International Journal of Public Opinion Research* 32(1): 1–24.

Röder, Antje, and Peter Mühlau. 2012. "Low Expectations or Different Evaluations: What Explains Immigrants' High Levels of Trust in Host-Country Institutions?" *Journal of Ethnic and Migration Studies* 38(5): 777–92.

Roller, Edeltraud. 1995. "The Welfare State: The Equality Dimension." In *The Scope of Government*, eds. Ole Borre and Elinor Scarbrough, 165–97. Oxford: Oxford University Press.

Roosma, Femke, John Gelissen and Wim van Oorschot. 2013. "The Multidimensionality of Welfare State Attitudes: A European Cross-National Study." *Social Indicators Research* 113(1): 235–55.

Roosma, Femke, Wim van Oorschot and John Gelissen. 2014. "The Weakest Link in Welfare State Legitimacy: European Perceptions of Moral and Administrative Failure in the Targeting of Social Benefits." *International Journal of Comparative Sociology* 55(6): 489–508.

Sainsbury, Diane. 2012. *Welfare States and Immigrant Rights: The Politics of Inclusion and Exclusion*. Oxford: Oxford University Press.

Schmidt-Catran, Alexander W. and Romana Careja. 2017. "Institutions, Culture and Migrants' Preference for State-Provided Welfare: Longitudinal Evidence from Germany." *Journal of European Social Policy* 27(2): 197–212.

Sihvo, Tuire, and Hannu Uusitalo. 1995. "Attitudes towards the Welfare State Have Several Dimensions: Evidence from Finland." *Scandinavian Journal of Social Welfare* 4: 215–23.
Smith, Heather J., Thomas F. Pettigrew, Gina M. Pippin and Silvana Bialosiewicz. 2012. "Relative Deprivation: A Theoretical and Meta-Analytic Review." *Personality and Social Psychology Review* 16(3): 203–32.
Staerklé, Christian, Tiina Likki and Régis Scheidegger. 2012. "A Normative Approach to Welfare Attitudes." In *Contested Welfare States: Welfare Attitudes in Europe and Beyond*, ed. Stefan Svallfors, 81–118. Stanford, CA: Stanford University Press.
Stellmacher, Jost, and Thomas Petzel. 2005. "Authoritarianism as a Group Phenomenon." *Political Psychology* 26(2): 245–74.
Svallfors, Stefan. 2004. "Class, Attitudes and the Welfare State: Sweden in Comparative Perspective." *Social Policy and Administration* 38(2): 119–38.
Svallfors, Stefan. 2012. *Contested Welfare States: Welfare Attitudes in Europe and Beyond*. Stanford, CA: Stanford University Press.
Swyngedouw, Marc, Bart Meuleman, Koen Abts, Hassan Bousetta and Jolien Galle. 2015. *Belgian Ethnic Minorities Election Study 2014: Codebook: Questions and Frequency Tables*. Leuven: ISPO-KU Leuven and CLEO/CEDEM-Université de Liège.
van der Meer, Tom, and Jochem Tolsma. 2014. "Ethnic Diversity and Its Effects on Social Cohesion." *Annual Review of Sociology* 40(1): 459–78.
van Dijk, Tobias K., Charles Agyemang, Matty de Wit and Karen Hosper. 2010. "The Relationship between Perceived Discrimination and Depressive Symptoms among Young Turkish–Dutch and Moroccan–Dutch." *European Journal of Public Health* 21(4): 477–83.
Van Hootegem, Arno, Koen Abts and Bart Meuleman. 2021. "The Welfare State Criticism of the Losers of Modernization: How Social Experiences of Resentment Shape Populist Welfare Critique." *Acta Sociologica*: 1–19.
van Oorschot, Wim. 2000. "Who Should Get What, and Why? On Deservingness Criteria and the Conditionality of Solidarity among the Public." *Policy and Politics* 28(1): 33–48.
van Oorschot, Wim. 2010. "Public Perceptions of the Economic, Moral, Social and Migration Consequences of the Welfare State: An Empirical Analysis of Welfare State Legitimacy." *Journal of European Social Policy* 20(1): 19–31.
van Oorschot, Wim, and Bart Meuleman. 2012. "Welfare Performance and Welfare Support." In *Contested Welfare States: Welfare Attitudes in Europe and Beyond*, ed. Stefan Svallfors, 25–57. Stanford, CA: Stanford University Press.
van Oorschot, Wim, Tim Reeskens and Bart Meuleman. 2012. "Popular Perceptions of Welfare State Consequences: A Multilevel, Cross-National Analysis of 25 European Countries." *Journal of European Social Policy* 22(2): 181–97.
van Stekelenburg, Jacquelien. 2013. "The Political Psychology of Protest: Sacrificing for a Cause." *European Psychologist* 18(4): 224–34.
Vandezande, Veronique, Fenella Fleischmann, Gülseli Baysu, Marc Swyngedouw and Karen Phalet. 2010. *De Integratie van de Europese Tweede Generatie: Resultaten van Het TIES Onderzoek in Antwerpen en Brussel*. Leuven: KU Leuven.
Wroe, Andrew. 2016. "Economic Insecurity and Political Trust in the United States." *American Politics Research* 44(1): 131–63.

APPENDIX

Table 22A.1 Measurement invariance for the latent concepts

	Chi²	Df	RMSEA	CFI	TLI	SRMR
Welfare criticism						
Configural invariance	126.805	48	0.037	0.965	0.947	0.035
Metric invariance	131.511	54	0.034	0.965	0.953	0.039
Scalar invariance	185.002	63	0.040	0.945	0.937	0.053
Societal resentment						
Configural invariance	62.501	34	0.026	0.992	0.987	0.027
Metric invariance	84.991	39	0.031	0.987	0.982	0.039
Scalar invariance	225.235	47	0.055	0.951	0.942	0.074
Ideology						
Configural invariance	45.121	16	0.038	0.972	0.947	0.027
Metric invariance	50.314	20	0.035	0.971	0.956	0.035
Scalar invariance	82.963	26	0.042	0.945	0.936	0.045

Table 22A.2 Question wordings and standardized factor loadings of the social experiences of resentment

	Ethnic minority RD	Ethnic minority EI	Ethnic minority SD	Majority RD	Majority EI	Majority SD
If we need something from the government, people like me always have to wait longer than others	0.725			0.778		
People like me are systematically disadvantaged, while other groups receive more than they are entitled to	0.810			0.849		
People like me are always the first victims of an economic crisis	0.690			0.774		
That your financial worries will increase the following years		0.827			0.800	
That your position in society will be hard to maintain in the future		0.868			0.847	
That your children or the next generation will have many more difficulties		0.626			0.551	
Nowadays it is hard to know who or what to trust			0.844			0.823
You cannot be too careful when dealing with other people			0.699			0.735
Correlation economic insecurity	0.219	1		0.391	1	
Correlation social distrust	0.320	0.370	1	0.709	0.376	1

Note: RD = group relative deprivation; EI = economic insecurity; SD = social distrust; Chi-square = 225.235; df = 47; RMSEA = 0.055; CFI = 0.951; TLI = 0.942; SRMR = 0.074.

440   Handbook on migration and welfare

Table 22A.3   Question wordings and standardized factor loadings of the ideological dimensions

	Ethnic minority AU	Ethnic minority EG	Majority AU	Majority EG
Most of our social problems would be solved if we could somehow get rid of the immoral, crooked people	0.415		0.483	
Obedience and respect for authority are the two most important virtues children have to learn	0.655		0.714	
Laws should become stricter because too much freedom is not good for people	0.523		0.653	
The differences between classes ought to be smaller than they are now		0.584		0.658
The differences between the high and the low incomes should stay as they are		−0.527		−0.559
The government should reduce income differentials		0.641		0.664
Correlation egalitarianism	−0.004	1	0.129	1

Note: AU = authoritarianism; EG = egalitarianism; Chi-square = 82.963; df = 26; RMSEA = 0.042; CFI = 0.945; TLI = 0.936; SRMR = 0.045.

Table 22A.4   Means and standard deviations of social characteristics for minority and majority sample

	Ethnic minority Mean	Ethnic minority SD	Majority Mean	Majority SD
Gender (woman = ref.)	0.520	0.500	0.482	0.500
Age	37.037	12.702	50.190	18.324
Education				
Lower (secondary)	0.393	0.489	0.357	0.479
Higher secondary	0.452	0.498	0.328	0.470
Tertiary	0.155	0.362	0.315	0.464
Occupation				
Blue collar	0.443	0.497	0.314	0.464
Service class	0.141	0.348	0.250	0.433
White collar	0.159	0.366	0.210	0.407
Self-employed	0.044	0.204	0.109	0.312
Inactive	0.213	0.410	0.117	0.321
Welfare dependency (no benefit = ref.)	0.486	0.500	0.245	0.430
Region (French-speaking = ref.)	0.769	0.421	0.628	0.484

PART V

THE VIEW FROM THE GLOBAL SOUTH: THE EFFECTS OF MIGRATION ON ORIGIN COUNTRIES

23. The Janus face of remittances: Do remittances support or undermine development in the Global South?
Farid Makhlouf and Oussama Ben Atta

INTRODUCTION

International migration is the subject of considerable discussion, both in host and home countries.[1] This is due to the fact that international migration affects several aspects: economic, as well as political, social and societal (Makhlouf 2013a; Edelbloude et al. 2017). Remittances can be considered among the most visible consequences between migration and the countries of origin. They are simultaneously influenced by shocks and uncertainties in the countries of origin and also influence the trends of macroeconomic variables in the countries of origin, namely consumption, investment and thus economic growth (Bahadir et al. 2018).

In 2019, according to United Nations data 3.5 percent of the world population are migrants and they remitted more than US$700 billion in the same year according to World Bank estimations. More than 75 percent of these remittances are destined for developing countries. Moreover, they have increased considerably since the 2000s (Makhlouf 2013a). The average annual growth rate was 24.32 percent over the 2000–2019 period for low- and middle-income countries according to the World Bank data. One of the major reasons behind the increasing remittances lies on the fact that migration flows continue to increase (Makhlouf and Kasmaoui 2017) despite restrictions on population movements (visas imposed by the main host countries).

Remittances have repercussions in the countries of origin. Their impact on countries of origin is manifested in several aspects: fertility rates (Beine et al. 2013; Mughal and Anwar 2014), knowledge transfer (Meyer 2001; Meyer and Brown 1999; Saxenian 2005; Hunger 2004) and productivity and labor market (Katseli et al. 2006; Makhlouf 2019). But the most visible aspect remains, without a doubt, the impact of remittances on economic growth.

Remittances are considered an essential financial source for the development of emigration countries (Makhlouf and Kasmaoui 2020). In addition, they are considered resilient in times of crisis (Sirkeci et al. 2012). Predominantly, the impact of remittances on countries of origin can be studied according to two approaches: short term and long term. The short-term approach focuses on the impact of remittances on prices, labor supply and consumer spending; the long-term approach focuses instead on the impact of remittances on the accumulation of physical and human capital, economic growth, inequality and poverty. The debate on the impact of remittances on the economies of the countries of origin is far from being conclusive. There are several reasons for these controversies about the impact of remittances on the economies of the countries of origin: remittances have an impact at the micro and macro levels, are generally uncontested, their uses are not controlled by governments and they are unpredictable.

This chapter empirically investigates the potential effects of remittances on economic growth by integrating into its empirical strategy the two aspects of remittances, which are the negative and positive effects of remittances on economic growth.

It is important to note that academic work on remittances is becoming increasingly important in the literature. However, this share is still marginal compared to the literature on other financial flows such as foreign direct investment (FDI)[2] and development aids (Makhlouf 2013a). With the increase in remittances, there has been a steadily increasing number of studies on remittances. This interest of academics in remittances can be explained by the importance of these flows. Indeed, they exceed FDI and development aid flows for most developing countries (Makhlouf and Mughal 2013).

Labor-exporting countries have understood that remittances generated by their workers abroad can be directed to productive projects. Several countries have implemented ideas to facilitate emigrants to repatriate their income (Makhlouf 2013a). Governments in developing countries are paying increasing attention to the potential impact of remittances with a view to integrating them into economic policies. Developing countries are acutely aware of the magnitude and consequences of these financial flows. Consequently, they are taking an increasingly important place in their economic policies (Makhlouf 2013b).

According to the World Bank data, in some countries, remittances represent an important weight in the economy. For example, more than one-third of national production is due to remittances in Tonga, Haiti and South Sudan, and more than 20 percent in the Kyrgyz Republic, Tajikistan, Nepal, Montenegro, Honduras, Lesotho and El Salvador. In terms of value, India, China, Mexico, the Philippines and Egypt represent about 45 percent of remittances, in current United States dollars, to developing countries. Regarding remittance outflows, the United States is both the world's leading recipient of migrants and source of remittances with more than $60 billion in remittances, which is equivalent to 8 percent of remittances to developing countries, followed by Saudi Arabia, Switzerland, Germany and the Russian Federation. As for the share of remittance outflows in gross domestic product, Luxembourg is at the top of the ranking with more than 19 percent followed by the Turks and Caicos Islands (12.6 percent), Oman (12.5 percent) and Kuwait (10.1 percent).

As the results of the studies on the economic impact of remittances differ, this chapter aims to address a new avenue to better understand the remittances–growth nexus.[3] More specifically, we question the linear design that has filled the empirical studies that examine the impact of remittances on economic growth. The idea is that there is a threshold level of the share of remittances in the GDP of recipient countries at which the effect of remittances shifts. Our results using a quadratic model and a dynamic threshold effect model show that remittances have a negative impact on growth, and it is only above a specific threshold that the effect becomes positive. This is very useful as it highlights the non-linearity of the remittances–growth nexus.

This chapter is structured as follows. The next section presents the stylized facts about remittances and discusses their evolution and compares the importance of remittances across regions. It also analyzes the behavior of remittances in terms of their cyclical properties vis-à-vis production in the home economies. The following section presents a literature review outlining the social and economic role of remittances and splits the literature into optimistic and pessimistic versions. The chapter then investigates the genuine effect of remittances on economic growth in sending countries, taking into account the contradictory findings of previous studies, and proposes a new estimation strategy based on non-linearity. It then discusses the results and threshold effects of the impact of remittances on economic growth.

REMITTANCES: FEATURES, STYLIZED FACTS AND BEHAVIOR

Features and Stylized Facts

According to United Nations data, in 2019, the stock of migrants in the world was more than 250 million, and they have generated more than 700 billion of remittances according to World Bank data. They are considered an important source of development (Makhlouf and Kasmaoui 2020) and are growing steadily. In 2020, according to World Bank estimates, remittances to developing countries were more than US$500 billion. By comparison, the value of remittances in 2007 to developing countries was about US$278 billion, a value that has almost doubled in the span of 10 years. The average annual growth rate over the same period was 5.43 percent, which is a significant performance. Migrant remittances are a complex phenomenon, particularly in terms of their impact on development in developing countries. The decision to remit money and how much is not the result of a decision made independently of the macroeconomic environment in the host country and the country of origin. The countries that benefit most from migration through remittances are not low-income countries[4] but rather upper middle-income countries,[5] as shown in Figure 23.1.

About 80 percent of remittances to developing countries are attracted by upper middle-income countries. For example, according to World Bank data in 2018 about US$75.79 billion of remittances were attracted to upper middle-income countries and only US$3.75 billion to low-income countries and US$14.74 billion to destinations in lower middle-income countries.[6] This can be explained by the cost of migration. Individuals living in low-income countries find it difficult to finance the costs of international mobility. The trend in remittances is up whatever the country's income level and this is mainly due to:

- the improvement of financial institutions in host countries;
- improving instruments to measure remittances (Ratha 2007);
- improving statistics related to the accounting of remittances; and
- lower remittance-related costs. For example, in the case of El Salvador, Aycinena et al. (2010) show that a reduction of US$1 in remittance costs can increase monthly remittances by US$25.

In terms of the weight of remittances in the economy, Figure 23.2 shows that low-income countries are more dependent on remittances. This dependence may have adverse effects on the economies of these countries. On average, the share of remittances in GDP in these countries varies between 7 and 8 percent over the 10-year period 2008 to 2018. With

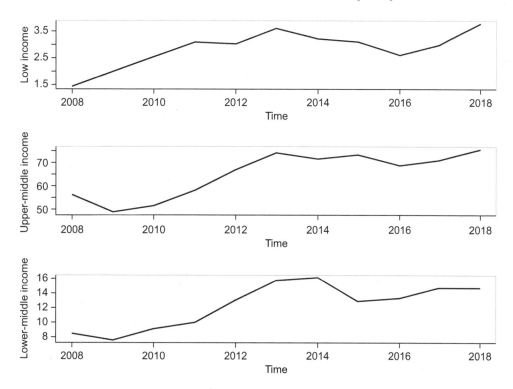

Figure 23.1 Remittances in US$ billion to countries according to their income classification, 2008–2018

regard to lower middle-income countries, remittances are increasingly important in the economy of these countries.

This share remains relatively low in upper middle-income countries and shows a downward trend. For example, in 2008, the share of remittances in GDP was between 5 and 6 percent (see Figure 23.2). It should be pointed out that Figure 23.2 depicts the average of the countries considered according to the availability of data. Some countries have a higher dependence on remittances such as Haiti, Kyrgyz Republic and Tajikistan where about one third of the national wealth is due to remittances. There is 20 to 30 percent of national wealth attributed to remittances in the following countries: Nepal, Lesotho, El Salvador and Fiji. In other countries remittances account for less than 1 percent of national wealth. Most of these countries are resource-based rentier countries.[7]

With regard to a disparity between regions, Figure 23.3 shows remittances received by region in the world. We can identify two regions with a large difference in the weight of remittances in the national economy. The first is Europe and Central Asia with an average of 10 percent of remittances in GDP and the second region is the sub-Saharan countries with an average of 5 percent of remittances in GDP. According to Figure 23.3, there is also a certain homogeneity with the rest of the remaining regions, namely: East Asia and Pacific, Latin America and Caribbean, Middle East and North Africa and South Asia.

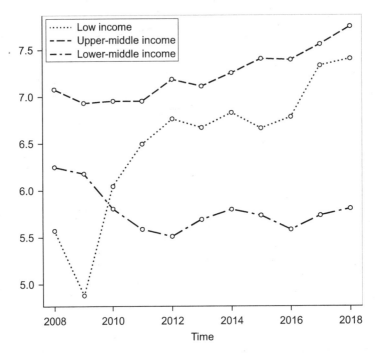

Figure 23.2 Remittances as percentage to GDP to countries according to their income classification, 2008–2018

Figure 23.3 also shows two types of dispersions: that between regions and dispersion intra-regions. Moreover, the intra-regional dispersion is greatest in South Asia. This region is characterized by an emigration that is quite diversified in terms of host countries (Persian Gulf, Western Europe and North America), which allows for a greater dispersion of remittances, unlike the sub-Saharan countries, which have a less significant dispersion of remittances compared to other regions.

Heterogeneity also manifests itself according to the level of economic development of the recipient countries, as shown in Figure 23.4. Economic conditions in host countries can impact the variability of remittances. For example, remittances from Europe are more stable than those from the Middle East and North America (Makhlouf and Mughal 2011). In other words, the variance of remittances from the latter two host regions is heteroskedastic. Moreover, the stability of remittances could be partly due to the fact that European economies are stable relative to other regions. In this way, Makhlouf and Mughal (2011) explain that remittances from countries with a more advanced social security system are stable in effect, so that when the migrant loses his job he receives support and aids that allow him to continue sending money.

Figure 23.5 compares financial inflows to developing countries,[8] in particular, it compares between FDI, net inflows (% of GDP) and personal remittances, received (% of GDP). It shows that the share of remittances in GDP is higher than FDI. In contrast to FDI, the share of remittances in GDP shows an upward trend. The gap between the two flows widens from 2013. However, scholarly work on remittances is still quite limited

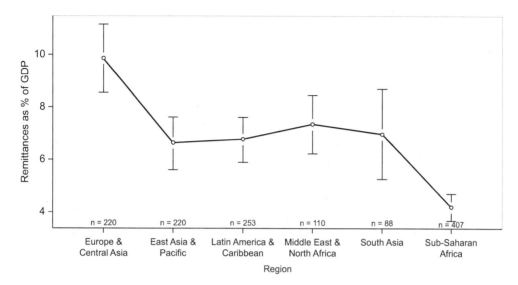

Figure 23.3   Heterogeneity across regions

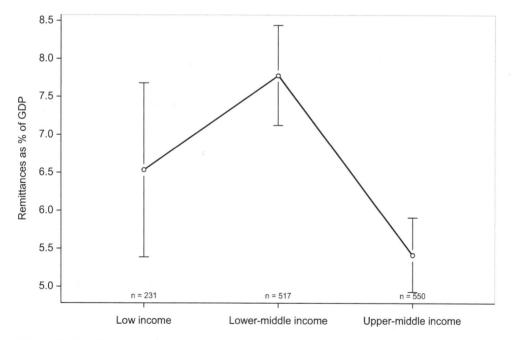

Figure 23.4   Heterogeneity by income

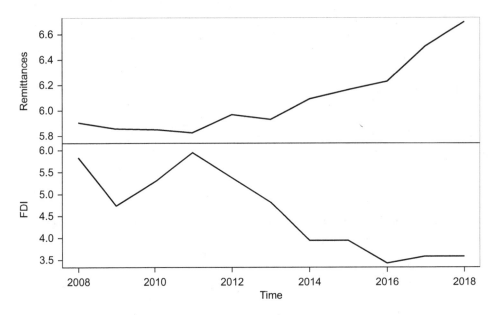

Figure 23.5 Foreign direct investment and remittances as percentage to GDP to developing countries, 2008–2018

compared to the literature on other financial flows to developing countries, particularly FDI (Makhlouf 2013a).

Moreover, remittances are less volatile than FDIs (Makhlouf and Mughal 2011), have no direct counterpart (Makhlouf 2013a) and generally increase in tough times such as economic crises and natural disasters. For example, in 2010 Haiti earthquake remittances reacted positively. In addition, Vargas-Silva (2008) points out that in the case of Mexico, remittances are counter-cyclical, while FDI is pro-cyclical. FDIs are rather pro-cyclical, which can aggravate the amplitudes of economic cycles in developing countries. This leads us to question the cyclical properties of remittances.

Remittance Behaviors

> Remittances may move countercyclically relative to the economic cycle of the recipient country. Remittances may rise when the recipient economy suffers a downturn in activity or macroeconomic shocks due to financial crisis, natural disaster, or political conflict, because migrants may send more funds during hard times to help their families and friends. Remittances may thus smooth consumption and contribute to the stability of recipient economies. (Schiantarelli 2005, 99)

But the literature has also shown that remittances can be pro-cyclical with the domestic production of the countries of origin in some cases (Makhlouf and Kasmaoui 2020). Sayan et al. (2010) argue that the cyclical properties of remittances are impacted by the characteristics of business cycles in Mexico and the United States. The nature of the interaction between the home economy and the host country can therefore

Table 23.1   Cyclical properties of remittances

Authors	Conclusion
Bouhga-Hagbe (2006)	Counter-cyclical
Chami et al. (2008)	Counter-cyclical
Vargas-Silva (2008)	Counter-cyclical
Mandelman and Zlate (2012)	Counter-cyclical
Sayan et al. (2010)	Counter-cyclical
Frankel (2011)	Counter-cyclical
Mughal and Ahmed (2014)	Counter-cyclical
Sayan (2004)	Pro-cyclical
Sayan and Tekin-Koru (2007)	Pro-cyclical
Akkoyunlu and Kholodilin (2006)	A-cyclical
Makhlouf and Kasmaoui (2020)	Co-existence (counter-cyclical and pro-cyclical)

play on the cyclical properties of remittances. Similarly, Akkoyunlu and Kholodilin (2006) studied the interaction of remittances of Turkish migrants residing in Germany with the GDP of Turkey and Germany. They find that remittances respond positively to changes in Germany's GDP. On the other hand, they are not sensitive to changes in Turkey's GDP. Table 23.1 summarizes the main findings on the cyclical properties of remittances.

We can assume that the families of migrants who remain at home request money from their relatives living abroad. This demand may depend, among other factors, on the income of the families who stay behind. On the other hand, the supply of remittances is dependent on the migrants' income. If there is an economic crisis specific to the country of origin that does not extend between the country of origin and the host countries, the financial resources of the migrants' families will tend to decrease but not those of the migrants. As a result, families will ask for more help than usual from their relatives abroad. In this case, the demand for remittances will be greater than the supply. If migrants respond favorably to this demand, remittance cycles will be counter-cyclical with economic activity. In the opposite case, a favorable economic situation in the country of origin will lead to a decrease in the demand for family support. In this case, migrants will generate a surplus of remittances. The cycles of remittances will then be pro-cyclical. In this case the migrant can send money to invest. Therefore, the cyclical properties of remittances can be impacted by the country of origin, the host countries and the degree of interdependence between the two countries. For countries of origin, generally, economic, political and natural shocks are at the origin of fluctuations in remittances because migrants are permanently connected to their country of origin mainly through their families, the media, etc. The reaction of migrants can be immediate or spread out over time, depending on the type of shock.

Migrant remittances are a multifaceted phenomenon, particularly from the point of view of their cyclical properties. They are not the result of a decision taken independently of the macroeconomic environment in the host country and the country of origin. Shocks and unexpected events in countries of origin can also affect the behavior of remittances.

LITERATURE REVIEW

The Social Role of Remittances

Various scholars have pointed out the social and economic implications of remittances (Durand et al. 1996; Ratha 2007; Edelbloude et al. 2017, among others). Remittances can have positive effects on overall well-being in the origin countries (Taylor and Wyatt 1996; Rozelle et al. 1999). This includes improving the living conditions of families receiving remittances. They also influence fiscal policies (Ebeke 2011), impact government spending (Kapur and Singer 2006) and influence the fertility rate (Mughal and Anwar 2014). They can replace traditional insurance mechanisms in countries that do not have sufficiently efficient insurance systems. Indeed, the migrant will play an important role in crisis situations, i.e. a sudden drop in family income due to a natural disaster, job loss or illness. Remittances are also used in health and education spending (Makhlouf et al. 2019). They can play a significant role in the health and education of children (Lindstrom and Munoz-Franco 2006; Bouoiyour and Miftah 2014). Remittances play an important role in absorbing social crises.

The Economic Contribution of Remittances

The answer to the question as to how remittances influence economic growth in the countries of origin is not obvious because remittances are multidimensional and affect several macroeconomic aspects, namely: consumption and investment of recipient households (Wahba 1991; Combes and Ebeke 2011; Încalțărău and Maha 2012; Zhu et al. 2014; Bouoiyour et al. 2019), productivity (Rozelle et al. 1999; Senbeta 2013; Makhlouf 2019), exchange rate (Amuedo-Dorantes and Pozo 2004; Acosta et al. 2009; Makhlouf 2013b; Makhlouf and Mughal 2013; Kim 2019; Hien et al. 2020), exchange rate regime (Singer 2010), financial development (Giuliano and Ruiz-Arranz 2009; Aggarwal et al. 2011; Deisting et al. 2012; Brown et al. 2013; Azizi 2020), competitiveness (Makhlouf 2013b), corruption and institutions (Abdih et al. 2012; Tyburski 2012; Ahmed 2013; Ajide and Olayiwola 2020), emigration (Van Dalen et al. 2005), labor market (Kim 2007; Mughal and Makhlouf 2013; Asiedu and Chimbar 2020), government expenditures (Kapur and Singer 2006) and health and education (Adams and Cuecuecha 2010; Terrelonge 2014; Gyimah-Brempong and Asiedu 2015; Kan 2020). This makes the task even more difficult with regard to the effect of remittances on economic growth. In other words, remittances have both micro and macroeconomic effects. Empirical results yield mixed evidence of the effect of remittances on economic growth in countries (Makhlouf 2019). We distinguish between two different views: the first is a pessimistic view of remittances which considers that the latter have a negative impact on origin countries by associating remittances with the misuse of natural resources. The second is the optimistic view which considers that remittances contribute to the development of emigration countries by considering remittances as an insurance and an income that alleviates budgetary constraints. In this way, Cazachevici et al. (2020) in collecting 95 articles on the effect of remittances on the economy state that 40 percent of these studies found a positive effect, 40 percent reveal a negative one, and the remaining 20 percent demonstrate an insignificant impact of remittances. In this literature review, we will discuss the two visions.

A pessimistic view of remittances
In one of the pioneering works on the impact of remittances, Russell (1986) highlights that the costs associated to remittances are unpredictable, they increase inflation and deteriorate the balance of payment. Yet, under this vision, Keely and Tran (1989) highlight that the negative effects of remittances could be an increase in dependency and a contribution to economic and political instability as well as a development distortion. Chami et al. (2005) find that remittances have a negative effect on economic growth and conclude that remittances cannot be seen as a source of capital for economic development. Three years later, Chami et al. (2008) show that remittances are not necessarily associated with increased investment in the countries of origin and therefore have a negative effect on economic growth. In addition, Le (2009) empirically investigates the relationship between remittances and economic growth in a large sample of developing countries and finds that remittances hamper it. Rao and Hassan (2012) show that remittances have no direct effect on growth. In another context related to that of sub-Saharan African countries, Singh at al. (2011) find that remittances have a negative impact on economic growth. In the same African context, Nyamongo et al. (2012) find that the volatility of remittances seems to have a negative effect on the economic growth. This result has been confirmed by Adams and Klobodu (2016). In addition, Jawaid and Raza (2016) find the same conclusions in the following countries: Pakistan, India, Bangladesh and Sri Lanka. Bettin and Zazzaro (2012) stipulate that the positive effect of remittances on economic growth requires the quality of the financial system. Another study by Lartey (2017) states that the effect of remittances on economic growth will depend on the exchange rate regime, and for Mim and Mabrouk (2014) the level of public spending on education conditions the impact of remittances on growth. Again, on the mechanisms that promote the effect of remittances on economic growth, Senbeta (2013) analyzes the transmission mechanisms between remittances and GDP and argues that remittances have an entirely contradictory effect, i.e. remittances have a significant positive impact on capital accumulation while the impact on total factor productivity growth is insignificant. In the Small Island Developing States, Feeny et al. (2014) find that there is no association between remittances and economic growth. Moreover, Valdivia López and Ascencio (2010) analyze the Mexican case, which can be an example of an interesting study given its migratory history, and find that remittances do not promote the growth of states. In fact, their study is interesting because it analyzes the growth of states in Mexico through a spatial analysis, taking into account the heterogeneity of the states in terms of their migration history. Considering another level, Verter and Osakwe (2015) find that migrant remittances were positively associated with economic performance, albeit only in the short term. In the case of Tunisia, Jouini (2015) does not find a strong long-term correlation between remittances and economic growth. This result is confirmed by Shukralla (2016) who shows that the link between remittances and economic growth is weak. In the case of China, Jawaid and Raza (2016) find a negative relationship between remittances and economic growth. To summarize, the pessimistic view of remittances states that remittances have a negative impact on economic growth or the positive effect of remittances on growth is conditioned by other variables, namely financial development, level of education and the quality of institutions in the origin.

An optimistic view of remittances

We have seen in the previous sub-section the main studies that show a negative link between remittances and economic growth in developing countries and other studies that postulate certain conditions for remittances to have a significant and positive effect on growth and consequently development. In this sub-section, we summarize the most relevant studies that show the positive aspect of remittances on development through economic growth. Among the research on the link between remittances and domestic production, Taylor et al. (1996) assume that remittances positively affect the demand for goods and services, which involves an increase in economic growth. They can also be a stabilizing factor for financial equilibrium in times of crisis (Yang 2003). In this vein, Massey and Parrado (1998) and Griffin (1978) consider that remittances contribute to productive investment. Catrinescu et al. (2009) find that remittances are more likely to contribute to long-term growth in countries with higher-quality economic and political institutions. Pradhan et al. (2008), using 39 developing countries, find that remittances have a positive effect on economic growth. Moreover, Giuliano and Ruiz-Arranz (2009), based on 100 developing countries, find that remittances promote growth in nations with fewer developed financial systems by providing an alternative means of financing investment and helping to overcome liquidity constraints. Considering more than 20 countries of Latin America and the Caribbean, Vargas-Silva et al. (2009), find that a 10 percent raise in remittances as a percentage of GDP leads to a 0.9–1.2 percent increase in GDP growth. Mundaca (2009) finds, among other things, that remittances can have significant positive long-term effects on growth. In the case of the Philippines, this result is further supported by the study by Tchantchane et al. (2013), which finds that there is a positive relationship between economic growth and remittances as well as a positive relationship between remittances and education expenditures. In the case of India, Jayaraman et al. (2011) find that remittances and the interaction between remittances and financial development have a positive and significant effect on economic growth. For the Middle East and North Africa countries, Mohamed and Sidiropoulos (2010) find a positive effect of remittances on economic growth. Using a dynamic equilibrium-correction mechanism model, Adenutsi (2011) in Ghana finds that remittances have a positive impact on economic growth in both the short and long term. Still in the same case in Ghana by using the fully modified ordinary least squares estimator, Agbola (2013) confirms this result by showing that remittances are a key determinant of economic growth. In the context of small Pacific island countries, Jayaraman et al. (2012) find a positive relationship between remittances and economic growth. This result is confirmed by Makun (2018) for the Republic of the Fiji Islands in concluding that remittances and FDI are positively associated with economic growth. Comes et al. (2018) empirically investigate the relationship between remittances and GDP in seven Central and Eastern European countries and find a positive and significant relationship. Kumar et al. (2018) explore the link between economic growth and remittances in Kyrgyzstan and Macedonia and they clearly demonstrate a positive long-term impact. In South Asian countries, Strielkowski (2013) shows that the effect of remittances on per capita GDP growth is greater than that of official development assistance. In the same context, Azam et al. (2014) find a positive effect in seven Asian countries, namely Bangladesh, Pakistan, Malaysia, Philippines, Singapore, Thailand and Vietnam. In selected high- and low-income countries in Latin America and the Caribbean, Ramirez (2013) finds that remittances have a positive and significant effect on economic growth. Imai et al. (2014) re-examine the effects of remittances on GDP per capita growth for 24 countries in Asia and the Pacific. The results broadly support that remittance flows have been beneficial for economic growth. Using time series techniques Jawaid and Saleem (2017) confirm Imai et al.'s study for Pakistan. In 10 selected former post-Soviet republics, Abduvaliev and Bustillo (2020) find that, on average, a 1 percent increase in remittance flows leads to an increase in GDP per capita of about 0.25 percent.

In this section on research on the impact of remittances on economic growth, we have seen the main studies that show three effects: a negative effect, a positive effect and a positive effect under certain conditions, namely a better quality of economic and political institutions. In the empirical part we will try to take into account these effects in order to better estimate the relationship between remittances and growth. Most of the studies estimate linear relationships; we estimate a non-linear relationship in order to take into account the two potential effects of remittances on economic growth.

EMPIRICAL FRAMEWORK

This section assesses the effect of remittances on economic growth and by ricochet on economic development. It should be emphasized that there is a clear difference between economic growth, which is a quantitative measure, and development, which is a qualitative measure. The general premise of this chapter is that a positive effect of remittances on development can be achieved through two channels. The first channel is economic growth, where an increase in wealth can boost economic development. The second channel can be presented as a direct effect of remittances on development by enabling recipient households to access health and education services and other essential products. A positive effect of remittances on economic growth can lead to economic development as long as the wealth created is well distributed. A negative effect of remittances on economic growth does not necessarily mean a negative link between remittances and economic development, which is a wider notion than economic growth.

The Model

Our analysis of the relationship between remittances and economic growth is based on the standard Cobb–Douglas-type production function in the augmented Solow model (Solow 1956; Mankiw et al. 1992). The aggregate production function for country i in time t is expressed as follows:

$$Y_{it} = A_{it} K_{it}^{\alpha} L_{it}^{\beta}. \tag{23.1}$$

Where A_{it} denotes the total factor productivity the stock of technology, K_{it} is capital and L_{it} is labor. α and β are the production elasticities of capital and labor, respectively. Given constant returns to scale, we divide (23.1) by L and obtain the following equation:

$$y_{it} = A_{it} k_{it}^{\alpha}. \tag{23.2}$$

The Solow model implies that the evolution of the technology is defined by:

$$A_{it} = A_t e^{\varphi}, \varphi \geq 0. \tag{23.3}$$

In (23.3), A represents the stock of technology that depends on autonomous factors. It is assumed to be constant ($\Delta \ln A = 0$) and to grow at a constant autonomous rate of g:

$$A_{it} = A_0 e^{git}. \tag{23.4}$$

A_0 denotes the initial stock of technology. The time variant technology A_{it} is expanded to include other derivers of growth, besides k. More specifically, we include workers' remittances R, human capital HC, trade openness O and government expenditure G. We therefore obtain the following expression:

$$A_{it} = f(R, HC, O, G). \tag{23.5}$$

Where R denotes remittances as a share of GDP, HC is the human capital index based on years of schooling, O is trade openness measured by the sum of exports and imports expressed as a share of GDP and G denotes government expenditures relative to GDP. The effects of our variable of interest R, as well as other growth determinants, are detected when they are included as shift variables in the production function (Rao 2010), such that:

$$A_{it} = A_0 e^{git} R_{it}^{\gamma} H_{it}^{\delta} O_{it}^{\theta} G_{it}^{\rho} \tag{23.6}$$

and

$$y_{it} = (A_0 e^{git} R_{it}^{\gamma} H_{it}^{\delta} O_{it}^{\theta} G_{it}^{\rho}) k_{it}^{\alpha}. \tag{23.7}$$

We transform (23.7) into a natural logarithm and obtain the following specification of the economic growth determinants for country i in time t:

$$\ln y_{it} = \tau + \gamma \ln R + \alpha \ln k_{it} + \delta \ln H_{it} + \theta \ln O_{it} + \rho \ln G_{it} + \varepsilon_{it}, \tag{23.8}$$

where τ is the constant. Our coefficient of interest, γ, indicates the impact of remittances on economic growth. α, δ, θ and ρ represent the associated coefficients of the remaining variables contained in the specification. ε_{it} is the error term (*iid*). We decompose the latter in a time variant v_{it} a time invariant component ω_i to account for time invariant effects at the country level:

$$\varepsilon_{it} = \omega_i + v_{it}. \tag{23.9}$$

The panel equation that allows us to identify the effect of remittances on growth is therefore written as follows:[9]

$$\ln y_{it} = \tau + \gamma \ln R + \alpha \ln k_{it} + \delta \ln H_{it} + \theta \ln O_{it} + \rho \ln G_{it} + \omega_i + v_{it}. \tag{23.10}$$

Identification Strategy

Benchmark regression

As a starting exercise, we estimate (23.10) using an ordinary least square (OLS). In fact, under the assumption that remittances are exogenous, an OLS model would give an unbiased estimate of the remittances effect. However, since the amount of remittances may be linked to unobserved country-level confounders or encounter a reverse causality and measurement error issues, we expect that the estimates of the coefficient of interest, γ, will be skewed using standard regression models and can no longer be given a causal interpretation.

The identification of the workers' remittances impact on economic growth is therefore plagued by the endogeneity of remittances, a concern often mentioned in the literature. First, we may encounter the unobservable heterogeneity issue. Specifically, there may be unobservable country-level factors that may affect jointly workers' remittances and economic growth. Second, there exists a reverse causality concern. While remittances might affect economic growth, the latter may also determine the level of remittances. If the economic situation in the countries of origin deteriorates as a result of negative shocks, the migrant can support his or her family by providing more remittances (*altruistic behavior*). Similarly, if the economic conditions are conducive to sustained economic growth, the migrant may act as an investor and would enjoy taking advantage of the economic opportunities in his or her country of origin and therefore remitting (*self-interested behavior*). Finally, the third source of endogeneity is measurement error. The remittances we consider in our study are those of the World Bank and include only remittances sent through official, formal channels. Consequently, in such cases, the magnitude of remittances may be underestimated.

Although the first source of endogeneity related to unobservable heterogeneity is potentially addressed since we integrate the time invariant component in (23.10), we still have to deal with the other two possible causes of endogeneity. To benchmark our estimates with existing literature that has addressed the endogeneity issue of remittances, we follow Barajas et al. (2009) and consider the amount of remittances to the rest of the world as an exogenous variation of remittances received by each country. In other studies, endogeneity has been dealt with either by using as instruments the lagged values of remittances (*internal instruments*) or migrants' host country characteristics such as GDP per capita. The results obviously differ and the question of identification of the causal effect of remittances is still one of the major concerns and partially explains the divergence of the workers' remittances growth effects.[10]

Non-Linear Effect

The relationship between workers' remittances and economic growth is not obvious. As noted earlier, the objective of this chapter is to contribute to the existing literature on the effects of remittances on recipient economies. The results are mixed and partly due to the identification strategy taken in empirical studies. Previous empirical literature, however, may neglect an important aspect, which is the nature of the relationship that may provide insights regarding the heterogeneous effects of remittances on economic growth. More particularly, while previous studies support empirical investigations on the linearity of the relationship, we hypothesize that the connection may be non-monotonic. Our study, therefore, investigates the non-linear effects of workers' remittances on economic growth. The idea is that for countries whose remittances are not massive, the effect on growth may be negative. There is a threshold level of remittances relative to GDP at which remittances may lead to a positive effect. To investigate the issue of non-linearity of effect, we adopt two complementary empirical strategies. First, we include a quadratic polynomial of remittances as a determinant of economic growth and follow the approach of Lind and Mehlum (2010), which provides a test for the existence of U or inverted U-shaped connection. The Lind and Mehlum (2010) test enables us to investigate the necessary and sufficient conditions for the presence of a U-shaped relationship. Second, we adopt the first-differenced generalized method of moments (GMM) estimation of the dynamic panel threshold model proposed by Seo and Shin (2016). Since remittances are both endogenous and constitute the threshold variable, the approach of Seo and Shin (2016) provides an adequate framework to question the nature of the relationship between remittances and economic growth since it allows both the threshold variable and the regressors to be endogenous. Hence, the main advantage of this approach compared to the Hansen (1999) and Kremer et al. (2013) estimators is to investigate the non-linear asymmetric connections within a dynamic panel setting when one or all of the regressors are endogenous.

Quadratic polynomial of remittances

The first approach employed to investigate the non-linear effect of remittances is to include a quadratic term of workers' remittances in (23.10) such that:

$$\ln y_{it} = \tau + \gamma_1 R_{it} + \gamma_2 R_{it}^2 + \alpha k_{it} + \delta H_{it} + \theta O_{it} + \rho G_{it} + \omega_i + v_{it}. \tag{23.11}$$

We estimate (23.11) via pooled OLS and FE models. We expect γ_1 and γ_2 to be negative and positive, respectively. This suggests that the relationship between remittances and economic growth is U-shaped.

Next, we follow the approach of Lind and Mehlum (2010) that highlights that including a quadratic term in conventional regression specification is not sufficient. In their paper, they propose a test of the presence of U or inverted U-shaped connection.

We therefore test the joint hypothesis:

$$H_0: (\gamma_1 + \gamma_{22} R_{min} \geq 0) \cup (\gamma_1 + \gamma_{22} R_{max} \leq 0)$$

against the alternative hypothesis:

$$H_1: (\gamma_1 + \gamma_{22} R_{min} < 0) \cup (\gamma_1 + \gamma_{22} R_{max} > 0),$$

where R_{max} and R_{min} represent the maximum and minimum values of remittances, respectively. If the null is rejected, this supports the existence of a U-shaped association between remittances and growth.

Dynamic panel with threshold effect and endogeneity

The second strategy to check the presence of a threshold effect of workers' remittances is to rely on the dynamic panel threshold model developed by Seo and Shin (2016) that proposes an extension of the Hansen (1999) and Kremer et al. (2013) estimators. In a seminal paper, Hansen (1999) provides a panel threshold model that is appropriate for a static panel setting. However, most of the macroeconomic variables, including our outcome of GDP per capita growth, are highly persistent, implying that the dynamic panel format is more suitable. Accordingly, Hansen's model was later developed by Kremer et al. (2013) to explore the potential presence of a discrete shift in a dynamic panel setting.

One major limitation of the Kremer et al. (2013) approach is that the threshold variable regressors need to be exogenous. In this respect, Seo and Shin (2016) propose a dynamic estimator that allows both the threshold variable and contemporaneous covariates to be endogenous. This is an important point in our case. As we have underlined, the endogeneity of workers' remittances is a serious matter and ignoring it may lead to biased estimates. More precisely, Seo and Shin (2016) propose a first-differenced GMM (FD-GMM) transformation that eliminates the unobserved country effect and therefore overcomes the exogeneity assumption on threshold variable and covariates while ensuring that the estimators follow a normal distribution asymptotically.

Thus, we follow Seo and Shin (2016) and consider the following the panel threshold model to explore the non-linear remittances–growth nexus:

$$Y_{it} = (1, Z_{it}) \varnothing_1 I(R_{it} \leq \pi) + (1, Z_{it}) \varnothing_2 I(R_{it} > \pi) + \omega_i + v_{it}. \quad (23.12)$$

In (23.12), the remittances variable is treated as a threshold variable and π represents the hypothetical threshold value. $I(.)$ denotes the indicator function. Z is the matrix of control variables mentioned above including the one-period lag of GDP per capita. $\varnothing_1$ and $\varnothing_2$ correspond to slope parameters for the lower and upper regimes, respectively. ω_i denotes the individual component that captures country heterogeneity and v_{it} is the standard error term. To assess the existence of a threshold effect, we rely on a sup-Wald test provided by Seo and Shin (2016). In line with Hansen (1996), critical values are generated by a bootstrap method. In particular, the null hypothesis of the sup-Wald test is the absence of a threshold effect ($\varnothing_1 - \varnothing_2 = 0$).

Data

This chapter is based on panel data covering 37 developing countries,[11] as ranked by the World Bank in 2019, across the period 1985–2018. Our dependent variable is the per capita GDP growth. Regarding the control variables, we considered a broad set of controls commonly employed in the literature on the determinants of economic growth: gross fixed capital formation (percentage of GDP), trade openness (percentage of GDP), government expenditure (percentage of GDP) and human capital index. Our variable of interest is workers' remittances. We employ the remittances to GDP ratio as a measure of remittance flows. Data on per capita GDP, workers' remittances and controls are drawn from World Bank indicators and the World Penn Table. Table 23.2 reports the descriptive statistics for the variables covered in our empirical model. The countries

Table 23.2 Descriptive statistics

Variable	Obs	Mean	Std. Dev.	Min	Max
GDP per capita (log)	1,178	7.465	.929	5.334	9.392
Remittances relative to GDP	1,178	3.839	4.734	.001	24.899
Investment relative to GDP	1,178	20.801	6.258	5.539	46.589
Human capital	1,178	1.826	.473	1.014	3.035
Trade openness	1,178	58.409	28.373	11.087	149.453
Government expenditure relative to GDP	1,178	.167	.074	.030	.494

included in our sample show an average of about 4 percent in terms of the share of remittances relative to GDP. This figure can be as high as 25 percent for some countries.

RESULTS

Benchmark Estimates

This section describes benchmark findings when using OLS, FE and IV estimators. Table 23.3 reports the correlation between workers' remittances and economic growth. The first column links remittances (percentage of GDP) and economic growth without any controls. The coefficient of remittances in this first specification is statically insignificant. The second column of Table 23.3 relates economic growth to remittances, gross fixed capital formation, human capital, trade openness and government expenditures. We also include country fixed effects to limit the unobservable heterogeneity concern. In this case, the variable of interest is statistically significant, suggesting a negative correlation between workers' remittances and growth.

The estimates we have presented cannot be interpreted as causal due to the issue of endogeneity of remittances. In fact, the estimated relationships provided in Table 23.3 between remittances and growth may, in some ways, capture a "third" independent variable effect. In Table 23.4, we display results when employing an instrumental variable approach. Column 1 of Table 23.4 reports the results for the first-stage regression. The estimated effect of the instrument on remittances is positively and statistically significant. This suggests that remittances at the world level account for the variation in workers' remittances received for each country, particularly via cost reduction and remitting facility. The first-stage F-statistic for excluded instruments is higher than 10 showing that the remittances at the global level satisfy the instrument relevance. Next, column 2 presents the second-stage estimates. They document a positive and significant impact of remittances on growth. It is worth noting that the IV estimates are different from those obtained with fixed effects in Table 23.3. Thus, without addressing the endogeneity concern, the true effect of workers' remittances on growth is biased.

As the literature does not fully agree on the nature of the relationship between remittances and economic growth, our estimates are in line with this discrepancy. As we noted in Table 23.3, by relating remittances only to growth without any controls, the

Table 23.3 Remittances and economic growth: OLS and FE estimates

Variables	(1)	(2)
	\multicolumn{2}{c}{GDP per capita (log)}	
Remittances relative to GDP	−0.000637	−0.00423***
	(0.00400)	(0.00162)
Investment relative to GDP		0.00579***
		(0.00101)
Human capital		0.661***
		(0.0241)
Trade openness		0.00221***
		(0.000409)
Government expenditure relative to GDP		0.252***
		(0.0882)
Constant	7.448***	6.736***
	(0.0346)	(0.0665)
Country FE	NO	YES
Observations	1,443	1,319
R-squared	0.0006	0.974

Note: Robust standard errors in parentheses; *** $p < 0.01$, ** $p < 0.05$, * $p < 0.1$.

relationship is not significant. Second, including fixed effects to capture country-time invariant effects as well as control variables leads to a negative and significant correlation. Lastly, instrumenting remittances and addressing the three sources of endogeneity leads to estimates of a positive effect of remittances on economic growth.

Non-Linear Effect of Workers' Remittances

The estimates provided above are premised on the linearity of the effect of workers' remittances on economic growth. Indeed, one of the targets of our study is to question the linear approach that predominates previous empirical studies on the remittances–growth nexus. In fact, assuming linearity of the association between remittances and economic growth may be misleading. The rationale is that the effect of remittances differs according to the magnitude of these financial flows within the size of the recipient economies. To examine the non-linearity dimension, we first include a quadratic term of workers' remittances in the growth regression. The results are provided in Table 23.5. They indicate that remittances have a negative and significant impact, while remittances SQ has a positive and significant one.

Based on the two specifications given in Table 23.5, we perform the Lind and Mehlum (2010) test. The findings provided in Table 23.6 show that the lower-bound slope of remittances is negative and the upper-bound slope of remittances is positive. Both bounds are statistically significant. The Sasabushi test in the bottom panel of Table 23.6 suggests that the null hypothesis is rejected at the 1 percent level revealing that the estimates are consistent with the presence of a U-shaped relationship between remittances and growth.

Table 23.4 *Remittances and economic growth: OLS and IV-FE estimates*

Variables	(1) Remittances relative to GDP	(2) GDP per capita (log)
Global remittances relative to world GDP	5.484*** (0.606)	
Remittances relative to GDP		0.0494*** (0.0107)
Investment relative to GDP	0.0157 (0.0107)	0.00351*** (0.00104)
Human capital	−2.519*** (0.537)	0.578*** (0.0349)
Trade openness	0.0526*** (0.00666)	−0.000975 (0.000858)
Government expenditure relative to GDP	−1.892** (0.861)	0.343*** (0.0985)
Constant	0.742 (0.925)	7.046*** (0.0996)
Country FE	Yes	Yes
Observations	1,314	1,314
R-squared	0.733	0.954
F-test	97.84	

Note: Robust standard errors in parentheses; *** $p < 0.01$, ** $p < 0.05$, * $p < 0.1$.

Next, we discuss the threshold regressions when remittances are treated as the threshold variable. The non-linear hypothesis is accepted at the 1 percent significance level in both the static and dynamic threshold models in Table 23.7. The estimation of the static and dynamic models (with a lagged independent variable of growth) shows that the threshold parameter is significant reconfirming that there is a threshold effect of remittances on growth across countries. Concerning the threshold value, we note that the threshold level of workers' remittances is between 4 and 6 percent of GDP. We find that the impact of remittances on growth is estimated to be negative under the first regime and positive in the second regime. From these findings, it is clear that a U-shaped association occurs between remittances and economic growth implying that a low level of remittances is harmful to growth. When moving beyond the threshold level, workers' remittances may be beneficial for growth. This is confirmed when we divide the sample in two according to the 4 percent threshold identified in the dynamic model. The results are reported in Table 23.8 and show that for the first group of countries remittances have a negative effect while for the second group the effect is positive.

These findings must obviously be interpreted in a microeconomic setting. In an economy where the level of remittances is low, households will channel the use of remittances into consumption. This can have adverse effects in terms of growth if domestic production is failing to cover internal demand, thereby making it necessary to seek out

Table 23.5 Non-linear remittances–growth nexus: OLS and FE estimates

Variables	(1)	(2)
	\multicolumn{2}{c}{GDP per capita (log)}	
Remittances relative to GDP	−0.0852***	−0.0170***
	(0.0149)	(0.00398)
Remittances relative to GDP SQ	0.00488***	0.000746***
	(0.000814)	(0.000216)
Investment relative to GDP		0.00573***
		(0.00103)
Human capital		0.671***
		(0.0230)
Trade openness		0.00228***
		(0.000402)
Government expenditure relative to GDP		0.223**
		(0.0876)
Constant	7.593***	6.738***
	(0.0450)	(0.0660)
Country FE	No	Yes
Observations	1,443	1,319
R-squared	0.029	0.975

Note: Robust standard errors in parentheses; *** p < 0.01, ** p < 0.05, * p < 0.1.

Table 23.6 Lind and Mehlum U test

	(1)	(2)
Slope at R_{min}	−0.0851***	−0.0170***
	[−5.7180]	[−4.2798]
Slope at R_{max}	0.1898***	0.0250***
	[5.9531]	[2.8947]
Sasabuchi test for inverse U shape	5.72	2.89
	(0.0000)	(0.0019)
Extremum point	8.7214	11.4037
95% confidence interval, Fieller method	[7.8137; 9.6193]	[9.3123; 16.2761]

Note: P-values in square brackets and T-values in parentheses; *** p < 0.01, ** p < 0.05, * p <0.1.

the global market. Conversely, if remittances represent a significant share of the recipient economy, households can initiate investments, which will boost economic growth. Another possible explanation is that countries with large amounts of remittances treat these financial flows as a driver of economic and social development through a clear scheme to channel remittances and to avoid the adverse effects that could lead to inappropriate practices.

Table 23.7 *Remittances and economic growth: dynamic threshold regressions*

Variables	(1)	(2)
	GDP per capita (log)	
Lower regime		
Remittances relative to GDP	−0.0962***	−0.117**
	(0.0155)	(0.0473)
GDP per capita (log) in t−1		0.195
		(0.356)
Investment relative to GDP	0.00600*	0.0174*
	(0.00350)	(0.00944)
Human capital	0.635***	0.517
	(0.135)	(0.438)
Trade openness	0.000954*	−0.00201
	(0.000504)	(0.00152)
Government expenditure relative to GDP	−0.0894	−0.280
	(0.356)	(0.831)
Upper regime		
Remittances relative to GDP	0.112***	0.158***
	(0.0175)	(0.0530)
GDP per capita (log) in t−1		0.0173
		(0.187)
Investment relative to GDP	−0.00273	−0.0268*
	(0.00500)	(0.0153)
Human capital	0.258***	0.578*
	(0.0632)	(0.305)
Trade openness	−0.00155*	0.00375
	(0.000802)	(0.00280)
Government expenditure relative to GDP	1.685***	3.276***
	(0.608)	(1.154)
Constant	−1.249***	−1.852
	(0.211)	(1.168)
Threshold	6.538***	4.045**
	(1.634)	(1.816)
Upper regime (%)	20.11	31.06
Bootstrapped p-value	0.000	0.000
Observations	1178	1178

Note: Standard errors in parentheses; *** $p < 0.01$, ** $p < 0.05$, * $p < 0.1$.

CONCLUSION

Developing countries have a very large number of migrants who can play a crucial economic and social role, particularly through remittances. This role deserves special attention from academics, researchers and policy makers. Despite their geographical remoteness, migrants have maintained strong ties with their countries of origin. This is reflected, in part, by the volume of remittances made. These are not only for consumption

Table 23.8 *Remittances and economic growth: subsamples*

Variables	(1)	(2)
	GDP per capita (log)	
	= < Threshold	≻ Threshold
Remittances relative to GDP	−0.0459***	0.00656**
	(0.00708)	(0.00269)
Investment relative to GDP	0.0124***	0.0118***
	(0.00127)	(0.00263)
Human capital	0.548***	0.754***
	(0.0299)	(0.0394)
Trade openness	0.00435***	−0.000936
	(0.000527)	(0.000709)
Government expenditure relative to GDP	0.415***	0.438***
	(0.117)	(0.155)
Constant	6.626***	4.883***
	(0.0727)	(0.118)
Country FE	Yes	Yes
Observations	812	366
R-squared	0.982	0.973

Note: Robust standard errors in parentheses; *** $p < 0.01$, ** $p < 0.05$, * $p < 0.1$.

but also for investment. Moreover, their impact can change on two dimensions: spatial and temporal. The objective of this chapter was therefore to analyze remittances more closely on economic growth and to understand their behavior and why their impact varies according to the country of origin.

The empirical literature on remittances and economic growth does not lead to a conclusion on the nature of the effect due to the endogeneity of remittances and the multiple identification strategies implemented. In this chapter, we propose another empirical vision by focusing on the non-linearity of the remittances–growth nexus. Estimates show that remittances have a negative effect on economic growth but that there is a certain threshold at which remittances can be a catalyst for economic development.

Moreover, it should be noted that the questions raised in this chapter are highly relevant and reflect some of the debates recently raised by economists, academics and politicians. The purpose of this chapter was to enrich the empirical literature on remittances by further refining the understanding of their impact on economic growth. Beyond the empirical contribution that this chapter can bring to the literature, the results show that countries that receive few remittances are the ones that struggle in terms of economic growth. In the case of a relatively low remittance intensity, our results do not exclude the direct positive effects that remittances have on recipient households, such as access to education and health and certain basic needs. Despite this finding, remittances, while not contributing to economic growth, can nonetheless help improve the economic situation of recipient households in the broadest sense.

464 *Handbook on migration and welfare*

Developing countries need to encourage migrants abroad to send more remittances by improving ties but also need to consider these financial flows in their economic and social development strategies. This requires reducing remittance transfer costs and providing institutional and organizational incentives for migrants to send more remittances.

NOTES

1. The authors would like to thank Refk Selmi and Markus M.L. Crepaz for their comments on earlier versions of this chapter.
2. For example, search results on Google Scholar give for the words "remittances" and "FDI" in November 2020 about 351,000 references for remittances and 1,040,000 for FDIs.
3. This matter is discussed in the third section of this chapter.
4. Countries considered: Afghanistan, Tajikistan, Yemen, Burkina Faso, Burundi, Democratic Republic of the Congo, Ethiopia, Gambia, Guinea, Guinea-Bissau, Liberia, Madagascar, Malawi, Mali, Mozambique, Niger, Sierra Leone, Sudan, Togo, Uganda and Haiti.
5. Countries considered: Maldives, Albania, Armenia, Azerbaijan, Belarus, Bosnia and Herzegovina, Bulgaria, Georgia, Kazakhstan, Kosovo, Montenegro, North Macedonia, Russian Federation, Serbia, Turkey, Turkmenistan, Iraq, Jordan, Lebanon, China, Fiji, Indonesia, Malaysia, Marshall Islands, Samoa, Thailand, Tonga, Tuvalu, Botswana, Gabon, Namibia, South Africa, Argentina, Belize, Brazil, Colombia, Costa Rica, Dominica, Dominican Republic, Ecuador, Grenada, Guatemala, Guyana, Jamaica, Mexico, Paraguay, Peru, St. Lucia, St. Vincent and the Grenadines and Suriname.
6. The considered countries include Bangladesh, Bhutan, India, Nepal, Pakistan, Sri Lanka, Kyrgyz Republic, Moldova, Ukraine, Uzbekistan, Algeria, Djibouti, Morocco, Tunisia, West Bank and Gaza, Cambodia, Kiribati, Lao PDR, Mongolia, Myanmar, Papua New Guinea, Philippines, Solomon Islands, Timor-Leste, Vanuatu, Vietnam, Angola, Benin, Cabo Verde, Cameroon, Comoros, Cote d'Ivoire, Eswatini, Ghana, Kenya, Lesotho, Nigeria, Sao Tome and Principe, Senegal, Tanzania, Zambia, Zimbabwe, Bolivia, El Salvador, Honduras and Nicaragua.
7. These incorporate Angola, Turkmenistan, Suriname, Cambodia, Maldives, Argentina, Gabon, Algeria, Iraq, Turkey, Brazil, Botswana, China, Guinea, South Africa, Kazakhstan, Zambia, Namibia, Tonga, Ethiopia, Russian Federation, Cote d'Ivoire, Tanzania, Cameroon, Costa Rica and Indonesia.
8. For comparison purposes, the following countries were considered: Afghanistan, Albania, Algeria, Angola, Argentina, Armenia, Azerbaijan, Bangladesh, Belarus, Belize, Benin, Bhutan, Bolivia, Bosnia and Herzegovina, Botswana, Brazil, Bulgaria, Burkina Faso, Burundi, Cabo Verde, Cambodia, Cameroon, China, Colombia, Comoros, Congo, Dem. Rep., Costa Rica, Cote d'Ivoire, Djibouti, Dominica, Dominican Republic, Ecuador, Egypt, Arab Rep., El Salvador, Eswatini, Ethiopia, Fiji, Gabon, Gambia, Georgia, Ghana, Grenada, Guatemala, Guinea, Guinea-Bissau, Guyana, Haiti, Honduras, India, Indonesia, Iraq, Jamaica, Jordan, Kazakhstan, Kenya, Kiribati, Kosovo, Kyrgyz Republic, Lao PDR, Lebanon, Lesotho, Liberia, Madagascar, Malawi, Malaysia, Maldives, Mali, Marshall Islands, Mexico, Moldova, Mongolia, Montenegro, Morocco, Mozambique, Myanmar, Namibia, Nepal, Nicaragua, Niger, Nigeria, North Macedonia, Pakistan, Papua New Guinea, Paraguay, Peru, Philippines, Russian Federation, Samoa, Sao Tome and Principe, Senegal, Serbia, Sierra Leone, Solomon Islands, South Africa, Sri Lanka, St. Lucia, St. Vincent and the Grenadines, Sudan, Suriname, Tajikistan, Tanzania, Thailand, Timor-Leste, Togo, Tonga, Tunisia, Turkey, Turkmenistan, Tuvalu, Uganda, Ukraine, Uzbekistan, Vanuatu, Vietnam, West Bank and Gaza, Yemen, and Zambia.
9. Since most variables are expressed as a percentage of GDP, we do not take the natural log to make simplicity in terms of interpretation. Estimates with or without the log are similar.
10. Barajas et al. (2009) provide an excellent analysis of the constraints of the instruments that have been used in the literature examining the impact of remittances on economic growth.
11. The countries used in the study are: Algeria, Argentina, Bangladesh, Benin, Bolivia, Botswana, Brazil, Burkina-Faso, Cameroon, Cape Verde, Colombia, Dominican Republic, Egypt, El Salvador, Ghana, Guatemala, Honduras, India, Ivory Coast, Jordan, Kenya, Madagascar, Mali, Morocco, Niger, Nigeria, Pakistan, Paraguay, Philippines, Rwanda, Senegal, South Africa, Sudan, Thailand, Togo, Tunisia and Turkey.

REFERENCES

Abdih, Yasser, Ralph Chami, Jihad Dagher and Peter Montiel. 2012. "Remittances and institutions: Are remittances a curse?" *World Development* 40(4): 657–666.

Abduvaliev, Mubinzhon and Ricardo Bustillo. 2020. "Impact of remittances on economic growth and poverty reduction amongst CIS countries." *Post-Communist Economies* 32(4): 525–546.

Acosta, Pablo A., Emmanuel K.K. Lartey and Federico S. Mandelman. 2009. "Remittances and the Dutch disease." *Journal of International Economics* 79(1): 102–116.

Adams, Jr., Richard H. and Alfredo Cuecuecha. 2010. "Remittances, household expenditure and investment in Guatemala." *World Development* 38(11): 1626–1641.

Adams, Samuel and Edem Kwame Mensah Klobodu. 2016. "Remittances, regime durability and economic growth in Sub-Saharan Africa (SSA)." *Economic Analysis and Policy* 50(1): 1–8.

Adenutsi, Deodat E. 2011. "Financial development, international migrant remittances and endogenous growth in Ghana." *Studies in Economics and Finance* 28(1): 68–89.

Agbola, Frank Wogbe. 2013. "Does human capital constrain the impact of foreign direct investment and remittances on economic growth in Ghana?" *Applied Economics* 45(19): 2853–2862.

Aggarwal, Reena, Asli Demirgüç-Kunt and Maria Soledad Martínez Pería. 2011. "Do remittances promote financial development?" *Journal of Development Economics* 96(2): 255–264.

Ahmed, Faisal Z. 2013. "Remittances deteriorate governance." *Review of Economics and Statistics* 95(4): 1166–1182.

Ajide, Folorunsho M. and John A. Olayiwola. 2020. "Remittances and corruption in Nigeria." *Journal of Economics and Development* 23(1): 19–33.

Akkoyunlu, Sule and Konstantin Arkadievich Kholodilin. 2006. "What affects the remittances of Turkish workers: Turkish or German output?" Technical report DIW Discussion Papers.

Amuedo-Dorantes, Catalina and Susan Pozo. 2004. "Workers' remittances and the real exchange rate: A paradox of gifts." *World Development* 32(8): 1407–1417.

Asiedu, Edward and Nurokinan Chimbar. 2020. "Impact of remittances on male and female labor force participation patterns in Africa: Quasi-experimental evidence from Ghana." *Review of Development Economics* 24(3): 1009–1026.

Aycinena, Diego, Claudia Martinez and Dean Yang. 2010. "The impact of remittance fees on remittance flows: Evidence from a field experiment among Salvadoran migrants." Report, University of Michigan.

Azam, Muhammad, Yusnidah Ibrahim and Bardia Bakhtyar. 2014. "Foreign direct investment and economic growth in Asia." Актуальні проблеми економіки 11: 58–67.

Azizi, Seyed Soroosh. 2020. "Impacts of remittances on financial development." *Journal of Economic Studies* 47(3): 467–477.

Bahadir, Berrak, Santanu Chatterjee and Thomas Lebesmuehlbacher. 2018. "The macroeconomic consequences of remittances." *Journal of International Economics* 111: 214–232.

Barajas, Adolfo, Ralph Chami, Connel Fullenkamp, Michael Gapen and Peter J. Montiel. 2009. "Do workers' remittances promote economic growth?" IMF Working Papers, 1–22.

Beine, Michel, Frédéric Docquier and Maurice Schi. 2013. "International migration, transfer of norms and home country fertility." *Canadian Journal of Economics/Revue canadienne d'économique* 46(4): 1406–1430.

Bettin, Giulia and Alberto Zazzaro. 2012. "Remittances and financial development: Substitutes or complements in economic growth?" *Bulletin of Economic Research* 64(4): 509–536.

Bouhga-Hagbe, Jacques. 2006. "Altruism and workers' remittances: Evidence from selected countries in the Middle East and Central Asia." Working Paper 06/130.

Bouoiyour, Jamal and Amal Miftah. 2014. "Household welfare, international migration and children time allocation in rural Morocco." *Journal of Economic Development* 39(2): 75–95.

Bouoiyour, Jamal, Refk Selmi and Amal Miftah. 2019. "The relationship between remittances and macroeconomic variables in times of political and social upheaval: Evidence from Tunisia's Arab Spring." *Economics of Transition and Institutional Change* 27(2): 355–394.

Brown, Richard P.C., Fabrizio Carmignani and Ghada Fayad. 2013. "Migrants remittances and financial development: Macro-and micro level evidence of a perverse relationship." *The World Economy* 36(5): 636–660.

Catrinescu, Natalia, Miguel Leon-Ledesma, Matloob Piracha and Bryce Quillin. 2009. "Remittances, institutions, and economic growth." *World Development* 37(1): 81–92.

Cazachevici, Alina, Tomas Havranek and Roman Horvath. 2020. "Remittances and economic growth: A meta-analysis." *World Development* 134: 105–121.

Chami, Ralph, Connel Fullenkamp and Samir Jahjah. 2005. "Are immigrant remittance flows a source of capital for development?" *IMF Sta Papers* 52(1): 55–81.

Chami, Ralph, Adolfo Barajas, Thomas Cosimano, Connel Fullenkamp, Michael Gapen and Peter Montiel. 2008. "Macroeconomic consequences of remittances." Washington, DC: International Monetary Fund.
Combes, Jean-Louis and Christian Ebeke. 2011. "Remittances and household consumption instability in developing countries." *World Development* 39(7): 1076–1089.
Comes, Calin-Adrian, Elena Bunduchi and Valentina Vasile. 2018. "The impact of foreign direct investments and remittances on economic growth: A case study in central and eastern Europe." *Sustainability* 10(1): 238.
Deisting, Florent, Farid Makhlouf and Adil Naamane. 2012. "Développement financier et croissance économique." Technical report.
Durand, Jorge, William Kandel, Emilio A. Parrado and Douglas S. Massey. 1996. "International migration and development in Mexican communities." *Demography* 33(2): 249–264.
Ebeke, Christian Hubert. 2011. "Remittances, countercyclicality, openness and government size." *Louvain Economic Review* 77(4): 89–114.
Edelbloude, Johanna, Charlotte Fontan Sers and Farid Makhlouf. 2017. "Do remittances respond to revolutions? The evidence from Tunisia." *Research in International Business and Finance* 42: 94–101.
Feeny, Simon, Sasi Iamsiraroj and Mark McGillivray. 2014. "Remittances and economic growth: Larger impacts in smaller countries?" *Journal of Development Studies* 50(8): 1055–1066.
Frankel, Jeffrey. 2011. "Are bilateral remittances countercyclical?" *Open Economies Review* 22(1): 1–16.
Giuliano, Paola and Marta Ruiz-Arranz. 2009. "Remittances, financial development, and growth." *Journal of Development Economics* 90(1): 144–152.
Griffin, Keith. 1978. "On the emigration of the peasantry." In *International Inequality and National Poverty*. New York: Springer, 81–96.
Gyimah-Brempong, Kwabena and Elizabeth Asiedu. 2015. "Remittances and investment in education: Evidence from Ghana." *Journal of International Trade and Economic Development* 24(2): 173–200.
Hansen, Bruce E. 1996. "Inference when a nuisance parameter is not identified under the null hypothesis." *Econometrica: Journal of the Econometric Society* 64(2): 413–430.
Hansen, Bruce E. 1999. "Threshold effects in non-dynamic panels: Estimation, testing, and inference." *Journal of Econometrics* 93(2): 345–368.
Hien, Nguyen Phuc, Cao Thi Hong Vinh and Vu Thi Phuong Mai. 2020. "Remittances, real exchange rate and the Dutch disease in Asian developing countries." *Quarterly Review of Economics and Finance* 77: 131–143.
Hunger, Uwe. 2004. "Indian IT entrepreneurs in the US and in India: An illustration of the brain gain hypothesis." *Journal of Comparative Policy Analysis: Research and Practice* 6(2): 99–109.
Imai, Katsushi S., Raghav Gaiha, Abdilahi Ali and Nidhi Kaicker. 2014. "Remittances, growth and poverty: New evidence from Asian countries." *Journal of Policy Modeling* 36(3): 524–538.
Încalțărău, Cristian and Liviu-George Maha. 2012. "The impact of remittances on consumption and investment in Romania." *Eastern Journal of European Studies* 3(2): 61–86.
Jawaid, Syed Tehseen and S.A. Raza. 2016. "Effects of workers' remittances and its volatility on economic growth in South Asia." *International Migration*, 54(2): 50–68.
Jawaid, Syed Tehseen and Shaikh Muhammad Saleem. 2017. "Foreign capital inflows and economic growth of Pakistan." *Journal of Transnational Management* 22(2): 121–149.
Jayaraman, Tiruvalangadu K., Chee-Keong Choong and Ronald Ravinesh Kumar. 2011. "Financial sector development and remittances in Pacific island economies: How do they help the world's two most recipient-dependent countries?" *Perspectives on Global Development and Technology* 10(3–4): 386–405.
Jayaraman, Tiruvalangadu K., Chee-Keong Choong and Ronald Ravinesh Kumar. 2012. "Role of remittances in India's economic growth." *Global Business and Economics Review* 14(3): 159–177.
Jouini, Jamel. 2015. "Economic growth and remittances in Tunisia: Bidirectional causal links." *Journal of Policy Modeling* 37(2): 355–373.
Kan, Sophia. 2020. "Is an ounce of remittance worth a pound of health? The case of Tajikistan." *International Migration Review* 55(2): 347–381.
Kapur, Devesh and David Singer. 2006. "Remittances, government spending, and the global economy." Annual Meeting, San Diego, CA, 22–25.
Katseli, Louka T., Robert E.B. Lucas and Theodora Xenogiani. 2006. "Effects of migration on sending countries: What do we know?" www.un.org/en/development/desa/population/events/pdf/other/turin/P11_Katseli.pdf.
Keely, Charles B. and Bao Nga Tran. 1989. "Remittances from labor migration: Evaluations, performance and implications." *International Migration Review* 23(3): 500–525.
Kim, Jounghyeon. 2019. "The impact of remittances on exchange rate and money supply: Does openness matter in developing countries?" *Emerging Markets Finance and Trade* 55(15): 3682–3707.
Kim, Namsuk. 2007. "The impact of remittances on labor supply: The case of Jamaica." Washington, DC: World Bank.
Kremer, Stephanie, Alexander Bick and Dieter Nautz. 2013. "Inflation and growth: New evidence from a dynamic panel threshold analysis." *Empirical Economics* 44(2): 861–878.

Kumar, Ronald Ravinesh, Peter Josef Stauvermann, Arvind Patel and Selvin Prasad. 2018. "The effect of remittances on economic growth in Kyrgyzstan and Macedonia: Accounting for financial development." *International Migration* 56(1): 95–126.

Lartey, Emmanuel K.K. 2017. "Exchange rate flexibility and the effect of remittances on economic growth." *Review of Development Economics* 21(1): 103–125.

Le, Thanh. 2009. "Trade, remittances, institutions, and economic growth." *International Economic Journal* 23(3): 391–408.

Lind, Jo Thori and Halvor Mehlum. 2010. "With or without U? The appropriate test for a U-shaped relationship." *Oxford Bulletin of Economics and Statistics* 72(1): 109–118.

Lindstrom, David P. and Elisa Munoz-Franco. 2006. "Migration and maternal health services utilization in rural Guatemala." *Social Science and Medicine* 63(3): 706–721.

Makhlouf, Farid. 2013a. *Transferts de fonds vers le Maroc, enjeux, comportement et impacts*. PhD thesis, Pau.

Makhlouf, Farid. 2013b. "Remittances and Dutch disease: A meta-analysis." Technical report.

Makhlouf, Farid. 2019. "Is productivity affected by remittances? The evidence from Morocco." *Journal of International Development* 31(2): 211–222.

Makhlouf, Farid and Kamal Kasmaoui. 2017. "The impact of oil price on remittances." *Journal of Energy and Development* 43(1/2): 293–310.

Makhlouf, Farid and Kamal Kasmaoui. 2020. "Remittances and business cycle in Morocco." *Economics Bulletin* 40(2): 1431–1445.

Makhlouf, Farid and Mazhar Mughal. 2011. "Volatility of remittances to Pakistan: What do the data tell?" *Economics Bulletin* 31(1): 605–612.

Makhlouf, Farid and Mazhar Mughal. 2013. "Remittances, Dutch disease, and competitiveness: A Bayesian analysis." *Journal of Economic Development* 38(2): 67–97.

Makhlouf, Farid, Kamal Kasmaoui and Johanna Edelbloude. 2019. "Voting with the wallet: The response of remittances to political systems." *Economics Bulletin* 39(2): 1639–1650.

Makun, Keshmeer Kanewar. 2018. "Imports, remittances, direct foreign investment and economic growth in Republic of the Fiji Islands: An empirical analysis using ARDL approach." *Kasetsart Journal of Social Sciences* 39(3): 439–447.

Mandelman, Federico S. and Andrei Zlate. 2012. "Immigration, remittances and business cycles." *Journal of Monetary Economics* 59(2): 196–213.

Mankiw, N. Gregory, David Romer and David N. Weil. 1992. "A contribution to the empirics of economic growth." *Quarterly Journal of Economics* 107(2): 407–437.

Massey, Douglas S. and Emilio A. Parrado. 1998. "International migration and business formation in Mexico." *Social Science Quarterly*: 1–20.

Meyer, Jean-Baptiste. 2001. "Network approach versus brain drain: Lessons from the diaspora." *International Migration* 39(5): 91–110.

Meyer, Jean-Baptiste and Mercy Brown. 1999. "Scientific diasporas: A new approach to the brain drain." Management of Social Transformations Programme.

Mim, Sami Ben and Fatma Mabrouk. 2014. "Through which channels do remittances promote human capital and growth?" *Mondes en developpement* 3: 131–147.

Mohamed, Sufian Eltayeb and Moise G. Sidiropoulos. 2010. "Does workers' remittances affect growth: Evidence from seven MENA labor exporting countries." *International Research Journal of Finance and Economics* 46(14): 181–194.

Mughal, Mazhar and Junaid Ahmed. 2014. "Remittances and business cycles: Comparison of South Asian countries." *International Economic Journal* 28(4): 513–541.

Mughal, Mazhar and Amar Anwar. 2014. "Fertility responses to migrant remittances in Pakistan." In *Migrant Remittances in South Asia*. New York: Springer, 235–254.

Mughal, Mazhar and Farid Makhlouf. 2013. "Labour effects of foreign and domestic remittances evidence from Pakistan." *International Review of Applied Economics* 27(6): 798–821.

Mundaca, B. Gabriela. 2009. "Remittances, financial market development, and economic growth: The case of Latin America and the Caribbean." *Review of Development Economics* 13(2): 288–303.

Nyamongo, Esman Morekwa, Roseline N. Misati, Leonard Kipyegon and Lydia Ndirangu. 2012. "Remittances, financial development and economic growth in Africa." *Journal of Economics and Business* 64(3): 240–260.

Pradhan, Gyan, Mukti Upadhyay and Kamal Upadhyaya. 2008. "Remittances and economic growth in developing countries." *European Journal of Development Research* 20(3): 497–506.

Ramirez, Miguel D. 2013. "Do financial and institutional variables enhance the impact of remittances on economic growth in Latin America and the Caribbean? A panel cointegration analysis." *International Advances in Economic Research* 19(3): 273–288.

Rao, B. Bhaskara. 2010. "Time-series econometrics of growth-models: A guide for applied economists." *Applied Economics* 42(1): 73–86.

Rao, B. Bhaskara and Gazi Mainul Hassan. 2012. "Are the direct and indirect growth effects of remittances significant?" *The World Economy* 35(3): 351–372.

Ratha, Dilip. 2007. "Leveraging remittances for development." *Policy Brief* 3(11): 1–16.

Rozelle, Scott, J. Edward Taylor and Alan DeBrauw. 1999. "Migration, remittances, and agricultural productivity in China." *American Economic Review* 89(2): 287–291.

Russell, Sharon Stanton. 1986. "Remittances from international migration: A review in perspective." *World Development* 14(6): 677–696.

Saxenian, Anna Lee. 2005. "From brain drain to brain circulation: Transnational communities and regional upgrading in India and China." *Studies in Comparative International Development* 40(2): 35–61.

Sayan, Serdar. 2004. "Guest workers' remittances and output fluctuations in host and home countries: The case of remittances from Turkish workers in Germany." *Emerging Markets Finance and Trade* 40(6): 68–81.

Sayan, Serdar and Ayca Tekin-Koru. 2007. "Business cycles and remittances: A comparison of the cases of Turkish workers in Germany and Mexican workers in the US." www.researchgate.net/publication/24114739_Business_Cycles_and_Remittances_A_Comparison_of_the_Cases_of_Turkish_Workers_in_Germany_and_Mexican_Workers_in_the_US.

Sayan, Serdar, Bedri Tas and Ayse Yalta. 2010. "Cyclical behavior of Mexican remittances over the Mexican and the US business cycles." Technical report, TOBB University of Economics and Technology, Department of Economics.

Schiantarelli, Fabio. 2005. "Global economic prospects 2006: Economic implications of remittances and migration." Washington, DC: World Bank.

Senbeta, Aberra. 2013. "Remittances and the sources of growth." *Applied Economics Letters* 20(6): 572–580.

Seo, Myung Hwan and Yongcheol Shin. 2016. "Dynamic panels with threshold effect and endogeneity." *Journal of Econometrics* 195(2): 169–186.

Shukralla, Elias. 2016. "Remittances, institutions and economic growth: A closer look at some proxies for institutions." *Economics Bulletin* 36(1): 298–312.

Singer, David Andrew. 2010. "Migrant remittances and exchange rate regimes in the developing world." *American Political Science Review* 104(2): 307–323.

Singh, Raju Jan, Markus Haacker and Kyung-Woo Lee. 2011. "Determinants and macroeconomic impact of remittances in Sub-Saharan Africa." *Journal of African Economies* 20(2): 312–340.

Sirkeci, Ibrahim, Jeffrey H. Cohen and Dilip Ratha. 2012. "Migration and remittances during the global financial crisis and beyond." Washington, DC: World Bank.

Solow, Robert M. 1956. "A contribution to the theory of economic growth." *Quarterly Journal of Economics* 70(1): 65–94.

Strielkowski, Wadim. 2013. "Economic potential of remittances: Evidence from the South Asian Countries." *Journal of Applied Economic Sciences* 8(23): 120–126.

Taylor, J. Edward and Tom Jeffrey Wyatt. 1996. "The shadow value of migrant remittances, income and inequality in a household-farm economy." *Journal of Development Studies* 32(6): 899–912.

Taylor, J. Edward, Joaquin Arango, Graeme Hugo, Ali Kouaouci, Douglas S. Massey and Adela Pellegrino. 1996. "International migration and community development." *Population Index*: 397–418.

Tchantchane, Abdellatif, Gwendolyn Rodrigues and Pauline Carolyne Fortes. 2013. "An empirical study of the impact of remittance, educational expenditure and investment on growth in the Philippines." *Applied Econometrics and International Development* 13(1): 173–186.

Terrelonge, Sophia C. 2014. "For health, strength, and daily food: The dual impact of remittances and public health expenditure on household health spending and child health outcomes." *Journal of Development Studies* 50(10): 1397–1410.

Tyburski, Michael D. 2012. "The resource curse reversed? Remittances and corruption in Mexico." *International Studies Quarterly* 56(2): 339–350.

Valdivia López, Marcos and Fernando Lozano Ascencio. 2010. "A spatial approach to the link between remittances and regional growth in Mexico." *Migraciones internacionales* 5(3): 7–41.

Van Dalen, Hendrik P., George Groenewold and Tineke Fokkema. 2005. "The effect of remittances on emigration intentions in Egypt, Morocco, and Turkey." *Population Studies* 59(3): 375–392.

Vargas-Silva, Carlos. 2008. "Are remittances manna from heaven? A look at the business cycle properties of remittances." *North American Journal of Economics and Finance* 19(3): 290–303.

Vargas-Silva, Carlos, Shikha Jha and Guntur Sugiyarto. 2009. "Remittances in Asia: Implications for the fight against poverty and the pursuit of economic growth." Asian Development Bank Economics Working Paper Series 182.

Verter, Nahanga and Christian Nedu Osakwe. 2015. "Economic globalization and economic performance dynamics: Some new empirical evidence from Nigeria." *Mediterranean Journal of Social Sciences* 6(1): 87–96.

Wahba, Sadek. 1991. "What determines workers' remittances?" *Finance and Development* 28(4): 41–44.

Yang, Dean. 2003. "Remittances and human capital investment: Child schooling and child labor in the origin households of overseas Filipino workers." Unpublished manuscript, Gerald R. Ford School of Public Policy and Department of Economics.

Zhu, Yu, Zhongmin Wu, Liquan Peng and Laiyun Sheng. 2014. "Where did all the remittances go? Understanding the impact of remittances on consumption patterns in rural China." *Applied Economics* 46(12): 1312–1322.

24. Tracing the links between migration and food security in Bangladesh
Mohammad Moniruzzaman and Margaret Walton-Roberts

INTRODUCTION

The number of international migrants has reached 281 million (United Nations 2020). The stock of migrants is more widely distributed across countries and often considered one of the most visible manifestations of globalization (Favell et al. 2007; Sassen 1998). Some of the notable outcomes of international migration are transfer of financial remittances, return migration and utilization of knowledge, skills in migrants' home countries, diaspora involvement in development through trade, investment, networks and migrants' "collective remittances" (Kapur 2010; Massey and Taylor 2004). Remittances are the most substantial and measurable benefits of international migration. Internationally, $714 billion was transferred in 2019 with low and middle-income countries receiving $554 billion (World Bank 2020). However, since remittances in cash or in kind are often carried by migrants themselves or sent through unrecorded informal channels, actual figures are potentially much higher. Globally these "unrequited transfers" are the second largest source of external finance, twice the size of Official Development Assistance and almost as large as Foreign Direct Investment. The significance of remittances for migrants' families has become more apparent with both the increase in their value, but also in terms of how economic and financial shocks influence the magnitude of remittance flows. During the global financial crisis migrant remittances proved to be relatively more resilient than other financial flows to developing countries, declining only 6 percent in 2008–2009 (Ratha and Sirkeci 2011). During the COVID-19 pandemic it is clear that the amount of remittances will decrease as migrant income declines, but the channels for sending funds have also been negatively influenced by travel restrictions and closures that have restricted the actual transfer of funds, particularly in remittance corridors that are not well served by larger formal financial agencies or are negatively affected by onerous anti-money-laundering legislation (*Economist* 2020).

As a result of the rapid increase in global remittances, research on remittances gained momentum, resulting in a mushrooming of literature on their impact. However, theoretical and empirical research on the impact of remittances has produced mixed results. Migrants' remittances form a substantial resource to households to raise the quality of life in many low and middle-income countries. Remittances might have direct income effects on the receiving households that mitigate income shocks and other spatially covariant risks and raise the household's ability to access important nutritional inputs like food, sanitation facilities and health services. These resources allow poor households to obtain higher living standards and contribute to the reduction of poverty, reduce the variability of household food consumption and therefore positively influence their food and nutrition security outcomes. Surprisingly, the existing economic literature largely ignores their impact on households' food security and their long-term human development impact. The objective of this chapter is to examine the impact of migrants' remittances on household food security in Bangladesh.

Cash remittances are private resource transfers and are spent partly on consumption and partly on investment, therefore their impact on development is dauntingly complex. Empirical research focuses mostly on their positive impact on poverty reduction (Adams and Page 2005; Adams 2011; Imran et al. 2020; Lokshin et al. 2010), education, healthcare and better housing provisions (Askarov and Doucouliagos 2020; Edwards and Ureta 2003; Yang 2008), impact on inequality (Adams 1989; Koechlin and Leon 2007) and their impact on smoothing income shocks (Jones 1998; Kapur 2003). A large body of research investigated their role in facilitating access to formal financial sector services, their role in promoting the financial inclusion of the marginalized and their influence on financial development (Anzoategui et al. 2014; Gupta et al. 2009; Sobiech 2019). There is also evidence that cash remittances can assist credit-constrained entrepreneurs in inefficient and fragile credit markets (Kakhkharov 2019; Giuliano and Ruiz-Arranz 2009; Woodruff and Zenteno 2001). In the economic literature cash remittances are sometimes viewed as a "moral hazard problem" and examined in terms of their negative impact on economic growth. As non-market private transfers, cash remittances may reduce the recipient's labor market and civic participation (Acosta et al. 2009; Chami et al. 2005). The traditional view in the economic literature is that remittances are mostly used for basic livelihood needs and consumption, therefore their impacts are non-developmental (Crush 2013). Such a viewpoint fails to recognize consumption smoothing and the risk-coping mechanisms remittances offer in regard to food and nutritional insecurity.

While empirical research on migration and development is burgeoning, with few exceptions the relationship between migration and food security has been underexplored until recently (Crush 2013; Karamba et al. 2011; Moniruzzaman 2020; Nguyen and Winters 2011; Obi et al. 2020). With some national variability, remittances are estimated to constitute approximately 30 to 40 percent of migrants' household income (Adams 2011). As a result, these resources help to secure and smooth the recipients' consumption and are a critical component of household food security.

Some more recent empirical studies investigate the impact of migration and remittances on households' food and nutritional security. Based on their focus and methodological approaches these can be grouped into three categories. The first category follows purely quantitative approaches and uses secondary aggregate national data as well as multitopic household survey data to investigate linkages between migration and food security (Babatunde and Qaim 2010; Combes and Ebeke 2011; De Brauw 2011; Regmi and Paudel 2016; Jimenez 2009; Nguyen and Winters 2011; Zahonogo 2011; Quinn 2009). The second category of studies uses both qualitative and quantitative approaches to explore different dimensions of migration and food security (Crush 2013; Gray 2009; Jokisch 2002). The third category of studies uses a qualitative approach to investigate the impact of migration and remittances on agricultural intensification, landscape-related practices and migrants' social capital in creating agricultural businesses (Davis and Lopez-Carr 2014; Taylor 2004).

Most of these empirical studies use data from multipurpose secondary surveys. Caution should be taken in examining the impact of remittances on household food security using multipurpose secondary survey data for two reasons. First, the objectives of multipurpose surveys are varied and contain a vast amount of information on a wide range of variables, but may lack adequate information on migration, remittances and food security. Second, the impact of remittances on rural migrant households (MHs) will be different than urban ones. Similarly, food security experiences of temporary and circular MHs differ from those of permanent MHs. Secondary survey data do not contain disaggregated information on migration and remittances, so it is challenging to map out the role of migration and remittances in influencing household food security. This chapter addresses these problems using primary data from a survey in Bangladesh.

The remainder of the chapter proceeds as follows. Following this introduction, we describe the materials and method used in the study. We then report the descriptive results and statistical analysis, followed by a discussion of the empirical results.

MATERIALS AND METHOD

The primary data used in this chapter were collected in 2014–2015 from a small-scale household survey conducted in the south-east region of Bangladesh. There is no comprehensive database or list of MHs from which to draw a sample. However, available literature shows that outmigration is highly concentrated in southern Bangladesh. Comilla and Chandpur districts located in the south-east are two leading districts for outmigration with about 15 and 6.23 percent of the outmigrants from the country (ILO 2010; Islam 2014). Locations of the survey area were then identified from the existing literature, personal knowledge and discussions with the Upazila Nirbahi officers (chief executive officers of Upazila), the district statistical officer and Union Parishad chairmen who are familiar with the magnitude and trend of outmigration from those districts. Through these consultation processes, four villages with a high concentration of MHs from Comilla and Chandpur districts were identified for the survey.

As there was no comprehensive database or list of MHs, it was not possible to select households for interview based on any protocol or rigorous probability sampling method. Therefore, this research relied on a methodology called the Expanded Program on Immunization (EPI) cluster sampling approach developed by the World Health Organization (Bennett et al. 1991; Flynn et al. 2013; Henderson and Sundaresan 1982; Lemeshow and Robinson 1985; Lemeshow et al. 1985; Turner et al. 1996; World Health Organization 1991). The households were selected for interview following the protocols of the "random walk" approach suggested in the literature.

First, each of the villages was divided into four segments, approximately equal in size, and based on locally known informal neighborhood segmentation; Uttar para, Dakshin para, Paschim para and Purba para. For meaningful inference of migration and food security linkages, it was necessary to compare the food security situation of remittance-receiving and non-receiving households and, therefore, data were collected from both household types.

Second, a junction of two roads in a central location in each of the segments of the village was first identified for the start of the survey. The household nearest to the starting point was included for an interview. Then from that specific location of the household, a walking direction was chosen randomly for selecting households for interview.

Third, proximity selection was used to select subsequent households as the next nearest. Households were selected randomly from the direction of the walk. Every eligible household had a known (non-zero) chance of being selected. Information on the ratio of migrant and non-migrant populations in the district level was neither available nor feasible to estimate. Moreover, the villages were heavily concentrated with MHs. Therefore, one non-migrant, who had never been involved in international migration, was interviewed after interviewing every three MHs that had at least one member living abroad during the research. Through this process, data were collected from a total of 753 households while 526 were migrant remittance-receiving and 227 non-migrant households (NMHs). Five locally based enumerators were hired and trained to conduct the survey.

The study employed the local concept of "households," *Khana*, as the unit of analysis, which consists of a group of people who share living quarters and their principal meals (BBS 2017). The respondent was the head of the household or person most responsible for food acquisition and preparation in the household.

A retrospective questionnaire was designed that included questions on demographic characteristics, dwelling conditions, household size, number of children, level of education, asset and land holding, income and expenditure profile and remittances utilization pattern. Considering the multifaceted dimensions of both migration and food security, it is unlikely that any single measurement indicator or approach can effectively assess migration and food security linkages. Use of multiple measurement indicators allows a more complete and holistic understanding of these linkages. To identify and select adequate indicators, different aspects were taken into consideration, including measurability, reliability, efficiency and cost-effectiveness. In addition, the simplicity of interpretation, level of disaggregation and credibility in Bangladesh cultural contexts were considered for selecting food security assessment tools (Table 24.1).

After critically evaluating the purpose of the different metrics and their underlying constructs, four categories of food security assessment tools were included in the questionnaire: (1) a perception-based indicator, the Household Food Insecurity Access Scale (HFIAS), was used to assess food access; (2) a dietary diversity and micronutrient sufficiency indicator, the Household Dietary Diversity Score (HDDS); (3) the Coping Strategies Index (CSI) was used to compare the level and degree of food-related coping strategies, vulnerability, risk and consumption fluctuation in MHs and NMHs; and (4) specific questions were included in the questionnaire on food-related expenditure and family size to estimate the per capita food consumption expenditure. Moreover, a self-assessment question on how food remittances improved the food consumption pattern in the households was included.

The survey was conducted in the local language, Bangla. All translations were done by the first author who followed established practices of cross-language research to ensure the accuracy of data (Bracken and Barona 1991; Chang et al. 1999; Harkness 2003; McDermott and Palchanes 1994; Temple 1997; Temple and Young 2004).

Table 24.1 Comparing different food security measurement indicators

Domain/ loci measured	Metrics	Degree of sensitivity to cultural context	Cost of data collection	Required timeframe	Complicity/ skill in data collection	Susceptibility for misinterpretation
		1	2	3	4	5
Self-reported behaviors, experiences and conditions	HFIAS	L	M	M	M	M
Diversity, quality of diet	HDDS	L	L	L	L	L
Coping strategies	CSI	L	L	L	L	H
Economic gauge	Per capita food expenditure	L	L	L	M	H

Note: HFIAS: Household Food Insecurity Access Scale; HDDS: Household Dietary Diversity Score; CSI: Coping Strategies Index.

Source: Authors' own construction based on different empirical literature including Hoddinott (1999); Hoddinott and Yohannes (2002); Santeramo (2015); Jones et al. (2013).

RESULTS

Descriptive Results

The average size of the MHs was 6.1 compared with 6.2 for the NMHs. The age range of the MH sample varied from 19 to 78 years old, with the mean 45.17 years old. A slightly different dispersion was found for NMHs, where the age range was from 21 to 75 years old, with the mean 47.44 years old. More than 57 percent of MHs was female-headed, compared with 16 percent for NMHs. This higher number of female-headed MHs is an outcome of the migration of the male household heads. Irrespective of their gender, household heads had a low level of education. Over 37.2 percent of MH heads reported that they had never received any formal education compared with 56 percent for NMH heads. Some 37 percent of MH heads had completed primary school, compared with 22 percent for NMH heads, while 25 percent of MH heads reported they had completed secondary school certificates, diplomas and degrees compared with 22 percent for NMH heads. The survey did not find any significant difference between the demographic profiles of MHs and NMHs except for the gender dimension.

The two main components of net wealth in the surveyed region are homestead and farming land. Possession of homesteads and land ownership are used as proxy variables to indicate the economic status of MHs and NMHs. For subsistence farmers, land is a

Table 24.2 Distribution of land ownership

Amount of agricultural land	Migrant households No.	Migrant households % of households	Non-migrant households No.	Non-migrant households % of households
Landless	32	6.08	32	14.1
0.01–0.25	108	20.53	69	30.4
0.26–0.50	159	30.23	24	10.57
0.51–0.75	113	21.48	65	28.63
0.76–1	42	7.98	18	7.93
More than 1	72	13.69	19	8.37
Total	526	100	227	100

Note: Amount of land reported in acres (100 decimal = 1 acre and 1 acre = 4046.86 square meters).

stable source of income compared to other rural casual occupations, and the entitlement of food often depends on households' own production and access to land in the surveyed region. The amount of cultivable land owned by a household was reported in decimals in the survey and converted into acres. MHs were mostly lower middle-income and middle-income earners. The majority of MHs had homestead land (97 percent) compared with 90.3 percent of NMHs. The survey shows, however, that 6.08 percent of MHs and 14.1 percent of households do not have any farming land (Table 24.2).

For MHs, mean landholding size per household is 0.53 acres, ranging from 0.01 to more than 1 acre, compared with 0.44 acres, ranging from 0.01 to more than 1 acre for NMHs. Despite the fact that agriculture is the largest source of non-remittance income for both MHs and NMHs, more than 56.84 percent of MHs and 55.07 percent of NMHs have less than 0.5 acres of land.

Household income largely shapes the food security situation (Guo 2011; Leete and Bania 2010; Loopstra and Tarasuk 2013). All sources of income were included when calculating household income. The average total gross monthly income of MHs is Bangladeshi taka (BDTK) 14,830 ($190), and the median and mode is BDTK 13,800 and BDTK 12,000, respectively. For the NMHs, mean, median and mode income is BDTK 11,916, BDTK 1,200 and BDTK 1,000, respectively. A total of 27.9 percent of MHs reported a combined household income of less than BDTK 10,000 ($150), while 46.7 percent of NMHs reported their income was less than BDTK 10,000. A total of 10.26 percent of MHs reported a household income of more than BDTK 20,000 compared with only 1.76 percent of NMHs. The results show that the MHs are better off in terms of income and wealth as compared to the NMHs (Figure 24.1).

Both MHs and NMHs are engaged in a mixture of on- and off-farm work, such as seasonal and part-time work, and seasonal small-scale crop trading. Although a large number of the households (more than 50 percent) in the survey are farmers by profession, their livelihood depends significantly on other sources of income. Subsistence production is often insufficient to feed family members. Additional resources are necessary to procure food from the local market. NMHs lack any supplementary source of income, which makes their income-smoothing ability volatile and particularly susceptible to economic hardship. On the other hand, household remittances make up from 40 to 100 percent of

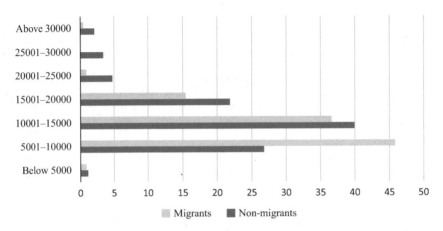

Note: In Bangladeshi taka (BDTK), $1 = 78 BDTK (approx.).

Figure 24.1 Percentage distribution of the respondents' household monthly income

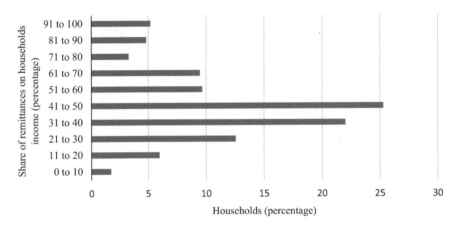

Figure 24.2 Share of remittances in recipient household incomes

total household income for more than 57 percent of MHs (Figure 24.2). As remittances constitute a significant source of income for MHs, the latter can potentially reduce their income uncertainty.

Migrant members of the surveyed households were overwhelmingly male (94 percent). Male-dominant migration may be due to the restrictive policies of the sending government and conservative values, as well as socioeconomic and cultural conditions. The average age of the migrants was approximately 33.64 years old. Forty-six percent of migrants were between 15 and 29 years, almost 39 percent between 30 and 40 years and the remaining (7.41 percent) were older than 40 years. Most of the migrants were not highly educated. More than half of the migrants had up to secondary school education, while 6 percent had graduate-level education.

Both MHs and NMHs rely on their off-farm income to purchase their food and groceries. In the current study, a major proportion of household income is spent on purchasing

Table 24.3 Food consumption expenditure of migrant and non-migrant households

Food consumption expenditure (percentage of household total income)	Migrant households No.	Migrant households % of households	Non-migrant households No.	Non-migrant households % of households
< 30	9	1.71	0	0.00
31–40	53	10.08	4	1.77
41–50	115	21.86	13	5.75
51–60	124	23.57	33	14.60
61–70	152	28.90	69	30.53
71–80	52	9.89	67	29.65
81–90	18	3.42	40	17.70
91–100	3	0.57	0	0.00
Total	526	100.00	226	100.00

food (61.88 percent) (Table 24.3). Average household expenditure on food was BDTK 8,128 ($104) per month, which is significantly higher than the amount spent on other common categories, including education and medical expenses. This situation reflects the fact that, without remittances, the amount spent on food would drop significantly. Remittances are, therefore, a critical device for household food security. About 46.2 percent of the total earnings of the MHs is contributed by remittances. This overwhelming dependence on remittances means that households' food security depends largely on migration and the remittances it provides.

Although different scientifically validated food security measurement metrics were used in the survey, a variable named "per capita food expenditure" was created to assess and compare the expenditure on food per person. MHs spent slightly more money per person per month for food compared to NMHs (Figure 24.3). MHs in the surveyed area spend BDTK 1,454 on average per person on food in a month. The median share of food consumption expenditure in (gross) income for MHs is 60 percent, compared with NMHs, for which the median is 70 percent. This difference means that migrants might be able to have some additional resources to allocate to other expenditures, including education and healthcare.

The HFIAS was used to assess household food security status, specifically the severity of food access problems of MHs and NMHs. Interviewees in both MHs and NMHs were asked nine widely accepted and validated questions regarding food consumption, thus providing insight into their subjective experiences of four domains of food insecurity: food-related anxiety and uncertainty; perceptions that the quality or quantity of accessible food is not adequate; reduced food intake by adults; and reduced food intake by children. Based on the responses concerning the perception and experience of food vulnerability, a score was generated on a 0 (most secure) to 27 (most insecure) point scale.

MHs are more likely to be food secure than are NMHs (Figure 24.4). A total of 69.2 percent of MHs had a score between 0 to 4, compared with 48.9 percent of NMHs. Twenty-seven percent of MHs had a score between 5 to 10 compared with 44.5 percent of NMHs. The remaining 3 percent of MHs had a score greater than 11, compared with 6.6 percent of NMHs.

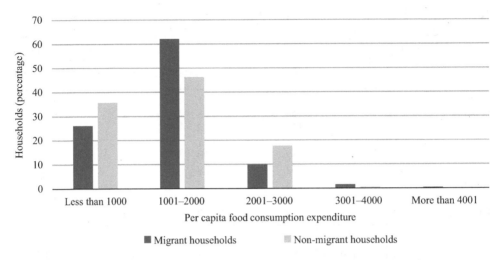

Figure 24.3 Per capita food consumption expenditure of migrant and non-migrant households

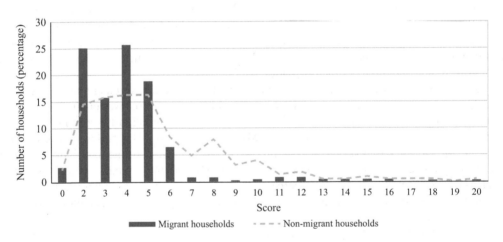

Figure 24.4 HFIAS of migrant and non-migrant households

HDDS is one of the most widely used measures to determine how many food groups were eaten by household members in the previous 24 hours. A standard list of 12 food groups is used for this indicator (Hoddinott 1999; Swindale and Bilinsky 2006). Information for each group is of a bivariate type (yes/no). All food groups have the same importance (relative weight equal to 1), with each group consumed providing one point. The score was calculated by summing equally weighted response data on the consumption of 12 food groups: cereal grain staples, roots and tubers, vegetables, fruits, meat, eggs, fish, nuts and pulses, dairy products, oils and fats, sugar and condiments.

The economic ability of a household influences its access to a wide range of food items. An increase in dietary diversity is associated with improved socioeconomic status (Hatløy

Migration and food security in Bangladesh 479

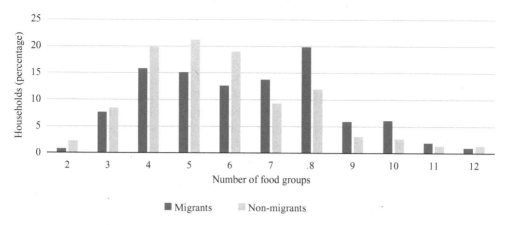

Figure 24.5 HDDS for migrant and non-migrant households

et al. 2000; Hoddinott and Yohannes 2002; Ruel 2002). A more diversified diet is associated with a number of improved health and nutritional outcomes thus making HDDS a robust indicator to assess the income effects of remittances in household food security (Hoddinott 1999; Thorne-Lyman et al. 2010). This method, however, does not capture the corresponding weighting of each food group or items, meaning that all food groups are equally weighted, regardless of their caloric or nutritional value. MHs had a more diversified diet compared with NMHs. Nearly 60.84 percent of MHs consumed more than six food groups, compared with 48.64 percent of NMHs (Figure 24.5).

The CSI, a quick and simple index, was used to assess how households adapt to food-related shocks and food shortages. The interviewees, in some cases the person with primary responsibility for preparing and serving meals, were asked a series of questions on coping strategies for food-related uncertainties. Based on the responses, a score was generated on a weighted sum of different coping strategies where the weighting reflected the frequency of use by each member of the household. This means that the higher the CSI value, the more insecure the household is. Four general categories of coping strategies were measured in the survey: dietary change (e.g., eating less nutritious and less expensive foods); increasing short-term food access (e.g., borrowing food, receiving gifts of food, obtaining food on credit); decreasing the number of people to feed (e.g., through migration); and rationing food (e.g., skipping meals or reducing the amount of food consumed per meal). For MHs, the mean CSI score was 6.6, compared with 11 for NMHs. The result shows that MHs face comparatively fewer shocks related to food insecurity than those of NMHs. Although remittances are a transitory income, these resources act as a cushion against income shocks to the household. Remittance-receiving households are likely to adopt fewer coping strategies to stabilize their consumption. MHs might be able to alter the risk profile of the household income utilizing remittances, which largely influences the state of their food security. The study also found that procuring food and other groceries on credit from a local store is a widely used food arrangement system in the surveyed region. This system works through an informal contract between the store and the consumers in rural settings. Remittance-receiving households are less dependent on this coping strategy.

Results of Statistical Analysis

Bivariate statistical analysis was conducted to assess the association and measure the strength of association between remittances and four food security indicators: food consumption expenditure, HFIAS, HDDS and CSI. The distribution of the variables was analyzed to select appropriate statistical tools (Figure 24.6). Kolmogorov–Smirnov tests showed that the distributions of the variables differed significantly from normal ($p < 0.001$). Therefore, Spearman's correlation was used to analyze the relationship between remittances and the four food security indicators.

The results show that the correlation between remittance and household food consumption expenditure is positive and statistically significant (Spearman's $\rho = 0.33$, $p < 0.001$). This indicates that as remittances increase, household food consumption expenditure tends to increase. The positive and significant correlation is probably due to the fact that remittances contribute to higher household income and therefore ensure better economic access to food.

The estimated result also indicates that the correlation between remittances and HFIAS is negative and statistically significant (Spearman's $\rho = -0.23$, $p < 0.001$); if remittances increase, households' food access problem (HFIAS) tends to decrease. This is probably due to the fact that remittances form a substantial part of household income and their presence reduces problems associated with food access and counterbalances food-related uncertainty, moving the household toward sufficient food intake. A household with access to remittances might manage economic access to food utilizing remittances compared to NMHs.

The correlation between remittances and HDDS is positive and significant (Spearman's $\rho = 0.22$, $p < 0.001$). The household dietary diversity score rises in response to increases in remittances. The reason might be remittances improve the household's economic ability to access a wider range of food items and improve the quality of their diet.

The result shows a negative and statistically significant correlation between remittances and household coping strategies (Spearman's $\rho = -0.25$, $p < 0.001$). That means if remittances increase, the number of food-related coping strategies (CSI) tend to decrease. The probable reason is that remittances act as a cushion against income shocks for the household. Therefore, receiving households need fewer food-related coping strategies. Remittances help to counterbalance against food-related shocks and reduce the need for coping strategies such as short-term dietary changes, rationing or altering food consumption, altering the intra-household distribution of food or reliance on credit for food procurement.

DISCUSSION

Bangladesh presents a good case to investigate the reciprocal relationship between migration and food security as it is one of the top 10 emigrant and remittance-receiving countries in the world (World Bank 2019) and one of the most food-insecure countries in the world. Migration from Bangladesh can be divided into three major streams: low-skilled contract-based migration to the Arab Gulf; low- and semi-skilled labor migration to emerging Southeast Asian countries, including Singapore and Malaysia; and high-skilled

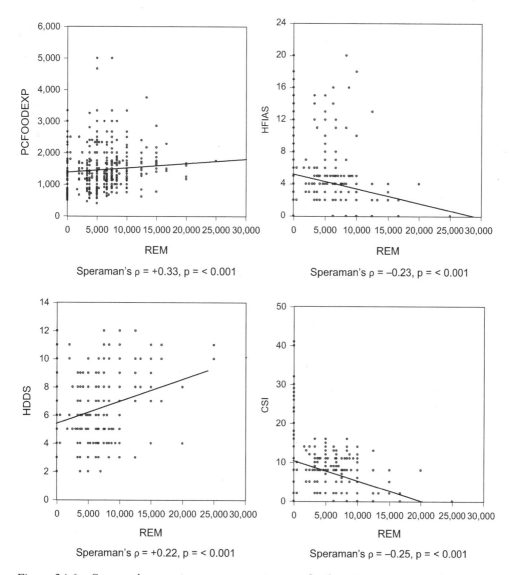

Figure 24.6 Scatterplot matrices among remittance, food consumption expenditure, HFIAS, HDDS and CSI

migration to traditional immigrant-destination Organisation for Economic Co-operation and Development (OECD) member countries. Remittances in Bangladesh come from these distinct destinations. In contrast to migration to OECD countries, migration to the Middle East and Southeast Asia are mostly short-term employment involving specific contracts with migrants returning home after completion of the contract. Outmigration from the surveyed villages predominantly falls within the first two categories. The lack of year-round employment and disguised underemployment, as well as widespread poverty in rural areas, all have contributed to the predominance of economically motivated international migration from this region. The findings of the research indicates a number of different channels and mechanisms through which migration and remittances can influence food and nutrition security.

First, income from remittances provides security for the household against the risks of "consumption instability." Since remittances constitute a substantial portion of households' income, they help to raise and improve households' ability to access sufficient, safe and nutritious food to meet their dietary and nutritional needs.

Second, cash remittances improve household dietary diversity. Sudden increases in food prices and other income-related shocks could reduce households' dietary diversity. To counterbalance the impact of these shocks, affected households usually switch from more expensive, nutritious food to cheaper and less healthy foods. Remittances are predominantly altruistic transfers that are resilient during financial crises and during income shocks (Sugiyarto et al. 2012). Increasing the purchasing power of households through cash remittances may improve their dietary diversity status thus mitigating micronutrient malnutrition. Increased expenditure from remittances on consumption has a positive impact on health and nutritional outcomes in the long run which has been evident in other empirical literature (Azzarri and Zezza 2011; De Brauw 2011).

Third, migrants' remittances have a direct income effect on food consumption. The findings of the study also suggest that remittances help the household to counterbalance against food-related shocks and remittance-receiving households tend to adopt fewer coping strategies related to food such as short-term dietary changes, rationing or altering food consumption, affecting the intra-household distribution of food or reliance on credit for food procurement.

Surprisingly, food security issues are largely absent in the global agenda on migration and development (Crush 2013) and are unexplored in the Asian context. According to the World Food Programme, remittance is the primary income for around 8 million households in Bangladesh (WFP 2012). Therefore, the findings of this research have important policy implications. Globally, the food security-related policy landscape, particularly the Sustainable Development Goals, has exclusively focused on production dimensions of food security such as targets to double the agricultural production and incomes of small-scale food producers, secure equal access to land, productive resources and inputs, knowledge, financial services, markets and implementation of resilient agricultural practices (United Nations 2015). However, the findings of this research suggest that food security of the large number of households in developing countries is not merely a simple function of what is produced and how much is produced. Rather, off-farm income sources such as remittances are a critical component of household food security. Without remittances the food security condition of a large number of households will deteriorate. Therefore, policy intervention should acknowledge the role of remittances as a critical component of household food security. On the other hand, policy intervention should also target a reduction in remittance transfer costs and broaden the networks of payment and distribution systems to maximize their benefits in ensuring household food security.

It is evident that as remittances are a transitory income, these resources help to improve economic access to food, reduce household food-related anxieties and improve dietary quality in the short term. However, remittances may also influence food security by increasing capital investment in the agricultural sector in receiving countries in the long run. In the context of fragile financial markets in developing countries, remittances may increase agricultural investment and help bypass high borrowing costs from formal credit and insurance institutions (Chiodi et al. 2012; Jokisch 2002). They may also ease credit constraints and aid the adoption of new technology (Findley and Sow 1998; Taylor and Martin 2001) and high-yielding varieties (Quinn 2009), as well as encourage efficient irrigation (Konseiga 2004) and accelerate agricultural production. The adoption of new technology in the agricultural sector may also influence non-migrant farming practices through spillover effects (Taylor and Martin 2001). Future research should investigate whether remittances can potentially compensate the loss of outmigration by providing capital to hire labor from surplus labor markets.

While this study can inform the analysis of migration and food security links in settings with similar conditions related to South–South migration, there are some shortcomings. The relatively small sample size may limit the ability to use these findings in larger policy decisions. As there was no comprehensive database or list of MHs, it was not possible to select households for an interview following the protocol of any rigorous probability sampling method. Although some of the widely used and scientifically validated food security measurement tools were used for the study, these indices also have their own limitations. Collection of food security-related information is entirely dependent on "recall." As a result, these tools may suffer from "shortfall-in-memory" bias. The food security-related behavior and experience of MHs in circular migration to and from the Arab Gulf might not be similar to the food security experience in other migration circuits, such as that of skilled migration to OECD countries. Moreover, the food security experience of MHs in the rural context, who also are subsistence producers, clearly differs from the food security experience of MHs in urban regions. Despite these limitations, however, the study has shed some light on the association between migration and household food security. The influence of remittances on household food security is a relatively underinvestigated area of research. As remittances are mostly used for basic livelihood, their impact on development is a topic of some debate. Although remittances primarily are used for food procurement for households, households also utilize remittances efficiently for "merit goods," such as education and healthcare, and housing provisions. Thus, these remittance spending patterns increase the efficiency of investment and remittance transfers, and form a strategy that helps to mitigate production constraints in imperfect market environments by securing and smoothing the recipients' consumption.

CONCLUSION

This chapter has examined the food security status of remittance-receiving and non-receiving households using a sample of 753 households from four villages in the southeast region in Bangladesh collected in 2014–2015.

The study used different food security indicators and scientifically validated measurement tools and analyzed the correlation between remittances and different food security measurement tools. Descriptive analysis of the data and statistical analysis indicate that, as remittances constitute a substantial portion of many households' income, they help to raise and improve a household's ability to sustain economic access to sufficient, safe and nutritious food to meet their dietary and nutritional diversity needs. Without remittances, the total amount spent on food might drop significantly, which would result in greater food-related insecurity. The study also showed that remittances influence household purchasing power and smooth the acquisition and consumption of more diversified food and improved nutrition. The correlation analysis indicates that remittances are positively and significantly correlated with household per capita food consumption expenditure and dietary diversity. The study also indicates that remittances have a negative and statistically significant correlation with household coping strategies and the food insecurity access scale. The result indicates that remittance contributes to higher household income and therefore ensures households have better economic access to food. While the study contributes to understanding migration and food security links, it cannot answer questions about some dimensions of the links, such as the role of remittances in reducing structural food security problems. It is also important to investigate the role of remittances in agricultural asset accumulation, and improving agricultural input investment, all of which are important to increase productivity and reduce long-term food insecurity. Future research should investigate this aspect with a larger representative sample. Gaining a more detailed understanding of how migration affects agricultural productivity and local labor markets would be helpful for the critical assessment of the migration–food security link.

REFERENCES

Acosta, Pablo A., Emmanuel K.K. Lartey and Federico S. Mandelman. 2009. "Remittances and the Dutch disease." *Journal of International Economics* 79(1): 102–116.
Adams, Richard. 1989. "Workers' remittances and inequality." *Development and Cultural Change* 38(1): 45–71.
Adams, Richard. 2011. "Evaluating the economic impact of international remittances on developing countries using household surveys: A literature review." *Journal of Development Studies* 47(6): 809–828.
Adams, Jr., Richard H., and John Page. 2005. "Do international migration and remittances reduce poverty in developing countries?" *World Development* 33(10): 1645–1669.
Anzoategui, Diego, Asli Demirgüç-Kunt and María Soledad Martínez Pería. 2014. "Remittances and financial inclusion: Evidence from El Salvador." *World Development* 54: 338–349.
Askarov, Zohid, and Hristos Doucouliagos. 2020. "A meta-analysis of the effects of remittances on household education expenditure." *World Development* 129: 104860. https://doi.org/10.1016/j.worlddev.2019.10 4860.
Azzarri, Carlo, and Alberto Zezza. 2011. "International migration and nutritional outcomes in Tajikistan." *Food Policy* 36(1): 54–70.
Babatunde, Raphael O., and Matin Qaim. 2010. "Impact of off-farm income on food security and nutrition in Nigeria." *Food Policy* 35(4): 303–311.
BBS. 2017. Statistical terms/concepts/definitions used in census/surveys of BBS and other national/international agencies. https://unstats.un.org/unsd/dnss/docViewer.aspx?docID=1774.
Bennett, Steve, Tony Woods, Winitha M. Liyanage and Duane L. Smith. 1991. "A simplified general method for cluster-sample surveys of health in developing countries." *World Health Statistics Quarterly* 44: 98–106.
Bracken, Bruce A., and Andrers Barona. 1991. "State of the art procedures for translating, validating and using psychoeducational tests in cross-cultural assessment." *School Psychology International* 12(1–2): 119–132.
Chami, Ralph, Connel Fullenkamp and Samir Jahjah. 2005. "Are immigrant remittance flows a source of capital for development?" *IMF Working Paper* 52(1). Washington, DC: International Monetary Fund.
Chang, Anne M., Janita P.C. Chau and Eleanor Holroyd. 1999. "Translation of questionnaires and issues of equivalence." *Journal of Advanced Nursing* 29(2): 316–322.
Chiodi, Vera, Esteban Jaimovich and Gabriel Montes-Rojas. 2012. "Migration, remittances and capital accumulation: Evidence from rural Mexico." *Journal of Development Studies* 48(8): 1139–1155.
Combes, Jean-Louis, and Christian Ebeke. 2011. "Remittances and household consumption instability in developing countries." *World Development* 39(7): 1076–1089.

Crush, Jonathan. 2013. "Linking food security, migration and development." *International Migration* 51(5): 61–75.
Davis, Jason, and David Lopez-Carr. 2014. "Migration, remittances and smallholder decision-making: Implications for land use and livelihood change in Central America." *Land Use Policy* 36: 319–329.
De Brauw, Alan. 2011. "Migration and child development during the food price crisis in El Salvador." *Food Policy* 36(1): 28–40.
Economist. 2020. "Covid dries up a cash cow." April 18: 34.
Edwards, Alejandra Cox, and Manuelita Ureta. 2003. "International migration, remittances, and schooling: Evidence from El Salvador." *Journal of Development Economics* 72(2): 429–461.
Favell, Adrian, Mirian Feldblum and Michael Peter Smith. 2007. "The human face of global mobility: A research agenda." *Society* 44(2): 15–25.
Findley, Sally, and Salif Sow. 1998. "From season to season: Agriculture, poverty and migration in the Senegal River Valley, Mali." In Reginald Appleyard, ed., *Emigration Dynamics in Developing Countries, Volume 1: Sub-Saharan Africa*. Aldershot: Ashgate, 69–114.
Flynn, Andrea, Paul F. Tremblay, Jürgen Rehm and Samantha Wells. 2013. "A modified random walk door-to-door recruitment strategy for collecting social and biological data relating to mental health, substance use, addiction, and violence problems in a Canadian community." *International Journal of Alcohol and Drug Research* 2(2): 7–16.
Giuliano, Paola, and Marta Ruiz-Arranz. 2009. "Remittances, financial development, and growth." *Journal of Development Economics* 90(1): 144–152.
Gray, Clark. L. 2009. "Rural out-migration and smallholder agriculture in the southern Ecuadorian Andes." *Journal of Population and Environment* 30: 193–217.
Guo, Baorong. 2011. "Household assets and food security: Evidence from the survey of program dynamics." *Journal of Family and Economic Issues* 32(1): 98–110.
Gupta, Sanjeev, Catherine A. Pattillo and Smita Wagh. 2009. "Effect of remittances on poverty and financial development in Sub-Saharan Africa." *World Development* 37(1): 104–115.
Harkness, Janet A. 2003. "Questionnaire translation." In Janet A. Harkness, Fons J.R. van de Vijer and Peter Ph. Mohler, eds, *Cross-Cultural Survey Methods*. New York: Wiley, 35–36.
Hatløy, Anne, Jesper Hallund, Modibo M. Diarra and Arne Oshaug. 2000. "Food variety, socioeconomic status and nutritional status in urban and rural areas in Koutiala (Mali)." *Public Health Nutrition* 3(1): 57–65.
Henderson, Ralph H., and Thalanayar Sundaresan. 1982. "Cluster sampling to assess immunization coverage: A review of experience with a simplified sampling method." *Bulletin of the World Health Organization* 60(2): 253–260.
Hoddinott, John. 1999. "Choosing outcome indicators of household food security." Washington, DC: International Food Policy Research Institute.
Hoddinott, John, and Yisehac Yohannes. 2002. "Dietary diversity as a food security indicator." *Food Consumption and Nutrition Division Discussion Paper* 136.
ILO. 2010. "Study on the international demand for semi-skilled and skilled Bangladeshi workers: TVET reform project report." Dhaka: Maxwell Stamp.
Imran, K., E.S. Devadason and C. Kee Cheok. 2020. "Foreign remittances and regional poverty: Evidence from household data." *International Migration* 58(4): 214–230.
Islam, Md Nurul. 2014. "Migration scenario: Nature, patterns and trends." Country Paper Migration. Dhaka: Bangladesh Bureau of Manpower Employment and Training.
Jimenez, Miguel Angel Corona. 2009. "Household development in Tlapanalá: A comparative study between households receiving remittances and households not receiving remittances." *Journal of Poverty* 13(3): 331–349.
Jokisch, Brad. 2002. "Migration and agricultural change: The case of smallholder agriculture in highland Ecuador." *Human Ecology* 30(4): 523–550.
Jones, Andrew D., Francis M. Ngure, Gretel Pelto and Sera L. Young. 2013. "What are we assessing when we measure food security? A compendium and review of current metrics." *Advances in Nutrition* 4(5): 481–505.
Jones, Richard C. 1998. "Introduction: The renewed role of remittances in the new world order." *Economic Geography* 74(1): 1–7.
Kakhkharov, Jakhongir. 2019. "Migrant remittances as a source of financing for entrepreneurship." *International Migration* 57(5): 37–55.
Kapur, Devesh. 2003. "Remittances: The new development mantra?" Paper prepared for the G-24 Technical Group Meeting, September 15–16. New York: United Nations.
Kapur, Devesh. 2010. *Diaspora, Development, and Democracy: The Domestic Impact of International Migration from India*. Princeton, NJ: Princeton University Press.
Karamba, Wendy R., Esteban J. Quiñones and Paul Winters. 2011. "Migration and food consumption patterns in Ghana." *Food Policy* 36(1): 41–53.

Koechlin, Valerie, and Gianmarco Leon. 2007. "International remittances and income inequality: An empirical investigation." *Journal of Economic Policy Reform* 10(2): 123–141.

Konseiga, Adama. 2004. "Adoption of agricultural innovations. In the Sahel: The role of migration in food security." Paper presented on the 38th Annual Meeting of the Canadian Economics Association, June 4–6. Ryerson University, Toronto, Ontario. http://economics.ca/2004/papers/0072.pdf.

Leete, Laura, and Neil Bania. 2010. "The effect of income shocks on food insufficiency." *Review of Economics of the Household* 8(4): 505–526.

Lemeshow, Stanley, and David Robinson. 1985. "Surveys to measure programme coverage and impact: A review of the methodology used by the expanded programme on immunization." *World Health Statistics Quarterly* 38: 65–75.

Lemeshow, Stanley, Alexandre Tserkonvi, James Leonard Tulloch, John Dowd, Steven Lwanga and Jacobus Keja. 1985. "A computer simulation of the EPI survey strategy." *International Journal of Epidemiology* 14(3): 473–481.

Lokshin, Michael, Mikhail Bontch-Osmolovski and Elena Glinskaya. 2010. "Work-related migration and poverty reduction in Nepal." *Review of Development Economics* 14(2): 323–332.

Loopstra, Rachel, and Valerie Tarasuk. 2013. "Severity of household food insecurity is sensitive to change in household income and employment status among low-income families." *Journal of Nutrition* 143(8): 1316–1323.

Massey, Douglas S., and J. Edward Taylor, eds. 2004. *International Migration: Prospects and Policies in a Global Market*. Oxford: Oxford University Press.

McDermott, Mary Anne Nelson and Kathleen Palchanes. 1994. "A literature review of the critical elements in translation theory." *Journal of Nursing Scholarship* 26(2): 113–117.

Moniruzzaman, Mohammad. 2020. "The impact of remittances on household food security: Evidence from a survey in Bangladesh." *Migration and Development*: 1–20. https://doi.org/10.1080/21632324.2020.1787097.

Nguyen, Minh Cong, and Paul Winters. 2011. "The impact of migration on food consumption patterns: The case of Vietnam." *Food Policy* 36(1): 71–87.

Obi, Chinedu, Fabio Bartolini and Marijke D'Haese. 2020. "International migration, remittance and food security during food crises: The case study of Nigeria." *Food Security* 12(1): 207–220.

Quinn, Michael A. 2009. "Estimating the impact of migration and remittances on agricultural technology." *Journal of Developing Areas* 43(1): 199–216.

Ratha, Dilip and Ibrahim Sirkeci. 2011. "Remittances and the global financial crisis." *Migration Letters* 7(2): 125–131.

Regmi, Madhav, and Krishna P. Paudel. 2016. "Impact of remittance on food security in Bangladesh." In A. Schmitz, P.L. Kennedy and T.G. Schmitz, eds, *Food Security in a Food Abundant World*. London: Emerald Group Publishing, 145–158.

Ruel, Marie. 2002. "Is dietary diversity an indicator of food security or dietary quality: A review of measurement issues and research needs?" *FCND Discussion Paper* 140. Washington, DC: International Food Policy Research Institute.

Santeramo, Fabio Gaetano. 2015. "On the composite indicators for food security: Decisions matter!" *Food Reviews International* 31(1): 63–73.

Sassen, Saskia. 1998. *Globalization and its Discontents: Essays on the New Mobility of People and Money*. New York: New Press.

Sobiech, Izabela. 2019. "Remittances, finance and growth: Does financial development foster the impact of remittances on economic growth?" *World Development* 113: 44–59.

Sugiyarto, Gunter, S. Selim Raihan, Carlos Vargas-Silva and Shika Jha. 2012. "Impacts of the crisis on migrants and their families: A case study from Bangladesh." In I. Sirkeici, J.H. Cohen and D. Ratha, eds, *Migration and Remittances during Global Financial Crisis and Beyond*. Washington DC: World Bank, 171–179.

Swindale, Anne, and Paul Bilinsky. 2006. "Development of a universally applicable household food insecurity measurement tool: Process, current status, and outstanding issues." *Journal of Nutrition* 136(5): 1449S–1452S.

Taylor, J. Edward. 2004. "Remittances, savings, and development in migrant-sending areas." In Douglas Massey and J. Edward Taylor, eds, *International Migration: Prospects and Policies in a Global Market*. Oxford: Oxford University Press, 157–174.

Taylor, J. Edward, and Philip L. Martin. 2001. "Human capital: Migration and rural population change." In *Handbook of Agricultural Economics*. New York: Elsevier Science, 457–511.

Temple, Bogusia. 1997. "Watch your tongue: Issues in translation and cross-cultural research." *Sociology* 31: 607–618.

Temple, Bogusia, and Alys Young. 2004. "Qualitative research and translation dilemmas." *Qualitative Research* 4(2): 161–178.

Thorne-Lyman, Andrew L., Natalie Valpiani, Kai Sun, Richard D. Semba, Christine L. Klotz, Klaus Kraemer, Nasima Akhter, Saskia de Pee, Regina Moench-Pfanner, Mayang Sari and Martin W. Bloem. 2010.

"Household dietary diversity and food expenditures are closely linked in rural Bangladesh, increasing the risk of malnutrition due to the financial crisis." *Journal of Nutrition* 140(1): 182S–188S.

Turner, Anthony G., Robert J. Magnani and Muhammad Shuaib. 1996. "A not quite as quick but much cleaner alternative to the Expanded Programme on Immunization (EPI) cluster survey design." *International Journal of Epidemiology* 25(1): 198–203.

United Nations. 2015. "Transforming Our World: The 2030 Agenda for Sustainable Development." Resolution adopted by the General Assembly on September 25. https://sustainabledevelopment.un.org/post2015/transformingourworld on April 12, 2016.

United Nations. 2020. "International migration 2020 highlights." www.un.org/development/desa/pd/sites/www.un.org.development.desa.pd/files/undesa_pd_2020_international_migration_highlights.pdf.

WFP. 2012. *Bangladesh Food Security Monitoring Bulletin* 9(April–June). Dhaka: World Food Programme.

Woodruff, Christopher M., and Rene Zenteno. 2001. "Remittances and microenterprises in Mexico." UCSD, Graduate School of International Relations and Pacific Studies Working Paper.

World Bank. 2019. "Migration and remittances: Recent developments and outlook." Migration and Remittances Team Social Protection and Jobs. www.knomad.org/sites/default/files/2019-04/Migrationanddevelopmentbrief31.pdf.

World Bank. 2020. COVID-19 "Crisis through a migration lens." *Migration and Development Brief* 32. www.knomad.org/sites/default/files/2020-06/R8_Migration%26Remittances_brief32.pdf.

World Health Organization. 1991. *Training for Mid-level Managers: The EPI Coverage Survey*. Geneva: WHO Expanded Programme on Immunization.

Yang, Dean. 2008. "Coping with disaster: The impact of hurricanes on international financial flows, 1970–2002." *B.E. Journal of Economic Analysis and Policy* 8(1): 1–43.

Zahonogo, Pam. 2011. "Migration and agricultural production in Burkina Faso." *African Journal of Agricultural Research* 6(7): 1844–1852.

25. Migration as a development strategy: Debating the role that migrants and those in diaspora can play
Elizabeth Mavroudi

INTRODUCTION

This chapter explores how migrants and those in diaspora contribute to their homeland's development through a focus on the relationships between migration and development. It will critically assess the migration–development nexus and the idea that migration always leads to development. It will thus question the extent to which migration can be used as a tool and strategy for homeland or sending-country development and improved welfare. In order to do this, it will outline how governments have used migration as a means to increase development in sending contexts and that the focus has primarily been an economic one. However, this optimism also needs to be balanced with caution. Thus the chapter will do the following: (1) provide an overview of the relationship between migration and development; (2) explore the role of remittances, the loss of key workers and the brain drain that this can cause especially for some contexts – this section will also discuss diaspora strategies and how remittances are used in the homeland; (3) explore the value and role of return migration and brain circulation; and (4) explore the wider impacts and role of transnational and diasporic connections. Finally, it will discuss more liberal systems of migration so that both sending and receiving contexts can benefit as much as possible from migration. This final point stresses that even though this chapter is primarily about the sending context or homeland, the receiving context is important and the relationships between migration and development should be considered from both perspectives, but also, crucially, from the perspective of migrants and those in diaspora, and their families (Sinatti 2019). The chapter will argue that these relationships need to be viewed ethically, with a commitment to reducing inequalities between places and people, in order to potentially achieve justice and increased welfare as well as economic development.

Any discussion on the relationships between migration and development needs to begin with the reminder of the contested nature of development. For the purposes of this chapter, development is used in broad and not just in narrow economic terms. This is relevant especially for a book on welfare and migration because it highlights development as a tool for justice and change (Rahnema and Bawtree 1997). Others have also highlighted the need to examine development in broader, moral terms and the unequal relationships between the Global North (hereafter GN) and the Global South (hereafter GS) in the context of migration (Anderson 2017; Castles 2004; de Haas 2005; Hickey 2016; Phillips 2009; Raghuram 2009; Suliman 2017). Such an approach necessitates critical discussions around power inequalities between the GN and GS (and the inadequacy of such terms). It also requires engagement with the ongoing and pervasive impact of colonialism, racism and of neoliberalism and, finally, the complex relationships between sending and receiving contexts which can be viewed through a diasporic and transnational migration lens and for which migration policies are often poorly suited (Castles 2017; Mavroudi and Nagel 2016).

It is important to set up such a backdrop in this analysis because of the positive role that such migration has been seen as playing in more recent years, especially by institutions such as the International Monetary Fund and World Bank (hereafter WB) (Ratha et al. 2011). Such optimistic accounts also have to be viewed as part of the migration–development nexus which calls into question any easy and uncomplicated assumptions about the relationships between migration and development (Bastia 2013; Gamlen 2014; Portes 2009).

So, on the one hand, there is a need to view the relationships between migration and development from a macro perspective which privileges economics and global financial and trade linkages. The ways in which countries in the GS are differentially positioned globally can impact their economic and political development because of core–periphery relationships.

On the other hand, and equally importantly, there is a need to examine how migrants are affected by such structures, interactions and relationships by listening to their views and unravelling their experiences and actions through time and space. This can reveal the realities of precarity and vulnerability for migrants (Silvey and Parreñas 2020). It also demonstrates the dynamicism and fluctuations in migrant/diasporic homeland-oriented activity (Koinova 2018), whereby it is useful to conceptualize such processes as a craft (Page and Tanyi 2015), which take place within people's everyday lives (Page and Mercer 2012) and not as a given. It is therefore important to focus more on people and their everyday lives, transnational/diasporic connections and the structural constraints and opportunities that affect what they are able to do in material ways. To sum up, it is necessary to explore top-down and bottom-up perspectives in any discussion of the relationships between migration and development.

CRITIQUING REMITTANCES: FROM BRAIN DRAIN TO HARNESSING DIASPORAS AND THE VALUE OF ECONOMIC AND NON-ECONOMIC REMITTANCES

It makes sense to begin the discussion on remittances because these are most often cited in policy and literature as one of the main ways in which migrants can help homeland development. However, before this happens, there is a need to briefly outline that this view has not always been prevalent and there are still scholars who view the loss of key workers and the brain drain that is seen to accompany it in negative ways because of the sheer numbers involved, such as in the South African and Greek context (see e.g. Mlambo and Adetiba 2019; Labrianidis and Pratsinakis 2017). This is accompanied by concerns around brain waste, or the untapped talent of highly skilled immigrants in host countries (Batalova et al. 2016), and de-skilling, which is often gendered, pervasive and problematic (Elo et al. 2020), despite women's agency and coping strategies (Korzeniewska and Erdal 2019).

These issues are seen as less problematic now by institutions and governments because of the remittances that are sent back but it is still an issue if a country is losing a high percentage of its skilled and key workers. These are people educated and trained in the home country who are subsequently not able to use those skills to help with development in their home country. Their brain drain is the GN's brain gain.

While some scholars and politicians continue to raise concerns about the outflow of skilled workers to the GN, such concerns have been largely superseded since the 1990s by the idea that both skilled and unskilled migrations are far more beneficial than detrimental to the GS. Sending countries have moved from seeing emigrants as traitors and deserters to members of the nation abroad and have increasingly attempted to harness what they see as "their" diasporic members.

Diaspora Strategies

This has entailed the creation of diaspora strategies such as the fostering of diasporic consciousness, practical assistance, enabling investment, easier channelling of remittances and the encouragement of dual citizenship, which states aim to create productive investments and economic growth. Diaspora strategies are also seen by states as a way to encourage the return of skilled and professional emigrants and brain circulation but all sorts of assumptions are made by states in such pursuits. States are thus keen to "cultivate" the diaspora for economic gain (Ho 2011). According to Ancien et al. (2009: 3): "A diaspora strategy is an explicit and systematic policy initiative or series of policy initiatives aimed at developing and managing relationships with a diaspora." They go on to stress that these are best thought of as diverse frameworks, rather than a one-size-fits-all approach. There is therefore considerable variation in the approach that states take (Ancien et al. 2009) and it is important to compare different approaches (Délano and Gamlen 2014). What then becomes apparent is that ethno-national belonging, obligation and loyalty to the homeland is not the sole factor which influences how successful such policies are (Ragazzi 2014). Indeed, one needs to also explore the processes of diaspora formation and how groups negotiate who they are (Fischer 2015). States often make assumptions around who constitutes "their" diaspora based on simplistic notions of ethno-national belonging and attachment (Jöns et al. 2015; Ho and Boyle 2015; Sinatti and Horst 2015) which they feel connects migrants and those in diasporas to their homeland state and which they can also try to explicitly cultivate (see Abramson 2017 on the case of the Taglit-Birthright programme in Israel). However, it is important to question such assumptions and to differentiate between nation and state (Larner 2007) because although emigrants might negotiate belonging towards their homeland, they do not necessarily want to support the state. For example, Kang (2017) outlines how those in diaspora can subvert and resist government diaspora strategies, for example the People's Republic of China's online attempts to engage its diaspora, which did not necessarily result in the engagement they anticipated because of diasporic feelings of mistrust and because they did not think the strategies were useful or helpful. In addition, Erdal's (2016) case study on the Pakistani diaspora in Norway demonstrates the mismatch between state and nation: the Pakistani state is keen to woo its diaspora but the reality is that emigrants distrust the state and its corruption and they send money back in a personal capacity rather than as part of formal state channels. Therefore, although they continue to feel a sense of belonging towards their homeland nation, they can be ambivalent about state strategies which makes it harder for such policies to be effective. Feelings of belonging and attachment to the homeland do not necessarily translate into either homeland-oriented economic or political action or mobilization. Governments need to be aware of how those in diaspora view the homeland and the state rather than make assumptions that their policies and strategies will work because of "loyalty" and obligation towards the homeland (Mavroudi 2018).

This process of naming and "claiming" a diaspora and deciding who is included or excluded (Ho 2011) is one which ends up targeting particular individuals and groups often for economic reasons and is based around essentialized notions of ethno-nationalism and diasporic "success." As a result of narrow interpretations of who constitutes a diaspora or emigrant population and how they are able to potentially contribute, states are not able to fully capitalize or include all those who may wish to help a homeland or place of origin (Ancien et al. 2009; Jöns et al. 2015).

This vision of economic success can exclude refugees and other more marginalized or poorer groups, their potential for sending remittances (Lindley 2009) and the role that they too can play in homeland development. There is a need for a broader conceptualization of the skills and knowledge that different generations and groups of migrants can use to contribute to development. Lulle et al.'s (2019) discussion of the "knowledgeable" migrant demonstrates that it is important to view migrant human capital in broader and more holistic terms, especially when it comes to younger generations.

Nonetheless, sending states continue to encourage emigrants and diasporas to contribute to homeland development but with varying levels of success. Williams (2018) succinctly illustrates in his comparative work on Kosovo, Montenegro and Bosnia how diaspora strategies of different countries vary in their approach and success for particular reasons. He argues that there is fragmentation in the approach by these governments to their diasporas but that they have a long-term vision which needs to be maintained. This highlights an additional challenge: strategies, policies and frameworks to support homeland-oriented economic investment take time to build and materialize.

In terms of thinking through the ability of emigrants to contribute to homeland development and increased welfare, it is arguably necessary to have more honest and critical discussions around the role that governments play, the assumptions they make, who they target with their diaspora strategies and why. Emigrant and diasporic contributions to homeland development constitute complex processes which are dependent on context, wider international power relations and connections between states (such as immigration policies, past colonial relations and so forth) and the realities on the ground for migrants and those in diaspora and what they feel able to do. This can be seen in Brinkerhoff's (2009) analysis of conditions which help those in diaspora to contribute to their homeland's development. Such contributions are helped when those in diaspora have access to economic, social, political, moral and informational power resources and tend to be more prevalent when the homeland (and host country) is democratic and economically productive.

Labrianidis and Pratsinakis, in their case study on diasporic Greeks in the United Kingdom and the Greek state stress the need for sending states to develop non-patronizing relationships and attitudes with those in diaspora and to have a broader view of them so that they are not just perceived as a passive group waiting to "be tapped" (2017: 42). My own research (Mavroudi 2015; Mavroudi forthcoming) on Greeks in Australia and the United Kingdom confirms this as many spoke of feeling ignored by the Greek state who they felt made assumptions about them and what they were willing to do. Like in Erdal's

(2016) work, they remained very attached culturally and emotionally to their homeland even if this was not translated into formal action. It is therefore not surprising that Ho and Boyle (2015) remain sceptical about diaspora strategies in their examination of Singapore and this serves as an important note of caution: diaspora strategies are not necessarily the panacea they are made out to be.

Economic Remittances

International organizations such as the WB have increasingly recognized the potential of migration in creating development through different forms of remittances (Ratha 2007): economic (through remittances, investments, entrepreneurship), cultural/human (through migrants' knowledge and "know-how"), expertise (academics and scientists), social (established social networks) and political (political networks and groups). However, it is often economic remittances that are honed in on by states and international organizations and this has also contributed to narrow interpretations of both remittances and development. As a result, they have potentially ignored and marginalized non-economic flows and practices of both migrants and those in the sending country, which are often informal and can be hard to trace.

This enthusiasm around economic remittances comes primarily from the reality that the numbers involved are huge. In 2019, annual remittance flows to low- and middle-income countries (LMICs hereafter) are likely to reach $550 billion. Remittance flows are larger than foreign direct investment and official development assistance flows to LMICs (World Bank 2019: vii). In 2018, remittance flows to LMICs reached $529 billion, an increase of 9.6 per cent over 2017 (World Bank 2019: vii). In addition, these numbers do not include informal remittances and gifts, which means that in reality the amount of money flowing as remittances is even larger (Pieke et al. 2007). The sending of remittances has also become a large part of migrant livelihoods and practices in receiving contexts.

The WB stresses the role that migrants can play in welfare: "Global welfare gains from an increase in cross-border labor mobility could be several times larger than those from full trade liberalization" (World Bank 2019: 17). However, the report goes on to state that "Migration is not a substitute for development at home, but it can be leveraged for development" (World Bank 2019: 20). This suggests that the WB is aware of the limits of remittances and of the role that migration can play in homeland development even as it continues to stress its potential in increasing welfare.

Thus, remittances can be seen as very important to the development process and to the welfare of individuals and families in sending contexts (Adams and Page 2005; de Haas 2005). This is because they can help people "on the ground" in sending countries in terms of improving living conditions and it does not mean that people and states are "passively" depending on remittances (see de Haas 2012). In addition, remittances are much more important for low-income countries such as Jamaica (Joseph and Hamilton 2014) and for family incomes in Africa and Asia (Siddiqui 2012). Kusunose and Rignall (2018) for example illustrate what can be seen as a positive case study in Morocco where remittances have been both useful and productive for migrant-sending families and they also have wider positive ramifications for the economy. However, challenges and limitations still remain because of "broader political-economic conditions and deeply entrenched inequalities" (Joseph and Hamilton 2014: 149).

There is debate, therefore, on the wider impacts of such remittances and what such money is actually spent on. Work by the WB paints a positive picture of such money predominantly being used on education and health rather than just on consumption (Ratha et al. 2011). However, in Zimbabwe, for example, although remittances have been crucial in helping to alleviate poverty, the money received is not necessarily reaching the poorest households and can increase or exacerbate existing inequalities within sending communities. Other studies have shown that remittances can create dependencies as in the case of the Philippines (Siddiqui 2012). Therefore, the benefits of emigration and remittances are not evenly distributed socially or geographically, and thus emigration tends to exacerbate, rather than to alleviate, uneven patterns of development (Fitzgerald 2009).

The issue of what people in the sending country "do" with remittances is also contested (Glytsos 2002), but the ideal is that there should be a positive multiplier effect: "Households receiving remittances ... are more likely to invest ... and help to raise incomes elsewhere in [the] economy ... Because of multiplier effects, [the] economic impact of remittances [is] mostly found in [the] broader economy and depends on [the] ability of households to make productive investments" (United Nations General Assembly 2006: 13).

This is a difficult issue to discuss because it is not easy to see how the money sent back is used or what the wider effects are (Taylor 2004). Migration should not be seen as a substitute for macro-economic and "well-designed" development strategies in sending contexts which are aimed less at increasing remittances and aimed more at what happens to this money once it reaches the sending country and how it can be put to best and "productive" use to support economic development (Taylor 2004; Newland and Patrick 2004). There is also the wider issue of whether countries should be depending on remittances so much, which can be uneven and dynamic. As de Haas (2012) reminds us, migrants cannot do it all, and they cannot be blamed for development not occurring.

Remittances need to be seen within a broader personal context of helping families and local communities back in the homeland, which can impact positively on their welfare, but it is important to question how useful and reliable such relationships are e.g. at times of crisis like pandemics. This dependency on remittances also ignores the often precarious labour and insecure livelihoods of many low and unskilled migrants who are doing their best to send money back (see e.g. Datta et al. 2007 and their work on migrant working conditions in London and the sacrifices they have to make). Women overall have been an important component of labour export strategies, with millions emigrating to work in the Gulf Arab states and highly developed Asian economies, often in precarious conditions (Silvey and Parreñas 2020). Asian states have been leaders in encouraging and facilitating labour export as a development strategy, in parallel with broader export-oriented industrialization policies. Such gendered policies of the Philippines and Indonesia are also a form of control over women (Oishi 2005) and are a reminder that migration policies can be gender blind and either explicitly or inadvertently exploitative and marginalizing for migrants and their families. So the question remains: at what personal and emotional cost has the "neo-optimism" (Bastia 2013) of the relationships between migration and development occurred?

As outlined earlier in relation to diaspora strategies, sending states need to reflect on wider constraints that emigrants face but also the realities in their own states which can limit remittances and their effectiveness. States, both sending and receiving, need to look beyond narrow economic development and purely economic remittances. The nature of the relationships between migration and development means that they are complex and the economic is often connected to the cultural, social and political aspects of people's lives and identities (Siddiqui 2012).

Non-Economic Remittances: Social and Political

It is important to recognize and research non-economic remittances, namely social and political ones, and the ways in which migrants and those in diaspora are involved in these. This is because there are interconnections between economic, political and social development and there is a need for broader conceptualizations of development based around justice and welfare, in which people's lives, practices and emotions are brought to the fore.

Non-economic remittances can be useful as they change ideas and perceptions in the homeland. Social remittances are the transmission by emigrants of new and potentially beneficial ideas, information and expertise through their communications with friends and family and visits home (see Levitt and Lamba-Nieves 2011). Peth and Sakdapolrak (2020) provide a good example of the importance of social remittances and how they may be lost or not fully utilized in a case study of Thailand and Singapore. They also stress, as others have done (e.g. Yeoh and Huang 2000), that migration needs to be seen as ongoing, and does not necessarily have specific start and end points. Such realities of social remittances and migration as a journey also complicate the role that migrants can and do play in development. Their actions and practices as well as their lives are dynamic and "on the move." However, there is an assumption that Western ideas are superior to those in the GS so the GS should be happy to be the recipient of them. The same applies to the Western model of economic development which is often imposed on countries in the GS. It may not necessarily be easy or even morally and culturally acceptable to transmit non-economic flows and ideas back to the homeland.

This is very well demonstrated by the complexities and controversies around the sending of what Müller-Funk (2019) calls "political remittances" and the debate as to whether emigrants and those in diaspora are "peace makers" or "wreckers" (Shain 2002; Toivanen and Baser Ozturk 2020). Therefore, this raises questions about political mobilization (Koinova 2018) and whether such processes actually help bring about positive socio-political change in the homeland. A good example of the complexities around this is provided by Lampert's (2009) case study of Nigerian diasporic organizations and the ways in which they reinforce rather than resist gender and socio-economic inequalities in the homeland.

On the positive side, we have Brinkerhoff's (2012) work, Bernal's (2006) work on the Eritrean diasporas' online activism to promote democracy in the homeland and Hammond et al.'s (2011) case study on Somalia, which can be seen as a potential success story. One of the reasons that the diaspora has been as successful as it has in helping communities in the country of origin has to do with the fact that the support network is entirely run by Somalis, which helps to build trust and is a bottom-up approach. However, it is important not to paint a simplistic picture of diasporic politics and political mobilization, which is dynamic (Koinova 2018), complex (Fischer 2018) and which, like with economic remittances, also depends on the situation migrants and those in diaspora find themselves within host communities. This is demonstrated by Müller-Funk's work (2016) on young Egyptian political mobilization in France and Austria and Toivanen's (2016) case study on Kurds in Finland. This work also stresses the links between politics and identity, particularly for young people with a migrant/diasporic background (also see Fiddian-Qasmiyeh 2013). In turn, this suggests that young people can have an important role in helping the homeland but that their identities need to be taken into account as well (see also Mavroudi and Silva Huxter 2020; Mavroudi forthcoming).

A key issue to consider therefore is the nature of political remittances and the reality that for many in diaspora, politics occurs informally, within everyday spaces, identities and lives (Mavroudi 2008). This is something that was evident in my recent research on young people in the Greek, Jewish and Palestinian diasporas in England; young people had political opinions and thoughts about how to make a difference to the lives of themselves and their peers but felt that politicians and those in positions of power (both in their own diasporic communities and in sending/receiving contexts) did not listen to them (Mavroudi forthcoming). They had multiple and complex identities and loyalties and were just as likely to be interested in global justice issues such as climate change as they were on solely homeland issues (as Toivanen also discusses in relation to her work on youth in diaspora in Baser and Toivanen 2020; see also Blachnicka-Ciacek 2018 and Salih et al. 2020 on Palestinian diasporic youth). This again stresses that states (both sending and receiving) must not have assumptions about diasporas and those from migrant backgrounds in terms of their identities, belonging and allegiances, particularly for the younger generation. There is increasing work on the role that young people in diaspora play in political mobilization and homeland politics with the aim to create social and political change (see Baser 2015) and the role of virtual spaces in particular (NurMuhammad et al. 2016; Leurs 2015; Godin and Doná 2016; Nagel and Staeheli 2010). However, such online spaces are not necessarily emancipatory, as work by Moss (2018) on Syrian government attempts to control online diasporic voices outlines.

There is often a tendency towards a much more nuanced approach in terms of relationships to diasporic mobilization and the role that diasporas can play. There is an appreciation that the situation is dynamic, context specific and that there are ambivalences, tensions and contradictions. Cochrane's (2007) work in Northern Ireland, Antwi-Boateng's work (2012) on the Liberian diaspora and Orjuela's (2008) study of the Sri Lankan diaspora all demonstrate the negative and positive role diasporas can play in homeland political development and peace. By discussing the many ways in which diasporas engage in homeland politics, Orjuela challenges simplified understandings of diasporas as either "warriors" or "peace workers" in relation to their homeland conflicts. Power relations and inequalities can exacerbate the situation and Orjuela also stresses that more work is needed on the role of women and younger generations.

The migration-as-development model rests on the idea that migrants will always be willing to support their places of origin, but the reality of diasporic networks and belonging is much more complex (Féron and Lefort 2019). We cannot make assumptions about the role, practices and contributions of emigrants and those in diaspora on homeland development.

FROM RETURN MIGRATION TO BRAIN CIRCULATION AND TRANSNATIONAL NETWORKS

Return migration can be seen as part of the diasporic and transnational networks that migrants and those in diaspora have with their homeland. It also needs to be seen within the wider reality of circular mobilities that often accompanies transnational migrant and diasporic life in the form of social and family visits, business and work-related trips and other material and symbolic physical and virtual connections. However, care is needed over assumptions around the linkages between transnationalism and return migration (Carling and Erdal 2014) and over whether it is always a positive experience.

Return migration has been viewed by states and organizations in positive ways (see Cassarino 2004; United Nations General Assembly 2006) because return is linked to the return of (and possibly an increase in) skills, which can arguably lead to social and political change (e.g. better gender equality, peace building, political change and so forth): "Migrants who return home often bring expertise and savings ... use savings to start businesses that contribute to job creation ... pass expertise along to others as teachers or trainers ... [this] new critical mass of skilled workers may launch new ventures in their countries and promote economic development" (United Nations General Assembly 2006: 14).

This is the ideal scenario in many ways but such processes and motivations for and realities of return need to be unpacked because people often return for multiple cultural, social and economic reasons. Return is not necessarily helpful or positive but depends on conditions in the homeland such as exclusion, the ability to find a job and the emotional toll of return (see Lee 2015 on the Korean diaspora and Christou 2011 who focuses on Greek diasporic return to Greece). Koh's work (2015) shows the complexities in relation to the skilled Malaysian Chinese diasporas going back to Malaysia and the complications in terms of citizenship, inclusion and exclusion in terms of which groups are favoured by the state. Another critical perspective on return can be seen in Poland whereby it can be hard for returnees to find a job and reintegrate into the homeland labour market and economy (Coniglio and Brzozowski 2018). Research by Baser and Toivanen (2019) on Kurdish diasporic return also highlights that despite the fact that those who returned did so in order to explicitly help homeland political and economic development, they encountered difficulties and did not receive practical state support even though the government professed to want such returns to occur. Their work also outlines that those who were successful were so because of personal and family networks, not state strategies or policies.

However, there are examples where return has had a more positive outcome. Sinatti's (2019) work focuses on returning Senegalese businessmen and the wider impacts and linkages of their activities, which utilized the local as well as transnational connections they had. This stresses the connections between the economic, social and political development that returning migrants can contribute to directly and indirectly. Mullings (2011) focuses on how the Jamaican government has tried to encourage skilled Jamaicans returning as a way to reverse brain drain. This work demonstrates the economic and social changes that such returnees can bring because they are more likely to be innovators and "potentially challenge the inequalities and inefficiencies produced by Jamaica's postplantation labour market culture, precisely because they are not bound by the norms and established practices that insiders are expected to uphold" (Mullings 2011: 39). However, she stresses the governments also need to pay attention to continued gender, race and class inequalities if such return is to be inclusionary and fulfil its potential for transformation. The process of return is one full of negotiations and tensions, and is not necessarily smooth. According to Wong (2014) in a case study on the return of Ghanaian highly skilled migrants, this is because of the need to deal with a new context and gender expectations intersected with class differences. However, the paper also stresses the need to further recognize the valuable role that highly skilled women can play in the homeland development process but also the challenges that they face. Thus, these personal endeavours and challenges need to be seen as part of the complex relationships between migration and development and a reminder that scholars and governments need to view the situation from the perspective of migrants and their agency and the wider structural constraints they face in sending and receiving contexts.

Viewing the links between migration and development in this way stresses the intense, but also uneven connections between sending and receiving contexts which migrants have to negotiate and in which they themselves are also differentially placed. This can be seen in the concept and reality of brain circulation. This has been put forward as a way for both sending and receiving contexts to benefit from skilled and highly skilled migrants who by virtue of their knowledge and skills are able to contribute "here" and "there" and in the process further the myriad connections between them (Robertson 2006; Portes 2009). Such knowledge transfer is often associated with the work of Saxenian (2002) on Silicon Valley and the links back to South East Asia in the information technology and engineering industries. It emphasized the ability of highly skilled migrants to participate in economic and human capital development without permanently returning to countries of origin (Jöns 2009).

However, the potential of this so-called "brain exchange" (Pellegrino 2001) is not necessarily realized and can be hard to measure in reality. Pellegrino states that for Latin America, brain circulation is difficult to ascertain in this context because of a lack of data, but what data there is suggest that brain circulation does not happen in the Latin American migration context. Similarly, Ortiga et al. (2018) comment that for academics, brain circulation in Singapore does not necessarily happen. Harvey's (2008) work on Indian and British scientists working in Boston, Massachusetts stresses that they are contributing to a brain drain rather than brain circulation. More recent work by Harvey (2012) on highly skilled British emigrants in Vancouver also did not find much evidence of brain circulation. Other scholars acknowledge that there is potential for possible brain circulation such as in Bacchi's (2016) work on highly skilled Egyptians in Austria, but there is also ambivalence over how they can help the homeland. A related reality is that of so-called diaspora tourism, which sits across the fields of economic remittances, return visits and diaspora strategies. Here, migrants and those in diaspora come and go and purposefully spend money as a means to help the homeland (Scheyvens 2007). Coles and Timothy's edited book (2004) provides numerous case studies on the reality of doing so in relation to space and highlights that the relationships between diasporas, homelands, visits, tourism and development are often ambiguous and far from straightforward. The last sections of the book stress the difficulties around the role that diasporas play in tourism and related diaspora tourism strategies and economies. Part of this is linked to the discussion above on the need for sending governments to appreciate the diversity of the diasporic experience before putting together and implementing strategies to enlist their help and support.

RETHINKING DIASPORIC AND MIGRANT "OBLIGATIONS" TOWARDS THE HOMELAND: COMPLEX BELONGING AND THE NEED FOR LIBERAL MIGRATION SYSTEMS

This section will conclude the chapter by stressing the complex realities which enable and constrain the relationships between migration and development and which in turn impact the ability of migration to create economic, social and political justice and development in the homeland. It will then go on to discuss ways forward by outlining the need for liberal migration systems and a rethink of migration policies and diaspora strategies.

I want to start this section with a more detailed case study by Giles Mohan (2008), who paints a complex picture of the Ghanaian diaspora and the ways in which they relate and contribute to the homeland. His work stresses that we need to rethink the contribution on "national" development because the reality is that it is not necessarily national, especially in Africa where nation building is quite new and arbitrary in many ways due to its colonial past. Tribal, regional and religious affiliations are still very important even in diaspora. These identities create hybrid, multiple identities and attachments which do not map easily into top-down, one-size-fits-all (sending and receiving) state approaches. The transnational activities that Ghanaians do get involved in are also themselves bound by class and power relations and occur along elitist lines, which limits their capacity to create meaningful institutional change. This reminds us that diasporas and migration are made up of people who themselves are positioned and have vested interests and personal connections and affiliations, in which there are tensions and power inequalities.

In addition, a large challenge may be the reality that remittances and the enthusiasm about the relationships between migration and development can be seen as part of a neoliberal system of governance in which individuals are moving around and taking responsibility for sending money back in transnational, diasporic ways as the responsibility and protection of the state decreases (Khanal and Todorova 2019). This leads to a fragmented approach and response by states and puts the onus (and precarity and vulnerability) on everyday people rather than governments.

This helps to explain why states can find it hard to appreciate or formally/openly recognize why their diaspora and migration policies do not always work as they anticipated (Castles 2004) and why efforts can be limited in their positive impacts on homeland development. There is a tension between the role of the state as a top-down entity which tries to control through policies on the one hand, and the messy realities of neoliberalism and migration in which people do not move in the way that money does.

What is arguably missing is a strategy to protect people caught up in this tension. This points to a need for receiving states to reflect more critically on the role they play in limiting migration and sending states in their role in encouraging emigration in the name of development. In an age of globalization, transnational connections and multiple, plural identities and loyalties, state assumptions around national belonging need to be unpacked

(Sinatti and Horst 2015). Diaspora strategies should be more flexible and inclusive and recognize the diversity of emigrant and diaspora lives, identities and potential contributions to the homeland (Ho 2011).

According to de Haas (2012: 21): "Instead of uselessly and harmfully trying to stop inevitable migration, immigration policies allowing for greater circulation can enhance the vital contribution of migrants to the development of migration sending and receiving societies." He goes on to stress the need for states to design immigration policies that empower (instead of exploit) migrants. So, for example, states should make conditions in origin countries attractive for emigrants to invest in and allow freer flow of skills and capital between sending and receiving countries. Managed migration policies should encourage circular migration and migration corridors and there should be global agreements and policies over international migration and meaningful inclusion of participant voices in such policy making (Castles 2004). States therefore need to move beyond narrow country-specific blinkers to consider the benefits of working together in meaningful ways, through diasporic, global and transnational fields which arguably better capture and account for the material realities of what is occurring "on the ground."

At the same time, it is important for states to recognize the personal, embodied endeavour that migration entails, which is played out in relation to intersectionalities of class, gender, race, age and so forth, which both limit and enable migrant lives and activities. Migration, for many, is complex, embodied and situated. Such people-centred approaches act as an important antidote to top-down assumptions over migration and development. Quantitative research on patterns and research on policies have their role in providing useful data from such macro-economic and state perspectives. However, it is research with migrants themselves and from a micro perspective that provides necessary insights into why such policies and state strategies may not work. It can also demonstrate the many small but important ways migrants can and do help homelands in incremental and dynamic ways.

Migration can potentially have both positive and negative impacts on development outcomes. However, the migration–development nexus needs to be recognized as a complex, contested, ambiguous relationship between emigration, economic growth, social and political well-being, change and prosperity. There is a need as Castles (2017) and Anderson (2017) stress to reduce inequalities, not focusing just on "migrants" as a category but on making lives better for all. Such an approach is a human(e) one. As Ho et al. (2015: 207) stress: "we see the economy and care existing in a symbiotic manner captured in the concept of 'diaspora economies of care,'" which occurs for the public good both "here" and "there" and which is based on meaningful interactions and nurturing relationships which can help build more "sustainable and equitable" social relations (Ho et al. 2015). In turn, this necessitates a deeper and more critical examination and dismantling and rethinking of the state (Dickinson 2017; Cohen 2017), what it does, who it involves and how it impacts upon people's daily lives.

REFERENCES

Abramson, Yehonatan. 2017. "Making a Homeland, Constructing a Diaspora: The Case of Taglit-Birthright Israel." *Political Geography* 58: 14–23.

Adams, Richard H. and Page, John. 2005. "Do International Migration and Remittances Reduce Poverty in Developing Countries?" *World Development* 33(10): 1645–1669.

Ancien, Delphine, Boyle, Mark and Kitchin, Rob. 2009. *Exploring Diaspora Strategies: An International Comparison*, January 26–28, NUI Maynooth, Workshop report.

Anderson, Bridget. 2017. "Towards a New Politics of Migration?" *Ethnic and Racial Studies* 40(9): 1527–1537.

Antwi-Boateng, Osman. 2012. "After War Then Peace: The US-Based Liberian Diaspora as Peace-Building Norm Entrepreneurs." *Journal of Refugee Studies* 25: 93–112.

Bacchi, Alessia. 2016. "Highly Skilled Egyptian Migrants in Austria: A Case of Brain Drain or Brain Gain?" *Journal of Immigrant and Refugee Studies* 14(2): 198–219.

Baser, Bahar. 2015. "Komkar: The Unheard Voice in the Kurdish Diaspora." In *Dismantling Diasporas: Rethinking the Geographies of Diasporic Identity, Connection and Development*, eds. Anastasia Christou and Elizabeth Mavroudi, 113–128. London: Ashgate.

Baser, Bahar and Toivanen, Mari. 2019. "Diasporic Homecomings to the Kurdistan Region of Iraq: Pre- and Post-Return Experiences Shaping Motivations to Re-Return." *Ethnicities* 19(5): 901–924.

Baser, Bahar and Toivanen, Mari. 2020. *MENA Diasporas in Peace, Conflict and Development: Mobilization, Impact and Generational Dynamics*. Presentation for Arab Reform Initiative, September 29.

Bastia, Tanja. 2013. "The Migration–Development Nexus: Current Challenges and Future Research Agenda." *Geography Compass* 7(7): 464–477.

Batalova, Jeanne, Fix, Michael and Bachmeier, James D. 2016. *Untapped Talent: The Costs of Brain Waste among Highly Skilled Immigrants in the United States*. Washington, DC: Migration Policy Institute, New American Economy and World Education Services. Available at: www.migrationpolicy.org/research/untapped-talent-costs-brain-waste-among-highly-skilled-immigrants-united-states.

Bernal, Victoria. 2006. "Diaspora, Cyberspace and Political Imagination: The Eritrean Diaspora Online." *Global Networks* 6(2): 161–179.

Blachnicka-Ciacek, Dominika. 2018. "Palestine as 'a State of Mind': Second-Generation Polish and British Palestinians' Search for Home and Belonging." *Journal of Ethnic and Migration Studies* 44(11): 1915–1931.

Brinkerhoff, Jennifer M. 2009. *Digital Diasporas: Identity and Transnational Engagement*. Cambridge: Cambridge University Press.

Brinkerhoff, Jennifer M. 2012. "Creating an Enabling Environment for Diasporas' Participation in Homeland Development." *International Migration* 50: 75–95.

Carling, Jørgen and Erdal, Marta Bivand. 2014. "Return Migration and Transnationalism: How Are the Two Connected?" *International Migration* 52: 2–12.

Cassarino, Jean-Pierre. 2004. "Theorising Return Migration: The Conceptual Approach to Return Migrants Revisited." *International Journal on Multicultural Societies* 6(2): 253–279.

Castles, Stephen. 2004. "The Factors That Make and Unmake Migration Policies." *International Migration Review* 38(3): 852–884.

Castles, Stephen. 2017. "Migration Policies Are Problematic – Because They Are about Migration." *Ethnic and Racial Studies* 40(9): 1538–1543.

Christou, Anastasia. 2011. "Narrating Lives in (E)motion: Embodiment, Belongingness and Displacement in Diasporic Spaces of Home and Return." *Emotion, Space and Society* 4: 249–257.

Cochrane, Feargal. 2007. "Civil Society beyond the State: The Impact of Diaspora Communities on Peace Building." *Global Media Journal: Mediterranean Edition* 2: 19–29.

Cohen, Nir. 2017. "Diaspora Strategies: Actors, Members, and Spaces." *Geography Compass* 11: e12308.

Coles, Tim and Timothy, Dallen J., eds. 2004. *Tourism, Diasporas and Space*. London: Routledge.

Coniglio, Nicola D. and Brzozowski, Jan. 2018. "Migration and Development at Home: Bitter or Sweet Return? Evidence from Poland." *European Urban and Regional Studies* 25(1): 85–105.

Datta, Kavita, McIlwaine, Cathy, Evans, Yara, Herbert, Joanna, May, Jon and Wills, Jane. 2007. "From Coping Strategies to Tactics: London's Low-Pay Economy and Migrant Labour." *British Journal of Industrial Relations* 45: 404–432.

de Haas, Hein. 2005. "International Migration, Remittances and Development: Myths and Facts." *Third World Quarterly* 26(8): 1269–1284.

de Haas, Hein. 2012. "The Migration and Development Pendulum: A Critical View on Research and Policy." *International Migration* 50(3): 8–25.

Délano, Alexandra and Gamlen, Alan. 2014. "Comparing and Theorizing State–Diaspora Relations." *Political Geography* 41: 43–53.

Dickinson, Jen. 2017. "The Political Geographies of Diaspora Strategies: Rethinking the 'Sending State.'" *Geography Compass* 11: e12305.

Elo, Maria, Aman, Raushan and Täube, Florian. 2020. "Female Migrants and Brain Waste: A Conceptual Challenge with Societal Implications." *International Migration*. https://doi.org/10.1111/imig.12783.

Erdal, Marta Bivand. 2016. "Juxtaposing Pakistani Diaspora Policy with Migrants' Transnational Citizenship Practices." *Geoforum* 76: 1–10.

Féron, Élise and Lefort, Bruno. 2019. "Diasporas and Conflicts: Understanding the Nexus." *Diaspora Studies* 12(1): 34–51.

Fiddian-Qasmiyeh, Elena. 2013. "Transnational Childhood and Adolescence: Mobilizing Sahrawi Identity and Politics across Time and Space." *Ethnic and Racial Studies* 36(5): 875–895.

Fischer, Carolin. 2015. "Exploring the Dynamics of Diaspora Formation among Afghans in Germany." In *Dismantling Diasporas: Rethinking the Geographies of Diasporic Identity, Connection and Development*, eds. Anastasia Christou and Elizabeth Mavroudi, 154–161. London: Routledge.

Fischer, Carolin. 2018. "Reframing Transnational Engagement: A Relational Analysis of Afghan Diasporic Groups." *Global Networks* 18: 399–417.

Fitzgerald, David. 2009. *A Nation of Emigrants: How Mexico Manages Its Migration*. Berkeley, CA: University of California Press.

Gamlen, Alan. 2014. "The New Migration-and-Development Pessimism." *Progress in Human Geography* 38(4): 581–597.

Glytsos, Nicholas P. 2002. "The Role of Migrant Remittances in Development: Evidence from Mediterranean Countries." *International Migration* 40: 5–26.

Godin, Marie and Doná, Giorgia. 2016. "New Social Media and Politics of Representation: Young Congolese in the Diaspora and Beyond." *Refuge* 32(1): 1–12.

Hammond, Laura, Awad, Mustafa, Dagane, Ali I., Hansen, Peter, Horst, Cindy, Menkhaus, Ken and Obare, Lynette. 2011. *Cash and Compassion: The Role of the Somali Diaspora in Relief, Development and Peace-Building*. Available at: http://eprints.soas.ac.uk/11710/1/Cash_and_Compassion_Draft_for_comments.pdf.

Harvey, William. S. 2008. "Brain Circulation?" *Asian Population Studies* 4(3): 293–309.

Harvey, William S. 2012. "Brain Circulation to the UK? Knowledge and Investment Flows from Highly Skilled British Expatriates in Vancouver." *Journal of Management Development* 31(2): 173–186.

Hickey, Maureen. 2016. "Modernisation, Migration, and Mobilisation: Relinking Internal and International Migrations in the 'Migration and Development Nexus.'" *Population, Space and Place* 22: 681–692.

Ho, Elaine. 2011. "'Claiming' the Diaspora: Elite Mobility Sending State Strategies and the Spatialities of Citizenship." *Progress in Human Geography* 35: 757–772.

Ho, Elaine and Boyle, Mark. 2015. "Migration-as-Development Repackaged?" *Singapore Journal of Tropical Geography* 36: 164–182.

Ho, Elaine, Boyle, Mark and Yeoh, Brenda. 2015. "Recasting Diaspora Strategies through Feminist Care Ethics." *Geoforum* 59: 206–214.

Jöns, Heike. 2009. "'Brain Circulation' and Transnational Knowledge Networks: Studying Long-term Effects of Academic Mobility to Germany, 1954–2000." *Global Networks* 9: 315–338.

Jöns, Heike, Mavroudi, Elizabeth and Heffernan, Michael. 2015. "Mobilising the Elective Diaspora: German-American Academic Exchanges in the Postwar Period." *Transactions of the Institute of British Geographers* 40: 113–127.

Joseph, Samarth and Hamilton, Trina. 2014. "Development and Dependence along the New York–Haiti Remittance Corridor." *The Professional Geographer* 66(1): 149–159.

Kang, Tingyu. 2017. "The Digitization of Diaspora Engagement: Managing Extraterritorial Talent using the Internet." *Global Networks* 17: 537–553.

Khanal, Kalpana and Todorova, Zdravka. 2019. "Remittances and Households in the Age of Neoliberal Uncertainty." *Journal of Economic Issues* 53(2): 515–522.

Koh, Sin Yee. 2015. "Unpacking 'Malaysia' and 'Malaysian Citizenship': Perspectives of Malaysian-Chinese Skilled Diasporas." In *Rethinking the Geographies of Diasporic Identity, Connection and Development*, eds. Anastasia Christou and Elizabeth Mavroudi, 129–145. London: Ashgate.

Koinova, Maria. 2018. "Diaspora Mobilisation for Conflict and Post-Conflict Reconstruction: Contextual and Comparative Dimensions." *Journal of Ethnic and Migration Studies* 44(8): 1251–1269.

Korzeniewska, Lubomila and Erdal, Marta Bivand. 2019. "Deskilling Unpacked: Comparing Filipino and Polish Migrant Nurses' Professional Experiences in Norway." *Migration Studies*, mnz053.

Kusunose, Yoko and Rignall, Karen. 2018. "The Long-Term Development Impacts of International Migration Remittances for Sending Households: Evidence from Morocco." *Migration and Development* 7(3): 412–434.

Labrianidis, Lois and Pratsinakis, Manolis. 2017. "Crisis Brain Drain: Short-Term Pain/Long Term Gain?" In *Greece in Crisis: The Cultural Politics of Austerity*, ed. Dimitris Tziovas, 87–107. London: I.B. Tauris.

Lampert, Ben. 2009. "Diaspora and Development? Nigerian Organizations in London and the Transnational Politics of Belonging." *Global Networks* 9: 162–184.

Larner, Wendy. 2007. "Expatriate Experts and Globalizing Governmentalities: The New Zealand Diaspora Strategy." *Transactions of the Institute of British Geographers* 32: 331–345.

Lee, Jane Y. 2015. "Returning Diasporas: Korean New Zealander Returnees' Journeys of Searching 'Home' and Identity." In *Rethinking the Geographies of Diasporic Identity, Connection and Development*, eds. Anastasia Christou and Elizabeth Mavroudi, 161–175. London: Ashgate.

Leurs, Koen. 2015. *Digital Passages: Migrant Youth 2.0 Diaspora, Gender and Youth Cultural Intersections*. Amsterdam: Amsterdam University Press.
Levitt, Peggy. and Lamba-Nieves, Deepak. 2011. "Social Remittances Revisited." *Journal of Ethnic and Migration Studies* 37(1): 1–22.
Lindley, Anna. 2009. "The Early-Morning Phonecall: Remittances from a Refugee Diaspora Perspective." *Journal of Ethnic and Migration Studies* 35(8): 1315–1334.
Lulle, Aija, Janta, Hania and Emilsson, Henrik. 2019. "Introduction to the Special Issue: European Youth Migration: Human Capital Outcomes, Skills and Competences." *Journal of Ethnic and Migration Studies*. DOI: 10.1080/1369183X.2019.1679407.
Mavroudi, Elizabeth. 2008. "Palestinians in Diaspora, Empowerment and Informal Political Space." *Political Geography* 27: 57–73.
Mavroudi, Elizabeth. 2015. "Helping the Homeland? Diasporic Greeks in Australia and the Potential for Homeland-Oriented Development at a Time of Economic Crisis." In *Rethinking the Geographies of Diasporic Identity, Connection and Development*, eds. Anastasia Christou and Elizabeth Mavroudi, 175–189. London: Ashgate.
Mavroudi, Elizabeth. 2018. "Deconstructing Diasporic Mobilisation at a Time of Crisis: Perspectives from the Palestinian and Greek Diasporas." *Journal of Ethnic and Migration Studies* 44(8): 1309–1324.
Mavroudi, Elizabeth. forthcoming. "The Greek Diaspora and the Role of Younger Generations in Helping the Homeland: Opportunities and Challenges." In *Homeland-Diaspora Engagement in Times of Severe Economic Crisis: The Case of Greece*, eds. Fotini Kalantzi, Manolis Pratsinakis, Antonis Kamaras and Othon Anastasakis. Basingstoke: Palgrave Macmillan.
Mavroudi, Elizabeth and Nagel, Caroline. 2016. *Global Migration: Patterns, Processes, and Policies*. London: Routledge.
Mavroudi, Elizabeth and Silva Huxter, Cintia. 2020. "Migrant Youth and Politics: A Workshop." *Migration Letters* 17(5): 747–752.
Mlambo, Victor H. and Adetiba, Toyin C. 2019. "Brain Drain and South Africa's Socioeconomic Development: The Waves and Its Effects." *Journal of Public Affairs* 19: e1942.
Mohan, Giles. 2008. "Making Neoliberal States of Development: The Ghanaian Diaspora and the Politics of Homelands." *Environment and Planning D: Society and Space* 26: 464–479.
Moss, Dana M. 2018. "The Ties That Bind: Internet Communication Technologies, Networked Authoritarianism, and 'Voice' in the Syrian Diaspora." *Globalizations* 15(2): 265–282.
Müller-Funk, Lea. 2016. "Diaspora Mobilizations in the Egyptian (Post)Revolutionary Process: Comparing Transnational Political Participation in Paris and Vienna." *Journal of Immigrant & Refugee Studies* 14(3): 353–370. DOI: 10.1080/15562948.2016.1180471.
Müller-Funk, Lea. 2019. "Diaspora Politics and Political Remittances: A Conceptual Reflection." In *Routledge Handbook of Diaspora Studies*, eds. Robin Cohen and Carolin Fischer, 251–260. Abingdon: Routledge.
Mullings, Beverley. 2011. "Diaspora Strategies, Skilled Migrants and Human Capital Enhancement in Jamaica." *Global Networks* 11: 24–42.
Nagel, Caroline and Staeheli, Lynn. 2010. "ICT and Geographies of British Arab and Arab American Activism." *Global Networks* 10: 262–281.
Newland, Kathleen and Patrick, Erin. 2004. *Beyond Remittances: The Role of Diaspora in Poverty Reduction in Their Countries of Origin: A Scoping Study*. Migration Policy Institute for the Department of International Development. Available at: www.migrationpolicy.org/pubs/Beyond_Remittances_0704.pdf.
NurMuhammad, Rizwangul, Horst, Heather A., Papoutsaki, Evangelia and Dodson, Giles. 2016. "Uyghur Transnational Identity on Facebook: On the Development of a Young Diaspora." *Identities: Global Studies in Culture and Power* 23(4): 485–499.
Oishi, N. 2005. *Women in Motion: Globalization, State Policies, and Labor Migration in Asia*. Stanford, CA: Stanford University Press.
Orjuela, Camilla. 2008. "Distant Warriors, Distant Peace Workers? Multiple Diaspora Roles in Sri Lanka's Violent Conflict." *Global Networks* 8: 436–452.
Ortiga, Yasmin Y., Chou, Meng-Hsuan, Sondhi Gunjan and Wand, Jue. 2018. "Academic 'Centres,' Epistemic Differences and Brain Circulation." *International Migration* 56(5): 90–105.
Page, Ben and Mercer, Claire. 2012. "Why Do People Do Stuff? Reconceptualising Remittance Behaviour in Diaspora-Development Research and Policy." *Progress in Development Studies* 12(1): 1–18.
Page, Ben and Tanyi, Ralph. 2015. "Engaging the African Diaspora in the Fight against Malaria." In *Rethinking the Geographies of Diasporic Identity, Connection and Development*, eds. Anastasia Christou and Elizabeth Mavroudi, 189–203. London: Ashgate.
Pellegrino, Adela. 2001. "Trends in Latin American Skilled Migration: 'Brain Drain' or 'Brain Exchange'?" *International Migration* 39(5): 111–132.

Peth, Simon A. and Sakdapolrak, Patrick. 2020. "When the Origin Becomes the Destination: Lost Remittances and Social Resilience of Return Labour Migrants in Thailand." *Area* 52: 547–557.

Phillips, Nicola. 2009. "Migration as Development Strategy? The New Political Economy of Dispossession and Inequality in the Americas." *Review of International Political Economy* 16(2): 231–259.

Pieke, Frank N., Van Hear, Nicholas and Lindley, Anna. 2007. "Beyond Control? The Mechanics and Dynamics of 'Informal' Remittances between Europe and Africa." *Global Networks* 7(3): 348–366.

Portes, Alejandro. 2009. "Migration and Development: Reconciling Opposite Views." *Ethnic and Racial Studies* 32(1): 5–22.

Ragazzi, Francesco. 2014. "A Comparative Analysis of Diaspora Policies." *Political Geography* 41: 74–89.

Raghuram, Parvati. 2009. "Which Migration, What Development? Unsettling the Edifice of Migration and Development." *Population, Space and Place* 15: 103–117.

Rahnema, Majid and Bawtree, Victoria. 1997. *The Post-Development Reader*. London: Zed Books.

Ratha, Dilip. 2007. *Leveraging Remittances for Development*. Policy Brief. Washington, DC: Migration Policy Institute.

Ratha, Dilip, Mohapatra, Sanket, Ozden, Caglar, Plaza, Sonia, Shaw, William and Shimeles, Abebe. 2011. *Leveraging Migration for Africa: Remittances, Skills, and Investments*. Washington, DC: World Bank. Available at: https://openknowledge.worldbank.org/handle/10986/2300 License: CC BY 3.0 IGO.

Robertson, Susan L. 2006. "Editorial: Brain Drain, Brain Gain and Brain Circulation." *Globalisation, Societies and Education* 4(1): 1–5.

Salih, Ruba, Zambelli, Elena and Welchman, Lynn. 2020. "'From Standing Rock to Palestine We Are United': Diaspora Politics, Decolonization and the Intersectionality of Struggles." *Ethnic and Racial Studies*. DOI: 10.1080/01419870.2020.1779948.

Saxenian, Anna Lee. 2002. "Brain Circulation: How High Skill Immigration Makes Everyone Better Off." *Brookings Review* 20(1): 28–31.

Scheyvens, Regina. 2007. "Poor Cousins No More: Valuing the Development Potential of Domestic and Diaspora Tourism." *Progress in Development Studies* 7: 307–325.

Shain, Yoshi. 2002. "The Role of Diasporas in Conflict Perpetuation or Resolution." *SAIS Review* 22: 115–144.

Siddiqui, Tasneem. 2012. *Impact of Migration on Poverty and Development*. Migrating out of Poverty Research Programme Consortium Working Paper 2. Available at: https://opendocs.ids.ac.uk/opendocs/handle/20.500.12413/14824.

Silvey, Rachel and Parreñas, Rhacel. 2020. "Precarity Chains: Cycles of Domestic Worker Migration from Southeast Asia to the Middle East." *Journal of Ethnic and Migration Studies* 46(16): 3457–3471.

Sinatti, Giulia. 2019. "Return Migration, Entrepreneurship and Development: Contrasting the Economic Growth Perspective of Senegal's Diaspora Policy through a Migrant-Centred Approach." *African Studies* 78(4): 609–623.

Sinatti, Giulia and Horst, Cindy. 2015. "Migrants as Agents of Development: Diaspora Engagement Discourse and Practice in Europe." *Ethnicities* 15(1): 134–152.

Suliman, Samid. 2017. "Migration and Development after 2015." *Globalizations* 14(3): 415–431.

Taylor, J. Edward. 2004. "Remittances, Savings and Development in Migrant-Sending Areas." In *International Migration: Prospects and Policies*, eds. J.E. Taylor and D. Massey, 157–174. Oxford: Oxford University Press.

Toivanen, Mari. 2016. "Political Transnationalism as a Matter of Belonging: Young Kurds in Finland." In *Dislocations of Civic Cultural Borderlines: Methodological Nationalism, Transnational Reality and Cosmopolitan Dreams*, eds. Pirkkoliisa Ahponen, Päivi Harinen and Ville-Samuli Haverinen, 87–107. Heidelberg: Springer.

Toivanen, Mari and Baser Ozturk, Bahar. 2020. "Diasporas' Multiple Roles in Peace and Conflict: A Review of Current Debates." *Migration Letters* 17(1): 47–57.

United Nations General Assembly. 2006. *International Migration and Development*. Report of the Secretary-General, May 18, A/60/871. Available at: www.refworld.org/docid/44ca2d934.html.

Williams, Nick. 2018. "Mobilising Diaspora to Promote Homeland Investment: The Progress of Policy in Post-Conflict Economies." *Environment and Planning C: Politics and Space* 36(7): 1256–1279.

Wong, Madeleine. 2014. "Navigating Return: The Gendered Geographies of Skilled Return Migration to Ghana." *Global Networks* 14: 438–457.

World Bank. 2019. *Migration and Remittances: Recent Developments and Outlook*. Migration and Development Brief 31. Available at: www.knomad.org/sites/default/files/2019-04/Migrationanddevelopmentbrief31.

Yeoh, Brenda and Huang, Shirlena. 2000. "Home and Away: Foreign Domestic Workers and Negotiations of Diasporic Identity in Singapore." *Women's Studies International Forum* 4: 413–429.

26. The migration–development nexus under scrutiny
Raúl Delgado Wise

THE THEORETICAL BATTLEFRONT

In the realm of the economic restructuring and labor precarization processes, i.e. the decline of wages, part-time or temporary jobs and diminishing working rights that characterize contemporary migration flows, the debate regarding the relationship between migration and development has been dominated by the almost sacrosanct belief that migration contributes to development of the country of origin. This view—promoted by the World Bank in line with the implementation of neoliberal policies—posits that remittances sent by international migrants have a positive effect on development within countries and regions of origin. Rooted in neoclassical and monetarist economic theories, this approach conceives of migration as an independent variable, and the link between migration and development is approached as a one-way scheme in which remittances serve as a key source of development for countries of origin. This optimistic line of reasoning portrays the global market as the culmination of capitalist modernity and the end point of an inevitable process that has no reasonable alternative. Social concerns associated with development are overlooked or ignored, as it is generally assumed that a "free" global market—ignoring the outrageous concentration and centralization of capital in a handful of large multinational corporations that control and regulate the global market in contemporary capitalism—will operate as an inexhaustible source of economic growth and social welfare. In this regard, "neoliberal globalization" refers to the current stage of capitalism, characterized by the increasing monopolization of finance, production, services and trade, leaving every major global industry dominated by a handful of large multinational corporations. In the expansion of their operations, the agents of corporations, or monopolistic engines of capitalism, have created a global network and process of production, finance, distribution and investment that has allowed them to seize the strategic and profitable segments of peripheral economies and appropriate the economic surplus produced at enormous and unbearable social and environmental cost (Delgado Wise, 2020).

The dominant approach encompasses the following core propositions:

1. Remittances are an *instrument* for development: in the absence of effective development policies in less developed, migrant-sending nations, the migrants themselves become agents and catalysts for development in places of origin. Remittances serve as the primary tool.
2. Financial instruments should be *democratized*: massive remittance flows across the globe produce an attractive market for financial enterprises offering banking services to marginalized groups. Remittance-based savings and credit are viewed as an attractive platform for development under micro-finance schemes.

3. *The poor have economic power*: remittances provide migrants and their dependents at home in the origin countries with access to resources that can bring them out of poverty, transforming them into agents of global capitalist development.

Ultimately, the dominant approach, supported by the main principles and postulates of the neoliberal school of thought, is conceptually limited. It ignores the historical and political context of contemporary capitalism and fails to consider critical aspects of the relationship between migration and development. It disregards the root causes of migration, ignores the human rights of migrants, downplays the contributions of migrants to receiving societies and overlooks the risks and adversities they face in countries of transit. This approach encompasses an optimistic view that fails to address the meager—and often unbearable—living and working conditions experienced by migrants in receiving societies and the high socioeconomic costs that migration imposes on sending countries. It also fails to appreciate any potential connection between internal and international migration.

This approach has also been referred to as *migration management* (Geiger and Pécoud, 2010). In fact,

> [t]hrough the umbrella of an apparently "neutral" notion ... new narratives have been promoted. These narratives attempt to depoliticize migration, obfuscate the existence of divergent interests or asymmetries of power and conflicts, avoid obligations imposed by international law, and promote the idea that managing migration can be beneficial for all stakeholders: countries of destination, countries of origin, the migrants themselves and their families. This unrealistic triple win scenario clearly favors the interests of the migrant-receiving countries and the large multinational corporations based in such countries. (Delgado Wise et al., 2013: 433–434)

It is an approach to the relationship between migration and development that engenders—as mentioned before—contrasting views of migrants. In origin countries, they are portrayed as national heroes with the political purpose of ensuring the flow of remittances; in transit and destination countries, they are characterized as a burden and, more often, as a negative and polluting cultural and racial influence. The underlying purpose of this stigmatization is to guarantee the supply of cheap and disposable labor.

From this viewpoint, international migration has been analyzed in destination countries in a decontextualized manner. This ethnocentric and individualistic stance has resulted in an incomplete understanding of the complex and multidimensional nexus between migration and development. It has promoted a kind of methodological imperialism with a nativist focus on salary disparities, the displacement of native workers, illegality and border security. This vision not only distorts reality but also obscures the underlying causes of migration and development-related problems that are intrinsic to neoliberal globalization. In a nutshell, through this lens "remittances have become a new 'development mantra': The belief that remittances can be channeled into economic investments that will overcome underdevelopment. Or to put it less positively, the idea is that some of the most exploited workers in the world can make up for the failure of mainstream development policies" (Castles and Delgado Wise, 2008: 7).

A COUNTERHEGEMONIC OR SOUTHERN PERSPECTIVE

In contrast to the dominant view, an alternative, counterhegemonic approach to conceptualizing the relationship between migration and development rooted on the Latin American critical development school of thought has been brought into the debate. This school of thought has left an indelible mark on the field of development studies:

> ECLAC's [Economic Commission for Latin America and the Caribbean] structural school introduced a fundamental paradigmatic shift in the field. For the first time, the theory and practice of development was analyzed from a Southern perspective. This paradigmatic turn did not merely imply a negation of the North, but a negation of the negation in dialectical terms: a search for a more systematic analysis of the dynamics of development and underdevelopment, and for a more equitable form of development or post-development. With the advent of the dependency school, an emancipatory angle was incorporated into the debate: the necessity to transcend the limits of capitalism. (Veltmeyer and Delgado Wise, 2018: 347–348)

This perspective, also referred to as a *southern perspective*, was incorporated into the field of migration and development studies in an attempt to build a comprehensive, inclusive, emancipatory and libertarian approach to the nexus between migration and development (Delgado Wise, 2014).

This alternative perspective is based on a deep understanding of the nature and contrasting characteristics of neoliberal globalization along the North–South divide and between social classes. From this analytical prism the nexus between migration and development is characterized as a dialectical rather than a unidirectional relationship and approached from a multidimensional framework that encompasses economic, political, social, environmental, cultural, racial, ethnic, gender, geographical and demographic factors (Castles and Delgado Wise, 2008).

While the mainstream perspective—also regarded as the dominant approach—only focuses on the horizontal axis of Figure 26.1, from a decontextualized, ahistorical, reductionist and unilateral standpoint, the alternative/counterhegemonic perspective attempts to cover the whole spectrum of dialectical relationships. It also considers the ample spectrum of impacts along countries of origin, transit and destination, and incorporates, as a key analytical dimension, the vertical axis. This axis—intentionally hidden by the dominant/conservative approach—incorporates two fundamental dimensions: (1) an analysis of the multiple violations of human and labor rights suffered by the migrants themselves and their families in origin, transit and destination countries; and (2) the root causes of the complex relationships between migration and development under neoliberal globalization.

NEOLIBERAL GLOBALIZATION

A major and inescapable feature of the current form of capitalism, neoliberal globalization, is uneven development (Emmanuel, 1972; Amin, 1974; Marini, 1974; Katz, 2018). The global and national dynamics of capitalist development, the international division of labor, the imperialist system of international power relations, and the conflicts that surround the capital–labor relation and the dynamics of extractive capital have made

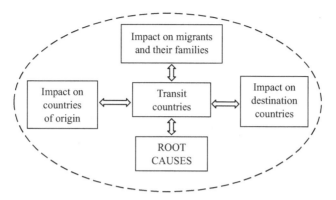

Figure 26.1   The counterhegemonic perspective: key analytical dimensions

economic, social, political and cultural polarization more extreme between geographical spaces and social classes than ever before in human history. A conspicuous output of this scenario is the disproportionate concentration of capital, power and wealth in the hands of a small elite within the capitalist class. Nowadays, the richest 1 percent of the world's population controls 40 percent of total global assets (Davies et al., 2008). Moreover, "from 1970 to 2009, the per capita GDP of developing countries (excluding China) averaged a mere 6.3 percent of the per capita GDP of the G8 countries" (Foster et al., 2011).

Global labor arbitrage, i.e. wage differentials among countries and regions, has become a key pillar of the new global architecture. This allows capital to appropriate enormous monopolistic returns, or imperial rents, by taking advantage of the huge national wage differentials existing across the North–South divide, and the existence of subsistence (and below) wages in much of the Global South. Through the mechanism of global labor arbitrage (Delgado Wise and Martin, 2015), social and geographic asymmetries are reproduced on a global scale.

Social inequalities are one of the most distressing aspects of this process, given the unprecedented concentration and centralization of capital, power and wealth in a few hands while a growing segment of the population suffers poverty, (super)exploitation and exclusion. Increasing disparities are also expressed, ever more strongly, in terms of racial, ethnic and gender relations; reduced access to production and employment; a sharp decline in living and working conditions; and the progressive dismantling of social safety nets (Davidai et al., 2018; Kiely, 2018).

The referred features imply an unprecedented attack on the labor and living conditions of the working class. With the dismantling of the former Soviet Union, the integration of China and India into the world economy and the implementation of structural adjustment programs (including the opening of tariff barriers, privatizations and labor reforms) in the Global South, the supply of labor available to capital over the last two decades has more than doubled from 1.5 to 3.25 billion, in what Richard Freeman calls the "Great Doubling" (Freeman, 2005). This has led to an exorbitant oversupply of labor that has scaled down the global wage structure and increased the overall precariousness of labor. According to estimates of the International Labour Organization, the number of workers in conditions of labor insecurity rose to 1.5 billion in 2017—encompassing nearly half of the world's labor force—with 800 million receiving a salary of less than 3 US dollars per day, while the global number of unemployed continues to rise (ILO, 2018). These conditions—which are unevenly distributed worldwide—have led to growing structural pressures to emigrate internally and/or internationally under circumstances of extreme vulnerability.

THE NEW FACE OF HUMAN MOBILITY: FORCED MIGRATION

Under the conditions engendered by contemporary capitalism, migration cannot be conceived as the product of individual or family decisions—as postulated by the neoclassical school of thought—and essentially becomes a phenomenon with its own patterns, embedded in a set of social networks and transnational relations. The massive scale of migration in the neoliberal era and the bond between domestic and international flows are fundamentally determined by the contradictory and disorderly dynamics of uneven development.

Migration thus adopts the mode of "compulsive displacement", i.e. a new modality of forced migration, possessing the following two characteristics: first, migration is largely an expulsion process resulting from a downward spiral of social regression triggered by the deprivation of production means and subsistence, pillaging, violence and catastrophes that jeopardize the survival of large segments of the population in places of origin. This is not simply a cumulative or gradual process, but an actual breakdown of the social order brought about by structural adjustment policies, domination and wealth concentration strategies, which have attained extreme levels and are forcing massive contingents of the population—through accumulation by dispossession mechanisms (Harvey, 2005)—to sell their labor power both nationally and internationally to guarantee their families' subsistence.

Second, compulsive displacement imposes restrictions on the mobility of the migrant workforce, depreciating and subjecting it to conditions of high vulnerability, precariousness and extreme exploitation. If the process of expulsion is a reprisal of the original accumulation modes characteristic of the first historical stages of capitalism, the current liberalization of the workforce is fated to face obstacles in the labor market internationally. Migrant-receiving states regulate immigrant entry with punitive and coercive instruments that devalue labor, in addition to violating human rights and criminalizing migrants. Conditions for labor exploitation and social exclusion, as well as risks experienced at different stages of transit and settling, jeopardize the lives of migrants (Márquez and Delgado Wise, 2011).

Under these circumstances, migration has acquired a new role in the national and international division of labor. Uneven development generates a new type of migration that can broadly be characterized as forced migration. Although the conventional concept of "forced migration" does not apply to all migrants (Castles, 2003), most current migration flows are forced displacements, and therefore require a more accurate descriptor. In the field of human rights, the term "forced migration" refers specifically to asylum seekers, refugees or displaced people. However, as previously argued, the dynamics of uneven development have led to structural conditions that foster the massive migration of dispossessed, marginalized and excluded populations. Thus, migration has essentially turned into a forced population displacement encompassing the following modalities (Delgado Wise and Márquez, 2009).

Migration due to violence, conflict and catastrophe. Social, political and ethnic conflicts, natural disasters, major infrastructure developments and urbanization can severely affect communities, social groups, families and individuals, to the point of forcing them to abandon their place of origin and sometimes their country. This category includes refugees, asylum seekers and displaced people. These modalities, which tend to mainly affect populations in the Global South, have been acknowledged in international law and there are protection instruments in place. According to figures from the United Nations (UN) High Commissioner for Refugees, there are 79.4 million worldwide, including 20.2 million refugees, 43.9 million internally displaced and 3.7 million asylum seekers (UNHCR, 2019).

Human trafficking and smuggling. This modality of forced displacement has increased at an alarming rate in recent years, becoming a highly lucrative business due to the restrictive policies of receiving countries and increasing hardship in less developed ones. Human trafficking is associated with coercion, abduction and fraud, and includes sexual exploitation and illicit adoptions among other serious violations of human rights. The global response to the sustained increase in this form of criminal activity—which has become increasingly profitable for organized crime—includes the UN Convention against Transnational Organized Crime, signed in Palermo in 2000, and the subsequent Protocol to prevent, suppress and punish the trafficking of people, especially women and children. It is estimated that at least 40 million people are currently engaged in forced labor because of internal and international human trafficking (IOM, 2019).

Migration due to dispossession, exclusion, and unemployment. As argued in this section, most current labor migration falls under this category, which is characterized by extreme vulnerability, criminalization, discrimination and exploitation. It is by far the largest category of forced migration, encompassing around 120 million international "economic" migrants. Instead of adequately categorizing the problems and risks to which these migrants are exposed, they are generally subsumed under the notion of "economic migrants", which assumes they travel in a context of freedom and opportunities for social mobility in transit and destination countries, ignoring the growing vulnerability, insecurity and forced disappearances to which these migrants are subjected.

Return migration in response to massive deportations. This is a growing trend in international migration associated with the irregular status faced by an increasing proportion of migrants derived from a state policy by destination countries—not a criminal act. It entails a process of double forced migration: they were forced to leave their countries of origin and then forced to return under increasingly vulnerable and insecure conditions.

In a less strict sense, migration due to overqualification and a lack of opportunities can be considered as a fifth type of forced migration. It ensues from the restructuring of innovation systems and structural imbalances in the labor market as well as limited institutional backing in peripheral countries which result in many highly qualified workers being unable to find suitable occupation opportunities in their own country. This category of forced migration encompasses nearly 30 million professionals (OECD-UNDESA, 2013). While these migrants do not face serious problems when moving or seeking to cover their basic needs, they migrate to fulfil their labor and intellectual capacities in a context in which the demand of skilled and highly skilled labor has grown exponentially in the United States (US) and European countries, particularly in areas associated with innovation and knowledge-intensive activities: science, technology, engineering and mathematics.

The international debate on migration and development—associated with the need to establish a global governance migration regime—has not been linear. Several disruptive events have influenced the course of the debate: the fall of the Berlin Wall in 1989 and the subsequent dismantling of the former Soviet Union; the attacks on the twin towers of September 11, 2011; and the refugee crisis in Europe triggered in 2015. These events have contributed to accentuate nationalistic, xenophobic and racial prejudices in the main migrant-receiving countries, positing the need to address an increasingly important and pressing topic in the debate: the securitization issue.

DEMYSTIFYING INDICATORS

Regardless of the strategic importance of migration and development in the contemporary policy agenda, public perceptions of human mobility are fraught with myths that distort reality under a unilateral, decontextualized, reductionist and biased view. The dominant political and research agendas in the field tend to reproduce—not disinterestedly—much of the prevailing mythology, disregarding the context in which contemporary migration takes place and its root causes. Human mobility is assumed to be a free and voluntary act oblivious to any kind of structural conditioning and/or national or supranational agents. The multiple economic, demographic, social and cultural contributions made by migrants to host societies and nations are often ignored, hidden or even distorted, regardless of their legal status and categorization (economic migrants, refugees, asylum seekers and so on), to the point where the former are portrayed as a socioeconomic burden for destination countries and in times of crisis are turned into public scapegoats.

In order to reverse or at least confront these distorted views, an effort has been made to build an alternative, solidly grounded, critical, comprehensive and inclusive vision of the main drivers and consequences of contemporary migration through a series of strategic indicators in several critical areas (Puentes et al., 2010). An example of these indicators related to the Mexico–US migration system is the following: it is usually thought that immigrant contributions to the host country are minimal or marginal and that, conversely, immigrant integration to the labor market constitutes an act of "generosity" that eventually leads to a decrease in economic productivity and the loss of jobs for native workers. The truth, however, is very different, even though it has been concealed and distorted in public discourse and, in such a guise, tended to negatively influence public opinion. This topic has been left off bilateral and multilateral agendas between sending and receiving countries, but more importantly perhaps, it has been pushed aside because of the decision to address the issue unilaterally by arguing border control is a matter of national sovereignty. Ultimately, this reflects the way in which the doctrine of national security, which tends to criminalize migrants, has become the benchmark for public migration policies.

The fact is, from 2000 to 2015, the main lever of growth for the US economy—at the time the largest in the world—was constituted by Latin American immigrants and their descendants. As shown in Figure 26.2, their contribution to national gross domestic product (GDP) was 45.3 percent vis-à-vis 54.7 percent by white non-Latino natives. The group with the greatest contribution by national origin was that of Mexican natives (14.3 percent) which, when added to the contributions of Mexican descendants, reaches 31.3 percent.

The main economic sectors for the employment of Mexicans in the US changed between 1994 and 2020; although the numbers in manufacturing grew in absolute terms despite a widespread collapse in employment in said area due to the transfer of assembly plants to countries with a cheap workforce (e.g. Mexico), Mexican participation in the sector fell 13.8 percent in relative terms. Meanwhile, construction became the main source of jobs for Mexican immigrants, rising from 5.9 to 19.5 percent despite a significant drop due to the crisis (including the health crisis due to Covid-19). Overall, and in terms of significance regarding economic dynamism, Mexican immigrant participation in the US industrial sector was 30.7 percent in 2020. An additional 25.3 percent work in professional services, business, education and health; 13.8 percent in leisure and hospitality; and 10.2 percent in commercial activities. Another important sector is agriculture: even though it only amounted to 5.5 percent in 2020, the vast majority of agricultural workers are of Mexican origin, mostly indigenous (see Figure 26.3).

It is important to add that Mexican highly skilled migration to the US has increased exponentially in the last three decades (see Table 26.1). In this period, the number of Mexicans with masters and Ph.D. degrees grew from 47,000 in 1990 to 207,000 in 2019, positioning Mexico in third place of foreign graduates in 2019 (together with the Republic of Korea). This trend is of noteworthy importance given the increasingly conspicuous role played by foreigners in innovation (53 percent of US patents were granted to foreign

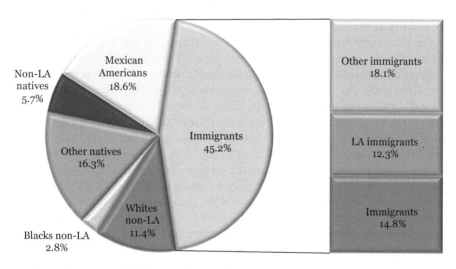

Source: Estimation based on US Bureau of Economic Analysis, Gross Domestic Product by Industry Accounts, and US Bureau of Census, Current Population Survey, March Supplement 2000 and 2015.

Figure 26.2 United States gross domestic product contribution by worker ethnicity and migration origin, 2000–2015

512 *Handbook on migration and welfare*

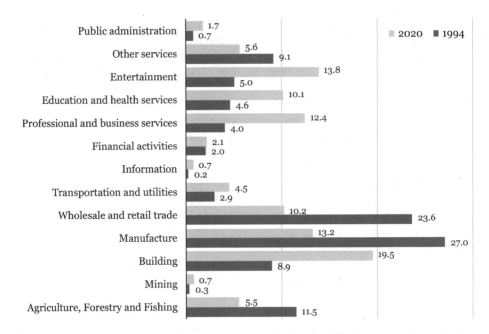

Source: SIMDE, UAZ, estimation based on the Bureau of the Census; BLS, Current Population Survey, March Supplement 1994, 2020.

Figure 26.3   Main sectors of economic activity for Mexicans in the United States, 1994–2020

inventors in 2019) and knowledge-intensive activities in the US, particularly in high technology manufacture (30 percent in 2019).

Despite their significant contributions to the growth of the US economy, Mexican immigrants had the worst wage levels when compared to other ethnic immigrant groups. This implies an ominous wage discrimination associated to the stigma of "illegality"; it must be highlighted that 5.8 million Mexican immigrants (52 percent) bear that stigma (Passel and Cohn 2016). The fact that the Mexican workforce has the lowest US earnings is conspicuous. In global terms, we can say that Mexican labor is among the cheapest in the world and exploited by transnational (mainly US) capital both in Mexico and the US.

Another area of demystification relevant to the Mexico–US migration system lies with the widespread notion of remittances based on monetary fetishism; money is taken for granted without being related to the modes of social production that generate it. For orthodox discourse, the problem is to channel the cash sent by migrants to their relatives in the countries of origin and use them to promote development and stabilize national accounts. The emphasis has been on "family remittances" as an instrument presumed to reduce poverty because it is incorrectly assumed that these improve recipients' consumption capacity (Canales 2008). Most remittances are essentially wage earnings sent by workers to their financial dependents. Mexico is the largest recipient of remittances in Latin America and the fourth globally.

As evidenced by Canales (2011), the economic impact attributed to remittances is disproportionate: the growth of GDP through the multiplying effect of remittances is 0.47

Table 26.1 *Mexican highly skilled immigrants residing in the US, 1990–2019 (growth rates)*

	Master	Ph.D.
1990–2000	10.3	7.2
2000–2010	2.5	3.5
2010–2015	11.6	10.8
2015–2019	9.6	19.0

Source: SIMDE UAZ, estimation based on US Bureau of Census, Dataferret, Percent Samples 1990–2000; 2001–2017 on the American Community Survey; and 2018–2019 on the Current Population Survey.

percent; the elasticity of GDP with regard to remittances is 0.036; the impact of remittances in poverty reduction is 1.3 percentage points; the impact of remittances in reducing inequality (Gini) is 1.3 percent; the elasticity of poverty with regard to remittances is 0.221; and inequality elasticity (Gini) with respect to remittances is 0.221. The fact is that remittances represent a fraction of the wages earned by migrant workers, most often in conditions of labor overexploitation, and which are directed to support financial dependents in places of origin while contributing to family reproduction. This includes the formation of a new workforce with a high propensity to migrate (for example, children, siblings or other relatives) and support for the elderly and sick. Remittances play an essential role in ensuring social reproduction in conditions of poverty and social exclusion. Overexploited migrant workers sending part of their wages to their poor dependents caught in a spiral of family and community degradation is a far cry from the apologist discourse on migration.

Considering the educational level of Mexican immigrants upon initial arrival in the US and the implicit educational cost, I estimate that, between 1994 and 2008, Mexico transferred 83 billion US dollars (in 2008 prices). If said education had been undertaken in US public schools, the cost would have been 613 billion US dollars at constant 2008 prices over the same period. As a reference, remittances channeled to Mexico—often seen as a waste of resources for the US—were only 30 percent of the educational resources transferred to the US via labor migration (see Figure 26.4).

Despite the claims made by certain international bodies and governments, there is no empirical evidence of the alleged positive effects of migration and remittances as catalysts of development in countries of origin. While "successful case studies" have been proffered in an attempt to support these claims, these usually involve self-help micro projects that hardly contribute to sustainable local development initiatives, let alone national ones. In fact, the dominant discourse has been forced to take an increasingly cautious stance.

Many other examples of demystifying indicators can be given and expanded to other migration corridors (Delgado Wise and Gaspar, 2017); however, at this point, it should be evident that the mythology surrounding the dominant narrative in the field encompasses an attempt to obscure the power relations, class relations and modalities of unequal exchange (as well as imperialist domination) underlying the dialectical relationship between migration and development.

Education and social reproduction cost   Remittances sent to México

Source: Estimates based on Current Population Survey, 1994–2008; CONEVAL, Poverty Lines in Mexico; and Educational Statistics Yearbook in Mexico, 2008.

Figure 26.4 Mexico: cost of education and social reproduction (food and housing costs) of immigrants who entered the United States between 1994 and 2008 versus remittances (billions of 2008 United States dollars)

TOWARDS AN INCLUSIVE AGENDA

The efforts to build an institutional framework for the global governance of migration have followed a complex and uncertain route. The non-ratification of the 1990 UN Convention on the Rights of All Migrant Workers and Their Families by most migrant-receiving countries exemplifies the inherent complexity and limitations of this endeavor. Derived from the need to discuss pressing issues on the international migration agenda, a broader initiative for building a global migration regime was envisaged at the UN General Assembly in 2006 with its launch of the High-Level Dialogue on Migration and Development (UN-HLD). This initiative entailed focusing on the relationship between migration and development, in an attempt to avoid the negative connotations surrounding human mobility, particularly across the North–South divide. The first UN-HLD gave rise to the creation of a yearly state-led, non-binding, related forum, alternatively hosted by migrant-receiving and migrant-sending countries: The Global Forum on Migration and Development. In September 2016, the New York UN Declaration for Refugees and Migrants was adopted, giving rise to an intergovernmental consultation and negotiation process that culminated with the adoption of the Global Compact for Refugees and the Global Compact for Safe, Orderly and Secure Migration on December 18, 2018. The US did not participate in the negotiation process and 14 countries did not attend the international conference in Marrakesh where these non-binding agreements were embraced. At the heart of the debates surrounding the final adoption of the Global Compact for

Migration was the attempt to reconcile two positions: a human rights-centered approach and the securitization question which reaffirms the right of states to criminalize migrants under the façade of the right of states to control "illegal" migration (Schierup et al., 2019).

The concept of human development coined by Amartya Sen and adopted by the UN in the 2030 Sustainable Development Agenda represents a positive step in the furthering of the development debate; it cannot, however, adequately address the complex dynamics of unequal development, forced migration and human rights infringements under contemporary capitalism. There is a need for further contextualization; a clear identification of the competing social projects; the creation of viable pathways that lead to the political and institutional strengthening of social organizations, movements and networks; and the definition of alternative and transformative agendas. This implies the need to rethink development in a much deeper way so as to understand the dynamics of uneven development. In this regard, the Latin American critical development school of thought has made important contributions for advancing towards a counterhegemonic agenda on migration and development, capable of envisioning, in theory and practice, avenues to overcome—and transcend—Latin America's asymmetrical and subordinated integration into the world capitalist system (Delgado Wise, 2014). At the same time and counterposed with the regressive model of development propelled by neoliberal globalization, it is crucial to rethink development from a post-neoliberal perspective.

The consequences of the Covid-19 pandemic are uncertain. An immediate effect of the pandemic has been the mass unemployment of broad segments of the population, exacerbating nationalist, xenophobic and racial prejudices. Most likely, this situation will be further aggravated by the strong tendency to deepen automation in the face of population confinement. It will also accelerate the current trend towards monopolization. The pandemic is likewise having devastating effects on social security, health systems and all sectors associated with human mobility; a situation that is already having severe repercussions for millions of migrants and refugees, including fatal victims of the disease. Beyond its adverse implications for the working class and particularly for its most vulnerable segments such as that made up of forced migrants, it is engendering the worst economic recession in the history of capitalism. The impacts of the recession on the migrants' countries of origin will be even more devastating due to their structural weaknesses. Paradoxically, contrary to what the World Bank predicted, remittances have not decreased and represent an invaluable source of income for both the migrants' families and to support the deteriorated balance of payments in the migrant-sending countries. Access to foreign exchange becomes particularly critical in the time of Covid-19 not only to confront the public health emergency, but also for a possible economic recovery in the medium and long term.

What may come from this epochal crisis—for its metabolic relation with nature (Foster, 2013)—is unpredictable, but what is certain is that it will radically transform the current economic and geopolitical global landscape.

REFERENCES

Amin, S. 1974. *Accumulation on a World Scale: A Critique of the Theory of Underdevelopment*. New York: Monthly Review Press.

Canales, A. 2008. *Vivir del Norte. Remesas, desarrollo y pobreza en México*. Mexico, DF: Conapo.
Canales, A. 2011. "Hacia una visión comprehensiva del nexo entre migración, desarrollo y derechos humanos". *Migración y Desarrollo*, 9 (16): 43–78.
Castles, S. 2003. "Towards a sociology of forced migration and social transformation". *Sociology*, 37: 13–34.
Castles, S. and Delgado Wise, R., eds. 2008. *Migration and Development: Perspectives from the South*. Geneva: IOM.
Davidai, S., Klasen, S., Cornia, G.A. et al. 2018. "Economic inequality and social progress", in International Panel on Social Progress, ed. *Rethinking Society for the 21st Century*. Cambridge: Cambridge University Press, 83–140.
Davies, J., Sandström, S., Shorrocks, A. and Wolff, E. 2008. "The world distribution of household wealth". United Nations University: World Institute for Development Economics Research (Discussion Paper No. 2008/03). http://citeseerx.ist.psu.edu/viewdoc/download?doi=10.1.1.337.440&rep=rep1&type=pdf.
Delgado Wise, R. 2014. "A critical overview of migration and development: The Latin American challenge". *Annual Review of Sociology*, 40: 643–663.
Delgado Wise, R. 2020. "Unravelling monopoly capital in the 21st century and the role of the imperial innovation system: Silicon Valley and counter-hegemonies", in Hosseini, H., Goodman, J., Motta, S.C. and Gills, B.K., eds. *The Routledge Handbook of Transformative Global Studies*. London: Routledge, 331–342.
Delgado Wise, R. and Gaspar, S. 2017. "Pacto mundial: migrantes mexicanos frente al espejo de la economía estadounidense". *Migración y Desarrollo*, 15 (29): 7–28.
Delgado Wise, R. and Márquez, H. 2009. "Understanding the relationship between migration and development: Toward a new theoretical approach". *Social Analysis*, 53: 85–105.
Delgado Wise, R. and Martin, D. 2015. "The political economy of global labour arbitrage", in van der Pijl, K., ed., *Handbook of the International Political Economy of Production*. Cheltenham, UK and Northampton, MA, USA: Edward Elgar Publishing, 59–75.
Delgado Wise, R., Márquez, H. and Puentes, R. 2013. "Reframing the debate on migration, development and human rights". *Population, Space and Place*, 19 (4): 430–443.
Emmanuel, A. 1972. *Unequal Exchange: A Study of the Imperialism of Trade*. New York: Monthly Review Press.
Foster, J.B. 2013. "The epochal crisis". *Monthly Review*, 65 (6): 1–12.
Foster, J.B., McChesney, R.W. and Jonna, J. 2011. "The internationalization of monopoly capital". *Monthly Review*, 63 (2): 3–18.
Freeman, R.B. 2005. "What really ails Europe and America: The doubling of the global workforce". *The Globalist*, June 3. www.theglobalist.com/StoryId.aspx?StoryId=5026.
Geiger, M. and Pécoud, A. 2010. *The Politics of International Migration Management*. London: Palgrave Macmillan.
Harvey, D. 2005. *The New Imperialism*. Oxford: Oxford University Press.
ILO (International Labour Organization). 2018. *World Employment and Social Outlook: Trends 2018*. Geneva: ILO.
IOM (International Organization for Migration). 2019. *World Migration Report 2020*. Geneva: IOM.
Katz, C. 2018. *La Teoría de la Dependencia, cincuenta años después*. Buenos Aires: Batalla de Ideas.
Kiely, R. 2018. "Development and inequality: A critical analysis", in Fagan, G.H. and Munck, R., eds. *Development and Inequality: A Critical Analysis*. Cheltenham, UK and Northampton, MA, USA: Edward Elgar Publishing.
Marini, R.M. 1974. *Dialéctica de la Dependencia*. México: Era.
Márquez, H. and Delgado Wise, R. 2011. "Una perspectiva del sur sobre capital global, migración forzada y desarrollo alternativo." *Migración y Desarrollo*, 9 (16): 3–42.
OECD-UNDESA. 2013. "World migration in figures". www.oecd.org/els/mig/WorldMigration-in-Figures.pdf.
Passel, J.S. and Cohn, D. 2016. *Overall Number of U.S. Unauthorized Immigrants Holds Steady since 2009*. Pew Research Center. www.pewhispanic.org/2016/09/20/overall-number-of-u-s-unauthorized-immigrants-holds-steady-since-2009/.
Puentes, R., Canales, A., Rodriguez, H. et al. 2010. "Towards an assessment of migration, development and human rights links: Conceptual framework and new strategic indicators". http://148.217.94.54/secciones_documentos/119TOWARDS_AN_ASSESSMENT_OF_MIGRATION_V.pdf.
Schierup, K.-U., Likić-Brborić, B., Delgado Wise, R. and Toksöz, G. 2019. *Migration, Civil Society and Global Governance*. London: Routledge.
UNHCR. 2019. "Figures at a glance". www.unhcr.org/figures-at-a-glance.html.
Veltmeyer, H. and Delgado Wise, R. 2018. "Rethinking development from a Latin American perspective". *Canadian Journal of Development Studies*, 39 (3): 335–352.

Index

Aaroe, Lene 106–7
Abduvaliev, Mubinzhon 453
Abou-Chadi, Tarik 58, 131–2
Abts, Koen 8–9
Adams, Richard H. 451
Adams, Samuel 451
Adenutsi, Deodat E. 452
Adsera, Alicia 47
Afghanistan 25
Agbola, Frank W. 452
age 15, 26, 31–2, 47, 161–2, 184, 219, 236, 287, 303, 310–11, 359, 393, 395, 398, 430, 432, 476, 499
  see also population aging
Akkerman, Agnes 8
Akkoyunlu, Sule 449
Alba, Richard 301
Aleksynska, Mariya 200–201
Alesina, Alberto 4, 65, 92, 118–19, 121–5, 132, 298, 323, 409
Ali, Sundas 413–14
Allport, Gordon 123, 177, 368–70, 383, 385–6
Altheide, David 361
American Dream 357
American Exceptionalism 91
Americanization of European welfare politics 204, 217, 323, 325
Americanness 91
Ancien, Delphine 490
Andersen, Jørgen 157–8, 175–6
Anderson, Benedict 105
Anderson, Bridget 499
Ang, Alvin 452
anti-immigrant sentiment 4, 7, 45, 58, 88, 90–91, 123, 129–32, 139–42, 148, 156–8, 160, 164–5, 178–81, 223, 232–5, 245, 248–9, 255, 258, 273, 285, 288, 302, 339–46, 351–3, 355, 358, 375, 382, 417
  see also nativism
Antwi-Boateng, Osman 495
Applebaum, Lauren 107
apprenticeships 35
Argentina 34
artificial intelligence 355
Ascencio, Fernando L. 451
asylum seeking 2, 7, 13, 16–20, 24, 26–8, 31, 35, 37–9, 47–9, 58, 64, 73–6, 79, 113, 131, 140, 175, 188, 201, 216, 223, 230, 248–9, 258, 321, 326, 328–31, 334, 351, 508–10

asylum tourism 360
Australia 16–17, 19, 23, 31, 34, 213–14, 225, 302–3, 305–6, 330, 359, 361, 491
Austria 14, 17, 19, 22–3, 33, 35, 37–8, 52, 55, 74–9, 130, 144, 158, 166, 213, 220, 225, 255, 261–71, 285–7, 330, 495
authoritarianism 9, 161–4, 167, 175, 179–80, 259, 424–5, 427, 430–34
automation 355
Avdagic, Sabina 124
Aycinena, Diego 444
Aydemir, A. 27
Azam, Muhammad 452

Bacchi, Alessia 497
backlash against immigration 338–47
  see also anti-immigrant sentiment
balance of power 156, 165–6, 168
Bale, Tim 165, 255
Bangladesh 9, 451–2, 470–84
Banting, Keith 4, 21, 290, 326, 409–10, 413, 415
Barajas, Adolfo 454
Baser, Bahar 496
basic income scheme see universal basic income
Bay, Ann-Helén 142
Beck, Ulrich 359
Beckfield, Jason 257
Beine, Michel 29
Belgium 8–9, 14, 17, 19, 22–3, 33–4, 37, 74–6, 78–9, 144, 158, 165–6, 201, 213, 220, 285–6, 303, 305–6, 315, 330, 410, 420–35
Ben Atta, Oussama 9
Benhabib, Seyla 21
Bentley, Lee 181
Bernal, Victoria 494
Bettin, Giulia 451
Betz, Hans-Georg 7
Bevelander, Pieter 2–3, 24–5, 28, 32, 34
Beveridge health system 74
biases 56, 59, 67, 72, 180, 182, 291, 341, 344–5, 483, 510
  see also prejudice
big data 355
Bilgili, Özge 201
Bjørklund, Tor 157–8, 175–6
Blalock, Hubert M. 370
Blocher, Christoph 358

517

Bloemraad, Irene 21, 197, 282, 290
Blomberg, Helena 422
Boeri, Tito 52
Boräng, Frida 6, 328–9
Borevi, Karin 415
Borjas, George 18, 20, 22, 29–30, 51
Bösch, Frank 50
Bosnia 25, 491
boundaries of generosity 102–15
bounded solidarity 102
Boyle, Mark 492
Brady, David 122, 324, 326
brain exchange 497
Brazil 34
Brexit 16, 38, 156, 211, 338
Breznau, Nate 122, 140, 180–82
Brinkerhoff, Jennifer M. 491, 494
Brochmann, Grete 21
Brubaker, Rogers 104
Brücker, Herbert 30, 51–2
Bulgaria 17
Burgoon, Brian 122–3, 142, 301, 324
Burkhardt, Christoph 324, 410
Bustillo, Ricardo 453

Caicos Islands 443
Cameron, Adrian C. 303
Cameron, David 211
Canada 4, 16–17, 19, 23, 27–8, 31, 34, 67–8, 73–5, 77–9, 105, 107, 109, 112–13, 139, 198, 213–14, 216, 218, 220, 223, 282, 302–3, 305–6, 330, 407, 409–10, 413, 417
Canales, Alejandro I. 512–13
capitalism 10, 255, 351, 357, 361, 363, 504–5
Cappelen, Cornelius 124
Careja, Romana 5, 425
CARIN criteria 69–71
Castles, Stephen 499
Castronova, Edward J. 52
Catrinescu, Natalia 452
causality 332–3
Cazachevici, Alina 450
Celeste, Laura 201
Chami, Ralph 451
Chapel Hill Expert Survey 58
Chile 17
China 354–5, 443, 451, 490, 507
Chiswick, Barry R. 47
Christa, Oliver 367–8
citizenship 14, 33, 103–4, 106, 113, 183, 197, 199, 201–2, 211, 353, 358, 416, 421, 433
Citrin, Jack 188, 199
civic engagement 196–7, 202–4, 277, 406
civic nationalism 102, 104–5, 108, 114, 212, 214

civil rights 13, 198, 211
Clark, Rebecca 31
cleavage 119, 132, 175, 183, 259, 284, 356, 358, 360, 424
closing-the-doors-to-the-welfare-state approach 325–7
Cochraine, Feargal 495
Coenders, Marcel 178
Coles, Tim 497
Collins, Mary E. 369–70
Colombia 17
colonialism 488
Comes, Calin-Adrian 452
Common European Framework of Reference for Languages 33
Comparative Manifesto Project 262
comradeship 105–6, 113
conflict theory 68, 123, 161, 167, 177, 180, 278, 292, 368
constructivism 406, 415
contact theory 7, 198, 200, 359, 367–79, 382–402, 408
contact with strangers 367–79
Coping Strategies Index 473–4, 479–80
corruption 255, 450, 480, 490
Council of Europe 212, 216
countries of origin 2, 9, 28, 32, 39, 72, 273, 442–64, 504
    see also individual countries
COVID-19 pandemic 13, 15, 73, 470, 511, 515
Crepaz, Markus M. L. 21, 161, 182, 218, 281, 290, 325, 328, 369, 373, 375, 378, 433
Croatia 17
crowding out 89, 217, 219–20
crowdsourcing 70
cultural diversity 21, 36, 66, 128, 195, 197, 199–201, 204, 298, 373, 406
cultural threat 7, 90, 96, 119, 198–9, 259, 292, 338–9, 341–6, 352
Curran, Michaela 122, 218
Czech Republic 17, 22–3, 33, 49, 55

Dahlberg, Matz 92, 123
d'Albis, Hippolyte 48
Dallen, Timothy 497
Damron, Regan 182, 328
Dancygier, Rafaela 425
De Giorgi, Giacomo 30
de Haas, Hein 493, 499
De Koster, Willem 164–5
de Vroome, Thomas 27, 199
deep horizontal comradeship 105–6, 108, 113
demystifying indicators 510–14

Denmark 14, 17, 22–5, 27–8, 33–4, 36, 38, 49, 52, 58, 71, 105, 119, 130–31, 175–6, 213–14, 218, 220, 223, 225, 255, 265, 268, 270–72, 278, 280, 283, 285–6, 303, 305, 330, 351, 413
Dermont, Clau 142
deservingness 4, 68–73, 92–3, 97–8, 102–3, 106–9, 112–14, 138–40, 160, 164, 224, 226, 283, 290, 327
"designer immigrants" 73
Deutsch, Karl 10
Deutsch, Morton 369–70
diaspora 2, 9, 470, 488–99
Dinesen, Peter T. 293, 298
disabilities 72, 106, 125
discrimination 13, 28, 33, 36, 49–50, 69, 72, 114, 129–31, 139, 148, 158, 179, 204, 211, 218, 277, 280, 282–4, 286, 289–90, 293, 357, 421–2, 424, 429, 432–4, 509, 512
distributive justice 21, 132, 249, 424
diversity 1, 20–22, 38, 45, 58, 87, 92, 118, 122, 161, 181, 195, 198, 204, 210, 212, 216–17, 223, 230, 233, 297–300, 322, 324, 326, 358–9, 377, 497–8
  contact with strangers 367–79
  see also contact theory
  cultural diversity 21, 36, 66, 128, 195, 197, 199–201, 204, 298, 373, 406
  ethnic diversity 21, 45, 65, 67, 95, 118, 120, 181, 187–8, 204, 230–32, 276–80, 283, 291–2, 298–300, 323, 326–7, 329, 353, 360, 382–401, 407, 420, 433
  and trust 276–93, 298, 323, 405–18
  and the welfare state 64–79
  in the workplace 382–401
dress codes 212, 214
dual citizenship 113, 212–14, 490
Dustmann, Christian 30, 49, 58, 130

economic anxiety 338–41, 343–6
Economic Commission for Latin America and the Caribbean 505
economic growth 9, 14, 32, 46–7, 49, 126, 181, 287, 289, 442–4, 450–63, 490, 499, 504
economic migration 22–6, 31, 140
economic shocks 9, 343–5, 448
Edo, Anthony 130
"educated preferences" theory 128
education, levels of 3–5, 10, 26–8, 30–31, 39, 47, 49–50, 89, 96–7, 137–8, 143–8, 162, 164, 167, 180, 184–6, 236, 259, 287–8, 291, 293, 303, 311, 340, 346–7, 357, 359–60, 370, 387, 390, 392–3, 395, 398, 423–4, 430, 432, 473–4, 476–7, 489

education system 14, 21, 48, 121, 129, 211, 223, 415, 417, 450, 453, 471, 493, 512
egalitarianism 9, 91, 94, 132, 178, 281, 327, 372, 415, 424, 427, 430–34, 440
Eger, Maureen 3, 5–6, 56, 58, 122–3, 140, 180–82
Egypt 443, 495
Ekberg, Jan 31, 48
El Salvador 443–5
Elsner, Benjamin 120
Emilsson, Henrik 32, 34
emotions 7, 171, 178, 196, 347, 352, 355, 361–3, 391, 424, 492–3, 496
empathy 93, 96, 231, 362, 382, 384–8
employment 13, 16–29, 31–2, 38, 46–9, 52, 72, 74, 122–3, 127, 131, 137–48, 151, 154–5, 181–2, 184–5, 211, 287–9, 301, 303, 310–11, 315, 319–20, 324, 329, 338–40, 408, 450, 481, 507, 511
  see also unemployment
Erdal, Marta B. 490–91
Eritrea 25, 494
Esping-Anderson, Gøsta 37, 297, 303, 325, 327
Estonia 17, 19, 23, 33, 144
Ethiopia 25
ethnic competition theory 177
ethnic diversity 21, 45, 65, 67, 95, 118, 120, 181, 187–8, 204, 230–32, 276–80, 283, 291–2, 298–300, 323, 326–7, 329, 353, 360, 382–401, 407, 420, 433
ethnic minorities 69, 198, 211, 227, 232, 281, 323, 356, 385, 390, 396, 407, 420–25, 427, 429–30, 433–5, 439–40
ethnic nationalism 102, 104–6
ethnic threat theory 177, 179
ethnic tolerance 8, 382–3, 386–90, 392, 396–7, 400–401
ethnonationalism 211
European Agenda for Migration 32
European Community Household Panel 47
European Economic Area 30–31
European Migration Network 36
European Monetary Union 261
European Social Survey 4–6, 49, 53–7, 69–70, 121, 123, 126, 138, 142, 144, 148, 156, 158–60, 162, 165, 175–6, 183–8, 231, 233–5, 237, 239, 241, 244, 262, 277, 284, 286–7, 356, 408, 410, 413
European Union 6, 10, 15, 17–18, 22–6, 30–32, 34, 37, 48–9, 51–2, 58, 70, 75, 125, 128, 139, 212, 230, 256–8, 260–61, 263–5, 272–3, 299, 344, 358, 360
  see also Brexit
European Values Survey 408, 410
Euroscepticism 160, 162, 164, 167, 171, 173

Eurostat 18, 144, 184
exclusive solidarity *see* welfare chauvinism
external boundaries 102–3, 105–6, 113–14

family reunion migration 19–20, 24, 27–8, 33, 198, 223, 329
far right *see* radical right; right-wing parties
Feeny, Simon 451
Fernández, Eva 183
Ferrera, Maurizio 178
Fiji Islands 445, 452
Filindra, Alexandra 202
Finland 14, 17, 23, 34, 52, 142, 144, 158–9, 165–6, 213, 220, 225, 280, 285–6, 303, 305, 330, 495
Finnigan, Ryan 122, 324, 326
Finseraas, Henning 58, 123, 232–3, 301
first-generation migrants 13–16, 20–21, 31, 49, 432
fiscal burden 2, 28–32, 39, 46–50, 178, 340
fiscal leakage 123, 128
Fix, Michael 51
Foged, Mette 49
Foner, Nancy 301
food security 9, 470–84
Forbes, Hugh D. 123
forced migration 15, 17, 27–8, 37, 329, 508–10, 515
  see also refugees
Ford, Robert 125, 233
foreign direct investment 443, 446, 448, 470, 492
framing 195–205, 339
France 14, 16–17, 19, 22–4, 33–4, 52, 74–5, 78–9, 105, 109–12, 128–30, 144, 158–60, 165–6, 211, 213, 216, 220, 223, 225, 285–6, 303, 305, 330, 359, 495
Frattini, Tomasso 30
fraud 138–9, 327, 509
Freeman, Gary 18, 20–21, 29, 215, 217, 322–4, 328–9
Freeman, Richard 507
free-movers 15–16, 30, 51
free-riders 175
Friedman, Milton 45, 118, 137, 142, 147–8

gap hypothesis 71
Garand, James C. 141
GDP 14, 19, 29–31, 48, 50, 52, 122, 126, 144, 181, 184, 219, 287, 290, 304, 307, 443, 445–7, 449, 452–4, 456–63, 507, 511–13
gender 24, 48, 219, 287–8, 303, 311, 355, 362, 390, 392–3, 395, 425, 430, 474, 493, 497, 499, 505, 507
General Social Survey 5, 58, 231, 235, 239, 372–4

Geneva Convention 16, 329
Gerber, Alan S. 141, 178
Germany 6, 14, 16–17, 19–20, 22–4, 30, 33, 35, 37–9, 49–50, 52, 55, 58, 71, 73–5, 78–9, 109–11, 123, 126, 129, 131, 144, 156, 158, 160, 165–6, 181–2, 211, 213–14, 220, 223, 230–34, 236, 238, 245, 247–8, 283–7, 303, 305, 330, 351, 353, 362–3, 369, 373, 375, 378, 443, 449
Ghana 452, 497–8
Gilens, Martin 107
Giuliano, Paola 123, 452
Giulietti, Corrado 30, 51
Gladwell, Malcolm 367, 371–2
Glaeser, Edward 65, 132, 298, 323, 409
global cities 359
Global Compact for Migration 514–15
Global Compact for Refugees 514
global financial crisis 470
Global North 2, 9, 13, 73, 488, 490
Global South 2, 9, 13, 409, 442, 488–90, 494, 507, 509
  see also individual countries
globalization 2, 64, 119, 132, 177, 216, 255, 259, 352, 355–7, 360, 362, 423, 498, 504, 506–8
Goldschmidt, Tina 232–3
Goodhart, David 58, 230, 298, 323, 353, 409
Gorodzeisky, Anastasia 49
Great Doubling 507
Great Recession 66
Greece 17, 52, 55, 130, 213, 220, 489, 491, 495
Green, Eva G.T. 198–9
Griffin, Keith 452
group conflict 123, 175, 181, 278, 292
group empathy 93, 96
group identity 87, 90, 95–6
  see also in-groups; out-groups
group loyalty 67, 92, 95, 98, 124, 128
group membership 95, 372, 384
group-centrism 89–90, 92–5
Guimond, Serge 198–9

H1N1 73
Hacker, Jacob S. 215
Haider, Jörg 130
Hainmueller, Jens 89, 96, 201, 338
Haiti 73, 443, 445, 448
Halla, Martin 130
Hamilton, David L. 370
Hammond, Laura 494
Hangartner, Dominik 130
Hansen, Bruce E. 456–7
Hansen, Jorgen 52
Hansen, Peo 31–2

Hanson, Pauline 361
Harell, Allison 4
Harvey, William S. 497
Hassan, Gazi M. 451
Häusermann, Silja 183
health care 14–15, 51, 59, 64, 72–9, 107, 121, 223, 286, 291, 347, 357, 450, 453, 471, 477, 493, 512
health insurance 74, 76–7
health policies 76
Heisenberg, Werner 1, 10
Heizmann, Boris 188
Hero, Rodney E. 300
heterogeneity 24, 28, 71, 118, 127, 148, 182, 184, 186–8, 230, 232, 276–7, 280–81, 283–4, 287, 290, 292, 298, 322–3, 344, 407, 446–7, 451, 455, 457–8
Hewstone, Miles 373
"hidden consensus" argument 89, 96
high-income countries 64–5, 73–4, 78, 122, 130
see also individual countries
high-skilled migrants 51, 73, 89, 178, 201, 340, 359, 489
Hilton, Lynette 51
HIV/AIDS 73–4
Hjerm, Mikael 181
Hjorth, Frederik 178
Ho, Elaine 492, 499
Hobolt, Sara B. 344
Hochschild, Arlie 357, 362
Hofer, Johannes 360
Hollifield, James 2–3, 326–7
home countries *see* countries of origin
Honduras 443
Hooghe, Marc 199, 408
Hopkins, Daniel J. 89, 96, 338
Household Dietary Diversity Score 473–4, 479–80
Household Food Insecurity Access Scale 473–4, 480
housing 14, 29, 52, 121, 131, 211, 286, 471
Huang, Xiaoning 51
Huddle, Donald L. 31
human rights 356, 508, 515
human trafficking 509
humanitarianism 15–16, 25, 37–8, 91, 93, 102, 113
Hungary 17, 22–4, 144
hunkering-down argument 277–8, 282–3, 293, 298

Iceland 17, 19, 34, 144, 158–60, 166, 285–6, 303, 305
illegal immigration *see* undocumented migrants
imagined community 104

Imai, Katsushi S. 453
Immigrant Exclusion to Social Programs Index 6, 224–5, 285–7, 289–91
immigrant integration 6, 13, 21–2, 24, 26, 28, 33–5, 112, 183–4, 195–205, 234, 285, 316, 510
immigration
see also migration
backlash against 338–47
see also anti-immigrant sentiment
boundaries of generosity 102–15
as challenge to welfare state 45–59
contact with strangers 367–79
see also contact theory
and diversity *see* diversity
effect on trust *see* trust
inequality and welfare regimes 297–316
integration/multiculturalist policy 195–205, 210–27, *see also* integration policy; multiculturalist policy
and migration policy 321–35
opposition to 338–47
see also anti-immigrant sentiment; nativism; xenophobia
politicization of 230–50
and preferences for redistribution 118–32
remittances 2, 9, 442–64, 471–3, 475–6, 482–4, 492–3, 504, 512
shaping support for a UBI 4, 137–48, 153–5
sharing with strangers 87–98
see also strangers
social democratic dilemma 255–71
sources of trust resilience 276–93
welfare chauvinism *see* welfare chauvinism
income inequality 6, 55, 66–7, 120, 181–2, 262, 265, 289, 303–6, 308, 310, 312–14, 405
India 355, 443, 451–2, 507
individualism 37, 91, 94–5
Indonesia 493
inequality 297–316, 362, 372
inflation 219, 221, 451
in-groups 56, 59, 67, 90, 93, 102, 128, 141, 177, 179, 182, 278, 341–2, 344–5, 374, 406, 411, 421
integration policy 2, 5, 10, 20, 22, 26–7, 32–9, 183–6, 188, 195–205, 279, 281, 285
see also multiculturalist policy
interculturalism 212, 216
interethnic contact 21, 64, 68, 382–401
interethnic social resources 387–97, 400
internal hierarchies 102–3, 106, 113–14
International Labour Organization 13, 507–8
International Monetary Fund 489
International Social Survey Program 6, 70, 122, 302, 306

Iran 25
Iraq 25, 249
Ireland 17, 19, 23–4, 34, 128, 144, 158, 166, 213, 285–6, 303, 305–6, 330, 354–5, 495
Ireland, Patrick 3
Islam 90, 105, 195, 198, 204, 212, 358, 361, 374–5, 377
Islamophobia 212–13, 215, 226
Israel 17, 19, 22–3, 55, 302–3, 305, 309, 490
Italy 14–17, 23–4, 34–5, 37, 109–11, 129, 144, 158, 160, 165–6, 213, 220, 265, 268, 270, 272, 285–6, 303, 305, 330, 354–5, 408
Iyengar, Shanto 378–9

Jamaica 492, 496
Japan 15, 17, 213, 220, 330, 355
Jawaid, Syed T. 451, 453
Jayaraman, Tiruvalangadu K. 452
job security 343, 356
Johnston, Richard 413
Joppke, Christian 21
justice 20–21, 68, 132, 249, 261, 414, 423–4, 488, 494–5, 498

Kalm, Sara 6
Kang, Tingyu 490
Kauff, Mathias 198
Kayran, Elif N. 6
Keely, Charles B. 451
Kennedy, John F. 75
Kesler, Christel 6, 197
Kevins, Anthony 4–5
Key, V.O. 368
Kholodilin, Konstantin A. 449
Kim, Dowon 59
Kitschelt, Herbert 176, 259
Kleider, Hanna 7
Klobodu, Edem K.M. 451
Know Nothings 353–4
Koh, Sin Y. 496
Kokkonen, Andrej 387
Kolbe, Melanie 6, 433
Koning, Edward 4–6, 131, 183, 223–4, 286
Koopmans, Ruud 21, 201, 298
Korpi, Walter 325, 329–30
Koseki, Shin 359–60
Kosovo 491
Krause, Werner 131–2
Kremer, Stephanie 456
Kriesi, Hanspeter 183
Kros, Mathijs 178
Kuk, J. 345
Kulin, Joakim 5–6, 58, 233
Kumar, Ronald R. 452
Kusunose, Yoko 492

Kuwait 443
Kwon, Ronald 122, 218
Kymlicka, Will 4–5, 21, 70–71, 290
Kyrgyzstan 443, 445, 452

La Ferrara, Eliana 125
labor market competition 89, 123–4, 128, 177, 181, 339–40, 358
labor migration 7, 16, 19, 24, 48, 321, 326, 328–31, 334, 480, 509, 513
Labrianidis, Lois 491
laissez-faire approach 13, 32, 35, 38, 424
Lampert, Ben 494
language 21, 33, 35, 65, 87, 89, 96–7, 104, 106, 131, 195–6, 212, 342, 355–6, 369, 412, 416
Larsen, Christian A. 182, 283, 290
Lartey, Emmanuel K.K. 451
Latvia 17
Laurence, James 181, 373
laziness 107–9, 111, 119, 121, 126, 132, 171, 426–7
Le, Thanh 451
Le Pen, Marine 131
Lee, Dongwon 59
Lefkofridi, Zoe 6, 257
left-wing parties 6–7, 45, 57–8, 119, 132, 165, 168, 175, 183, 231, 233–4, 236–8, 240–45, 249–50, 265, 351, 356
   see also social democratic parties
legalism 91, 94
Lenard, Patti 8
Lesotho 443, 445
Levy, Morris E. 300
liberal nationalism 104, 108
Liberia 495
libertarianism 424
life expectancies 15
Lind, Jo T. 456, 459
Lindvall, Johannes 6
Linnander, Erika 368
Lithuania 17, 144
living conditions 78, 354, 406
living standards 27, 126, 301
Lofstrom, Magnus 52
low-skilled migrants 48, 89, 130, 164, 322, 339–40, 493
Luik, Marc-André 24–5
Lulle, Aija 491
Luttmer, Erzo F.P. 92, 124, 323
Lutz, Philipp 36
Luxembourg 17, 19, 22–3, 34, 292, 410, 443
Luxembourg Income Study 6, 302–3

Mabrouk, Fatma 451
Macedonia 452

magnet hypothesis *see* welfare magnets hypothesis
Magni-Berton, Raul 123
Mair, Peter 6, 256–7
majority 8–9, 33, 92–3, 104, 108, 129, 176–7, 196–7, 199–200, 203, 205, 235, 247–8, 278, 281, 283–4, 300, 327, 353, 357, 359, 363, 369, 390, 396, 407–8, 420–35, 439–40, 475, 511
Makhlouf, Farid 9, 446
Malaysia 452, 480
Manatschal, Anita 5, 202
Manevska, Katerina 8
Marcus, George 362
Margalit, Yotam 352
market research 70
Marshall, Thomas H. 91
Marx, Paul 181–2
Masgoret, Anne-Marie 199
Massey, Douglas S. 452
Mau, Steffen 177, 182, 324, 410
Mavroudi, Elizabeth 9
Mayda, Anna M. 130
McClelland, Katherine 368
McGann, Anthony J. 176, 259
McLaren, Lauren 198
McPherson, Miller 370
meaningful contact 382–401
means-tested programs 4, 51–2, 107, 138, 148, 182, 234, 324, 327, 410
measurement 4, 96, 120–21, 156–9, 164, 167–8, 175–6, 261, 276, 284, 292–3, 390–91, 396, 428, 439, 455, 473–4, 477, 483
Medicaid 51, 76–7
Medicare 75
Melhum, Halvor 456, 459
Meltzer-Richard effect 66
membership 4, 90, 95, 102–4, 108–14, 144, 160–62, 164, 203, 226, 235–6, 256–8, 261, 264, 268, 360, 372, 384, 416
membership perceptions 102–3, 108–12, 226
mental health issues 27–8, 203
Merkel, Angela 38, 211, 248
Meuleman, Bart 8–9
Mewes, Jan 177, 182
Mexico 17, 22–3, 34, 443, 448, 510–11, 513–14
micro-finance schemes 504
Midtbø, Tor 124
migrant integration 22, 32–3, 38, 72, 74, 184, 198, 200
Migrant Integration Policy Index *see* MIPEX
migrant remittances 2, 9, 442–64, 471–3, 475–6, 482–4, 492–3, 504, 512
migration
  see also immigration
  as a development strategy 488–99, 504–15
  and diversity *see* diversity
  and food security 470–84
  managing in welfare states 13–39
  remittances 2, 9, 442–64, 471–3, 475–6, 482–4, 492–3, 504, 512
  types of 328–30
migration policy 321–35
migration shocks 48
Miller, David 109, 413–14
Miller, Timothy. 31
Mim, Sami B. 451
minimum wage 27
Minkenberg, Michael 131
MIPEX 5, 22, 33–4, 78–9, 184–5, 200–201
Mohamed, Sufian E. 452
Mohan, Giles 498
Moller, Stephanie 303
Moniruzzaman, Mohammad 9
Montenegro 443, 491
moral hazard 138, 471
Moriconi, Simone 58, 130
Morocco 387, 390–91, 421, 428, 432–3, 492
Morrison, Kimberly R. 199
Moss, Dana M. 495
Mouritsen, Per 105
Mughal, Mazhar 446
Müller-Funk, Lea 494–5
Mullings, Beverley 496
multicultural societies 8, 122, 215, 278, 421
multiculturalism 21, 38, 70, 74, 112, 195–6, 204, 211, 230, 258–9, 277, 279, 293, 375, 412, 420
Multiculturalism Policy Index 5, 212–14, 219
multiculturalist policy 2, 5, 10, 73, 122, 140, 195, 197–9, 201, 210–27, 281–2, 298, 412
  see also integration policy
multi-level governance 32–3, 35, 37–8
multilevel regression 184–5, 188, 392, 395
Mundaca, Gabriela B. 452
Murard, Elie 4, 125, 130

Nannestad, Peter 52, 120
National Academies of Sciences, Engineering, and Medicine 47, 49, 52
national identity 8, 64, 67–9, 90, 96, 102–6, 112, 198–9, 212, 218, 223, 259, 344, 353, 359–60, 400, 405–18
national security 347, 510
nationhood 66, 96, 102, 104–5, 109, 113, 255
native attitudes 195, 202–5
nativism 3, 7, 10–11, 18, 38–9, 97, 119, 130, 132, 175, 255, 282, 351–62, 505
  see also anti-immigrant sentiment; xenophobia

naturalization 8, 14, 38, 51, 113, 140, 196, 201–3, 355, 415–16
Naumann, Elias 124, 181–2
neoliberalism 2, 4, 6, 10, 69, 156–9, 161–7, 171, 173–4, 216, 231, 234, 258, 424, 488, 498, 505, 508
Nepal 443, 445
Netherlands 14, 16–17, 19–20, 22–5, 27, 33–8, 52, 109–11, 119, 130, 144, 158–60, 164–6, 178, 213–14, 219, 223, 225, 255, 278, 283–6, 303, 305–6, 315, 326, 330, 338, 342, 383, 387, 390–91, 400, 422
new liberal dilemma *see* progressive's dilemma
New Zealand 17, 19, 23, 34, 199, 213–14, 220, 225, 302–3, 305–6, 330
Nezi, Roula 257
Nigeria 18, 494
non-governmental organizations 35, 37–8, 76–8
normative-power-of-welfare-states approach 327–8
norms 3–4, 21, 91, 94–6, 98, 104, 106, 108, 114, 120, 125, 179, 195, 197–200, 202, 211, 214, 256, 277–8, 280, 322, 327–9, 331, 342, 354, 362, 405–7, 420–25, 434, 496
see also values
North America 64, 69, 75, 78–9, 87, 188, 277, 284, 298, 446
Norway 14, 17, 19, 23–4, 27–8, 34, 36, 38, 55, 144, 158, 165–6, 175–6, 213–14, 220, 225, 280, 285–6, 303, 305, 330, 490
Nowrasteh, Alex 51
Nyamongo, Esman M. 451

Oesch, Daniel 356
official development assistance 9, 452, 470, 492
Oman 443
Oorschot, Wim J.H. 410, 413
open migration 29, 322, 325, 327, 334
Organisation for Economic Co-operation and Development 13–20, 22–3, 32, 34, 50, 52, 59, 143–4, 219, 284, 302–3, 413, 481, 483
Orjuela, Camilla 495
Orloff, Ann S. 297
Orr, Robert 51
Ortiga, Yasmin Y. 497
Osakwe, Christian N. 451
Österman, M. 30–31
out-groups 3, 8, 54, 56, 68, 90, 102, 114, 124, 128, 139, 141, 160–61, 177, 179, 183, 187, 204, 278, 282–3, 290, 292, 323, 341–2, 345, 351, 368, 370–71, 374–8, 387–8, 421

Pakistan 451–3, 490
Palme, Joakim 325, 329–30
panel surveys 51, 390, 400
Parolin, Zachary 142
Parrado, Emilio A. 452
partisanship 112, 262, 344, 346, 372, 379
Passel, Jeffrey 31, 51
patriotism 179
Patten, Alan 104
Pedersen, Axel W. 142
Pedersen, Peder J. 50
Pellegata, Alessandro 178
Pellizzari, Michele 30
Pempel, T.J. 215
Pendakur, Ravi 28
pensions 14–15, 29, 121, 286
Peri, Giovanni 49
permanent residency 18–20, 33–4, 75, 113
Peters, Margaret E. 329–30
Petersen, Michael B. 106–7
Peth, Simon A. 494
Pettigrew, Thomas F. 131, 367–8
Pew Center for the People and the Press 374
Philippines 443, 452, 493
Plaut, Victoria C. 199
Poland 17–18, 22–4, 31, 109–11, 144, 496
policy outcomes 3, 57, 59, 94, 195–6, 200, 202, 214
policy preferences 58, 70, 140–41, 148, 256, 259, 262, 422
political economy 29, 37, 66, 293, 297, 301
population aging 15, 32, 47, 322
population diversity 122, 124–5
population growth 47
populism 18, 38, 69, 97, 211–13, 215–16, 226, 357, 422
Portes, Alejandro 298
Portugal 14, 17, 22–3, 34, 144, 158, 160, 166, 213, 220, 225, 285–6, 303, 305, 309
post-migration trauma 27
poverty 52, 106–7, 218, 232, 304, 323, 353, 362, 409, 426–7, 442, 470–71, 481, 493, 505, 507, 512–14
power relations 9, 491, 495, 498, 506, 513
Pradhan, Gyan 452
Pratsinakis, Manolis 491
prejudice 8, 28, 50, 54, 92, 114, 125, 132, 157, 160, 176–80, 195, 198–9, 203, 205, 232, 341–2, 345, 353, 359, 368–70, 373, 382–9, 392, 396–8, 400–401, 510, 515
progressive's dilemma 5, 11, 45, 56, 58–9, 66, 105, 118–32, 217, 220, 223, 226, 230–50, 298, 322–4, 326, 353, 409–10, 412
Protestant work ethic 91
Protestantism 91–2, 353–4, 374

psychology of acquisition 97
public culture 109, 405
public opinion 3, 57, 71, 94–5, 97, 107, 137–42, 181, 187–8, 199, 204, 218, 224, 299–300, 304, 324, 326–7, 409, 421, 510
Putnam, Robert 8, 20–21, 68, 277–8, 293, 298, 371, 373–4, 378, 407–8

race 108
racism 8, 72, 92, 95, 107, 109, 114, 132, 160, 176, 211, 217, 223, 343, 345, 353, 355, 357–8, 368–9, 409, 488, 507, 510
radical right 7, 68, 71–2, 129–32, 183, 211–12, 215–16, 234, 236, 240–44, 249, 255–6, 258–60, 262, 265, 269–73, 323, 327, 338, 351–3, 356–8, 360–61, 363, 375
Rafferty, Anthony 50
Rainwater, Lee 31
Ramirez, Miguel D. 453
Rao, B. Bhaskara 451
Rapoport, Hillel 4, 125
rational actor model 88, 92
Raza, Syed A. 451
Razin, Assaf 29–30, 51
redistribution 6, 21, 45, 55–6, 58, 64–6, 68, 71, 73, 323–4, 327, 413, 420, 425
  see also welfare state
  boundaries of generosity 102–15
  immigration and preferences for 118–32
  politics of (MCPs) 210–27
  progressive's dilemma see progressive's dilemma
  sharing with strangers 87–98
    see also progressive's dilemma; strangers; welfare chauvinism
  social democratic dilemma 255–71
  universal basic income 4, 137–48, 153–5
  welfare chauvinism see welfare chauvinism
redistributive solidarity 218, 273, 420–21, 433
Reeskens, Tim 181–2, 198, 326, 329, 413, 432
refugee crisis 66, 181–2, 188, 234, 249, 363
refugees 2, 7, 15–17, 20, 22–8, 31–2, 37–9, 49, 51, 58, 64, 66, 74–6, 79, 92, 123, 130, 201, 216, 321, 326–31, 334, 351, 362
  see also forced migration
regression models 67, 70–71, 112, 143, 145, 154, 161, 163–4, 173–4, 185–6, 188, 219, 222, 231, 236–8, 240, 242, 246, 303, 392, 395, 398, 455
relative deprivation 50, 178, 184, 187, 421, 423–4, 426, 430–32, 434, 439
religion 87, 90, 105, 195–8, 211–12, 214, 287–8, 346–7, 353–8, 369–71, 374, 377–9, 407, 416

remittances 2, 9, 442–64, 471–3, 475–6, 482–4, 492–3, 504, 512
resentment 7, 69, 293, 345, 351–63, 423–4, 426, 428–30, 432–4, 439
responsibility 6, 33, 36–7, 51, 75, 77, 107, 121, 182, 256–7, 263–5, 272, 302, 310, 343–4, 362, 372, 422, 479, 498
responsiveness 6, 79, 256–7, 259, 263, 265, 272
Rhein, Suzanne 6
right to care 78–9
right-wing parties 7, 68–9, 71–2, 95, 129–32, 165, 168, 183, 211–13, 215–16, 226, 231, 234, 236–8, 240–47, 249, 255–6, 258–60, 262, 265, 269–73, 323, 327, 338, 351–3, 356–8, 360–61, 363, 375, 424
Rignall, Karen 492
Riphahn, Regina T. 30
Robinson, Vaughan 196
Rodrik, Dani 357–9
Romania 17, 109–11
Römer, Friederike 328
Roodenburg, Hans 31
Rooduijn, Matthijs 123, 142
Rothstein, Bo 280, 325
Rowthorn, Robert 31, 52
Ruhs, Martin 19
Ruist, Joakim 31, 48–9
Ruiz-Arranz, Marta 452
Runst, Petrik 124
rural residence 161–4, 167, 172, 245–6, 287, 289, 358–62, 374
Russell, Sharon S. 451
Russia 443

Sainsbury, Diane 223, 328
Sakdapolrak, Patrick 494
Saleem, Shaikh M. 453
Samuelson, Paul A. 29
Sarkozy, Nicolas 211
SARS 73
Saudi Arabia 443
Saunders, Elizabeth N. 425
Savage, Lee 124
Saxenian, Anna L. 497
Sayan, Serdar 448
Scheff, Thomas 362
Schildkraut, Deborah J. 342
Schmidt-Catran, Alexander W. 123, 425
Scholten, Peter 36
Schwartz, Shalom 184
second-generation migrants 15, 32, 47–9, 66, 120, 171, 202, 421
segregation 8, 21, 27, 64, 68, 119, 128, 211, 281, 368–70, 372–4, 376–9, 412
Sekulić, Duško 396

selective solidarity *see* welfare chauvinism
self-employment 127, 143, 288, 303, 310–11, 319–20, 390, 392–3, 395, 398, 428, 430–31, 440
self-interest 69, 87, 89, 141, 178, 280, 340–43, 420, 422–4, 429, 433–4
self-selection 18, 26–7, 126, 359, 384
Semynov, Moshe 49
Sen, Amartya 515
Senbeta, Aberra 451
sending societies *see* countries of origin
Senik, Claudia 123, 141
Seo, Myung H. 456–7
Shin, Adrian J. 329–30
Shin, Yongcheol 456–7
Shukralla, Elias 451
Sibley, Chris G. 188
sick leave 29, 52, 125
Sidiropoulos, Moise G. 452
Silicon Valley 89, 497
Sinatti, Giulia 496
Singapore 452, 480, 492, 494
Singh, Raju J. 451
Siöland, Linus 142
Sirin, Cigdem V. 93
skill level of migrants 51–2, 96, 130
  high-skilled migrants 51, 73, 89, 178, 201, 340, 359, 489
  low-skilled migrants 48, 89, 130, 164, 322, 339–40, 493
  unskilled migrants 29, 39, 51, 58, 322, 493
Slovak Republic 17, 22–3
Slovenia 17, 23, 144
Sluiter, Roderick 8
Smith, Anthony 103
Sniderman, Paul M. 342
social capital 3, 18, 27–8, 39, 64, 68, 125, 196–7, 230, 278, 284, 297–8, 323, 373, 376–7, 387, 406–7, 411, 420, 471
Social Capital Benchmark Survey 373, 376–7
social cohesion 3, 13, 20–21, 64, 67–8, 72, 92, 95, 120, 125, 217, 230–31, 276–82, 290, 292–3, 298–300, 420
social contract 13, 20–21, 39, 90–91, 93, 95, 97, 423
social democratic parties 6, 57–8, 172, 231, 236, 245, 248–9, 255–73
social dominance theory 180
social identity 3, 89–90, 93, 124, 179–80, 198, 204, 341–2, 344
social insurance 132, 139, 301, 329–30, 333
social justice 68, 414
social media 121, 357
social mobility 180, 509,
  see also upward mobility

social networks 29, 97, 374, 378–9, 406–7, 492, 508
social rights 2, 13, 19–22, 48, 53, 56–7, 69, 73, 103, 129, 176, 180, 183, 187–8, 198, 223, 232–4, 285, 413
social security 13, 19, 108, 131, 148, 175, 182–3, 217, 234, 262, 329, 421–2, 433, 446, 515
social services 19, 29–32, 39, 71, 75, 128, 157, 262, 340, 355
social solidarity 20, 37, 45, 64, 67–8, 72, 109, 137, 140, 142, 148, 230, 276, 282, 297, 315, 327–8, 421
social transfers 14–15, 29
social trust 64, 67–8, 72, 197–8, 231, 277, 280, 298, 387, 406, 434
socialization 4, 8, 97, 105, 198, 343, 345, 373, 386
sociotropic concerns 178–9, 187, 278, 341
Solodoch, Omer 178
Somalia 25, 494
Somerville, Will 31
Soroka, Stuart N. 59, 219, 325
South Africa 489
South Korea 15, 17
South Sudan 443
Soviet Union 510
Spain 14–17, 19, 23–4, 34, 52, 109–11, 158–60, 165–6, 213, 220, 225, 285–6, 303, 305, 309
Spies, Dennis C. 123, 323–4
Sri Lanka 451, 495
Stadelmann-Steffen, Isabelle 142
Standing, Guy 361–2
Stein, Arlene 362
stereotypes 8, 92–3, 107, 109, 119, 125, 132, 178, 180, 233, 341, 368–9
Stetler, Henry G. 369
Stichnoth, Holger 120, 123
Stoetzer, Lukas F. 124
Stolle, Dietlind 280
Stolper, Wolfgang F. 29
strangers 3, 7–8, 87–98, 102, 113, 205, 357, 359, 362, 367–79
Straubhaar, Thomas 31
Strielkowski, Wadim 452
Su, Phi H. 50
Supplemental Security Income 51
Sustainable Development Goals 482, 515
Sweden 14, 16–17, 19, 22–8, 31–2, 34–9, 48–9, 52, 58, 92, 122–3, 125, 142, 144, 158, 166, 178, 213–14, 220, 223, 230–32, 234–5, 238, 245, 247–9, 280, 285–6, 303, 305–6, 330, 357–8, 413
Switzerland 16–17, 19, 23–4, 31, 72, 144, 158, 160, 166, 201, 213, 261–71, 278, 285–6, 292, 303, 305–6, 330, 346, 359–60, 410, 443

symbolic threat 180, 342
Syria 17–18, 25, 73, 130, 249, 495

Tabellini, Marco 49, 59, 92
Tajfel, Henri 323
Tajikistan 443, 445
Tamborini, Christopher R. 47
Tampubolon, Gindo 197
taxation 72, 74, 89, 103, 120, 130, 138, 143, 249, 259, 340
Taylor, J.E. 452
Taylor-Gooby, Peter 325
Tchantchane, Abdellatif 452
technological innovation 355, 362
Temporary Protected Status 73, 76
Thailand 452, 494
Thatcher, Margaret 353
Tilley, James 344
Toivanen, Mari 495–6
Tolsma, Jochem 298
Tomlinson, John 356
Tonga 443
transnational connections 496, 498
Tritah, Ahmed 200–201
Tropp, Linda R. 367–8
Trudeau, Justin 73, 79
Trump, Donald 38, 73, 79, 156, 238, 248, 362
Trumpism 97
trust 2, 6, 20, 45, 161, 164, 167, 197–8, 202, 205, 217–18, 230, 276–93, 371–7, 387–8, 423, 490
 and diversity 276–93, 298, 323, 405–18
 measuring 406–7
 social trust 64, 67–8, 72, 197–8, 231, 277, 280, 298, 387, 406, 434
Tsai, Ming-Chang 178
tuberculosis 73
Tuli, Sajeda 359
Tunisia 451
Turkey 17, 23, 30, 346, 387, 390–91, 421, 428, 432–3, 443, 449
Tzeng, Rueyling 178

UBI 4, 137–48, 153–5
Ukraine 18, 55
underemployment 49
undocumented migrants 38, 45, 64, 73, 76–9, 93, 203–4, 223, 347
unemployment 48–9, 145–8, 177, 181, 184–5, 188, 201, 219, 232, 287–9, 302–7, 310–15, 408, 423, 509
unemployment benefits 14, 29, 51–2, 106, 125, 138, 140, 286
unemployment insurance 72, 120–21, 138

United Kingdom 14, 16–19, 23–4, 27, 30–31, 33–8, 50, 52, 55, 68, 71, 107, 109–13, 119, 125, 128, 130–31, 139, 144, 156, 158–9, 165–6, 178, 211, 213, 220, 223, 225, 233, 265, 268–72, 285–6, 303, 305–6, 330, 359, 373–5, 377, 408, 417, 491, 495
 see also Brexit
United Nations 13, 442, 444, 515
 Convention against Transnational Organized Crime 509
 Convention on the Rights of All Migrant Workers and Their Families 514
 Declaration for Refugees and Migrants 514
 General Assembly 514
 High Commissioner for Refugees 73, 509
United States 6, 13–14, 16–21, 23, 27–31, 34, 38–9, 45, 47, 49–51, 58–9, 65–8, 71–9, 89, 91–2, 95, 97, 107–8, 118, 122, 130, 132, 139, 141, 156, 198, 202–4, 211, 213–14, 217–18, 220, 223, 225, 230–32, 234–6, 238, 245, 247–8, 298–300, 302–3, 305–6, 309, 323–5, 330, 338, 345, 347, 352–6, 358–9, 361–2, 368–70, 372–5, 378–9, 407, 409, 416, 425, 443, 448, 497, 510–11, 513–14
universal basic income 4, 137–48, 153–5
universalism 21, 73, 105, 139, 180, 183, 356
unskilled migrants 29, 39, 51, 58, 322, 493
upward mobility 88, 126, 180
 see also social mobility
urbanization 355, 358–9, 509
U.S. Census Bureau 47, 51
Uslander, Eric 7–8
utility maximization 3, 88–9, 92, 94, 96–7
Uunk, Wilfred G.J. 410

Vadlamannati, Krishna Chaitanya 327
Valdivia Lopez, Marcos 451
values 3, 33, 53–5, 58, 87, 90–91, 93–6, 98, 104–5, 108–9, 114, 145–7, 179–80, 184–8, 199, 204, 214, 218, 230, 238, 245, 257, 262–3, 265–6, 269–70, 278, 284–6, 290, 298, 303, 309, 312–13, 322, 327, 352, 354, 357–60, 362, 371, 377, 383, 386, 400, 405, 408–10, 414, 416, 424–5, 455–7, 461, 476
Van der Meer, Tom 181, 298, 326, 329
Van der Straeten, Karine 120
Van der Waal, Jeroen 180–82
Van Hootegem, Arno 8–9
Van Oorschot, Wim 106–9, 114, 125, 182, 198, 224, 422, 432
Van Spanje, Joost 131
Van Tubergen, Frank 27, 50
Vargas-Silva, Carlos 448, 452

Verter, Nahanga 451
Vickstrom, Erik 298
Vietnam 50, 452
Villarreal, Andrés 47
voting 5, 57–8, 66, 129–30, 157, 164–6, 195, 197, 231, 233–4, 238, 240, 242, 245–6, 249–50, 343, 412
voting behavior 5, 57–8, 66, 157, 164–6, 195, 197, 233–4, 238, 240, 242, 245, 250, 259, 262, 340, 363

Wagner, Markus 58
Wahba, Jackline 29–30, 51
Walton-Roberts, Margaret 9
Walzer, Michael 20–21
Ward, Colleen 199
Weber, René 31
Weis, Hilde 396
welfare chauvinism 4–5, 10, 64, 68–70, 72, 88–90, 92–3, 97–8, 119, 124–5, 128, 131, 138–40, 142, 198, 210, 223–4, 226, 232, 256, 282, 293, 299, 322, 326–7, 360, 566
   importance of measurement in study of 156–68
   personal and contextual foundations of 175–89
welfare deservingness theory 69–71
welfare magnet hypothesis 29–30, 50–52, 78, 121, 126, 322
welfare nationalism *see* welfare chauvinism
welfare populism *see* welfare chauvinism
welfare restrictiveness *see* welfare chauvinism
welfare state 1–10, 102, 105–6, 109, 125, 137, 157, 159, 164, 166–7, 175, 182, 187, 203, 210, 214, 219–20, 223, 257, 260, 262–6, 405, 409–10, 415
   see also redistribution; *individual countries*
   criticism, roots of 420–35
   definition of 14
   diversity and 64–79
      see also diversity
   expansion 58, 137, 220, 258, 262–9
   explaining 322–5
   immigration as a challenge to 45–59

inequality and welfare regimes 297–316
managing migration in 13–39
and migration policy 321–35
mitigating role of institutions 276–93
politicization of immigration 230–50
welfare system 3, 13, 15, 20, 22, 28–9, 73, 102, 119, 121, 123, 125–6, 128–30, 156–9, 167, 182–3, 224, 413, 422
Western Europe 14, 22, 30–31, 38, 50–52, 65, 125, 132, 158–9, 175–89, 198–9, 230, 298, 302, 351, 361, 407, 446
Westlake, Daniel 5
Westwood, Sean 378–9
Wieseltier, Leon 357
Wilkinson, Will 358
Williams, Nick 491
Williams, Robin M. 368
Windrush scandal 113
Wise, Raúl D. 9–10
Wodak, Ruth 361
Wong, Madeleine 497
Work and Politics Panel Study 390
working class 58, 90, 245, 250, 255, 257, 259–60, 273, 353, 356, 507, 515
workplace ethnic diversity 382–401
World Bank 6, 302–3, 442–4, 454, 457, 489, 492–3, 504, 515
World Development Indicator Database 6
World Food Programme 482
Wright, Matthew 3–4, 21, 198–9
Wuthnow, Robert 362

xenophobia 10, 18, 38, 114, 156, 161–3, 171, 195, 198–9, 202, 205, 357, 360, 510, 515
   see also nativism

Yugoslavia 17, 346

Zazzaro, Alberto 451
Ziller, Conrad 5
Zimbabwe 493
Zimdars, Anna 197
Zimmermann, Klaus F. 52
zombie theory 89